LATIN DIC

10631527

Chuck Freeman

TEACH YOURSELF BOOKS

LATIN DICTIONARY

Alastair Wilson
B.A.

TEACH YOURSELF BOOKS
Hodder and Stoughton

First edition 1965
Sixth impression 1983

Copyright © 1965
Hodder and Stoughton Ltd

All rights reserved. No part of this publication may be reproduced or transmitted in any form or by any means, electronic or mechanical, including photocopy, recording, or any information storage and retrieval system without permission in writing from the publisher.

This volume is published in the U.S.A. by David McKay Company Inc., 750 Third Avenue, New York, N.Y. 10017

ISBN 0 340 26166 8

Printed in Great Britain
for Hodder and Stoughton Educational,
a division of Hodder and Stoughton Ltd,
Mill Road, Dunton Green, Sevenoaks, Kent
by Richard Clay (The Chaucer Press) Ltd., Bungay, Suffolk

CONTENTS

1. Introduction and Advice on Learning Vocabulary 1–2

2. Abbreviations Used 3–4

3. Latin–English 5–130

4. Proper Names (Latin–English) . . . 131–147

5. English–Latin 149–291

6. Proper Names (English–Latin) . . . 293

7. Concise Grammar:

Alphabet and Pronunciation . . . 294

Nouns and Declensions 294–297

Adjectives and Declensions—Comparison of Adjectives 297–299

Verbs. Tables of Regular Verbs . . . 300–307

Tables of Irregular Verbs . . . 307–310

Deponent Verbs 310

Impersonal Verbs 311

Defective Verbs 312

Pronouns—Personal, Reflexive, Demonstrative, Emphatic, Relative, List of other Pronouns 313–314

Prepositions 314

Conjunctions 315

Adverbs—Comparison of Adverbs . . 316

Numerals—Cardinal, Ordinal, Distributive, Reflexive 316–318

Roman Calendar—Dating 318–319

Money, Weights, Measures 319

Time, Place, Space 320

INTRODUCTION

THE chief benefit that a knowledge of Latin confers is the ability to read the works of the Roman authors, particularly those of the Golden and Silver Ages of Latin Literature, i.e. 60 B.C.–A.D. 100. This Dictionary has been compiled with this in mind, and also with an eye to the "non-specialist". To this end, the equivalents in the Latin–English section of the Dictionary have been presented in as simple and "modern" a form as possible, while at the same time the most important distinctions in meaning which each Latin word bears have been indicated. The vocabulary has been based on that commonly used by the authors of the period mentioned above, and a person who is acquainted with Latin grammar and the common forms of the Latin language should be able, with a little help from this Dictionary, to read them without much difficulty. For those not so acquainted, for those whose memory may have dimmed with the passage of time, and for those who have never been fully conversant with a highly inflected language like Latin, a Concise Latin Grammar has been provided. This contains, in tabulated form and with simple explanations, all the basic regular and irregular word-forms needed for translation from the commoner Latin authors.

In the English–Latin section, the Latin equivalent given is that which represents the best *general* meaning of the English, and which is used in that sense by a Classical author. Occasionally, however, where no exact Latin equivalent for an English word exists, it has been necessary to give a short circumlocution: in this case the phrase given is always translated into English, e.g. **disinterested**, neutri favens (**favouring neither side**). Where several different meanings are borne by the same word, or where ambiguity may occur, care has been taken to differentiate between the various meanings, e.g. **order**, *nn*, (**arrangement**), ordo, *m*; (**in —**), *adj*, dispŏsĭtus; (**command, direction**), iussum, *n*; (**class, rank**), ordo, *m*; (**in — to**), ut.

Where fuller information is required about any of the words given in the Dictionary, reference should be made to the following standard works upon the subject: A Latin Dictionary by Charlton T. Lewis and Charles Short and Smaller English–Latin Dictionary by Dr. William Smith.

ADVICE ON LEARNING VOCABULARY

If you are gifted with a good memory, you will find it particularly easy to learn Latin vocabulary, especially if you try to link in your mind new Latin words and any English derivatives of them which you can think of, e.g. **mare**—sea—marine; **nauta**—ship—nautical. A high proportion of Latin words have quite common English derivatives. If you do this, not only will your interest in both languages grow, but you will begin to form an impression of the debt which our language owes to that of the Romans.

If on the other hand, you are one of those who find it "difficult to make words stick" in schoolboy phraseology, then here is a piece of simple advice —not to be despised because of its simplicity—which might help you to retain words in your memory. To learn a new word it is not only essential to find out and to understand its meaning, but also to see it working in relationship to other words, and to "meet" it as many times as possible immediately after first acquaintance. It is therefore advisable to *re-read* the piece in which you originally met the word two or three times after you have learned it, and to make an effort to find the same word again within a day or two of first meeting it, otherwise you may find, on ultimately seeing it again, that it has "gone". Above all, try to maintain your interest in learning new vocabulary, for without such interest no learning of real or lasting nature can take place.

ABBREVIATIONS USED

( ) Brackets are used to indicate alternative forms.

a, um, see adj.
abl. ablative case; see page 295.
acc. accusative case; see page 295.
acis } genitive singular ending of nouns indicating that they belong to the
atis } third declension.
adj. adjective, **a, um era, erum** after an adjective indicates that it belongs to the First Class, "e" that it belongs to the Second Class; see page 297.
adv. adverb. The adverb ending is often given, e.g. **e, iter, nter, um, o,** and should be attached to the *stem* of the adjective, e.g. **abditus** (*adj*); **abdite** (*adv*). See page 316.
ae. genitive singular ending of a noun, indicating that it belongs to the first declension.
arum, genitive plural ending, indicating that the noun belongs to the first declension.
auxil. auxiliary verb.
c. common gender.
c. comp. comparative adjective or adverb, see pages 299–316.
conj. conjunction; see p. 315.
cris, cre. nominative feminine and neuter endings, indicating that an adjective belongs to the Second Class; see page 298.
cl. clause.
dat. dative case; see page 295; also some verbs take a dative case after them.
defect. a defective verb, i.e. it has not all its parts; see page 312.
demonst. demonstrative pronoun.
dep, see v. dep.
e, see adj.
ei. genitive singular ending of noun, indicating that it belongs to the fifth declension.
enis } genitive singular endings of nouns indicating that they belong to the
etis } third declension.
exclam. exclamation.
f. feminine gender.
f.pl. feminine plural.
fut. future.
i, ii. genitive singular ending of noun, indicating that it belongs to the second declension.
icis } genitive singular endings of nouns indicating that they belong to the
inis } third declension.
impers. impersonal verb; see page 311.
indecl. indeclinable.
inf. infinitive.
interj. interjective.
interr. interrogative.
irreg. irregular verb; see pages 307–310.
is. genitive singular of noun, indicating that it belongs to the third declension.
iter, see adv.

itis. genitive singular ending of noun, indicating that it belongs to the third declension.
ium. genitive plural ending of noun, indicating that it belongs to the third declension.
m. masculine gender.
m.pl. masculine plural.
n. neuter gender.
nn. noun.
nter, see adv.
ntis. genitive singular ending of some nouns and adjectives of the third declension.
num. numeral.
n.pl. neuter plural.
onis / **oris** } genitive singular noun ending, indicating that the noun belongs to the third declension.
orum. genitive plural ending, indicating that a noun belongs to the second declension.
partic. participle.
pass. a passive verb, conjugated in the passive voice only.
perf. perfect.
pers. personal.
phr. phrase.
pl. plural.
poss. possessive.
prep. preposition; see page 314: the case taken by the preposition is usually indicated.
pres. present.
pron. pronoun; see pages 312–314.
pron. adj. pronominal adjective; a pronoun which declines and agrees like an adjective.
reflex. reflexive.
rel. relative.
semi-dep. semi-deponent; verbs which are deponent in some of their tenses.
sup(erl). superlative adjective or adverb.
tis / **tris** } genitive singular ending of some nouns and adjs. of the third declension.
um. genitive plural ending of noun, indicating that it belongs to the third declension.
ūs. genitive singular ending of noun, indicating that it belongs to the fourth declension.
v. vb. verb. The conjugation to which a verb belongs is indicated by the figure 1, 2, 3, or 4; see page 299. In the case of 3rd conjugation verbs, and other verbs whose Perfect stem and Supine are not regular, these are given with the verb, e.g. **aboleo, evi, itum.** If none of these parts are given, it may be assumed that the verb is regularly conjugated; if some, but not all parts are given, it may be assumed that the ones not given are not in regular use.
v. dep. verb deponent; see page 310.
v.i. verb intransitive, i.e. a verb which does not have a direct object.
v. impers. verb impersonal; see page 311.
v.i.t. a verb which can be used intransitively or transitively. The separate uses are indicated by the use of the semi-colon, e.g. **abhorreo,** *v.i.t.* 2, to shrink back (intransitive); to disagree with (transitive).
voc. vocative case, see page 295.
v.t. verb transitive, i.e. a verb which has a direct object.

LATIN - ENGLISH

For List of Abbreviations used, turn to pages 3, 4

A

ā, ăb, *prep. with abl,* by (agent); from (place, time); in, at (position); since
ăbăcus, i, *m,* sideboard, counting or gaming board, slab
ăbăliēno, *v.t.* 1, to estrange, make a legal transfer
ăbăvus, i, *m,* great-great-grandfather, ancestor
abdĭcātio, ōnis, *f,* renunciation of office
abdĭco, *v.t.* 1, to resign
abdĭco, xi, ctum, *v.t.* 3, to refuse assent
abdĭtus, a, um, *adj, adv,* **ē,** hidden, secret
abdo, didi, dĭtum, *v.t.* 3, to conceal
abdōmĕn, ĭnis, *n,* belly
abdūco, xi, ctum, *v.t.* 3, to lead away
ăbĕo, *v.i.* 4, to go away
ăberro, *v.i.* 1, to go astray
ăbhinc, *adv,* ago
ăbhorrĕo, *v.i.t.* 2, to shrink back; disagree with
ăbi, see **ăbĕo**
ăbĭcio, iēci, iectum, *v.t.* 3, to throw away
abiectus, a, um, *adj, adv,* **ē,** downcast
ăbiēgnus, a um, *adj,* made of fir
ăbiēs, ĕtis, *f,* fir
ăbĭgo, ĕre, ēgi, actum, *v.t.* 3, to drive away
ăbĭtio, ōnis, *f,* departure
ăbĭtus, ūs, *m,* departure
abiūdico, *v.t.* 1, to deprive by legal sentence
abiungo, nxi, nctum, *v.t.* 3, to unyoke
abiūro, *v.t.* 1, to deny on oath
ablātus, a, um, *adj.* from **auferō,** taken away
ablēgātio, ōnis, *f,* banishment
ablēgo, *v.t.* 1, to send away
ablŭo, ŭi, ūtum, *v.t.* 3, to wash away
ablūtio, ōnis, *f,* ablution, washing
abnĕgo, *v.t.* 1, to refuse
abnormis, e, *adj,* irregular
abnŭo, ŭi, ūtum, *v.i.t.* 3, to refuse
ăbŏlĕo, ēvi, ĭtum, *v.t.* 2, to destroy
ăbŏlesco, ēvi, *v.i.* 3, to decay
ăbŏlĭtio, ōnis, *f,* abolition
ăbolla, ae, *f,* cloak
ăbōminor, *v.t.* 1, *dep.* to wish away (being ominous)
ăbŏrīgines, um, *m.pl,* natives
ăbortio, ōnis, *f,* miscarriage
ăbortus, ūs, *m,* abortion
abrādo, si, sum, *v.t.* 3, to scrape off
abrĭpio, ŭi, reptum, *v.t.* 3, to drag away
abrōdo, si, sum, *v.t.* 3, to gnaw away
abrŏgātio, ōnis, *f,* repeal
abrŏgo, *v.t.* 1, to repeal
abrumpo, rūpi, ruptum, *v.t.* 3, to break off
abruptus, a, um, *adj,* steep
abscēdo, cessi, cessum, *v.i.* 3, to go away
abscīdo, cīdi, scīsum, *v.t.* 3, to cut off
abscindo, scĭdi, scissum, *v.t.* 3, to tear away
abscīsus, a, um, *adj, adv,* **ē,** steep
abscondĭtus, a, um, *adj, adv,* **ē,** hidden
abscondo, di, dĭtum, *v.t.* 3, to conceal
absens, entis, *adj,* absent
absentia, ae, *f,* absence
absilio, *v.i.* 4, to jump away
absĭmilis, e, *adj,* unlike
absinthium, ii, *n,* absinth
absisto, stĭti, *v.i.* 3, to stand aloof
absŏlūtio, ōnis, *f,* acquittal
absŏlūtus, a, um, *adj, adv,* **ē,** complete
absolvo, vi, sŏlūtum, *v.t.* 3, to unfasten, acquit
absŏnus, a, um, *adj, adv,* **ē,** discordant
absorbĕo, bŭi, ptum, *v.t.* 2, to swallow up
absquĕ, *prep. with abl,* without
abstēmius, a, um, *adj,* sober
abstergĕo, rsi, rsum, *v.t.* 2, to wipe off
absterrĕo, *v.t.* 2, to frighten away
abstinens, ntis, *adj, adv,* **nter,** temperate
abstĭnentia, ae, *f,* self-restraint
abstĭnĕo, ŭi, tentum, *v.i.t.* 2, to abstain from; restrain
abstrăho, xi, ctum, *v.t.* 3, to drag away
abstrūdo, si, sum, *v.t.* 3, to push away

abstrūsus, a, um, *adj, adv,* **ē,** hidden
absum, esse, abfui (afui), *v.i. irreg,* to be absent
absūmo, mpsi, mptum, *v.t.* 3, to take away, use up
absurdus, a, um, *adj, adv,* **ē,** stupid, tuneless
ăbundans, ntis, *adj, adv,* **nter,** plentiful
ăbundantia, ae, *f,* plenty
ăbundo, *v.i.* 1, to overflow
ăbūtor, i, usus sum, *v.* 3, *dep. with abl,* to use up, abuse
ac, *conj,* and
ăcācia, ae, *f,* acacia
ăcădēmia, ae, *f,* academy
accēdo, cessi, cessum, *v.i.* 3, to approach
accĕlĕro, *v.i.t.* 1, to hurry; quicken
accendo, ndi, nsum, *v.t.* 3, to set on fire
accensĕo, ŭi, nsum, *v.t.* 2, to add to
accensus, i, *m,* attendant
accentus, ūs, *m,* accentuation
acceptio, ōnis, *f,* acceptance
acceptum, i, *n,* receipt
acceptus, a, um, *adj,* agreeable
accessio, ōnis, *f,* approach, increase
accessus, ūs, *m,* approach
accīdo, cīdi, cīsum, *v.t.* 3, to cut
accĭdo, cĭdi, *v.i.* 3, to fall upon, happen
accingo, nxi, nctum, *v.t.* 3, to equip, put on
accĭo, *v.t.* 4, to summon
accĭpio, cēpi, ceptum, *v.t.* 3, to receive
accĭpiter, tris, *m,* hawk
accĭtus, ūs, *m,* summons
acclāmātio, ōnis, *f,* shout
acclāmo, *v.t.* 1, to shout at
acclīnis, e, *adj,* leaning on
acclino, *v.t.* 1, to lean
acclīvis, e, *adj,* uphill
acclīvitas, ātis, *f,* ascent
accŏla, ae, *c,* neighbour
accŏlo, cŏlui, cultum, *v.t.* 3, to live near
accommŏdātus, a, um, *adj, adv,* **ē,** suitable
accommŏdātio, ōnis, *f,* compliance
accommŏdo, *v.t.* 1, to adapt
accommŏdus, a, um, *adj,* suitable
accresco, crēvi, crētum, *v.i.* 3, to grow
accrētio, ōnis, *f,* increase
accŭbĭtio, ōnis, *f,* reclining
accŭbo, *v.i.* 1, to lie near, recline at table
accumbo, cŭbŭi, cŭbĭtum, *v.i.* 3, to lie near, recline at table
accŭmŭlo, *v.t.* 1, to heap up
accūro, *v.t.* 1, to take care of
accūrātus, a, um, *adj, adv,* **ē,** prepared carefully, precise
accurro, curri, cursum, *v.i.* 3, to run to
accūsātio, ōnis, *f,* accusation
accūsātor, ōris, *m,* accuser
accūso, *v.t.* 1, to accuse
ăcer, cris, e, *adj, adv,* **iter,** keen
ăcer, ĕris, *n,* maple tree
ăcerbĭtas, ātis, *f,* bitterness
ăcerbo, *v.t.* 1, to embitter
ăcerbus, a, um, *adj,* bitter, keen
ăcernus, a, um, *adj,* made of maple
ăcerra, ae, *f,* incense-box
ăcervo, *v.t.* 1, to heap up
ăcervus, i, *m,* heap
ăcētăria, ōrum, *n.pl,* salad
ăcētum, i, *n,* vinegar
ăcĭdus, a, um, *adj, adv,* **ē,** sour
ăcies, ēi, *f,* edge, pupil of eye, battle-line, keenness
ăcĭnăces, is, *m,* scimitar
ăcĭnus, i, *m* (**um, i,** *n*), berry
ăcipenser, ĕris, *m,* sturgeon
aclys, ўdis, *f,* small javelin
ăcŏnĭtum, i, *n,* aconite
acquiesco, ēvi, ētum, *v.i.* 3, to rest, aquiesce
acquīro, sīvi, sītum, *v.t.* 3, to procure
ăcrimōnia, ae, *f,* sharpness
ăcriter, *adv,* keenly
acta, ōrum, *n.pl,* acts, records
actio, ōnis, *f,* act, legal action
actor, ōris, *m,* driver, plaintiff, performer
actŭārius, a, um, *adj,* swift
actŭārius, i, *m,* notary
actum, i, *n,* deed
actus, a, um, see **ăgo**
actus, ūs, *m,* impulse, act (of drama)
ăcŭlĕātus, a, um, *adj,* prickly
ăcŭlĕus, i, *m,* sting
ăcūmĕn, ĭnis, *n,* point, sting
ăcŭo, ŭi, ūtum, *v.t.* 3, to sharpen
ăcus, ūs, *f,* needle, pin
ăcūtus, a, um, *adj, adv,* **ē,** sharp
ad, *prep. with acc,* to, towards, near (place), about (time), for (purpose)
ădaequo, *v.i.t.* 1, to be equal; to make equal
ădămas, ntis, *m,* steel, diamond
ădămo, *v.t.* 1, to love deeply
ădăpĕrio, ŭi, rtum, *v.t.* 4, to open fully
ădaugĕo, xi, ctum, *v.t.* 2, to increase
addīco, xi, ctum, *v.t.* 3, to assent, award
addictio, ōnis, *f,* adjudication
addictus, a, um, *adj,* dedicated
addo, dĭdi, dĭtum, *v.t.* 3, to add to
addŭbĭto, *v.i.t.* 1, to doubt
addūco, xi, ctum, *v.t.* 3, to lead to, influence
ădemptio, ōnis, *f,* seizure

ădĕo, *v.i.* 4, to approach, attack
ădĕo, *adv,* so much, so long
ădeps, ĭpis, *c,* fat
ădeptĭo, ōnis, *f,* attainment
ădĕquĭto, *v.i.* 1, to gallop up
ădhaerĕo, si, sum, *v.i.* 2, to cling to
ădhaeresco, si, sum, *v.i.* 3, to cling to
ădhĭbĕo, *v.t.* 2, to apply, invite
ădhortātĭo, ōnis, *f,* encouragement
ădhortor, *v.t.* 1, *dep,* to encourage
ădhuc, *adv,* still
adiăcĕo, *v.i.* 2, to adjoin
adĭcĭo, iēci, iectum, *v.t.* 3, to throw to, add to
ădĭgo, ēgi, actum, *v.t.* 3, to drive to, compel
ădĭmo, ēmi, emptum, *v.t.* 3, to take away
ădĭpiscor, eptus, *v.t.* 3, *dep,* to obtain
ăditus, ūs, *m,* approach
adiūdĭco, *v.t.* 1, to assign
adiūmentum, i, *n,* assistance
adiunctĭo, ōnis, *f,* union
adiungo, xi, ctum, *v.t.* 3, to join to
adiūro, *v.t.* 1, to swear, confirm
adiūtor, ōris, *m,* helper
adiūvo, iūvi, iūtum, *v.t.* 1, to help
admātūro, *v.t.* 1, to precipitate
admētĭor, mensus, *v.t.* 4, *dep,* to measure out
adminĭcŭlum, i, *n,* prop
administer, tri, *m,* servant
administrātĭo, ōnis, *f,* aid, management, arrangement
administro, *v.t.* 1, to assist, manage
admīrābilis, e, *adj, adv,* **iter,** wonderful
admīrātĭo, ōnis, *f,* admiration
admīror, *v.t.* 1, *dep,* to wonder at
admiscĕo, scŭi, xtum, *v.t.* 2, to mix with
admissārĭus, ii, *m,* stallion
admissĭo, ōnis, *f,* reception
admissum, i, *n,* fault
admitto, mīsi, ssum, *v.t.* 3, to let in, let go, incur, commit
admixtĭo, ōnis, *f,* mixture
admŏdum, *adv,* up to the limit, very much, nearly
admŏnĕo, *v.t.* 2, to remind
admŏnĭtĭo, ōnis, *f,* warning
admŏnĭtus, ūs, *m,* suggestion
admordĕo, di, sum, *v.t.* 2, to bite at
admŏtĭo, ōnis, *f,* application
admŏvĕo, mōvi, mōtum, *v.t.* 2, to conduct, assault
admurmŭrātĭo, ōnis, *f,* murmur
admurmŭro, *v.i.* 1, to murmur at
adn- see **ann-**
ădŏlĕo, ŭi, ultum, *v.i.* 3, to grow up
ădŏlescens, ntis, *adj,* young
ădŏlescens, ntis, *c,* young person
ădŏlescentĭa, ae, *f,* youth
ădŏlescentŭlus, i, *m,* very young man
ădŏlesco, ēvi, ultum, *v.i,*3, to grow up
ădŏpĕrĭo, ŭi, rtum, *v.t.* 4, to cover up
ădoptātĭo, ōnis, *f,* adoption
ădoptĭo, ōnis, *f,* adoption
ădoptīvus, a, um, *adj,* adoptive
ădopto, *v.t.* 1, to choose, adopt
ădor, ōris, *n,* grain
ădōrātĭo, ōnis, *f,* adoration
ădōrĕa, ae, *f,* reward for bravery
ădōrĭor, ortus, *v.t.* 4, *dep,* to attack, undertake
ădorno, *v.t.* 1, to equip, decorate
ădōro, *v.t.* 1, to worship, entreat
adrādo, si, sum, *v.t.* 3, to shave
adsum, esse, adfui, *v.i, irreg,* to be near
ads . . . see **ass . . .**
ădūlātĭo, ōnis, *f,* flattery
ădūlātor, ōris, *m,* flatterer
ădūlor, *v.t.* 1, *dep,* to flatter
ădulter, ĕri, *m,* adulterer
ădultĕra, ae, *f,* adulteress
ădultĕrātĭo, ōnis, *f,* adulteration
ădultĕrīnus, a, um, *adj,* false
ădultĕrĭum, ii, *n,* adultery
ădultĕro, *v.i.t.* 1, to commit adultery; to falsify, pollute
ădultus, a, um, *adj,* grown up
ădumbrātĭo, ōnis, *f,* sketch
ădumbro, *v.t.* 1, to sketch
ăduncus, a, um, *adj,* hooked
ădurgĕo, *v.t.* 2, to press
ădūro, ssi, stum, *v.t.* 3, to scorch
ădusque, *prep. with acc,* right up to
ădusta, ōrum, *n.pl,* burns
ădustus, a, um, *adj,* burnt
ădvĕho, xi, ctum, *v.t.* 3, to carry to
ădvĕna, ae, *c,* stranger
ădvĕnio, vēni, ventum, *v.t.* 4, to reach
ădvento, *v.t.* 1, to approach
ădventus, ūs, *m,* arrival
adversārĭus, ii, *m,* opponent
adversārĭus, a, um, *adj,* opposite, opposing
adversor, *v.* 1, *dep. with dat,* to oppose
ădversus, a, um, *adj,* opposite; (of winds) contrary
adversus, *prep. with acc,* opposite
adversum, *adv,* opposite
adverto, ti, sum, *v.t.* 3, to direct towards
ădvespĕrascit, avit, *v. impers,* evening approaches
ădvĭgilo, *v.i.* 1, to keep watch
ădvŏcātĭo, ōnis, *f,* summons, legal assistance
ădvŏcātus, i, *m,* legal adviser
ădvŏco, *v.t.* 1, to call, summon help

For List of Abbreviations used, turn to pages 3, 4

advŏlo, *v.i.* 1, to fly towards
advolvo, vi, ūtum, *v.t.* 3, to roll, grovel before
ădȳtum, i, *n,* sanctuary
aedēs, is, *f,* temple, house
aedĭcŭla, ae, *f,* shrine, niche
aedĭficātor, ōris, *m,* builder
aedĭficĭum, ii, *n,* building
aedĭficātio, ōnis, *f,* constructing
aedĭfico, *v.t.* 1, to build
aedĭlĭcius, a, um, *adj,* of an aedile
aedĭlis, is, *m,* aedile—Roman magistrate
aedĭlĭtas, ātis, *f,* aedileship
aedĭtŭus, i, *m,* verger
aeger, ra, rum, *adj,* ill, sad
aegis, idis, *f,* shield
aegrē, *adv,* with difficulty, scarcely, amiss, with displeasure
aegresco, *v.i.* 3, to fall ill
aegrĭtūdo, ĭnis, *f,* illness, grief
aegrōtātio, ōnis, *f,* sickness
aegrōto, *v.i.* 1, to be ill
aegrōtus, a, um, *adj,* ill
aemŭlātio, ōnis, *f,* rivalry
aemŭlor, *v.t.* 1, *dep,* to rival, envy
aemŭlus, a, um, *adj,* rivalling
āēnĕus, a, um, *adj,* of bronze
aenigma, ătis, *n,* riddle
aequābĭlis, e, *adj, adv,* **ĭter,** similar, uniform
aequābĭlĭtas, ātis, *f,* equality
aequaevus, a, um, *adj,* of equal age
aequālis, e, *adj, adv,* **iter,** level, contemporary
aequālĭtas, ātis, *f,* uniformity
aequē, *adv,* equally, justly
aequilĭbrium, ii, *n,* horizontal position
aequĭnoctium, i, *n,* equinox
aequĭpăro, *v.i.t.* 1, to equal; compare
aequĭtas, ātis, *f,* equality, fairness, calmness
aequo, *v.i.t.* 1, to equalize; match, raze
aequor, ŏris, *n,* even surface, sea
aequum, i, *n,* plain, justice
aequus, a, um, *adj,* flat, friendly, equal, reasonable
āēr, ris, *m,* air
aerāria, ae, *f,* mine
aerārium, i, *n,* treasury
aerārius, a, um, *adj,* of bronze, of the treasury
aerātus, a, um, *adj,* bronze-covered
aerĕus, a, um, *adj,* of bronze
aerĭpes, ĕdis, *adj,* bronze-footed
āĕrius, a, um, *adj,* lofty
aerūgo, ĭnis, *f,* rust, envy
aerumna, ae, *f,* suffering
aerumnōsus, a, um, *adj,* wretched
aes, aeris, *n,* copper, money
aescŭlētum, i, *n,* oak-forest
aescŭlĕus, a, um, *adj,* oaken
aescŭlus, i, *f,* oak
aestas, ātis, *f,* summer
aestĭfer, ĕra, ĕrum, *adj,* hot, sultry
aestĭmābĭlis, e, *adj,* valuable
aestĭmātio, ōnis ,*f,* valuation
aestĭmātor, ōris, *m,* valuer
aestĭmo, *v.t.* 1, to value, assess
aestīva, ōrum, *n.pl,* summer-camp
aestīvus, a, um, *adj, adv,* **ē,** summer-like
aestŭārium, ii, *n,* creek, air-hole
aestŭo, *v.i.* 1, to seethe, glow
aestŭōsus, a, um, *adj, adv,* **ē,** sweltering
aestus, ūs, *m,* heat, tide, rage, excitement
aetas, ātis, *f,* age, life-time
aetātŭla, ae, *f,* tender age
aeternĭtas, ātis, *f,* eternity
aeternus, a, um, *adj, adv,* **um,** everlasting
aether, ĕris, *m,* upper air, heaven
aethĕrius, a, um, *adj,* celestial
Aethiops, ŏpis, *m,* Aethiopian, negro
aethra, ae, *f,* upper air
aevum, i, *n,* lifetime, generation
affābĭlis, e, *adj, adv,* **iter,** courteous
affātim, *adv,* enough
affātus, *partic. from* **affor**
affectātio, ōnis, *f,* pretension, whim
affectātus, a, um, *adj,* far-fetched
affectio, ōnis, *f,* disposition, whim
affecto, *v.t.* 1, to strive after
affectus, ūs, *m,* mood, sympathy
affĕro, afferre, attŭli, allātum, *v.t, irreg,* to bring to, announce, help, produce, confer
afficio, affēci, ctum, *v.t.* 3, to influence, seize
affīgo, xi, xum, *v.t.* 3, to fasten to
affingo, nxi, ictum, *v.t.* 3, to add to, fabricate
affīnis, e, *adj,* neighbouring, related
affinĭtas, ātis, *f,* kinship
affirmātē, *adv,* explicitly
affirmātio, ōnis, *f,* assertion
affirmo, *v.t.* 1, to assert
affixus, a, um, *adj,* fastened to
afflātus, ūs, *m,* breath, blast
afflicto, *v.t.* 1, to trouble, shatter
afflictus, a, um, *adj,* damaged, prostrate
affligo, xi, ctum, *v.t.* 3, to dash to the ground, damage

afflo, *v.t.* 1, to breathe on, inspire
afflŭens, ntis, *adj, adv,* **nter,** rich in
afflŭo, xi, xum, *v.i.* 3, to flow towards, flock in
affor, *v.t.* 1, *dep,* to speak to, accost
affulgĕo, ulsi, *v.i.* 2, to shine on
affundo, ūdi, ūsum, *v.t.* 3, to pour on, in
Āfrĭcus (ventus), S.W. wind
āfui, see **absum**
ăgāso, ōnis, *m,* groom
ăgĕ!, come on!
ăgellus, i, *m,* small field
ăgens, ntis, *adj,* powerful
ăger, gri, *m,* field, territory
agger, ĕris, *m,* mound, rampart
aggĕro, ssi, stum, *v.t.* 3, to convey
aggĕro, *v.t.* 1, to heap up
agglŏmĕro, *v.t.* 1, to add to
aggrăvo, *v.t.* 1, to make heavier or worse
aggrĕdĭor, grĕssus, *v.t.* 3, *dep,* to approach, attack, undertake
aggrĕgo, *v.t.* 1, to adhere, join
aggressus, see **aggrĕdĭor**
ăgilis, e, *adj, adv,* **iter,** active
ăgilĭtas, ātis, *f,* activity
ăgitātio, ōnis, *f,* quick movement, contemplation
ăgĭtātor, ōris, *m,* charioteer
ăgĭtātus, a, um, *adj,* driven, dogged
ăgito, *v.t.* 1, to drive, shake, swing, torment, mock, consider
agmen, ĭnis, *n,* marching column
agna, ae, *f,* ewe lamb
agnātus, a, um, *adj,* related (male line)
agnĭtio, ōnis, *f,* recognition
agnōmen, ĭnis, *n,* surname, additional name
agnosco, nōvi, ĭtum, *v.t.* 3, to recognize, acknowledge
agnus, i, *m,* lamb
ăgo, ēgi, actum, *v.t.* 3, to drive, steal, bring, do, negotiate, pass (time), act, lead (life)
ăgrārius, a, um, *adj,* agrarian
ăgrārii, ōrum, *m.pl,* land reformers
ăgrestis, is, *m,* peasant
ăgrestis, e, *adj,* rural, coarse
agrĭcŏla, ae, *m,* farmer, countryman
agrĭcultūra, ae, *f,* agriculture
āio (parts only), to assert
āla, ae, *f,* wing, armpit, porch
ălăcer, cris, e, *adj, adv,* **iter,** brisk, vigorous
ălăcrĭtas, ātis, *f,* briskness
ălăpa, ae, *f,* slap
ălauda, ae, *f,* lark
albārium, ii, *n,* whitewash
albātus, a, um, *adj,* clothed in white
albĕo, *v.i.* 2, to be white
albesco, *v.i.* 3, to become white
album, i, *n,* whiteness, register
albus, a, um, *adj,* white
alces, is, *f,* elk
alcēdo, ĭnis, *f,* kingfisher
alcȳon, ōnis, *f,* kingfisher
alcȳŏnēus, a, um, *adj,* halcyon
ālĕa, ae, *f,* gambling, a game with dice, chance, hazard
ālĕātor, ōris, *m,* gambler
ālĕs, ĭtis, *adj,* winged
ālĕs, ĭtis, *c,* bird
alga, ae, *f,* sea-weed
algĕo, si, *v.i.* 2, to feel cold
algĭdus, a, um, *adj,* cold
algor, ōris, *m,* coldness
ălĭā, *adv,* in a different way
ălĭās . . . ălĭās, *adv,* at one time . . . at another time, otherwise
ălĭbi, *adv,* elsewhere
ălĭcŭbi, *adv,* somewhere
ălĭcunde, *adv,* from somewhere
ăliēnātio, ōnis, *f,* transfer, aversion, delirium
ăliēnātus, a, um, *adj,* alienated
ăliēnĭgĕna, ae, *m,* foreigner
ăliēno, *v.t.* 1, to transfer, estrange
ăliēnus, a, um, *adj,* someone else's, strange, hostile, unsuitable
ăliēnus, i, *m,* stranger
ăliēnum, i, *n,* stranger's property
ālĭger, ĕra, ĕrum, *adj,* winged
ălii, see **ălius**
ălĭmentum, i, *n,* nourishment
ălĭmōnium, ii, *n,* nourishment
ăliō, *adv,* to another place
ăliōquĭ(n), *adv,* in other respects
ālĭpēs, ĕdis, *adj,* wing-footed
ăliquā, *adv,* somehow
ăliquamdiū, *adv,* for some time
ăliquando, *adv,* at some time
ăliquantus, a, um, *adj, adv,* **ō, um,** somewhat, some
ăliqui, qua, quod, *pron, adj,* some, any
ăliquis, quid, *pron,* someone, something
ăliquō, *adv,* to some place
ăliquot, *adj,* several
ăliquŏties, *adv,* at different times
ălĭter, *adv,* otherwise
ăliunde, *adv,* from elsewhere
ălius, a, ud, *pron, adj,* other, different
allābor, psus, *v.* 3, *dep,* to glide, flow towards
allapsus, ūs, *m,* stealthy approach
allātro, *v.t.* 1, to bark at
allecto, *v.t.* 1, to entice
allĕgo, *v.t.* 1, to commission
allĕgo, ēgi, ectum, *v.t.* 3, to elect

allēgŏrĭa, ae, *f,* allegory
allĕvātio, ōnis, *f,* raising up
allĕvo, *v.t.* 1, to lift up, relieve
allĭcĭo, exi, ectum, *v.t.* 3, to attract
allĭdo, si, sum, *v.t.* 3, to strike
allĭgo, *v.t.* 1, to bind, fasten
allĭno, ēvi, ĭtum, *v.t.* 3, to bedaub
allĭum, i, *n,* garlic
allŏcūtio, ōnis, *f,* address
allŏquĭum, ii, *n,* exhortation
allŏquor, lŏcūtus, *v.t.* 3, *dep,* to speak to, exhort, console
allūdo, si, sum, *v.i.t.* 3, to play, joke; sport with
allŭo, ŭi, *v.t.* 3, to wash against, bathe
allŭvies, ēi, *f,* pool
allŭvio, ōnis, *f,* inundation
almus, a, um, *adj,* nourishing, kind
alnus, i, *f,* alder
ălo, ŭi, altum, *v.t.* 3, to nourish, cherish, encourage
alŏē, ēs, *f,* aloe
alpīnus, a, um, *adj,* Alpine
alsĭus, a, um, *adj,* cold, chilly
alsus, a, um, *adj,* cold, chilly
altāre, altāris, *n,* high altar
altārĭa, ĭum, *n.pl,* high altar
alter, ĕra, ĕrum, *adj,* one or the other of two, second
altercātio, ōnis, *f,* dispute
altercor, *v.i.* 1, *dep,* to quarrel
alterno, *v.i.t.* 1, to hesitate; alternate
alternus, a, um, *adj,* alternate
altĕrŭter, ra, rum, *adj,* one or the other, either
altĭlis, e, *adj,* fattened, rich
altĭsŏnus, a, um, *adj,* high sounding
altĭtūdo, ĭnis, *f,* height, depth
altor, ōris, *m,* foster-father
altrix, īcis, *f,* foster-mother
altum, i, *n,* the deep (sea)
altus, a, um, *adj,* high, deep, great
ālūcĭnor, *v.i.* 1, *dep,* to wander in the mind
ălumna, ae, *f,* foster-child
ălumnus, i, *m,* foster-child
ălūta, ae, *f,* soft leather
alvĕārĭum, ii, *n,* beehive
alvĕus, i, *m,* salver, channel, canoe
alvus, i, *f,* belly, stomach
āmābĭlis, e, *adj, adv,* **ĭter,** lovable, amiable
āmandō, *v.t.* 1, to remove
ămans, ntis, *adj,* fond
ămans, ntis, *m,* lover
ămārĭties, ēi, *f,* bitterness
ămārus, a, um, *adj,* bitter
ămātor, ōris, *m,* lover
ămātōrĭum, ii, *n,* love-philtre
ămātōrĭus, a, um, *adj,* amatory
ambactus, i, *m,* vassal
ambāges, is, *f,* roundabout way
ambĭgo, *v.i.* 3, to waver, go about
ambĭgŭĭtas, ātis, *f,* double sense
ambĭgŭum, i, *n,* uncertainty
ambĭgŭus, a, um, *adj, adv,* **ē,** doubtful, changeable
ambĭo, *v.i.t.* 4, to go round; solicit
ambĭtĭo, ōnis, *f,* canvassing
ambĭtĭōsus, a, um, *adj, adv,* **ē,** embracing, fawning
ambĭtus, ūs, *m,* going round, circuit, bribery
ambō, ae, ō, *adj,* both
ambrŏsĭa, ae, *f,* food of the gods
ambrŏsĭus, a, um, *adj,* immortal
ambŭlātio, ōnis, *f,* walk
ambŭlātor, ōris, *m,* walker
ambŭlo, *v.i.* 1, to walk, lounge
ambūro, ssi, stum, *v.t.* 3, to singe
ambustum, i, *n,* burn
amellus, i, *m,* star-wort
āmens, ntis, *adj,* out of one's mind
āmentĭa, ae, *f,* madness
āmentum, i, *n,* strap
ămēs, ĭtis, *m,* pole, shaft
ămĕthystus, i, *f,* amethyst
ămĭca, ae, *f,* mistress
ămĭcio, ŭi, ctum, *v.t.* 4, to wrap
ămĭcĭtĭa, ae, *f,* friendship
ămictus, ūs, *m,* cloak
ămĭcŭlum, i, *n,* cloak
ămĭcus, i, *m,* friend
ămĭcus, a, um, *adj, adv,* **ē,** friendly
āmissio, ōnis, *f,* loss
ămĭta, ae, *f,* paternal aunt
āmitto, misi, missum, *v.t.* 3, to let go, dismiss, lose
amnis, is, *m,* river
ămo, *v.t.* 1, to love, like
ămoenĭtas, ātis, *f,* pleasantness
ămoenus, a, um, *adj, adv,* **ē,** charming
āmŏlior, *v.t.* 4, *dep,* to remove, refute
ămor, ōris, *m,* love, desire
āmŏvĕo, mōvi, tum, *v.t.* 2, to remove
amphithĕātrum, i, *n,* amphitheatre
amphŏra, ae, *f,* two-handled jar
amplector, xus, *v.t.* 3, *dep,* to embrace
amplexus, ūs, *m,* embrace
amplĭfĭcātio, ōnis, *f,* enlargement
amplĭfĭco, *v.t.* 1, to enlarge
amplio, *v.t.* 1, to enlarge
amplĭtūdo, ĭnis, *f,* width, size
amplĭus, *comp. adv,* more
amplus, a, um, *adj, adv,* **ē, ĭter,** spacious, great, glorious
ampulla, ae, *f,* bottle
ampŭtātio, ōnis, *f,* pruning
ampŭto, *v.t.* 1, to cut away
ămurca, ae, *f,* dregs of oil

ămȳlum, i, *n,* starch
ăn, *conj,* or: also used to introduce a question
ănăphŏrā, ae, *f,* recurrence
ănăs, ătis, *f,* duck
ănăticŭla, ae, *f,* duckling
anceps, cipitis, *adj,* two-headed, doubtful
ancīle, is, *n,* oval shield
ancilla, ae, *f,* maidservant
ancŏra, ae, *f,* anchor
ancŏrāle, is, *n,* cable
ānellus, i, *m,* small ring
anfractus, ūs, *m,* circuitous route, digression
angīna, ae, *f,* quinsy
angiportus, ūs, *m,* alley
ango, xi, ctum, *v.t.* 3, to strangle, torment
angor, ōris, *m,* strangling, distress
anguilla, ae, *f,* eel
anguīnĕus, a, um, *adj,* snaky
anguipēs, ĕdis, *adj,* snake-footed
anguis, is, *c,* snake
angŭlātus, a, um, *adj,* angular
angŭlāris, e, *adj,* angular
angŭlus, i, *m,* corner
angustĭae, ārum, *f.pl,* defile, straits, difficulties
angustus, a, um, *adj, adv,* **ē,** narrow, difficult
ănhēlĭtus, ūs, *m,* panting, vapour
ănhēlo, *v.i.t.* 1, to pant; exhale
ănhēlus, a, um, *adj,* panting
ănĭcŭla, ae, *f,* little old woman
ănĭlis, e, *adj, adv,* iter, old womanish
ănĭma, ae, *f,* breeze, breath, life, soul
ănĭmadversĭo, ōnis, *f,* attention, reproof
ănĭmadverto, ti, sum, *v.t.* 3, to pay attention to, notice, punish
ănĭmăl, ālis, *n,* animal
ănĭmālis, e, *adj, adv,* iter of air, living
ănĭmans, ntis, *adj,* living
ănĭmātus, a, um, *adj,* disposed, courageous
ănĭmo, *v.i.t.* 1, to have life; revive, give life to
ănĭmōsus, a, um, *adj, adv,* **ē,** bold
ănĭmōsus, a, um, *adj,* gusty, living, spirited
ănĭmus, i, *m,* soul, mind, memory, opinion, anger, purpose, courage, attitude
annāles, ĭum, *m.pl,* chronicles
annālis, e, *adj,* annual
annĕ—introduces a question
annecto, xŭi, xum, *v.t.* 3, to fasten to, add
annĭtor, nĭsus (nixus), *v.i.* 3, *dep,* to lean against, exert oneself
ănniversārĭus, a, um, *adj,* anniversary
anno, *v.i.* 1, to swim to
annon, *conj,* or not
annōna, ae, *f,* annual produce, grain price
annōsus, a, um, *adj,* old
annōtātĭo, ōnis, *f,* annotation, note
annōto, *v.t.* 1, to note down
annŭa, ōrum, *n.pl,* annuity
annŭmĕro, *v.t.* 1, to pay, include
annŭo, ŭi, ūtum, *v.i.* 3, to nod, assent
annus, i, *m,* year
annŭus, a, um, *adj,* annual, yearly
ănōmălĭa, ae, *f,* anomaly
anquīro, sīvi, sītum, *v.t.* 3, to search for
ansa, ae, *f,* handle, opportunity
anser, ĕris, *m,* goose
antĕ, *prep. with acc,* before, in front of
antĕ (antĕā), *adv,* before
antĕcēdo, ssi, ssum, *v.i.t.* 3, to distinguish oneself; precede
antĕcello, *v.i.t.* 3, to be outstanding; surpass
antĕcessĭo, ōnis, *f,* antecedent
antĕcursor, ōris, *m,* advanced guard
antĕ-ĕo, *v.i.* 4, to go before, excel
antĕfĕro, ferre, tŭli, lātum, *v.t., irreg,* to carry in front, prefer
antĕgrĕdĭor, gressus, *v.t.* 3, *dep,* to go in front
antĕhāc, *adv,* previously
antĕlūcānus, a, um, *adj,* before daybreak
antĕmĕrīdiānus, a, um, *adj,* before midday
antĕmitto, mĭsi, missum, *v.t.* 3, to send on
antenna, ae, *f,* sail-yard
antĕpōno, pŏsŭi, ĭtum, *v.t.* 3, to place in front
antĕquam, *conj,* before
antĕris, ĭdis, *f,* buttress (*pl.*)
antes, ĭum, *m.pl,* ranks
antĕsignānus, i, *m,* in front of the standard, selected soldier
antesto, ĕti, *v.i.* 1, to stand before, excel
antestor, *v.* 1, *dep,* to call a witness
antĕverto, ti, sum, *v.t.* 3, to precede, anticipate
anthrōpŏphăgus, i, *m,* cannibal
antĭcus, a, um, *adj,* foremost
anticĭpo, *v.t.* 1, to anticipate
antidŏtum, i, *n,* remedy
antipŏdes, um, *m.pl,* antipodes
antĭquĭtas, ātis, *f,* age, olden times
antĭqui, ōrum, *m.pl,* old writers

For List of Abbreviations used, turn to pages 3, 4

antĭquus, a, um, *adj, adv,* **ē,** old
antistēs, ĭtis, *m, f,* high priest
antistĭta, ae, *f,* high priestess
antlĭa, ae, *f,* pump
antrum, i, *n,* cave
ănŭlus, i, *m,* ring
ănus, ūs, *f,* old woman
anxiĕtas, ātis, *f,* anxiety
anxĭus, a, um, *adj, adv,* **ē,** troubled
ăpăgē!, *interj,* begone!
ăper, pri, *m,* wild boar
ăpĕrio, rŭi, rtum, *v.t.* 4, to open, explain
ăpertus, a, um, *adj, adv,* **ē,** open, frank
ăpex, ĭcis, *m,* summit, crown
ăpis, is, *f,* bee
ăpiscor, aptus, *v.t.* 3, *dep,* to reach for, acquire
ăpĭum, ii, *n,* parsley
āplustre, is, *n,* stern
ăpo, — aptum, *v.t.* 3, to fasten
ăpŏcha, ae, *f,* receipt
ăpŏthēca, ae, *f,* store-place
appărātio, ōnis, *f,* preparation
appărātus, a, um, *adj, adv,* **ē,** ready, elaborate
appărātus, ūs, *m,* preparation, apparatus, pomp
appārĕo, *v.i.* 2, to appear
appāritio, ōnis, *f,* service
appāritor, ōris, *m,* public servant
appăro, *v.t.* 1, to prepare
appellātio, ōnis, *f,* calling, appeal, title
appellātor, ōris, *m,* appellant
appellātus, a, um, *adj,* called
appello, ŭli, ulsum, *v.t.* 3, to drive towards, land
appello, *v.t.* 1, to speak to, appeal to, name
appendix, ĭcis, *f,* supplement
appendo, ndi, nsum, *v.t.* 3, to weigh
appĕtens, ntis, *adj, adv,* **nter,** eager for
appĕtentĭa, ae, *f,* desire
appĕtĭtio, ōnis, *f,* desire
appĕtĭtus, ūs, *m,* attack, passion
appĕto, ii, ĭtum, *v.i.t.* 3, to approach; strive after
applĭcātio, ōnis, *f,* inclination
applĭco, *v.t.* 1, to affix, attach, steer
appōno, pŏsŭi, sĭtum, *v.t.* 3, to put near, apply, add
apporto, *v.t.* 1, to conduct
appŏsĭtus, *adj, adv,* **ē,** bordering, suitable
apprĕhendo, di, sum, *v.t.* 3, to seize, understand
apprīmus, a, um, *adj, adv,* **ē,** very first
approbātio, ōnis, *f,* sanction
approbo, *v.t.* 1, to approve, make satisfactory
appropĕro, *v.i.t.* 1, to hurry; speed up
appropinquātio, ōnis, *f,* approach
appropinquo, *v.i.* 1, to approach
appulsus, ūs, *m,* landing, approach
āprīcātio, ōnis, *f,* sunning
āprīcor, *v.i.* 1, *dep,* to sun oneself
āprīcus, a, um, *adj,* sunny
Āprīlis (mensis), April
aptātus, a, um, *adj,* suitable
apto, *v.t.* 1, to adjust
aptus, a, um, *adj, adv,* **ē,** suitable
ăpŭd, *with acc,* at the house of, in the works of, amongst, near
ăqua, ae, *f,* water, rain; *pl.* spa
ăquaeductus, ūs, *m,* aqueduct
ăquālis, is, *c,* wash-basin
ăquārĭus, ii, *m,* water-bearer, a Sign of the Zodiac
ăquātĭcus, a, um, *adj,* watery
ăquātĭlis, e, *adj,* aquatic
ăquātio, ōnis, *f,* water-fetching
ăquātor, ōris, *m,* water-carrier
ăquĭla, ae, *f,* eagle, standard
ăquĭlĭfer, ĕri, *m,* standard-bearer
ăquĭlīnus, a, um, *adj,* aquiline
ăquĭlo, ōnis, *m,* north wind, north
ăquĭlōnāris, e, *adj,* northern
ăquor, *v.i.* 1, *dep,* to fetch water
ăquōsus, a, um, *adj,* moist, rainy
ăra, ae, *f,* altar
ărānĕa, ae, *f,* spider, web
ărānĕus, i, *m,* spider, web
ărātio, ōnis, *f,* cultivation
ărātor, ōris, *m,* ploughman
ărātrum, i, *n,* plough
arbĭter, tri, *m,* witness, umpire
arbĭtrātus, ūs, *m,* free-will
arbĭtrĭum, ii, *n,* verdict, power, inclination
arbĭtror, *v.i.* 1, *dep,* to think, decide
arbor, ŏris, *f,* tree
arbŏrĕus, a, um, *adj,* tree-like
arbustum, i, *n,* plantation
arbŭtum, i, *n,* wild strawberry
arbŭtus, i, *f,* wild strawberry tree
arca, ae, *f,* box, dungeon
arcānus, a, um, *adj, adv,* **ō,** secret
arcĕo, *v.t.* 2, to confine, keep off
arcessĭtus, a, um, *adj,* sent for, far-fetched
arcesso, sīvi, sĭtum, *v.t.* 3, to send for
architector, *v.t.* 1, *dep,* to design
architectūra, ae, *f,* architecture
architectus, i, *m,* architect

arcĭtĕnens, ntis, *adj*, armed with bow
arctŏs, i, *f*, Bear, North Pole
arctūrus, i, *m*, chief star in constellation Boötes
arcŭla, ae, *f*, small box
arcŭo, *v.t.* 1, to bend
arcus, ūs, *m*, rainbow, arch
ardĕa, ae, *f*, heron
ardens, ntis, *adj*, *adv*, **nter,** burning, eager
ardĕo, arsi, sum, *v.i.* 2, to burn, be eager
ardesco, arsi, *v.i.* 3, to catch fire
ardor, ōris, *m*, blaze, desire
ardŭus, a, um, *adj*, high, difficult
ārĕa, ae, *f*, open space, threshing-floor
ārēna, ae, *f*, sand, arena
ārēnātum, i, *n*, mortar, plaster
ārēnōsus, a, um, *adj*, sandy
ārens, ntis, *adj*, parched
ārĕo, *v.i.* 2, to be dry
āresco, ŭi, *v.i.* 3, to dry up
argentāria, ae, *f*, bank, silver-mine
argentārius, ii, *m*, banker, broker
argentātus, a, um, *adj*, silver-plated
argentĕus, a, um, *adj*, silver
argentum, i, *n*, silver, money
argilla, ae, *f*, white clay
argūmentātio, ōnis, *f*, proof
argūmentor, *v.i.* 1, *dep*, to prove
argūmentum, i, *n*, proof, content, artistic aim
argŭo, ŭi, ūtum, *v.t.* 3, to prove, accuse, convict
argūtiae, ārum, *f.pl*, liveliness
argūtus, a, um, *adj*, *adv*, **ē,** clear, witty, rattling
ārĭdĭtas, ātis, *f*, dryness
ārĭdum, i, *n*, dry land
ārĭdus, a, um, *adj*, dry
ărĭēs, tis, *m*, ram, battering-ram
ărista, ae, *f*, ear of corn
ărĭthmētica, ōrum, *n.pl*, arithmetic
arma, ōrum, *n.pl*, armour, shield, weapons, army, equipment
armāmenta, ōrum, *n.pl*, gear, tackle
armāmentārium, ii, *n*, arsenal
armāmentum, i, *n*, ship's tackle
armārium, ii, *n*, cupboard
armātura, ae, *f*, equipment, (light-) armed troops
armātus, a, um, *adj*, equipped
armentārius, ii, *m*, herdsman
armentum, i, *n*, plough-animal, herd
armifer, ĕra, ĕrum, *adj*, warlike, armoured
armiger, ĕra, ĕrum, *adj*, warlike, armoured
armilla, ae, *f*, bracelet
armipŏtens, ntis, *adj*, valiant
armisŏnus, a, um, *adj*, with clashing armour
armo, *v.t.* 1, to arm, equip
armus, i, *m*, shoulder, side
ăro, *v.t.* 1, to plough
arquātus, a, um, *adj*, bent
arrectus, a, um, *adj*, steep
arrēpo, psi, ptum, *v.i.* 3, to creep towards
arrha, ae, *f*, money given as a pledge
arrĭdĕo, si, sum, *v.i.* 2, to laugh at, favour
arrĭgo, rexi, rectum, *v.t.* 3, to erect, excite
arripio, ŭi, reptum, *v.t.* 3, to seize, indict
arrŏgans, ntis, *pres. partic*, *adj*, *adv*, **nter,** haughty
arrŏgantia, ae, *f*, haughtiness
arrŏgo, *v.t.* 1, to claim, confer
ars, tis, *f*, art, skill, theory, habit, stratagem
artē, *adv*, closely
arthrĭticus, a, um, *adj*, arthritic
articŭlātim, *adv*, piece by piece
articŭlo, *v.t.* 1, to articulate
articŭlus, i, *m*, joint, movement
artĭfex, ficis, *m*, artist, author
artificiōsus, a, um, *adj*, *adv*, **ē,** skilful
artĭficium, ii, *n*, trade, skill; (*pl*) intrigue
arto, *v.t.* 1, to compress
artus, ūs, *m*, limb
artus, a, um, *adj*, *adv*, **ē,** confined
ărun, ărus . . . see **hărun, hărus . .**
arvīna, ae, *f*, grease
arvum, i, *n*, cultivated land
arvus, a, um, *adj*, ploughed
arx, cis, *f*, citadel
as, assis, *m*, pound weight, coin
ascendo, ndi, nsum, *v.i.t.* 3, to climb
ascensus, ūs, *m*, ascent
ascĭa, ae, *f*, adze
ascĭo, *v.t.* 4, to receive
ascisco, īvi, ītum, *v.t.* 3, to admit
ascītus, ūs, *m*, reception
ascrĭbo, psi, ptum, *v.t.* 3, to insert, enrol, attribute
ascriptīvus, a, um, *adj*, supernumerary
ascriptus, a, um, *adj*, appointed
ăsella, ae, *f*, small ass
ăsellus, i, *m*, small ass
ăsinus, i, *m*, ass, simpleton
aspectābilis, e, *adj*, visible
aspecto, *v.t.* 1, to look at eagerly
aspectus, ūs, *m*, look, sight
asper, ĕra, ĕrum, *adj*, *adv*, **ē,** rough, bitter, austere, adverse
aspĕrĭtas, ātis, *f*, roughness
aspĕrum, i, *n*, rough ground

aspergo, si, sum, *v.t.* 3, to scatter, sprinkle, defile
aspergo, ĭnis, *f*, sprinkling, spray
aspĕritas, ātis, *f*, roughness
aspernātio, ōnis, *f*, disdain
aspernor, *v.t.* 1, *dep*, to despise
aspĕro, *v.t.* 1, to roughen, rouse
aspersio, ōnis, *f*, sprinkling
aspĭcio, exi, ectum, *v.t.* 3, to look at
aspīrātio, ōnis, *f*, exhalation
aspīro, *v.i.t.* 1, to aspire to; breathe on
aspis, ĭdis, *f*, adder
asporto, *v.t.* 1, to carry away
assĕcla, ae, *c*, attendant
assectātio, ōnis, *f*, attendance
assectātor, ōris, *m*, follower
assector, *v.t.* 1, *dep*, to wait upon
assensio, ōnis, *f*, approval
assensus, ūs, *m*, approval
assentātio, ōnis, *f*, flattery
assentātor, ōris, *m*, flatterer
assentior, sus, *v.* 4, *dep. with dat*, to agree with
assentor, *v.* 1, *dep. with dat*, to flatter
assĕquor, sĕcūtus, *v.t.* 3, *dep*, to pursue, overtake, comprehend
asser, ĕris, *m*, stake
assĕro, rŭi, sertum, *v.t.* 3, to claim, set free
assertor, ōris, *m*, protector
asservo, *v.t.* 1, to keep, guard
assessor, ōris, *m*, assessor
assĕvĕrātio, ōnis, *f*, assertion
assĕvĕro, *v.t.* 1, to assert
assĭdĕo, sēdi, sessum, *v.i.* 2, to sit by, wait upon, blockade, resemble
assĭdŭitas, ātis, *f*, constant presence
assĭdŭus, a, um, *adj, adv*, ē, constantly present
assignātio, ōnis, *f*, allotment
assigno, *v.t.* 1, to distribute
assĭlio, ŭi, sultum, *v.i.* 4, to spring upon
assĭmĭlis, e, *adj, adv*, ĭter, like
assĭmŭlo, *v.i.t.* 1, to resemble; imitate
assĭmŭlātus, a, um, *adj*, similar
assisto, astĭti, *v.i.* 3, to stand near, aid
assŏlĕo, *v.i.* 2, to be in the habit of doing
assŭefăcio, fēci, factum, *v.t.* 3, to make someone used to
assŭesco, ēvi, ētum, *v.i.t.* 3, to become used to; familiarise
assŭētūdo, ĭnis, *f*, habit
assŭētus, a, um, *adj*, customary
assulto, *v.t.* 1, to jump on, attack
assultus, ūs, *m*, attack
assūmo, mpsi, mptum, *v.t.* 3, to take up, adopt
assŭo, *v.t.* 3, to sew on
assurgo, surrexi, rectum, *v.i.* 3, to rise, stand up
assŭla, ae, *f*, splinter, chip
assus, a, um, *adj*, roasted; **assa, ōrum,** *n.pl*, turkish bath
ast, see **at**
astĭpŭlātor, ōris, *m*, assistant
astĭpŭlor, *v.* 1, *dep. with dat.* to bargain with
asto, stĭti, *v.i.* 1, to stand near
astrĕpo, *v.i.t.* 3, to make a noise; applaud
astringo, nxi, ctum, *v.t.* 3, to bind, fasten, cool, limit
astrictus, a, um, *adj, adv*, ē, tight, concise
astrŏlŏgĭa, ae, *f*, astronomy
astrŏlŏgus, i, *m*, astronomer
astrum, i, *n*, star, constellation
astrŭo, xi, ctum, *v.t.* 3, to build near, add
astŭpĕo, *v.i.* 2, to be astonished
astus, ūs, *m*, dexterity, craft
astūtia, ae, *f*, dexterity, slyness
astūtus, a, um, *adj, adv*, ē, shrewd, sly
ăsylum, i, *n*, place of refuge
at, *conj*, but, on the other hand
ătăvĭa, ae, *f*, ancestor
ătăvus, i, *m*, ancestor
āter, tra, trum, *adj*, black, deadly
ăthĕos, i, *m*, atheist
athlēta, ae, *c*, wrestler, athlete
ătŏmus, i, *f*, atom
atque, *conj*, and, and also
atqui, *conj*, but, nevertheless
ātrāmentum, i, *n*, ink, varnish
ātrātus, a, um, *adj*, in mourning
ātrĭensis, is, *m*, house-steward
ātrĭŏlum, i, *n*, ante-room
ātrium, ii, *n*, hall, forecourt
ătrōcitas, ātis, harshness, cruelty
ătrox, ōcis, *adj, adv*, ĭter, horrible, fierce, stern
attactus, ūs, *m*, touch
attămen, *adv*, but nevertheless
attendo, di, tum, *v.t.* 3, to stretch out, give attention to
attentio, ōnis, *f*, attention
attento, *v.t.* 1, to try, attack
attentus, a, um, *adj, adv*, ē, engrossed, frugal
attĕnŭo, *v.t.* 1, to impair, reduce
attĕro, trīvi, trĭtum, *v.t.* 3, to rub away, exhaust
attĭnĕo, ŭi, tentum, *v.i.t.* 2, to stretch, concern; retain
attingo, tigi, tactum, *v.t.* 3, to touch, reach, attack
attollo, *v.t.* 3, to raise
attondĕo, di, sum, *v.t.* 2, to shear

attŏnĭtus, a, um, *adj, adv,* **ē,** astonished
attŏno, ŭi, ĭtum, *v.t.* 1, to stun
attorquĕo, *v.t.* 2, to hurl
attrăho, xi, ctum, *v.t.* 3, to drag towards, attract
attrecto, *v.t.* 1, to handle
attrĭbŭo, ŭi, ūtum, *v.t.* 3, to assign
attrĭbūtum, i, *n,* predicate
attrĭtus, ūs, *m,* rubbing against
auceps, ŭpis, *c,* bird-catcher, eavesdropper
auctio, ōnis, *f,* auction, increase
auctiōnor, *v.i.* 1, *dep,* to hold an auction
auctor, ōris, *c,* creator, master, witness, supporter, author
auctŏritas, ātis, *f,* influence, power
auctumnālis, e, *adj,* autumnal
auctumnus, a, um, *adj,* autumnal
auctumnus, i, *m,* autumn
auctus, a, um, *adj,* enlarged
auctus, ūs, *m,* increase
aucŭpium, ii, *n,* bird-catching
aucŭpor, *v.i.t.* 1, *dep,* to go bird-catching; pursue, watch for
audācia, ae, *f,* boldness, insolence
audax, ācis, *adj, adv,* **cter,** bold, rash
audens, ntis, *adj, adv,* **nter,** bold
audentia, ae, *f,* boldness
audĕo, ausus, *v.i.t.* 2 (*semi-dep.*), to dare
audientia, ae, *f,* hearing, audience
audio, *v.t.* 4, to hear, understand, obey
auditio, ōnis, *f,* a hearing, report
auditor, ōris, *m,* hearer, pupil
auditus, ūs, *m,* sense of hearing
aufĕro, ferre, abstŭli, ablātum, *v.t, irreg,* to take away, rob, obtain
aufŭgio, fūgi, ĭtum, *v.i.* 3, to run away
augĕo, xi, ctum, *v.i.t.* 2, to grow; enlarge
augesco, *v.i.* 3, to grow
augur, ŭris, *c,* diviner, prophet
augŭrālis, e, *adj,* prophetic
augŭrātus, ūs, *m,* office of augur
augŭrium, ii, *n,* omen, augury
augŭrius, a, um, *adj,* augural
augŭror, *v.t.* 1, *dep,* to prophesy, suppose
augustus, a, um, *adj, adv,* **ē,** venerable
aula, ae, *f,* palace, court
aulaeum, i, *n,* curtain
aulicus, i, *m,* courtier
aura, ae, *f,* air, soft breeze, sky, publicity, gleam
aurāria, ae, *f,* gold mine
aurātus, a, um, *adj,* gilded
aurĕus, i, *m,* gold piece
auricŏmus, a, um, *adj,* golden-haired
auricŭla, ae, *f,* ear
aurifer, ĕra, ĕrum, *adj,* gold-producing
aurifex, ĭcis, *m,* goldsmith
auriga, ae, *c,* charioteer
auriger, ĕra, ĕrum, *adj,* bearing gold
auris, is, *f,* ear
aurītus, a, um, *adj,* long-eared
aurōra, ae, *f,* dawn
aurum, i, *n,* gold
ausculto, *v.i.t.* 1, to listen
auspex, ĭcis, *c,* diviner
auspicātō, *adv,* after taking the auspices
auspicium, ii, *n,* divination
auspicor, *v.i.t.* 1, *dep,* to take the auspices, begin
auster, tri, *m,* south wind
austērus, a, um, *adj, adv,* **ē,** harsh, severe
austrālis, e, *adj,* southern
austrīnus, a, um, *adj,* southern
ausum, i, *n,* bold attempt
aut, *conj,* or, **aut . . . aut,** either . . . or
autem, *conj,* but
autumnālis, *adj,* autumnal
autumnus, a, um, *adj,* autumnal
autūmo, *v.i.* 1, to assert
auxilĭa, ōrum, *n.pl,* auxiliary troops
auxiliāris, e, *adj,* helping
auxiliāres, ium, *m.pl,* auxiliary troops
auxilĭor, *v.* 1, *dep. with dat.* to help
auxilium ii, *n,* help
āvāritia, ae, *f,* greediness
āvārus, a, um, *adj, adv,* **ē,** greedy
āve! (*pl,* **āvete**), hail! farewell!
āvĕho, vexi, ctum, *v.t.* 3, to carry away
āvello, velli, vulsum, *v.t.* 3, to tear away
āvēna, ae, *f,* oats, shepherd's pipe
āvēnācĕus, a, um, *adj,* oaten
āvĕo, *v.t.* 2, to long for
āvĕo, *v.i.* 2, to be well
āversor, *v.t.* 1, *dep,* to turn away from, avoid
āversor, ōris, *m,* embezzler
āversus, a, um, *adj,* backwards, hostile
āverto, ti, sum, *v.t.* 3, to push aside, steal, estrange
āvĭa, ae, *f,* grandmother
āvĭārium, ii, *n,* bird-haunts
āvĭditas, ātis, *f,* eagerness, desire
āvĭdus, a, um, *adj, adv,* **ē,** greedy
āvis, is, *f,* bird
āvĭtus, a, um, *adj,* ancestral
āvĭum, ii, *n,* pathless place
āvĭus, a, um, *adj,* pathless
āvŏcātio, ōnis, *f,* calling away, distraction

For List of Abbreviations used, turn to pages 3, 4

āvŏco, *v.t.* 1, to call away
āvŏlo, *v.i.* 1, to fly away
ăvuncŭlus, i, *m*, uncle
ăvus, i, *m*, grandfather
axis, is, *m*, axle, chariot, region

B

bāca, ae, *f*, berry
bācātus, a, um, *adj*, pearl-set
baccar, ăris, *n*, fox-glove
baccha, ae, *f*, bacchanal
bacchānālia, ĭum, *n.pl*, orgies of Bacchus
bacchātio, ōnis, *f*, orgy
bacchor, *v.i.* 1, *dep*, to rave
bācifer, ĕra, ĕrum, *adj*, berry-bearing
băcillum, i, *n*, stick
băcŭlum, i, *n*, stick, sceptre
bāiŭlo, *v.t.* 1, to carry a load
bāiŭlus, i, *m*, porter
bālaena, ae, *f*, whale
bălănus, i, *f*, acorn
bălātro, ōnis, *m*, comedian
bālātus, ūs, *m*, bleating
balbus, a, um, *adj*, *adv*, **ē**, stammering
balbūtio, *v.i.t.* 4, to stammer
ballista, ae, *f*, artillery engine
balnĕae, ārum, *f.pl*, baths
balnĕātor, ōris, *m*, bath-keeper
balnĕum, i, *n*, bath
bālo, *v.i.* 1, to bleat
balsămum, i, *n*, balm
baltĕus, i, *m*, belt, sword-belt
bărāthrum, i, *n*, abyss
barba, ae, *f*, beard
barbăria, ae, *f*, foreign country, rudeness
barbărus, i, *m*, foreigner, stranger
barbărus, a, um, *adj*, *adv*, **ē**, foreign, rude, savage
barbātus, a, um, *adj*, bearded
barbĭtos, *m*, *f*, (*pl*, **a**), lute, lyre
bardus, a, um, *adj*, stupid
bāro, ōnis, *m*, blockhead
barrus, i, *m*, elephant
băsĭlica, ae, *f*, town-hall
băsĭlĭcus, a, um, *adj*, royal
bāsio, *v.t.* 1, to kiss
băsis, is, *f*, pedestal, base
bāsium, ii, *n*, kiss
battŭo, ūi, *v.i.t.* 3, to fence; beat
bĕātĭtas, ātis, *f*, happiness
bĕātĭtūdo, ĭnis, *f*, happiness
bĕātus, a, um, *adj*, *adv*, **ē**, happy, fortunate
bellans, see **bello**
bellāria, ōrum, *n.pl*, dessert
bellātor, ōris, *m*, warrior
bellātrix, īcis, *f*, female-warrior
bellē, *adv*, prettily
bellĭcōsus, a, um, *adj*, warlike
bellĭcum, i, *n*, signal for march or attack
bellĭcus, a, um, *adj*, military
belliger, ĕra, ĕrum, *adj*, warlike
belligĕro, *v.t.* 1, to wage war
bellis, ĭdis, *f*, daisy
bello, *v.i.* 1 (**bellor**, *v.* 1, *dep*), to make war
bellum, i, *n*, war
bellus, a, um, *adj*, pretty
bēlŭa, ae, *f*, beast
bĕnĕ, *adv*, well, very
bĕnĕdīco, xi, ctum, *v.i.t.* 3, to praise
bĕnĕdictio, ōnis, *f*, blessing
bĕnĕfăcio, fēci, factum, *v.t.* 3, to do well, oblige
bĕnĕfactum, i, *n*, good deed
bĕnĕficentia, ae, *f*, kind treatment
bĕnĕficiārii, ōrum, *m.pl*, privileged soldiers (excused fatigues)
bĕnĕficium, ii, *n*, a kindness
bĕnĕficus, a, um, *adj*, obliging
bĕnĕvŏlentia, ae, *f*, good will
bĕnĕvŏlus, a, um, *adj*, *adv*, **ē**, well-disposed
bĕnignē, *adv*, thank you; no thank you; courteously
bĕnignus, a, um, *adj*, kind, fruitful
bĕnignĭtas, ātis, *f*, kindness
bĕo, *v.t.* 1, to bless, enrich
bes, bessis, *m*, eight ounces
bestia, ae, *f*, wild beast
bestiārius, ii, *m*, wild-beast fighter
bestiŏla, ae, *f*, small animal
bēta, ae, *f*, beet
betŭla, ae, *f*, birch
biblĭa, ōrum, *n.pl*, the Bible
bibliŏpōla, ae, *m*, bookseller
bibliŏthēca, ae, *f*, library
bibliŏthēcārius, ii, *m*, librarian
bĭbo, bĭbi, ĭtum, *v.t.* 3, to drink
bĭbŭlus, a, um, *adj*, given to drink, porous
bĭceps, cĭpĭtis, *adj*, two-headed
bĭcŏlōr, ōris, *adj*, two-coloured
bĭcornis, e, *adj*, two-horned
bĭdens, ntis, *adj*, two-pronged
bĭdens, ntis, *m*, hoe
bĭdŭum, ii, *n*, space of two days
bĭennĭum, ii, *n*, space of two years
bĭfārĭam, *adv*, in two ways
bĭfer, ĕra, ĕrum, *adj*, blooming or fruiting twice a year
bĭfĭdus, a, um, *adj*, cut in two

bĭfŏris, e, *adj*, with double opening
bĭformis, e, *adj*, two-shaped
bĭfrons, ntis, *adj*, two-headed
bĭfurcus, a, um, *adj*, two-pronged
bīgae, ārum, *f.pl*, pair of horses, two-horsed chariot
bīgātus, a, um, *adj*, stamped with a two-horsed chariot (of coins)
bĭiŭgus, a, um, *adj*, yoked two together
bĭlĭbris, e, *adj*, weighing two pounds
bĭlinguis, e, *adj*, bilingual
bĭliōsus, a, um, *adj*, bilious
bīlis, is, *f*, bile
bĭmăris, e, *adj*, lying between two seas
bĭmăritus, i, *m*, bigamist
bĭmembris, e, *adj*, half-man, half-beast
bĭmestris, e, *adj*, two months old
bĭmus, a, um, *adj*, two years old
bĭni, ae, a, *adj*, two each, a pair
bĭpartĭo, *v.t.* 4, to bisect
bĭpartĭto, *adv*, in two ways
bĭpĕdālis, e, *adj*, measuring two feet
bĭpennĭfer, ĕra, ĕrum, *adj*, carrying a double-edged axe
bĭpennis, e, *adj*, double-edged
bĭpēs, ĕdis, *adj*, two-legged
bĭrēmis, e, *adj*, two-oared
bĭrēmis, is, *f*, a galley with two banks of oars
bis, *adv*, twice
bĭsextĭlis, e, *adj* (of years) leap
bĭsulcus, a, um, *adj*, cloven
bĭtūmen, ĭnis, *n*, bitumen
bĭvĭum, ii, *n*, cross-road
bĭvĭus, a, um, *adj*, going in two directions
blaesus, a, um, *adj*, stammering
blandĭmentum, i, *n*, flattery
blandĭor, *v.* 4, *dep. with dat*, to flatter
blanditia, ae, *f*, flattery
blandus, a, um, *adj, adv,* **ē,** smooth-tongued, enticing
blasphēmo, *v.t.* 1, to revile
blătĕro, *v.t.* 1, to babble
blătĕro, ōnis, *m*, gabbler
blatta, ae, *f*, cockroach, moth
bŏārius, a, um, *adj*, of cattle
bŏlētus, i, *m*, mushroom
bombyx, ȳcis, *m*, silk, silk-worm
bŏnĭtas, ātis, *f*, excellence
bŏna, ōrum, *n.pl*, goods, property
bŏnum, i, *n*, goodness, profit
bŏnus, a, um, *adj*, good
bŏrĕas, ae, *m*, north wind
bŏrĕus, a, um, *adj*, northern
bōs, bŏvis, *c*, ox; *pl*, cattle
bŏvārius, see **boārius**
brăcae, ārum, *f.pl*, trousers
brăcātus, a, um, *adj*, wearing trousers, foreign
bracchium, ii, *n*, fore-arm, branch, dike
bractĕa, ae, *f*, thin metal plate
branchĭae, ārum, *f.pl*, fish-gills
brassĭca, ae, *f*, cabbage
brĕvī, *adv*, in a short time, in a few words
brĕviārĭum, ii, *n*, summary
brĕvis, e, *adj, adv,* **ĭter,** short, brief
brĕvĭtas, ātis, *f*, conciseness, shortness
brūma, ae, *f*, shortest day, winter
brūmālis, e, *adj*, wintry
brūtus, a, um, *adj*, unwieldy, dull
būbo, ōnis, *m*, owl
būbulcus, i, *m*, ploughman
būbŭlus, a, um, *adj*, of cattle
bucca, ae, *f*, the cheek
buccŭla, ae, *f*, small mouth, helmet
būcĭna, ae, *f*, trumpet
būcŭla, ae, *f*, heifer
būfo, ōnis, *m*, toad
bulbus, i, *m*, bulb
bulla, ae, *f*, bubble, knob, amulet
bullo, *v.i.* 1, to bubble
būmastus, i, *f*, grape which grows in large bunches
būris, is, *m*, plough-beam
bustum, i, *n*, funeral pyre, grave
būtȳrum, i, *n*, butter
buxifer, ĕra, ĕrum, *adj*, growing box-trees
buxum, i, *n*, box-wood
buxus, i, *f*, box-tree
byssus, i, *f*, cotton

C

căballus, i, *m*, pack-horse
căcăbus, i, *m*, saucepan
căchinnātĭo, ōnis, *f*, guffaw
căchinno, *v.i.* 1, to laugh aloud
căchinnus, i, *m*, laughter, jeering
căcūmen, ĭnis, *n*, extremity, peak
căcūmĭno, *v.t.* 1, to make into a point
cădāver, ĕris, *n*, corpse
cădo, cĕcĭdi, căsum, *v.i.* 3, to fall, wane, occur, decay
cādūcĕātor, ōris, *m*, herald
cādūcĕum, i, *n* (**us, i,** *m*), herald's staff, Mercury's wand
cādūcĭfer, ĕra, ĕrum, *adj*, carrying a herald's staff (Mercury)
cădūcus, a, um, *adj*, falling, doomed
cădus, i, *m*, large jar (for liquids)
caecĭtas, ātis, *f*, blindness
caeco, *v.t.* 1, to blind
caecus, a, um, *adj*, blind, hidden
caedēs, is, *f*, slaughter

caedo, cĕcīdi, caesum, *v.t.* 3, to cut, strike, slaughter
caelātor, ōris, *m,* engraver
caelātūra, ae, *f,* carving
caelebs, lĭbis, *adj,* unmarried
caelēs, ĭtis, *adj,* heavenly
caelites, um, *pl,* gods
caelestia, ĭum, *n.pl.,* the heavenly bodies
caelestis, e, *adj,* heavenly
caelestis, is, *m,* god
caelibātus, ūs, *m,* celibacy
caelicŏla, ae, *m. f,* inhabitant of heaven
caelifer, ĕra, ĕrum, *adj,* supporting the heavens (Atlas)
caelo, *v.t.* 1, to engrave
caelum, i, *n,* heaven, climate
caelum, i, *n,* chisel
caementum, i, *n,* quarry-stone
caenum, i, *n,* dirt
caepa, ae, *f* (e, is, *n*), onion
caerimōnia, ae, *f,* religious ceremony, awe
caerŭlĕus(lus), a, um, *adj,* dark blue
caesăriēs, ēi, *f,* the hair
caesim, *adv,* by cutting
caesĭus, a, um, *adj,* green or grey-eyed
caespĕs, ĭtis, *m,* a turf
caestus, ūs, *m,* boxing-glove
caetra, ae, *f,* native shield
cālămister, tri, *m,* curling-iron; *pl,* flourishes
cālămitas, ātis, *f,* disaster
cālămitōsus, a, um, *adj, adv,* **ē,** destructive, unhappy
cālămus, i, *m,* cane, reed-pen
cālăthus, i, *m,* basket
calcăr, āris, *n,* spur, stimulus
calcĕāmentum, i, *n,* shoe
calcĕo, *v.t.* 1, to shoe
calcĕus, i, *m,* shoe
calcĭtrātus, ūs, *m,* kicking
calcĭtro, *v.i.* 1, to kick, resist
calco, *v.t.* 1, to tread on, oppress
calcŭlātor, ōris, *m,* accountant
calcŭlus, i, *m,* pebble, calculation, vote, piece (chess, draughts)
cālĕfăcio, fēci, factum, *v.t.* 3, to heat, excite
cālĕo, *v.i.* 2, to be warm, roused
cālesco, *v.i.* 3, to become warm
cālĭdus, a, um, *adj,* warm, hot, hot-headed
cāliga, ae, *f,* leather boot
cālīgātus, a, um, *adj,* wearing soldier's boots
cālīginōsus, a, um, *adj,* obscure
cālīgo, ĭnis, *f,* mist, gloom
cālīgo, *v.i.* 1, to steam, be dark
călix, ĭcis, *m,* cup
calyx, see **calix**
callĕo, *v.i.t.* 2, to be callous, insensible; to know by experience
callĭdĭtas, ātis, *f,* skill, cunning
callĭdus, a, um, *adj, adv,* **ē,** skilful, sly
callis, is, *m,* footpath
callum, i, *n,* hard or thick skin
cālo, ōnis, *m,* soldier's servant, menial
călor, ōris, *m,* heat, ardour
caltha, ae, *f,* marigold
cālumnĭa, ae, *f,* trickery, libel
cālumniātor, ōris, *m,* slanderer
cālumnior, *v.t.* 1, *dep,* to blame or accuse unjustly
calva, ae, *f,* scalp
calvāria, ae, *f,* skull
calvĭtĭum, i, *n,* baldness
calvus, a, um, *adj,* bald
calx, cis, *f,* heel
calx, cis, *f,* limestone, chalk
cămēlōpardālis, is, *f,* giraffe
cămēlus, i, *m,* camel
cămēna, ae, *f,* muse
căměra, ae, *f,* vault
cămīnus, i, *m,* forge, furnace
campester, tris, e, *adj,* on level ground
campestre, is, *n,* wrestling trunks
campus, i, *m,* plain, open country, opportunity, scope
cămŭr, ŭra, ŭrum, *adj,* curved inwards
cănālis, is, *m,* pipe, groove
cancelli, ōrum, *m.pl,* railings
cancer, cri, *m,* crab
candēla, ae, *f,* candle
candēlābrum, i, *n,* candlestick
candens, ntis, *adj,* shining white, glowing hot
candĕo, *v.i.* 2, to shine, glow
candesco, ŭi, *v.i.* 3, to glisten
candĭdātus, i, *m,* candidate
candĭdus, a, um, *adj, adv,* **e,** dazzling white, beautiful, honest
candor, ōris, *m,* whiteness, beauty, honesty
cănens, ntis, *adj,* grey, white
cănĕo, *v.i.* 2, to be white, grey
cănesco, *v.i.* 3, to grow white
cănĭcŭla, ae, *f,* small dog, Dog-star
cănīnus, a, um, *adj,* dog-like
cănis, is, *c,* dog, Dog-star
cănistrum, i, *n,* open basket
cănities, (*no genitive*) *f,* grey hair, old age
canna, ae, *f,* reed, flute
cannăbis, is, *f,* hemp

cănō, cĕcĭnī, cantum, *v.i.t.* 3, to sing, play; prophesy
cănor, ōris, *m,* tune
cănōrus, a, um, *adj,* melodious
cantērius, see **canthērius**
cantātor, ōris, *m,* singer
canthăris, ĭdis, *f,* beetle
canthārus, i, *m,* tankard
canthērius, ii, *m,* mule, rafter
cantĭcum, i, *n,* song
cantĭlēna, ae, *f,* hackneyed song
canto, *v.i.t.* 1, to sing, act; predict
cantor, ōris, *m,* singer, actor
cantus, ūs, *m,* music, prophecy, singing
cānus, a, um, *adj,* white, old
căpăcĭtas, ātis, *f,* capacity
căpax, ācis, *adj,* roomy, capable
căpella, ae, *f,* she-goat
căper, pri, *m,* goat
căpesso, īvi, ĭtum, *v.t.* 3, to seize, undertake, reach for
căpillāmentum, i, *n,* wig
căpillāre, is, *n,* hair-oil
căpillātus, a, um, *adj,* hairy
căpillus, i, *m,* the hair
căpĭo, cēpi, captum, *v.t.* 3, to take, capture, tempt, choose, obtain, undertake, hold, grasp
căpistrum, i, *n,* halter
căpĭtālis, e, *adj,* of life and death, criminal, dangerous
capra, ae, *f,* she-goat
căprĕa, ae, *f,* wild she-goat, roe
căprĕŏlus, i, *m,* roebuck, prop
căpricornus, i. *m,* capricorn
căprĭficus, i, *f,* wild fig-tree
căprĭgĕnus, a, um, *adj,* goat-born
căprīnus, a, um, *adj,* of a goat
capsa, ae, *f,* box, satchel
captātor, ōris, *m,* fortune-hunter
captĭo, ōnis, *f,* fraud, quibble
captīvitas, ātis, *f,* captivity
captīvus, a, um, *adj* (**i,** *m*), prisoner
capto, *v.t.* 1, to chase, entice
captus, ūs, *m,* grasp, capacity
captus, a, um, *adj,* taken, disabled
căpŭlus, i, *m,* tomb, handle
căpŭt, ĭtis, *n,* head, person, chief, origin, summit, status, paragraph, chapter
carbăsĕus, a, um, *adj,* made of flax, linen
carbăsus, i, *f,* flax, linen
carbo, ōnis, *m,* charcoal, coal
carbuncŭlus, i, *m,* ruby, carbuncle
carcer, ĕris, *m,* prison, jail-bird
carchēsium, ii, *n,* goblet, mast-head
cardiăcus, a, um, *adj,* dyspeptic
cardo, ĭnis, *m,* hinge, crisis
cardŭus, i, *m,* thistle
cărĕo, *v.i.* 2 (*with abl.*), to lack
cārex, ĭcis, *f,* reed-grass
cāries, (*no genitive*) *f,* decay
cārica, ae, *f,* dried fig
cārīna, ae, *f,* hull, keel, boat
cāriōsus, a, um, *adj,* decayed
cāritas, ātis, *f,* costliness, affection
carmen, ĭnis, *n,* song, poem
carnārium, ii, *n,* larder
carnĭfex, ĭcis, *m,* executioner
carnĭfĭcīna, ae, *f,* execution, torment
carnĭfĭco, *v.t.* 1, to execute
carnĭvŏrus, a, um, *adj,* carnivorous
carnōsus, a, um, *adj,* fleshy
cāro, carnis, *f,* flesh, meat
carpentum, i, *n,* chariot
carpo, psi, ptum, *v.t.* 3, to pluck, graze, slander, weaken, pass over
carptim, *adv,* separately
carrus, i, *m,* two-wheeled cart
cartilāgo, ĭnis, *f,* cartilage
cārus, a, um, *adj, adv,* **ē,** dear
căsa, ae, *f,* cottage, hut
căsĕus, i, *m,* cheese
căsĭa, ae, *f,* cinnamon (tree)
casses, ĭum, *m.pl,* hunting-net, spider's web
cassis, ĭdis, *f,* helmet
cassĭda, ae, *f,* helmet
cassus, a, um, *adj,* empty, vain
castănĕa, ae, *f,* chestnut
castē, *adv,* purely
castellum, i, *n,* stronghold
castīgātio, ōnis, *f,* punishment
castīgātor, ōris, *m,* critic
castīgo, *v.t.* 1, to correct, punish
castĭmōnĭa, ae, *f,* purity
castĭtas, ātis, *f,* chastity
castor, ōris, *m,* beaver
castra, ōrum, *n.pl,* camp
castrensis, e, *adj,* of the camp, military
castro, *v.t.* 1, to castrate
castrum, i, *n,* fort
castus, a, um, *adj,* pure, virtuous
cāsū, *adv,* accidentally
cāsus, ūs, *m,* fall, chance, mishap
cătăpulta, ae, *f,* catapult
cătăracta, ae, *f,* waterfall, portcullis
cătellus, i, *m* (**a, ae,** *f*), puppy
cătēna, ae, *f,* chain, fetter
cătēnātus, a, um, *adj,* chained
căterva, ae, *f,* crowd, company
cătervātim, *adv,* by companies
căthēdra, ae, *f,* chair
cătillus, i, *m,* dish
cătīnus, i, *m,* bowl, dish
cătŭlus, i, *m,* puppy, young animal
cătus, a, um, *adj, adv,* **ē,** intelligent, sly

For List of Abbreviations used, turn to pages 3, 4

cauda, ae, *f*, tail
caudex, ĭcis, *m*, tree-trunk, ledger
caulae, ārum, *f.pl*, hole, enclosure
caulis, is, *m*, stem, cabbage
caupo, ōnis, *m*, retailer, innkeeper
caupōna, ae, *f*, shop, inn
caupōnor, *v.t.* 1, *dep*, to trade
causa, ae, *f*, reason, cause, motive; *abl.* **causā** for the sake of
causidĭcus, i, *m*, counsel
causor, *v.i.t.* 1, *dep*, to make excuses; plead
cautē, *adv*, cautiously
cautēs, is, *f*, crag, rock
cautio, ōnis, *f*, precaution
cautus, a, um, *adj*, safe, cautious
căvĕa, ae, *f*, den, coop
căvĕo, cāvi, cautum, *v.i.t.* 2, to be on one's guard; stipulate
căverna, ae, *f*, cave, ship's hold
căvillātio, ōnis, *f*, jeering
căvillor, *v.i.t.* 1, *dep*, to jeer; taunt, quibble
căvo, *v.t.* 1, to hollow out
căvum, i, *n* (**us, i,** *m*), hole
căvus, a, um, *adj*, hollow
cēdo, cessi, cessum, *v.i.t.* 3, to move, yield, happen; befall
cĕdo, *imperative*, here! say! give!
cēdrus, i, *f*, cedar (wood, tree, oil)
cĕlĕbĕr, ĕbris, ĕbre, *adj*, much frequented, crowded, famous
cĕlĕbrātio, ōnis, *f*, crowd, festival,
cĕlĕbrātus, a, um, *adj*, popular, usual, well-known
cĕlĕbrĭtas, ātis, *f*, crowd, fame
cĕlĕbro, *v.t.* 1, to frequent, use, celebrate, praise, proclaim, solemnize
cĕlĕr, ĕris, ĕre, *adj*, *adv*, **ĭter,** swift, lively, rash
cĕlĕrĭtas, ātis, *f*, speed
cĕlĕro, *v.i.t.* 1, to hurry; quicken
cella, ae, *f*, store-room
cellārius, i, *m*, butler
cēlo, *v.t.* 1, to conceal
cĕlox, ōcis, *f*, yacht
celsus, a, um, *adj*, high, eminent
cēna, ae, *f*, dinner
cēnācŭlum, i, *n*, attic, refectory
cēnātio, ōnis, *f*, dining-room
cēnātus, a, um, *adj*, having dined
cēno, *v.i.t.* 1, to dine; eat
censĕo, ŭi, censum, *v.t.* 2, to assess, give an opinion
censor, ōris, *m*, censor
censōrius, a, um, *adj*, censorial
censūra, ae, *f*, censorship
census, ūs, *m*, census, wealth
centaurēum, i, *n*, herb (centaury)
centaurus, i, *m*, a Centaur
centēni, ae, a, *adj*, a hundred each
centēsĭmus, a, um, *adj*, hundredth
centĭens (centĭes), *adv*, a hundred times
centĭmănus, a, um, *adj*, hundred-handed
cento, ōnis, *m*, patchwork
centum, a hundred
centumgĕmĭnus, a, um, *adj*, a hundredfold
centumpondĭum, ii, *n*, weight of a hundred pounds
centŭplex, plĭcis, *adj*, hundredfold
centŭria, ae, *f*, division, century
centŭriātim, *adv*, by hundreds
centŭrio, ōnis, *m*, centurion
centŭrio, *v.t.* 1, to divide into centuries
cēnŭla, ae, *f*, small dinner
cēra, ae, *f*, wax, writing-tablet
cĕrăsus, i, *f*, cherry (tree)
cerdo, ōnis, *m*, handicraftsman
cĕrĕbrōsus, a, um, *adj*, hot-headed
cĕrĕbrum, i, *n*, brain, understanding
cērĕus, a, um, *adj*, of wax
cērĕus, i, *m*, wax taper
cerevisia, ae, *f*, beer
cērintha, ae, *f*, wax-flower
cerno, crēvi, crētum, *v.t.* 3, to perceive, decide
cernŭus, a, um, *adj*, headfirst
cēro, *v.t.* 1, to smear with wax
cerrĭtus, a, um, *adj*, frantic, crazy
certāmen, ĭnis, *n*, struggle
certātim, *adv*, eagerly
certātio, ōnis, *f*, contest
certē, *adv*, undoubtedly
certĭōrem făcio, to inform
certō, *adv*, certainly
certo, *v.i.t.* 1, to struggle; contest
certus, a, um, *adj*, certain, fixed
cērussa, ae, *f*, white lead
cerva, ae, *f*, doe
cervĭcal, ālis, *n*, pillow
cervĭnus, a, um, *adj*, of a deer
cervisia, see **cerevisia**
cervix, ĭcis, *f*, neck
cervus, i, *m*, deer
cessātio, ōnis, *f*, loitering
cessātor, ōris, *m*, idler
cessātrix, īcis, *f*, idler
cesso, *v.i.t.* 1, to loiter, cease; fail
cētārium, ii, *n*, fish-pond
cētārius, ii, *m*, fishmonger
cētĕrōqui, *adv*, in other respects

cētĕrum, *adv.* otherwise, but yet
cētĕrus, a, um, *adj, adv*, **um**, the rest, remainder
cētus, i, *m*, sea-monster, whale
ceu, *adv.* as, just as
chălybs, ȳbis, *m*, steel
charta, ae, *f*, writing paper
chĕlȳdrus, i, *m*, water-snake
chĕrăgra, ae, *f*, gout in the hand
chīrŏgrăphum, i, *n*, handwriting
chīrurgia, ae, *f*, surgery
chīrurgus, i, *m*, surgeon
chlămys, ȳdis, *f*, military cloak
chorda, ae, *f*, string of a musical instrument
chŏrēa, ae, *f*, dance
chŏrus, i, *m*, dance, chorus, group
Christus, i, *m*, Christ
Christiānus, a, um, *adj*, Christian
cibāria, ōrum, *n.pl*, food
cibārius, a, um, *adj*, of food
cibōrium, ii, *n*, drinking-cup
cibus, i, *m*, food
cicāda, ae, *f*, grasshopper
cicātrix, īcis, *f*, scar
cicer, ĕris, *n*, chick pea
cicĭnus, a, um, *adj*, of the cici tree
cicōnia, ae, *f*, stork
cicur, ūris, *adj*, tame
cicūta, ae, *f*, hemlock
ciĕo, cīvi, citum, *v.t.* 2, to rouse, move, summon
cilicium, ii, *n*, coarse cloth
cimex, īcis, *m*, bug
cincinnātus, a, um, *adj*, with ringlets
cincinnus, i, *m*, lock of hair
cinctus, ūs, *m*, girdle
cinĕrĕus, a, um, *adj*, ash-coloured
cingo, nxi, nctum, *v.t.* 3, to enclose, encircle, fasten on, crown, besiege
cingŭla, ae, *f*, (**um, i**, *n*), girdle
cinis, ĕris, *m*, ashes, death
cippus, i, *m*, stake
circā, *adv. and prep. with acc*, round about
circenses, ĭum, *m.pl*, The Games
circĭnus, i, *m*, pair of compasses
circiter, *adv. and prep. with acc*, round about, near
circitor, ōris, *m*, patrol
circŭĭtio, ōnis, *f*, patrolling
circŭĭtus, ūs, *m*, circuit
circŭlor, *v.i.* 1, *dep*, to form a group
circŭlus, i, *m*, circle, orbit
circum, *adv. and prep. with acc*, around, near
circŭmăgo, ēgi, actum, *v.t.* 3, to wheel, drive round, pass (time)
circumcīdo, cīdi, cīsum, *v.t.* 3, to cut around, reduce
circumcīsus, a, um, *adj*, cut off
circumclūdo, si, sum, *v.t.* 3, to shut in, surround
circumdātus, a, um, *adj*, surrounded
circumdo, dĕdi, dătum, *v.t.* 1, to put around, shut in, surround
circumdūco, xi, ctum, *v.t.* 3, to lead around
circŭmĕo, circŭĭtum, *v.i.t.* 4, to go around; surround, canvass
circumfĕro, ferre, tŭli, lātum, *v.t.*, *irreg*, to carry or pass around
circumflecto, xi, xum, *v.t.* 3, to bend, turn round
circumflŭo, xi, ctum, *v.i.t.* 3, to flow round; overflow with
circumfŏrānĕus, a, um, *adj*, movable
circumfundo, fūdi, fūsum, *v.t.* 3, to pour around, envelop, hem in
circumgrĕdior, gressus, *v.i.t.* 3, *dep*, to go around
circumĭcio, iēci, ctum, *v.t.* 3, to throw or set round
circumiectus, a, um, *adj*, surrounding
circumlīgo, *v.t.* 1, to tie round
circumlĭno,—ĭtum, *v.t.* 3, to besmear
circummitto, mīsi, missum, *v.t.* 3, to send around
circummūnio, *v.t.* 4, to fortify round
circumplector, xus, *v.t.* 3, *dep*, to embrace, surround
circumplĭco, *v.t.* 1, to wind round
circumrōdo, di, *v.t.* 3, to nibble round
circumscrĭbo, psi, ptum, *v.t.* 3, to draw a line round, restrict, deceive
circumscriptio, ōnis, *f*, circle, outline
circumsĕdĕo, sēdi, sessum, *v.t.* 2, to surround, blockade
circumsisto, stĕti, *v.i.t.* 3, to stand around; surround
circumsŏno, *v.i.t.* 1, to resound; fill with sound
circumspecto, *v.i.t.* 1, to look round; survey carefully
circumspectus, a, um, *adj*. guarded, considered
circumspectus, ūs, *m*, contemplation, spying
circumspĭcio, spexi, ctum, *v.i.t.* 3, to look around, take care; survey, search for
circumsto, stĕti, *v.i.t.* 1, to stand around; surround, besiege
circumtextus, a, um, *adj*, woven round
circumtŏno, ŭi, *v.t.* 1, to thunder around
circumvādo, si, *v.t.* 3, to envelop
circumvallo, *v.t.* 1, to surround with a wall, blockade

circumvector, *v.* 1, *dep,* to ride around
circumvĕhor, vectus, *v.i.t.* 3, *dep,* to ride around
circumvēnio, vēni, ventum, *v.t.* 4, to surround
circumvŏlĭto, *v.i.t.* 1, to flit; fly around
circumvŏlo, *v.t.* 1, to fly around
circumvolvo—vŏlūtum, *v.t.* 3, to roll around
circus, i, *m,* circle, ring
cĭris, is, *f,* sea-bird
cirrus, i, *m,* curl
cis, *prep, with acc,* on this side of, within
cĭsium, ii, *n,* two-wheeled vehicle
cista, ae, *f,* box, chest
cisterna, ae, *f,* cistern
citātus, a, um, *adj,* urged on, quick
citĕrior, *comp. adj,* on this side
cithăra, ae, *f,* guitar, lute
cithărista, ae, *m,* guitar-player
cithăroedus, i, *m,* a singing guitar-player
cĭto, *adv,* soon, quickly
cĭto, *v.t.* 1, to incite, call
cĭtrā, *adv. and prep. with acc,* on this side (of)
cĭtrĕus, a, um, *adj,* of citrus-wood, of the citrus tree
cĭtrō, *adv.* (*with* **ultro**), to and fro, backwards and forwards
cĭtrus, i, *f,* citrus-tree
cĭtus, a, um, *adj,* swift, quick
civĭcus, a, um, *adj,* of a citizen, civic, civil
cĭvĭlis, e, *adj, adv,* **ĭter,** of a citizen, civic, civil
cĭvis, is, *c,* citizen
cĭvĭtas, ātis, *f,* citizenship, the state, the citizens
clādes, is, *f,* disaster, massacre
clam, *adv. and prep. with acc,* secretly; unknown to
clāmĭto, *v.i.t.* 1, to call out
clāmo, *v.i.t.* 1, to shout; declare
clāmor, ōris, *m,* shout, applause
clāmōsus, a, um, *adj,* noisy, bawling
clandestĭnus, a, um, *adj, adv,* **o,** secret, hidden, furtive
clangor, ōris, *m,* noise, clash
clārĕo, *v.i.* 2, to shine, be famous
clāresco, clārŭi, *v.i.* 3, to become clear or famous
clārĭtas, ātis, *f,* brightness, renown
clārĭtūdo, ĭnis, *f,* renown
clārus, a, um, *adj, adv,* **e,** clear, bright, plain, famous
classiārĭi, ōrum, *m. pl,* marines
classicum, i, *n,* battle-signal
classis, is, *f,* fleet, class or muster of citizens
claudĕo, *v.i.* 2 (*no perf*), to limp, be lame
claudĭco, *v.i.* 1, to limp, be lame
claudĭcātio, ōnis, *f,* limping
claudo, si, sum, *v.t.* 3, to shut, cut off, enclose, blockade
claudus, a, um, *adj,* lame
claustra, ōrum, *n. pl,* lock, bolt, barricade
clausŭla, ae, *f,* conclusion, end
clausum, i, *n,* enclosed space
clāva, ae, *f,* club, cudgel
clāvĭger, ĕra, ĕrum, *adj,* club-armed
clāvĭger, ĕri, *m,* key-bearer
clāvis, is, *f,* key
clāvŭlus, i, *m,* small nail
clāvus, i, *m,* nail, tiller, stripe
clēmens, ntis, *adj, adv,* **nter,** gentle, mild, merciful
clēmentia, ae, *f,* mildness, mercy
clĕpo, psi, ptum, *v.t.* 3, to steal
clepsydra, ae, *f,* water-clock
cliens, ntis, *c,* retainer, follower
clientēla, ae, *f,* patronage, train of dependants
clĭpĕus, i, *m,* Roman round shield
clĭtellae, ārum, *f. pl,* saddle-bags
clĭvōsus, a, um, *adj,* hilly
clĭvus, i, *m,* slope, hill
clŏāca, ae, *f,* sewer, drain
clūnis, is, *m, f,* buttock, haunch
cŏăcervo, *v.t.* 1, to pile together
cŏactor, ōris, *m,* money-collector
cŏactum, i, *n,* a thick covering
cŏactus, a, um, *adj, adv,* **e,** forced
cŏaequo, *v.t.* 1, to level, equalize
cŏagmento, *v.t.* 1, to join together
cŏagŭlo, *v.t.* 1, to coagulate
cŏālesco, ălŭi, ălĭtum, *v.i.* 3, to grow together, combine
cŏargŭo, ŭi, *v.t.* 3, to convict, refute, demonstrate
cŏarto, *v.t.* 1, to compress
coccinĕus, a, um, *adj,* scarlet
coccum, i, *n,* scarlet colour
cochlĕa, ae, *f,* snail, spiral
cŏclĕa, ae, *f,* snail, spiral
cŏclĕar, āris, *n,* spoon
coctĭlis, e, *adj,* baked, burned
cŏcus, i, *m,* cook
cŏdex, ĭcis, *m,* tree-trunk, ledger
cŏdĭcilli, ōrum, *m. pl,* note-book
cŏĕmo, ēmi, emptum, *v.t.* 3, to buy up
coenum, i, *n,* dirt
cŏĕo, *v.i.* 4, to assemble, unite, encounter, conspire
(coepio) coepi, coeptum, *v.i.t.* 3, *defect,* to begin

coeptum, i, *n*, attempt
coeptus, ūs, *m*, undertaking
cŏercĕo, *v.t.* 2, to confine, curb
cŏercĭtio, ōnis, *f*, coercion, restraint
coetus, ūs, *m*, meeting, crowd
cōgĭtātio, ōnis, *f*, thought, reflection, purpose
cōgĭtātum, i, *n*, idea, thought
cōgĭtātus, a, um, *adj*, thought out
cōgĭto, *v.t.* 1, to consider, think, be disposed towards, plan
cognātio, ōnis, *f*, blood relationship, family
cognātus, a, um, *adj*, related by birth; (*as a noun*) blood-relative
cognĭtio, ōnis, *f*, study, knowledge, recognition, idea, trial
cognĭtor, ōris, *m*, legal representative
cognĭtus, a, um, *adj*, known, approved
cognōmen, ĭnis, *n*, surname
cognōminis, e, *adj*, of the same name
cognosco, gnōvi, gnĭtum, *v.t.* 3, to learn, understand, inquire
cŏgo, cŏēgi, cŏactum, *v.t.* 3, to collect, compel, restrict
cŏhaerens, see **cohaerĕo**
cŏhaerĕo, si, sum, *v.i.* 2, to cling together, agree with
cŏhēres, ēdis, *c*, fellow-heir
cŏhĭbĕo, *v.t.* 2, to hold together, confine, restrain
cŏhŏnesto, *v.t.* 1, to honour
cŏhorresco, horrŭi, *v.i.* 3, to shudder
cŏhors, tis, *f*, company of soldiers ($\frac{1}{10}$ of a legion); enclosure
cŏhortālis, e, *adj*, of the poultry-farm
cŏhortātio, ōnis, *f*, encouragement
cŏhortor, *v.t.* 1, *dep*, to encourage
cŏĭtio, ōnis, *f*, meeting, conspiracy
cŏĭtus, ūs, *m*, meeting, crowd, sexual intercourse
cŏlăphus, i, *m*, blow, cuff
collăbĕfacto, *v.t.* 1, to dislodge
collăbĕfio, fieri, factus, *v. irreg*, to be overthrown, disabled
collābor, psus, *v.i.* 3, *dep*, to fall, faint, decay
collăcrĭmo, *v.i.t.* 1, to weep; deplore
collactĕus, i, *m*, (**a, ae,** *f.*) foster-brother (sister)
collātio, ōnis, *f*, collection, encounter, comparison
collaudo, *v.t.* 1, to praise highly
collēga, ae, *m*, partner, colleague
collēgium, ii, *n*, organization, body of officials
collibet, *v. impers*, 2, it is agreeable
collido, si, sum, *v.t.* 3, to beat or strike together
collĭgo, lēgi, ctum, *v.t.* 3, to collect, compress, consider
colligo, *v.t.* 1, to tie together
collĭno, lēvi, lĭtum, *v.t.* 3, to besmear, defile
collĭnus, a, um, *adj*, hilly
collis, is, *m*, hill, high ground
collŏcātio, ōnis, *f*, setting up, giving in marriage
collŏco, *v.t.* 1, to arrange, give in marriage, invest, employ
collŏquium, ii, *n*, conversation
collŏquor, cūtus, *v.i.* 3, *dep*, to hold a conversation, discuss
collūcĕo, *v.i*, 2, to shine
collūdo, si, sum, *v.i.* 3, to play with, be in collusion with
collum, i, *n*, neck, throat
columna, see **columna**
collŭo, lŭi, lūtuma, *v.t.* 3, to rinse
collūsio, ōnis, *f*, collusion
collūsor, ōris, *m*. playmate
collustro, *v.t.* 1, to illumine
collŭvio, ōnis, *f*, heap of rubbish
collŭvies, —, *f*, heap of rubbish
cŏlo, ŭi, cultum, *v.t.* 3, to cultivate improve, worship, study
cŏlo, *v.t.* 1, to filter
cŏlŏcāsia, ae, *f*, marsh-lily
cŏlon, i, *n*, colon
cŏlōna, ae, *f*, farmer's wife
cŏlōnia, ae, *f*, Roman outpost, colonial settlement, farm
cŏlōnus, i, *m*, farmer, colonist
cŏlor, ōris, *m*, colour, dye, beauty
cŏlōrātus, a, um, *adj*, coloured
cŏlōro, *v.t.* 1, to colour, dye
cŏlossus, i, *m*, gigantic statue
cŏlŭber, bri, *m* (**bra, ae,** *f*), snake
cŏlum, i, *n*, strainer, colander
cŏlumba, ae, *f*. (**us, i,** *m*), dove
cŏlumbārium, ii, *n*, dove-cot
cŏlumbĭnus, a, um, *adj*, of a dove, dove-coloured
cŏlŭmella, ae, *f*, small pillar
cŏlŭmen, ĭnis, *n*, summit, prop
cŏlumna, ae, *f*, pillar, post
cŏlurnus, a, um, *adj*, of hazel
cŏlus, ūs, *f*, distaff
cŏma, ae, *f*, hair, crest, foliage
cŏmans, ntis, *adj*, hairy
cŏmātus, a, um, *adj*, long-haired
combĭbo, bĭbi, *v.t.* 3, to drink up
combūro, ussi, ustum, *v.t.* 3, to burn, consume completely
cŏmĕdo, ēdi, ēsum, *v.t.* 3, to eat up, waste
cŏmes, ĭtis, *c*, companion, attendant
cŏmĕtes, ae, *m*, comet
cŏmĭcus, a, um, *adj*, *adv*, **ē,** comic

For List of Abbreviations used, turn to pages 3, 4

cōmĭcus, i, *m*, comedian
cōmis, e, *adj, adv,* **iter,** courteous, obliging
cōmissātio, ōnis, *f*, drinking-party
cōmissātor, ōris, *m*, reveller
cōmissor, *v.i.* 1, *dep*, to have a party
cōmitas, ātis, *f*, affability
cŏmitātus, a, um, *adj*, accompanied
cōmitātus, ūs, *m*, escort, retinue
cōmitĭa, ōrum, *n.pl*, Roman assembly for electing magistrates
cŏmitiālis, e, *adj*, of the elections; (with **morbus**) epilepsy
cŏmitĭum, ii, *n*, assembly place for voting
cŏmitor, *v.t.* 1, *dep*, to accompany
commăcŭlo, *v.t.* 1, to stain
commēātus, ūs, *m*, expedition, leave of absence, convoy, supplies
commĕmŏrātio, ōnis, *f*, mention
commĕmŏro, *v.t.* 1, to remember, relate
commendātĭcius, a, um, *adj*, commendatory
commendātio, ōnis, *f*, recommendation
commendo, *v.t.* 1, to entrust, recommend
commentārĭus, ii, *m* (**ium, ii,** *n*), notebook, record
commentātio, ōnis, *f*, careful study
commentĭcius, a, um, *adj*, thought-out, imaginary, false
commentor, *v.i.t.* 1, *dep*, to study
commentor, ōris, *m*, inventor
commentum, i, *n*, fabrication
commĕo, *v.i.* 1, to come and go, frequent
commercĭum, ii, *n*, commerce, trade, a relationship with
commĕrĕo, *v.t.* 2, to deserve fully, be guilty of
commigro, *v.t.* 1, to migrate
commilĭtium, ii, *n*, comradeship
commĭlĭto, ōnis, *m*, comrade
comminātio, ōnis, *f*, threats
comminiscor, mentus, *v.t.* 3, *dep*, to devise, invent
comminor, *v.t.* 1, *dep*, to threaten
comminŭo, ŭi, ūtum, *v.t.* 3, to crush, lessen, weaken
comminus, *adv*, at close quarters
commiscĕo, scŭi, xtum, *v.t.* 2, to mix together
commisĕror, *v.t.* 1, *dep*, to pity
commissio, ōnis, *f*, opening of the games, prepared speech
commissum, i, *n*, offence, secret
commissūra, ae, *f*, knot, joint
committo, mīsi, ssum, *v.t.* 3, to connect, engage in, begin, entrust, do something wrong, bring together in combat
commŏdātum, i, *n*, loan
commŏdē, *adv*, appropriately, just in time
commŏdĭtas, ātis, *f*, benefit
commŏdo, *v.t.* 1, to adjust, lend, be kind to, oblige
commŏdum, i, *n*, convenient time or opportunity, advantage
commŏdus, a, um, *adj*, suitable, obliging, advantageous
commŏnĕfăcio, fēci, factum, *v.t.* 3, to remind, impress upon
commŏnĕo, *v.t.* 2, to impress upon
commonstro, *v.t.* 1, to point out
commŏrātio, ōnis, *f*, delay
commŏror, *v.i.t.* 1, *dep*, to wait, stay
commŏtio, ōnis, *f*, commotion, excitement
commŏtus, a, um, *adj*, aroused
commŏvĕo, mōvi, mŏtum, *v.t.* 2, to shake, move, arouse, disturb
commūnicātio, ōnis, *f*, communication
commūnĭco, *v.t.* 1, to share with another, consult, unite, partake
commūnio, *v.t.* 4, to fortify strongly
commūnio, ōnis, *f*, partnership
commūnē, is, *n*, community, state
commūnis, e, *adj, adv,* **iter,** common, general
commūnĭtas, ātis, *f*, fellowship
commūtābilis, e, *adj*, changeable
commūtātio, ōnis, *f*, change
commūto, *v.t.* 1, to change, exchange
cōmo, mpsi, mptum, *v.t.* 3, to arrange comb, braid, adorn
cōmoedĭa, ae, *f*, comedy
cōmoedus, a, um, *adj*, comic
cōmoedus, i, *m*, comic actor
compactum, i, *n*, agreement
compactus, a, um, *adj*, thick-set
compāges, is, *f*, joint, structure
compār, ăris, *adj*, equal, like
compār, ăris, *m*, companion
compărātio, ōnis, *f*, comparison, preparation
compărātivus, a, um, *adj*, comparative
compārĕo, *v.i.* 2, to be evident
compăro, *v.t.* 1, to pair off, compare, make ready, provide
compello, pŭli, pulsum, *v.t.* 3, to collect, compel
compello, *v.t.* 1, to address, rebuke

compendiārius, a, um, *adj*, short
compendium, ii, *n*, gain, saving, abbreviation
compensātio, ōnis, *f*, compensation
compenso, *v.t.* 1, to make things balance, compensate
compĕrendĭno, *v.t.* 1, to remand
compĕrio, pĕri, pertum, *v.t.* 4, to ascertain
compertus, a, um, *adj*, proved
compēs, ĕdis, *f*, chain, shackle for the feet
compesco, scŭi, *v.t.* 3, to restrain
compĕtitor, ōris, *m*, rival
compĕto, īvi, ĭtum, *v.i.* 3, to correspond, coincide
compīlo, *v.t.* 1, to plunder
compingo, pēgi, pactum, *v.t.* 3, to construct, fasten together
compĭtum, i, *n*, cross-road
complāno, *v.t.* 1, to level
complector, xus, *v.t.* 3, *dep*, to embrace, value, enclose, understand
complēmentum, i, *n*, complement
complĕo, ēvi, ētum, *v.t.* 2, to fill up, supply
complexio, ōnis, *f*, combination
complexus, ūs, *m*, embrace, love
complico, *v.t.* 1, to fold up
complōrātio, ōnis, *f*, lamentation
complōrātus, ūs, *m*, lamentation
complōro, *v.t.* 1, to lament
complūres, a, *pl. adj*, several
compōno, pŏsŭi, pŏsĭtum, *v.t.* 3, to put together, unite, build, arrange, compare, put to sleep, adjust, pretend, agree upon
comporto, *v.t.* 1, to bring together
compŏs, ŏtis, *adj*, *with genit. or abl*, having control of
compŏsĭtio, ōnis, *f*, arranging
compŏsĭtus, a, um, *adj*, *adv*, **ē,** well-arranged, suitable: **ex compŏsĭto,** by previous agreement
comprĕhendo, di, sum, *v.t.* 3, to seize, perceive, recount, understand
comprĕhensio, ōnis, *f*, arrest
comprĭmo, pressi, pressum, *v.t.* 3, to press together, restrain
comprŏbo, *v.t.* 1, to approve, prove
comptus, a, um, *m*, *adj*, dressed-up
compulsus, a, um, *adj*, collected, driven
compungo, nxi, nctum, *v.t.* 3, to prick, sting
compŭto, *v.t.* 1, to calculate
cōnāmen, inis, *n*, effort
cōnāta, ōrum, *n.pl*, undertaking
cōnātum, i, *n*, attempt
cōnātus, ūs, *m*, effort, enterprise
concăvus, a, um, *adj*, hollow, arched
concēdo, cessi, ssum, *v.i.t.* 3, to go away, yield; permit
concēlĕbro, *v.t.* 1, to frequent, celebrate, notify
concentus, ūs, *m*, harmony
conceptio, ōnis, *f*, comprehension, conception
conceptus, ūs, *m*, gathering
concertātio, ōnis, *f*, dispute
concerto, *v.t.* 1, to dispute
concessio, ōnis, *f*, permission
concessu (*abl*), by permission
concessus, a, um, *adj*, yielded, confirmed
concha, ae, *f*, shell-fish, oyster-shell, Triton's trumpet
conchȳlium, ii, *n*, shell-fish
concĭdo, cĭdi, *v.i.* 3, to collapse
concīdo, cīdi, cīsum, *v.t.* 3, to cut up, kill, annihilate
concĭĕo, īvi, ĭtum, *v.t.* 2, to bring together
conciliābŭlum, i, *n*, assembly-place
concĭliātio, ōnis, *f*, union
concĭliātor, ōris, *m*, promoter
concĭlio, *v.t.* 1, to unite, win over, bring about
concĭlium, ii, *n*, meeting, assembly
concinnitas, ātis, *f*, elegance
concinnus, a, um, *adj*, *adv*, **ē,** well-adjusted, graceful
concino, nŭi, *v.i.t.* 3, to harmonize; celebrate
concĭpio, cēpi, ceptum, *v.t.* 3, to take hold of, become pregnant, understand, formulate, designate
concīsus, a, um, *adj*, *adv*, **ē,** cut short
concĭtātio, ōnis, *f*, quick motion
concĭtātus, a, um, *adj*, *adv*, **ē,** swift, roused
concĭto, *v.t.* 1, to stir up, rouse
conclāmo, *v.i.t.* 1, to shout out; call upon
conclāve, is, *n*, room
conclūdo, si, sum, *v.t.* 3, to enclose, include, conclude
concoctio, ōnis, *f*, digestion
concŏlor, ōris, *adj*, similar in colour
concŏquo, xi, ctum, *v.t.* 3, to boil together, digest, put up with
concordia, ae, *f*, agreement
concordo, *v.i.* 1, to agree
concors, cordis, *adj*, *adv*, **iter,** of the same mind
concrēdo, didi, ditum, *v.t.* 3, to entrust
concrĕmo, *v.t.* 1, to burn up
concrĕpo, ŭi, ĭtum, *v.i.t.* 3, to creak, crack; 2 rattle, clash

concresco, crēvi, tum, *v.i.* 3, to grow together, harden
concrētus, a, um, *adj*, hardened
concŭbīna, ae, *f*, concubine
concŭbius, a, um, *adj*, (with **nox**) at dead of night
conculco, *v.t.* 1, to trample on
concŭpisco, cŭpīvi, ītum, *v.t.* 3, to long for, strive after
concurro, curri, cursum, *v.i.* 3, to rush together, assemble, join battle
concursātio, ōnis, *f*, running together
concursio, ōnis, *f*, running together
concurso, *v.i.t.* 1, to run, travel about, skirmish; frequent
concursus, ūs, *m*, rush, collision
concŭtio, cussi, ssum, *v.t.* 3, to shake, disturb, terrify, examine
condemno, *v.t.* 1, to convict
condenso, *v.t.* 1, to condense
condensus, a, um, *adj*, thick
condicio, ōnis, *f*, agreement, proposition, terms, alliance, rank, situation
condimentum, i, *n*, seasoning
condio, *v.t.* 4, to pickle
condiscipŭlus, i, *m*, school-friend
condisco, didici, *v.t.* 3, to learn carefully
conditor, ōris, *m*, builder, author, founder
conditus, a, um, *adj*, fashioned, composed
conditus . a, um, *adj*, savoury
condo, didi, ditum, *v.t.* 3, to construct, found, store up, hide, thrust in
condŏlesco, lŭi, *v.i.* 3, to suffer pain
condōno, *v.t.* 1, to present, give up, surrender, pardon
condūco, xi, ctum, *v.i.t.* 3, to be useful; collect, connect, hire
conductio, ōnis, *f*, hiring
conductor, ōris, *m*, tenant, contractor
conductum, i, *n*, tenement
conductus, a, um, *adj*, hired
cōnecto, xŭi, xum, *v.t.* 3, to tie together, involve
confarrēātio, ōnis, *f*, marriage
confectio, ōnis, *f*, arrangement, completion
confectus, a, um, *adj*, completed, exhausted
confercio, (*no perf.*) **fertum,** *v.t.* 4, to cram, stuff together
confĕro, ferre, tŭli, collātum, *v.t, irreg*, to bring together, contribute, confer, talk about, engage, fight, compare, condense, convey, postpone; (*reflex.*) to betake oneself, go
confertus, a, um, *adj, adv,* **e,** crowded
confessio, ōnis, *f*, confession
confessus, a, um, *adj*, admitted
confestim, *adv*, immediately
conficio, fēci, fectum, *v.t.* 3, to complete, produce, exhaust, kill
confidens, ntis, *adj, adv,* **nter,** bold, impudent
confidentia, ae, *f*, boldness
confido, fisus sum, *v.i.* 3, *semi-dep*, to feel confident; *with dat*, to trust
confīgo, xi, xum, *v.t.* 3, to nail, fasten together, transfix
confingo, nxi, ctum, *v.t.* 3, to fashion, invent
confinis, e, *adj*, adjoining
confinium, ii, *n*, border
confirmātio, ōnis, *f*, encouragement, confirming
confirmātus, a, um, *adj*, resolute
confirmo, *v.t.* 1, to strengthen, encourage, prove
confisus, a, um, *adj*, trusting
confitĕor, fessus, *v.t.* 2, *dep*, to acknowledge, own
conflāgro, *v.i.* 1, to burn
conflicto, *v.t.* 1, to strike or dash together, ruin, harass
confligo, xi, ctum, *v.i.t.* 3, to fight, struggle; strike or dash together
conflo, *v.t.* 1, to kindle, cause
conflŭens, ntis, *m*, confluence of rivers
conflŭo, xi, *v.i.* 3, to flow together, unite, come in crowds
confŏdio, fōdi, fossum, *v.t.* 3, to dig thoroughly, stab, pierce
conformātio, ōnis, *f*, shaping
conformo, *v.t.* 1, to form, fashion
confrăgōsus, a, um, *adj*, broken
confringo, frēgi, fractum, *v.t.* 3, to smash up
confŭgio, fŭgi, *v.i.* 3, to run away for help, take refuge
confundo, fūdi, sum, *v.t.* 3, to pour together, confuse
confūsio, ōnis, *f*, blending, disorder
confūsus, a, um, *adj, adv,* **ē,** disorderly
confūto, *v.t.* 1, to repress, silence
congēlo, *v.i.t.* 1, to freeze; thicken
congĕmino, *v.t.* 1, to redouble
congĕmo, ŭi, *v.i.t.* 3, to sigh; mourn
congĕries, ēi, *f*, heap
congĕro, ssi, stum, *v.t.* 3, to bring together, accumulate
congestus, ūs, *m*, heap
congiārium, ii, *n*, gratuity
congius, ii, *m*, 6-pint measure
conglŏbo, *v.t.* 1, to gather, press into a ball

conglūtĭno, *v.t.* 1, to glue or cement together, unite
congrĕdior, gressus, *v.i.* 3, *dep*, to meet, encounter
congrĕgātĭo, ōnis, *f*, assembly
congrĕgo, *v.t.* 1, to collect into a flock, unite
congressus, ūs, *m*, meeting, combat
congrŭens, ntis, *adj*, *adv*, **nter,** appropriate, proper, consistent
congrŭentĭa, ae, *f*, agreement
congrŭo, ŭi, *v.i.* 3, to meet, coincide
cōnĭcĭo, iēci, iectum, *v.t.* 3, to hurl, infer, drive
coniecto, *v.t.* 1, to hurl, foretell
coniectūra, ae, *f*, inference
coniectus, ūs, *m*, throwing, heap
coniectus, a, um, *adj*, thrown together
cōnĭfer, ĕra, ĕrum, *adj*, cone-bearing
cōnĭtor, nĭsus (nixus), *v.i.* 3, *dep*, to strive, struggle towards
cōnīvĕo, nīvi, *v.i.* 2, to wink, blink
coniŭgĭum, ii, *n*, union, marriage
coniunctĭo, ōnis, *f*, uniting, junction
coniunctus, a, um, *adj*, *adv.* **e,** near, connected, allied
coniungo, nxi, nctum, *v.t.* 3, to join together, marry
coniunx, iŭgis, *m*, *f*, husband, wife
coniūrātĭo, ōnis, *f*, conspiracy
coniūrātus, i, *m*, conspirator
coniūro, *v.i.* 1, to conspire, band together
conl . . . see **coll . . .**
connecto, . . . see **cōnecto**
connīvĕo, see **cōnīvĕo**
connŭbĭum, ii, *n*, marriage
cōnŏpĕum, i, *n*, gauze-net
cōnor, *v.t.* 1, *dep*, to try, undertake
conquĕror, questus, *v.i.t.* 3, *dep*, to complain (of)
conquĭesco, quiēvi, quiētum, *v.i.* 3, to rest, pause
conquīro, quīsīvi, sītum, *v.t.* 3, to search for
conquīsītĭo, ōnis, *f*, search
conquīsītus, a, um, *adj*, sought after
consălūto, *v.t.* 1, to greet
consānesco, ŭi, *v.i.* 3, to heal
consanguĭnĕus, a, um, *adj*, related by blood
consanguĭnĭtas, ātis, *f*, blood-relationship
conscendo, di, sum, *v.i.t.* 3, to embark; mount
conscientĭa, ae, *f*, joint knowledge, moral sense
conscindo, ĭdi, issum, *v.t.* 3, to tear in pieces
conscisco, scīvi, ĭtum, *v.t.* 3, to make a joint resolution, decree, inflict
conscĭus, a, um, *adj*, sharing knowledge of, (with **sibi**) conscious of
conscĭus, i, *m*, accomplice
conscrĭbo, psi, ptum, *v.t.* 3, to enroll, enlist, compose
conscriptus, i, *m*, senator
consĕco, cŭi, ctum, *v.t.* 1, to cut up
consecrātĭo, ōnis, *f*, consecration
consecro, *v.t.* 1, to dedicate, doom
consector, *v.t.* 1, *dep*, to pursue eagerly, imitate
consĕnesco, nŭi, *v.i.* 3, to grow old or weak
consensĭo, ōnis, *f*, agreement, plot
consensus, ūs, *m*, agreement, plot
consentānĕus, a, um, *adj*, suited
consentĭo, sensi, sum, *v.i.t.* 4, to agree, conspire, resolve; plot
consĕquens, ntis, *adj*, according to reason, fit
consĕquor, sĕcūtus, *v.t.* 3, *dep*, to follow, pursue, overtake, attain, obtain
consĕro, sēvi, sĭtum (sătum), *v.t.* 3, to plant, sow
consĕro, rŭi, rtum, *v.t.* 3, to fasten together
consertus, a, um, *adj*, *adv*, **ē,** joined, close, serried
conservātĭo, ōnis, *f*, maintenance
conservo, *v.t.* 1, to maintain, keep safe
conservus, i, *m*, fellow-slave
consessus, ūs, *m*, assembly
consĭdĕrātus, a, um, *adj*, *adv*, **e,** well-considered, cautious, discreet
consĭdĕrātĭo, ōnis, *f*, consideration
consĭdĕro, *v.t.* 1, to examine, contemplate
consĭdo, sēdi, sessum, *v.i.* 3, to sit down, take up position, subside
consigno, *v.t.* 1, to seal, certify
consiliārĭus, ii, *m*, adviser
consilĭor, *v.i.* 1, *dep*, to consult
consilĭum, ii, *n*, plan, deliberation, policy, advice, assembly, wisdom
consĭmĭlis, e, *adj*, quite like
consisto, stĭti, stĭtum, *v.i.* 3, to stand, halt, take up position, endure, exist, settle
consōbrīnus, i, *m* (**a, ae,** *f*), cousin
consŏcĭātus, a, um, *adj*, united
consŏcĭo, *v.t.* 1, to share, unite
consōlātĭo, ōnis, *f*, comfort
consōlātor, ōris, *m*, comforter
consōlor, *v.t.* 1, *dep*, to comfort
consŏnans, ntis (with **littera**), consonant

For List of Abbreviations used, turn to pages 3, 4

consŏno, ŭi, *v.i.* 1, to resound, harmonize, agree
consŏnus, a, um, *adj, adv,* **ē,** fit, harmonious
consōpĭo, *v.t.* 4, to put to sleep
consors, rtis, *adj,* partner
consortĭo, ōnis, *f,* association
conspectus, ūs, *m,* look, sight, view, presence
conspectus, a, um, *adj,* distinguished, visible
conspergo, si, sum, *v.t.* 3, to sprinkle
conspĭcĭo, spexi, ctum, *v.t.* 3, to look at, understand
conspĭcor, *v.t.* 1, *dep,* to catch sight of
conspĭcŭus, a, um, *adj,* visible, striking
conspīrātĭo, ōnis, *f,* agreement, plot
conspīro, *v.i.* 1, to agree, plot
consponsor, ōris, *m,* joint surety
conspŭo, —, ūtum, *v.t.* 3, to spit on, cover
constans, ntis, *adj, adv,* **nter,** firm, resolute, consistent
constantĭa, ae, *f,* firmness, consistency
constat, *v. impers,* it is agreed
consternātĭo, ōnis, *f,* dismay
consterno, strāvi, strātum, *v.t.* 3, to cover over
consterno, *v.t.* 1, to alarm, provoke
constĭtŭo, ŭi, ūtum, *v.t.* 3, to put, place, draw up, halt, establish, arrange, determine, decide
constĭtūtĭo, ōnis, *f,* arrangement, establishment
constĭtūtum, i, *n,* agreement
constĭtūtus, a, um, *adj,* arranged
consto, stĭti, stātum, *v.i.* 1, to agree with, endure, be established, exist, consist of, cost
constrātus, a, um, *adj,* covered
constringo, nxi, ctum, *v.t.* 3, to tie up, restrain
constrŭo, xi, ctum, *v.t.* 3, to heap up, build
constūpro, *v.t.* 1, to ravish
consŭēfăcio, fēci, factum, *v.t.* 3, to accustom
consŭesco, sŭēvi, sŭētum, *v.i.t.* 3, to be accustomed; train
consŭētūdo, ĭnis, *f,* habit, custom, intimacy
consŭētus, a, um, *adj,* customary
consŭl, ŭlis, *m,* consul (highest Roman magistrate)
consŭlāris, e, *adj,* of a consul
consŭlātus, ūs, *m,* consulship
consŭlo, ŭi, sultum, *v.i.t.* 3, to consider, consult; *with dat.* promote the interests of
consulto, *v.i.t.* 1, to deliberate; consult
consultor, ōris, *m,* adviser, client
consultum, i, *n,* decision, decree
consultus, a, um, *adj, adv,* **e, o,** well-considered
consummātĭo, ōnis, *f,* summing-up, completion
consūmo, mpsi, mptum, *v.t.* 3, to use, eat up, consume, waste, destroy
consumptĭo, ōnis, *f,* wasting, use
consurgo, surrexi, surrectum, *v.i.* 3, to stand up, rise
contăbŭlātĭo, ōnis, *f,* flooring
contăbŭlo, *v.t.* 1, to board over
contactus, ūs, *m,* touch, contact, contagion
contāgio, ōnis, *f,* touch, contact, contagion
contāmĭnātus, a, um, *adj,* impure
contāmĭno, *v.t.* 1, to blend, stain
contĕgo, xi, ctum, *v.t.* 3, to cover up, hide
contemnendus, a, um, *adj,* contemptible
contemno, mpsi, mptum, *v.t.* 3, to despise
contemplātĭo, ōnis, *f,* observation
contemplor, *v.t.* 1, *dep,* to observe
contemptor, ōris, *m,* despiser
contemptus, ūs, *m,* contempt
contemptus, a, um, *adj,* despicable
contendo, di, tum, *v.i.t.* 3, to strive, march, fight, stretch; compare, make a bid for
contentĭo, ōnis, *f,* struggle, effort, contrast, dispute
contentus, a, um, *adj,* strained
contentus, a, um, *adj,* satisfied
conterminus, a, um, *adj,* bordering on
contĕro, trīvi, trītum, *v.t.* 3, to grind, wear away, waste
conterrĕo, *v.t.* 2, to frighten
contestor, *v.t.* 1, *dep,* to call to witness
contexo, ŭi, xtum, *v.i.t.* 3, to weave together; build, compose
contextus, ūs, *m,* connection
conticesco, ticŭi, *v.i.* 3, to be silent, cease
contignātĭo, ōnis, *f,* wooden floor
contigŭus, a, um, *adj,* adjoining
continens, ntis, *f,* continent
continens, ntis, *adj, adv,* **nter,** moderate, adjacent, unbroken
continentĭa, ae, *f,* self-restraint

contĭnĕo, ŭi, tentum, *v.t.* 2, to keep together, contain, enclose, restrain
contingo, tĭgi, tactum, *v.i.t.* 3, to happen; touch, border on, reach
contĭnŭātio, ōnis, *f*, succession
contĭnŭō, *adv*, immediately
contĭnŭo, *v.t.* 1, to connect, to do one thing after another
contĭnŭus, a, um, *adj*, unbroken
contiō, ōnis, *f*, meeting, speech
contiōnātor, ōris, *m*, demagogue
contiōnor, *v.* 1, *dep*, to expound
contorquĕo, tōrsi, tortum, *v.t.* 2, to twist, brandish, hurl
contortio, ōnis, *f*, twisting, intricacy
contortus, a, um, *adj*, *adv*, **ē,** energetic, complicated
contrā, *adv*, *prep. with acc*, opposite, facing, contrary to
contractio, ōnis, *f*, contraction
contractus, a, um, *adj*, compressed
contrādĭco, xi, ctum, *v.t.* 3, to reply
contrādictio, ōnis, *f*, reply
contrāho, xi, ctum, *v.t.* 3, to bring together, shorten, produce, check
contrārĭum, ii, *n*, the contrary
contrārĭus, a, um, *adj*, *adv*, **ē,** opposite, injurious
contrecto, *v.t.* 1, to handle, feel
contrĕmisco, mŭi, *v.i.t.* 3, to quake; tremble at
contribŭo, ŭi, ūtum, *v.t.* 3, to incorporate, unite
contristo, *v.t.* 1, to sadden, cloud
contrĭtus, a, um, *adj*, worn out
controversia, ae, *f*, dispute
controvērsus, a, um, *adj*, questionable
contrŭcido, *v.t.* 1, to slash
contŭbernālis, is, *c*, messmate
contŭbernium, ii, *n*, companionship
contŭĕor, *v.t.* 2, *dep*, to survey
contŭmācia, ae, *f*, obstinacy
contŭmax, ācis, *adj*, *adv*, **iter,** stubborn, insolent
contŭmēlia, ae, *f*, insult
contŭmēliōsus, a, um, *adj*, abusive
contŭmŭlo, *v.t.* 1, to bury
contundo, tŭdi, tūsum, *v.t.* 3, to grind, crush, subdue
conturbo, *v.t.* 1, to confuse
contus, i, *m*, pole
contūsum, i, *n*, bruise
cōnŭbĭum, ii, *n*, marriage
cōnus, i, *m*, cone, helmet-tip
convālesco, lŭi, *v.i.* 3, to regain strength or health
convallis, is, *f*, valley
convecto, *v.t.* 1, to to collect
convĕho, xi, ctum, *v.t.* 3, to bring together
convello, velli, vulsum, *v.t.* 3, to tear up
convĕniens, ntis, *adj*, *adv*, **nter,** consistent, appropriate
convĕnientia, ae, *f*, consistency, symmetry
convĕnio, vēni, ventum, *v.i.t.* 4, to assemble, agree with; meet
convĕnit, *impers*, it is agreed, it is right, it suits
conventum, i, *n*, agreement
conventus, ūs, *m*, meeting, assizes
conversio, ōnis, *f*, revolution
conversus, a, um, *adj*, reversed, turned, transposed
converto, ti, sum, *v.i.t.* 3, to turn; change, alter
convexus, a, um, *adj*, arched
convĭcium, ii, *n*, outcry, squabbling, abuse
convictor, ōris, *m*, close friend
convictus, ūs, *m*, intimacy
convinco, vĭci, victum, *v.t.* 3, to conquer, prove
convīva, ae, *c*, guest
convīvium, ii, *n*, dinner-party
convīvor, *v.i.* 1, *dep*, to banquet
convŏco, *v.t.* 1, to call together
convŏlo, *v.i.* 1, to flock together
convolvo, volvi, vŏlūtum, *v.t.* 3, to roll up, interweave
convulsio, ōnis, *f*, convulsion
convulsus, a, um, *adj*, torn-up
cŏŏpĕrĭo, rŭi, rtum, *v.t.* 4, to cover up, overwhelm
cŏoptātio, ōnis, *f*, election
cŏopto, *v.t.* 1, to nominate, elect
cŏŏrior, ortus, *v.i.* 4, *dep*, to arise, break out
cŏphinus, i, *m*, wicker basket
cōpia, ae, *f*, abundance, power, supply, opportunity; (*pl*) forces
cōpĭōsus, a, um, *adj*, *adv*, **ē,** well-supplied, eloquent
cōpŭla, ae, *f*, thong, grappling-iron
cōpŭlo, *v.t.* 1, to link, join
cŏquo, xi, ctum, *v.t.* 3, to cook, burn, ripen, devise, harass
cŏquus, i, *m*, cook
cŏr, cordis, *n*, heart, mind
cŏrālium, ii, *n*, coral
cōram, *adv. and prep. with abl*, in the presence of, openly
corbis, is, *c*, basket
corbĭta, ae, *f*, merchant ship
cordātus, a, um, *adj*, shrewd
cŏrĭārius, ii, *m*, tanner
cŏrium, ii, *n*, skin, hide, leather, layer, stratum
cornĕus, a, um, *adj*, horny

cornĕus, a, um, *adj*, of cornel-wood
cornĭcen, ĭnis, *m*, horn-player
cornĭcŭla, ae, *f*, jackdaw
cornĭcŭlum, i, *n*, little horn, feeler
corniger, ĕra, ĕrum, *adj*, horned
cornĭpēs, ĕdis, *adj*, hoofed
cornix, īcis, *f*, crow
cornū, ūs, *n*, horn, hoof, beak, tributary, promontory, knob, wing of army, bow, trumpet, drinking horn
cornum, i, *n*, cornel-cherry
cornus, i, *f*, cornel-cherry tree, cornel-wood javelin
cŏrōna, ae, *f*, garland, wreath, crown, ring, circle, crowd
cŏrōno, *v.t.* 1, to crown, encircle
corpŏrĕus, a, um, *adj*, physical
corpŭlentus, a, um, *adj*, corpulent
corpus, ŏris, *n*, body
correctio, ōnis, *f*, improvement
corrector, ōris, *m*, reformer
corrēpo, psi, *v.i.* 3, to creep
corrīgia, ae, *f*, shoe-lace
corrīgo, rexi, ctum, *v.t.* 3, to put right, improve
corripio, pŭi, reptum, *v.t.* 3, to snatch, plunder, attack, shorten
corrōbŏro, *v.t.* 1, to strengthen
corrūgo, *v.t.* 1, to wrinkle
corrumpo, rūpi, ptum, *v.t.* 3, to destroy, corrupt, spoil
corrŭo, ŭi, *v.i.t.* 3, to collapse; overthrow
corruptēla, ae, *f*, corruption
corruptor, ōris, *m*, corruptor, seducer
corruptus, a, um, *adj, adv,* ē, spoiled, damaged, tainted
cortex, icis, *m*, bark, rind
cortīna, ae, *f*, kettle, cauldron
cŏrusco, *v.i.t.* 1, to glitter; shake
cŏruscus, a, um, *adj*, glittering, vibrating
corvus, i, *m*, raven
cŏrȳlus, i, *f*, hazel shrub
cŏrymbus, i, *m*, cluster of fruit or flowers
cŏrȳtŏs, i, *m*, quiver
cŏs, cŏtis, *f*, flintstone
costa, ae, *f*, rib, wall
cŏthurnus, i, *m*, hunting-boot, buskin (worn by tragic actors)
cottĭdiānus, a, um, *adj, adv,* ō, daily, usual
cottĭdiē, *adv*, daily
cŏturnix, īcis, *f*, quail
coxendix, īcis, *f*, hip
crabro, ōnis, *m*, hornet
crambē, es, *f*, cabbage, kale
crāpŭla, ae, *f*, intoxication
crās, *adv*, tomorrow
crassĭtūdo, ĭnis, *f*, thickness
crassus, a, um, *adj, adv,* ē, thick, fat, solid
crastīnus, a, um, *adj*, of tomorrow
crātēr, ĕris, *m*, mixing-bowl, basin
crātēra, ae, *f*, mixing-bowl, basin
crātĭcŭla, ae, *f*, gridiron
crātis, is, *f*, wicker-work, hurdle
crĕātio, ōnis, *f*, appointing
crĕātor, ōris, *m*, founder, creator
crĕātrix, īcis, *f*, mother
crēber, bra, brum, *adj, adv,* o, thick, numerous, repeated
crēbresco, brŭi, *v.i.* 3, to become frequent, gain strength
crēdens, ntis, *c*, believer
crēdibilis, e, *adj, adv,* ĭter, credible, probable
crēditor, ōris, *m*, creditor
crēdo, dĭdi, dĭtum, *v.t.* 3, to lend, entrust, trust, believe in (*with dat*); suppose
crēdŭlitas, ātis, *f*, credulity
crēdŭlus, a, um, *adj*, ready to believe
crĕmo, *v.t.* 1, to burn
crĕo, *v.t.* 1, to produce, appoint
crĕpĭda, ae, *f*, sandal
crĕpĭdo, ĭnis, *f*, pedestal, dike
crĕpĭtăcŭlum, i, *n*, rattle
crĕpĭto, *v.i.* 1, to rattle, rustle
crĕpĭtus, ūs, *m*, rattling, clashing, cracking
crĕpo, ŭi, ĭtum, *v.i.t.* 1, to rattle, creak, jingle; prattle about
crĕpundia, ōrum, *n.pl*, child's rattle
crĕpuscŭlum, i, *n*, twilight, dusk
cresco, crēvi, crētum, *v.i.* 3, to arise, grow, appear, thrive
crēta, ae, *f*, chalk
crētus, a, um, *adj*, arisen, born of
crĭbro, *v.t.* 1, to sift
crĭbrum, i, *n*, sieve
crĭmen, ĭnis, *n*, accusation, offence
crĭminātio, ōnis, *f*, accusation, calumny
crĭminor, *v.t.* 1, *dep*, to accuse
crĭminōsus, a, um, *adj, adv,* ē, slanderous, culpable
crĭnālis, e, *adj*, of the hair
crĭnis, is, *m*, the hair
crĭnītus, a, um, *adj*, long-haired
crispo, *v.i.t.* 1, to curl; brandish
crispus, a, um, *adj*, curled, quivering
crista, ae, *f*, crest, plume
cristātus, a, um, *adj*, crested
crĭticus, i, *m*, critic
crŏcĕus, a, um, *adj*, of saffron or yellow
crŏcio, *v.i.* 4, to croak
crŏcŏdīlus, i, *m*, crocodile

crŏcus, i, *m* (**um, i,** *n*), crocus
crŭcĭātus, ūs, *m*, torture, pain
crŭcio, *v.t.* 1, to torture
crūdēlis, e, *adj, adv,* **ĭter,** cruel
crūdēlĭtas, ātis, *f*, cruelty
crūdesco, dŭi, *v.i.* 3, to get worse
crūdĭtas, ātis, *f*, indigestion
crūdus, a, um, *adj*, raw, fresh, unripe, cruel
crŭento, *v.t.* 1, to stain with blood
crŭentus, a, um, *adj*, blood-stained, blood-thirsty
crŭmēna, ae, *f*, small purse
crŭor, ōris, *m*, blood (from a wound), murder
crūs, ūris, *n*, leg, shin
crusta, ae, *f*, crust, bark, mosaic
crustŭlārius, ii, *m*, confectioner
crustŭlum, i, *n*, confectionery
crustum, i, *n*, confectionery
crux, ŭcis, *f*, cross
crypta, ae, *f*, cloister, vault
crystallum, i, *n*, crystal
cŭbĭcŭlārius, ii, *m*, chamber-servant
cŭbĭcŭlum, i, *n*, bedroom
cŭbĭcus, a, um, *adj*, cubic
cŭbīle, is, *n*, bed, lair
cŭbĭtăl, ālis, *n*, cushion
cŭbĭtum, i, *n*, elbow
cŭbĭtus, i, *m*, elbow
cŭbĭtum, see **cŭbo**
cŭbo, ŭi, ĭtum, *v.i.* 1, to lie down, sleep, lie ill, slant
cŭcullus, i, *m*, hood
cŭcūlus, i, *m*, cuckoo
cŭcūmis, ĕris, *m*, cucumber
cŭcurbĭta, ae, *f*, cup
cūdo, *v.t.* 3, to beat, strike, stamp
cūius, a, um, *interr. adj*, whose?
cūius, *genit*, of **qui, quis**
culcĭta, ae, *f*, mattress, cushion
cŭlex, ĭcis, *m*, gnat, mosquito
cŭlĭna, ae, *f*, kitchen, food
cullĕus, i, *m*, leather bag
culmen, ĭnis, *n*, summit, roof
culmus, i, *m*, stem, stalk
culpa, ae, *f*, blame, fault, weakness
culpābĭlis, e, *adj*, culpable
culpandus, a, um, *adj*, culpable
culpo, *v.t.* 1, to blame
culter, tri, *m*, knife, ploughshare
cultor, ōris, *m*, cultivator, supporter, inhabitant
cultrix, īcis, *f*, female inhabitant
cultūra, ae, *f*, cultivation, care
cultus, a, um, *adj*, cultivated, elegant
cultus, ūs, *m*, farming, education, culture-pattern, reverence, dress
cŭlullus, i, *m*, drinking-cup
cum, *conj*, when, whenever, since, although, **cum ... tum,** both ... and, not only ... but also
cum, *prep. with abl*, with, together with; *it is attached to the abl. case of personal prons*, e.g. **mecum,** with me
cumba, ae, *f*, small boat
cŭmĕra, ae, *f*, box, chest
cŭmīnum, i, *n*, cumin (plant)
cumquĕ, *adv*, however, whenever
cŭmŭlātus, a, um, *adj, adv,* **ē,** full, increased
cŭmŭlo, *v.t.* 1, to heap up, complete
cŭmŭlus, i, *m*, heap, "last straw"
cūnābŭla, ōrum, *n.pl*, cradle
cūnae, ārum, *f. pl*, cradle
cunctans, ntis, *adj, adv,* **nter,** loitering, sluggish
cunctātio, ōnis, *f*, delay, doubt
cunctātor, ōris, *m*, loiterer, cautious person
cunctor, *v.i.* 1, *dep*, to hesitate, delay
cunctus, a, um, *adj*, all together
cŭnĕātim, *adv*, wedge-shaped
cŭnĕo, *v.t.* 1, to fasten with wedges
cŭnĕus, i, *m*, wedge, wedge-shaped block of theatre-seats or troop-formation
cŭnīcŭlum, i, *n*, tunnel, mine
cŭnīcŭlus, i, *m*, rabbit
cūpa, ae, *f*, barrel, cask
cūpēdĭa, ōrum, *n.pl*, delicacies
cŭpĭdē, *adv*, eagerly
cŭpĭditas, ātis, *f*, desire, longing
cŭpĭdo, ĭnis, *f*, lust, greed
cŭpĭdus, a, um, *adj*, eager, longing for, greedy, passionate
cŭpĭens, ntis, *adj, adv,* **nter,** eager or longing for
cŭpio, īvi, ītum, *v.t.* 3, to desire
cŭpressus, i, *f*, cypress tree
cūr, *adv*, why
cūra, ae, *f*, care, attention, management, anxiety
cūrātio, ōnis, *f*, administration, cure
cūrātor, ōris, *m*, manager
cūrātus, a, um, *adj*, urgent
curcŭlio, ōnis, *m*, weevil
cūrĭa, ae, *f*, senate-house, city-ward
cūrĭālis, e, *adj*, of the same ward
cūrĭōsus, a, um, *adj, adv,* **e,** careful, inquisitive
cūro, *v.t.* 1, to take care of; *with acc. and gerundive*, to see to it that ... to arrange, command
currĭcŭlum, i, *n*, race-course, chariot, racing, career
curro, cŭcurri, cursum, *v.i.* 3, to run
currus, ūs, *m*, chariot
cursim, *adv*, swiftly

For List of Abbreviations used, turn to pages 3, 4

curso, *v.i.* 1, to run to and fro
cursor, ōris, *m,* runner, courier
cursus, ūs, *m,* running, journey, speed, direction
curtus, a, um, *adj,* shortened, humble
cŭrŭlis, e, *adj,* of a chariot; **sella cŭrŭlis,** ivory chair of office used by high magistrates
curvāmen, inis, *n,* curve
curvo, *v.t.* 1, to bend
curvus, a, um, *adj,* bent, stooping
cuspis, ĭdis, *f,* point, lance, spit, sting
custōdĭa, ae, *f,* watch, guard, imprisonment, guard-room
custōdio, *v.t.* 4, to guard, watch, keep, preserve
custos, ōdis, *c,* guardian, goaler
cūtis, is, *f,* skin, surface
cȳăthus, i, *m,* small ladle
cȳcnēus, a, um, *adj,* of a swan
cȳcnus, i, *m,* swan
cȳlindrus, i, *m,* roller, cylinder
cymba, ae, *f,* small boat
cymbălum, i, *n,* cymbal, bell
cymbĭum, ii, *n,* bowl, basin
Cȳnĭcus, i, *m,* a Cynic philosopher
cȳpărissus, i, *f,* cypress tree

D

dactȳlus, i, *m,* dactyl (metrical foot consisting of 1 long and 2 short syllables)
daedălus, a, um, *adj,* skilful
daemōnĭum, ii, *n,* demon
damma (dāma), ae, *f,* deer
damnātio, ōnis, *f,* condemnation
damnātōrius, a, um, *adj,* condemnatory
damnātus, a, um, *adj,* guilty
damno, *v.t.* 1, to condemn
damnōsus, a, um, *adj, adv,* **e,** destructive
damnum, i, *n,* damage, loss, fine
daps, dăpis, *f,* formal banquet
dătio, ōnis, *f,* distribution
dător, ōris, *m,* giver
dē, *prep. with abl,* from, down from, about, concerning, on account of
dĕa, ae, *f,* goddess
dĕalbo, *v.t.* 1, to whitewash
dĕambŭlo, *v.i.* 1, to take a walk
dĕarmo, *v.t.* 1, to disarm
dēbacchor, *v.i.* 1, *dep,* to rage
dēbellātor, ōris, *m,* conqueror
dēbello, *v.i.t.* 1, to finish a war; subdue
dēbĕo, *v.i.t.* 2, to be indebted; owe, (one) ought
dēbĭlis, e, *adj,* disabled, weak
dēbĭlĭtas, ātis, *f,* weakness
dēbĭlĭtātio, ōnis, *f,* maiming, enervating
dēbĭlĭto, *v.t.* 1, to cripple, weaken
dēbĭtor, ōris, *m,* debtor
dēbĭtum, i, *n,* debt
dēbĭtus, a, um, *adj,* owed
dēcanto, *v.i.* 1, to sing repeatedly
dēcēdo, ssi, ssum, *v.i.* 3, to go away, cease, yield, resign
dĕcem, *indecl. adj,* ten
Dĕcember (mensis), December
dĕcempēda, ae, *f,* measuring rod (ten feet long)
dĕcempēdātor, ōris, *m,* surveyor
dĕcemvĭrālis, e, *adj,* of the decemviri
dĕcemvĭrātus, ūs, *m,* the rank of decemvir
dĕcemvĭri, ōrum, *m.pl,* commission of ten (early rulers of Rome)
dĕcens, ntis, *adj, adv,* **nter,** proper, graceful
dĕcentĭa, ae, *f,* comeliness
dēceptus, a, um, *adj,* deceived
dēcerno, crēvi, crētum, *v.i.t.* 3, to decide, resolve; fight
dēcerpo, psi, ptum, *v.t.* 3, to pluck, gather
dēcertātio, ōnis, *f,* struggle
dēcerto, *v.i.t.* 1, to fight it out; struggle for
dēcessio, ōnis, *f,* departure
dēcessus, ūs, *m,* departure
dĕcet, cŭit, *v.* 2, *impers,* it is becoming or proper
dēcĭdo, cĭdi, *v.i.* 3, to fall down, die, perish
dēcīdo, cīdi, cīsum, *v.t.* 3, to cut off, settle
dĕcĭēs (dĕcĭens), *adv,* ten times
dĕcĭma, ae, *f,* tenth part, tithe
dĕcĭmānus, a, um, *adj,* of tithes, of the tenth legion; **porta dĕcĭmāna,** main camp-gate
dĕcĭmo, *v.t.* 1, to punish every tenth man, decimate
dĕcĭmus, a, um, *adj,* tenth
dēcĭpio, cēpi, ptum, *v.t.* 3, to deceive
dēcisio, ōnis, *f,* decision
dēclāmātio, ōnis, *f,* practice in public speaking
dēclāmātor, ōris, *m,* speech-expert
dēclāmātōrius, a, um, *adj,* rhetorical
dēclāmo, *v.i.* 1, to practise speaking
dēclāro, *v.t.* 1, to make clear
dēclīnātio, ōnis, *f,* avoidance, bending
dēclīno, *v.i.t.* 1, to turn aside

dēclīve, is, *n*, slope
dēclīvis, e, *adj*, sloping downwards
dēclīvitas, ātis, *f*, slope
dēcoctor, ōris, *m*, bankrupt
dēcoctus, a, um, *adj*, boiled, refined
dēcŏlor, ōris, *adj*, discoloured
dēcŏlōro, *v.t.* 1, to discolour
dēcŏquo, xi, ctum, *v.t.* 3, to boil down, go bankrupt
dĕcor, ōris, *m*, elegance
dĕcŏro, *v.t.* 1, to adorn
dĕcōrum, i, *n*, decency
dĕcōrus, a, um, *adj*, *adv*, **ē,** becoming, proper, elegant
dēcrĕpĭtus, a, um, *adj*, decrepit
dēcresco, crēvi, tum, *v.i.* 3, to diminish, wane
dēcrētum, i, *n*, decree, decision
dĕcŭma, dĕcŭmānus, see **decim . . .**
dēcumbo, cŭbŭi, *v.i.* 3, to lie down, lie ill
dĕcŭrĭa, ae, *f*, section of ten
dĕcŭrio, *v.t.* 1, to divide into sections
dĕcŭrio, ōnis, *m*, the head of ten, superintendent
dēcurro, cŭcurri, cursum, *v.i.* 3, to run down, complete a course, manoeuvre, have recourse to
dēcursus, ūs, *m*, descent, course, manoeuvre, attack
dĕcus, ŏris, *n*, ornament, splendour
dēcussātio, ōnis, *f*, intersection
dēcŭtio, cussi, ssum, *v.t.* 3, to shake off, beat off
dēdĕcet, cŭit, *v.* 2, *impers*, it is unbecoming
dēdĕcŏro, *v.t.* 1, to disgrace
dēdĕcus, ŏris, *n*, disgrace, shame
dēdĭcātio, ōnis, *f*, dedication
dēdĭco, *v.t.* 1, to dedicate
dēdignor, *v.t.* 1, *dep*, to disdain
dēdisco, didĭci, *v.t.* 3, to forget
dēdĭtĭcĭus, ii, *m*, prisoner-of-war
dēdĭtio, ōnis, *f*, surrender
dēditus, a, um, *adj*, addicted to
dēdo, dēdidi, dĭtum, *v.t.* 3, to give up, surrender, devote
dēdŏcĕo, *v.t.* 2, to teach one not to . . .
dēdŏlĕo, *v.i.* 2, to stop grieving
dēdūco, xi, ctum, *v.t.* 3, to bring, lead down, withdraw, conduct, escort, mislead, subtract, launch
dēductio, ōnis, *f*, diversion, transplanting, inference
dēductus, a, um, *adj*, fine-spun
dēerro, *v.i.* 1, to go astray
dēfătīgātio, ōnis, *f*, exhaustion
dēfătīgo, *v.t.* 1, to exhaust
dēfectio, ōnis, *f*, rebellion, failure, eclipse
dēfectus, ūs, *m*, rebellion, failure, eclipse
dēfectus, a, um, *adj*, worn out
dēfendo, di, sum, *v.t.* 3, to repel, defend, support
dēfensio, ōnis, *f*, defence
dēfensor, ōris, *m*, protector
dēfĕro, ferre, tŭli, lātum, *v.t. irreg*, to bring down or away, convey, refer, announce, indict, offer
dēfervesco, fervi, *v.i.* 3, to cool down
dēfessus, a, um, *adj*, weary
dēfĕtiscor, fessus, *v.i.* 3, *dep*, to grow tired
dēfĭcio, fēci, fectum, *v.i.t.* 3, to fail, disappear, revolt; desert
dēfīgo, xi, xum, *v.t.* 3, to fasten down, astound
dēfingo, nxi, *v.t.* 3, to shape
dēfīnio, *v.t.* 4, to mark off, restrict, define
dēfīnĭtio, ōnis, *f*, definition
dēfīnītus, a, um, *adj*, *adv*, **ē,** precise
dēfixus, a, um, *adj*, fixed
dēflāgrātio, ōnis, *f*, destruction by fire
dēflāgro, *v.i.* 1, to burn out
dēflecto, xi, xum, *v.i.t.* 3, to swerve; divert
dēflĕo, ēvi, ētum, *v.t.* 2, to deplore
dēflōresco, rŭi, *v.i.* 3, to wither
dēflŭo, xi, xum, *v.i.* 3, to flow down, vanish
dēfŏdio, fōdi, ssum, *v.t.* 3, to dig deep, bury
dēfŏre, *fut. infinitive* (**dēsum**)
dēformis, e, *adj*, deformed, ugly
dēformĭtas, ātis, *f*, ugliness
dēformo, *v.t.* 1, to shape
dēformo, *v.t.* 1, to disfigure
dēfossus, a, um, *adj*, buried
dēfraudo, *v.t.* 1, to cheat
dēfrico, cŭi, ctum, *v.t.* 1, to rub hard
dēfringo, frēgi, fractum, *v.t.* 3, to break up, break off
dēfrŭtum, i, *n*, syrup
dēfŭgio, fūgi, *v.i.t.* 3, to escape; avoid
dēfunctus, a, um, *adj*, having finished, deceased
dēfundo, fūdi, fūsum, *v.t.* 3, to pour out
dēfungor, functus, *v.* 3, *dep. with abl*, to bring to an end
dēgĕner, ĕris, *adj*, unworthy of one's birth, ignoble
dēgĕnĕro, *v.i.t.* 1, to deteriorate; impair
dēgo, dēgi, *v.i.t.* 3, to live; spend
dēgrandinat, *v. impers*, it is hailing, ceasing to hail
dēgrăvo, *v.t.* 1, to weigh down

dēgrĕdĭor, gressus, *v.i.* 3, *dep,* to step down, dismount
dēgusto, *v.t.* 1, to taste, graze
dēhinc, *adv,* from here, hence, next, afterwards
dēhisco, hīvi, *v.i.* 3, to split open, gape
dēhŏnesto, *v.t.* 1, to disgrace
dēhortor, *v.t.* 1, *dep,* to dissuade
dēĭcĭo, iēci, iectum, *v.t.* 3, to throw down, drive out, lower
dēiectus, a, um, *adj,* downcast
dēiectus, ūs, *m,* descent, felling
dēin, *adv,* from there, after that, afterwards
dēindĕ, *adv,* from there, after that, afterwards
dēinceps, *adv,* in succession
dēlābor, lapsus, *v.i.* 3, *dep,* to fall, sink, glide down
dēlasso, *v.t.* 1, to tire out
dēlātĭo, ōnis, *f,* accusation
dēlātor, ōris, *m,* informer
dēlectābĭlis, e, *adj,* delightful
dēlectātĭo, ōnis, *f,* delight, pleasure
dēlecto, *v.t.* 1, to allure, charm
dēlectus, a, um, *adj,* chosen
dēlectus, ūs, *m,* choice, selection, levy
dēlectum hăbere, to hold a levy
dēlĕgo, *v.t.* 1, to dispatch, assign, attribute
dēlēnīmentum, i, *n,* allurement
dēlēnĭo, *v.t.* 4, to soothe, charm
dēlĕo, lēvi, lētum, *v.t.* 2, to destroy, finish
dēlĭbĕrātĭo, ōnis, *f,* careful thought
dēlĭbĕrātus, a, um, *adj,* settled
dēlĭbĕro, *v.t.* 1, to consider, consult, resolve
dēlĭbo, *v.t.* 1, to taste, pluck, detract from
dēlĭbūtus, a, um, *adj,* smeared
dēlĭcātus, a, um, *adj, adv,* **e,** charming, luxurious
dēlĭcĭae, ārum, *f. pl,* pleasure, luxury, sweetheart, pet
dēlictum, i, *n,* crime, offence
dēlĭgo, lēgi, lectum, *v.t.* 3, to pick, choose, gather
dēlĭgo, *v.t.* 1, to tie down
dēlinquo, līqui, lictum, *v.i.* 3, to fail, offend
dēlīrātĭo, ōnis, *f,* silliness
dēlīrĭum, ii, *n,* delirium
dēlīro, *v.i.* 1, to be out of one's mind
dēlīrus, a, um, *adj,* crazy
dēlitesco, tŭi, *v.i.* 3, to lurk
delphīnus, i, *m,* dolphin
dēlūbrum, i, *n,* sanctuary
dēlūdo, si, sum, *v.t.* 3, to mock
dēmando, *v.t.* 1, to entrust
dēmens, ntis, *adj, adv,* **nter,** out of one's mind
dēmensum, i, *n,* ration
dēmentĭa, ae, *f,* insanity
dēmĕrĕo, *v.t.* 2, to deserve, oblige
dēmergo, si, sum, *v.t.* 3, to immerse, sink
dēmētĭor, mensus, *v.t.* 4, *dep,* to measure off
dēmĕto, messŭi, ssum, *v.t.* 3, to mow, reap, gather
dēmigro, *v.i.* 1, to emigrate
dēmĭnŭo, ŭi, ūtum, *v.t.* 3, to lessen, infringe
dēmĭnūtĭo, ōnis, *f,* decrease
dēmīror, *v.t.* 1, *dep,* to wonder
dēmissĭo, ōnis, *f,* abasement
dēmissus, a, um, *adj, adv,* **ē,** low-lying, drooping, downcast, shy
dēmitto, mīsi, ssum, *v.t.* 3, to send down, lower, descend, enter upon, lose heart
dēmo, mpsi, mptum, *v.t.* 3, to take away, remove
dēmōlĭor, *v.t.* 4, *dep,* to pull down, destroy
dēmonstrātĭo, ōnis, *f,* indication
dēmonstro, *v.t.* 1, to point out
dēmŏrĭor, mortŭus, *v.i.* 3, *dep,* to die
dēmŏror, *v.i.t.* 1, *dep,* to loiter; restrain
dēmŏvĕo, mōvi, mōtum, *v.t.* 2, to remove, put aside
dēmum, *adv,* at last, not until then, only
dēmūto, *v.i.t.* 1, to change
dēnārĭus, ii, *m,* small Roman silver coin
dēnăto, *v.i.* 1, to swim down
dēnĕgo, *v.t.* 1, to deny completely
dēni, ae, a, *adj,* ten each, ten
dēnique, *adv,* and then, at last, in short
dēnōmĭno, *v.t.* 1, to name
dēnormo, *v.t.* 1, to disfigure
dēnŏto, *v.t.* 1, to mark out, point out
dens, ntis, *m,* tooth, prong
denso, *v.t.* 1, to thicken, close up
densus, a, um, *adj,* thick, frequent
dentālĭa, ĭum, *n.pl,* plough-beam
dentātus, a, um, *adj,* with teeth
dentĭfrĭcĭum, ii, *n,* tooth-powder
dentĭo, *v.i.* 4, to teethe
dentĭtĭo, ōnis, *f,* teething
dentiscalpĭum, ii, *n,* toothpick
dēnūbo, psi, ptum, *v.i.* 3, to marry
dēnūdo, *v.t.* 1, to lay bare
dēnuntĭātĭo, ōnis, *f,* declaration
dēnuntĭo, *v.t.* 1, to announce, command, warn

dēnŭō, *adv*, anew, again
dĕorsum, *adv*, downwards
dēpăciscor, see **dēpĕciscor**
dēpasco, pāvi, pastum, *v.t.* 3, to feed on, consume
dēpĕciscor, pectus (pactus), *v.t.* 3, *dep*, to bargain for
dēpĕcūlor, *v.t.* 1, *dep*, to plunder
dēpello, pŭli, pulsum, *v.t.* 3, to drive away, dissuade
dēpendĕo, *v.i.* 2, to hang down, depend on
dēpendo, di, sum, *v.t.* 3, to spend, pay
dēperdo, didi, ditum, *v.t.* 3, to destroy, lose
dēpĕrĕo, *v.i.* 4, to perish completely, die with love for
dēpingo, pinxi, pictum, *v.t.* 3, to paint, portray, sketch
dēplōro, *v.i.t.* 1, to lament; deplore
dēpōno, pŏsŭi, pŏsĭtum, *v.t.* 3, to put aside, entrust, bet, get rid of
dēpŏpŭlātio, ōnis, *f*, pillaging
dēpŏpŭlor, *v.t.* 1, *dep*, to plunder
dēporto, *v.t.* 1, to carry down, carry away, banish, earn
dēposco, pŏposci, *v.t.* 3, to demand, challenge
dēpŏsĭtum, i, *n*, deposit, trust
dēprāvātio, ōnis, *f*, corruption
dēprāvo, *v.t.* 1, to pervert, corrupt
dēprĕcātio, ōnis, *f*, pleading, intercession
dēprĕcātor, ōris, *m*, pleader
dēprĕcor, *v.t.* 1, *dep*, to avert by prayer, beseech, plead for
dēprĕhendo, di, sum, *v.t.* 3, to catch, overtake, discover
dēpressus, a, um, *adj*, low-lying
dēprĭmo, pressi, pressum, *v.t.* 3, to press down, sink, suppress
dēproelior, *v.i.* 1, *dep*, to battle fiercely
dēprōmo, mpsi, mptum, *v.t.* 3, to fetch out
dēprŏpĕro, *v.i.t.* 1, to hasten; prepare hastily
dēpugno, *v.i.* 1, to fight it out
dēpulsio, ōnis, *f*, warding off
dēpŭto, *v.t.* 1, to prune
dērĕlinquo, lĭqui, lictum, *v.t.* 3, to abandon completely
dērīdĕo, si, sum, *v.t.* 2, to mock
dērigesco, gŭi, *v.i.* 3, to stiffen
dēripio, ripŭi, reptum, *v.t.* 3, to tear off, pull down
dērisor, ōris, *m*, scoffer
dērīvātio, ōnis, *f*, turning off
dērīvo, *v.t.* 1, to divert water
dērŏgo, *v.t.* 1, to remove, restrict
dērōsus, a, um, *adj*, nibbled
dērūptus, a, um, *adj*, broken, steep
dēsaevio, *v.i.* 4, to rage
dēscendo, di, sum, *v.i.* 3, to go down, come down, go into battle, penetrate, resort to
dēscensus, ūs, *m*, descent
dēscisco, īvi, ītum, *v.i.* 3, to revolt, desert, degenerate
dēscribo, psi, ptum, *v.t.* 3, to transcribe, describe, define, arrange
dēscripta, ōrum, *n.pl*, records
dēscriptio, ōnis, *f*, sketch, description, arrangement
dēsĕco, cŭi, ctum, *v.t.* 1, to cut off
dēsĕro, rŭi, rtum, *v.t.* 3, to abandon
dēserta, ōrum, *n.pl*, desert
dēsertor, ōris, *m*, deserter
dēsertus, a, um, *adj*, abandoned
dēservio, *v.i.* 4, to serve wholeheartedly
dēses, ĭdis, *adj*, indolent
dēsidĕo, sēdi, *v.i.* 2, to sit idle
dēsīdĕrium, ii, *n*, longing, grief, request
dēsīdĕro, *v.t.* 1, to miss, crave for
dēsidia, ae, *f*, idleness
dēsidiōsus, a, um, *adj*, lazy
dēsīdo, sēdi, *v.i.* 3, to sink down
dēsignātio, ōnis, *f*, description, arrangement
dēsignātor, ōris, *m*, master of ceremonies, undertaker
dēsignātus, a, um, *adj*, elect
dēsigno, *v.t.* 1, to mark out, indicate, appoint
dēsilio, sĭlŭi, sultum, *v.i.* 4, to jump down
dēsino, sĭi, ĭtum, *v.i.t.* 3, to cease; put an end to
dēsipio, *v.i.* 3, to be foolish
dēsisto, stĭti, stĭtum, *v.i.* 3, to leave off, halt
dēsōlātus, a, um, *adj*, forsaken
dēsōlo, *v.t.* 1, to abandon
dēspecto, *v.t.* 1, to look down on
dēspectus, ūs, *m*, view down on
dēspectus, a, um, *adj*, despicable
dēspērātio, ōnis, *f*, hopelessness
dēspērātus, a, um, *adj*, past hope
dēspēro, *v.i.t.* 1, to despair; give up as lost
dēspicio, exi, ctum, *v.i.t.* 3, to look down; despise
dēspŏlio, *v.t.* 1, to plunder
dēspondĕo, di, nsum, *v.t.* 2, to promise (in marriage)
dēspūmo, *v.t.* 1, to skim off
dēspŭo, *v.i.t.* 3, to spit; reject
dēstillo, *v.i.* 1, to trickle, drip
dēstinātio, ōnis, *f*, purpose

For List of Abbreviations used, turn to pages 3, 4

dēstīnātum, i, *n*, aim, intention
dēstīnātus, a, um, *adj*, fixed
dēstīno, *v.t.* 1, to secure, intend
dēstĭtŭo, ŭi, ūtum, *v.t.* 3, to place, desert
dēstĭtūtus, a, um, *adj*, abandoned
dēstringo, nxi, ctum, *v.t.* 3, to strip off, unsheath, graze
dēstrŭo, xi, ctum, *v.t.* 3, to demolish
dēsŭesco, sŭēvi, sŭētum, *v.i.t.* 3, to become unused; cease to use
dēsŭētus, a, um, *adj*, disused
dēsultor, ōris, *m*, acrobat on horseback
dēsum, dēesse, dēfŭi, *v.i*, to be lacking, fail, desert
dēsūmo, mpsi, mptum, *v.t.* 3, to select
dēsŭpēr, *adv*, from above
dēsurgo, *v.i.* 3, to rise from
dētĕgo, xi, ctum, *v.t.* 3, to expose
dētentus, a, um, *adj*, kept back
dētergĕo, si, sum, *v.t.* 2, to wipe clean
dētĕrior, ĭus, *adj*, lower, worse
dētĕrius, *adv*, worse, less
dētermino, *v.t.* 1, to fix limits
dētĕro, trīvi, trītum, *v.t.* 3, to rub or wear away, impair
dēterrĕo, *v.t.* 2, to discourage
dētestābilis, e, *adj*, detestable
dētestātio, ōnis, *f*, cursing
dētestor, *v.t.* 1, *dep*, to curse, loathe, ward off
dētexo, xŭi, xtum, *v.t.* 3, to weave, finish
dētĭnĕo, tĭnŭi, tentum, *v.t.* 2, to keep back, delay, lengthen
dētŏno, ŭi, *v.i.* 1, to thunder, cease thundering
dētorquĕo, si, tum, *v.t.* 2, to turn aside, distort
dētrăho, xi, ctum, *v.t.* 3, to pull down, remove, deprecate
dētrecto, *v.t.* 1, to reject, detract from
dētrīmentum, i, *n*, loss, damage, defeat
dētrūdo, si, sum, *v.t.* 3, to push down, dislodge
dētrunco, *v.t.* 1, to lop off
dēturbo, *v.t.* 1, to throw down
dēūro, ussi, ustum, *v.t.* 3, to burn
dĕus, i, *m*, god
dēvasto, *v.t.* 1, to devastate
dēvĕho, xi, ctum, *v.t.* 3, to carry down, carry away
dēvĕnio, vēni, ventum, *v.i.* 4, to come down, arrive at
dēversor, *vi.* 1, *dep*, to lodge
dēversor, ōris, *m*, lodger
dēversōrium, ii, *n*, inn
dēverto, ti, sum, *v.i.t.* 3, to lodge, stay; turn aside
dēvexus, a, um, *adj*, sloping down
dēvĭa, ōrum, *n.pl*, lonely places
dēvincio, nxi, nctum, *v.t.* 4, to tie up, endear
dēvinco, vĭci, ctum, *v.t.* 3, to conquer completely
dēvinctus, see **dēvincio**
dēvĭto, *v.t.* 1, to avoid
dēvĭus, a, um, *adj*, out-of-the-way
dēvŏco, *v.t.* 1, to call away
dēvŏlo, *v.i.* 1, to fly down
dēvolvo, volvi, vŏlūtum, *v.t.* 3, to roll down
dēvŏro, *v.t.* 1, to gulp down
dēvōtio, ōnis, *f*, consecration
dēvōtus, a, um, *adj*, devoted
dēvŏvĕo, vōvi, vōtum, *v.t.* 2, to dedicate, doom, devote
dexter, tĕra, tĕrum (tra, trum), *adj*, on the right, skilful, suitable
dextĕra (dextra), ae, *f*, right hand
dextĕritas, ātis, *f*, dexterity
dextrorsum, *adv*, to the right
di, *pl.* of **dĕus**
diădēma, ătis, *n*, crown, diadem
diāgōnālis, e, *adj*, diagonal
diălecticus, a, um, *adj*, of debate
diălŏgus, i, *m*, conversation
diāria, ōrum, *n.pl*, rations
dĭca, ae, *f*, lawsuit
dĭcācĭtas, ātis, *f*, wit
dĭcax, ācis, *adj*, witty
dĭcio, ōnis, *f*, dominion, power
dĭco, *v.t.* 1, to dedicate, devote
dĭco, xi, ctum, *v.t.* 3, to say, tell, appoint
dicta, see **dictum**
dictāta, ōrum, *n.pl*, written exercises
dictātio, ōnis, *f*, dictation
dictātor, ōris, *m*, dictator (Roman magistrate appointed in emergencies)
dictātūra, ae, *f*, dictatorship
dictio, ōnis, *f*, speaking, style
dictĭto, *v.t.* 1, to repeat, dictate, compose
dicto, *v.t.* 1, to declare, dictate
dictum, i, *n*, saying, proverb, order
dictus, a, um, *adj*, said, told
dĭdo, dĭdĭdi, dĭdĭtum, *v.t.* 3, to distribute
dĭdūco, xi, ctum, *v.t.* 3, to divide, scatter
diēs, diēi, *m, f*, day
diffĕro, differre, distŭli, dīlātum, *v.i.t., irreg*, to differ; scatter, publish, defer

differtus, a, um, *adj*, crowded
diffibŭlo, *v.t.* 1, to unbuckle
difficĭlis, e, *adj, adv,* **ē, ĭter,** difficult, surly
difficultas, ātis, *f*, difficulty, obstinacy
diffĭdens, ntis, *adj*, distrustful
diffidentĭa, ae, *f*, mistrust, despair
diffīdo, fisus sum, *v.i.* 3, *semi-dep. with dative*, to mistrust, despair
diffindo, fĭdi, fĭsum, *v.t.* 3, to split, divide
diffingo, *v.t.* 3, to re-shape
diffitĕor, *v.t.* 2, *dep*, to deny
difflŭo, *v.i.* 3, to flow away
diffŭgio, fūgi, *v.i.* 3, to disperse
diffundo, fūdi, fūsum, *v.t.* 3, to pour out, scatter
diffūsus, a, um, *adj, adv,* **ē,** spread out, wide
dīgĕro, gessi, gestum, *v.t.* 3, to separate, arrange, interpret
dīgesta, ōrum, *n.pl*, digest of writings
dīgĭtus, i, *m*, finger, toe, inch
dīglădior, *v.i.* 1, *dep*, to fight fiercely
dignātio, ōnis, *f*, reputation
dignĭtas, ātis, *f*, worthiness, rank, authority
dignor, *v.t.* 1, *dep*, to consider someone worthy
dignus, a, um, *adj, adv,* **ē,** *with abl*, worthy, suitable
dīgrĕdior, gressus, *v.i.* 3, *dep*, to go away
dīgressio, ōnis, *f*, digression
dīgressus, ūs, *m*, departure
diiūdico, *v.t.* 1, to decide
diiun . . . see **disiun . . .**
dīlābor, lapsus, *v.i.* 3, *dep*, to dissolve, scatter, perish
dīlăcĕro, *v.t.* 1, to tear apart, or to pieces
dīlănio, *v.t.* 1, to tear apart, or to pieces
dīlātio, ōnis, *f*, delay
dīlāto, *v.t.* 1, to enlarge
dīlātor, ōris, *m*, delayer
dīlātus, a, um, *adj*, scattered
dilectus, a, um, *adj*, beloved
dĭligens, ntis, *adj, adv,* **nter,** scrupulous, thrifty
dĭligentĭa, ae, *f*, care, economy
dĭligo, lexi, lectum, *v.t.* 3, to value highly
dīlūcesco, luxi, *v.i.* 3, to grow light, dawn
dīlūcĭdus, a, um, *adj*, clear
dīlūcŭlum, i, *n*, dawn
dīlŭo, ŭi, ūtum, *v.t.* 3, to wash away, dilute, drench, weaken
dīlūtum, i, *n*, solution
dīlŭvies, ēi, *f* (**. . . ĭum, ii,** *n*), flood, destruction
dīmētior, mensus, *v.t.* 4, *dep*, to measure out
dīmicātio, ōnis, *f*, struggle
dīmico, *v.i.* 1, to struggle
dīmidiātus, a, um, *adj*, halved
dīmidĭum, ii, *n*, a half
dīmidĭus, a, um, *adj*, half
dīmissio, ōnis, *f*, sending out
dīmitto, mīsi, missum, *v.t.* 3, to send away, break up, disband, throw away, give up
dīmŏvĕo, mōvi, mōtum, *v.t.* 2, to divide, part, remove
dīnŭmĕro, *v.t.* 1, to count up
dĭplōma, ātis, *n*, official letter of recommendation
dīra, ōrum, *n.pl*, curses
dīrectus, a, um, *adj, adv,* **ē,** straight, level
dīreptio, ōnis, *f*, plundering
dīreptor, ōris, *m*, plunderer
dīrigo, rexi, ctum, *v.t.* 3, to put in a straight line, arrange
dīrĭmo, ēmi, emptum, *v.t.* 3, to part, divide, interrupt
dīripio, ŭi, reptum, *v.t.* 3, to tear apart, plunder
dīrumpo, rūpi, ptum, *v.t.* 3, to break in pieces, sever
dīrŭo, ŭi, ŭtum, *v.t.* 3, to destroy
dīrus, a, um, *adj*, fearful, ill-omened
discēdo, cessi, cessum, *v.i.* 3, to depart, abandon, gape, deviate
disceptātio, ōnis, *f*, discussion
discepto, *v.t.* 1, to debate
discerno, crēvi, tum, *v.t.* 3, to separate, distinguish between
discerpo, psi, ptum, *v.t.* 3, to tear in pieces
discessus, ūs, *m*, departure
discĭdium, ii, *n*, separation
discinctus, a, um, *adj*, casually-dressed, slovenly
dīscindo, cĭdi, cissum, *v.t.* 3, to cut to pieces, divide
discingo, nxi, nctum, *v.t.* 3, to take off or undo (clothing)
disciplīna, ae, *f*, teaching, knowledge, system, tactics
discipŭlus, i, *m*, pupil
disclūdo, si, sum, *v.t.* 3, to keep apart, separate
disco, dĭdĭci, *v.t.* 3, to learn
discŏlor, ōris, *adj*, of different colours
discordĭa, ae, *f*, disagreement
discordo, *v.i.* 1, to differ
discors, dis, *adj*, disagreeing
discrĕpantĭa, ae, *f*, discrepancy

discrĕpo, ŭi, *v.i.* 1, to differ
dĭscrĭbo, scrĭpsi, ptum, *v.t.* 3, to distribute
discrĭmen, ĭnis, *n,* division, distinction, crisis, danger
discrĭmĭno, *v.t.* 1, to divide
discrŭcio, *v.t.* 1, to torture
discumbo, cŭbŭi, cŭbĭtum, *v.i.* 3, to recline at table
discurro, curri, cursum, *v.i.* 3, to run about
discursus, ūs, *m,* bustle, activity
discus, i, *m,* discus, quoit
discŭtio, cussi, ssum, *v.t.* 3, to shatter, disperse
dĭsertus, a, um, *adj, adv,* **ē,** fluent, clear
dĭsĭcio, īēci, ctum, *v.t.* 3, to scatter, destroy
disiunctus, a, um, *adj, adv,* **ē,** distant, abrupt
disiungo, nxi, nctum, *v.t.* 3, to separate, unyoke
dispar, ăris, *adj,* unlike, unequal
dispăro, *v.t.* 1, to divide
dispello, pŭli, pulsum, *v.t.* 3, to drive away, scatter
dispendĭum, ii, *n,* expense, cost
dispenso, *v.t.* 1, to pay out, distribute, manage
disperdo, dĭdi, dĭtum, *v.t.* 3, to spoil, ruin
dispĕrĕo, *v.i.* 4, to perish
dispergo, si, sum, *v.t.* 3, to scatter about
dispertio, *v.t.* 4, to distribute
dispĭcio, spexi, ctum, *v.i.t.* 3, to look around; discern, reflect on
displĭcĕo, *v.i.* 2, to displease
dispōno, pŏsŭi, pŏsĭtum, *v.t.* 3, to arrange, dispose
dispŏsĭtus, a, um, *adj,* arranged
dispungo, xi, ctum, *v.t.* 3, to check
dispŭtātio, ōnis, *f,* debate, dispute
dispŭtātor, ōris, *m,* debater
dispŭto, *v.i.t.* 1, to theorise; examine, discuss
dissēmĭno, *v.t.* 1, to spread about
dissensio, ōnis, *f,* disagreement
dissentio, si, sum, *v.i.* 4, to disagree, differ
dissĕrēnat, *v. impers.* 1, to be clear
dissĕro, rŭi, rtum, *v.t.* 3, to discuss, argue
dissĭdĕo, ēdi, essum, *v.i.* 2, to differ, disagree
dissĭlio, ŭi, *v.i.* 4, to leap apart, split
dissĭmilis, e, *adj, adv,* **ĭter,** unlike, different
dissĭmĭlĭtūdo, ĭnis, *f,* unlikeness
dissĭmŭlātus, a, um, *adj,* disguised
dissĭmŭlo, *v.t.* 1, to disguise, hide
dissĭpātio, ōnis, *f,* scattering, destruction
dissĭpo, *v.t.* 1, to scatter, rout
dissŏcĭābĭlis, e, *adj,* dividing
dissŏcio, *v.t.* 1, to estrange
dissŏlūtio, ōnis, *f,* break-up, destruction
dissŏlūtus, a, um, *adj,* loose
dissolvo, solvi, sŏlūtum, *v.t.* 3, to unloose, separate, pay, annul, destroy
dissŏnus, a, um, *adj,* discordant
dissuādĕo, si, sum, *v.t.* 2, to advise against
dissulto, *v.i.* 1, to burst apart
distans, ntis, *adj,* distant
distendo, di, tum, *v.t.* 3, to stretch out, distend, torture
distentus, a, um, *adj,* full
distentus, a, um, *adj,* busy
distinctio, ōnis, *f,* difference
distinctus, a, um, *adj, adv,* **ē,** separate, clear, adorned
distĭnĕo, tĭnŭi, tentum, *v.t.* 2, to keep apart, perplex, hinder
distinguo, nxi, nctum, *v.t.* 3, to separate, discriminate, adorn
disto, *v.i.* 1, to be distant, differ
distorquĕo, rsi, rtum, *v.t.* 2, to twist, distort, torture
distortio, ōnis, *f,* distortion
distortus, a, um, *adj,* deformed
distractio, ōnis, *f,* division
distractus, a, um, *adj,* bewildered
distrăho, xi, ctum, *v.t.* 3, to pull apart, divide, distract, perplex
distrĭbŭo, ŭi, ūtum, *v.t.* 3, to distribute
distrĭbūtē, *adv,* methodically
distrĭbūtio, ōnis, *f,* distribution
districtus, a, um, *adj,* busy, strict
distringo, nxi, ctum, *v.t.* 3, to stretch tight, distract the attention
disturbo, *v.t.* 1, to disturb, demolish, frustrate
dĭto, *v.t.* 1, to enrich
dĭŭ, *adv,* a long time
dĭurnus, a, um, *adj,* daily
dĭurna, ōrum, *n.pl,* records
dĭŭtĭnus, a, um, *adj,* long-lasting
dĭŭtĭus, *comp. adv,* longer
dĭŭturnĭtas, ātis, *f,* long duration
dĭŭturnus, a, um, *adj, adv,* **ē,** long-lasting
dīva, ae, *f,* goddess
dīvello, velli, vulsum, *v.t.* 3, to tear to pieces, destroy
dīvendo, (*no perfect*), **itum,** *v.t.* 3, to retail
dīverbĕro, *v.t.* 1, to cut

dĭversĭtas, ātis, *f*, disagreement
dĭversus, a, um, *adj, adv,* **ē**, opposite, contrary, hostile, separate, different
dĭverto, ti, sum, *v.i.* 3, to diverge
dĭves, ĭtis, *adj*, rich
dĭvĭdo, vĭsi, sum, *v.t.* 3, to separate, distribute, destroy
dĭvĭdŭus, a, um, *adj*, divisible
dĭvīnĭtas, ātis, *f*, divinity
dĭvīnĭtus, *adv*, providentially
dĭvīno, *v.t.* 1, to prophesy
dĭvīnus, a, um, *adj, adv,* **ē**, divine, prophetic, superhuman
dĭvīnus, i, *m*, prophet
dĭvĭsĭo, ōnis, *f*, division
dĭvĭsor, ōris, *m*, distributor of bribes to electors
dĭvĭtĭae, ārum, *f.pl.* wealth
dĭvortĭum, ii, *n*, separation
dĭvulgo, *v.t.* 1, to make known
dĭvum, i, *n*, sky
dĭvus, a, um, *adj*, divine
dĭvus, i, *m* (**a, ae,** *f*), god, (goddess)
do, dĕdi, dătum, *v.t.* 1, to give
dŏcĕo, ŭi, doctum, *v.t.* 2, to teach, inform
dŏcĭlis, e, *adj*, easily taught
doctor, ōris, *m*, teacher
doctrīna, ae, *f*, teaching, education, learning
doctus, a, um, *adj, adv,* **ē**, learned, skilled
dŏcŭmentum, i, *n*, lesson, example
dōdrans, ntis, *m*, three quarters
dogma, ătis, *n*, doctrine, dogma
dŏlābra, ae, *f*, pick-axe
dŏlĕo, *v.i.t.* 2, to suffer pain; grieve, deplore
dŏlĭum, ii, *n*, large jar
dŏlo, *v.t.* 1, to chop, beat
dŏlor, ōris, *m*, pain, sorrow
dŏlōsus, a, um, *adj*, deceitful
dŏlus, i, *m*, fraud, trick
dŏmābĭlis, e, *adj*, tamable
dŏmestĭcus, a, um, *adj*, of the home
dŏmestĭci, ōrum, *m. pl*, family, servants, escort
dŏmi, *adv*, at home
dŏmĭcĭlĭum, ii, *n*, dwelling place
dŏmĭna, ae, *f*, mistress, lady
dŏmĭnans, ntis, *adj*, ruling
dŏmĭnātĭo, ōnis, *f*, absolute rule
dŏmĭnātus, ūs, *m*, absolute rule
dŏmĭnĭum, ii, *n*, banquet, property-ownership
dŏmĭnor, *v.i.* 1, *dep*, to reign
dŏmĭnus, i, *m*, master, owner
dŏmĭto, *v.t.* 1, to tame
dŏmĭtor, ōris, *m*, tamer
dŏmĭtus, a, um, *adj*, tamed
dŏmo, ŭi, ĭtum, *v.t.* 1, to tame, conquer
dŏmus, ūs, *f*, house, home
dōnārĭum, ii, *n*, altar, sanctuary
dōnātĭo, ōnis, *f*, donation
dōnātus, a, um, *adj*, presented
dōnĕc, *conj*, while, until
dōno, *v.t.* 1, to present, remit
dōnum, i, *n*, gift, present
dorcas, ădis, *m*, gazelle
dormĭo, *v.i.* 4, to sleep
dormĭto, *v.i.* 1, to fall asleep
dorsum, i, *n*, the back, ridge, ledge
dōs, dōtis, *f*, dowry
dōtālis, e, *adj*, of a dowry
dōtātus, a, um, *adj*, endowed
dōto, *v.t.* 1, to endow
drachma, ae, *f*, small Greek silver coin
drăco, ōnis, *m*, water-snake
drŏmas, ădis, *m*, dromedary
drŷas, ădis, *f*, wood-nymph
dŭbĭē, *adv*, doubtfully
dŭbĭtātĭo, ōnis, *f*, doubt, uncertainty
dŭbĭto, *v.i.t.* 1, to hesitate; doubt
dŭbĭum, ii, *n*, doubt
dŭbĭus, a, um, *adj*, doubtful, dangerous
dŭcēni, ae, a, *adj*, two hundred each
dŭcenti, ae, a, *adj*, two hundred
dŭco, xi, ctum, *v.t.* 3, to lead, marry, construct, receive, prolong, consider
ductĭlis, e, *adj*, moveable, malleable
ductor, ōris, *m*, leader
ductus, ūs, *m*, bringing, leadership
dŭdum, *adv*, some time ago, formerly
dulcē, *adv*, sweetly
dulcēdo, ĭnis, *f*, sweetness, charm
dulcĭtūdo, ĭnis, *f*, sweetness, charm
dulcis, e, *adj, adv,* **ĭter,** sweet, pleasant, dear
dum, *conj*, while, until, provided that
dūmētum, i, *n*, thicket
dummŏdo, *adv*, as long as
dūmōsus, a, um, *adj*, bushy
dūmus, i, *m*, bramble
dumtaxat, *adv*, in so far as, merely, at least
dŭŏ, ae, ŏ, *adj*, two
dŭŏdĕcies, *adv*, twelve times
dŭŏdĕcim, *adj*, twelve
dŭŏdĕcimus, a, um, *adj*, twelfth
dŭŏdēni, ae, a, *adj*, twelve each
dŭŏdēvīcensĭmus, a, um, *adj*, eighteenth
dŭŏdēvīginti, *adj*, eighteen
dŭŏvĭri, ōrum, *m.pl*, board or commission of two men
dŭplex, ĭcis, *adj, adv,* **ĭter,** double, deceitful

For List of Abbreviations used, turn to pages 3, 4

dŭplĭco, *v.t.* 1, to double
dŭplus, a um, *adj*, double
dūra, ōrum, *n.pl*, hardship
dūrābĭlis, e, *adj*, durable
dūrātus, a, um, *adj*, hardened
dūrē, *adv*, roughly
dūresco, rŭi, *v.i.* 3, to harden
dūrĭtĭa, ae, *f*, hardness, strictness, austerity
dūro, *v.i.t.* 1, to be hard, endure; harden
dūrus, a, um, *adj, adv,* **ē, ĭter,** hard, rough, harsh, stern
dux, dŭcis, *m*, leader, commander
dȳnastes, ae, *m*, chieftain
dȳsentĕrĭa, ae, *f*, dysentery
dyspnoea, ae, *f*, asthma

E

ē, *prep. with abl*, out of, from, since
ĕa, see **is**
ĕādem, see **idem**
ĕātĕnus, *adv*, so far
ĕbĕnus, i, *f*, ebony (tree)
ēbĭbo, bi, bĭtum, *v.t.* 3, to drink up, absorb, squander
ēblandĭor, *v. t.* 4, *dep*, to obtain by flattery
ēbrĭĕtas, ātis, *f*, drunkenness
ēbrĭŏsus, a, um, *adj*, addicted to drink
ēbrĭus, a, um, *adj*, drunk
ēbullĭo, *v.t.* 4, to boast about
ēbŭlum, i, *n*, dwarf-elder
ēbŭr, ŏris, *n*, ivory
ĕburnĕus, a, um, *adj*, of ivory
ecce, *demonstrative adv*, see!
ĕchĭnus, i, *m*, hedgehog, sea-urchin, rinsing bowl
ēchō, ūs, *f*, echo
ecquando, *interr. adv*, at any time?
ecqui, ae, od, *interr. pron, adj*, any? anyone?
ecquis, id, *interr. pron*, anyone? anything?
ĕdācĭtas, ātis, *f*, gluttony
ĕdax, ācis, *adj*, greedy
ēdentŭlus, a, um, *adj*, toothless
ēdĭco, xi, ctum, *v.t.* 3, to publish, declare
ēdictum, i, *n*, proclamation
ēdisco, dĭdĭci, *v.t.* 3, to learn by heart, study
ēdissĕro, rŭi, rtum, *v.t.* 3, to explain in full
ēdĭtĭo, ōnis, *f*, bringing out, publishing
ēditus, a, um, *adj*, high, raised, brought out
ĕdo, ēdi, ēsum, *v.t.* 3, to eat
ēdo, dĭdi, dĭtum, *v.t.* 3, to produce, bring out, declare, cause, erect
ēdŏcĕo, cŭi, ctum, *v.t.* 2, to teach thoroughly
ēdŏmo, ŭi, ĭtum, *v.t.* 1, to subdue
ēdŭcātĭo, ōnis, *f*, bringing up, education
ēdūco, xi, ctum, *v.t.* 3, to lead or bring out, summon, educate, erect
ēdŭco, *v.t.* 1, to bring up (child)
ēdŭlis, e, *adj*, eatable
effātus, a, um, *adj*, established
effectĭo, ōnis, *f*, doing, performing
effectus, a, um, *adj*, completed
effectus, ūs, *m*, accomplishment
effēmĭnātus, a, um, *adj*, effeminate
effĕrātus, a, um, *adj*, wild
effĕro, efferre, extŭli, ēlātum, *v.t. irreg*, to bring out, bury, declare, raise; *in passive or with* **se**, to be haughty
effĕro, *v.t.* 1, to brutalize
effĕrus, a, um, *adj*, savage
effervesco, fĕrbŭi, *v.i.* 3, to boil up, rage
effervo, *v.i.* 3, to boil over
effĕtus, a, um, *adj*, exhausted
efficax, ācis, *adj*, efficient
efficĭens, ntis, *adj, adv,* **nter,** efficient
efficio, fēci, fectum, *v.t.* 3, to bring about, complete, produce
effictus, a, um, *adj*, fashioned
effigies, ēi, *f*, portrait, copy
effingo, nxi, ctum, *v.t.* 3, to shape, fashion, portray
efflāgĭto, *v.t.* 1, to request urgently
efflo, *v.t.* 1, to breathe out
efflōresco, rŭi, *v.i.* 3, to bloom
efflŭo, xi, *v.i.* 3, to flow out, vanish
effŏdĭo, fōdi, fossum, *v.t.* 3, to dig out, dig up
effor, *v. t.* 1, *dep*, to speak out
effrēnātus, a, um, *adj*, unruly
effrēnus, a, um, *adj*, unrestrained
effringo, frēgi, fractum, *v.t.* 3, to break open, smash
effŭgĭo, fūgi, *v.i.t.* 3, to escape; flee from, avoid
effŭgĭum, ii, *n*, escape
effulgĕo, si, *v.i.* 2, to gleam
effundo, fūdi, fūsum, *v.t.* 3, to pour out, let loose, squander; *in pass. or with reflexive*, to rush out
effūsĭo, ōnis, *f*, outpouring, profusion
effūsus, a, um, *adj, adv,* **ē,** poured out, spread out, wide, loosened
effŭtĭo, *v.t.* 4, to blurt out
ēgĕlĭdus, a, um, *adj*, cool

ĕgens, ntis, *adj,* in want of
ĕgēnus, a, um, *adj,* in want of
ĕgĕo, *v.i.* 2, *with abl,* to be in need of
ēgĕro, ssi, stum, *v.t.* 3, to bring out
ĕgestas, ātis, *f,* poverty
ĕgō, *pers. pron,* I
ĕgŏmet, *pron,* I myself
ēgrĕdĭor, gressus, *v.i.t.* 3, *dep,* to go or come out; leave, exceed
ēgrĕgĭus, a, um, *adj, adv,* **ē,** distinguished
ēgressus, ūs, *m,* departure, passage
ēheu! alas!
ēiă! hey! I say!
ēiăcŭlor, *v. t.* 1, *dep,* to shoot out
ēĭcĭo, iēci, iectum, *v.t.* 3, to drive out, expel, wreck; *with reflexive,* to rush out
ēiecto, *v.t.* 1, to vomit
ēiūro, *v.t.* 1, to reject on oath, abandon
ēius, *genit. of* **is, ea, id**
ēiusmŏdi, in such a manner
ēlābor, lapsus, *v.i.* 3, *dep,* to slip away, escape
ēlăbōrātus, a, um, *adj,* elaborate
ēlăbōro, *v.i.t.* 1, to make an effort; take pains with
ēlanguesco, gŭi, *v.i.* 3, to grow feeble
ēlātio, ōnis, *f,* lifting up, passion
ēlātro, *v.t.* 1, to bark loudly
ēlātus, a, um, *adj,* raised, lofty
ēlectio, ōnis, *f,* selection
ēlectrum, i, *n,* amber
ēlectus, a, um, *adj,* selected
ēlĕgans, ntis, *adj, adv,* **nter,** refined, tasteful
ēlĕgantia, ae, *f,* refinement
ēlĕgi, ōrum, *m. pl,* elegy
ēlĕgĭa, ae, *f,* elegy
ēlĕmentum, i, *n,* element, first principle; *pl,* rudiments
ēlĕphantus, i, *m,* elephant, ivory
ēlĕvo, *v.t.* 1, to lift up, weaken, disparage
ēlĭcio, cŭi, cĭtum, *v.t.* 3, to lure out, call out
ēlĭdo, si, sum, *v.t.* 3, to knock or force out, shatter
ēlĭgo, lēgi, ctum, *v.t.* 3, to choose
ēlinguis, e, *adj,* speechless
ēlixus, a, um, *adj,* boiled
ellychnium, ii, *n,* lampwick
ēlŏco, *v.t.* 1, to let (a farm)
ēlŏcūtio, ōnis, *f,* expression, elocution
ēlŏgium, ii, *n,* saying, inscription
ēlŏquens, ntis, *adj,* eloquent
ēlŏquentia, ae, *f,* eloquence
ēlŏquor, ēlŏcūtus, *v. t.* 3, *dep,* to speak out, declare
ēlūcĕo, xi, *v.i.* 2, to shine out
ēluctor, *v.i.t.* 1, *dep,* to struggle out; struggle out of
ēlūdo, si, sum, *v.t.* 3, to evade, cheat, frustrate
ēlūgĕo, xi, *v.t.* 2, to mourn for
ēlŭo, ŭi, ūtum, *v.t.* 3, to wash off, clean
ēlūtus, a, um, *adj,* insipid
ēlŭvies, *no genit, f,* inundation
ēlŭvio, ōnis, *f,* inundation
ēmancipo, *v.t.* 1, to set free, transfer, sell
ēmāno, *v.i.* 1, to flow out, arise from
embŏlium ii, *n,* interlude
ēmendātio, ōnis, *f,* correction
ēmendātor, ōris, *m,* corrector
ēmendātus, a, um, *adj,* faultless
ēmendo, *v.t.* 1, to correct
ēmentior, *v. t.* 4, *dep,* to assert falsely
ēmercor, *v. t.* 1, *dep,* to purchase
ēmĕrĕo, *v.t.* 2 (**ēmĕrĕor,** *v.t.* 2, *dep*), to deserve, earn, complete one's military service
ēmergo, si, sum, *v.i.* 3, to come out, escape
ēmĕritus, a, um, *adj,* worn out
ēmētior, mensus, *v.t.* 4, *dep,* to measure out, travel over
ēmĭco, ŭi, ātum, *v.i.* 1, to spring out, appear
ēmĭgro, *v.i.* 1, to depart
ēmĭnens, ntis, *adj,* projecting, distinguished
ēmĭnentia, ae, *f,* prominence
ēmĭnĕo, *v.i.* 2, to stand out, excel
ēmĭnus, *adv,* from or at a distance
ēmissārium, ii, *n,* drain, vent
ēmissārius, ii, *m,* spy
ēmissio, ōnis, *f,* sending out, hurling (of missiles)
ēmitto, mĭsi, ssum, *v.t.* 3, to send out, produce, publish; with **manū,** to set free
ĕmo, ēmi, emptum, *v.t.* 3, to buy
ēmŏdŭlor, *v. t.* 1, *dep,* to sing
ēmollio, *v.t.* 4, to soften
ēmŏlŭmentum, i, *n,* effort, profit
ēmŏrĭor, mortuus, *v.i.* 3, *dep,* to die
ēmŏvĕo, mōvi, tum, *v.t.* 2, to remove, shake
empĭricus, a, um, *adj,* empirical
emplastrum, i, *n,* plaster
empŏrium, ii, *n,* market
emptio, ōnis, *f,* purchase
emptor, ōris, *m,* buyer
ēmunctus, a, um, *adj,* clean, shrewd
ēmungo, nxi, nctum, *v.t.* 3, to wipe the nose
ēmūnio, *v.t.* 4, to fortify

ēn! see! come!
ēnarro, *v.t.* 1, to expound
ēnascor, nātus, *v. i.* 3, *dep,* to spring up, be born
ēnāto, *v.i.* 1, to swim away
ēnectus, a, um, *adj,* killed
ēnĕco, ŭi, ctum, *v.t.* 1, to kill, exhaust
ēnervo, *v.t.* 1, to weaken
ēnim, *conj,* for, indeed
ēnimvēro, *conj,* certainly
ēnīsus, a, um, *adj,* strenuous
ēnĭtĕo, *v.i.* 2, to shine out
ēnĭtesco, tŭi, *v.i.* 3, to shine out
ēnĭtor, nīsus (nixus), *v. i. t.* 3, *dep,* to struggle upwards, climb, strive; give birth to, ascend
ēnixus, a, um, *adj, adv,* **ē,** strenuous, earnest
ēno, *v.i.* 1, to swim out or away
ēnōdātĭo, ōnis, *f,* explanation
ēnōdis, e, *adj,* smooth, clear
ēnōdo, *v.t.* 1, to elucidate
ēnormis, e, *adj,* enormous, shapeless
ēnormĭtas, ātis, *f,* shapelessness
ēnōto, *v.t.* 1, to note down
ensĭger, ĕra, ĕrum, *adj,* carrying a sword
ensis, is, *m,* sword
ēnŭclĕātus, a, um, *adj, adv,* **ē,** pure, clear, simple
ēnŭmĕrātĭo, ōnis, *f,* counting, recapitulation
ēnŭmĕro, *v.t.* 1, to count, relate
ēnuntĭo, *v.t.* 1, to disclose, declare
ĕo, īre, īvi (ii), ĭtum, *v.i. irreg,* to go; with **pedibus,** to vote for
ĕō, *adv,* to that place, to such an extent, so long, besides
eo . . . quo, (*with comparatives*) the more . . . the more
ĕōdem, *adv,* to the same place, to the same point or purpose
ĕōus, i, *m,* (**a, um,** *adj*), east
ĕphēbus, i, *m,* a youth
ĕphippĭum, ii, *n,* saddle
ĕphŏrus, i, *m,* Spartan magistrate
ĕpĭcus, a, um, *adj,* epic
ĕpiscŏpus, i, *m,* bishop
ĕpĭgramma, ătis, *n,* inscription
ĕpistŏla, ae, *f,* letter
ĕpistŏmium, ii, *n,* valve
ĕpĭtŏmē (ĕpĭtŏma), ēs, *f,* abridgement
ĕpŏs, *n,* epic poem
ĕpōto, pōtum, *v.t.* 1, to drink up
ĕpŭlae, ārum, *f. pl,* food, banquet
ĕpŭlor, *v.i.t.* 1, *dep,* to banquet; eat
ĕqua, ae, *f,* mare
ĕquāria, ae, *f,* stud of horses
ĕques, ĭtis, *m,* horseman, Knight
ĕquester, tris, tre, *adj,* of a horseman, of cavalry
ĕquĭdem, *adv,* indeed, of course, for my part
ĕquīnus, a, um, *adj,* of horses
ĕquĭtātĭo, ōnis, *f,* riding on horseback
ĕquĭtātus, ūs, *m,* cavalry
ĕquĭto, *v.i.* 1, to ride
ĕquŭlĕus, i, *m,* colt, the rack
ĕquus, i, *m,* horse
ĕra, ae, *f,* lady of the house
ērādĭco, *v.t.* 1, to root out
ērādo, si, sum, *v.t.* 3, to scrape out, abolish
ērectus, a, um, *adj,* upright, noble, haughty, resolute
ērēpo, psi, *v.i.t.* 3, to creep out; creep over
ergā, *prep. with acc,* towards
ergastŭlum, i, *n,* detention centre
ergō, *adv,* therefore; *prep. following genit,* on account of
ērĭgo, rexi, rectum, *v.t.* 3, to raise up, encourage
ĕrĭlis, e, *adj,* of the master, or mistress
ērĭpĭo, rĭpŭi, reptum, *v.t.* 3, to snatch, take away; *with reflexive,* to escape
ērŏgātĭo, ōnis, *f,* paying out
ērŏgo, *v.t.* 1, to pay out, squander
errābundus, a, um, *adj,* wandering
errāticus, a, um, *adj,* rambling
errātum, i, *n,* mistake
erro, *v.i.* 1, to stray, err
erro, ōnis, *m,* wanderer
error, ōris, *m,* straying, mistake
ērŭbesco, bŭi, *v.i.* 3, to blush, feel ashamed
ērŭca, ae, *f,* caterpillar
ēructo, *v.t.* 1, to belch, emit
ērŭdĭo, *v.t.* 4, to polish, instruct
ērŭdĭtĭo, ōnis, *f,* learning
ērŭdĭtus, a, um, *adj, adv,* **ē,** learned, skilled
ērumpo, rūpi, ptum, *v.i.t.* 3, to break out; burst
ērŭo, ŭi, ūtum, *v.t.* 3, to throw out, dig out, destroy, rescue
ēruptĭo, ōnis, *f,* break-out
ĕrus, i, *m,* master of the house
ervum, i, *n,* wild pea
esca, ae, *f,* food, bait
ēscendo, di, sum, *v.i.* 3, to climb
ēscensĭo, ōnis, *f,* ascent
escŭlentus, a, um, *adj,* eatable
esse, see **sum**
essĕdārius, i, *m,* chariot-fighter
essĕdum, i, *n,* war-chariot
ēsŭrĭens, ntis, *adj,* hungry

ēsŭrĭo, *v.i.t.* 4, to be hungry; long for
ĕt, *conj,* and, as
ĕtĕnim, *conj,* and indeed
ĕtĭam, *conj,* also, even, still
ĕtĭamnum, ĕtĭamnunc, *adv,* even then, till now
etsi, *conj,* although, even if
eu!, well done!
eurĭpus, i, *m,* canal
eurōus, a, um, *adj,* eastern
eurus, i, *m,* east wind
ēvādo, si, sum, *v.i.t.* 3, to go out, escape; leave behind
ēvăgor, *v.i.t.* 1, *dep.* to stray; overstep
ēvălesco, lŭi, *v.i.* 3, to grow strong, to be able
ēvānesco, nŭi, *v.i.* 3, to vanish
ēvānĭdus, a, um, *adj,* vanishing
ēvasto, *v.t.* 1, to devastate
ēvĕho, xi, ctum, *v.t.* 3, to carry out; *in passive,* to ride or move out
ēvello, velli, vulsum, *v.t.* 3, to tear out, eradicate
ēvĕnĭo, vēni, ventum, *v.i.* 4, to come out, turn out, result
ēventum, i, *n,* occurrence, result, fortune
ēventus, ūs, *m,* occurrence, result, fortune
ēverbĕro, *v.t.* 1, to strike hard
ēverro, verri, versum, *v.t.* 3, to sweep out
ēversĭo, ōnis, *f,* destruction
ēversor, ōris, *m,* destroyer
ēversus, a, um, *adj,* overthrown
ēverto, ti, sum, *v.t.* 3, to overthrow, ruin
ēvĭdens, ntis, *adj,* apparent
ēvĭgĭlo, *v.i.t.* 1, to wake up; keep awake, keep watch through
ēvincĭo, nxi, nctum, *v.t.* 4, to bind round
ēvinco, vīci, ctum, *v.t.* 3, to conquer completely, succeed
ēviscĕro, *v.t.* 1, to tear apart
ēvĭto, *v.t.* 1, to avoid
ēvŏcāti, ōrum, *m. pl,* reservists
ēvŏco, *v.t.* 1, to call out
ēvŏlo, *v.i.* 1, to fly away
ēvolvo, vi, vŏlūtum, *v.t.* 3, to unroll (and read a book), disclose
ēvŏmo, ŭi, ĭtum, *v.t.* 3, to spit out, vomit
ēvulsĭo, ōnis, *f,* pulling out
ex(ē), *prep. with abl,* out of, from, after, since, on account of, according to, made of
exăcerbo, *v.t.* 1, to irritate
exactio, ōnis, *f,* debt or tax collecting, expelling
exactor, ōris, *m,* expeller, superintendent, tax-collector
exactus, a, um, *adj,* accurate
exăcŭo, ŭi, ūtum, *v.t.* 3, to sharpen, stimulate
exadversum (. . . **us**), *adv. and prep. with acc,* opposite
exaedĭfico, *v.t.* 1, to construct
exaequo, *v.t.* 1, to place equal
exaestŭo, *v.i.* 1, to seethe
exaggĕro, *v.t.* 1, to heap up
exăgito, *v.t.* 1, to disturb
exalbesco, bŭi, *v.i.* 3, to turn pale
exāmen, ĭnis, *n,* crowd, swarm
exāmĭno, *v.t.* 1, to weigh, test
exănĭmātio, ōnis, *f,* terror
exănĭmātus, a, um, *adj,* out of breath
exănĭmis, e, *adj,* lifeless
exănĭmus, a, um, *adj,* lifeless
exănĭmo, *v.t.* 1, to deprive of breath, kill, terrify
exardesco, arsi, sum, *v.i.* 3, to be inflamed
exāresco, rŭi, *v.i.* 3, to dry up
exăro, *v.t.* 1, to plough, write
exaspĕro, *v.t.* 1, to roughen, provoke
exauctōro, *v.t.* 1, to discharge honourably or dishonourably from army
exaudĭo, *v.t.* 4, to hear, grant
excandesco, dŭi, *v.i.* 3, to glow
excēdo, ssi, ssum, *v.i.t.* 3, to depart, die; leave, exceed
excellens, ntis, *adj, adv,* **nter,** distinguished, excellent
excello, cellŭi, lsum, *v.i.* 3, to be eminent, excel
excelsus, a, um, *adj,* distinguished
exceptio, ōnis, *f,* restriction
excepto, *v.t.* 1, to catch
excerno, crēvi, crētum, *v.t.* 3, to separate
excerpo, psi, ptum, *v.t.* 3, to select
excessus, ūs, *m,* departure
excĭdium, ii, *n,* destruction
excĭdo, cĭdi, *v.i.* 3, to fall from, escape, disappear, slip the memory, fail in
excīdo, cīdi, cīsum, *v.t.* 3, to cut down, destroy
excĭo, *v.t.* 4, to call or bring out.
excĭpĭo, cēpi, ceptum, *v.t.* 3, to take out, make an exception, receive, capture, follow after, overhear, intercept
excĭtātus, a, um, *adj,* roused, vigorous
excĭto, *v.t.* 1, to rouse up, excite
exclāmātio, ōnis, *f,* exclamation
exclāmo, *v.i.t.* 1, to call out
exclūdo, si, sum, *v.t.* 3, to shut out, drive out, remove, hinder, hatch
exclūsio, ōnis, *f,* exclusion

For List of Abbreviations used, turn to pages 3, 4

excōgĭto, *v.t.* 1, to think out
excŏlo, cŏlŭi, cultum, *v.t.* 3, to cultivate, improve, refine
excŏquo, xi, ctum, *v.t.* 3, to boil away, purify
excors, dis, *adj*, stupid
excresco, crēvi, crētum, *v.i.* 3, to grow up
excrētus, a, um, *adj*, full grown
excrētus, a, um, *adj*, separated
excrŭcio, *v.t.* 1, to torture
excŭbiae, ārum, *f. pl*, watch, guard
excŭbitor, ōris, *m*, watchman
excŭbo, ŭi, ĭtum, *v.i.* 1, to sleep out of doors, keep watch
excŭdo, di, sum, *v.t.* 3, to hammer out
exculco, *v.t.* 1, to trample down
excurro, cŭcurri, cursum, *v.i.* 3, to run out, make a sortie, extend
excursio, ōnis, *f*, attack, invasion, sally
excursus, ūs, *m*, attack, invasion, sally
excūsābilis, e, *adj*, excusable
excūsātio, ōnis, *f*, excuse
excūso, *v.t.* 1, to excuse, plead in excuse
excŭtio, cussi, cussum, *v.t.* 3, to shake off, get rid of, hurl, examine
exēdo, ēdi, ēsum, *v.t.* 3, to eat up
exemplar, āris, *n*, copy, model
exemplum, i, *n*, copy, model, precedent, warning, example
exemptus, a, um, *adj*, removed
exĕo, *v.i.t.* 4, to depart, run out (time), die; cross, avoid
exercĕo, *v.t.* 2, to keep busy, train, exercise, pester
exercĭtātio, ōnis, *f*, practice
exercĭtātus, a, um, *adj*, trained
exercĭtor, ōris, *m*, trainer
exercĭtus, ūs, *m*, army
exercĭtus, a, um, *adj*, trained, harrassed
exhālātio, ōnis, *f*, exhalation
exhālo, *v.t.* 1, to breathe out
exhaurio, si, stum, *v.t.* 4, to draw out, exhaust, empty
exhaustus, a, um, *adj*, drained, worn out
exhērēdo, *v.t.* 1, to disinherit
exhibĕo, *v.t.* 2, to present, display, procure, cause
exhibĭtus, a, um, *adj*, produced
exhilăro, *v.t.* 1, to delight
exhorresco, rŭi, *v.i.t.* 3, to tremble; shrink from, dread
exhortor, *v. t.* 1, *dep*, to encourage
exiens, see **exeo**
exĭgo, ēgi, actum, *v.t.* 3, to drive out, enforce, demand, complete, examine, estimate, spend (time)
exĭgŭĭtas, ātis, *f*, small size
exĭgŭus, a, um, *adj*, *adv*, **ē,** small, short
exĭlis, e, *adj*, *adv*, **ĭter,** small, thin, feeble, insignificant
exĭlium, ii, *n*, exile
eximius, a, um, *adj*, *adv*, **ē,** unusual, distinguished
eximo, ēmi, emptum, *v.t.* 3, to take away, free, waste
exinānio, *v.t.* 4, to empty
exindē (exin), *adv*, from there, then, next, accordingly
existimātio, ōnis, *f*, opinion, reputation, character
existimātor, ōris, *m*, critic
existimo, *v.t.* 1, to estimate, think
exitiābilis, e, *adj*, fatal, deadly
exitiālis, e, *adj*, fatal, deadly
exitiōsus, a, um, *adj*, destructive
exitium, ii, *n*, destruction
exitus, ūs, *m*, departure, outlet, conclusion, result, death
exŏlesco, ŏlēvi, lētum, *v.i.* 3, to grow up, disappear
exŏnĕro, *v.t.* 1, to unload
exoptātus, a, um, *adj*, longed for
exopto, *v.t.* 1, to long for
exōrābilis, e, *adj*, easily persuaded
exordior, orsus, *v. t.* 4, *dep*, to begin, weave
exordĭum, ii, *n*, beginning, introduction
exŏrior, ortus, *v. i.* 4, *dep*, to spring up, arise, appear
exornātio, ōnis, *f*, decoration
exorno, *v.t.* 1, to equip, adorn
exōro, *v.t.* 1, to prevail upon
exorsus, a, um, *adj*, begun
exortus, ūs, *m*, rising
exōsus, a, um, *adj*, hating, detested
expăvesco, pāvi, *v.i.t.* 3, to be afraid; dread
expect, see **exspect**
expĕdio, *v.t.* 4, to set free, prepare, arrange, explain; *impers*, it is expedient
expĕditio, ōnis, *f*, campaign
expĕditē, *adv*, promptly
expĕditus, a, um, *adj*, ready
expĕditus, i, *m*, soldier in light-marching-order
expello, pŭli, pulsum, *v.t.* 3, to drive away
expendo, di, sum, *v.t.* 3, to pay out, consider, pay the penalty

expergēfăcĭo, fēci, factum, *v.t.* 3, to arouse
expergiscor, perrectus, *v.i.* 3, *dep.* to awake
expĕrĭens, ntis, *adj*, enterprising
expĕrĭentĭa, ae, *f*, experiment, practice
expĕrīmentum, i, *n*, proof, experience
expĕrĭor, pertus, *v. t.* 4, *dep*, to prove, test, try; *perf*, know from experience
expers, rtis, *adj*, devoid of
expertus, a, um, *adj*, proved
expĕto, īvi (ii), ītum, *v.t.* 3, to long for, aim at, reach
expĭātĭo, ōnis, *f*, atonement
expīlo, *v.t.* 1, to plunder
expīlātĭo, ōnis, *f*, plundering
expingo, nxi, ctum, *v.t.* 3, to paint
expĭo, *v.t.* 1, to atone for
expiscor, *v. t.* 1, *dep*, to search out
explānātĭo, ōnis, *f*, explanation
explāno, *v.t.* 1, to explain
explĕo, ēvi, ētum, *v.t.* 2, to fill up, fulfil, finish
explētĭo, ōnis, *f*, satisfying
explētus, a, um, *adj*, full, complete
explĭcātĭo, ōnis, *f*, unfolding, explanation
explĭcātus, a, um, *adj*, spread-out, plain
explĭco, *v.t.* 1, (or . . . **ŭi** . . . **ĭtum**) to unfold, spread out, deploy, arrange, explain
explōdo, si, sum, *v.t.* 3, to hiss off the stage, disapprove
explōrātor, ōris, *m*, spy, scout
explōrātus, a, um, *adj*, *adv*, **ē**, established, certain
explōro, *v.t.* 1, to search out, spy, test
expŏlĭo, *v.t.* 4, to polish
expōno, pŏsŭi, pŏsĭtum, *v.t.* 3, to expose, put on shore, explain
exporto, *v.t.* 1, to carry away
exposco, pŏposci, *v.t.* 3, to implore, require
expŏsĭtĭo, ōnis, *f*, elucidation
expŏsĭtus, a, um, *adj*, accessible
expostŭlātĭo, ōnis, *f*, complaint
expostŭlo, *v.t.* 1, to demand, upbraid, complain
expressus, a, um, *adj*, clear
exprĭmo, pressi, pressum, *v.t.* 3, to press out, model, extort
exprŏbrātĭo, ōnis, *f*, reproach
exprŏbro, *v.t.* 1, to reproach
exprōmo, mpsi, mptum, *v.t.* 3, to fetch out, display, explain
expugnātĭo, ōnis, *f*, capture by assault
expugno, *v.t.* 1, to storm, capture
expurgo, *v.t.* 1, to purify, justify
exquīro, sīvi, sītum, *v.t.* 3, to search out
exquĭsĭtus, a, um, *adj*, *adv*, **ē**, choice, excellent
exsanguis, e, *adj*, bloodless, weak
exsătĭo, *v.t.* 1, to satisfy
exsătŭro, *v.t.* 1, to satiate
exscensĭo, ōnis, *f*, landing
exscindo, ĭdi, issum, *v.t.* 3, to destroy completely
exscrĭbo, psi, ptum, *v.t.* 3, to write out, copy
exsĕco, cŭi, ctum, *v.t.* 1, to cut out, cut off
exsĕcrābĭlis, e, *adj*, accursed
exsĕcrātĭo, ōnis, *f*, curse
exsĕcrātus, a, um, *adj*, accursed
exsĕcror, *v. i.t.* 1, *dep*, to take an oath; curse,
exsĕcūtĭo, ōnis, *f*, execution
exsĕquĭae, ārum, *f. pl*, funeral
exsĕquor, sĕcūtus, *v.t.* 3, *dep*, to pursue, follow, carry out, describe, avenge
exsĕro, rŭi, rtum, *v.t.* 3, to put out, uncover, protrude
exserto, *v.t.* 1, to stretch out
exsicco, *v.t.* 1, to dry up
exsĭlĭo, ĭlŭi, *v.i.* 4, to leap out, jump up
exsĭlĭum, ii, *n*, exile
exsisto, stĭti, stĭtum, *v.i.* 3, to come out, appear, arise, exist
exsolvo, solvi, sŏlūtum, *v.t.* 3, to unloose, free, discharge
exsomnis, e, *adj*, sleepless
exsorbĕo, *v.t.* 2, to suck up
exsors, rtis, *adj*, specially chosen, deprived of
exspătĭor, *v.i.* 1, *dep*, to digress, launch out
exspectātĭo, ōnis, *f*, expectation
exspectātus, a, um, *adj*, desired
exspecto, *v.t.* 1, to look out for, wait for, hope for
exspergo (spargo), *no perfect*, **spersus** *v.t.* 3, to scatter
exspīrātĭo, ōnis, *f*, breathing out
exspīro, *v.i.t.* 1, to rush out, expire, cease; breathe out
exspŏlĭo, *v.t.* 1, to plunder
exstĭmŭlo, *v.t.* 1, to goad on
exstinctor, ōris, *m*, destroyer
exstinctus, a, um, *adj*, destroyed, extinct
exstinguo, nxi, nctum, *v.t.* 3, to quench, kill, destroy
exstirpo, *v.t.* 1, to uproot

exsto, *v.i.* 1, to project, be conspicuous, exist
exstructio, **ōnis**, *f*, structure
exstrŭo, **xi**, **ctum**, *v.t.* 3, to heap up, build up
exsūdo, *v.t.* 1, to toil or sweat at
exsul (exul), **ŭlis**, *c*, an exile
exsŭlo (exulo), *v.i.* 1, to live in exile
exsultans, **ntis**, *adj*, boastful
exsultātio, **ōnis**, *f*, rapture
exsultim, *adv*, friskingly
exsulto, *v.i.* 1, to jump about, run riot, boast
exsŭpĕrābilis, **e**, *adj*, surmountable
exsŭpĕro, *v.i.t.* 1, to get the upper hand; pass over, exceed
exsurdo, *v.t.* 1, to deafen, dull
exsurgo, **surrexi**, *v.i.* 3, to rise, stand up
exsuscĭto, *v.t.* 1, to awaken
exta, **ōrum**, *n.pl*, the inwards
extemplō, *adv*, immediately
extendo, **di**, **tum**, *v.t.* 3, to stretch out, enlarge, prolong
extentus, **a**, **um**, *adj*, extensive
extĕnŭātio, **ōnis**, *f*, attenuation
extĕnŭo, *v.t.* 1, to diminish, weaken
exter (extĕrus), **ĕra**, **ĕrum**, *adj*, external, strange, foreign
extergĕo, **si**, **sum**, *v.t.* 2, to plunder
extĕrior, **us**, *comp. adj*, outer
extermino, *v.t.* 1, to expel
externus, **a**, **um**, *adj*, external, foreign
extĕro, **trīvi**, **trītum**, *v.t.* 3, to rub off, wear away
exterrĕo, *v.t.* 2, to frighten
extĭmesco, **mŭi**, *v.i.t.* 2, to be afraid; to dread
extollo, **sustŭli**, *v.t.* 3, to raise
extorquĕo, **si**, **sum**, *v.t.* 2, to wrench away from, extort
extorris, **e**, *adj*, exiled
extrā, *adv. and prep. with acc.* outside, beyond, except
extrăho, **xi**, **ctum**, *v.t.* 3, to drag out, release, prolong
extrānĕus, **i**, *m*, stranger
extrăordinārius, **a**, **um**, *adj*, extraordinary
extrēma, **ōrum**, *n.pl*, last resort
extrēmĭtas, **ātis**, *f*, extremity
extrēmum, **i**, *n*, the end
extrēmum, *adv*, for the last time, finally
extrēmus, **a**, **um**, *adj*, furthest, the end of, or extremity of
extrīco, *v.t.* 1, to disentangle
extrinsĕcus, *adv*, from, or on, the outside
extrūdo, **si**, **sum**, *v.t.* 3, to push out
extundo, **tŭdi**, **tūsum**, *v.t.* 3, to force out, hammer out
exturbo, *v.t.* 1, to drive away
exŭbĕro, *v.i.* 1, to be abundant
exul, see **exsul**
exulcĕro, *v.t.* 1, to aggravate
exŭlŭlo, *v.i.* 1, to howl
exundo, *v.i.* 1, to overflow
exŭo, **ŭi**, **ūtum**, *v.t.* 3, to strip, deprive of, discard
exūro, **ussi**, **ustum**, *v.t.* 3, to burn up, consume
exustio, **ōnis**, *f*, conflagration
exŭviae, **ārum**, *f. pl*, stripped-off clothing or equipment

F

făba, **ae**, *f*, bean
fābella, **ae**, *f*, short story
făber, **bri**, *m*, smith, carpenter
făbrĭca, **ae**, *f*, workshop, a trade, a skilled work
făbrĭcātio, **ōnis**, *f*, structure
făbrĭcātor, **ōris**, *m*, maker
făbrĭcor, *v.t.* 1, *dep* (**fabrico**, *v.t.* 1), to construct, form
făbrĭlis, **e**, *adj*, of a craftsman
fābŭla, **ae**, *f*, story, play
fābŭlor, *v.t.* 1, *dep*, to talk, chat
fābŭlōsus, **a**, **um**, *adj*, legendary
făcesso, **cessi**, **ītum**, *v.i.t.* 3, to depart; perform, cause
făcētiae, **ārum**, *f. pl*, witticisms
făcētus, **a**, **um**, *adj*, *adv*, **ē**, courteous, elegant, witty
făcies, **ēi**, *f*, face, shape, appearance
făcilē, *adv*, easily
făcĭlis, **e**, *adj*, easy, quick, good-natured
făcĭlĭtas, **ātis**, *f*, ease, affability
făcinus, **ŏris**, *n*, deed, crime
făcio, **fēci**, **factum**, *v.i.t.* 3, to do, act, to side with (**cum**, **ab**), or against (**contra**), to be useful; to make, do, produce, assert, pretend, practise (trade)
factio, **ōnis**, *f*, faction, party
factiōsus, **a**, **um**, *adj*, mutinous
factĭto, *v.t.* 1, to keep doing
factum, **i**, *n*, deed
făcultas, **ātis**, *f*, power, opportunity, supply
fācundĭa, **ae**, *f*, eloquence
fācundus, **a**, **um**, *adj*, *adv*, **ē**, eloquent
faecŭla, **ae**, *f*, wine-dregs
faenĕrātio, **ōnis**, *f*, money-lending
faenĕrātor, **ōris**, *m*, money-lender
faenĕrātōrius, **a**, **um**, *adj*, usurious

faenĕror, *v.t.* 1, *dep* (**faenĕro,** *v.t.* 1), to lend on interest
faenīlĭa, ĭum, *n. pl,* hay-loft
faenum, i, *n,* hay
faenus, ŏris, *n,* interest, profit
faex, cis, *f,* dregs, sediment
fāgĭnĕus (nus), a, um, *adj,* of beech
fāgus, i, *f,* beech-tree
fălārĭca, ae, *f,* burning missile
falcātus, a, um, *adj,* armed with scythes, curved
falcĭfer, ĕra, ĕrum, *adj,* holding a sickle
falco, ōnis, *m,* falcon
fallācĭa, ae, *f,* trick, deceit
fallax, ācis, *adj, adv,* **ĭter,** deceitful, fallacious
fallo, fĕfelli, falsum, *v.t.* 3, to deceive, betray, escape the notice of, appear
falsum, i, *n,* falsehood
falsus, a, um, *adj, adv,* **ē,** or **o,** false, counterfeit, deceptive
falx, cis, *f,* scythe, hook
fāma, ae, *f,* rumour, public opinion, reputation, fame
fămes, is, *f,* hunger, famine
fămĭlĭa, ae, *f,* domestic servants, family property, crowd or set
fămĭlĭāris, e, *adj, adv,* **ĭter,** domestic, intimate
fămĭlĭāris, is, *m,* friend
fămĭlĭārĭtas, ātis, *f,* friendship
fāmōsus, a, um, *adj,* notorious
fămŭla, ae, *f,* maid-servant
fămŭlātus, ūs, *m,* servitude
fămŭlor, *v.i.* 1, *dep,* to serve, wait on
fămŭlus, i, *m,* servant
fānātĭcus, a, um, *adj,* inspired, frantic
fandus, a, um, *adj,* lawful
fānum, i, *n,* temple, shrine
fār, farris, *n,* grain, corn
farcĭmen, ĭnis, *n,* sausage
farcĭo, rsi, rtum, *v.t.* 4, to cram
fārĭna, ae, *f,* flour
farrāgo, ĭnis, *f,* hotchpotch
fartor, ōris, *m,* poultry-farmer
fartum, i, *n,* stuffing
fartūra, ae, *f,* cramming, padding
fās, *n* (*indeclinable*), divine law, right
fascēs, ĭum, *m. pl,* bundle of rods and axes; symbol of magistrates' power of scourging and beheading
fascĭa, ae, *f,* band, head-band
fascĭcŭlus, i, *m,* small bundle
fascĭnātĭo, ōnis, *f,* bewitching
fascĭno, *v.t.* 1, to charm, enchant
fascĭnum, i, *n,* lucky charm
fasciŏla, ae, *f,* small bandage
fascis, is, *m,* bundle, pack
fassus, a, um, *participle,* having acknowledged
fasti, ōrum, *m. pl,* working days, calendar
fastīdĭo, *v.i.t.* 4, to be disgusted; to loathe
fastīdĭōsus, a, um, *adj, adv,* **ē,** scornful, squeamish, disagreeable
fastīdĭum, ii, *n,* loathing, scorn
fastīgātus, a, um, *adj, adv,* **e,** sloping
fastīgĭum, ii, *n,* gable, top, bottom, slope
fastīgo, *v.t.* 1, to make jointed
fastus, a, um (**diēs**), court-day
fastus, ūs, *m,* arrogance
fātālis, e, *adj, adv,* **ĭter,** destined, deadly
fătĕor, fassus, *v.t.* 2, *dep,* to admit confess
fātĭdĭcus, a, um, *adj,* prophetic
fātĭfer, ĕra, ĕrum, *adj,* deadly
fātīgātĭo, ōnis, *f,* exhaustion
fātīgātus, a, um, *adj,* exhausted
fātīgo, *v.t.* 1, to weary, harass, torment
fātĭsco, *v.i.* 3, to fall apart
fātŭĭtas, ātis, *f,* foolishness
fātum, i, *n,* destiny, calamity, prophetic saying
fătŭus, a, um, *adj,* foolish
faucēs, ĭum, *f. pl,* throat, narrow passage
faustus, a, um, *adj, adv,* **ē,** fortunate
fautor, ōris, *m,* supporter
fautrix, īcis, *f,* patroness
făvĕo, fāvi, fautum, *v.i.* 2, *with dat;* to favour, befriend
făvilla, ae, *f,* embers
făvor, ōris, *m,* good-will, applause
făvōrābĭlis, e, *adj,* popular
făvus, i, *m,* honey-comb
fax, făcis, *f,* torch, stimulus
febrĭcŭlōsus, a, um, *adj,* feverish
fĕbris, is, *f,* fever
Fĕbrŭārĭus (mensis), February
fēbrŭum, i, *n,* atonement
fēcundĭtas, ātis, *f,* fertility
fēcundo, *v.t.* 1, to fertilize
fēcundus, a, um, *adj,* fertile, abundant
fel, fellis, *n,* gall-bladder, poison, bitterness
fēles, is, *f,* cat
fēlĭcĭtas, ātis, *f,* happiness
fēlix, īcis, *adj, adv,* **ĭter,** happy, fortunate, abundant
fēmĭna, ae, *f,* woman
fēmĭnĕus, a, um, *adj,* feminine
fĕmur, ŏris (**ĭnis**), *n,* thigh
fēn. . . see **faen**

For List of Abbr viations used, turn to pages 3, 4

fĕnestra, ae, *f*, window
fĕra, ae, *f*, wild animal
fĕrālis, e, *adj*, of the dead
fĕrax, ācis, *adj*, fertile
fercŭlum, i, *n*, barrow, dish
fĕrē, *adv*, almost, nearly, usually
fĕrentārius, ii, *m*, light-armed soldier
fĕrĕtrum, i, *n*, bier
fĕrĭae, ārum, *f. pl*, holidays
fĕrĭātus, a, um, *adj*, on holiday
fĕrīnus, a, um, *adj*, of wild animals
fĕrĭo, *v.t.* 4, to strike, kill; with **foedus,** to make a treaty
fĕrĭtas, ātis, *f*, wildness
fermē, *adv*, almost, usually
fermentum, i, *n*, yeast, beer
fĕro, ferre, tŭli, lātum, *v.t. irreg*, to bear, bring, move, produce, plunder, offer, tolerate, show, assert; **fertur, ferunt,** it is said
fĕrōcĭa, ae, *f*, high spirits, ferocity
fĕrōcĭtas, ātis, *f*, high spirits, ferocity
fĕrōcĭter, *adv*, bravely, fiercely
fĕrox, ōcis, *adj*, brave, fierce
ferrāmentum, i, *n*, iron tool
ferrātus, a, um, *adj*, iron-clad
ferrĕus, a, um, *adj*, made of iron
ferrūgĭnĕus, a, um, *adj*, rusty, dark red
ferrūgo, ĭnis, *f*, rust, dark red
ferrum, i, *n*, iron, sword
ferrūmen, ĭnis, *n*, cement, glue, solder
ferrūmino, *v.t.* 1, to cement, solder
fertĭlis, e, *adj*, fertile
fertĭlĭtas, ātis, *f*, fertility
fĕrŭla, ae, *f*, stalk, rod
fĕrus, a, um, *adj*, wild, cruel
fĕrus, i, *m*, wild animal
fervĕfăcio, fēci, factum, *v.t.* 3, to heat, melt
fervens, ntis, *adj, adv*, **nter,** burning, boiling, hot
fervĕo, būi, *v.i.* 2, to boil, burn, rage, swarm
fervĭdus, a, um, *adj*, burning, impetuous
fervor, ōris, *m*, heat, passion
fessus, a, um, *adj*, tired
festīnans, ntis, *adj, adv*, **nter,** in haste
festīnātio, ōnis, *f*, haste
festīno, *v.i.t.* 1, to hurry
festīnus, a, um, *adj*, quick
festīvĭtas, ātis, *f*, humour
festīvus, a, um, *adj, adv*, **ē,** witty, lively, cheerful
festum, i, *n*, holiday, banquet
festus, a, um, *adj*, festive, gay
fētĕo, *v.i.* 2, to stink
fētiāles, ĭum, *m, pl*, college of priests concerned with war-ceremonies
fētĭdus, a, um, *adj*, stinking
fētor, ōris, *m*, stench
fētūra, ae, *f*, bearing of young, young brood
fētus, ūs, *m*, bearing of young, young brood
fētus, a, um, *adj*, pregnant, fruitful, newly delivered
fĭbra, ae, *f*, fibre, nerve
fĭbŭla, ae, *f*, brooch, pin
fĭbŭlo, *v.t.* 1, to fasten
fictilis, e, *adj*, made of clay
fictile, is (ia, ĭum), *n*, earthen pottery
fictor, ōris, *m*, designer
fictus, a, um, *adj*, imagined
fĭcus, i, or, **ūs,** *f*, fig-tree
fĭdēlis, e, *adj, adv*, **iter,** faithful, true, sure
fĭdēlĭtas, ātis, *f*, faithfulness
fĭdens, ntis, *adj, adv*, **nter,** self-confident
fĭdentĭa, ae, *f*, confidence
fĭdes, ĕi, *f*, trust, faith, confidence, honesty, promise
fĭdes, ĭum, *f. pl*, lute, guitar
fĭdĭcen, ĭnis, *m*, lute-player
fĭdo, fĭsus sum, *v.* 3, *semi-dep. with dat*; to trust
fĭdŭcĭa, ae, *f*, confidence
fĭdus, a, um, *adj*, trustworthy
fĭĕri, see **fio**
fĭgo, xi, xum, *v.t.* 3, to fix, fasten, transfix
fĭgŭlāris, e, *adj*, of a potter
fĭgŭlus, i, *m*, potter
fĭgūra, ae, *f*, shape, phantom, atom, nature
fĭgūrātus, a, um, *adj*, shaped
fĭgūro, *v.t.* 1, to shape
filia, ae, *f*, daughter
filiŏla, ae, *f*, little daughter
filiŏlus, i, *m*, little son
filius, i, *m*, son
filix, ĭcis, *f*, hair, fern
filum, i, *n*, thread, texture
fimbriae, ārum, *f. pl*, threads, fringe
fimus, i, *m*, manure
findo, fĭdi, ssum, *v.t.* 3, to split
fines, ĭum, *m. pl*, territory
fingo, nxi, ctum, *v.t.* 3, to shape, adorn, imagine, devise
finĭo, *v.t.* 4, to enclose, limit, prescribe, end, die
finis, is, *m*, boundary, limit, end
finĭtĭmus, a, um, *adj*, adjoining
finĭtĭmi, ōrum, *m. pl*, neighbours

fĭnĭtor, ōris, *m,* surveyor
fio, fĭĕri, factus sum, *v, irreg,* to become, happen
firmāmen, ĭnis, *n,* prop, support
firmāmentum, i, *n,* prop, support
firmĭtas, ātis, *f,* strength, firmness
firmĭtūdo, ĭnis, *f,* strength, firmness
firmo, *v.t.* 1, to strengthen, encourage, promise
firmus, a, um, *adj, adv,* **ē, ĭter,** strong, stable, constant, true
fiscella, ae, *f,* small basket, muzzle
fiscĭna, ae, *f,* small basket
fiscus, i, *m,* purse, imperial treasury
fissĭlis, e, *adj,* breakable
fissum, i, *n,* cleft, chink
fissūra, ae, *f,* split, chink
fistūca, ae, *f,* rammer
fistŭla, ae, *f,* pipe, tube
fistŭlātor, ōris, *m,* piper
fĭsus, a, um, *adj,* trusting, relying on
flābellum, i, *n,* small fan
flābra, ōrum, *n. pl,* gusts
flaccĭdus, a, um, *adj,* flabby
flăgello, *v.t.* 1, to whip
flăgellum, i, *n,* whip, thong
flăgĭtātio, ōnis, *f,* demand
flăgĭtiōsus, a, um, *adj, adv,* **e,** disgraceful
flăgĭtium, ii, *n,* disgraceful conduct, shame
flăgĭto, *v.t.* 1, to demand
flăgrans, ntis, *adj,* burning
flăgro, *v.i.* 1, to blaze, glow
flăgrum, i, *n,* whip
flāmen, ĭnis, *m,* priest
flāmen, ĭnis, *n,* blast
flāmĭnium, ii, *n,* priesthood
flamma, ae, *f,* flame, blaze
flammĕum, i, *n,* bridal-veil
flammĕus, a, um, *adj,* flaming
flammĭfer, ĕra, ĕrum, *adj,* flame-carrying
flammo, *v.i.t.* 1, to burn
flātus, ūs, *m,* blowing, bluster
flāvens, ntis, *adj,* yellow
flāvĕo, *v.i.* 2, to be golden, yellow
flāvesco, *v.i.* 3, to turn golden
flāvus, a, um, *adj,* golden, yellow
flĕbĭlis, e, *adj, adv,* **iter,** lamentable, tearful
flecto, xi, xum, *v.i.t.* 3, to turn; bend, curve, wheel, persuade
flĕo, ēvi, tum, *v.i.t.* 2, to weep; mourn
flĕtus, ūs, *m,* weeping
flexĭbĭlis, e, *adj,* flexible
flexio, ōnis, *f,* curve
flexŭōsus, a, um, *adj,* crooked
flexus, ūs, *m,* bend, turning
flictus, ūs, *m,* collision
flō, *v.i.t.* 1, to blow
floccus, i, *m,* lock of wool
flōrens, ntis, *adj,* shining, flourishing
flōrĕo, *v.i.* 2, to bloom, flourish
flōresco, *v.i.* 3, to come into flower, flourish
flōrĕus, a, um, *adj,* made of flowers
flōrĭdus, a, um, *adj,* blooming
flōs, ōris, *m,* flower, ornament
floscŭlus, i, *m,* small flower
fluctŭo, *v.i.* 1, to ripple, undulate, hesitate
fluctŭōsus, a, um, *adj,* billowy
fluctus, ūs, *m,* wave
flŭens, ntis, *adj,* lax, fluent
flŭentum, i, *n,* stream, flood
flŭĭdus, a, um, *adj,* flowing, slack
flŭĭto, *v.i.* 1, to flow, float
flūmen, ĭnis, *n,* river, flood
flūmĭnĕus, a, um, *adj,* of a river
flŭo, xi, xum, *v.i.* 3, to flow, wave, vanish
flŭvĭālis, e, *adj,* of a river
flŭvĭus, ii, *m,* river
fluxio, ōnis, *f,* flowing
fluxus, a, um, *adj,* fluid, slack
fŏcāle, is, *n,* neck-tie
fŏcŭlus, i, *m,* brazier
fŏcus, i, *m,* fire-place, home
fŏdĭco, *v.t.* 1, to dig, nudge, stab
fŏdio, fōdi, fossum, *v.i.t.* 3, to dig; dig up, prick, stab
foedĕrātus, a, um, *adj,* allied
foedĭtas, ātis, *f,* filthiness
foedo, *v.t.* 1, to disfigure, disgrace, stain
foedus, a, um, *adj, adv,* **ē,** filthy, shameful
foedus, ĕris, *n,* treaty, contract
foet . . . see **fet . . .**
fŏlĭum, ii, *n,* leaf
follĭcŭlus, i, *m,* small bag
follis, is, *m,* pair of bellows
fŏmentum, i, *n,* poultice, comfort
fōmes, ĭtis, *m,* firewood
fons, ntis, *m,* fountain, origin
fontĭcŭlus, i, *m,* small fountain
for, *v.i.t.* 1, *dep,* to speak; say, predict
fŏrāmen, ĭnis, *n,* hole
fŏrās, *adv,* out-of-doors
forceps, ĭpis, *m, f,* tongs, pincers
fŏrĕ = futurum esse see **esse**
fŏrem = essem,
fŏrensis, e, *adj,* concerning the courts of law
fŏres, um , *f. pl,* door, entrance
forfex, ĭcis, *f,* scissors (*usually in pl.*)
fŏrica, ae, *f,* public convenience

fŏrĭcŭlae, ārum, *f. pl,* shutters
fōris, is, *f,* door, entrance
fōris, *adv,* outside, from outside
forma, ae, *f,* form, shape, beauty
formĭca, ae, *f,* ant
formidābĭlis, e, *adj,* fearful
formīdo, *v.i.t.* 1, to be afraid; fear
formīdo, ĭnis, *f,* fear, terror
formidŭlōsus, a, um, *adj, adv,* **ē,** dreadful, fearful
formo, *v.t.* 1, to shape
formōsus, a, um, *adj,* beautiful
formŭla, ae, *f,* rule, principle, agreement, lawsuit
fornax, ācis, *f,* oven
fornix, ĭcis, *m,* arch, vault
fors, rtis, *f,* chance, luck
fors, *adv,* perhaps
forsan, *adv,* perhaps
forsĭtan, *adv,* perhaps
fortassē, *adv,* perhaps
fortē, *adv,* by chance
fortis, e, *adj, adv,* **ĭter,** strong, brave
fortĭtūdo, ĭnis, *f,* bravery
fortŭĭtō(ū), *adv,* by chance
fortŭĭtus, a, um, *adj,* accidental
fortūna, ae, *f,* luck, fate, fortune (good or bad), circumstances, property
fortūnātus, a, um, *adj, adv,* **ē,** lucky, happy
fortūno, *v.t.* 1, to enrich, bless
fŏrum, i, *n,* market-place, business
fŏrus, i, *m,* gangway, passage, row of seats
fossa, ae, *f,* ditch
fossĭo, ōnis, *f,* excavation
fossor, ōris, *m,* digger, miner
fŏvĕa, ae, *f,* pit, pitfall
fŏvĕo, fōvi, fōtum, *v.t.* 2, to warm, caress, love
fractūra, ae, *f,* fracture
fractus, a, um, *adj,* weak, feeble
frāga, ōrum, *n. pl,* strawberries
frăgĭlis, e. *adj,* brittle, frail
frăgĭlĭtas, ātis, *f,* frailty
fragmen, ĭnis, *n,* fracture, splinter
fragmentum, i, *n,* fragment
frăgor, ōris, *m,* crash
frăgōsus, a, um, *adj,* rugged, crashing
fragro, *v.i.* 1, to smell
frāgum, i, *n,* strawberry plant
frango, frēgi, fractum, *v.t.* 3, to break, crush, weaken
frāter, tris, *m,* brother
frāternĭtas, ātis, *f,* brotherhood
frāternus, a, um, *adj, adv,* **ē,** brotherly
frātrĭcīda, ae, *m,* a fratricide
fraudātio, ōnis, *f,* deceit
fraudātor, ōris, *m,* deceiver
fraudo, *v.t.* 1, to cheat, defraud
fraudŭlentus, a, um, *adj,* deceitful
fraus, dis, *f,* deceit, crime, mistake, injury
fraxĭnĕus, a, um, *adj,* of ash
fraxĭnus, i, *f,* ash-tree
frĕmĭtus, ūs, *m,* murmur, roar
frĕmo, ŭi, ĭtum, *v.i.t.* 3, to roar, murmur, howl; grumble at
frĕmor, ōris, *m,* murmuring
frendĕo, ŭi, frēsum, *v.i.* 2, to gnash the teeth, crush
frēno, *v.t.* 1, to bridle, curb
frēnum, i, *n,* bridle, restraint
frĕquens, ntis, *adj, adv,* **nter,** usual, repeated, crowded
frĕquentātio, ōnis, *f,* frequency
frĕquentĭa, ae, *f,* crowd
frĕquento, *v.t.* 1, to frequent, repeat, crowd, celebrate
frĕtum, i, *n,* channel, strait
frĕtus, a, um, *adj. with abl,* relying on
frĭco, cŭi, ctum, *v.t.* 1, to rub
frictus, a, um, *adj,* rubbed, (**frico**); roasted (**frigo**)
frīgĕo, *v.i.* 2, to be cold or languid, to be slighted
frīgesco, frixi, *v.i.* 3, to grow cold, become languid
frīgĭdus, a, um, *adj,* cold, stiff, feeble, spiritless
frīgĭda, ae, *f,* cold water
frīgo, xi, ctum, *v.t.* 3, to roast
frīgus, ŏris, *n,* cold, winter
fringilla, ae, *f,* small bird, robin, chaffinch
frondātor, ōris, *m,* pruner
frondĕo, *v.i.* 2, to be in leaf
frondesco, dŭi, *v.i.* 3, to come into leaf
frondĕus, a, um, *adj,* leafy
frondōsus, a, um, *adj,* leafy
frons, dis, *f,* foliage, leaf
frons, ntis, *f,* forehead, front, appearance
fructŭōsus, a, um, *adj,* fruitful, advantageous
fructus, ūs, *m,* enjoyment, fruit, profit
frūgālis, e, *adj, adv,* **ĭter,** thrifty, careful
frūgālĭtas, ātis, *f,* thrift, worth
frūges, um, *f. pl,* see **frux**
frūgi, *indecl. adj,* worthy, useful
frūgĭfer, ĕra, ĕrum, *adj,* fertile
frūmentārius, a, um, *adj,* of corn
frūmentor, *v.i.* 1, *dep,* to fetch corn
frūmentum, i, *n,* corn
frŭor, fructus, *v.* 3, *dep. with abl,* to enjoy

frustrā, *adv*, in vain
frustrātĭo, ōnis, *f*, deception, frustration
frustror, *v.t.* 1, *dep*, to deceive
frustum, i, *n*, piece
frŭtex, ĭcis, *m*, bush
frŭtĭcētum, i, *n*, thicket
frŭtĭcōsus, a, um, *adj*, bushy
frux, frūgis, *f*, fruit, crops, value, result
fŭcātus, a, um, *adj*, painted, counterfeit
fŭco, *v.t.* 1, to paint, dye
fŭcōsus, a, um, *adj*, coloured, spurious
fŭcus, i, *m*, rouge, disguise
fŭcus, i, *m*, drone
fŭga, ae, *f*, flight, exile
fŭgax, ācis, *adj*, runaway, swift
fŭgiens, ntis, *adj*, fleeing
fŭgĭo, fūgi, fŭgĭtum, *v.i.t.* 3, to run away; flee from, avoid
fŭgĭtīvus, a, um, *adj*, fugitive
fŭgĭtīvus, i, *m*, runaway slave, deserter
fŭgĭto, *v.t.* 1, to flee, avoid
fŭgo, *v.t.* 1, to rout, chase
fulcio, fulsi, fultum, *v.t.* 4, to prop up, strengthen
fulcrum, i, *n*, foot (of couch)
fulgens, ntis, *adj*, shining
fulgĕo, lsi, *v.i.* 2, to flash, shine
fulgĭdus, a, um, *adj*, flashing, shining
fulgor, ōris, *m*, lightning, gleam, splendour
fulgur, ŭris, *n*, lightning
fulgŭrat, *v*, *impers*, it lightens
fŭlĭca, ae, *f*, moor-hen
fūlĭgo, ĭnis, *f*, soot
fūlĭgĭnōsus, a, um, *adj*, sootY
fulmen, ĭnis, *n*, thunderbolt, lightning
fulmĭnĕus, a, um, *adj*, of lightning, destructive, brilliant
fulmĭno, *v.i.* 1, to thunder
fultūra, ae, *f*, prop, tonic
fulvus, a, um, *adj*, deep yellow
fūmĕus, a, um, *adj*, smoky
fūmĭdus, a, um, *adj*, smoky
fūmĭfer, ĕra, ĕrum, *adj*, smoking, steaming
fūmĭfĭcus, a, um, *adj*, smoking, steaming
fūmĭgo, *v.t.* 1, to smoke out, fumigate
fūmo, *v.i.* 1, to smoke
fūmōsus, a, um, *adj*, smoky, smoke-dried
fūmus, i, *m*, smoke
fūnāle, is, *n*, cord, torch
functĭo, ōnis, *f*, performing
functus, a, um, *partic. adj*, *with abl*, having completed
funda, ae, *f*, sling, missile
fundāmen, ĭnis, *n*, foundation
fundāmentum, i, *n*, foundation
funditor, ōris, *m*, slinger
funditus, *adv*, from the bottom, completely
fundo, fūdi, fūsum, *v.t.* 3, to pour out, spread out, scatter, overthrow, produce
fundo, *v.t.* 1, to found, fix
fundus, i, *m*, the bottom, a farm
fundus, i, *m*, guarantor
fūnĕbris, e, *adj*, of a funeral
fūnĕrĕus, a, um, *adj*, of a funeral
fūnĕro, *v.t.* 1, to bury, kill
fūnesto, *v.t.* 1, to pollute
fūnestus, a, um, *adj*, fatal, sad
fungor, functus, *v.* 3, *dep*, *with abl*, to perform, complete
fungus, i, *m*, mushroom, fungus
fūnis, is, *m*, rope
fūnus, ĕris, *n*, funeral, death, ruin
fūr, fūris, *c*, thief, rogue
fūrax, ācis, *adj*, light-fingered
furca, ae, *f*, two-pronged fork or pole for punishment
furcifer, ĕri, *m*, gallows-bird
furcilla, ae, *f*, small fork
furcŭla, ae, *f*, fork-shaped prop, ravine
fūrens, ntis, *adj*, raging
furfur, ŭris, *m*, bran
fūrĭae, ārum, *f. pl*, rage, frenzy, avenging Furies
fūrĭālis, e, *adj*, *adv*, **ĭter**, raging, wild
fūrĭbundus, a, um, *adj*, raging
fūrĭo, *v.t.* 1, to enrage
fūrĭōsus, a, um, *adj*, raging
furnus, i, *m*, oven
fūro, ŭi, *v.i.* 3, to rage, be mad
fūror, *v.t.* 1, *dep*, to steal
fūror, ōris, *m*, rage, fury
furtim, *adv*, stealthily
furtīvus, a, um, *adj*, stolen, secret
furtum, i, *n*, theft, trick
furtō, *adv*, secretly
fūruncŭlus, i, *m*, pilferer, sore, boil
furvus, a, um, *adj*, gloomy, swarthy
fuscĭna, ae, *f*, trident
fusco, *v.t.* 1, to blacken, darken
fuscus, a, um, *adj*, dark, swarthy
fūsĭlis, e, *adj*, fluid, soft
fustis, is, *m*, cudgel, club
fūsus, a, um, *adj*, spread out, wide
fūsus, i, *m*, spindle
futtilis (fūtĭlis), e, *adj*, worthless
futtilĭtas (fūtĭlitas), ātis, *f*, worthlessness
fūtūra, ōrum, *n. pl*, the future
fūtūrum, i, *n*, the future

For List of Abbreviations used, turn to pages 3, 4

fŭtūrus, a, um, *adj*, future

G

gaesum, i, *n*, heavy Gallic javelin
galbĭnus, a, um, *adj*, greenish-yellow
gălĕa, ae, *f*, helmet
gălĕo, *v.t.* 1, to issue with helmets
gălērum, i, *n* (**us, i,** *m*), hat
galla, ae, *f*, oak-apple
gallĭna, ae, *f*, hen
gallĭnārĭŭm, ii, *n*, hen-house
gallus, i, *m*, cock
gănĕa, ae, *f*, eating-house
gănĕo, ōnis, *m*, glutton
gannĭo, *v.i.* 4, to bark, snarl
gannĭtus, ūs, *m*, chattering
garrĭo, *v.t.* 4, to chatter
garrŭlĭtas, ātis, *f*, chattering
garrŭlus, a, um, *adj*, talkative
gărum (garon), i, *n*, fish-sauce
gaudĕo, gāvīsus, *v.i.t.* 2, *semi-dep*, to rejoice
gaudĭum, ii, *n*, joy, delight
gausăpa, ae, *f*, rough cloth
gāvĭa, ae, *f*, sea-bird
gāza, ae, *f*, treasure (of Persia)
gĕlĭdus, a, um, *adj*, *adv*, **ē,** ice-cold, frosty
gĕlo, *v.i.t.* 1, to freeze
gĕlum, i (gĕlu, ūs), *n*, frost, cold
gĕmellus, a, um, *adj*, (**us, i,** *m*), twin
gĕmĭno, *v.t.* 1, to double, pair
gĕmĭnus, a, um, *adj*, twin
gĕmĭni, ōrum, *m. pl*, twins
gĕmĭtus, ūs, *m*, lamentation
gemma, ae, *f*, bud, jewel, goblet, signet-ring
gemmārĭus, ii, *m*, jeweller
gemmātus, a. um *adj*, set with jewels
gemmĕus, a, um, *adj*, set with jewels
gemmo, *v.i.* 1, to come into bud
gĕmo, ŭi, ĭtum, *v.i.t.* 3, to groan, creak; deplore
gĕna, ae, *f*, the cheek
gĕner, ĕri, *m*, son-in-law
gĕnĕrālis, e, *adj*, of a certain kind, general
gĕnĕrātim, *adv*, in classes, in general
gĕnĕrātor, ōris, *m*, breeder
gĕnĕro, *v.t.* 1, to create, produce, be born (passive)
gĕnĕrōsus, a, um, *adj*, *adv*, **ē,** of noble birth, generous
gĕnesta, ae, *f*, small shrub with yellow flowers, broom
gĕnĕtīvus, a, um, *adj*, inborn
gĕnĕtrix, īcis, *f*, mother
gĕnĭālis, e, *adj*, *adv*, **ĭter,** bridal, cheerful
gĕnĭtālis, e, *adj*, of birth, fruitful
gĕnĭtor, ōris, *m*, father
gĕnĭus, ii, *m*, guardian angel
gens, ntis, *f*, clan, race, descendant, nation
gentilĭcĭus, a, um, *adj*, of the same clan
gentīlis, e, *adj*, of the same clan
gentīlis, is, *c*, relative
gĕnu, ūs, *n*, knee
gĕnŭĭnus, a, um, *adj*, innate
gĕnŭĭnus, a, um, *adj*, of the cheek or jaw
gĕnus, ĕris, *n*, birth, race, kind, type, descendant
gĕōgrăphĭa, ae, *f*, geography
gĕōmĕtres, ae, *m*, mathematician
gĕōmĕtrĭa, ae, *f*, geometry
germānĭtas, ātis, *f*, brotherhood
germānus, a, um, *adj*, own
germānus, i, *m* (**a, ae,** *f*), brother, (sister)
germen, ĭnis, *n*, bud, sprig
germĭno, *v.i.* 1, to bud
gĕro, gessi, stum, *v.t.* 3, to bear, wear, bring, produce, behave, display, carry on, honour
gerrae, ārum, *f.pl*, nonsense
gĕrŭlus, i, *m*, porter
gestāmen, ĭnis, *n*, load
gestātĭo, ōnis, *f*, riding, driving
gestĭo, *v.i.* 4, to be joyful, desire passionately
gesto, *v.t.* 1, to carry, wear, have
gestus, ūs, *m*, posture, gesture
gestus, a, um, *adj*, achieved, carried
gibber, ĕris, *m*, hump; *as adj*, hunch-backed
gibbus, i, *m*, hump; *as adj*, hunch-backed
gigantēus, a, um, *adj*, of giants
gigās, ntis, *m*, giant
gigno, gĕnŭi, gĕnĭtum, *v.t.* 3, to give birth to; (*passive*) be born
gilvus, a, um, *adj*, pale yellow
gingīva, ae, *f*, gum
glăber, bra, brum, *adj*, bald
glăcĭālis, e, *adj*, frozen
glăcĭes, ēi, *f*, ice
glăcĭo, *v.t.* 1, to freeze
glădĭātor, ōris, *m*, gladiator
glădĭātōrĭus, a, um, *adj*, gladiatorial
glădĭus, ii, *m*, sword
glaeba (glēba), ae, *f*, clod
glans, ndis, *f*, acorn, bullet
glārĕa, ae, *f*, gravel

glaucus, a, um, *adj,* blue-grey
glēba, see **glaeba**
glis, glĭris, *m,* dormouse
glisco,–*v.i.* 3, to swell, grow
glŏbōsus, a, um, *adj,* spherical
glŏbus, i, *m,* ball, crowd
glŏmĕro, *v.t.* 1, to gather into a heap, crowd together
glŏmus, ĕris, *n,* ball of thread
glōrĭa, ae, *f,* glory, boasting
glōrĭātĭo, ōnis, *f,* boasting
glōrĭor, *v.i.t.* 1, *dep,* to boast
glōrĭōsus, a, um, *adj, adv,* **ē,** famous, conceited
glossārĭum, ii, *n,* glossary
glūten, ĭnis, *n,* glue
glūtĭnātor, ōris, *m,* bookbinder
glūtĭno, *v.t.* 1, to glue
gluttĭo, *v.t.* 4, to gulp
gnārus, a, um, *adj.* *with genit,* acquainted with, expert in
gnātus, a, um, *adj,* born
gnāv . . . see **nāv . . .**
gossypĭum, ii, *n,* cotton
grăcĭlis, e, *adj,* slender
grăcĭlĭtas, ātis, *f,* slenderness
grăcŭlus, i, *m,* jackdaw
grădātim, *adv,* gradually
grădātĭo, ōnis, *f,* gradation, climax
grădĭor, gressus, *v.i.* 3, *dep,* to walk, go, move
grădus, ūs, *m,* pace, step, rank, position, station, stair, plait
graecor, *v.i.* 1, *dep,* to live like the Greeks
grallae, ārum, *f. pl,* stilts
grāmen, ĭnis, *n,* grass
grāmĭnĕus, a, um, *adj,* grassy
grammătĭca, ae, *f,* grammar
grammătĭcus, i, *m,* grammarian
grānārĭa, ōrum, *n. pl,* granary
grānātus, a, um, *adj,* with many seeds
grandaevus, a, um, *adj,* old
grandilŏquus, a, um, *adj,* boastful
grandĭnat, *v.* 1, *impers,* it is hailing
grandis, e, *adj,* full-grown, large, old, strong, noble
grando, ĭnis, *f,* hail, hail-storm
grānum, i, *n,* grain, seed
grānōsus, a, um, *adj,* seedy
grassātor, ōris, *m,* idler, footpad
grassor, *v.i.* 1, *dep,* to hang about, attack, rage
grātē, *adv,* gratefully, willingly
grātes, *f. pl,* thanks
grātĭa, ae, *f,* esteem, friendship, charm, beauty, kindness, favour, gratitude; *in abl,* for the sake of; **grātĭīs (grātis),** as a favour; *pl,* thanks
grātĭfĭcātĭo, ōnis, *f,* doing favours
grātĭfĭcor, *v.* 1, *dep,* to do as a favour, oblige
grātĭōsus, a, um, *adj,* popular
grātor, *v. i.t.* 1, *dep,* to congratulate
grātŭĭtus, a, um, *adj,* voluntary
grātŭlātĭo, ōnis, *f,* rejoicing
grātŭlor, *v.i.t.* 1, *dep,* to congratulate
grātus, a, um, *adj,* pleasing, grateful
grăvāte, *adv,* unwillingly
grăvēdo, ĭnis, *f,* cold, catarrh
grăvĕŏlens, ntis, *adj,* stinking
grăvesco, *v.i.* 3, to grow heavy
grăvĭdus, a, um, *adj,* pregnant
grăvis, e, *adj, adv,* **ĭter,** heavy, loaded, low, pregnant, severe, unpleasant, serious, urgent, important
grăvĭtas, ātis, *f,* weight, heaviness, severity, dignity, urgency
grăvo, *v.t.* 1, to load, oppress
grăvor, *v.i.t.* 1, *dep,* to be irritated or reluctant; not to tolerate
grĕgālis, e, *adj,* of the herd, gregarious
grĕgārĭus, a, um, *adj,* common
grĕgātim, *adv,* in herds
grĕmĭum, ii, *n,* bosom, lap
gressus, ūs, *m,* step, way
grex, grĕgis, *m,* flock, herd
grūmus, i, *m,* hillock
grunnĭo, *v.i.* 4, to grunt
grunnĭtus, ūs, *m,* grunt
grus, grŭis, *m, f,* crane
grȳllus, i, *m,* grasshopper
gryps, gryphis, *m,* griffin
gŭbernācŭlum, i, *n,* rudder
gŭbernātĭo, ōnis, *f,* management
gŭbernātor, ōris, *m,* steersman
gŭberno, *v.t.* 1, to, steer, manage
gŭla, ae, *f,* throat, appetite
gŭlōsus, a, um, *adj,* gluttonous
gummi, *n,* (*indecl.*), gum
gurges, ĭtis, *m,* whirlpool, abyss
gustātĭo, ōnis, *f,* taste
gustātus, ūs, *m,* sense of taste
gusto, *v.t.* 1, to taste
gustus, ūs, *m,* tasting, snack
gutta, ae, *f,* drop, spot
guttur, ŭris, *n,* throat
gutus (guttus), i, *m,* flask
gymnāsĭum, ii, *m,* gymnasium
gymnĭcus, a, um, *adj,* gymnastic
gypsātus, a, um, *adj,* covered with lime
gypso, *v.t.* 1, to plaster
gypsum, i, *n,* white lime
gȳrus, i, *m,* circuit, ring

H

hăbēna, ae, *f,* thong, rein

hăbĕo, *v.t.* 2, to have, keep, be able, render, esteem, use, deal with, know; with **in animo,** to intend
hăbĭlis, e, *adj,* convenient, expert
hăbĭtābĭlis, e, *adj,* habitable
hăbĭtātio, ōnis, *f,* residence
hăbĭto, *v.i.t.* 1, to live; inhabit
hăbĭtus, ūs, *m,* condition, bearing, state, dress, shape
hāc, *adv,* by this way, here
hactĕnus, *adv,* up to this point
haec, see **hic**
haedus, i, *m,* young goat
haemorrhăgia, ae, *f,* haemorrhage
haerĕo, si, sum, *v.i.* 2, to hang, cling, hesitate
haesĭtans, ntis, *adj,* hesitant
haesĭtantia, ae, *f,* stammering
haesĭtātio, ōnis, *f,* embarrassment
haesĭto, *v.i.* 1, to hesitate
hālĭtus, ūs, *m,* breath, steam
hālo, *v.i.t.* 1, to breathe; exhale
hăma, ae, *f,* bucket
hāmātus, a, um, *adj,* hooked
hāmus, i, *m,* hook, fish-hook
hăra, ae, *f,* coop, pen, sty
hărēna, ae, *f,* sand, arena
hărēnārius, a, um, *adj,* of sand
hărēnōsus, a, um, *adj,* sandy
hărĭŏlor, *v.i* 1, *dep,* to foretell
hărĭŏlus, i, *m,* prophet
harmōnia, ae, *f,* harmony
harpăgo, ōnis, *m,* grappling-hook
hărundo, ĭnis, *f,* reed, fishing-rod, shaft, shepherd's pipe
hăruspex, ĭcis, *m,* clairvoyant
hasta, ae, *f,* spear, lance
hastāti, ōrum, *m. pl,* pike-men; front line of a Roman army
hastĭle, is, *n,* spear-shaft
haud (haut), *adv,* not at all
haudquāquam, *adv,* by no means
haurĭo, si, stum, *v.t.* 4, to draw up, drink in, drain, exhaust
haustus, ūs, *m,* a drink, draught
hav . . . see **av . . .**
hēbēnus, i, *f,* ebony
hēbĕo, *v.i.* 2, to be dull
hēbes, ĕtis, *adj,* blunt, dull
hēbesco, *v.i.* 3, to grow dull
hēbĕto, *v.t.* 1, to blunt
hĕdĕra, ae, *f,* ivy
hei, *interj,* ah! alas!
hellŭo, ōnis, *m,* glutton
hellŭor, *v.* 1, *dep, with abl,* to squander
hem! (**em!**), *interj,* ah! indeed!
hēmicyclĭum, ii, *n,* semi-circle
hēmisphaerĭum, ii, *n,* hemisphere
hĕra, ae, *f,* lady of the house
herba, ae, *f,* grass, plant
herbārius, a, um, *adj,* of plants
herbĭdus, a, um, *adj,* grassy
herbōsus, a, um, *adj,* grassy
hercŭle (hercle)! by Hercules!
hĕrĕ, *adv,* yesterday
hērēdĭtārius, a, um, *adj,* inherited
hērēdĭtas, ātis, *f,* inheritance
hēres, ēdis, *c,* heir, heiress
hĕri, *adv,* yesterday
hĕrĭlis, e, *adj,* of the master or mistress
hernĭa, ae, *f,* rupture
hērōĭcus, a, um, *adj,* heroic
hēros, ōis, *m,* demigod
hĕrus, i, *m,* master of the house
hespĕris, idis, *adj,* western
hespĕrius, a, um, *adj,* western
hesternus, a, um, *adj,* yesterday's
heu!, *interj,* oh! alas!
heus!, *interj,* hallo there!
hexămĕter, tri, *m,* a verse metre consisting of six feet
hians, see **hio**
hiātus, ūs, *m,* aperture
hĭberna, ōrum, *n.pl,* winter-quarters
hĭbernācŭla, ōrum, *n.pl,* tents to spend winter in
hĭberno, *v.i.* 1, to spend the winter
hĭbernus, a, um, *adj,* of winter
hibrĭda, ae, *c,* cross-breed
hĭc, haec, hōc, *pron,* this
hĭc, *adv,* here
hĭĕmālis, e, *adj,* of winter
hĭĕmo, *v.i.t.* 1, to spend the winter; freeze
hĭems (hiemps), hĭĕmis, *f,* winter, stormy weather
hĭlăris, e, *adj, adv,* **ē,** cheerful
hĭlăritas, ātis, *f,* gaiety
hĭlāro, *v.t.* 1, to cheer up
hillae, ārum, *f. pl,* sausage
hinc, *adv,* from here, hence
hinnĭo, *v.i.* 4, to neigh
hinnĭtus, ūs, *m,* neighing
hinnŭlēus, i, *m,* young stag
hĭo, *v.i.* 1, to gape open
hippŏpŏtămus, i, *m,* hippopotamus
hircīnus, a, um, *adj,* of a goat
hircus, i, *m,* goat
hirsūtus, a, um, *adj,* shaggy
hirtus, a, um, *adj,* rough, shaggy
hirūdo, ĭnis, *f,* leech
hĭrundinīnus, a, um, *adj,* of swallows
hĭrundo, ĭnis, *f,* a swallow
hisco,– *v.i.t.* 3, to gape; whisper
hispĭdus, a, um, *adj,* rough, shaggy
hĭstŏria, ae, *f,* story, account
hĭstŏrĭcus, a, um, *adj,* historical
hĭstŏrĭcus, i, *m,* historian
histrĭo, ōnis, *m,* actor
hĭulcus, a, um, *adj,* gaping; (of speech) badly connected

hoc, see **hic**
hŏdiē, *adv,* today
hŏdiernus, a, um, *adj,* of today
hŏlus, ĕris, *n,* vegetables
hŏluscŭlum, i, *n,* small vegetable
hŏmĭcīda, ae, *c,* murderer
hŏmĭcīdium, ii, *n,* homicide
hŏmo, īnis, *c,* human being
hŏmullus, i, *m,* puny man
hŏmuncŭlus, i, *m,* puny man
hŏnestas, ātis, *f,* honour, good name, integrity
hŏnesto, *v.t.* 1, to honour, adorn
hŏnestum, i, *n,* integrity
hŏnestus, a, um, *adj, adv,* **ē,** respectable, esteemed, eminent
hŏnor (hŏnos), ōris, *m,* esteem, public office, reward, charm
hŏnōrārĭus, a, um, *adj,* honorary
hŏnōrātus, a, um, *adj,* respected
hŏnōrĭfĭcus, a, um, *adj, adv,* **ē,** complimentary
hŏnōro, *v.t.* 1, to honour, respect, adorn
hŏnos, see **hŏnor**
hŏnus . . . see **ŏnus . . .**
hōra, ae, *f,* hour, time, season
hōrārĭum, ii, *n,* hour-glass
hordĕŏlus, i, *m,* sty (eye)
hordĕum, i, *n,* barley
hŏrĭŏla, ae, *f,* fishing-boat
hornōtĭnus, a, um, *adj,* this year's
hornus, a, um, *adj,* this year's
hōrŏlŏgĭum, ii, *n,* clock
horrendus, a, um, *adj,* terrible
horrĕo, *v.i.t.* 2, to bristle, tremble; dread
horresco, horrŭi, *v.i.* 3, to become ruffled or frightened
horrĕum, i, *n,* barn, warehouse
horrĭbĭlis, e, *adj,* terrible
horrĭdŭlus, a, um, *adj,* rough
horrĭdus, a, um, *adj, adv,* **ē,** rough, bristly, wild, uncouth
horrĭfer, ĕra, ĕrum, *adj,* dreadful
horrĭfĭco, *v.t.* 1, to ruffle, terrify
horrĭfĭcus, a, um, *adj,* terrible
horrĭsŏnus, a, um, *adj,* with fearful sounds
horror, ōris, *m,* bristling, trembling, chill, terror
hortāmen, īnis, *n,* encouragement
hortātĭo, ōnis, *f,* encouragement
hortātor, ōris, *m,* encourager
hortātus, ūs, *m,* encouragement
hortor, *v.t.* 1, *dep,* to encourage, urge, cheer on
hortŭlus, i, *m,* little garden
hortus, i, *m,* garden
hospĕs, ĭtis, *m,* (**hospĭta, ae,** *f*), host(ess), guest, stranger
hospĭtālis, e, *adj,* hospitable
hospĭtĭum, ii, *n,* hospitality, friendship, lodgings
hostĭa, ae, *f,* sacrificial victim
hostĭcus, a, um, *adj,* of the enemy
hostĭlis, e, *adj, adv,* **iter,** hostile
hostis, is, *c,* enemy, stranger
hūc, *adv,* to this place or point
hui!, *interj,* oh!
huius, *genitive of* **hic**
hūiuscĕmŏdi, hūiusmŏdi, *pron. adj,* (indecl.) of this sort
hūmāna, ōrum, *n.pl,* human affairs
hūmānē, *adv,* like a reasonable human being, courteously
hūmānĭtas, ātis, *f,* humanity, gentleness, refinement
hūmānĭter, *adv,* see **hūmānē**
hūmānus, a, um, *adj,* human, mortal, humane, gentle, kind
hūmecto, *v.t.* 1, to moisten
hūmĕo, *v.i.* 2, to be wet
hŭmĕrus, i, *m,* shoulder, arm
hūmi, *adv,* on or to the ground
hūmĭdus, a, um, *adj,* damp, wet
hŭmĭlis, e, *adj, adv,* **iter,** low, humble, abject
hŭmĭlĭtas, ātis, *f,* lowness, insignificance, meanness
hŭmo, *v.t.* 1, to bury
hŭmor, ōris, *m,* liquid
hŭmus, i, *f,* the ground, region
hŭăcinthus(os), i, *m,* blue iris
hŭaena, ae, *f,* hyena
hŭălus, i, *m,* glass
hybrĭda, ae, *c,* cross-breed
hydra, ae, *f,* seven-headed water-snake
hydrĭa, ae, *f,* jug
hydrops, ōpis, *m,* dropsy
hydrus, i, *m,* water-snake
hŭmen, mĕnis, *m,* marriage
hŭperbŏlē, es, *f,* exaggeration, hyperbole
hystrix, īcis, *f,* porcupine

I

ĭambēus, a, um, *adj,* iambic
ĭambus, i, *m,* iambic foot (2 syllables, short followed by long)
ĭanthĭnus, a, um, *adj,* violet in colour
ĭāpyx, iapŭgis, *m,* West-North-West wind
ĭaspis, ĭdis, *f,* jasper
ĭbi, *adv,* there, then
ĭbĭdem, *adv,* in that same place, at that very moment
ĭbis, ĭdis, *f,* sacred bird, ibis
ĭcĭo (ĭco), īci, ictum, *v.t.* 3, to hit, strike (a bargain)

For List of Abbreviations used, turn to pages 3, 4

ĭctus, ŭs, *m,* blow, stroke, shot
id, see **is**
idcirco, *adv,* for that reason
īdem, ĕădem, ĭdem, *pron,* the same
īdentidem, *adv,* repeatedly
īdĕo, *adv,* for that reason
īdĭōta, ae, *m,* layman
īdōnĕus, a, um, *adj,* suitable, capable, sufficient
īdus, ŭum, *f. pl,* the Ides, 13th or 15th day of the month
ĭdyllĭum, ii, *n,* idyll
ĭgĭtur, *adv,* therefore, then
ignārus, a, um, *adj,* unaware
ignāvĭa, ae, *f,* laziness, cowardice
ignāvus, a, um, *adj, adv,* **ē,** lazy, cowardly
ignesco, *v.i.* 3, to catch fire
ignĕus, a, um, *adj,* burning
ignĭcŭlus, i, *m,* spark
ignĭfer, ĕra, ĕrum, *adj,* fiery
ignis, is, *m,* fire, glow
ignōbĭlis, e, *adj,* unknown, obscure
ignōbĭlĭtas, ātis, *f,* obscurity
ignōmĭnĭa, ae, *f,* disgrace
ignōmĭnĭōsus, a, um, *adj,* shameful
ignōrans, ntis, *adj,* unaware
ignōrantĭa, ae, *f,* ignorance
ignōrātĭo, ōnis, *f,* ignorance
ignōro, *v.i.t.* 1, to be unaware (of)
ignosco, nōvi, nōtum, *v.t.* 3 (*with dat. of person*), to forgive
ignōtus, a, um, *adj,* unknown, of low birth
ii, see **is**
ĭlex, ĭcis, *f,* evergreen oak
ĭlĭa, ĭum, *n.pl,* groin, flank
ĭlĭcet, *adv,* immediately
ĭlĭco, *adv,* immediately
ĭlignus, a, um, *adj,* of oak
illa, see **ille**
illăbĕfactus, a, um, *adj,* unbroken
illăbor, psus, *v.i.* 3, *dep,* to slip, glide, fall
illac, *adv,* on that side
illăcessĭtus, a, um, *adj,* unprovoked
illăcrĭmābĭlis, e, *adj,* unlamented
illăcrĭmo, *v.i.* 1, to weep over
illaesus, a, um, *adj,* unhurt
illaetābĭlis, e, *adj,* gloomy
illăquĕo, *v.t.* 1, to ensnare
illātus, see **infero**
ille, a, ud, *pron, adj,* that, he, she, it
illĕcĕbra, ae, *f,* charm, allurement, bait
illĕcĕbrōsus, a, um, *adj,* alluring
illĕpĭdus, a, um, *adj,* ill-mannered, rude
illex, ĭcis, *c,* decoy
illĭbātus, a, um, *adj,* unimpaired
illĭbĕrālis, e, *adj,* mean
illic, *adv,* there, over there
illĭcĭo, lexi, ctum, *v.t.* 3, to allure, entice
illĭcĭtus, a, um, *adj,* forbidden
illĭco, *adv,* there, immediately
illīdo, si, sum, *v.t.* 3, to strike, dash, beat
illĭgo, *v.t.* 1, to tie, fasten
illinc, *adv,* from there
illĭno, lēvi, lĭtum, *v.t.* 3, to smear, spread
illittĕrātus, a, um, *adj,* illiterate
illĭus, *genitive of* **ille**
illō, *adv,* to that place
illōtus, a, um, *adj,* dirty
illūc, *adv,* to that place
illūcesco, luxi, *v.i.* 3, to grow light, dawn, shine
illud, see **ille**
illūdo, si, sum, *v.i.t.* 3, to play; mock, ridicule
illūmĭno, *v.t.* 1, to light up
illustris, e, *adj,* lighted up, distinct, distinguished
illustro, *v.t.* 1, to elucidate, make famous
illŭvĭes, ēi, *f,* dirt
ĭmāgo, ĭnis, *f,* statue, picture, copy, echo, conception
imbĕcillĭtas, ātis, *f,* weakness
imbĕcillus, a, um, *adj,* weak
imbellis, e, *adj,* unwarlike
imber, bris, *m,* rain, shower
imberbis, e, *adj,* beardless
imbĭbo, bĭbi, *v.t.* 3, to drink in
imbrex, ĭcis, *f,* gutter, tile
imbrĭfer, ĕra, ĕrum, *adj,* rainy
imbŭo, ŭi, ūtum, *v.t.* 3, to soak, infect, instil, train
ĭmĭtābĭlis, e, *adj,* easily imitated
ĭmĭtātĭo, ōnis, *f,* imitation
ĭmĭtātor, ōris, *m,* imitator
ĭmĭtātrix, ĭcis, *f,* imitator
ĭmĭtor, *v.t.* 1, *dep,* to imitate
immādesco, dŭi, *v.i.* 3, to become wet
immānĭa, ĭum, *n.pl,* horrors
immanis, e, *adj, adv,* **ē, ĭter,** enormous, frightful, savage
immānĭtas, ātis, *f,* enormity, barbarism, vastness
immansuētus, a, um, *adj,* untamed
immātūrus, a, um, *adj,* untimely, immature
immĕdĭcābĭlis, e, *adj,* incurable
immĕmor, ŏris, *adj.* heedless
immĕmŏrātus, a, um, *adj,* unmentioned

immensĭtas, ātis, *f*, immensity
immensum, i, *n*, immensity
immensus, a, um, *adj*, measureless, endless
immĕrens, ntis, *adj*, undeserving, innocent
immergo, si, sum, *v.t.* 3, to dip, plunge, immerse
immĕrĭtus, a, um, *adj*, undeserved
immētātus, a, um, *adj*, unmeasured
immīgro, *v.i.* 1, to go into
immĭnĕo, *v.i.* 2, to overhang, overlook, threaten, strive for
immĭnŭo, ŭi, ūtum, *v.t.* 3, to reduce, weaken, destroy
immĭnūtio, ōnis, *f*, weakening
immĭnūtus, a, um, *adj*, unabated
immiscĕo, scŭi, xtum, *v.t.* 2, to mix in, blend, unite
immisĕrābĭlis, e, *adj*, unpitied
immisĕrĭcors, cordis, *adj*, merciless
immissio, ōnis, *f*, admission
immītis, e, *adj*, harsh, rough
immitto, misi, ssum, *v.t.* 3, to send in, let fly, incite, allow to grow wild
immo, *adv*, on the contrary
immōbĭlis, e, *adj*, immovable
immōbĭlĭtas, ātis, *f*, immobility
immŏdĕrātus, a, um, *adj*, *adv*, **ē,** excessive
immŏdĭcus, a, um, *adj*, excessive
immŏlātio, ōnis, *f*, sacrifice
immŏlo, *v.t.* 1, to sacrifice, kill
immŏrĭor, mortŭus, *v.i.* 3, *dep*, to die, die away
immortāles, ĭum, *m. pl*, the gods
immortālis, e, *adj*, immortal
immortālĭtas, ātis, *f*, immortality
immŏtus, a, um, *adj*, unmoved
immūgio, *v.i.* 4, to roar, resound
immundus, a, um, *adj*, dirty
immūnis, e, *adj*, exempt, idle, devoid of
immūnĭtas, ātis, *f*, exemption
immūnĭtus, a, um, *adj*, unfortified
immurmŭro, *v.i.* 1, to murmur at
immūtābĭlis, e, *adj*, unchangeable
immūtātio, ōnis, *f*, interchange
immūto, *v.t.* 1, to change, alter
impācātus, a, um, *adj*, unsubdued
impar, ăris, *adj*, *adv*, **ĭter,** unequal, uneven
impărātus, a, um, *adj*, unprepared
impastus, a, um, *adj*, hungry
impătĭens, ntis, *adj*, impatient
impăvĭdus, a, um, *adj*, fearless
impeccābĭlis, e, *adj*, faultless
impĕdīmenta, ōrum, *n.pl*, luggage
impĕdīmentum, i, *n*, obstacle
impĕdio, *v.t.* 4, to hinder, entangle, hamper
impĕdĭtus, a, um, *adj*, difficult; (soldiers) in full marching-kit
impĕdĭtio, ōnis, *f*, obstruction
impello, pŭli, pulsum, *v.t.* 3, to strike upon, drive on, urge, overthrow
impendens, ntis, *adj*, overhanging
impendĕo, *v.i.t.* 2, to overhang; threaten
impendĭum, ii, *n*, cost, expense
impendo, di, sum, *v.t.* 3, to expend, devote
impĕnĕtrābĭlis, e, *adj*, impenetrable
impensa, ae, *f*, cost, expense
impensus, a, um, *adj*, *adv*, **ē,** large, strong, expensive
impĕrātor, ōris, *m*, general
impĕrātōrius, a, um, *adj*, of a general
impĕrātum, i, *n*, order
imperfectus, a, um, *adj*, incomplete
impĕrĭōsus, a, um, *adj*, powerful, mighty, tyrannical
impĕrĭtia, ae, *f*, inexperience
impĕrĭto, *v.i.t.* 1, to command
impĕrĭtus, a, um, *adj*, *with genit*, unskilled, or inexperienced in
impĕrĭum, ii, *n*, power, command, control, dominion
impermissus, a, um, *adj*, forbidden
impĕro, *v.t.* 1, *with dat. of person*, to command, impose on, demand, requisition, rule
impertio, *v.t.* 4, to share
impervĭus, a, um, *adj*, impervious
impĕtĭbĭlis, e, *adj*, intolerable
impĕtrābĭlis, e, *adj*, attainable
impĕtro, *v.t.* 1, to obtain, get
impĕtus, ūs, *m*, attack, impetuosity, impulse
impexus, a, um, *adj*, uncombed
impiĕtas, ātis, *f*, lack of respect for duty, disloyalty
impĭger, gra, grum, *adj*, energetic
impingo, pēgi, pactum, *v.t.* 3, to thrust, drive, strike (something) against
impĭus, a, um, *adj*, undutiful, unpatriotic, disloyal, wicked
implācābĭlis, e, *adj*, implacable
implācātus, a, um, *adj*, unsatisfied
implăcĭdus, a, um, *adj*, rough
implecto, xi, xum, *v.t.* 3, to plait, interweave
implĕo, ēvi, ētum, *v.t.* 2, to fill, complete, fulfil
implĭcātio, ōnis, *f*, entwining, complication
implĭcātus, a, um, *adj*, entangled, confused
implĭco, *v.t.* 1, to entangle, involve, grasp, unite
implōrātio, ōnis, *f*, entreaty

implōro, *v.t.* 1, to implore, beg for
implūmis, e, *adj,* unfledged, callow
implŭvium, ii, *n,* rain-tank in floor of atrium of Roman house
impŏlītus, a, um, *adj,* unpolished
impōno, pŏsŭi, pŏsĭtum, *v.t.* 3, to place in or on, impose, assign
importo, *v.t.* 1, to carry in, import, cause
importūnĭtas, ātis, *f,* insolence
importūnus, a, um, *adj, adv,* **ē,** inconvenient, unsuitable, troublesome, rude
impŏtens, ntis, *adj,* powerless, weak, violent, headstrong
impŏtentĭa, ae, *f,* violence
impransus, a, um, *adj,* fasting
imprĕcātio, ōnis, *f,* imprecation, curse
imprĕcor, *v.t.* 1, *dep,* to pray for something for someone
impressio, ōnis, *f,* imprint, onset
impressus, a, um, *adj,* stamped, printed
imprīmis, *adv,* especially
imprĭmo, pressi, ssum, *v.t.* 3, to stamp, imprint, engrave
improbĭtas, ātis, *f,* wickedness
improbo, *v.t.* 1, to disapprove
improbus, a, um, *adj, adv,* **ē,** bad, wicked, violent, enormous, shameless
imprōvĭdus, a, um, *adj,* not anticipating
imprōvīsus, a, um, *adj, adv,* **o,** unexpected
imprūdens, ntis, *adj, adv,* **nter,** unsuspecting, unaware
imprūdentĭa, ae, *f,* lack of foresight
impŭbes, is, *adj,* youthful
impŭdens, ntis, *adj,* shameless
impŭdentĭa, ae, *f,* impudence
impŭdĭcitĭa, ae, *f,* shameful behaviour
impŭdĭcus, a, um, *adj,* shameless, lewd, disgusting
impugno, *v.t.* 1, to attack
impulsor, ōris, *m,* instigator
impulsus, ūs, *m,* pressure, impulse, suggestion
impūnĕ, *adv,* without punishment
impūnĭtas, ātis, *f,* impunity
impūnĭtus, a, um, *adj,* unpunished
impūrus, a, um, *adj,* filthy
impŭto, *v.t.* 1, to reckon, ascribe, impute
īmus, a, um, *adj,* lowest, last
in, *prep. with abl,* in, on, within, among; *with acc,* into, towards, till, against
ĭnaccessus, a, um, *adj,* inaccessible
ĭnaedĭfico, *v.t.* 1, to build on
ĭnaequābĭlis, e, *adj,* uneven, unlike
ĭnaequālis, e, *adj,* uneven, unlike
ĭnaequālĭtas, ātis, *f,* inequality
ĭnaestimābĭlis, e, *adj,* inestimable
ĭnămābĭlis, e, *adj,* hateful
ĭnămāresco, *v.i.* 3, to become bitter
ĭnambŭlo, *v.i.* 1, to walk up and down
ĭnāne, is, *n,* emptiness
ĭnănĭmus, a, um, *adj,* lifeless
ĭnānis, e, *adj, adv,* **ĭter,** empty, useless, vain
ĭnānĭtas, ātis, *f,* emptiness
ĭnārātus, a, um, *adj,* unploughed
ĭnardesco, arsi, *v.i.* 3, to catch fire, glow
ĭnassŭētus, a, um, *adj,* unaccustomed
ĭnaudax, ācis, *adj,* timid
ĭnaudio, *v.t.* 4, to hear
ĭnaudītus, a, um, *adj,* unheard of
ĭnaugŭro, *v.i.t.* 1, to divine omens; to consecrate, inaugurate
ĭnaurātus, a, um, *adj,* golden
ĭnauro, *v.t.* 1, to cover with gold
ĭnauspicātus, a, um, *adj,* without good omens
ĭnausus, a, um, *adj,* unattempted
incaedŭus, a, um, *adj,* uncut
incălesco, căluĭ, *v.i.* 3, to grow hot, glow
incallĭdus, a, um, *adj,* stupid
incandesco, dŭi, *v.i.* 3, to grow hot, glow
incānesco, nŭi, *v.i.* 3, to grow grey or white
incanto, *v.t.* 1, to chant, bewitch
incānus, a, um, *adj,* grey, white
incassum, *adv,* in vain
incastīgātus, a, um, *adj,* unpunished
incautus, a, um, *adj, adv,* **ē,** rash, careless, unexpected
incēdo, cessi, ssum, *v.i.* 3, to advance, appear, enter
incendiārius, ii, *m,* an incendiary
incendĭum, ii, *n,* fire, heat
incendo, cendi, censum, *v.t.* 3, to burn, excite, irritate
incensus, a, um, *adj,* unregistered
incensus, a, um, *adj,* burning, excited
inceptio, ōnis, *f,* an attempt, undertaking
inceptum, i, *n,* an attempt, undertaking
incertum, i, *n,* uncertainty
incertus, a, um, *adj,* uncertain, hesitating, doubtful
incesso, cessīvi, *v.t.* 3 to attack, accuse
incessus, ūs, *m,* walk, pace, approach
incesto, *v.t.* 1, to pollute
incestum, i, *n,* adultery, incest
incestus, a, um, *adj,* impure

incĭdo, cĭdi, cāsum, *v.i.* 3, to fall into or upon, meet, happen, occur
incĭdo, cĭdi, sum, *v.t.* 3, to cut into, carve, interrupt
incĭngo, nxi, nctum, *v.t.* 3, to encircle
incĭpio, cēpi, ceptum, *v.i.t.* 3, to begin; undertake
incīsio, ōnis, *f,* an incision
incĭtāmentum, i, *n,* incentive
incĭtātio, ōnis, *f,* instigation, energy
incīsūra, ae, *f,* cutting, incision
incĭtātus, a, um, *adj,* swift
incĭto, *v.t.* 1, to urge on, rouse, excite, inspire
incĭtus, a, um, *adj,* swift
inclāmo, *v.i.t.* 1, to cry out; call out, to rebuke, abuse
inclēmens, ntis, *adj, adv,* **nter,** harsh, severe
inclēmentĭa, ae, *f,* harshness
inclīnātio, ōnis, *f,* leaning, tendency
inclīno, *v.i.t.* 1, to sink, yield; bend, turn, change
inclīnātus, a, um, *adj,* bent, disposed
inclĭtus, a, um, *adj,* famous
inclūdo, si, sum, *v.t.* 3, to shut in, include, finish
inclūsio, ōnis, *f,* confinement
inclūtus, a, um, *adj,* famous
incoctus, a, um, *adj,* uncooked
incognĭtus, a, um, *adj,* unknown
incŏhātus, a, um, *adj,* incomplete
incŏho, *v.i.t.* 1, to begin; undertake
incŏla, ae, *c,* inhabitant
incŏlo, lŭi, *v.i.t.* 3, to settle; inhabit
incŏlŭmis, e, *adj,* safe, sound
incŏlŭmĭtas, ātis, *f,* safety
incŏmĭtātus, a, um, *adj,* unaccompanied
incommŏdĭtas, ātis, *f,* unsuitability
incommŏdo, *v.i.* 1, to be annoying
incommŏdum, i, *n,* disadvantage
incommŏdus, a, um, *adj, adv,* **ē,** troublesome, unsuitable
incompertus, a, um, *adj,* unknown
incompŏsĭtus, a, um, *adj,* badly-arranged
incomptus, a, um, *adj,* unadorned
inconcessus, a, um, *adj,* illicit
inconcinnus, a, um, *adj,* awkward
inconditus, a, um, *adj,* irregular, confused, rude
inconsĭdērātus, a, um, *adj, adv,* **ē,** thoughtless, inconsiderate
inconsōlābĭlis, e, *adj,* inconsolable
inconstans, ntis, *adj, adv,* **nter,** inconsistent, fickle
inconstantĭa, ae, *f,* inconstancy
inconsultus, a, um, *adj, adv,* **ē,** without advice, indiscreet
inconsumptus, a, um, *adj,* unconsumed
incontāmĭnātus, a, um, *adj,* uncontaminated
incontĭnens, ntis, *adj, adv,* **nter,** immoderate
incŏquo, xi, ctum, *v.t.* 3, to boil, dye
incorruptus, a, um, *adj,* unspoiled
incrēbresco, brŭi, *v.i.* 3, to increase, become prevalent
incrēdĭbĭlis, e, *adj, adv,* **ĭter,** incredible, unbelievable
incrēdŭlus, a, um, *adj,* unbelieving
incrēmentum, i, *n,* increase
incrĕpito, *v.t.* 1, to rebuke
incrĕpo, ŭi, ĭtum, *v.i.t.* 1, to rattle, clatter; blare out, rebuke, reprimand
increscо, ēvi, *v.i.* 3, to grow
incrūentus, a, um, *adj,* bloodless
incrusto, *v.t.* 1, to coat over
incŭbo, ŭi, ĭtum, *v.i.* 1, to lie in or on, rest on, fall upon
inculco, *v.t.* 1, to trample on, cram in, force on, obtrude
incultus, a, um, *adj, adv,* **ē,** uncultivated, unpolished
incumbo, cŭbŭi, ĭtum, *v.i.* 3, to lean or lie on, overhang, fall upon, take pains over, influence
incūnābŭla, ōrum, *n.pl,* cradle, birthplace, origin, swaddling-clothes
incūrĭa, ae, *f,* neglect
incūrĭōsus, a, um, *adj, adv,* **ē,** indifferent
incurro, curri, cursum, *v.i.t.* 3, to run at, happen; attack
incursio, ōnis, *f,* raid, attack
incurso, *v.i.t.* 1, to run to; attack, strike
incursus, ūs, *m,* attack
incurvo, *v.t.* 1, to bend
incurvus, a, um, *adj,* bent
incūs, ūdis, *f,* anvil
incūso, *v.t.* 1, to accuse, blame
incustōdĭtus, a, um, *adj,* unguarded
incŭtio, cussi, cussum, *v.t.* 3, to strike upon, hurl, inflict
indāgātio, ōnis, *f,* investigation
indāgo, *v.t.* 1, to track down
indāgo, ĭnis, *f,* enclosing
indĕ, *adv,* from there, then
indēbĭtus, a, um, *adj,* not due
indĕcor, ŏris, *adj,* disgraceful
indĕcŏro, *v.t.* 1, to disgrace
indĕcŏrus, a, um, *adj, adv,* **ē,** unbecoming, unsightly, disgraceful
indēfensus, a, um, *adj,* undefended
indēfessus, a, um, *adj,* unwearied
indēlēbĭlis, e, *adj,* indestructible
indēlĭbātus, a, um, *adj,* untouched

For List of Abbreviations used, turn to pages 3, 4

indemnātus, a, um, *adj,* unsentenced
indēprensus, a, um, *adj,* unnoticed
index, ĭcis, *m, f,* forefinger, informer, sign, list
indĭcĭum, ii, *n,* information, evidence, proof, indication
indĭco, *v.t.* 1, to show, indicate, give evidence
indĭco, xi, ctum, *v.t.* 3, to announce, appoint, impose
indictus, a, um, *adj,* unsaid
indĭdem, *adv,* from the same place
indies, *adv,* from day to day
indiffĕrĕns, ntis, *adj,* indifferent
indigĕna, ae, *adj,* native
indigĕo, *v.i.* 2, to need, want
indigestus, a, um, *adj,* confused
indignans, ntis, *adj,* enraged
indignātio, ōnis, *f,* indignation
indignitas, ātis, *f,* shameful behaviour, unworthiness
indignor, *v.t.* 1, *dep,* to be indignant at, scorn
indignus, a, um, *adj, adv,* **ē,** unworthy, shameful, cruel
indĭgus, a, um, *adj,* needing
indĭligens, ntis, *adj, adv,* **nter,** careless
indĭligentĭa, ae, *f,* carelessness
indiscrētus, a, um, *adj,* unseparated
indĭsertus, a, um, *adj,* at a loss for words
indĭvĭdŭus, a, um, *adj,* indivisible
indo, dĭdi, dĭtum, *v.t.* 3, to put or place upon or into, attach
indŏcĭlis, e, *adj,* unteachable, untaught
indoctus, a, um, *adj,* untaught
indŏles, is, *f,* inborn abilities
indŏlesco, lŭi, *v.i.* 3, to be in pain, to be troubled
indŏmĭtus, a, um, *adj,* untamed
indormio, *v.i.* 4, to fall asleep over
indŏtātus, a, um, *adj,* without a dowry, poor
indŭbĭto, *v.i.* 1, to distrust
indŭbĭus, a, um, *adj,* not doubtful
indūco, xi, ctum, *v.t.* 3, to lead in, conduct, exhibit, spread over, put on (clothes), induce, resolve, cancel
inductĭo, ōnis, *f,* introduction, exhibition, intention
indulgens, ntis, *adj, adv,* **nter,** kind, indulgent, fond
indulgentĭa, ae, *f,* indulgence
indulgĕo, si, tum, *v.i.t.* 2, *with dat,* to be kind to; permit, grant
indŭo, ŭi, ūtum, *v.t.* 3, to put on (garment), assume
indūro, *v.t.* 1, to harden
indūsĭum, ii, *n,* woman's petticoat
industrĭa, ae, *f,* diligence; *with* **de** *or* **ex,** on purpose
industrĭus, a, um, *adj,* diligent
indūtĭae, ārum, *f. pl,* truce
indūtus, a, um, *adj,* clothed
ĭnĕdĭa, ae, *f,* fasting
inĕlĕgans, ntis, *adj, adv,* **nter,** unrefined
ĭnĕluctābĭlis, e, *adj,* unavoidable
ĭnemptus, a, um, *adj,* unbought
ĭnĕnarrābĭlis, e, *adj,* indescribable
ĭnĕo, *v.i.t.* 4, to begin; enter, calculate, estimate, contrive
ĭneptĭae, ārum, *f. pl,* absurdities
ĭneptus, a, um, *adj, adv,* **ē,** improper, inept, foolish
ĭnermis, e, *adj,* unarmed
ĭners, rtis, *adj,* unskilful, idle, sluggish
ĭnertĭa, ae, *f,* ignorance, idleness
ĭnērŭdĭtus, a, um, *adj,* illiterate
ĭnēvĭtābĭlis, e, *adj,* unavoidable
ĭnexcūsābĭlis, e, *adj,* inexcusable
ĭnexercĭtātus, a, um, *adj,* untrained
ĭnexhaustus, a, um, *adj,* inexhaustible
ĭnexōrābĭlis, e, *adj,* inexorable
ĭnexpectātus, a, um, *adj,* unexpected
ĭnexpertus, a, um, *adj,* inexperienced, untried
ĭnexpĭābĭlis, e, *adj,* irreconcilable
ĭnexplēbĭlis, e, *adj,* insatiable
ĭnexplētus, a, um, *adj,* unsatisfied
ĭnexplĭcābĭlis, e, *adj,* inexplicable
ĭnexplōrātus, a, um, *adj,* unexplored
ĭnexpugnābĭlis, e, *adj,* impregnable
ĭnexstinctus, a, um, *adj,* imperishable
ĭnextrĭcābĭlis, e, *adj,* inextricable
infăbrē, *adv,* unskilfully
infăcētus, a, um, *adj,* coarse
infāmĭa, ae, *f,* disgrace
infāmis, e, *adj,* disreputable
infāmo, *v.t.* 1, to disgrace
infandus, a, um, *adj,* unutterable
infans, ntis, *adj,* speechless
infans, ntis, *c,* child, baby
infantĭa, ae, *f,* speechlessness, infancy
infātŭo, *v.t.* 1, to make a fool of
infaustus, a, um, *adj,* unfortunate
infector, ōris, *m,* dyer
infectus, a, um, *adj,* unfinished
infēcundus, a, um, *adj,* unfruitful
infēlix, īcis, *adj,* unhappy, unfortunate, barren
infensus, a, um, *adj,* enraged
infĕri, ōrum, *m. pl,* the dead
infĕrĭae, ārum, *f. pl,* sacrifices in honour of the dead
infĕrĭor, ĭus, *adv,* lower, later, younger, inferior

infĕrĭus, *adv*, lower
infernus, a, um, *adj*, lower, underground
infĕri, ōrum, *m. pl*, inhabitants of the underworld, the dead
infero, inferre, intŭli, illātum, *v.t. irreg*, to bring to or against, attack, produce, inflict
infĕrus, a, um, *adj*, below, lower
infervesco, ferbŭi, *v.i.* 3, to boil
infesto, *v.t.* 1, to attack, molest
infestus, a, um, *adj, adv*, **ē,** dangerous, hostile, unsafe
inficio, fēci, fectum, *v.t.* 3, to stain, dye, taint, corrupt
infidēlis, e, *adj*, untrustworthy
infidēlitas, ātis, *f*, treachery
infidus, a, um, *adj*, treacherous
infigo, xi, xum, *v.t.* 3, to fix into, drive in, imprint
infimus, a, um, *adj*, lowest
infindo, fĭdi, fissum, *v.t.* 3, to cut into
infīnĭtas, ātis, *f*, endlessness
infīnĭtus, a, um, *adj, adv*, **ē,** unlimited, endless
infirmātio, ōnis, *f*, weakening
infirmĭtas, ātis, *f*, weakness
infirmo, *v.t.* 1, to weaken, annul
infirmus, a, um, *adj, adv*, **ē,** weak
infit, *v, defect*, he (she, it) begins
infitĭas ĕo (ire, ii), to deny
infitiātio, ōnis, *f*, denial
infitiātor, ōris, *m*, bad debtor
infitior, *v.t.* 1, *dep*, to deny
inflammātio, ōnis, *f*, inflammation, setting on fire
inflammo, *v.t.* 1, to set on fire
inflātus, ūs, *m*, blast
inflātus, a, um, *adj*, puffed up, haughty, inflated
inflecto, xi, xum, *v.t.* 3, to bend
inflētus, a, um, *adj*, unmourned
inflexĭbĭlis, e, *adj*, inflexible
inflexio, ōnis, *f*, bending
inflīgo, xi, ctum, *v.t.* 3, to strike (something) against
inflo, *v.t.* 1, to blow into
influo, xi, xum, *v.i.* 3, to flow into, crowd in
infŏdio, fōdi, fossum, *v.t.* 3, to dig in, bury
informātio, ōnis, *f*, outline
informis, e, *adj*, shapeless
informo, *v.t.* 1, to shape, sketch, educate
infortūnātus, a, um, *adj*, unfortunate
infrā, *adv, and prep. with acc*, below, under
infractio, ōnis, *f*, breaking
infractus, a, um, *adj*, broken, exhausted
infrĕmo, ŭi, *v.i.* 3, to growl
infrendĕo, *v.i.* 2, to gnash the teeth, threaten
infrēnis, e (us, a, um), *adj*, unbridled
infrēno, *v.t.* 1, to bridle, curb
infrĕquens, ntis, *adj*, rare, not well filled
infrĕquentia, ae, *f*, scantiness
infringo, frēgi, fractum, *v.t.* 3, to break off, crush, weaken
infŭla, ae, *f*, head-band, ribbon
infundĭbŭlum, i, *n*, funnel
infundo, fūdi, fūsum, *v.t.* 3, to pour out, lay before, impart
infusco, *v.t.* 1, to darken, stain
infūsus, a, um, *adj*, streaming or falling over
ingĕmino, *v.i.t.* 1, to increase; repeat, redouble
ingĕmisco, mŭi, *v.i.* 3, to sigh
ingĕmo, ŭi, *v.i.t.* 3, to groan; lament, mourn
ingĕnĕro, *v.t.* 1, to produce
ingĕniōsus, a, um, *adj, adv*, **ē,** talented, adapted to
ingĕnium, ii, *n*, natural disposition, abilities, intelligence
ingens, ntis, *adj*, huge, famous
ingĕnŭĭtas, ātis, *f*, good birth, gentlemanly character
ingĕnŭus, a, um, *adj, adv*, **ē,** natural, in-born, free-born, frank, honourable
ingĕnŭus, i, *m* **(a, ae,** *f*), free-born man or woman
ingĕro, gessi, gestum, *v.t.* 3, to carry, throw or thrust into
ingigno, gĕnŭi, gĕnĭtum, *v.t.* 3, to implant, produce
inglōrĭus, a, um, *adj*, inglorious
inglŭvies, ēi, *f*, gizzard, maw
ingrātĭis, *adv*, unwillingly
ingrātus, a, um, *adj, adv*, **ē,** unpleasant, ungrateful
ingrăvesco, *v.i.* 3, to become heavy or worse
ingrăvo, *v.t.* 1, to aggravate
ingrĕdior, gressus, *v.i.t.* 3, *dep*, to advance; enter, upon
ingressio, ōnis, *f*, entering, pace
ingressus, ūs, *m*, entrance, inroad, commencement
ingrŭo, ŭi, *v.i.* 3, to attack
inguen, inis, *n*, groin, abdomen
ingurgito, *v.t.* 1, (*with* **se**) to gorge, addict one's self to
inhăbĭlis, e, *adj*, unwieldy, incapable
inhăbĭtābĭlis, e, *adj*, uninhabitable
inhaerĕo, si, sum, *v.i.* 2, to cling to, adhere to

inhaeresco, haesi, haesum, *v.i.* 3, to cling to, adhere to
inhibĕo, *v.t.* 2, to restrain
inhĭo, *v.i.* 1, to gape, gaze
inhŏnestus, a, um, *adj*, shameful
inhŏnōrātus, a, um, *adj*, unhonoured
inhorrĕo, *v.i.* 2, to bristle, shiver
inhorresco, *v.i.* 3, to bristle, shiver
inhospitālis, e, *adj*, inhospitable
inhospĭtus, a, um, *adj*, inhospitable
inhūmānitas, ātis, *f*, barbarity, niggardliness
inhūmānus, a, um, *adj, adv,* **ē, ĭter,** savage, uncivilized, rude
inhūmātus, a, um, *adj*, unburied
inĭbi, *adv*, there
inĭcio, iēci, iectum, *v.t.* 3, to throw into, seize, inspire
inĭmĭcĭtia, ae, *f*, enmity
inĭmĭco, *v.t.* 1, to make into enemies
inĭmĭcus, a, um, *adj, adv,* **ē,** unfriendly, hostile
inĭmĭcus, i, *m* (**a, ae,** *f*), enemy
inĭquitas, ātis, *f*, unevenness, difficulty, injustice
inĭquus, a, um, *adj, adv,* **ē,** uneven, unfair, unfortunate, hostile, disadvantageous
initĭo, *v.t.* 1, to initiate
initiŏ, *adv*, in the beginning
initĭum, ii, *n*, beginning, origin; (*in pl*) first principles, sacred rites
iniūcundus, a, um, *adj, adv,* **ē,** unpleasant
iniungo, nxi, nctum, *v.t.* 3, to join on to, inflict, impose
iniūrātus, a, um, *adj*, without taking an oath
iniūria, ae, *f*, injury, wrong
iniūriōsus, a, um, *adj*, wrongful
iniussu, *adv*, without orders
iniussus, a, um, *adj*, of one's accord
iniustĭtia, ae, *f*, injustice
iniustus, a, um, *adj, adv,* **ē,** unjust, wrongful, harsh
innascor, nātus, *v.i.* 3, *dep*, to be born in, grow up in
innăto, *v.t.* 1, to swim, float in
innātus, a, um, *adj*, innate
innāvigābilis, e, *adj*, unnavigable
innecto, xŭi, xum, *v.t.* 3, to tie, fasten, attach, contrive
innĭtor, nixus (nīsus), *v.* 3, *dep, with dat. or abl*, to lean on
inno, *v.i.* 1, to swim, float in
innŏcens, ntis, *adj*, harmless, blameless
innŏcentia, ae, *f*, integrity
innŏcŭus, a, um, *adj*, harmless
innoxĭus, a, um, *adj*, harmless, innocent, unhurt
innŭbus, a, um, *adj*, unmarried
innŭmĕrābilis, e, *adj*, countless
innŭmĕrus, a, um, *adj*, countless
innŭo, ŭi, ūtum, *v.i.* 3, to nod, hint
innuptus, a, um, *adj*, unmarried
inobservātus, a, um, *adj*, unperceived
inoffensus, a, um, *adj*, untouched, uninterrupted
inŏlesco, lēvi, lĭtum, *v.i.* 3, to grow in, take root
inŏpia, ae, *f*, lack, need
inŏpĭnans, ntis, *adj*, unaware
inŏpĭnātus, a, um, *adj, adv,* **ē, ō,** unexpected
inŏpĭnus, a, um, *adj*, unexpected
inopportūnus, a, um, *adj*, unfitting, inopportune
inops, ŏpis, *adj*, helpless, needy
inordĭnātus, a, um, *adj*, in disorder
inornātus, a, um, *adj*, unadorned
inquam, *v. irreg*, I say
inquies, ētis, *f*, restlessness
inquiētus, a, um, *adj*, restless
inquilīnus, i, *m*, lodger
inquĭnātus, a, um, *adj*, filthy
inquĭno, *v.t.* 1, to stain, corrupt
inquīro, sīvi, sītum, *v.t.* 3, to search for, examine
inquĭsitio, ōnis, *f*, legal investigation
insālŭbris, e, *adj*, unhealthy
insālūtātus, a, um, *adj*, without saying goodbye
insānābilis, e, *adj*, incurable
insānia, ae, *f*, madness, folly
insānio, *v.i.* 4, to be insane, to rage
insānitas, ātis, *f*, disease
insānus, a, um, *adj, adv,* **ē,** insane, frantic, excessive
insātiābilis, e, *adj*, insatiable
insciens, ntis, *adj*, unaware
inscientia, ae, *f*, ignorance, inexperience
inscĭtia, ae, *f*, ignorance, inexperience
inscĭtus, a, um, *adj, adv,* **ē,** ignorant, stupid
inscĭus, a, um, *adj*, unaware
inscribo, psi, ptum, *v.t.* 3, to write on, attribute
inscriptio, ōnis, *f*, title
insculpo, psi, ptum, *v.t.* 3, to engrave
insĕco, cŭi, ctum, *v.t.* 1, to cut up
insectātio, ōnis, *f*, pursuit
insectātor, ōris, *m*, pursuer
insector, *v.t.* 1, *dep*, to pursue, reproach
insectum, i, *n*, insect
insĕnesco, nŭi, *v.i.* 3, to grow old at
insĕpultus, a, um, *adj*, unburied
insĕquor, sĕcūtus, *v.i.t.* 3, *dep*, to follow; pursue, reproach
insĕro, sēvi, sītum, *v.t.* 3, to implant, ingraft

insĕro, rŭi, rtum, *v.t.* 3, to put in, introduce
inserto, *v.t.* 1, to insert
inservio, *v.i.* 4, to serve, be submissive to, attend to
insidĕo, sēdi, sessum, *v.i.t.* 2, to sit upon, be fixed; occupy, inhabit
insidĭae, ārum, *f. pl,* ambush, plot; *with* **ex** *or* **per,** craftily
insidior, *v.* 1, *dep, with dat,* to lie in ambush
insidiōsus, a, um, *adj, adv,* **ē,** cunning, dangerous
insīdo, sēdi, sessum, *v.i.t.* 3, to settle on or in; occupy
insigne, is, *n,* mark, sign, costume, signal, ornament
insignio, *v.t.* 4, to make distinguished
insignis, e, *adj,* conspicuous, famous, distinguished
insilĭo, ŭi, *v.i.* 4, to spring upon
insimŭlo, *v.t.* 1, to accuse
insincērus, a, um, *adj,* tainted
insinŭo, *v.i.t.* 1, to penetrate; insinuate
insĭpiens, ntis, *adj,* foolish
insĭpientia, ae, *f,* folly
insisto, stĭti, *v.i.t.* 3, to step, stand, begin, halt; devote oneself to
insĭtus, a, um, *adj,* inborn
insŏlens, ntis, *adj, adv,* **nter,** unusual, unaccustomed, haughty
insŏlentia, ae, *f,* strangeness, novelty, affectation, arrogance
insŏlĭtus, a, um, *adj,* unaccustomed, unusual
insomnia, ae, *f,* sleeplessness
insomnis, e, *adj,* sleepless
insomnium, ii, *n,* dream
insŏno, ŭi, *v.i.* 1, to resound
insons, ntis, *adj,* innocent, harmless
inspecto, *v.t.* 1, to look at
inspērans, ntis, *adj,* not hoping
inspērātus, a, um, *adj,* unhoped for, unexpected
inspergo, si, sum, *v.t.* 3, to sprinkle
inspĭcio, spexi, spectum, *v.t.* 3, to examine, consider
inspīro, *v.t.* 1, to breathe on, inspire
instăbĭlis, e, *adj,* unsteady, changeable
instans, ntis, *adj,* present
instar, *n, indecl,* resemblance, appearance, value; *with genit,* as big as, like
instauro, *v.t.* 1, to renew
insterno, strāvi, strātum, *v.t.* 3, to spread or cover over
instigo, *v.t.* 1, to incite
instillo, *v.t.* 1, to instil
instimŭlo, *v.t.* 1, to spur on
instinctus, ūs, *m,* impulse
instinctus, a, um, *adj,* incited
instĭtor, ōris, *m,* commercial-traveller
instĭtŭo, ŭi, ūtum, *v.t.* 3, to set up, appoint, undertake, resolve, arrange, train
instĭtūtio, ōnis, *f,* arrangement, custom, education
instĭtūtum, i, *n,* purpose, plan, custom
insto, stĭti, stātum, *v.i.* 1, to stand over, harass, impend, urge on, pursue
instructus, a, um, *adj,* arranged, provided with
instrūmentum, i, *n,* tool, stores
instrŭo, xi, ctum, *v.t.* 3, to erect, arrange, provide, teach
insŭăvis, e, *adj,* unpleasant
insuesco, ēvi, ētum, *v.i.t.* 3, to become accustomed; to accustom
insuētus, a, um, *adj,* unaccustomed to, unusual
insŭla, ae, *f,* island, block of flats
insŭlānus, i, *m,* islander
insulsĭtas, ātis, *f,* silliness
insulsus, a, um, *adj, adv,* **ē,** tasteless, silly
insulto, *v.i.t.* 1, to jump, leap; to spring at, abuse
insum, inesse, infŭi, *v.i, irreg,* to be in, be contained in
insūmo, mpsi, mptum, *v.t.* 3, to employ, expend
insŭo, ŭi, ūtum, *v.t.* 3, to sew on
insŭper, *adv, and prep. with acc,* moreover, besides; above
insŭpĕrābĭlis, e, *adj,* insurmountable
insurgo, surrexi, rectum, *v.i.* 3, to arise, rise to
insŭsurro, *v.i.t.* 1, to whisper
intābesco, bŭi, *v.i.* 3, to waste away
intactus, a, um, *adj,* untouched, unattempted, chaste
intāmĭnātus, a, um, *adj,* pure
intectus, a, um, *adj,* uncovered
intĕger, gra, grum, *adj, adv,* **ē,** untouched, perfect, blameless, unspoiled, undecided
intĕgo, xi, ctum, *v.t.* 3, to cover
intĕgrĭtas, ātis, *f,* completeness, uprightness
intĕgro, *v.t.* 1, to renew, refresh
intĕgŭmentum, i, *n,* covering, disguise
intellĕgens, ntis, *adj,* understanding
intellĕgentia, ae, *f,* understanding
intellĕgo, xi, ctum, *v.t.* 3, to understand, perceive
intĕmĕrātus, a, um, *adj,* pure
intempĕrans, ntis, *adj,* extravagant
intempĕrantia, ae, *f,* extravagance

For List of Abbreviations used, turn to pages 3, 4

intempĕrĭes, ēi, *f*, inclement weather, violence
intempestīvus, a, um, *adj, adv,* **ē,** untimely, inconvenient
intempestus, a, um, *adj,* unseasonable, unhealthy; (with **nox**) the dead of night
intendo, di, tum (sum), *v.t.* 3, to stretch or spread out, aim, direct, threaten, concentrate, intend
intentātus, a, um, *adj,* untried
intentio, ōnis, *f,* tension, effort, application
intentus, a, um, *adj, adv,* **ē,** stretched, bent, intent
intĕpesco, pŭi, *v.i.* 3, to grow warm
inter, *adv, and prep. with acc,* among, between, during
intercēdo, cessi, ssum, *v.i.* 3, to go between, intervene, occur
intercessio, ōnis, *f,* veto, intervention
intercessor, ōris, *m,* mediator, surety, user of the veto
intercīdo, di, sum, *v.t.* 3, to cut up
intercĭdo, di, *v.i.* 3, to happen, fall down, perish
intercĭpio, cēpi, ceptum, *v.t.* 3, to intercept, seize, steal
interclūdo, si, sum, *v.t.* 3, to block, cut off, hinder, separate, blockade
intercurro, curri, cursum, *v.i.* 3, to run between, intercede
interdĭco, dixi, dictum, *v.t.* 3, to prohibit, banish
interdictum, i, *n,* prohibition
interdiu, *adv,* in the daytime
interdum, *adv,* sometimes
intĕrĕā, *adv,* meanwhile
intĕrĕo, ii, ĭtum, *v.i.* 4, to perish, die, become lost
intĕrest, see **intersum**
interfector, ōris, *m,* murderer
interfĭcio, fēci, fēctum, *v.t.* 3, to kill, destroy
interflŭo, xi, *v.i.* 3, to flow between
interfūsus, a, um, *adj,* poured between, interposed, stained
intĕrim, *adv,* meanwhile
intĕrĭmo, ēmi, emptum, *v.t.* 3, to take away, destroy, kill
intĕrĭor, ĭus, *comp. adj,* inner
intĕrĭus, *adv,* inside
intĕrĭtus, ūs, *m,* annihilation
interiăcĕo, *v.i.* 2, to lie between
interĭcio, iēci, iectum, *v.t.* 3, to put or throw between
interiectus, a, um, *adj,* interposed
interlābor, lapsus, *v.i.* 3, *dep,* to glide or flow between
interlĕgo, lēgi, lectum, *v.t.* 3, to pluck, pick
interlūcĕo, luxi, *v.i.* 2, to shine out, appear
interlŭo, *v.t.* 3, to flow between
intermīnātus, a, um, *adj,* endless
intermiscĕo, scŭi, xtum, *v.t.* 2, to intermix
intermissio, ōnis, *f,* interruption, cessation
intermitto, mīsi, missum, *v.i.t.* 3, to cease; neglect, omit, stop, pause, interrupt
intermortŭus, a, um, *adj,* lifeless
internĕcīnus, a, um, *adj,* deadly, internecine
internĕcio, ōnis *f,* massacre
internecto, *v.t.* 3, to bind up
internosco, nōvi nōtum, *v.t.* 3, to distinguish between
internuntĭus, ii, *m,* negotiator
internus a, um *adj,* internal
interpellātio, ōnis, *f,* interruption
interpello, *v.t.* 1, to interrupt
interpŏlo, *v.t.* 1, to furbish
interpōno, pŏsŭi, ĭtum, *v.t.* 3, to put between, introduce; with **se,** to interfere; with **fidem,** to pledge
interpŏsitio, ōnis, *f,* insertion
interprĕs, ĕtis, *c,* negotiator
interprĕtātio, ōnis, *f,* explanation
interprĕtor, *v.t.* 1, *dep,* to explain
interpunctio, ōnis, *f,* punctuation
interpungo, nxi, ctum, *v.t.* 3, to punctuate
interquiesco, quiēvi, quiētum, *v.i.* 3, to rest for a while
interregnum, i, *n,* vacancy in the kingship or high office
interrex, rēgis, *m,* regent
interritus, a, um, *adj,* fearless
interrŏgātor, ōris, *m,* questioner
interrŏgātum, i, *n,* question
interrŏgo, *v.t.* 1, to inquire
interrumpo, rūpi, ruptum, *v.t.* 3, to break up, interrupt
intersaepio, psi, ptum, *v.t.* 4, to hedge in, cut off
interscĭndo, scĭdi, scissum, *v.t.* 3, to tear down, divide
intersĕro, rŭi, rtum, *v.t.* 3, to interpose
intersum, esse, fŭi, *v.i, irreg,* to lie between, differ, take part in; **interest,** *v. impers,* it concerns, it is of importance
intertexo, xŭi, xtum, *v.t.* 3, to intertwine
intervallum, i, *n,* space, pause

intervĕnĭo, vēni, ventum, *v.i.* 4, to interrupt, happen, prevent
interventus, ūs, *m*, intervention
intervīso, si, sum, *v.t.* 3, to inspect, visit occasionally
intestābĭlis, e, *adj*, abominable
intestīna, ōrum, *n.* pl, intestines
intestīnus, a, um, *adj*, internal
intexo, xŭi, xtum, *v.t.* 3, to interlacé
intĭmus, a, um, *adj*, inmost
intŏlĕrābĭlis, e, *adj*, intolerable
intŏlĕrandus, a, um, *adj*, intolerable
intŏlĕrans, ntis, *adj, adv,* **nter,** impatient, intolerable
intŏno, ŭi, *v.i.* 1, to thunder
intonsus, a, um, *adj*, unshaven
intorquĕo, si, sum, *v.t.* 2, to twist, sprain, hurl
intrā, *adv, and prep. with acc*, on the inside, within
intractābĭlis, e, *adj*, unmanageable
intractātus, a, um, *adj*, untried
intrĕmo, ŭi, *v.i.* 3, to tremble
intrĕpĭdus, a, um, *adj*, fearless
intrō, *adv*, within, inside
intro, *v.i.t.* 1, to enter
intrōdūco, xi, ctum, *v.t.* 3, to lead in, introduce
intrōductĭo, ōnis, *f*, introduction
intrōĕo, *v.i.* 4, to enter
intrōfĕro, ferre, tŭli, lātum, *v.t, irreg*, to bring in
intrōgrĕdĭor, gressus, *v.i.* 3, *dep*, to enter
intrŏĭtus, ūs *m*, entrance
intrōmitto, mĭ si, ssum, *v.t.* 3, to send in
introrsum (us), *adv*, within
intrōspĭcio, spexi, spectum, *v.t.* 3, to look into, examine
intŭĕor, *v.t.* 2, *dep*, to look at
intūmesco, mŭi, *v.i.* 3, to swell
intus, *adv*, within, inside
intūtus, a, um, *adj*, unguarded
inultus, a, um, *adj*, unavenged
inumbro, *v.t.* 1, to shade
inundātĭo, ōnis, *f*, flooding
inundo, *v.i.t.* 1, to overflow; flood
inungo, nxi, unctum, *v.t.* 3, to anoint
inurbānus, a, um, *adj*, rude
inūro, ssi, stum, *v.t.* 3, to brand
inūsĭtātus, a, um, *adj, adv,* **ē,** unusual, strange
inūtĭlis, e, *adj*, useless
inūtĭlĭtas, ātis, *f*, uselessness
invādo, si, sum, *v.i.t.* 3, to enter; attack, invade, seize
invălĭdus, a, um, *adj*, weak
invĕho, xi, ctum, *v.t.* 3, to carry, bring to; *passive or reflex*, to ride, drive, attack (with words)
invĕnĭo, vēni, ventum, *v.t.* 4, to find, meet with, devise
inventĭo, ōnis, *f*, invention
inventor, ōris, *m*, inventor
inventum, i, *n*, invention
invĕnustus, a, um, *adj*, unattractive
invĕrēcundus, a, um, *adj*, immodest
invergo, *v.t.* 3, to pour on
inversus, a, um, *adj*, inverted, perverted
inverto, ti, sum, *v.t.* 3, to turn upside down, exchange
invespĕrascit, *v. impers*, evening is approaching
investīgātĭo, ōnis, *f*, investigation
investīgo, *v.t.* 1, to search for
invĕtĕrasco, rāvi, *v.i.* 3, to grow old, become permanent
invĕtĕrātus, a, um, *adj*, old-established
invĕtĕro, *v.t.* 1, to endure
invĭcem, *adv*, alternately
invĭctus, a, um, *adj*, unconquered, invincible
invĭdĕo, vīdi, vīsum, *v.t.* 2, *with dat*; to envy, grudge
invĭdĭa, ae, *f*, envy, ill-will
invĭdĭōsus, a, um, *adj, adv,* **ē,** jealous, enviable
invĭdus, a, um, *adj*, envious
invĭgĭlo, *v.i.* 1, to be watchful
invĭŏlātus, a, um, *adj*, unharmed
invīso, si, sum, *v.t.* 3, to visit
invīsus, a, um, *adj*, hated
invĭsus, a, um, *adj*, unseen
invĭtātĭo, ōnis, *f*, challenge, invitation
invĭto, *v.t.* 1, to invite, challenge, tempt
invĭtus, a, um, *adj*, unwilling
invĭus, a, um, *adj*, pathless
invŏcātus, a, um, *adj*, uninvited
invŏco, *v.t.* 1, to appeal to
invŏlĭto, *v.i.* 1, to hover
invŏlo, *v.i.t.* 1, to fly at; attack
invŏlūcrum, i, *n*, wrapper
invŏlūtus, a, um, *adj*, intricate
involvo, volvi, vŏlūtum, *v.t.* 3, to roll on, wrap up, envelop
invulnĕrābĭlis, e, *adj*, invulnerable
iō, *interj*, oh! ah! ho!
ipse, a, um (*genit*, **ipsius,** *dat*, **ipsi**), *emphatic pron*, himself, herself, itself, precisely, just
īra, ae, *f*, anger
īrācundĭa, ae, *f*, rage, temper
īrācundus, a, um, *adj*, irritable
īrascor, īrātus, *v.* 3, *dep. with dat*, to be angry with
īrātus, a, um, *adj*, angry
ire, see **ĕo**
īris, ĭdis, *f*, iris
īrōnĭa, ae, *f*, irony

irpex, ĭcis, *m,* harrow
irrĕmĕābĭlis, e, *adj,* irretraceable
irrĕpĕrābĭlis, e, *adj,* irrecoverable
irrĕpertus, a, um, *adj,* undiscovered
irrēpo, psi, ptum, *v.i.* 3, to creep in, insinuate oneself
irrĕquiētus, a, um, *adj,* restless
irrētio, *v.t.* 4, to entangle
irrĕtortus, a, um, *adj,* not turned back
irrĕvŏcābĭlis, e, *adj,* irrevocable
irrĭdĕo, si, sum, *v.i.t.* 2, to joke, jeer; mock, ridicule
irrĭgātio, ōnis, *f,* irrigation
irrĭgo, *v.t.* 1, to water, refresh
irrĭgŭus, a, um, *adj,* well-watered, moistening
irrĭsio, ōnis, *f,* mockery
irrĭsus, ūs, *m,* mockery
irrĭsor, ōris, *m,* scoffer
irrĭtābĭlis, e, *adj,* irritable
irrĭtāmen, ĭnis, *n,* incentive
irrĭtāmentum, i, *n,* incentive
irrĭto, *v.t.* 1, to provoke
irrĭtus, a, um, *adj,* invalid, unsuccessful
irrŏgo, *v.t.* 1, to propose (against someone), inflict
irrōro, *v.t.* 1, to bedew
irrumpo, rūpi, ptum, *v.i.t.* 3, to break in; attack, interrupt
irrŭo, ŭi, *v.i.* 3, to rush in, seize
irruptus, a, um, *adj,* unbroken
is, ĕa, id, *demonst. pron,* he, she, it, that
ischias, ădis, *f,* sciatica
iste, a, ud, *demonst. pron,* that
isthmus, i, *m,* isthmus
istīc, *adv,* there
istinc, *adv,* from there
istūc, *adv,* to that place
ĭtă, *adv,* in such a way, so
ĭtăque, *conj,* and so, therefore
ĭtem, *adv,* likewise, also
iter, ĭtĭnĕris, *n,* route, journey, march
ĭtĕrātio, ōnis, *f,* repetition
ĭtĕro, *v.t.* 1, to repeat
ĭtĕrum, *adv,* again
ĭtidem, *adv,* in the same way
ĭtio, ōnis, *f,* travelling

J (consonantal i)

iăcĕo, *v.i.* 2, to lie (recumbent), lie sick
iăcio, iēci, iactum, *v.t.* 3, to throw, lay down
iactans, ntis, *pres. part, adj,* boastful
iactantia, ae, *f,* ostentation
iactātio, ōnis, *f,* tossing, bragging
iactātor, ōris, *m,* braggart
iacto, *v.t.* 1, to throw about, boast
iactūra, ae, *f,* throwing overboard, sacrifice
iactus, ūs, *m,* throw, shot
iăcŭlātor, ōris, *m,* thrower
iăcŭlātrix, īcis, *f,* huntress
iăcŭlor, *v.t.* 1, *dep,* to hurl
iăcŭlum, i, *n,* javelin
iam, *adv,* already, now
iamdūdum, *adv,* a long time ago
iamprīdem, *adv,* for a long time now
iānĭtor, ōris, *m,* doorkeeper
iānŭa, ae, *f,* door, entrance
Iānŭārius (mensis), January
iĕcur, ŏris, *n,* liver
iēiūnĭtas, ātis, *f,* meagreness
iēiūnium, ii, *n,* fast, hunger
iēiūnus, a, um, *adj,* hungry, barren
ientăcŭlum, i, *n,* breakfast
iento, *v.i.* 1, to breakfast
iŏcātio, ōnis, *f,* joke
iŏcor, *v.i.t.* 1, *dep,* to joke
iŏcōsus, a, um, *adj,* humorous
iŏcŭlāris, e, *adj,* amusing
iŏcŭlātor, ōris, *m,* joker
iŏcus, i, *m,* joke
iŭba, ae, *f,* mane, crest
iŭbar, ăris, *n,* radiance
iŭbĕo, iussi, iussum, *v.t.* 2, to order, tell
iūcunditas, ātis, *f,* pleasantness
iūcundus, a, um, *adj,* pleasant
iūdex, ĭcis, *m,* judge
iudicialis, e, *adj,* judicial
iudicatio ōnis, *f,* judgement
iūdĭcium, ii, *n,* trial, verdict, court discretion, judgement
iūdĭco, *v.t.* 1, to judge, decide
iūgālis, e, *adj,* yoked together
iūgāles, *m. pl,* chariot-horses
iūgĕrum, i, *n,* acre (approx.)
iūgis, e, *adj,* perpetual
iūglans, dis, *f,* walnut
iūgo, *v.t.* 1, to marry, connect
iūgōsus, a, um, *adj,* mountainous
iūgŭlo, *v.t.* 1, to cut the throat
iūgum, i, *n,* yoke, bench, mountain-ridge
Iūlius (mensis), July
iūmentum, i, *n,* pack-animal
iuncĕus, a, um, *adj,* made of rushes
iuncōsus, a, um, *adj,* full of rushes
iunctio, ōnis, *f,* junction
iunctūra, ae, *f,* joint
iuncus, i, *m,* bullrush
iungo, nxi, nctum, *v.t.* 3, to join
iūnĭor, *comp. adj,* from **iŭvĕnis,** younger
iūnĭpĕrus, i, *f,* juniper tree
Iūnius (mensis), June
iūrātor, ōris, *m,* commissioner of oaths

iūrātus, a, um, *adj*, bound by oath
iurgium, ii, *n*, quarrel
iurgo, *v.i.t.* 1, to quarrel; upbraid
iūris consultus, i, *m*, lawyer
iūris dictio, ōnis, *f*, jurisdiction
iūro, *v.i.t.* 1, to take an oath; to swear by
iūs, iūris, *n*, law, legal status, right, authority
iūs, iūris, *n*, soup
iusiūrandum, i, *n*, oath
iussum, i, *n*, order
iusta, ōrum, *n.pl*, due ceremonies
iustē, *adv*, rightly
iustĭtĭa, ae, *f*, justice
iustĭtĭum, *n*, holiday for lawcourts, public mourning
iustum, i, *n*, fairness
iustus, a, um, *adj*, fair, lawful
iŭvēnālis, e, *adj*, youthful
iŭvenca, ae, *f*, heifer
iŭvencus, i, *m*, bullock
iŭvēnesco, nŭi, *v.i.* 3, to reach youth
iŭvēnīlis, e, *adj*, youthful
iŭvēnis, is, *m, f*, young person; (*adj*) young
iŭvēnor, *v.i.* 1, *dep*, to act youthfully
iŭventa, ae, *f*, the age of youth
iŭventas, ātis, *f*, the age of youth
iŭventus, ūtis, *f*, the age of youth
iŭvo, iūvi, iūtum, *v.t.* 1, to help, gratify; **iŭvat** (*impers. with acc*), it pleases, it is of use
iuxtā, *adv, and prep. with acc*, near
iuxtim, *adv, and prep. with acc*, next to

K

Kalendae, ārum, *f. pl*, the Kalends, the first day of the month

L

lăbĕfăcio, fēci, factum, *v.t.* 3, to shake, loosen, overthrow
lăbĕfacto, *v.t.* 1, to shake, destroy
lăbellum, i, *n*, a lip
lăbellum, i, *n*, tub, basin
lābes, is, *f*, sinking, downfall
lābes, is, *f*, spot, blemish
lăbo, *v.i.* 1, to totter, waver
lăbor, lapsus, *v.i.* 3, *dep*, to slip, slide, glide, pass away, be mistaken
lăbor, ōris, *m*, work, toil, workmanship, distress
lăbōrĭōsus, a, um, *adj, adv*, **ē,** laborious, industrious
lăbōro, *v.i.t.* 1, to strive, be in trouble or difficulty; to make, prepare
lăbrum, i, *n*, lip
lābrum, i, *n*, tub, basin
lăbyrinthus, i, *m*, labyrinth
lac, lactis, *n*, milk
lăcer, ĕra, ĕrum, *adj*, mangled
lăcerna, ae, *f*, cloak
lăcĕrātio, ōnis, *f*, laceration
lăcĕro, *v.t.* 1, to tear, rend, censure, destroy
lăcerta, ae, *f* (**us, i,** *m*), lizard
lăcertōsus, a, um, *adj*, brawny
lăcertus, i, *m*, arm, strength
lăcertus, i, *m*, lizard, newt
lăcesso, īvi, ītum, *v.t.* 3, to provoke, attack, irritate, urge
lăcĭnia, ae, *f*, edge of garment
lăcrĭma, ae, *f*, tear
lăcrĭmābilis, e, *adj*, mournful
lăcrĭmo, *v.i.* 1, to weep
lăcrĭmōsus, a, um, *adj*, tearful
lactens, ntis, *f*, very young (unweaned) animal
lactĕus, a, um, *adj*, milky
lacto, *v.i.t.* 1, to have milk; suck
lactūca, ae, *f*, lettuce
lăcūna, ae, *f*, ditch, pond, gap
lăcūnar, āris, *n*, ceiling
lăcus, ūs, *m*, lake, tank, tub
laedo, si, sum, *v.t.* 3, to injure, offend
laena, ae, *f*, cloak
laetābilis, e, *adj*, joyful
laetĭfĭco, *v.t.* 1, to delight
laetĭtĭa, ae, *f*, joyfulness
laetor, *v.t.* 1, *dep*, to rejoice
laetus, a, um, *adj, adv*, **ē,** glad, cheerful, willing, pleased, prosperous, beautiful
laeva, ae, *f*, the left hand
laevus, a, um, *adj*, on the left side, unfortunate, foolish
lăgănum, i, *n*, a cake
lăgēna, ae, *f*, wine-jar
lăgōis, ĭdis, *f*, grouse
lăgōpūs, ŏdis, *f*, grouse
lăguncŭla, ae, *f*, small bottle
lambo, bi, bĭtum, *v.t.* 3, to lick
lāmentābĭlis, e, *adj*, mournful
lāmentātio, ōnis, *f*, mourning
lāmentor, *v.i.t.* 1, *dep*, to weep; mourn
lāmenta, ōrum, *n.pl*, moaning
lămia, ae, *f*, witch, vampire
lāmĭna, ae, *f*, thin metal plate
lampas, ădis, *f*, torch
lāna, ae, *f*, wool
lancĕa, ae, *f*, lance, spear
lānĕus, a, um, *adj*, woollen
languens, ntis, *adj*, faint, weak
languĕo, *v.i.* 2, to be faint or listless
languesco, gŭi, *v.i.* 3, to become faint or listless
languĭdus, a, um, *adj*, faint, weary, sluggish

For List of Abbreviations used, turn to pages 3, 4

languor, ōris, *m,* weakness, weariness, sluggishness
lăniātus, ūs, *m,* laceration
lānĭcĭum, ii, *n,* wool
lăniēna, ae, *f,* butcher's stall
lānĭfĭcus, a, um, *adj,* weaving
lāniger, ĕra, ĕrum, *adj,* fleecy
lānio, *v.t.* 1, to mutilate
lānista, ae, *m,* fencing-master
lānius, ii, *m,* butcher
lanterna, ae, *f,* lamp, torch
lānūgo, ĭnis, *f,* down, hair
lanx, ncis, *f,* dish, plate
lăpăthus, i, *f,* sorrel
lăpĭcīda, ae, *m,* quarryman
lăpĭcīdĭnae, ārum, *f. pl,* stone-quarries
lăpĭdātio, ōnis, *f,* stoning
lăpĭdĕus, a, um, *adj,* of stone
lăpĭdōsus, a, um, *adj,* stony
lăpillus, i, *m,* pebble, grain
lăpis, ĭdis, *m,* stone, milestone, jewel
lappa, ae, *f,* a bur
lapso, *v.i.* 1, to slip, stumble
lapsus, a, um, *adj,* fallen, sinking, ruined
lapsus, ūs, *m,* fall, slip, gliding
lăquĕar, āris, *n,* ceiling
lăquĕātus, a, um, *adj,* panelled
lăquĕus, i, *m,* noose, snare
lar, āris, *m,* guardian deity of a house, home
largĭor, *v.t.* 4, *dep,* to lavish, give
largĭtas, ātis, *f,* abundance
largĭtio, ōnis, *f,* generous distribution, bribery
largĭtor, ōris, *m,* briber, generous giver
largus, a, um, *adj, adv,* **ē, ĭter,** abundant, lavish, large
lārĭdum (lardum), i, *n,* lard
lărix, ĭcis, *f,* larch
larva, ae, *f,* ghost, mask
lascīvĭa, ae, *f,* playfulness
lascīvio, *v.i.* 4, to frolic
lascīvus, a, um, *adj,* playful, licentious
lassitūdo, ĭnis, *f,* weariness
lasso, *v.t.* 1, to tire, fatigue
lassus, a, um, *adj,* exhausted
lātē, *adv,* far and wide
lătĕbra, ae, *f,* hiding-place, subterfuge
lătĕbrōsus, a, um, *adj,* full of hiding-places, secret
lătens, ntis, *adj, adv,* **nter,** hidden, secret
lătĕo, *v.i.* 2, to lie hidden, keep out of sight
lăter, ĕris, *m,* brick, tile, ingot
lătĕrĭcĭus, a, um, *adj,* made of bricks
lătex, ĭcis, *m,* liquid
lătibŭlum, i, *n,* hiding-place
Lătīnē, *adv,* in Latin
lătĭto, *v.i.* 1, to lie hidden
lātĭtūdo, ĭnis, *f,* breadth
lātor, ōris, *m,* proposer of a law
lātrātor, ōris, *m,* a barker
lātrātus, ūs, *m,* barking
lātrīna, ae, *f,* water-closet
lātro, *v.i.t.* 1, to bark; bark at
lătro, ōnis, *m,* robber
lătrōcĭnĭum, ii, *n,* robbery, fraud, robber-band
lătrōcĭnor, *v.i.* 1, *dep,* to practise highway robbery
lătrunculus, i, *m,* robber
lātus, a, um, *adj, adv,* **ē,** wide
lătus, ĕris, *n,* the side, flank, lungs
laudābĭlis, e, *adj,* praiseworthy
laudātio, ōnis, *f,* praises, eulogy
laudātor, ōris, *m,* praiser
laudātus, a, um, *adj,* praiseworthy
laudo, *v.t.* 1, to praise, name
laurēa, ae, *f,* laurel (tree)
laurēātus, a, um, *adj,* crowned with laurel (of victory)
laurĕus, a, um, *adj,* of laurel
laurus, i, *f,* laurel
laus, dis, *f,* praise, merit
lautē, *adv,* elegantly
lautĭtĭa, ae, *f,* elegance
lautŭmĭae, ārum, *f. pl,* stone-quarry
lautus, a, um, *adj,* elegant, splendid, noble
lăvātio, ōnis, *f,* ablution, washing
lăvo, lāvi, lautum, *v.i.t.* 1 or 3, to wash or wet
laxĭtas, ātis, *f,* spaciousness
laxo, *v.t.* 1, to enlarge, loosen, relax, relieve, weaken
laxus, a, um, *adj,* wide, loose
lēa, ae, *f,* lioness
lēaena, ae, *f,* lioness
lēbes, ētis, *m,* copper basin
lectĭca, ae, *f,* sedan, litter
lectio, ōnis, *f,* selection, reading aloud
lector, ōris, *m,* reader
lectŭlus, i, *m,* sofa, couch
lectus, a, um, *adj,* chosen, excellent
lectus, i, *m,* bed, couch
lectus, ūs, *m,* reading
lēgātio, ōnis, *f,* delegation
lēgātum, i, *n,* legacy
lēgātus, i, *m,* ambassador, delegate, lieutenant-general
lēges, see **lex**
lēgĭfer, ĕra, ĕrum, *adj,* law-giving
lēgio, ōnis, *f,* Roman legion (4,000–6,000 soldiers)
lēgiōnārĭus, a, um, *adj,* of a legion

lēgĭtĭmus, a, um, *adj*, legal, legitimate, proper, right
lēgo, *v.t.* 1, to send with a commission, appoint as a deputy, leave as a legacy
lĕgo, lēgi, lectum, *v.t.* 3, to read, gather, select, steal, pass through, sail by, survey
lĕgūmen, ĭnis, *n*, pulse, beans
lembus, i, *m*, yacht, cutter
lĕmŭres, um, *m. pl*, ghosts, spirits
lēna, ae, *f*, bawd
lēnīmen, ĭnis, *n*, alleviation, palliative
lēnīmentum, i, *n*, alleviation, palliative
lēnĭo, *v.t.* 4, to soften, soothe
lēnis, e, *adj, adv,* **ĭter,** soft, smooth, gentle, calm
lēnĭtas, ātis, *f*, gentleness
lēno, ōnis, *m*, pimp, seducer
lēnŏcĭnĭum, ii, *n*, pandering, ornamentation
lēnŏcĭnor, *v.1, dep, with dat*, to flatter, promote
lens, ntis, *f*, lentil
lentesco, *v.i.* 3, to become soft or sticky
lentĭgo, ĭnis, *f*, freckle
lentĭtūdo, ĭnis, *f*, apathy, sluggishness
lento, *v.t.* 1, to bend
lentus, a, um, *adj, adv,* **ē,** slow, flexible, sticky, tedious, calm (of character)
lēnuncŭlus, i, *m*, boat
lĕo, lōnis, *m*, lion
lĕpĭdus, a, um, *adj, adv,* **ē,** charming, elegant, pleasant
lĕpor (lĕpos), ōris, *m*, charm, pleasantness, wit
lĕpŏrārĭum, ii, *n*, warren
leprae, ārum, *f. pl*, leprosy
lĕprōsus, a, um, *adj*, leprous
lĕpus, ŏris, *m*, a hare
lĕpuscŭlus, i, *m*, leveret
lētālis, e, *adj*, fatal
lēthargĭcus, a, um, *adj*, lethargic
lēthargus, i, *m*, stupor
lētĭfer, ĕra, ĕrum, *adj*, deadly
lētum, i, *n*, death
lĕvāmen, ĭnis, *n*, consolation, comfort
lĕvāmentum, i, *n*, consolation, comfort
lĕvātĭo, ōnis, *f*, raising
lĕvis, e, *adj, adv,* **ĭter,** light, mild, light-armed, agile, trivial, unreliable
lēvis, e, *adj*, smooth, soft
lĕvĭtas, ātis, *f*, inconstancy
lēvĭtas, ātis, *f*, smoothness
lĕvo, *v.t.* 1, to raise, relieve, take away, support, soothe, release
lēvo, *v.t.* 1, to smooth
lex, lēgis, *f*, law, condition
lĭbāmen, ĭnis, *n*, drink-offering
lĭbāmentum, i, *n*, drink-offering
lĭbella, ae, *f*, small coin
lĭbellus, i, *m*, small book, pamphlet, diary
lĭbens, ntis, *adj, adv,* **nter,** with pleasure, willing
lĭber, ĕra, ĕrum, *adj, adv,* **ē,** free, frank
1. **lĭber, ĕri,** *m*, wine
2. **lĭber, ĕri,** *m*, child
lĭber, bri, *m*, book, tree-bark
lĭbĕrālis, e, *adj, adv,* **ĭter,** honourable, generous
lĭbĕrālĭtas, ātis, *f*, generosity
lĭbĕrātĭo, ōnis, *f*, release
lĭbĕrātor, ōris, *m*, liberator
lĭbĕri, ōrum, *m. pl*, children
lĭbĕro, *v.t.* 1, to release, free from slavery, acquit
lĭbertas, ātis, *f*, freedom
lĭbertīnus, i, *m*, freedman
lĭbertĭnus, a, um, *adj*, of a freedman
lĭbertus, i, *m*, a freedman
lĭbet, lĭbŭit, lĭbĭtum est, *v. 2, impers*, it is agreeable
lĭbĭdĭnōsus, a, um, *adj*, lecherous
lĭbĭdo, ĭnis, *f*, desire, passion, whim
lĭbo, *v.t.* 1, to taste, touch, pour out an offering of wine
lĭbra, ae, *f*, Roman pound (12 oz.), pair of scales
lĭbrāmentum, i, *n*, a weight
lĭbrārĭus, i, *m*, secretary
lĭbrārĭus, a, um, *adj*, of books
lĭbrātus, a, um, *adj*, balanced
lĭbrĭlis, e, *adj*, weighing a pound
lĭbro, *v.t.* 1, to balance, hurl
lĭbum, i, *n*, pancake
lĭburna, ae, *f*, fast sailing-ship
licenter, *adv*, without restraint
licentĭa, ae, *f*, freedom, licence
licĕo, *v.i.* 2, to be for sale, be valued at
licĕor, *v.t.* 2, *dep*, to bid (for)
licet, cŭit, cĭtum est, *v.2, impers*, it is allowed, one may
licet, *conj*, although
licĭtus, a, um, *adj*, permitted
licĭtātĭo, ōnis, *f*, bidding
licĭum, ii, *n*, a thread
lictor, ōris, *m*, official attendant of high magistrates
liēn, ēnis, *m*, spleen
ligāmen, ĭnis, *n*, bandage
ligāmentum, i, *n*, ligament
lignārĭus, ii, *m*, carpenter, joiner
lignātĭo, ōnis, *f*, wood-gathering
lignātor, ōris, *m*, wood-cutter
lignĕus, a, um, *adj*, wooden
lignor, *v.i.* 1, *dep*, to collect wood

lignum, i, *n*, wood
ligo, *v.t.* 1, to tie, bind
ligo, ōnis, *m*, hoe
ligŭla, ae, *f*, small tongue (of land); tongue of a shoe
ligūrio, *v.t.* 4, to lick, desire
ligustrum, i, *n*, a plant, privet
lilium, ii, *n*, lily
lima, ae, *f*, file
limax, ācis, *f*, slug
limbus, i, *m*, border, edge
limen, ĭnis, *n*, door-step, door, lintel
limēs, ĭtis, *m*, boundary, track
limo, *v.t.* 1, to file, polish, finish
limōsus, a, um, *adj*, slimy, muddy
limpĭdus, a, um, *adj*, clear, bright
limus, a, um, *adj*, aslant
limus, i, *m*, slime, mud
linus, i, *m*, apron
lināmentum, i, *n*, linen, lint
lĭnĕa, ae, *f*, thread, string, line, end, goal
lĭnĕāmentum, i, *n*, line, feature
lĭnĕus, a, um, *adj*, linen
lingo, nxi, *v.t.* 3, to lick
lingua, ae, *f*, tongue, speech, language
lĭniger, ĕra, ĕrum, *adj*, clothed in linen
lĭno, lēvi, lĭtum, *v.t.* 3, to daub, smear over
lĭnquo, lĭqui, *v.t.* 3, to leave
lintĕo, ōnis, *m*, linen-weaver
linter, tris, *f*, boat, tray
lintĕum, i, *n*, linen
lintĕus, a, um, *adj*, of linen
lĭnum, i, *n*, flax, linen, thread, rope, net
lippĭtūdo, ĭnis, *f*, inflammation of the eyes
lippus, a, um, *adj*, blear-eyed
liquĕfăcio, fēci, factum, *v.t.* 3, to melt, dissolve
liquĕfactus, a, um, *adj*, molten
liquens, ntis, *adj*, liquid
liquĕo, lĭqui, *v.i.* 2, to be clear
liquesco, licŭi, *v.i.* 3, to melt
liquĭdus, a, um, *adj*, liquid, flowing, clear
liquo, *v.t.* 1, to melt, filter
liquor, *v.i.* 3, *dep*, to melt, flow
liquor, ōris, *m*, a liquid
lis, tis, *f*, dispute, lawsuit
lĭtigĭōsus, a, um, *adj*, quarrelsome
lĭtigo, *v.i.* 1, to quarrel
lĭto, *v.i.t.* 1, to make a sacrifice with favourable omens; appease
lĭtŏrĕus, a, um, *adj*, of the sea-shore
littĕra, ae, *f*, a letter of the alphabet
littĕrae, ārum, *f. pl*, a letter, document, literature, learning
littĕrātus, ā, um, *adj*, educated
littĕrŭla, ae, *f*, small letter, moderate literary knowledge
litūra, ae, *f*, smear, erasure
litus, ōris, *n*, sea-shore
lĭtŭus, i, *m*, augur's staff, trumpet
livens, ntis, *adj*, bluish
livĕo, *v.i.* 2, to be black and blue
lĭvĭdus, a, um, *adj*, bluish, black and blue, envious
lĭvor, ōris, *m*, leaden colour, envy, malice
lixa, ae, *m*, camp-follower
lŏca, ōrum, *n.pl*, a region
lŏcātio, ōnis, *f*, placing, arrangement, lease
lŏco, *v.t.* 1, to place, arrange, give in marriage, lease, contract for
lŏcŭlāmentum, i, *n*, box
lŏcŭlus, i, *m*, satchel, purse
lŏcŭplēs, ētis, *adj*, wealthy
lŏcŭplēto, *v.t.* 1, to enrich
lŏcus, i, *m*, place, position, topic, subject, cause, reason
lŏcusta, ae, *f*, locust
lŏcūtio, ōnis, *f*, speaking, pronunciation, phrase
lŏdix, ĭcis, *f*, blanket
lŏgica, ōrum, *n.pl*, logic
lŏgicus, a, um, *adj*, logical
lŏlīgo, ĭnis, *f*, cuttle-fish
lŏlium, ii, *n*, darnel
longaevus, a, um, *adj*, ancient
longē, *adv*, far off, greatly
longinquitas, ātis, *f*, duration, distance
longinquus, a, um, *adj*, distant, strange, prolonged
longitūdo, ĭnis, *f*, length
longūrius, ii, *m*, long pole
longus, a, um, *adj*, long, tall, vast, distant, tedious
lŏquācitas, ātis, *f*, talkativeness
lŏquax, ācis, *adj*, *adv*, **ĭter,** talkative, babbling
lŏquēla, ae, *f*, speech, discourse
lŏquor, lŏcūtus, *v.i.t.* 3, *dep*, to speak; tell, mention, declare
lōrīca, ae, *f*, breastplate
lōrīpēs, pĕdis, *adj*, bandy-legged
lōrum, i, *n*, strap, whip
lōtos (lōtus), i, *f*, lotus-tree
lūbens, lŭbet, see **libens, libet**
lūbrĭcus, a, um, *adj*, slippery, dangerous, deceitful
lŭcellum, i, *n*, slight profit
lūcĕo, xi, *v.i.* 2, to shine
lūcet, *v. impers*, day breaks
lūcerna, ae, *f*, lamp
lūcesco, *v.i.* 3, to dawn
lūcĭdus, a, um, *adj*, bright, clear
lūcĭfer, ĕra, ĕrum, *adj*, light-bringing;
lūcĭfer ĕri, *m*, morning-star

lūcĭfŭgus, a, um, *adj*, retiring
lŭcrātivus, a, um, *adj*, profitable
lŭcror, *v.t.* 1, *dep*, to gain, win
lŭcrum, i, *n*, profit, advantage
luctāmen, inis, *n*, wrestling, struggle
luctātio, ōnis, *f*, wrestling, struggle
luctātor, ōris, *m*, wrestler
luctĭfĭcus, a, um, *adj*, woeful
luctor, *v.i.* 1, *dep*, to struggle
luctŭōsus, a, um, *adj*, sorrowful
luctus, ūs, *m*, grief, mourning (clothes)
lūcŭbrātio, ōnis, *f*, night-work
lūcŭlentus, a, um, *adj*, bright
lūcus, i, *m*, wood, grove
lūdĭbrium, ii, *n*, mockery, jest, laughing-stock
lūdĭbundus, a, um, *adj*, playful
lūdĭcer, ĭcra, ĭcrum, *adj*, sportive, theatrical
lūdĭcrum, i, *n*, public show or games, a play
lūdĭfĭcātio, ōnis, *f*, mocking
lūdĭfĭcor, *v.i.t.* 1, *dep* (**lūdĭfĭco,** *v.t.* 1), to mock, deceive
lūdĭmăgister, tri, *m*, schoolmaster
lūdĭus, ii, *m*, pantomine-actor
lūdo, si, sum, *v.i.t.* 3, to play, frolic; mock, deceive
lūdus, i, *m*, a play, game, public games, school, joke
lŭes, is, *f*, an epidemic
lūgĕo, xi, ctum, *v.i.t.* 2, to mourn
lūgŭbris, e, *adj*, lamentable, disastrous
lumbus, i, *m*, loin
lūmen, ĭnis, *n*, light, lamp, gleam, life, eye, glory
lūna, ae, *f*, moon
lūnāris, e, *adj*, lunar
lūnātus, a, um, *adj*, crescent-shaped
lūno, *v.t.* 1, to bend into a crescent-shape
lŭo, lŭi, *v.t.* 3, to pay a debt or penalty, undergo, atone for
lŭpāta, ōrum, *n.pl*, horse-bit
lŭpātus, a, um, *adj*, jagged
lŭpīnus, a, um, *adj*, of the wolf
lŭpīnus, i, *m*, lupin (plant)
lŭpus, i, *m*, wolf, pike (fish), a jagged bit, hook
lūridus, a, um, *adj*, lurid, sallow
luscĭnia, ae, *f*, nightingale
lūsor, ōris, *m*, player, mocker
lustrālis, e, *adj*, expiatory
lustrātio, ōnis, *f*. purification by sacrifice
lustro, *v.t.* 1, to purify by sacrifice, wander over, review
lustrum, i, *n*, den, wood
lustrum, i, *n*, purificatory sacrifice, period of five years
lūsus, ūs, *m*, play, sport, game
lūtĕŏlus, a, um, *adj*, yellow
lūtĕus, a, um, *adj*, golden-yellow
lūtĕus, a, um, *adj*, muddy, worthless
lūtra, ae, *f*, otter
lūtŭlentus, a, um, *adj*, filthy
lūtum, i, *n*, yellow
lūtum, i, *n*, mud, clay
lux, lūcis, *f*, light, dawn, day, life, brightness, glory
luxŭria, ae, *f*, luxuriance, extravagance
luxŭrĭo, *v.i.* 1 (**luxŭrĭor,** *v.* 1, *dep*), to be overgrown, to have in excess, run riot
luxŭrĭōsus, a, um, *adj*, luxuriant, excessive
luxus, ūs, *m*, extravagance, pomp
lychnūcus, i, *m*, lamp-stand
lychnus, i, *m*, light, lamp
lympha, ae, *f*, water
lymphātus, a, um, *adj*, frenzied
lyncēus, a, um, *adj*, sharp-eyed
lynx, cis, *c*, lynx
lyra, ae, *f*, lute, poetry, song
lyricus, a, um, *adj*, of the lute, lyric

M

măcellum, i, *n*, food-market
măcer, cra, crum, *adj*, lean, thin
măcĕria, ae, *f*, wall
măcĕro, *v.t.* 1, to soften, weaken, torment
măchĭna, ae, *f*, engine, machine, battering-ram, trick, plan
măchĭnālis, e, *adj*, mechanical
măchĭnātio, ōnis, *f*, contrivance, machine, trick
măchĭnātor, ōris, *m*, engineer, inventor
măchĭnor, *v.t.* 1, *dep*, to design, plot
măcies, ēi, *f*, thinness, poverty
macte or **macti** (*voc. of* **mactus**), good luck! well done!
macto, *v.t.* 1, to sacrifice a victim, reward, honour, destroy
mactus, a, um, *adj*, worshipped
măcŭla, ae, *f*, spot, stain, fault, mesh
măcŭlo, *v.t.* 1, to stain, disgrace
măcŭlōsus, a, um, *adj*, spotted, dishonoured
mădĕfăcio, fēci, factum, *v.t.* 3, to soak, drench
mădens, ntis, *adj*, moist, drunk
mădĕo, *v.i.* 2, to be moist, to drip, to be boiled, softened
mădesco, dŭi, *v.i.* 3, to become wet
mădĭdus, a, um, *adj*, soaked
maena, ae, *f*, small salted fish

For List of Abbreviations used, turn to pages 3, 4

maeniānum, i, *n,* balcony
maerens, ntis, *adj,* mourning
maerĕo, *v.i.t.* 2, to mourn; bewail
maeror, ōris, *m,* grief, mourning
maestĭtia, ae, *f,* sadness
maestus, a, um, *adj,* sad
măga, ae, *f,* witch
măgālia, ium, *n.pl,* huts
măgĭcus, a, um, *adj,* magic
măgis, *comp. adv* (magnus), more, rather
măgister, tri, *m,* master, leader, director, teacher
măgistĕrium, ii, *n,* president's position
măgistra, ae, *f,* mistress
măgistrātus, ūs, *m,* magistracy, magistrate
magnănĭmĭtas, ātis, *f,* magnanimity
magnănĭmus, a, um, *adj,* great-hearted
magnes, ētis, *m,* magnet
magnēticus, a, um, *adj,* magnetic
magni, see magnus
magnifĭcentia, ae, *f,* nobleness, splendour, boasting
magnifĭcus, a, um, *adj, adv,* ē, noble, distinguished, sumptuous, bragging
magnĭlŏquentia, ae, *f,* high-sounding language
magnĭtūdo, ĭnis, *f,* size
magnŏpĕrē, *adv,* very much
magnus, a, um, *adj,* large, great; **magni** or **magno,** at a high price
măgus, i, *m,* magician
Māius (mensis), May
māiestas, ātis, *f,* greatness, grandeur, sovereignty, treason
māior, *comp. adj,* larger, greater; **māiōres, um,** *m. pl,* ancestors, the Senate; **maior nātu,** older
māla, ae, *f,* cheek-bone, jaw
mălăcia, ae, *f,* a calm at sea
mălagma, ătis, *n,* poultice
mălē, *adv,* badly, exceedingly; often reverses the meaning of an adj: **male sānus,** deranged
mălĕdĭcens, ntis, *adj,* abusive
mălĕdĭco, xi, ctum, *v.i.* 3, to abuse, slander
mălĕdĭctio, ōnis, *f,* abuse
mălĕdĭctum, i, *n,* abusive word
mălĕdĭcus, a, um, *adj,* abusive
mălĕfĭcium, ii, *n,* wrongdoing
mălĕfĭcus, a, um, *adj,* evil-doing
mălĕsuādus, a, um, *adj,* persuading towards wrong
mălĕvŏlens, ntis, *adj,* spiteful
mălĕvŏlentia, ae, *f,* malice
mălĕvŏlus, a, um, *adj,* spiteful
mălignus, a, um, *adj,* malicious
mălĭtia, ae, *f,* malice
mălĭtiōsus, a, um, *adj,* wicked
mallĕus, i, *m,* hammer
mālo, malle, mālŭi, *v.t. irreg,* to prefer
mālŏbăthrum, i, *n,* a costly ointment
mālum, i, *n,* apple, fruit
mălum, i, *n,* evil, misfortune
mălus, a, um, *adj,* bad, harmful
mālus, i, *m,* mast
malva, ae, *f,* the mallow
mamma, ae, *f,* breast, teat
manceps, cipis, *m,* contractor
mancĭpium, ii, *n,* legal purchase, right of ownership, slave
mancĭpo, *v.t.* 1, to sell, transfer
mancus, a, um, *adj,* maimed
mandātum, i, *n,* order, commission
mandātus, ūs, *m,* order, commission
mando, *v.t.* 1, to order, commission, commit
mandūco, *v.t.* 1, to chew
māne, *indecl. n,* morning; *adv,* in the morning
mănĕo, nsi, nsum, *v.i.t.* 2, to stay, remain, continue; await
mānes, ĭum, *m. pl,* deified ghosts of the dead
mănĭcae, ārum, *f. pl,* glove, gauntlet, handcuff
mănĭfestus, a, um, *adj, adv,* ō, clear, apparent
mănĭpŭlāris, e, *adj,* belonging to a company (a soldier)
mănĭpŭlus, i, *m,* handful, bundle, company of soldiers
mannus, i, *m,* coach-horse, pony
mano, *v.i.t.* 1, to flow, trickle; pour out
mansio, ōnis, *f,* a stay, inn
mansŭēfăcio, fēci, factum, *v.t.* 3, to tame, civilize
mansŭesco, sŭēvi, sŭētum, *v.i.* 3, to grow tame or gentle
mansŭētus, a, um, *adj,* gentle
mansŭētūdo, ĭnis, *f,* gentleness
mansūrus, a, um, *adj,* lasting
mantēle, is, *n,* towel, cloth
mantĭca, ae, *f,* suit-case
mănŭbĭae, ārum, *f. pl,* money from the sale of booty
mănŭbrium, ii, *n,* handle
mănūmissio, ōnis, *f,* the freeing of a slave
mănūmitto, mĭsi, missum, *v.t.* 3, to set free a slave
mănus, ūs, *f,* hand, bravery, combat, violence, grappling-iron, armed band
măpălia, ium, *n. pl,* African huts

mappa, ae, *f,* towel, napkin
marcēo, *v.i.* 2, to be weak
marcesco, *v.i.* 3, to wither
marcĭdus, a, um, *adj,* decayed
mare, is, *n,* the sea
marga, ae, *f,* marl
margărĭta, ae, *f,* pearl
margo, ĭnis, *m, f,* edge, border
mārĭnus, a, um, *adj,* of the sea
mārĭta, ae, *f,* wife
mārĭtālis, e, *adj,* matrimonial
mārĭtĭmus, a, um, *adj,* of the sea
mārĭtus, a, um, *adj,* matrimonial
mārĭtus, i, *m,* husband
marmor, ŏris, *n,* marble, statue; *in pl,* surface of the sea
marmŏrĕus, a, um, *adj,* of marble
martiālis, e, *adj,* sacred to Mars
martius, a, um, *adj,* sacred to Mars
Martius (mensis), March
martyr, yris, *c,* martyr
martyrium, ii, *n,* martyrdom
mās, măris, *adj,* male
mascŭlus, a, um, *adj,* male, bold
massa, ae, *f,* lump, mass
mātellio, ōnis, *m,* pot
māter, tris, *f,* mother
māterfămĭlias, mātrisfămĭlias, *f,* mistress of the house
mātĕrĭa, ae, *f,* timber, materials, topic, opportunity
matĕris, is, *f,* Celtic javelin
māternus, a, um, *adj,* maternal
mātertĕra, ae, *f,* maternal aunt
mathēmātica, ae, *f,* mathematics
mathēmātĭcus, a, um, *adj,* mathematical
mātrĭcīda, ae, *c,* murderer of his (her) mother
mātrĭmōnium, ii, *n,* marriage
mātrōna, ae, *f,* married woman
mātrōnālis, e, *adj,* of a married woman
mātūrē, *adv,* at the proper time, soon, quickly
mātūresco, rŭi, *v.i.* 3, to ripen
mātūrĭtas, ātis, *f,* ripeness
mātūro, *v.i.t.* 1, to ripen, hurry; bring to maturity
mātūrus, a, um, *adj,* mature, ripe, early
mātūtīnus, a, um, *adj,* of the morning
maxilla, ae, *f,* jawbone, jaw
maxĭmē, *adv,* especially, very
maximus, a, um, *sup. adj,* very large or great
māzŏnŏmus, i, *m,* dish
me, *acc. or abl.* of **ego** (1)
mĕātus, ūs, *m,* motion, course
mĕdĕor, *v.* 2, *dep. with dat,* to heal, remedy, amend
mĕdĭastīnus, i, *m,* drudge
mēdĭca, ae, *f,* a kind of clover
mĕdĭcābĭlis, e, *adj,* curable
mĕdĭcāmen, ĭnis, *n,* remedy, drug
mĕdĭcāmentum, i, *n,* remedy, drug
mĕdĭcāmentārĭus, a, um, *adj,* of drugs
mĕdĭcīna, ae, *f,* the art of medicine, remedy
mĕdĭco, *v.t.* 1, to heal, sprinkle, dye
mĕdĭcor, *v.t.* 1, *dep,* to heal
mĕdĭcus, a, um, *adj,* healing
mĕdĭcus, i, *m,* doctor, surgeon
mĕdĭmnum, i, *n,* bushel
mĕdĭŏcris, e, *adj, adv,* **ĭter,** ordinary, insignificant
mĕdĭŏcrĭtas, ātis, *f,* a middle state, insignificance
mĕdĭtātio, ōnis, *f,* contemplation, preparation
mĕdĭtātus, a, um, *adj,* considered
mĕdĭterrānĕus, a, um, *adj,* inland
mĕdĭtor, *v.i.t.* 1, *dep,* to consider, muse; study, intend, practise
mēdĭum, ii, *n,* middle, the public
mēdĭus, a, um, *adj,* middle, neutral
mēdĭus, i, *m,* mediator
mēdulla, ae, *f,* kernel, marrow
mēio, *v.i.* 3, to urinate
mĕl, mellis, *n,* honey
mĕlancholĭcus, a, um, *adj,* melancholic
mēles, is, *f,* badger
mĕlimēla, ōrum, *n. pl,* honey apples
mĕlĭor, us, *comp. adj,* better
mĕlisphyllum, i, *n,* balm
mĕlius, *comp. adv,* better
mellĭfer, ĕra, ĕrum, *adj,* honey-producing
mellĭfĭco ,*v.t.* 1, to make honey
mellĭtus, a, um, *adj,* of honey
mēlo, ōnis, *m,* melon
mēlos, i, *n,* tune, song
membrāna, ae, *f,* skin, parchment
membrātim, *adv,* piece by piece
membrum, i, *n,* limb, division
mĕmini, isse, *v.i. defective,* to remember
mĕmor, ŏris, *adj,* remembering, mindful
mĕmŏrābĭlis, e, *adj,* memorable
mĕmŏrandus, a, um, *adj,* memorable
mĕmŏrātus, a, um, *adj,* renowned
mĕmŏrĭa, ae, *f,* memory, posterity, historical account, tradition
mĕmŏro, *v.t.* 1, to mention
menda, ae, *f,* defect
mendācium, ii, *n,* a lie
mendax, ācis, *adj,* lying, false
mendĭcĭtas, ātis, *f,* poverty
mendĭco, *v.i.* 1, to beg
mendĭcus, a, um, *adj,* needy
mendĭcus, i, *m,* beggar

mendōsus, a, um, *adj, adv,* **ē,** faulty, false
mendum, i, *n,* blunder, defect, mistake
mens, ntis, *f,* mind, intellect, understanding, intention, courage
mensa, ae, *f,* table, course; **sĕcunda mensa,** dessert
mensārĭus, ii, *m,* banker
mensis, is, *m,* month
mensor, ōris, *m,* valuer, surveyor
menstrŭus, a, um, *adj,* monthly
mensūra, ae, *f,* measurement, quantity
mensus, a, um, *adj,* measured off
menta, ae, *f,* mint
mentio, ōnis, *f,* recollection, mention
mentior, *v.i.t.* 4, *dep,* to lie, cheat; counterfeit, imitate
mentītus, a, um, *adj,* counterfeit
mentum, i, *n,* chin
mĕo, *v.i.* 1, to go
mĕrācus, a, um, *adj,* unmixed
mercātor, ōris, *m,* wholesaler
mercātūra, ae, *f,* trade
mercātus, ūs, *m,* trade, market
mercēdŭla, ae, *f,* small wages
mercēnārĭus, a, um, *adj,* hired
merces, ēdis, *f,* pay, wages, rent, interest, reward
merces (*pl*), see **merx**
mercor, *v.t.* 1, *dep,* to buy
mĕrens, ntis, *adj,* deserving
mĕrĕo, *v.t.* (**mĕrĕor,** *v. dep*) 2, to deserve, earn; with **stīpendĭa,** to serve as a soldier
mĕrĕtrīcĭus, a, um, *adj,* of prostitutes
mĕrĕtrix, trīcis, *f,* prostitute
merges, ĭtis, *f,* sheaf
mergo, si, sum, *v.t.* 3, to immerse
mergus, i, *m,* sea-bird (diver)
mĕrĭdiānus, a, um, *adj,* of midday
mĕrĭdies, ēi, *m,* midday, south
mĕrĭtōrĭus, a, um, *adj,* bringing in money
mĕrĭtum, i, *n,* reward, benefit, fault, blame
mĕrĭtus, a, um, *adj, adv,* **ō,** deserved, deserving
mĕrops, ōpis, *m,* bee-eating bird
merso, *v.t.* 1, to immerse, drown
mĕrŭla, ae, *f,* blackbird
mĕrum, i, *n,* pure wine
mĕrus, a, um, *adj,* pure, only, genuine
merx, cis, *f,* goods, commodities
messis, is, *f,* harvest, crops
messor, ōris, *m,* harvester
mēta, ae, *f,* winning-post, end, cone
mĕtallĭcus, a, um, *adj,* metallic
mĕtallĭcus, i, *m,* miner
mĕtallum, i, *n,* mine, metal
mĕtātor, ōris, *m,* surveyor
mĕtĭor, mensus, *v.t.* 4, *dep,* to measure, distribute, traverse, estimate, value
mĕto, ssŭi, ssum, *v.t.* 3, to mow, gather, cut down
mĕtor, *v.t.* 1, *dep,* to measure, mark out, traverse
mĕtrĭcus, a, um, *adj,* metrical
mĕtŭendus, a, um, *adj,* formidable
mĕtŭo, ŭi, ūtum, *v.i.t.* 3, to be afraid; to fear
mĕtus, ūs, *m.* fear, awe
mĕus, a, um, *adj,* my, mine: **mĕi, ōrum,** *m. pl,* my relatives
mīca, ae, *f,* crumb
mĭco, ŭi, *v.i.* 1, to tremble, sparkle
mĭgrātio, ōnis, *f,* migration
mĭgro, *v.i.* 1, to depart, change
mĭlĕs, ĭtis, *c,* soldier, army
mīlia, see **mille**
mīlĭārĭum, ii, *n,* mile-stone
mīlĭtāris, e, *adj,* military
mīlĭtāris, is, *m,* soldier
mīlĭtĭa, ae, *f,* military service, warfare
mīlĭto, *v.i.* 1, to serve as a soldier
mīlĭum, ii, *n,* millet
mille (*pl,* **mīlia,** with *genit.*), a thousand; **mille passus,** or **passuum,** a mile
millēsĭmus, a, um, *adj,* the thousandth
millies (**milliens**), *adv,* a thousand times
mīlŭīnus, a, um, *adj,* kite-like
mīlŭus, i, *m,* kite, gurnard
mĭmĭcus, a, um, *adj,* farcical
mĭmus, i, *m,* mime, mimic actor
mina, ae, *f,* Greek silver coinage
mĭnae, ārum, *f. pl,* threats
mĭnax, ācis, *adj, adv,* **ĭter,** threatening, projecting
mĭnĭmē, *sup. adv,* very little
mĭnĭmus, a, um, *sup. adj,* very small
mĭnister, tri, *m,* **mĭnistra, ae,** *f,* servant, assistant
mĭnistērĭum, ii, *n,* service, occupation
mĭnistrātor, ōris, *m,* servant
mĭnistro, *v.t.* 1, to wait upon, serve, manage
mĭnĭtor, *v.i.t.* 1, *dep,* to threaten
mĭnĭum, ii, red-lead
mĭnor, *v.i.t.* 1, *dep,* to threaten
mĭnor, us, *comp. adj,* smaller
mĭnŭo, ŭi, ūtum, *v.i.t.* 3, to ebb; to reduce, weaken, chop up
mĭnus, *comp. adv,* less
mĭnuscŭlus, a, um, *adj,* rather small
mĭnūtal, ālis, *n,* mincemeat
mĭnūtātim, *adv,* little by little
mĭnūtus, a, um, *adj, adv,* **ē,** small
mīrābĭlis, e, *adj, adv,* **ĭter,** wonderful, strange

mīrācŭlum, i, *n,* a wonder, marvel
mīrandus, a, um, *adj,* wonderful
mīrātĭo, ōnis, *f,* surprise
mīrātor, ōris, *m,* admirer
mīrĭfĭcus, a, um, *adj, adv,* **ē,** marvellous, extraordinary
mīror, *v.i.t.* 1, *dep,* to be amazed; to marvel at, admire
mīrus, a, um, *adj, adv,* **ē,** marvellous, extraordinary
miscĕo, scŭi, xtum, *v.t.* 2, to mix, unite, disturb
mĭsellus, a, um, *adj,* wretched
miser, ĕra, ĕrum, *adj, adv,* **ē,** wretched, pitiable, worthless
misĕrābĭlis, e, *adj, adv,* **ĭter,** pitiable, sad
misĕrandus, a, um, *adj,* pitiable
misĕrātĭo, ōnis, *f,* pity
misĕrĕor, *v.* 2, *dep, with gen,* to pity
misĕret (me, te, etc.), *v.* 2, *impers,* it distresses (me), I pity, am sorry for
misĕresco, *v.i.* 3, to feel pity
misĕrĭa, ae, *f,* misfortune, wretchedness
misĕrĭcordĭa, ae, *f,* pity
misĕrĭcors, dis, *adj,* merciful
misĕror, *v.t.* 1, *dep,* to lament, pity
missĭle, is, *n,* missile, javelin
missĭlis, e, *adj,* that is thrown
missĭo, ōnis, *f,* throwing, discharge, release
missus, ūs, *m,* dispatching, throwing, shot
mitella, ae, *f,* turban, bandage
mītesco, *v.i.* 3, to grow mild or soft or ripe
mītigātĭo, ōnis, *f,* mitigation
mītigo, *v.t.* 1, to make soft or ripe, to tame, soothe
mītis, e, *adj,* mild, ripe, calm
mĭtra, ae, *f,* head-band
mitto, mīsi, missum, *v.t.* 3, to send, announce, cease, release, throw, escort
mītŭlus, i, *m,* sea-mussel
mixtūra, ae, *f,* mixture
mixtus, a, um, *adj,* mixed
mōbĭlis, e, *adj, adv,* **ĭter,** movable, agile, flexible, fickle
mōbĭlĭtas, ātis, *f,* speed, inconstancy
mŏdĕrāmen, ĭnis, *n,* rudder, management
mŏdĕrātĭo, ōnis, *f,* moderation, restraint
mŏdĕrātor, ōris, *m,* manager
mŏdĕrātus, a, um, *adj, adv,* **ē,** moderate
mŏdĕror, *v.t.* 1, *dep,* to restrain, govern
mŏdestĭa, ae, *f,* moderation, discretion, modesty
mŏdestus, a, um, *adj, adv,* **ē,** modest, gentle
mŏdĭcus, a, um, *adj, adv,* **ē,** modest, ordinary
mŏdĭfĭcātus, a, um, *adj,* measured
mŏdĭus, ii, *m,* peck, measure
mŏdŏ, *adv,* only, but, just, lately; **non mŏdŏ,** not only; **mŏdŏ . . . mŏdŏ,** at one time . . . at another time
mŏdŭlātor, ōris, *m,* musician
mŏdŭlor, *v.t.* 1, *dep,* to sing, play
mŏdŭlātus, a, um, *adj,* sung, played
mŏdŭlus, i, *m,* a small measure
mŏdus, i, *m,* measure, quantity, rhythm, limit, restriction, end, method, way
moechus, i, *m,* adulterer
moenĭa, ĭum, *n.pl,* ramparts
mŏla, ae, *f,* millstone, grain mixed with salt to be sprinkled on sacrificial animals
mŏlāris, is, *m,* millstone
mŏles, is, *f,* mass, bulk, dam, pier, power, difficulty
mŏlestĭa, ae, *f,* trouble, affectation
mŏlestus, a, um, *adj, adv,* **ē,** troublesome, affected
mōlĭmen, ĭnis, *n,* undertaking, attempt
mōlĭmentum, i, *n,* undertaking, attempt
mōlĭor, *v.i.t.* 4, to strive, depart; to rouse, construct, attempt
mŏlĭtor, ōris, *m,* miller
mōlĭtor, ōris, *m,* contriver
mollesco, *v.i.* 3, to grow soft
mollĭo, *v.t.* 4, to soften, restrain
mollis, a, *adj, adv,* **ĭter,** soft, supple, tender, effeminate
mollĭtĭa, ae, *f,* softness, weakness
mollĭtĭes, ēi, *f,* softness, weakness
mollĭtūdo, ĭnis, *f,* softness, weakness
mŏlo, ŭi, ĭtum, *v.t.* 3, to grind
mōmentum, i, *n,* movement, motion, moment, instant, cause, influence, importance
mŏnăcha, ae, *f,* nun
mŏnastērĭum, ii, *n,* monastery
mŏnēdŭla, ae, *f,* jackdaw
mŏnĕo, *v.t.* 2, to warn, advise, remind, instruct, tell
mŏnēta, ae, *f,* the mint, coin
mŏnētālis, e, *adj,* of the mint
mŏnĭle, is, *n,* necklace, collar
mŏnĭtĭo, ōnis, *f,* warning
mŏnĭtor, ōris, *m,* adviser, instructor
mŏnĭtum, i, *n,* advice
mŏnĭtus, ūs, *m,* warning, omen

For List of Abbreviations used, turn to pages 3, 4

mŏnŏcĕros, ōtis, *m,* unicorn
mŏnŏpōlium, ii, *n,* monopoly
mons, ntis, *m,* mountain
monstrātio, ōnis, *f,* showing, pointing out
monstrātor, ōris, *m,* teacher
monstro, *v.t.* 1, to show, tell
monstrum, i, *n,* omen, monster
monstrŭōsus, a, um, *adj,* strange, monstrous
montānus, a, um, *adj,* of a mountain, mountainous
monticōla, ae, *c,* mountain-dweller
montivāgus, a, um, *adj,* wandering in the mountains
montŭōsus, a, um, *adj,* mountainous
mōnūmentum, i, *n,* monument, memorial, written record
mŏra, ae, *f,* delay, hindrance
mōrālis, e, *adj,* moral
mōrātus, a, um, *adj,* mannered; **mōrātus** *partic.* from **mŏror,** having delayed
morbĭdus, a, um, *adj,* diseased
morbus, i, *m,* illness, disease
mordax, ācis, *adj,* biting, stinging
mordĕo, mōmordi, morsum, *v.t.* 2, to bite, clasp, sting
mordĭcus, a, um, *adj,* by biting
mōres, see **mos**
mōrētum, i, *n,* salad
mŏribundus, a, um, *adj,* dying
mŏriens, ntis, *adj,* dying
mŏrior, mortŭus, *v.i.* 3, *dep,* to die
mŏror, *v.i.t.* 1, *dep,* to delay
mōrōsĭtas, ātis, *f,* fretfulness
mōrōsus, a, um, *adj,* fretful, fastidious
mors, mortis, *f,* death
morsus, ūs, *m,* bite, pungency
mortālis, e, *adj,* mortal, human, temporary
mortālis, is, *c,* human being
mortālitas, ātis, *f,* mortality
mortārium, ii, *n,* a mortar
mortĭfer, ĕra, ĕrum, *adj,* fatal
mortŭus, a, um, *adj,* dead
mortŭus, i, *m,* a dead person
mōrum, i, *n,* blackberry
mōrus, i, *f,* blackberry-bush
mos, mōris, *m,* custom, manner, habit, fashion; *in pl,* character
mōtăcilla, ae, *f,* wagtail
mōtio, ōnis, *f,* motion
mōto, *v.t.* 1, to move about
mōtus, ūs, *m,* motion, movement, impulse, emotion, rebellion
mŏvĕo, mōvi, mōtum, *v.t.* 2, to move, stir, excite, cause
mox, *adv,* soon, immediately
mūcĭdus, a, um, *adj,* musty
mūcor, ōris, *m,* mouldiness
mūcōsus, a, um, *adj,* mucous
mūcro, ōnis, *m,* sword's point
mūgil, is, *m,* mullet
mūginor, *v.i.* 1, *dep,* to hesitate
mūgio, *v.i.* 4, to low, bellow, groan, crash
mūgitus, ūs, *m,* bellowing, roaring
mūla, ae, *f,* she-mule
mulcĕo, si, sum, *v.t.* 2, to stroke, soothe
mulco, *v.t.* 1, to maltreat
mulctra, ae, *f,* milk-bucket
mulctrārium, ii, *n,* milk-bucket
mulgĕo, si, sum, *v.t.* 2, to milk
mŭlĭĕbris, e, *adj, adv,* **iter,** female, effeminate
mŭlier, ĕris, *f,* woman, wife
mŭliercŭla, ae, *f,* girl
mŭlio, ōnis, *m,* mule-driver
mullus, i, *m,* mullet
mulsum, i, *n,* honey-wine
multa, ae, *f,* penalty, fine
multātio, ōnis, *f,* penalty, fine
multi, see **multus**
multifāriam, *adv,* on many sides
multĭplex, icis, *adj,* with many windings, numerous, many
multiplicātio, ōnis, *f,* multiplication
multĭplico, *v.t.* 1, to multiply
multitūdo, ĭnis, *f,* crowd, great number
multō, *adv,* a great deal
multo, *v.t.* 1, to punish
multum, *adv,* very much, greatly
multus, a, um, *adj,* much; *pl.* many
mūlus, i, *m,* mule
munditia, ae, *f,* cleanliness, neatness
mundities, ēi, *f,* cleanliness, neatness
mundo, *v.t.* 1, to cleanse
mundus, a, um, *adj,* clean, elegant
mundus, i, *m,* world, universe, ornaments
mūnĕro, *v.t.* 1 (**mūnĕror,** *v.t.* 1, *dep.*), to reward, honour
mūnia, ōrum, *n.pl,* duties
mūniceps, cĭpis, *c,* citizen
mūnicipālis, e, *adj,* municipal
mūnicipium, ii, *n,* self-governing town
mūnifĭcentia, ae, *f,* generosity
mūnifĭcus, a, um, *adj, adv,* **ē,** generous
mūnĭmen, ĭnis, *n,* rampart, protection
mūnĭmentum, i, *n,* rampart, protection
mūnio, *v.t.* 4, to fortify, secure, make a way

mūnĭtĭo, ōnis, *f,* fortification
mūnĭtor, ōris, *m,* engineer
mūnĭtus, a, um, *adj,* fortified
mūnus, ĕris, *n,* service, duty, employment, post, tax, gift, public show
mūnuscŭlum, i, *n,* small present
mūrālis, e, *adj,* of a wall
mūrex, ĭcis, *m,* purple fish, purple dye, pointed rock
mūrĭa, ae, *f,* brine, pickle
murmur, ŭris, *n,* murmur, crash
murmŭro, *v.i.* 1, to murmur, roar
murra, ae, *f,* myrrh (tree)
murrĕus, a, um, *adj,* perfumed with myrrh
mūrus, i, *m,* wall, defence
mūs, mūris, *c,* mouse
mūsa, ae, *f,* goddess of the arts
musca, ae, *f,* a fly
muscĭpŭlum, i, *n,* mouse-trap
muscōsus, a, um, *adj,* mossy
muscŭlus, i, *m,* little mouse, mussel, muscle, military shed
muscus, i, *m,* moss
mūsēum, i, *n,* museum
mūsica, ae, *f,* music
mūsicus, a, um, *adj,* musical
mūsicus, i, *m,* musician
musso, *v.i.* 1, to mutter, be silent, be in doubt
mustēla, ae, *f,* weasel
mustum, i, *n,* new wine
mūtābilis, e, *adj,* changeable
mūtābilitas, ātis, *f,* changeableness
mūtātio, ōnis, *f,* alteration
mūtĭlo, *v.t.* 1, to cut off, maim
mūtĭlus, a, um, *adj,* maimed
mūto, *v.i.t.* 1, to alter, change
mūtŭlus, i, *m,* bracket
mūtŭō, *adv,* in turns
mūtŭor, *v.t.* 1, *dep,* to borrow
mūtus, a, um, *adj,* dumb, mute
mūtŭum, i, *n,* loan
mūtŭus, a, um, *adj,* borrowed, mutual
mȳrĭca, ae, *f;* **mȳrĭce, es,** *f,* a shrub, tamarisk
myrr . . . see **murr . . .**
myrtētum, i, *n,* myrtle-grove
myrtĕus, a, um, *adj,* of myrtle
myrtum, i, *n,* myrtle-berry
myrtus, i, *f,* myrtle-tree
mysta (es), ae, *f,* priest of Ceres' mysteries
mystērium, ii, *n,* secret rites
mystĭcus, a, um, *adj,* mystical

N

naevus, i, *m,* wart, mole
Nāiās, ădis, *f,* water-nymph
nam, *conj,* for
namque, *conj,* for indeed
nanciscor, nactus, *v.t.* 3, *dep,* to obtain, meet with, find
nānus, i, *m,* dwarf
nāpus, i, *m,* turnip
narcissus, i, *m,* narcissus
nardus, i, *f,* perfumed balm
nāris, is, *f,* nostril; *pl,* nose
narrātio, ōnis, *f,* narrative
narrātor, ōris, *m,* narrator
narro, *v.t.* 1, to tell, relate
narthēcĭum, ii, *n,* medicine-chest
nascor, nātus, *v.i.* 3, *dep,* to be born, rise, proceed
nasturtĭum, ii, *n,* cress
nāsus, i, *m,* nose
nāsūtus, a, um, *adj,* large-nosed
nāta, ae, *f,* daughter
nātālĭcius, a, um, *adj,* birthday
nātālis, e, *adj,* of birth
nātālis, is, *m,* birthday
nătantes, um, *f. pl,* fish
nătātio, ōnis, *f,* swimming
nătātor, ōris, *m,* swimmer
nātio, ōnis, *f,* race, nation
nătis, is, *f,* buttock
nātīvus, a, um, *adj,* created, inborn, natural
năto, *v.i.* 1, to swim, float, waver
nătrix, ĭcis, *f,* water-snake
nātūra, ae, *f,* nature
nātūrālis, e, *adj, adv,* **ĭter,** by birth, natural
nātus, ūs, *m,* birth
nātus, i, *m,* son
nātus, a, um, *adj,* born, aged
nauarchus, i, *m,* ship's master
naufrăgium, ii, *n,* shipwreck
naufrăgus, a, um, *adj,* shipwrecked
naumăchia, ae, *f,* mock sea-fight
nausĕa, ae, *f,* sea-sickness
nausēābundus, a, um, *adj,* sea-sick
nausĕo, *v.i.* 1, to be sea-sick
nauta, ae, *m,* sailor
nautĭcus, a, um, *adj,* nautical
nāvālia, ium, *n.pl,* dockyard
nāvāle, is, *n,* dockyard
nāvālis, e, *adj,* naval
nāvĭcŭla, ae, *f,* boat
nāvĭcŭlārius, ii, *m,* ship-owner
nāvifrăgus, a, um, *adj,* ship-wrecking
nāvigābilis, e, *adj,* navigable
nāvigātio, ōnis, *f,* sailing
nāviger, ĕra, ĕrum, *adj,* navigable
nāvigia, ōrum, *n.pl,* ships, shipping
nāvigĭum, ii, *n,* ship, boat
nāvigo, *v.i.t.* 1, to sail; navigate
nāvis, is, *f,* ship; **nāvis longa,** warship
nāvita, ae, *m* (**nauta**), sailor
nāviter, *adv,* completely

nāvo, *v.t.* 1, to do vigorously
nāvus, a, um, *adj,* hard-working
nē, *conj,* lest; **nē . . . quidem,** not even . . .
-nĕ, attached to the first word of a sentence to form a question
nē, *interj,* indeed, truly
nĕbŭla, ae, *f,* mist, fog, smoke
nĕbŭlo, ōnis, *m,* rascal, wretch
nĕbŭlōsus, a, um, *adj,* misty
nĕc, *adv,* not; *conj,* and not; **nĕc . . . nĕc,** neither . . . nor
necdum, *conj,* not yet
nĕcessārĭus, a, um, *adj, adv,* **ō,** unavoidable, necessary, related
nĕcessārĭus, ii, *m,* relative
nĕcesse, *indecl. adj,* unavoidable
nĕcessĭtas, ātis, *f,* necessity, compulsion, destiny
nĕcessĭtūdo, ĭnis, *f,* necessity, relationship
necnĕ, *adv,* or not
nec-non, and also
nĕco, *v.t.* 1, to kill
nĕcŏpĭnans, ntis, *adj,* unaware
nĕcŏpĭnātus, a, um, *adj, adv,* **ō,** unexpected
nĕcŏpĭnus, a, um, *adj,* unexpected
nectar, ăris, *n,* the drink of the gods
nectărĕus, a, um, *adj,* of nectar
necto, xŭi, xum, *v.t.* 3, to tie, fasten together
nĕcŭbi, *adv,* so that nowhere
nēdum, *conj,* still less
nĕfandus, a, um, *adj,* abominable, heinous, wrong
nĕfārĭus, a, um *adj,* heinous, wrong
nĕfas, *n, indecl,* wrong, sin
nĕfastus, a, um, *adj,* with **dies,** a day on which neither trials nor public meetings could be held, wicked, unlucky
nĕgātĭo, ōnis, *f,* denial
nĕgĭto, *v.t.* 1, to persist in denying
neglectus, a, um, *adj,* despised
neglĕgens (negligens), ntis, *adj,* careless, indifferent
neglĕgentĭa, ae, *f,* carelessness
neglĕgo, xi, ctum, *v.t.* 3, to neglect, slight, despise
nĕgo, *v.i.t.* 1, to say no (not); refuse
nĕgōtĭātĭo, ōnis, *f,* wholesale-business, banking
nĕgōtĭātor, ōris, *m,* wholesaler, banker
nĕgōtĭor, *v.i.* 1, *dep,* to carry on business, trade or banking
nĕgōtĭōsus, a, um, *adj,* busy
nĕgōtĭum, ii, *n,* business, occupation, difficulty
nēmo, ĭnis, *m, f,* nobody
nĕmŏrālis, e, *adj,* woody
nĕmŏrōsus, a, um, *adj,* woody
nempĕ, *conj,* certainly
nĕmus, ŏris, *n,* wood, grove
nēnĭa, ae, *f,* funeral hymn, sad song, popular song
nĕo, nēvi, nētum, *v.t.* 2, to spin
nēpa, ae, *f,* scorpion
nēpos, ōtis, *m, f,* grandson (. . . daughter), descendant, spendthrift
neptis, is, *f,* grand-daughter
nēquam, *indecl. adj, adv,* **nēquĭter,** worthless, bad
nēquāquam, *adv,* not at all
nĕque, *adv,* not; *conj,* and not; **nĕque . . . nĕque,** neither . . . nor
nĕquĕo, īvi (ii), ĭtum, *v.i.* 4, to be unable
nēquĭquam, *adv,* in vain
nēquĭtĭa, ae, *f,* worthlessness, idleness, extravagance
nervōsus, a, um, *adj, adv,* **ē,** sinewy, energetic
nervus, i, *m,* sinew, string of musical instrument or bow
nescĭo, *v.t.* 4, not to know, to be unable
nescĭus, a, um, *adj,* unaware
neu, *adv,* and so that . . . not
neuter, tra, trum, *adj,* neither the one nor the other
neutĭquam, *adv,* not at all
neutrō, *adv,* neither way
nēve, *adv,* and so that . . . not
nex, nĕcis, *f,* death, slaughter
nexĭlis, e, *adj,* tied together
nexum, i, *n,* slavery for debt, obligation
nexus, ūs, *m,* tying together
nī, *conj,* unless
nictātĭo, ōnis, *f,* winking
nicto, *v.i.* 1, to wink, blink
nīdor, ōris, *m,* steam, smell
nĭdŭlus, i, *m,* little nest
nĭdus, i, *m,* nest, home; *in pl,* nestlings
nĭger, gra, grum, *adj,* black, dark, ill-omened, funereal
nigrans, ntis, *adj,* black
nigresco, grŭi, *v.i.* 3, to grow dark
nĭhil (nīl), *n, indecl,* nothing
nihili, of no value
nihilōmĭnus, *adj,* nevertheless
nĭhilum, i, *n,* nothing
nīl, *n, indecl,* nothing
nimbĭfer, ĕra, ĕrum, *adj,* stormy, rainy
nimbōsus, a, um, *adj,* stormy, rainy
nimbus, i, *m,* heavy rain, rain-cloud, cloud
nīmīrum, *adv,* without doubt
nimis, *adv,* too much

nĭmĭum, *adv*, too much
nĭmĭum, ii, *n*, excess
nĭmĭus, a, um, *adj*, excessive
ningit, *v.i.* 3, *impers*, it is snowing
nĭsi, *conj*, if not, unless
nĭsus, ūs, *m*, pressure, effort, labour of childbirth
nĭtēdŭla, ae, *f*, dormouse
nĭtens, ntis, *adj*, bright, shining, sleek, beautiful
nĭtĕo, *v.i.* 2, to shine, to look handsome, thrive
nĭtĕsco, tŭi, *v.i.* 3, to shine
nĭtĭdus, a, um, *adj*, shining, sleek, handsome, refined
nĭtor, nĭsus (nixus), *v.i.* 3, *dep*, to lean, press forward, fly, make an effort, argue
nĭtor, ōris, *m*, brightness, splendour, beauty, elegance
nĭtrum, i, *n*, soda
nĭvālis, e, *adj*, snowy, cold
nĭvĕus, a, um, *adj*, snowy, white
nĭvōsus, a, um, *adj*, snowy
nix, nĭvis, *f*, snow
nixor, *v.i.* 1, *dep*, to strive
nixus, ūs, *m*, pressure, effort, labour of childbirth
no, *v.i.* 1, to swim
nōbĭlis, e, *adj*, famous, noble
nōbĭlĭtas, ātis, *f*, fame, noble birth
nōbĭlĭto, *v.t.* 1, to make famous
nōbis, *dat. or abl. of* **nos**
nŏcens, ntis, *adj*, wicked, bad, harmful, injurious
nŏcĕo, *v.i.* 2, *with dat*, to harm
nocte, *adv*, at night
noctĭlūca, ae, *f*, moon
noctĭvăgus, a, um, *adj*, wandering at night
noctu, *adv*, at night
noctŭa, ae, *f*, night owl
nocturnus, a, um, *adj*, nocturnal
nōdo, *v.t.* 1, to tie in a knot
nōdōsus, a, um, *adj*, knotty, difficult
nōdus, i, *m*, knot, knob, band, obligation, difficulty
nōli, nōlĭte, *imper*, do not . . .
nōlo, nolle, nōlŭi, *v, irreg*, to be unwilling
nōmen, ĭnis, *n*, name, debt, fame, repute, excuse, reason
nōmenclātor, ōris, *m*, slave who reminded his master of the names of the people he met
nōmĭnātim, *adj*, by name
nōmĭnātio, ōnis, *f*, nomination
nōmĭnātus, a, um, *adj*, renowned
nōmĭno, *v.t.* 1, to name, make famous
nŏmisma, ătis, *n*, a coin
nōn, *adv*, not
nōnae, ārum, *f. pl*, the Nones; 5th or 7th day of the month
nōnāgēni, ae, *adj*, ninety each
nōnāgēsĭmus, a, um, *adj*, ninetieth
nōnāgies, *adv*, ninety times
nōnāgintā, *indecl. adj*, ninety
nondum, *adj*, not yet
nongenti, ae, a, *adj*, nine hundred
nonnĕ, *adv*, used to introduce a question expecting the answer "yes"
nonnēmo, ĭnis, *m*, someone
nonnĭhil, *n*, something
nonnisi, *adv.* only
nonnullus, a, um, *adj*, several
nonnumquam, *adv*, sometimes
nōnus, a, um, *adj*, ninth
norma, ae, *f*, rule, pattern, standard
nōs, *pron, pl. of* **ĕgō**, we, us
noscĭto, *v.t.* 1, to know, observe
nosco, nōvi, nōtum, *v.t.* 3, to get to know, know, recognise, acknowledge
noster, tra, trum, *adj*, our, ours
nostras, ātis, *adj*, of our country
nŏta, ae, *f*, mark, sign, brand
nŏtābĭlis, e, *adj*, noteworthy
nŏtātio, ōnis, *f*, branding, observation
nŏthus, a, um, *adj*, illegitimate, counterfeit
nōtio, ōnis, *f*, investigation
nōtitia, ae, *f*, fame, knowledge
nŏto, *v.t.* 1, to mark, write, indicate, brand, reprimand
nŏtus, a, um, *adj*, well-known
nŏtus, i, *m*, the south wind
nŏvācŭla, ae, *f*, razor
nŏvālis, is, *f*, fallow land
nŏvellus, a, um, *adj*, young, new
nŏvem, *indecl. adj*, nine
Nŏvember (mensis), November
nŏvendiālis, e, *adj*, lasting nine days
nŏvēnus, a, um, *adj*, nine each
nŏverca, ae, *f*, stepmother
nŏvĭcius, a, um, *adj*, new
nŏvĭens, *adv*, nine times
nŏvies, *adv*, nine times
nŏvissĭmus, a, um, *adj*, last; in *m. pl*, or **nŏvissĭmum agmen**, rear ranks
nŏvitas, ātis, *f*, novelty, unusualness
nŏvo, *v.t.* 1, to renew, refresh, change
nŏvus, a, um, *adj*, new, recent, fresh; **nŏvus hŏmo** an upstart; **nŏvae res**, revolution
nox, noctis, *f*, night
noxa, ae, *f*, injury, harm, fault, crime
noxĭa, ae, *f*, injury, harm, fault, crime
noxĭus, a, um, *adj*, harmful, guilty
nūbes, is, *f*, cloud
nūbĭfer, ĕra, ĕrum, *adj*, cloud-capped, cloud-bringing

For List of Abbreviations used, turn to pages 3, 4

nūbīla, ōrum, *n.pl,* the clouds
nūbĭlis, e, *adj,* marriageable
nūbĭlus, a, um, *adj,* overcast
nūbo, psi, ptum, *v.i.t.* 3, *with dat,* to marry
nŭclĕus, i, *m,* nut, kernel
nūdĭus, with a number **(tertĭus)** (three) days ago
nūdo, *v.t.* 1, to strip, expose
nūdus, a, um, *adj,* naked, destitute of, poor, simple
nūgae, ārum, *f. pl,* jokes, nonsense, trifles
nūgātor, ōris, *m,* silly person
nūgātōrius, a, um, *adj,* trifling
nūgor, *v.i.* 1, *dep,* to play the fool
nullus, a, um, *adj,* none, no
nullus, ĭus, *m,* no-one
num, *adv,* used to introduce a question expecting answer "no"; whether
nūmen, ĭnis, *n,* divine will, divine power, divinity
nūmĕrābĭlis, e, *adj,* able to be counted
nūmĕrātor, ōris, *m,* counter
nūmĕrātum, i, *n,* ready money
nūmĕro, *v.t.* 1, to count, pay out, number
nūmĕrō, *adv,* in number, just
nūmĕrōsus, a, um, *adj, adv,* **ē,** numerous, rhythmic
nūmĕrus, i, *m,* number, band (of soldiers), class, category, sequence, rhythm, poetic-metre
nummārĭus, a, um, *adj,* of money
nummātus, a, um, *adj,* rich
nummus, i, *m,* money, a Roman silver coin, farthing
numquam, *adv,* never
numquid, *interr. adv,* is there anything . . .?
nunc, *adv,* now, at present
nuncia, nuncius . . . see **nunt . . .**
nuncŭpo, *v.t.* 1, to call, name
nundĭnae, ārum, *f. pl,* ninth day, market-day
nundĭnātio, ōnis, *f,* trading
nundĭnor, *v.i.t.* 1, *dep,* to trade; buy, sell
nunquam, *adv,* never
nuntiātio, ōnis, *f,* announcement
nuntio, *v.t.* 1, to announce, tell
nuntĭus, i, *m,* messenger, message
nūper, *adv,* lately, recently
nupta, ae, *f,* wife, bride
nuptiae, ārum, *f. pl,* marriage
nuptiālis, e, *adj,* of marriage
nuptus, a, um, *adj,* married
nŭrus, ūs, *f,* daughter-in-law, young wife
nusquam, *adv,* nowhere
nūto, *v.i.* 1, to nod, waver
nūtrĭcĭus, a, um, *adj,* foster-father
nūtrĭco, *v.t,* 1, to nurse, rear
nūtrĭcula, ae, *f,* nurse
nūtrĭmen, ĭnis, *n,* nourishment
nūtrĭmentum, i, *n,* nourishment
nūtrĭo, *v.t.* 4, to feed, bring up, support
nūtrix, ĭcis, *f,* nurse
nūtus, ūs, *m,* nod, command
nux, nŭcis, *f,* nut
nympha, ae, *f,* bride, nymph (demi-goddess inhabiting woods, trees, fountains, etc.)

O

ŏb, *prep. with acc,* on account of, in front of
ŏbaerātus, a, um, *adj,* involved in debt
ŏbambŭlo, *v.i.* 1, to walk about
obdo, didi, ditum, *v.t.* 3, to shut, place, expose
obdormio, *v.i.* 4, to fall asleep
obdormisco, *v.i.* 3, to fall asleep
obdūco, xi, ctum, *v.t.* 3, to lead forward, bring forward, cover over, swallow
obdūresco, rŭi, *v.i.* 3, to become hardened
obdūro, *v.i.* 1, to persist
ŏbēdiens, ntis, *adj,* obedient
ŏbēdientia, ae, *f,* obedience
ŏbēdio, *v.i.* 4, to obey, be subject to
ŏbĕliscus, i, *m,* obelisk
ŏbĕo, *v.i.t.* 4, to go to meet, die, set (constellations); to go to, reach, travel over, visit, undertake, perform
ŏbĕquito, *v.i.* 1, to ride towards
ŏbēsitas, ātis, *f,* fatness
ŏbēsus, a, um, *adj,* fat, dull
ōbex, ĭcis, *m, f,* bolt, barrier
obiăcĕo, *v.i.* 2, to lie opposite
ōbĭcio, iēci, iectum, *v.t.* 3, to throw forward, expose, oppose, taunt, reproach
obiectātio, ōnis, *f,* reproach
obiecto, *v.t.* 1, to place against, expose, reproach, accuse
obiectus, ūs, *m,* opposing, putting in the way
obiectus, a, um, *adj,* lying opposite
ŏbĭtus, ūs, *m,* setting, downfall
obiurgātio, ōnis, *f,* rebuke

obiurgātor, ōris, *m*, blamer
obiurgātōrius, a, um, *adj*, reproachful
obiurgo, *v.t.* 1, to blame, rebuke
oblectāmen, ĭnis, *n*, pleasure, delight
oblectāmentum, i, *n*, pleasure, delight
oblecto, *v.t.* 1, to amuse, please
obligātio, ōnis, *f*, obligation
oblīgo, *v.t.* 1, to bind, put under obligation, render liable
oblīmo, *v.t.* 1, to cover with mud, squander
oblĭno, lēvi, lĭtum, *v.t.* 3, to besmear, defile
oblĭquo, *v.t.* 1, to bend aside
oblĭquus, a, um, *adj*, *adv*, **ē,** slanting, sideways
oblīvio, ōnis, *f*, oblivion
oblīviōsus, a, um, *adj*, forgetful, producing forgetfulness
oblīviscor, oblĭtus, *v.* 3, *dep*, *with genit*, to forget
oblīvium, ii, *n*, oblivion
oblŏquor, lŏcūtus, *v.i.* 3, *dep*, to contradict, accompany a song
obluctor, *v.i.* 1, *dep*, to struggle against
obmūtesco, tŭi, *v.i.* 3, to become speechless
obnĭtor, xus, *v.i.* 3, *dep*, to push or struggle against
obnixus, a, um, *adj*, resolute
obnoxĭus, a, um, *adj*, liable to, submissive, indebted
obnūbo, psi, ptum, *v.t.* 3, to veil
obnuntiātio, ōnis, *f*, announcement of bad omens
obnuntio, *v.t.* 1, to announce bad omens
ŏboedĭens, oboedĭo, see **obēd . . .**
ŏbŏrĭor, ortus, *v.i.* 4, *dep*, to arise, appear
obrēpo, psi, ptum, *v.t.* 3, to creep up to, surprise
obrĭgesco, gŭi, *v.i.* 3, to stiffen
obrŏgo, *v.t.* 1, to invalidate
obrŭo, ŭi, ŭtum, *v.t.* 3, to overwhelm, bury, hide
obsaepio, psi, ptum, *v.t.* 4, to fence in
obscēnĭtas, ātis, *f*, obscenity, foulness
obscēnus, a, um, *adj*, ominous, filthy, obscene
obscūrĭtas, ātis, *f*, uncertainty, lowness
obscūro, *v.t.* 1, to darken, hide
obscūrus, a, um, *adj*, *adv*, **ē,** dark, shady, indistinct, ignoble, humble, reserved
obsĕcrātio, ōnis, *f*, appeal
obsĕcro, *v.t.* 1, to implore
obsĕcundo, *v.t.* 1, to humour, obey
obsēp . . . see **obsaep . . .**
obsĕquens, ntis, *adj*, amenable
obsĕquĭum, ii, *n*, compliance, obedience
obsĕquor, sĕcūtus, *v.* 3, *dep*, *with dat.* to comply with, submit to, humour
obsĕro, *v.t.* 1, to fasten
obsĕro, sēvi, sĭtum, *v.t.* 3, to sow, plant
observans, ntis, *adj*, attentive
observantia, ae, *f*, attention, respect
observātio, ōnis, *f*, care, observation
observo, *v.t.* 1, to watch, take note of, respect, comply with
obses, ĭdis, *m*, *f*, hostage
obsessio, ōnis, *f*, blockade
obsessor, ōris, *m*, besieger
obsĭdĕo, sēdi, sessum, *v.t.* 2, to besiege, hem in, frequent
obsidio, ōnis, *f*, siege
obsĭdo, *v.t.* 3, to besiege
obsignātor, ōris, *m*, witness
obsigno, *v.t.* 1, to seal up
obsisto, stĭti, stĭtum, *v.i.* 3, to resist, oppose
obsĭtus, a, um, *adj*, covered over
obsŏlesco, lēvi, lētum, *v.i.* 3, to wear out, decay
obsŏlētus, a, um, *adj*, worn out, low, mean
obsōnĭum, ii, *n*, eatables
obsōnātor, ōris, *m*, caterer
obsōno, *v.t.* 1, (**obsōnor,** *v.*1, *dep*), to cater
obsorbĕo, *v.t.* 2, to swallow
obstĕtrix, īcis, *f*, midwife
obstĭnātio, ōnis, *f*, firmness, obstinacy
obstĭnātus, a, um, *adj*, *adv*, **ē,** determined, resolute, stubborn
obstĭpesco, pŭi, *v.i.* 3, to be amazed
obstĭpus, a, um, *adj*, bent
obsto, stĭti, ātum, *v.i.* 1, *with dat*, to obstruct, withstand
obstrĕpo, ŭi, ĭtum, *v.i.* 3 to roar at, resound
obstringo, nxi, ctum, *v.t.* 3, to tie up, put under obligation
obstrŭo, xi, ctum, *v.t.* 3, to build up, barricade, impede
obstŭpĕfăcio, fēci, factum, *v.t.* 3, to astonish
obstŭpesco, pŭi, *v.i.* 3, to be stupified, amazed
obsum, obesse, obfŭi, *v.i.*, *irreg*, to hinder, injure
obsŭo, ŭi, ūtum, *v.t.* 3, to sew up
obsurdesco, dŭi, *v.i.* 3, to grow deaf
obtĕgo, xi, ctum, *v.t.* 3, to cover up

obtempĕro, *v.t.* 1, *with dat,* to comply with
obtendo, di, tum, *v.t.* 3, to spread before, hide
obtentus, ūs, *m,* outspreading
obtĕro, trīvi, trĭtum, *v.t.* 3, to crush to pieces
obtestātĭo, ōnis, *f,* appeal
obtestor, *v.t.* 1, *dep,* to call as a witness, implore
obtexo, xŭi, *v.t.* 3, to cover
obtĭcesco, tĭcŭi, *v.i.* 3, to be struck dumb
obtĭnĕo, nŭi, tentum, *v.i.t.* 2, to prevail, continue; keep, hold, gain, obtain
obtingo, tĭgi, *v.i.* 3, to befall
obtorpesco, pŭi, *v.i.* 3, to become stiff
obtorquĕo, si, tum, *v.t.* 2, to twist, wrench
obtrectātĭo, ōnis, *f,* disparagement
obtrectātor, ōris, *m,* slanderer
obtrecto, *v.i.t.* 1, to disparage
obtrunco, *v.t.* 1, to trim, kill
obtundo, tŭdi, tūsum, *v.t.* 3, to blunt, weaken, deafen, annoy
obtūrāculum, i, *n,* stopper
obtūrāmentum, i, *n,* stopper
obturbo, *v.t,* 1, to disturb
obtūro, *v.t.* 1, to close
obtūsus, a, um, *adj,* blunt, dull
obtūtus, ūs, *m,* gaze, stare
ŏbumbro, *v.t.* 1, to overshadow
ŏbuncus, a, um, *adj,* hooked
ŏbustus, a, um, *adj,* hardened in fire
obvĕnio, vēni, ventum, *v.i.* 4, to meet, befall one, happen
obversor, *v.i.* 1, *dep,* to move to and fro, hover
obversus, a, um, *adj,* directed towards
obverto, ti, sum, *v.t.* 3, to turn towards
obvĭam, *adv, with verbs of motion;* towards, against
obvĭus, a, um, *adj,* in the way, so as to meet, courteous, exposed
obvolvo, volvi, vŏlūtum, *v.t.* 3, to wrap round, cover
occaeco, *v.t.* 1, to blind, hide
occāsio, ōnis, *f,* opportunity
occāsus, ūs, *m,* setting (of sun, etc.) downfall, ruin
occĭdens, ntis, *m,* the west
occĭdentālis, e, *adj,* west
occīdio, ōnis, *f,* massacre
occīdo, cīdi, cīsum, *v.t.* 3, to strike down, crush, kill
occĭdo, cĭdi, cāsum, *v.i.* 3, to fall, perish, set (of sun, etc.)
occĭdŭus, a, um, *adj,* setting, western
occīsio, ōnis, *f,* slaughter
occlūdo, si, sum, *v.t.* 3, to close
occo, *v.t.* 1, to harrow
occŭbo, *v.i.* 1, to lie down, rest
occŭlo, lŭi, ltum, *v.t.* 3, to hide
occultātio, ōnis, *f,* concealment
occulto, *v.t.* 1, to hide
occultus, a, um, *adj, adv,* ē, hidden, secret
occumbo, cŭbŭi, cŭbĭtum, *v.i.* 3, to die
occŭpātio, ōnis, *f,* employment
occŭpātus, a, um, *adj,* busy
occŭpo, *v.t.* 1, to seize, occupy, attack, anticipate, fill
occurro, curri, cursum, *v.i.* 3, to meet
occursātio, ōnis, *f,* greeting
occurso, *v.i.* 1, to meet, attack
occursus, ūs, *m,* meeting
ŏcĕănus, i, *m,* ocean
ŏcellus, i, *m,* small eye, darling
ŏchra, ae, *f,* ochre
ōcior, ĭus, *comp. adj,* swifter
ōcius, *adv,* more quickly
ŏcrĕa, ae, *f,* leg-shield, greave
octāvus, a, um, *adj,* eighth
octiens (octies), *adv,* eight times
octingenti, ae, a, *pl. adj,* eight hundred
octŏ, *indecl. adj,* eight
Octōber (mensis), October
octōgēsimus, a, um, *adj,* eightieth
octōginta, *indecl. adj,* eighty
octōgōnum, i, *n,* octagon
octōni, ae, a, *pl. adj,* eight each
octōphŏron, i, *m,* sedan carried by eight men
ŏcŭlārius, a, um, *adj,* of the eyes
ŏcŭlus, i, *m,* eye, bud
ŏdi, ŏdisse, *v.t. defect,* to hate
ŏdiōsus, a, um, *adj, adv,* ē, hateful, troublesome
ŏdium, ii, *n,* hatred
ŏdor, ōris, *m,* odour, smell
ŏdōrātio, ōnis, *f,* smell
ŏdōrātus, ūs, *m,* smelling
ŏdōrātus, a, um, *adj,* scented
ŏdōrifer, ĕra, ĕrum, *adj,* fragrant
ŏdōro, *v.t.* 1, to perfume
ŏdōror, *v.t.* 1, *dep,* to smell out, investigate
ŏdōrus, a, um, *adj,* fragrant
oestrus, i, *m,* gad-fly
offa, ae, *f,* morsel
offendo, di, sum, *v.i.t.* 3, to make a mistake; strike against, meet with, find, offend
offensa, ae, *f,* hatred, crime
offensio, ōnis, *f,* stumbling, dislike, displeasure
offensus, a, um, *adj,* offensive, offended

offĕro, offerre, obtŭli, oblātum, *v.t, irreg,* to offer, show, cause, bring
officīna, ae, *f,* workshop
offĭcio, fēci, fectum, *v.i.* 3, to obstruct, hinder
officiōsus, a, um, *adj, adv,* **ē,** obliging, courteous
officium, ii, *n,* kindness, duty, employment, office
offirmātus, a, um, *adj,* firm
offulgĕo, si, *v.i,* 2, to shine on, appear
offundo, fūdi, fūsum, *v.t.* 3, to pour out, spread over
ōhē, *interj,* ho there!
ōlĕa, ae, *f,* olive
ōlĕācĕus, a, um, *adj,* oily
ōlĕārius, a, um, *adj,* of oil; (. . **i,** *m*), oil-seller
ōlĕaster, stri, *m,* wild olive-tree
ōlens, ntis, *adj,* fragrant, rank
ōlĕo, ŭi, *v.i.t.* 2, to smell of
ōlĕum, i, *n,* olive-oil
olfăcio, fēci, factum, *v.t.* 3, to smell
ōlĭdus, a, um, *adj,* stinking
ōlim, *adv,* once upon a time, once, sometime in the future
ŏlĭtor, ōris, *m,* market-gardener
ŏliva, ae, *f,* olive tree, olive branch
ŏlīvētum, i, *n,* olive-grove
ŏlīvifer, ĕra, ĕrum, *adj,* olive-growing
ŏlīvum, i, *n,* oil
olla, ae, *f,* pot, jar
ŏlor, ōris, *m,* swan
ŏlōrĭnus, a, um, *adj,* of swans
ŏlus, ĕris, *n,* vegetables
ōmāsum, i, *n,* tripe
ōmen, ĭnis, *n,* omen, sign
ōmĭnor, *v.t.* 1, *dep,* to forbode
ōmitto, mīsi, missum, *v.t.* 3, to put aside, give up, leave out
omnĭgĕnus, a, um, *adj,* of all kinds
omnĭno, *adv,* altogether, entirely
omnĭpărens, ntis, *adj,* all-producing
omnĭpŏtens, ntis, *adj,* almighty
omnes, ĭum, *c, pl,* all men
omnia, ĭum, *n.pl,* all things
omnis, e, *adj,* all, every
omnivăgus, a, um, *adj,* wandering everywhere
ŏnăger (grus), i, *m,* wild ass
ŏnĕrāria, ae, *f,* merchant ship
ŏnĕrārius, a, um, *adj,* of, or for, freight
ŏnĕro, *v.t.* 1, to load, oppress
ŏnĕrōsus, a, um, *adj,* burdensome
ŏnŭs, ĕris, *n,* load, burden
ŏnustus, a, um, *adj,* loaded, full
ŏnyx, ychis, *m, f,* yellow marble
ŏpāco, *v.t.* 1, to cover, shade
ŏpācus, a, um, *adj,* shady
ŏpălus, i, *m.,* opal
ŏpem (*no nomin.*), *f,* power, wealth, help
ŏpĕra, ae, *f,* exertion, effort; *in pl,* workmen
ŏpĕram do, to give careful attention to
ŏpĕrārius, a, um, *adj,* of labour
ŏpĕrārius, ii, *m,* labourer
ŏpercŭlum, i, *n,* lid, cover
ŏpĕrĭmentum, i, *n,* lid, cover
ŏpĕrio, ŭi, ŏpertum, *v.t.* 4, to cover, hide
ŏpĕror, *v.i.* 1, *dep,* to work, labour, perform a sacrifice
ŏpĕrōsus, a, um, *adj, adv,* **ē,** painstaking, busy, troublesome
ŏpertus, a, um, *adj,* hidden
ŏpes, um, *f. pl,* wealth, resources
ŏpifer, ĕra, ĕrum, *adj,* helping
ŏpifex, icis, *c,* craftsman
ŏpīmus, a, um, *adj,* fat, rich, fertile; **spolia ŏpīma,** arms won by a general in single combat with opposing general
ŏpīnābĭlis, e, *adj,* imaginary
ŏpīnātio, ōnis, *f,* supposition
ŏpīnātus, a, um, *adj,* imagined
ŏpinio, ōnis, *f,* supposition, belief, reputation, rumour
ŏpīnor, *v.i.t.* 1, *dep,* to suppose
ŏpĭpărē, *adv,* sumptuously
ŏpitŭlor, *v.i.* 1, *dep,* to help
ŏpium, ii, *n,* opium
ŏportet, *v.* 2, *impers, with acc. of person,* it is necessary
oppĕrior, pertus, *v.i.t.* 4, *dep,* to wait; wait for
oppĕto, īvi, ītum, *v.t.* 3, to encounter (especially death)
oppĭdāni, ōrum, *m. pl,* townspeople
oppĭdānus, a, um, *adj,* provincial
oppĭdŭlum, i, *n,* small town
oppĭdum, i, *n,* town
oppignĕro, *v.t.* 1, to pledge
oppĭlo, *v.t.* 1, to shut, stop
opplĕo, ēvi, ētum, *v.t.* 2, to fill up
oppōno, pŏsŭi, sĭtum, *v.t.* 3, to place opposite, oppose, offer, expose, object
opportūnĭtas, ātis, *f,* convenience, advantage
opportūnus, a, um, *adj, adv,* **ē,** suitable, convenient
oppŏsĭtio, ōnis, *f,* opposition
oppŏsĭtus, a, um, *adj,* opposite
opprimo, pressi, ssum, *v.t.* 3, to suppress, close, surprise, hide
opprŏbrium, i, *n,* scandal, taunt
oppugnātio, ōnis, *f,* attack, siege

For List of Abbreviations used, turn to pages 3, 4

oppugnātor, ōris, *m*, attacker
oppugno, *v.t.* 1, to attack
ops, ŏpis, *f*, power, aid
optābĭlis, e, *adj*, desirable
optātio, ōnis, *f*, wish
optātum, i, *n*, wish
optātus, a, um, *adj*, *adv*, **ō,** desired, pleasant
optĭmas, ātis, *adj*, aristocratic
optĭmātes, um, *c*, *pl*, the aristocratic party
optĭmus, a, um, *adj*, *adv*, **ē,** best
optio, ōnis, *f*, choice
optio, ōnis, *m*, assistant
opto, *v.t.* 1, to choose, desire
ŏpŭlens, ntis, *adj*, rich
ŏpŭlentia, ae, *f*, wealth
ŏpŭlentus, a, um, *adj*, rich
ŏpus, ĕris, *n*, work, task; **ŏpus est,** there is need (a necessity)
ŏpuscŭlum, i, *n*, a small work
ōra, ae, *f*, border, sea-coast, region
ōrăcŭlum, i, *n*, oracle
ōrātio, ōnis, *f*, speech, language, eloquence
ōrātĭuncŭla, ae, *f*, brief speech
ōrātor, ōris, *m*, speaker, orator, ambassador
ōrātōrĭus, a, um, *adj*, oratorical
orbicŭlātus, a, um, *adj*, circular
orbis, is, *m*, circle; **orbis terrarum,** the world
orbĭta, ae, *f*, track, rut
orbĭtas, ātis, *f*, bereavement
orbo, *v.t.* 1, to bereave, deprive
orbus, a, um, *adj*, bereaved, destitute
orca, ae, *f*, large tub
orchas, ādis, *f*, olive
orchēstra, ae, *f*, a place at the front of the theatre
orchis, is, *f*, orchid
Orcus, i, *m*, death, the Lower World
ordinārius, a, um, *adj*, regular, usual, orderly
ordinātim, *adv*, in proper order
ordinātus, a, um, *adj*, orderly, regulated
ordĭne, *adv*, in order
ordino, *v.t.* 1, to arrange
ordior, orsus, *v.i.t.* 4, *dep*, to begin, undertake
ordo, ĭnis, *m*, row, rank, band or company of soldiers, series, class of society
Ŏrēăs, ādis, *f*, mountain-nymph
orgia, ōrum, *n.pl*, revels in honour of Bacchus
ŏrĭchalcum, i, *n*, copper ore
ŏrĭens, ntis, *m*, the east
ŏrĭgo, ĭnis, *f*, beginning, origin, family, ancestor
ŏrĭor, ortus, *v.i.* 4, *dep*, to arise, appear, originate
ŏrĭundus, a, um, *adj*, descended or sprung from
ornāmentum, i, *n*, equipment, decoration
ornātus, a, um, *adj*, *adv*, **ē,** equipped, decorated
ornātus, ūs, *m*, equipment, dress, ornament
orno, *v.t.* 1, to equip, adorn, praise
ornus, i, *f*, mountain-ash
ōro, *v.t.* 1, to plead, beg, pray
orsa, ōrum, *n.pl*, undertaking, speech
orsus, ūs, *m*, undertaking
ortus, ūs, *m*, rising (of sun, etc.), beginning, source
ŏrȳsa, ae, *f*, rice
ōs, ōris, *n*, mouth, face, opening
ŏs, ossis, *n*, bone
oscen, ĭnis, *m*, singing bird from whose notes omens were taken
oscillātio, ōnis, *f*, swinging
oscillum, i, *n*, small mask
oscitātio, ōnis, *f*, yawning
oscĭto, *v.i.* 1, to gape, yawn
oscŭlor, *v.i.t.* 1, *dep*, to kiss
oscŭlum, i, *n*, mouth, kiss
ossēus, a, um, *adj*, made of bone
ossĭfrăgus, i, *m*, sea-eagle
ostendo, di, sum, *v.t.* 3, to show, make known
ostentātio, ōnis, *f*, display
ostento, *v.t.* 1, to show, display
ostentum, i, *n*, prodigy
ostiārĭum, ii, *n*, door-tax
ostiātim, *adv*, from door to door
ostĭum, ii, *n*, door, entrance
ostrĕa, ae, *f*, oyster
ostrĕārĭum, ii, *n*, oyster-bed
ostrum, i, *n*, purple, purple coverings or dress
ōtĭor, *v.i.* 1, *dep*, to be on holiday
ōtiōsus, a, um, *adj*, *adv*, **ē,** at leisure, unemployed, quiet
ōtĭum, ii, *n*, leisure, peace
ōvans, ntis, *adj*, triumphant
ōvātus, a, um, *adj*, oval
ŏvillus, a, um, *adj*, of sheep
ŏvĭlis, e, *adj*, of sheep
ŏvile, is, *n*, sheepfold
ŏvis, is, *f*, sheep
ōvo, *v.i.* 1, to exult
ōvum, i, *n*, egg

P

păbo, ōnis, *m*, wheelbarrow
pābŭlātio, ōnis, *f*, collection of fodder
pābŭlātor, ōris, *m*, forager
pābŭlor, *v.i.* 1, *dep*, to look for fodder
pābŭlum, i, *n*, food, fodder
pācālis, e, *adj*, peaceful
pācātus, a, um, *adj*, peaceful
pācifer, ĕra, ĕrum, *adj*, peace-bringing
pācifĭcātio, ōnis, *f*, pacification
pācifĭco, *v.t.* 1, to make peace
pācifĭcus, a, um, *adj*, peaceable
păciscor, pactus, *v.i.t.* 3, *dep*, to make a bargain; barter
pāco, *v.t.* 1, to subdue, pacify
pactio, ōnis, *f*, an agreement
pactum, i, *n*, an agreement
pactus, a, um, *adj*, agreed
paean, ānis, *m*, hymn to Apollo
paedăgōgus, i, *m*, slave who took children to school, and looked after them at home
paedor, ōris, *m*, filth
paelex, ĭcis, *f*, concubine
paenĕ, *adv*, almost, nearly
paeninsŭla, ae, *f*, peninsula
paenĭtens, ntis, *adj*, repentant
paenĭtentĭa, ae, *f*, penitence
paenĭtet, *v.* 2, *impers, with acc. of person*, it grieves
paenŭla, ae, *f*, cloak
paenultĭmus, a, um, *adj*, penultimate
paetus, a, um, *adj*, with a slight cast in the eye
pāgānus, a, um, *adj*, rural
pāgānus, i, *m*, country-dweller
pāgĭna, ae, *f*, page, leaf, book
pāgus, i, *m*, village, district
pāla, ae, *f*, spade
pălaestra, ae, *f*, wrestling ground or school, wrestling, rhetorical exercise
pălam, *adv*, openly; *prep. with abl*, in the presence of
pălātĭum, ii, *n*, palace
pălātum, i, *n*, palate
pălĕa, ae, *f*, chaff
pălĭŭrus, i, *m*, Christ's thorn (plant)
palla, ae, *f*, stole, robe
pallens, ntis, *adj*, pale
pallĕo, *v.i.* 2, to be pale
pallesco, pallŭi, *v.i.* 3, to turn pale
palliātus, a, um, *adj*, cloaked like Greeks
pallĭdus, a, um, *adj*, pale
palliŏlum, i, *n*, hood
pallĭum, ii, *n*, coverlet, cloak
pallor, ōris, *m*, paleness
palma, ae, *f*, palm, hand, oar-blade, palm-tree, broom, palm-wreath, prize, glory
palmāris, e, *adj*, excellent, worthy of the palm
palmātus, a, um, *adj*, marked with the hand, decorated with palm
palmĕs, ĭtis, *m*, wine-shoot
palmētum, i, *n*, palm-grove
palmifer, ĕra, ĕrum, *adj*, palm-bearing
palmōsus, a, um, *adj*, with many palm trees
palmŭla, ae, *f*, oar-blade
palmus, i, *m*, palm of hand, span
pālor, *v.i.* 1, *dep*, to wander
palpĕbra, ae, *f*, eyelid
palpĭtātio, ōnis, *f*, palpitation
palpĭto, *v.i.* 1, to throb, pant
palpo, *v.t.* 1, to stroke, caress
pălūdāmentum, i, *n*, military cloak, general's cloak
pălūdātus, a, um, *adj*, dressed in general's cloak
pălūdōsus, a, um, *adj*, marshy
pălumbes, is, *m, f*, wood-pigeon
pālus, i, *m*, stake
pălus, ūdis, *f*, marsh
păluster, tris, tre, *adj*, marshy
pampĭnĕus, a, um, *adj*, full of vine-leaves
pampĭnus, i, *m, f*, vine-shoot, vine-leaf
pănăcēa, ae, *f*, a herb which healed all diseases
panchrestus, a, um, *adj*, good for anything
pando, di, nsum, *v.t.* 3, to unfold, open out, spread out, publish
pandus, a, um, *adj*, curved
pango, pĕpĭgi, pactum, *v.t.* 3, to fasten, settle, agree upon
pānis, is, *m*, bread
pannōsus, a, um, *adj*, tattered
pannus, i, *m*, garment, rags
panthēra, ae, *f*, panther
pantŏmīmus, i, *m*, ballet-dancer
păpāver, ĕris, *n*, poppy
pāpĭlio, ōnis, *m*, butterfly
păpilla, ae, *f*, breast, nipple
păpŭla, ae, *f*, pimple
păpȳrifer, ĕra, ĕrum, *adj*, papyrus-producing
păpȳrus, i, *m, f*, paper
pār, păris, *adj*, equal, suitable
pār, păris, *m*, companion
părābĭlis, e, *adj*, easily-procured
părăbŏla, ae, *f*, parable, comparison

părallēlus, a, um, *adj*, parallel
părălȳsis, is, *f*, paralysis, palsy
părăsītus, i, *m*, parasite
părātus, a, um, *adj*, prepared
părātus, ūs, *m*, preparation
parco, pĕperci, parsum, *v.i.* 3, *with dat*, to spare, desist
parcus, a, um, *adj, adv,* **ē,** thrifty, sparing, scanty
pārens, ntis, *adj*, obedient
pārens, ntis, *m, f*, parent, ancestor, founder
pārentālia, ĭum, *n.pl*, festival in honour of dead relations
pārentālis, e, *adj*, parental
pārento, *v.t.* 1, to honour dead relatives, avenge a relative's death by killing
pārĕo, *v.i.* 2, *with dat*, to obey, to appear
pāriēs, ĕtis, *m*, wall
pāriētinae, ārum, *f.pl*, ruins
pārilis, e, *adj*, equal
pārio, pĕpĕri, partum, *v.t.* 3, to bring forth, produce, acquire
pāriter, *adv*, equally, at the same time
parma, ae, *f*, small round shield
parmŭla, ae, *f*, small round shield
pāro, *v.t.* 1, to prepare, intend, obtain
pārŏchus, i, *m*, caterer
pāroecia, ae, *f*, parish
parra, ae, *f*, owl
parrĭcīda, ae, *c*, murderer of a parent or relative, assassin
parrĭcīdium, ii, *n*, murder of a parent or relative, treason
pars, partis, *f*, part, party, faction, part in a play; *in pl*, duty, office; **in utramque partem,** on both sides; **pro parte,** to the best of one's ability
parsĭmōnia, ae, *f*, thrift
particeps, cipis, *adj, with genit*, sharing; (*as noun*) sharer
particīpo, *v.t.* 1, to give a share of
particŭla, ae, *f*, small part
partim, *adv*, partly
partio, *v.t.* 4, to share, divide
partior, *v.t.* 4, *dep*, to share, divide
partitio, ōnis, *f*, division
partītus, a, um, *adj*, divided
partŭrio, *v.i.t.* 4, to be pregnant or in labour; produce
pārtus, ūs, *m*, birth, confinement, offspring
pārum, *adv*, too little
pārumper, *adv*, for a short time
parvitas, ātis, *f*, smallness
parvŭlus, a, um, *adj*, slight
parvus, a, um, *adj*, small, petty, short; **parvi,** of little value
pasco, pāvi, pastum, *v.i.t.* 3, to feed; pasture, nourish
pascor, pastus, *v.i.* 3, *dep*, to graze, feast
pascŭum, i, *n*, pasture
pascŭus, a, um, *adj*, for grazing
passer, ĕris, *m*, sparrow, turbot
passim, *adv*, in all directions
passum, i, *n*, raisin-wine
passus, a, um, *adj*, spread out, dried
passus, a, um, *partic. adj*, having suffered
passus, ūs, *m*, step, pace
pastillus, i, *m*, lozenge to dispel bad breath
pastor, ōris, *m*, shepherd
pastōrālis, e, *adj*, of shepherds, pastoral
pastōrĭcĭus, a, um, *adj*, of shepherds, pastoral
pastōrius, a, um, *adj*, of shepherds, pastoral
pastus, ūs, *m*, pasture, food
pătĕfăcio, fēci, factum, *v.t.* 3, to throw open, disclose
pătĕfactio, ōnis, *f*, opening up
pătella, ae, *f*, plate
pătens, ntis, *adj*, open
pătĕo, *v.i.* 2, to be open, to extend, to be evident
păter, tris, *m*, father; *in pl.* forefathers, senators
pătĕra, ae, *f*, saucer, bowl
păterfămilias, patrisfămilias, *m*, master of the house
păternus, a, um, *adj*, of a father
pătesco, pătŭi, *v.i.* 3, to be opened, to extend, be evident
pătĭbilis, e, *adj*, endurable
pătĭbŭlum, i, *n*, fork-shaped yoke or gibbet
pătĭens, ntis, *adj, adv,* **nter,** suffering, patient, hard
pătĭentia, ae, *f*, endurance
pătĭna, ae, *f*, pan, dish
pătior, passus, *v.t.* 3, *dep*, to suffer, bear, allow
pătria, ae, *f*, fatherland
pătriarcha, ae, *m*, patriarch
pătrĭcĭus, a, um, *adj*, noble
pătrĭcĭus, i, *m*, member of the Roman nobility
pătrĭmōnium, ii, *n*, inherited estate
pătrĭtus, a, um, *adj*, of one's father or ancestor
pătrĭus, a, um, *adj*, of a father, hereditary, established, native
pătro, *v.t.* 1, to perform, finish
pătrōcĭnium, ii, *n*, defence
pătrōna, ae, *f*, patroness

pătrōnus, i, *m,* protector, patron, counsel
pătrŭēlis, is, *c,* cousin
pătrŭus, i, *m,* uncle
pătrŭus, a, um, *adj,* of an uncle
pătŭlus, a, um, *adj,* open, wide
pauci, ae, a, *pl. adj,* few
paucitas, ātis, *f,* small number
paucŭlus, a, um, *adj,* very few
paucus, a, um, *adj,* few, little
paulātim, *adv,* gradually
paulisper, *adv,* for a short time
paulō, *adv,* a little, somewhat
paulŭlum, *adv,* a little, somewhat
paulum, *adv,* a little, somewhat
pauper, ĕris, *adj,* poor, meagre
pauper, ĕris, *c,* a poor man
paupĕries, ēi, *f,* poverty
paupertas, ātis, *f,* poverty
paupĕro, *v.t.* 1, to impoverish
pausa, ae, *f,* stop, end
pāvĕfăcio, fēci, factum, *v.t.* 3, to alarm
pāvĕo, pāvi, *v.i.t.* 2, to be afraid; dread
pāvesco, *v.i.* 3, to become alarmed
pāvĭdus, a, um, *adj,* terrified
pāvīmentum, i, *n,* pavement
pāvĭo, *v.t.* 4, to beat, strike
pāvĭto, *v.i.t.* 1, to tremble (at)
pāvo, ōnis, *m,* peacock
pāvor, ōris, *m,* anxiety, dread
pax, pācis, *f,* peace, grace, favour, tranquillity; *in abl,* by permission
peccans, ntis, *c,* offender
peccātor, ōris, *m,* sinner
peccātum, i, *n,* fault, mistake
pecco, *v.i.t.* 1, to make a mistake; to miss
pecten, ĭnis, *m,* comb, reed, rake, a plectrum to strike the strings of the lyre
pecto, pexi, xum, *v.t.* 3, to comb
pectŏrālis, e, *adj,* pectoral
pectus, ŏris, *n,* breast, heart, soul, mind
pĕcŭārius, a, um, *adj,* of cattle
pĕcŭārius, ii, *m,* cattle-breeder
pĕcŭlātor, ōris, *m,* embezzler
pĕcŭlātus, ūs, *m,* embezzlement
pĕcŭliāris, e, *adj,* one's own, special
pĕcŭlium, ii, *n,* property, savings
pĕcūnia, ae, *f,* money
pĕcūniārius, a, um, *adj,* pecuniary
pĕcūniōsus, a, um, *adj,* rich
pĕcus, ŏris, *n,* cattle, herd
pĕcus, ŭdis, *f,* an animal, beast
pĕdālis, e, *adj,* a foot in length or thickness
pĕdes, ĭtis, *m,* infantryman
pĕdes, see **pes**
pĕdester, tris, tre, *adj,* on foot, prosaic, plain
pĕdĕtemptim, *adv,* gradually
pĕdica, ae, *f,* shackle, snare
pĕdicŭlōsus, a, um, *adj,* lousy
pĕdicŭlus, i, *m,* louse
pĕdisĕquus, i, *m,* footman
pĕditātus, ūs, *m,* infantry
pĕdum, i, *n,* shepherd's crook
pēiĕro, *v.i.* 1, to swear falsely
pēior, *comp. adj,* worse
pēius, *comp. adv,* worse
pĕlăgus, i, *n,* open sea
pellax, ācis, *adj,* seductive
pellex, ĭcis, *f,* concubine
pellĭcio, lexi, lectum, *v.t.* 3, to allure, coax
pellĭcŭla, ae, *f,* small skin
pellis, is, *f,* skin, leather, tent
pellĭtus, a, um, *adj,* clothed in skins
pello, pĕpŭli, pulsum, *v.t.* 3, to strike, push, drive out, rout, affect, impress
pellŭcĕo, xi, *v.i.* 2, to shine through, be transparent
pellŭcidus, a, um, *adj,* transparent
pĕlŏris, ĭdis, *f,* mussel
pelta, ae, *f,* small shield
pelvis, is, *f,* basin
pĕnārius, a, um, *adj,* for provisions
pĕnātes, ĭum, *m. pl,* guardian deities of the home, home
pendĕo, pĕpendi, *v.i.* 2, to hang, float, loiter, depend upon, be interrupted, be in suspense
pendo, pĕpendi, pensum, *v.t.* 3, to weigh or pay out, ponder
pendŭlus, a, um, *adj,* hanging, uncertain
pĕnĕs, *prep. with acc,* in the power of
pĕnĕtrābilis, e, *adj,* penetrable, penetrating
pĕnĕtrālia, ĭum, *n. pl,* inner places or rooms
pĕnĕtrālis, e, *adj,* inner
pĕnĕtro, *v.i.t.* 1, to enter; penetrate
pēnicillum, i, *n,* painter's brush, pencil
pēnicŭlāmentum, i, *n,* train of a dress
pēnicŭlus, i, *m,* brush
pēnis, is, *m,* tail, penis
pēnitus, *adv,* inwardly, deep within, entirely
penna, ae, *f,* feather, wing
pennātus, a, um, *adj,* winged
penniger, ĕra, ĕrum, *adj,* winged
pensĭlis, e, *adj,* hanging
pensio, ōnis, *f,* payment
pensito, *v.t.* 1, to pay, weigh, ponder

For List of Abbreviations used, turn to pages 3, 4

penso, *v.t.* 1, to weigh out, repay, consider
pensum, i, *n,* a task
pēnūria, ae, *f,* need, want
pēnus, ūs (*or* **i**), *m, f,* store of food
pēpo, ōnis, *m,* pumpkin
per, *prep. with acc,* through, during, by means of, on account of
per . . . in compound words usually adds intensity: very. . . .
pĕractĭo, ōnis, *f,* completion
pĕrăgo, ēgi, actum, *v.t.* 3, to complete, relate, transfix
pĕrăgro, *v.t.* 1, to travel over
pĕrambŭlo, *v.t.* 1, to go through
pĕrăro, *v.t.* 1, to plough through
perbrĕvis, e, *adj,* very short
perca, ae, *f,* perch (fish)
percēlĕbro, *v.t.* 1, to say frequently
percello, cŭli, culsum, *v.t.* 3, to upset, destroy, dishearten
percensĕo, *v.t.* 2, to reckon up
perceptĭo, ōnis, *f,* perception
percĭpio, cēpi, ceptum, *v.t.* 3, to gather, perceive, understand
percontātio, ōnis, *f,* inquiry
percontor, *v.i.t.* 1, *dep,* to investigate
percŏquo, xi, ctum, *v.t.* 3, to boil, cook, heat
percrēbesco, bŭi, *v.i.* 3, to become prevalent
percrĕpo, ŭi, ĭtum, *v.i.* 1, to resound, ring
perculsus, a, um, *adj,* upset
percurro, curri, cursum, *v.i.t.* 3, to run; pass over, mention
percussio, ōnis, *f,* beating
percussor, ōris, *m,* assassin
percŭtio, cussi, cussum, *v.t.* 3, to thrust through, kill, strike, astound
perdisco, didici, *v.t.* 3, to learn thoroughly
perditor, ōris, *m,* destroyer
perditus, a, um, *adj, adv,* **ē,** ruined, desperate, corrupt
perdix, ĭcis, *c,* partridge
perdo, didi, ditum, *v.t.* 3, to destroy, waste, lose
perdŏcĕo, *v.t.* 2, to teach thoroughly
perdŏmo, ŭi, ĭtum, *v.t.* 1, to subdue completely
perdŭco, xi, ctum, *v.t.* 3, to conduct, bedaub, prolong, induce
perductor, ōris, *m,* pimp
perdŭellio, ōnis, *f,* treason
perdŭellis, is, *m,* public enemy
pĕrēdo, ēdi, sum, *v.t.* 3, to eat up
pĕrēgrē, *adv,* abroad
pĕrĕgrīnātio, ōnis, *f,* travel abroad
pĕrĕgrīnātor, ōris, *m,* traveller
pĕrĕgrīnor, *v.i.* 1, *dep,* to live or travel abroad
pĕrĕgrīnus, a, um, *adj,* foreign
pĕrĕgrīnus, i, *m,* foreigner
pĕrendiē, *adv,* on the day after tomorrow
pĕrennis, e, *adj,* everlasting
pĕrenno, *v.i.* 1, to last, endure
pĕrĕo, ĭi, ĭtum, *v.i.* 4, *irreg,* to pass away, disappear, die, to be ruined or wasted
pĕrĕquito, *v.i.* 1, to ride about
pĕrerro, *v.t.* 1, to wander through
perfectio, ōnis, *f,* completion
perfectus, a, um, *adj, adv,* **ē,** complete, perfect
perfĕro, ferre, tŭli, lātum, *v.t. irreg,* to bring or bear through, convey, announce, complete, suffer
perficio, fēci, fectum, *v.t.* 3, to complete, finish
perfidia, ae, *f,* treachery
perfidiōsus, a, um, *adj,* treacherous
perfidus, a, um, *adj,* treacherous
perflo, *v.t.* 1, to blow through
perflŭo, xi, *v.i.* 3, to flow through
perfŏdio, fōdi, fossum, *v.t.* 3, to dig through
perfŏro, *v.t.* 1, to bore through
perfrico, cŭi, cātum, *v.t.* 1, to rub all over, put on a bold front
perfringo, frēgi, fractum, *v.t.* 3, to shatter, infringe
perfrŭor, fructus, *v.* 3, *dep, with abl,* to enjoy thoroughly
perfŭga, ae, *m,* deserter
perfŭgio, fūgi, *v.i.* 3, to flee for refuge, desert
perfŭgium, ii, *n,* shelter
perfundo, fūdi, fūsum, *v.t.* 3, to pour over, besprinkle
perfungor, functus, *v.* 3, *dep, with abl,* to fulfil, discharge
perfŭro, —*v.i.* 3, to rage
pergo, perrexi, perrectum, *v.i.t.* 3, to proceed, go; continue
pĕrhibĕo, ŭi, ĭtum, *v.t.* 2, to extend, assert, name
pĕrhorresco, rŭi, *v.i.t.* 3, to tremble; shudder at
pĕrĭclitor, *v.i.t.* 1, *dep,* to try, be in danger; test, endanger
pĕrĭcŭlōsus, a, um, *adj, adv,* **ē,** dangerous
pĕrĭcŭlum, i, *n,* danger, proof, attempt

pĕrĭmo, ēmi, emptum, *v.t.* 3, to annihilate, prevent
pĕrĭnde, *adv,* just as, equally
pĕrĭŏdus, i, *f,* complete sentence
pĕrĭtĭa, ae, *f,* experience, skill
pĕrĭtus, a, um, *adj, adv,* **ē,** *with genit,* skilled, expert
periūrĭum, ii, *n,* perjury
periūro, see pēiĕro
periūrus, a, um, *adj,* perjured, lying
perlābor, lapsus, *v.i.* 3, *dep,* to glide through
perlectĭo, ōnis, *f,* reading through
perlĕgo, lēgi, lectum, *v.t.* 3, to survey, examine, read through
perlūcĕo, xi, *v.i.* 2, to shine through, be transparent
perlŭo, ŭi, ūtum, *v.t.* 3, to wash
perlūcĭdus, a, um, *adj,* transparent
perlustro, *v.t.* 1, to wander through
permănĕo, nsi, nsum, *v.i.* 2 to last, continue
permāno, *v.i.* 1, to flow through, penetrate
permansĭo, ōnis, *f,* persisting
permĕo, *v.t.* 1, to cross, penetrate
permētĭor, mensus, *v.t.* 4, *dep,* to measure out, travel over
permiscĕo, scŭi, xtum, *v.t.* 2, to mix together
permissĭo, ōnis, *f,* permission, surrender
permissū, *abl,* by permission
permitto, mīsi, missum, *v.t.* 3, to let loose, commit, entrust; allow (*with dat*)
permŏtĭo, ōnis, *f,* excitement
permŏvĕo, mōvi, mōtum, *v.t.* 2, to stir up, rouse
permulcĕo, mulsi, mulsum, *v.t.* 2, to stroke, charm, flatter
permultus, a, um, *adj, adv,* **ō,** or **um,** very much
permūtātio, ōnis, *f,* exchange
permūto, *v.t.* 1, to change
perna, ae, *f,* leg of pork
pernĕgo, *v.t.* 1, to deny flatly
pernĭcies, ēi, *f,* disaster
perniciōsus, a, um, *adj, adv,* **ē,** destructive
pernĭcĭtas, ātis, *f,* agility
pernix, īcis, *adj,* agile
pernocto, *v.i.* 1, to stay all night
pernox, ctis, *adj,* night-long
pēro, ōnis, *m,* rawhide boot
pĕrōsus, a, um, *adj,* detesting, detested
pĕrōro, *v.t.* 1, to wind up a speech
perpendĭcŭlum, i, *n,* plumb-line
perpendo, pendi, pensum, *v.t.* 3, to ponder, consider
perpĕram, *adv,* untruly
perpĕtĭor, pessus, *v.i.t.* 3, *dep,* to suffer; endure
perpĕtŭĭtas, ātis, *f,* continuity
perpĕtŭus, a, um, *adv,* **ō,** perpetual, entire, continuous
perplexus, a, um, *adj,* intricate
perpŏlĭo, *v.t.* 4, to perfect
perprĭmo, pressi, ssum, *v.t.* 3, to press hard
perpurgo, *v.t.* 1, to clean up
perquam, *adv,* very much
perquīro, sīvi, sītum, *v.t.* 3, to make a careful search for
perrārō, *adv,* very rarely
perrumpo, rūpi, ruptum, *v.i.t.* 3, to break through
perscrĭbo, psi, ptum, *v.t.* 3, to write in full
perscriptĭo, ōnis, *f,* written entry or note
perscrūtor, *v.t.* 1, *dep,* to examine
persĕco, cui, ctum, *v.t.* 1, to cut up
persentĭo, si, sum, *v.t.* 4, to perceive plainly, feel deeply
persĕquor, sĕcūtus, *v.t.* 3, *dep,* to pursue, overtake, revenge
persĕvĕrantĭa, ae, *f,* constancy
persĕvĕro, *v.i.t.* 1, to persevere; persist in
persīdo, sēdi, sessum, *v.i.* 3, to penetrate
persisto, stĭti, *v.i.* 3, to persist
persolvo, solvi, sŏlūtum, *v.t.* 3, to pay out, give
persōna, ae, *f,* mask, character, part, person
persōnātus, a, um, *adj,* fictitious
persŏno, ŭi, ĭtum, *v.i.t.* 1, to resound; fill with sound
perspectus, a, um, *adj,* well-known
perspĭcācĭtas, ātis, *f,* perspicacity
perspĭcax, ācis, *adj,* astute
perspĭcĭo, spexi, spectum, *v.t.* 3, to look at, examine, perceive
perspĭcŭĭtas, ātis, *f,* clearness, perspicuity
perspĭcŭus, a, um, *adj, adv,* **ē,** clear, evident
persto, stĭti, stātum, *v.i.* 1, to endure, continue, persist
perstringo, nxi, ctum, *v.t.* 3, to graze, blunt, stun, blame, allude to, slight
persuādĕo, si, sum, *v.t.* 2, *with dat,* to persuade
persuāsĭo, ōnis, *f,* conviction
persuāsus, a, um, *adj,* settled

persuāsum hăbēre, to be convinced
pertento, *v.t.* 1, to consider
pertĕrĕbro, *v.t.* 1, to bore through
perterrĕo, *v.t.* 2, to frighten thoroughly
pertica, ae, *f,* pole, rod
pertĭmesco, mŭi, *v.i.t.* 3, to be very afraid; to fear greatly
pertĭnācĭa, ae, *f,* obstinacy
pertĭnax, ācis, *adj,* firm, constant, stubborn
pertĭnĕo, *v.i.* 2, to extend, pertain, concern, be applicable
pertracto, *v.t.* 1, to touch
pertundo, tŭdi, tūsum, *v.t.* 3, to make a hole through
perturbātio, ōnis, *f,* confusion
perturbātus, a, um, *adj,* disturbed
perturbo, *v.t.* 1, to disturb
pĕrungo, nxi, nctum, *v.t.* 3, to besmear
pĕrūro, ssi, stum, *v.t.* 3, to burn up, rub sore, nip
pervādo, si, sum, *v.i.* 3, to spread through, pervade
pervăgātus, a, um, *adj,* well-known
pervăgor, *v.i.t.* 1, *dep,* to wander through; pervade
pervĕho, xi, ctum, *v.t.* 3, to carry through
pervello, velli, *v.t.* 3, to pull, disparage
pervĕnio, vēni, ventum, *v.i.* 4, to reach, arrive at
perversĭtas, ātis, *f,* obstinacy
perversus, a, um, *adj,* askew, perverse
perverto, ti, sum, *v.t.* 3, to overturn, destroy, corrupt
pervestīgo, *v.t.* 1, to investigate
pervĭcācĭa, ae, *f,* obstinacy
pervĭcax, ācis, *adj, adv,* **ĭter,** stubborn, wilful
pervĭdĕo, vīdi, vīsum, *v.t.* 2, to view, survey
pervĭgil, is, *adj,* ever-watchful
pervĭgilātio, ōnis, *f,* vigil
pervĭgilo, *v.i.* 1, to remain awake all night
pervĭnco, vīci, victum, *v.t.* 3, to gain victory over
pervĭus, a, um, *adj,* able to be crossed or passed
pervŏlito, *v.i.* 1, to flit about
pervŏlo, *v.i.* 1, to fly about or through or to
pervŏlo, velle, vŏlŭi, *v.i, irreg,* to wish greatly
pervulgo, *v.t.* 1, to spread about
pĕs, pĕdis, *m,* foot; rope attached to a sail, sheet
pessimē, *adv,* very badly
pessimus, a, um, *adj,* very bad
pessŭlus, i, *m,* latch
pessum, *adv,* to the ground; **pessum ire,** to go to ruin
pestĭfer, ĕra, ĕrum, *adj,* destructive, harmful
pestĭlens, ntis, *adj,* unhealthy
pestĭlentĭa, ae, *f,* infectious disease
pestis, is, *f,* disease, ruin
pĕtāsātus, a, um, *adj,* dressed for a journey
pĕtāsus, i, *m,* travelling-hat
pĕtĭtio, ōnis, *f,* blow, candidature for office
pĕtĭtor, ōris, *m,* candidate, plaintiff
pĕto, īvi, ĭtum, *v.t.* 3, to make for, seek, aim at, request
pĕtŏritum, i, *n,* four-wheeled carriage
pĕtŭlans, ntis, *adj,* impudent
pĕtŭlantĭa, ae, *f,* impudence
pexus, a, um, *adj,* new
phălanx, ngis, *f,* military formation
phălĕrae, ārum, *f. pl,* military decoration
phărĕtra, ae, *f,* quiver
phărĕtrātus, a, um, *adj,* wearing a quiver
pharmăcŏpōla, ae, *m,* quack
phărus, i, *f,* lighthouse
phăsēlus, i, *m, f,* kidney-bean, light boat, yacht
phengĭtes, ae, *m,* selenite, mica
philŏlŏgĭa, ae, *f,* love of learning
philŏlŏgus, i, *m,* man of learning
philŏmēla, ae, *f,* nightingale
philŏsŏphĭa, ae, *f,* philosophy
philŏsŏphor, *v.i.* 1, *dep,* to study philosophy
philŏsŏphus, i, *m,* philosopher
philyra, ae, *f,* bark of the linden-tree
phĭmus, i, *m,* dice-box
phōca, ae, *f,* seal, sea-dog
phoenix, īcis, *m,* bird which was said to live 500 years
phthĭsis, is, *f,* phthisis
phŷlarchus, i, *m,* chief, prince
phŷsica, ōrum, *n. pl,* physics
phŷsicus, i, *m,* naturalist
phŷsiŏlŏgĭa, ae, *f,* physiology
pĭăcŭlāris, e, *adj,* expiatory
pĭăcŭlum, i, *n,* sacrificial offering of atonement, victim, sin, crime
pĭca, ae, *f,* magpie
pĭcĕa, ae, *f,* pitch-pine
pĭcĕus, a, um, *adj,* pitch-black
pictor, ōris, *m,* painter
pictūra, ae, *f,* painting, picture
pictūrātus, a, um, *adj,* embroidered
pictus, a, um, *adj,* painted, decorated
pĭcus, i, *m,* woodpecker
pĭĕtas, ātis, *f,* sense of duty, loyalty, mercy

pĭger, gra, grum, *adj,* lazy, sluggish
pĭget (me, te), *v.* 2, *impers,* it annoys or displeases (me, you)
pigmentum, i, *n,* paint, pigment
pignĕro, *v.t.* 1, to pledge, pawn
pignĕror, *v.t.* 1, *dep,* to take possession of
pignus, ŏris (ĕris), *n,* security, mortgage, pledge, bet
pĭgrĭtĭa, ae, *f,* laziness, indolence
pĭgrĭtĭes, ēi, *f,* laziness, indolence
pīla, ae, *f,* pillar, pier
pīla, ae, *f,* ball
pīlātus, a, um, *adj,* armed with javelins
pīlentum, i, *n,* carriage
pillĕātus, a, um, *adj,* wearing a felt cap, *see below*
pillĕus, i, *m* (**pillĕum, i,** *n*), felt cap, worn by Romans at festivals, and by freed slaves
pīlōsus, a, um, *adj,* hairy
pīlŭla, ae, *f,* pill
pīlum, i, *n,* the heavy javelin of the Roman infantry
pīlus, i, *m,* a hair, the hair
pīlus, i, *m* (with **prīmus**), senior centurion, senior division of trĭārĭimen who fought in the 3rd rank
pīnētum, i, *n,* a wood of pines
pīnĕus, a, um, *adj,* of pinewood
pingo, nxi, ctum, *v.t.* 3, to paint, decorate
pinguesco, *v.i.* 3, to grow fat or fertile
pingue, is, *n,* fat
pinguis, e, *adj,* rich, fertile, plump, dull, stupid
pinguĭtūdo, ĭnis, *f,* plumpness, richness
pīnĭfer, ĕra, ĕrum, *adj,* pine-bearing
pīnĭger, ĕra, ĕrum, *adj,* pine-bearing
pinna, ae, *f,* feather, wing
pinnātus, a, um, *adj,* winged
pinnĭger, ĕra, ĕrum, *adj,* winged
pīnus, ūs (or **i,**) *f,* pine tree
pĭo, *v.t.* 1, to appease, atone for
pīpātus, ūs, *m,* chirping
pĭper, ĕris, *n,* pepper
pīpĭlo, *v.i.* 1, to chirp
pīpĭo, *v.i.* 4, to chirp
pīrāta, ae, *m,* pirate
pīrātĭcus, a, um, *adj,* of pirates
pĭrum, i, *n,* pear
pĭrus, i, *f,* pear-tree
piscātor, ōris, *m,* fisherman
piscātōrĭus, a, um, *adj,* of fishing or fishermen
piscātus, ūs, *m,* fishing
piscīna, ae, *f,* fish-pond
piscis, is, *m,* a fish
piscor, *v.i.* 1, *dep,* to fish
piscōsus, a, um, *adj,* full of fish
pistor, ōris, *m,* miller, baker
pistrīnum, i, *n,* mill
pistris, is (**pistrix, icis**), *f,* sea-monster
pĭsum, i, *n,* pea
pĭtŭĭta, ae, *f,* phlegm
pĭi, ōrum, *m. pl,* the departed
pĭus, a, um, *adj, adv,* **ē,** dutiful, loyal, kind, affectionate
pix, pĭcis, *f,* pitch
plăcābĭlis, e, *adj,* easily pacified, mild
plăcātus, a, um, *adj, adv,* **ē,** calmed, still
plăcens, ntis, *adj,* pleasing
plăcenta, ae, *f,* cake
plăcĕo, *v.i.* 2, *with dat,* to please, to be welcome
plăcĭdus, a, um, *adj, adv,* **ē,** quiet, calm, peaceful
plăcĭtus, a, um, *adj,* agreeable
plăco, *v.t.* 1, to reconcile, soothe
plāga, ae, *f,* wound, blow
plăga, ae, *f,* region
plāga, ae, *f,* hunting-net
plāgĭārĭus, ii, *m,* oppressor
plāgōsus, a, um, *adj,* fond of flogging
plāgŭla, ae, *f,* curtain
planctus, ūs, *m,* lamentation
plango, nxi, nctum, *v.t.* 3, to beat, strike, lament
plangor, ōris, *m,* lamentation
plānĭtĭes, ēi, *f,* plain
planta, ae, *f,* shoot, twig
plantārĭa, ĭum, *n. pl,* young trees
plantārĭum, ii, *n,* plantation
plānum, i, *n,* plain
plānus, a, um, *adj, adv,* **ē,** flat, level, clear
plānus, i, *m,* imposter, cheat
plătănus, i, *f,* plane-tree
plătēa, ae, *f,* street
plaudo, si, sum, *v.i.t.* 3, to applaud; strike, beat
plausĭbĭlis, e, *adj,* acceptable
plaustrum, i, *n,* cart, waggon
plausus, ūs, *m,* applause
plēbēcŭla, ae, *f,* the mob
plēbēĭus, a, um, *adj,* vulgar
plēbĭcŏla, ae, *c,* demagogue
plebs (plēbes), is, *f,* the common people
plecto, *v.t.* 3, to punish
plectrum, i, *n,* quill with which to strike a stringed instrument
plēnĭtūdo, ĭnis, *f,* fulness
plēnus, a, um, *adj, adv,* **ē,** full, laden, complete, plentiful

For List of Abbreviations used, turn to pages 3, 4

plērĭque, aeque, ăque, *adj*, most, very many
plērumque, *adv*, for the most part
pleurĭtis, ĭdis, *f*, pleurisy
plĭco, *v.t.* 1, to fold up
plinthus, i, *m, f*, plinth
plōrātus, ūs, *m*, weeping
plōro, *v.i.t.* 1, to weep; bewail
plostellum, i, *n*, small cart
plŭit, *v. impers*, it rains
plūma, ae, *f*, feather, down
plumbĕus, a, um, *adj*, made of lead, heavy
plumbum, i, *n*, lead, bullet
plūmĕus, a, um, *adj*, downy, soft
plūrālis, e, *adj*, plural
plūres, es, a, *comp. adj*, more
plūrĭmum, *adv*, very much
plūrĭmus, a, um, *adj*, very much
plūs, plūris, *n*, more
plūs, *adv*, more
pluscŭlum, i, *n*, somewhat more
plŭtĕus, i, *m*, shed, parapet, shelf
plŭvĭa, ae, *f*, rain
plŭvĭālis, e, *adj*, rainy
plŭvĭus, a, um, *adj*, rainy
pōcŭlum, i, *n*, cup, beaker
pŏdăgra, ae, *f*, gout
pŏdĭa, ae, *f*, sail-rope
pŏdĭum, ii, *n*, height, balcony
pŏēma, ătis, *n*, poem
poena, ae, *f*, punishment, penalty
poenālis, e, *adj*, penal
pŏēsis, is, *f*, poetry
pŏēta, ae, *m*, poet
pŏētĭcus, a, um, *adj*, poetical
poi!, *interj*, indeed!
pŏlĭo, *v.t.* 4, to polish, improve
pŏlĭtĭcus, a, um, *adj*, political
pŏlītus, a, um, *adj, adv*, **ē,** polished, refined
pollens, ntis, *adj*, powerful
pollĕo, *v.i.* 2, to be powerful, to prevail
pollex, ĭcis, *m*, thumb
pŏllicĕor, *v.i.t.* 2, *dep*, to promise
pollicĭtātio, ōnis, *f*, promise
pollicĭtum, i, *n*, promise
pollinctor, ōris, *m*, undertaker
pollŭo, ŭi, ūtum, *v.t.* 3, to pollute, contaminate
pŏlus, i, *m*, pole, north-pole
pŏlypus, i, *m*, polypus
pōmārĭum, ii, *n*, orchard
pōmārĭus, ii, *m*, fruiterer
pōmĕridĭānus, a, um, *adj*, in the afternoon
pōmifer, ĕra, ĕrum, *adj*, fruit-bearing
pōmoerĭum, ii, *n*, open space inside and outside city walls
pompa, ae, *f*, procession, retinue, pomp
pōmum, i, *n*, fruit
pōmus, i, *f*, fruit-tree
pondĕro, *v.t.* 1, to consider
pondĕrōsus, a, um, *adj*, ponderous
pondo, *adv*, by weight
pondus, ĕris, *n*, weight, mass, influence, authority
pōne, *adv. and prep. with acc*, behind, after
pōno, pŏsŭi, pŏsĭtum, *v.t.* 3, to put, place, set, plant, wager, invest, spend, lay aside, appoint, calm, allege, propose
pons, ntis, *m*, bridge
pontĭcŭlus, i, *m*, drawbridge
pontĭfex, ĭcis, *m*, high-priest
pontĭfĭcĭus, a, um, *adj*, of a high-priest
pontus, i, *m*, the sea
pŏpa, ae, *m*, priest's assistant
pōpīna, ae, *f*, restaurant
poplĕs, ĭtis, *m*, knee
pŏpŭlāris, e, *adj, adv*, **ĭter,** of the people, popular, democratic
pŏpŭlāris, *c*, fellow-countryman
pŏpŭlāres, ĭum, *m. pl*, the people's party
pŏpŭlātĭo, ōnis, *f*, devastation
pŏpŭlātor, ōris, *m*, plunderer
pŏpŭlĕus, a, um, *adj*, of poplars
pŏpŭlo, *v.t.* 1, to plunder, devastate
pŏpŭlor, *v.t.* 1, *dep*, to plunder, devastate
pŏpŭlus, i, *m*, the people
pŏpŭlus, i, *f*, poplar tree
porcīna, ae, *f*, pork
porcŭlus, i, *m*, young pig; (with **mărīnus**), porpoise
porcus, i, *m*, pig
porrectio, ōnis, *f*, extension
porrectus, a, um, *adj*, extended
porrĭcĭo, ēci, ctum, *v.t.* 3, to offer to the gods
porrĭgo, rexi, rectum, *v.t.* 3, to stretch out, offer
porrĭgo, ĭnis, *f*, dandruff
porro, *adv*, forwards, next, moreover
porrum, i, *n*, leek
porta, ae, *f*, gate, door
portendo, di, tum, *v.t.* 3, to foretell
portentum, i, *n*, omen, monster
porticus, ūs, *f*, colonnade
portĭo, *in phrase*, **pro portiōne,** in proportion

portĭtor, ōris, *m,* customs-officer
portĭtor, ōris, *m,* boatman
porto, *v.t.* 1, to carry, bring
portōrĭum, ii, *n,* customs-duty
portŭōsus, a, um, *adj,* with many harbours
portus, ūs, *m,* harbour, refuge
posco, pŏposci, *v.t.* 3, to demand
pŏsĭtio, ōnis, *f,* placing, situation
pŏsĭtus, a, um, *adj,* situated
pŏsĭtus, ūs, *m,* arrangement, disposition
possessio, ōnis, *f,* seizure, occupation
possessor, ōris, *m,* possessor
possidĕo, sēdi, sessum, *v.t.* 2, to be master of, possess
possīdo, sēdi, sessum, *v.t.* 3, to take possession of, occupy
possum, posse, pŏtŭi, *v.i, irreg,* to be able, to have power
post, *adv. and prep. with acc,* behind, backwards, after
postĕā, *adv,* afterwards
postĕāquam, *conj.* after
postĕri, ōrum, *m. pl,* posterity
postĕrĭor, ĭus, *comp. adj,* next, worse
postĕrĭtas, ātis, *f,* posterity
postĕrĭus, *adv,* later
postĕrus, a, um, *adj,* next
postgĕnĭti, ōrum, *m. pl,* posterity
posthăbĕo, *v.t.* 2, to postpone, neglect
posthāc, *adv,* in future
postĭcum, i, *n,* back door
postis, is, *m,* door-post
postmŏdo, *adv,* afterwards
postpōno, pŏsŭi, pŏsĭtum, *v.t.* 3, to postpone, neglect
postquam, *conj,* after, when
postrēmo, *adv,* at last
postrēmus, a, um, *adj,* the last
postrīdiē, *adv,* on the next day
postŭlāta, ōrum, *n. pl,* demand, request
postŭlātio, ōnis, *f,* demands, requests
postŭlo, *v.t.* 1, to demand, prosecute, accuse
postŭmus, a, um, *adj,* last-born, posthumous
pŏtātio, ōnis, *f,* drinking
pŏtātor, ōris, *m,* drinker
pŏtens, ntis, *adj,* powerful, master of (*with genit*)
pŏtentātus, ūs, *m,* power, rule
pŏtentĭa, ae, *f,* power, authority
pŏtestas, ātis, *f,* power, dominion, control, value, force, ability, permission, opportunity
pŏtio, ōnis, *f,* a drink
pŏtĭor, *v.* 4, *dep, with abl,* to obtain, hold, possess
pŏtĭor, ĭus, *comp. adj,* preferable
pŏtis, e, *adj,* possible
pŏtĭus, *adv,* preferably
pŏto, *v.i.t.* 1, to drink
pŏtor, ōris, *m,* drinker,
pŏtus, a, um, *adj,* intoxicated, drained
pŏtus, ūs, *m,* a drink
prae, *adv. and prep. with abl,* before, in comparison with
prae se ferre (**gĕrere**), to reveal
praeăcŭo, ŭi, ūtum, *v.t.* 3, to sharpen
praeăcūtus, a, um, *adj,* pointed
praebĕo, *v.t.* 2, to offer, give, show
praecăvĕo, cāvi, cautum, *v.i.t.* 2, to be on one's guard; prevent
praecēdo, cessi, cessum, *v.i.t.* 3, to lead the way; precede
praecellens, ntis, *adj,* excellent
praecelsus, a, um, *adj,* very high
praeceps, cipĭtis, *adj,* headlong
praeceps, cipĭtis, *n,* precipice, danger
praeceptor, ōris, *m,* teacher
praeceptum, i, *n,* rule, maxim, order, command
praecerpo, psi, ptum, *v.t.* 3, to gather before time
praecīdo, cīdi, cīsum, *v.t.* 3, to cut off, cut short
praecĭngo, nxi, nctum, *v.t.* 3, to encircle, gird
praecĭno, nŭi, centum, *v.i.t.* 3, to sing before; predict
praecĭpio, cēpi, ceptum, *v.t.* 3, to receive in advance, anticipate, advise, teach
praecĭpĭto, *v.i.t.* 1, to rush down; throw headlong
praecĭpŭus, a, um, *adj, adv,* **ē,** particular, especial, excellent
praeclārus, a, um, *adj, adv,* **ē,** splendid, excellent
praeclūdo, si, sum, *v.t.* 3, to close
praeco, ōnis, *m,* herald
praecōnĭum, ii, *n,* office of herald, proclamation
praecōnĭus, a, um, *adj,* of a herald
praecordĭa, ōrum, *n.pl,* midriff, heart
praecox, ŏcis, *adj,* premature
praecurro, cŭcurri, cursum, *v.i.t.* 3, to run in front; excel
praecursor, ōris, *m,* scout, spy
praecŭtio, cussi, cussum, *v.t.* 3, to brandish in front
praeda, ae, *f,* plunder, prey
praedātor, ōris, *m,* plunderer
praedātōrĭus, a, um, *adj,* predatory
praedĭātor, ōris, *m,* estate agent
praedĭcātio, ōnis, *f,* proclamation, commendation

praedīco, *v.t.* 1, to proclaim, declare, praise
praedīco, xi, ctum, *v.t.* 3, to predict, advise, command
praedictio, ōnis, *f,* prediction
praedictum, i, *n,* prediction
praedisco, *v.t.* 3, to learn beforehand
praeditus, a, um, *adj,* provided with
praedium, ii, *n,* farm, estate
praedīvēs, ĭtis, *adj,* very rich
praedo, ōnis, *m,* robber
praedor, *v.i.t.* 1, *dep,* to plunder
praedūco, xi, ctum, *v.t.* 3, to make or put in front
praedulcis, e, *adj,* very sweet
praedūrus, a, um, *adj,* very hard
praeĕo, ii, ĭtum, *v.i.t.* 4, to lead the way; recite, dictate
praefātio, ōnis, *f,* preface
praefectūra, ae, *f,* superintendence
praefectus, i, *m,* director, commander, governor
praefĕro, ferre, tŭli, lātum, *v.t, irreg,* to carry in front, offer, prefer, show
praefĭcio, fēci, fectum, *v.t.* 3, to put in command
praefĭdens, ntis, *adj,* over-confident
praefīgo, xi, xum, *v.t.* 3, to fix in front
praefīnio, *v.t.* 3, to fix, appoint
praefluo, *v.i.* 3, to flow past
praefŏdio, fōdi, *v.t.* 3, to dig in front
praefor, fātus, *v.i.t.* 1, *dep,* to say in advance
praefringo, frēgi, fractum, *v.t.* 3, to break off
praefulgĕo, si, *v.i.* 2, to glitter
praegestio, *v.i.* 4, to desire greatly
praegnans, ntis, *adj,* pregnant
praegrăvis, e, *adj,* very heavy
praegrĕdior, gressus, *v.i.t.* 3, *dep,* to go in advance
praeiūdicātus, a, um, *adj,* preconceived
praeiūdicium, ii, *n,* precedent (at law)
praeiūdico, *v.t.* 1, to pre-judge
praelābor, lapsus, *v.i.t.* 3. *dep,* to glide or flow along or past
praelambo, *v.t.* 3, to taste in advance
praelūcĕo, xi, *v.i.* 2, to carry a light in front
praemandāta, ōrum, *n. pl,* warrant of arrest
praemĕditātio, ōnis, *f,* premeditation
praemĕditor, *v.t.* 1, *dep,* to premeditate
praemitto, mīsi, missum, *v.t.* 3, to send in advance
praemium, ii, *n,* booty, reward
praemŏnĕo, *v.t.* 2, to forewarn
praemūnio, *v.t.* 4, to fortify
praenăto, *v.i.* 1, to flow past
praenitĕo, *v.i.* 2, to outshine
praenōmen, ĭnis, *n,* first (Christian) name
praenosco, *v.t.* 3, to learn in advance
praenuntio, *v.t.* 1, to predict
praenuntius, a, um, *adj,* foreboding
praenuntius, i, *m,* foreteller
praeoccūpo, *v.t.* 1, to seize in advance
praeopto, *v.t.* 1, to prefer
praepārātio, ōnis, *f,* preparation
praepăro, *v.t.* 1, to prepare
praepĕdio, *v.t.* 4, to bind, obstruct
praependĕo, *v.i.* 2, to hang down in front
praepes, ĕtis, *adj,* swift
praepes, ĕtis, *c,* bird
praepinguis, e, *adj,* very fat
praepōno, pŏsŭi, pŏsĭtum, *v.t.* 3, to put first, put in command, prefer
praepŏsitio, ōnis, *f,* preference
praepŏsĭtus, i, *m,* chief, head
praepostĕrus, a, um, *adj,* preposterous
praepŏtens, ntis, *adj,* very powerful
praeprŏpĕrus, a, um, *adj,* sudden, precipitate
praeripio, rĭpŭi, reptum, *v.t.* 3, to snatch away
praerōdo, rōsum, *v.t.* 3, to nibble
praerŏgātīva, ae, *f,* the Roman tribe to which the first vote was allotted
praerumpo, rūpi, ruptum, *v.t.* 3, to break off
praeruptus, a, um, *adj,* steep
praes, dis, *m,* security, bail
praesaepe, is, *n,* stable, pen
praesaepio, psi, ptum, *v.t.* 4, to barricade
praesāgio, *v.t.* 4, to have a presentiment or premonition
praesāgium, ii, *n,* a foreboding
praesāgus, a, um, *adj,* foretelling
praescisco, *v.t.* 3, to learn in advance
praescius, a, um, *adj,* knowing in advance
praescribo, psi, ptum, *v.t.* 3, to order, appoint, prescribe
praescriptio, ōnis, *f,* excuse, order, law
praescriptum, i, *n,* order, law
praesens, ntis, *adj,* present, prompt, powerful, resolute, helping
praesensio, ōnis, *f,* foreboding
praesentia, ae, *f,* presence
praesentia, ium, *n. pl,* present circumstances
praesentio, si, sum, *v.t.* 4, to have a premonition
praesēpe, see **praesaepe**
praesertim, *adv,* especially

praeses, ĭdis, *adj*, guarding
praeses, ĭdis, *c*, guardian, chief
praesidĕo, sēdi, *v.i.t.* 2, to guard, direct, superintend
praesidĭum, ii, *n*, garrison, fortification, camp
praesignis, e, *adj*, excellent, distinguished
praestābĭlis, e, *adj*, excellent, distinguished
praestans, ntis, *adj*, excellent, distinguished
praestantĭa, ae, *f*, excellence
praestat, *v.* 1, *impers*, it is preferable
praestĭgiae, ārum, *f. pl*, juggling-tricks
praestĭtŭo, ŭi, ūtum, *v.t.* 3, to appoint in advance
praesto, *adv*, ready, present
praesto, stĭti, stĭtum, *v.i.t.* 1, to be superior; surpass, vouch for, perform, fulfil, show, give, offer
praestringo, nxi, ctum, *v.t.* 3, to tie up, graze, blunt
praestrŭo, xi, ctum, *v.t.* 3, to build or block up
praesum praeesse, praefŭi, *v.i, irreg, with dat*, to be in command of
praesūmo, mpsi, mptum, *v.t.* 3, to anticipate, imagine in advance
praetendo, di, tum, *v.t.* 3, to hold out, pretend
praetento, *v.t.* 1, to examine in advance
praeter, *adv, and prep. with acc*, past, beyond, beside, except, unless
praetĕrĕā, *adv*, besides, henceforth
praetĕrĕo, ii, ĭtum, *v.i.t.* 4, to pass by; go past, omit, neglect
praeterflŭo, xi, ctum, *v.i.* 3, to flow past
praetergrĕdĭor, gressus, *v.i.t.* 3, *dep*, to pass beyond
praetĕritus, a, um, *adj*, past, gone
praeterlābor, lapsus, *v.i.t.* 3, *dep*, to glide or flow past
praetermissio, ōnis, *f*, omission
praetermitto, mīsi, missum, *v.t.* 3, to let pass, omit, neglect
praeterquam, *adv*, besides, except
praetervĕhor, vectus, *v.i.t.* 3, *dep*, to sail, ride or drive past
praetervŏlo, *v.i.t.* 1, to escape; fly past
praetexo, xŭi, xtum, *v.t.* 3, to edge, border, pretend
praetexta, ae, *f*, purple-edged toga worn by Roman magistrates and children
praetexta, ae, *f*, a tragedy
praetextātus, a, um, *adj*, wearing the toga praetexta
praetextus, a, um, *adj*, wearing the toga praetexta
praetor, ōris, *m*, chief, head, Roman magistrate concerned with administration of justice
praetōrĭum, ii, *n*, general's tent, governor's residence
praetōrĭus, a, um, *adj*, of the praetor or general
praetūra, ae, *f*, praetorship
praeūro, ussi, ustum, *v.t.* 3, to burn at the end
praeustus, a, um, *adj*, burnt, frost-bitten
praevălĕo, *v.i.* 2, to be superior
praevălĭdus, a, um, *adj*, very strong
praevĕhor, ctus, *v.i.t.* 3, *dep*, to ride, fly or flow in front
praevĕnio, vēni, ventum, *v.i.t.* 4, to come before; outstrip
praeverto, ti, *v.t.* 3, to outstrip, anticipate, prevent
praevertor, sus, *v.i.t.* 3, *dep*, to concentrate one's attention (on)
praevĭdĕo, vīdi, vīsum, *v.t.* 2, to anticipate, see in advance
praevĭus, a, um, *adj*, leading the way
prandĕo, di, sum, *v.i.t.* 2, to breakfast, lunch, (on)
prandĭum, ii, *n*, breakfast, luncheon
pransus, a, um, *adj*, having breakfasted
prātensis, e, *adj*, growing in meadows
prātŭlum, i, *n*, small meadow
prātum, i, *n*, meadow
prāvitas, ātis, *f*, deformity, depravity
prāvus, a, um, *adj, adv*, ē, wrong, bad, deformed
prĕcārĭus, a, um, *adj, adv*, ō, obtained by prayer
prĕcātio, ōnis, *f*, prayer
prĕciae, ārum, *f. pl*, grape-vine
prĕcor, *v.i.t.* 1, *dep*, to pray, beg
prĕhendo, di, sum, *v.t.* 3, to seize, detain, take by surprise
prĕhenso, *v.t.* 1, to grasp, detain
prēlum, i, *n*, wine-press
prĕmo, ssi, ssum, *v.t.* 3, to press, grasp, cover, close, pursue closely, load, overwhelm, plant, prune, check, repress
prendo, see **prĕhendo**
prensus, a, um, *adj*, grasped
presso, *v.t.* 1, to press
pressus, ūs, *m*, pressure
pressus, a, um, *adj*, subdued, compact
prĕtiōsus, a, um, *adj, adv*, ē, valuable, costly

For List of Abbreviations used, turn to pages 3, 4

prĕtĭum, ii, *n*, price, value, money, wages, reward
prex, prĕcis, *f*, prayer, request
prĭdem, *adv*, long ago
prĭdiē, *adv*, on the day before
prĭmaevus, a, um, *adj*, youthful
prĭmārius, a, um, *adj*, of the first rank, chief
prĭmĭgĕnus, a, um, *adj*, primitive
prĭmĭpĭlus, *see* **pilus**
prĭmĭtĭae, ārum, *f. pl*, first-fruits
prĭmō, *adv*, at first
prĭmordĭa, ōrum, *n. pl*, origin
prĭmōris, e, *adj*, first, front end
prĭmōres, um, *m. pl*, nobles
prĭmum, *adv*, at first; **cum prĭmum,** as soon as; **quam prĭmum,** as soon as possible
prĭmus, a, um, *adj*, first, chief
princeps, cĭpis, *adj*, first, chief
princeps, cĭpis, *m*, chief, originator
principālis, e, *adj*, original, primitive, principal
principālis, is, *m*, overseer
principātus, ūs, *m*, the first place, command, rule
principĭo, *adv*, in the beginning
principĭum, ii, *n*, origin; *in pl*, principles, elements
prĭor, ĭus, *comp. adj*, previous, former
prĭōres, um, *m. pl*, ancestors
priscus, a, um, *adj*, ancient
prisma, ătis, *n*, prism
pristĭnus, a, um, *adj*, primitive
prĭus, *comp. adv*, previously
prĭusquam, *conj*, before
prĭvātim, *adv*, privately
prĭvātio, ōnis, *f*, taking-away
prĭvātus, a, um, *adj*, private
prĭvātus, i, *m*, private citizen
prĭvigna, ae, *f*, step-daughter
prĭvignus, i, *m*, step-son
prĭvilēgium, ii, *n*, bill or law concerned with an individual
prĭvo, *v.t.* 1, to deprive, release
prĭvus, a, um, *adj*, one's own
prō, *prep. with abl*, before, in front of, on behalf of, instead of, just as, on account of, according to, in relation to
prō! (prōh!), *interj*, Ah! Alas!
prŏăvus, i, *m*, great-grandfather
prŏbābĭlis, e, *adj, adv,* **ĭter,** likely, pleasing
prŏbābĭlĭtas, ātis, *f*, probability
prŏbātio, ōnis, *f*, trial, proving
prŏbātus, a, um, *adj*, tried, good
prŏbĭtas, ātis, *f*, honesty
prŏbo, *v.t.* 1, to try, test, approve of, recommend, prove
prŏboscis, ĭdis, *f*, elephant's trunk
prŏbrōsus, a, um, *adj*, shameful
prŏbrum, i, *n*, disgraceful deed, lechery, disgrace, abuse
prŏbus, a, um, *adj, adv,* **ē,** good, honest, virtuous
prŏcăcĭtas, ātis, *f*, impudence
prŏcax, ācis, *adj*, impudent
prŏcēdo, cessi, cessum, *v.i.* 3, to go forward, advance, turn out, prosper
prŏcella, ae, *f*, storm, violence
prŏcellōsus, a, um, *adj*, tempestuous
prŏcer, ĕris, *m*, chief, prince
prŏcērĭtas, ātis, *f*, height
prŏcērus, a, um, *adj*, tall
prŏcessus, ūs, *m*, advance
prŏcĭdo, di, *v.i.* 3, to fall flat
prŏcinctus, ūs, *m*, readiness for battle
prŏclāmo, *v.t.* 1, to cry out
prŏclīno, *v.t.* 1, to bend forwards
prŏclīve, is, *n*, slope, descent
prŏclīvis, e, *adj*, sloping downhill, liable, willing
prŏconsul, is, *m*, provincial governor
prŏcrastino, *v.t.* 1, to defer
prŏcrĕātio, ōnis, *f*, procreation
prŏcrĕātor, ōris, *m*, creator
prŏcrĕo, *v.t.* 1, to produce
prŏcŭbo, *v.i.* 1, to lie stretched-out
prŏcūdo, di, sum, *v.t.* 3, to forge
prŏcul, *adv*, in the distance
prŏculco, *v.t.* 1, to trample on
prŏcumbo, cŭbŭi, cŭbĭtum, *v.i.* 3, to lean or fall forwards, sink
prŏcūrātio, ōnis, *f*, administration
prŏcūrātor, ōris, *m*, manager, agent
prŏcūro, *v.t.* 1, to look after
prŏcurro, curri, cursum, *v.i.* 3, to run forward, project
prŏcus, i, *m*, suitor
prŏdĕo, ii, ĭtum, *v.i.* 3, to come forward, appear
prŏdesse, see **prŏsum**
prŏdĭgĭōsus, a, um, *adj*, strange, marvellous
prŏdĭgium, ii, *n*, omen, monster
prŏdĭgus, a, um, *adj*, wasteful
prŏdĭtio, ōnis, *f*, treachery
prŏdĭtor, ōris, *m*, traitor
prŏdo, didi, ditum, *v.t.* 3, to bring out, relate, betray, bequeath
prŏdūco, xi, ctum, *v.t.* 3, to lead forward, prolong, produce, promote
prŏductus, a, um, *adj, adv,* **ē,** prolonged
proelĭor, *v.i.* 1, *dep*, to join battle

proelĭum, ii, *n*, battle
prŏfāno, *v.t.* 1, to desecrate
prŏfānus, a, um, *adj*, wicked, common
prŏfectĭo, ōnis, *f*, departure
prŏfectō, *adv*, certainly
prŏfectus, ūs, *m*, advance
prŏfectus, a, um, *adj*, having advanced
prŏfĕro, ferre, tŭli, lātum, *v.t, irreg*, to bring out, extend, defer, reveal, mention; with **gradum**, to proceed; with **signa**, to march forward
prŏfessor, ōris, *m*, teacher, professor
prŏfessĭo, ōnis, *f*, declaration
prŏfessus, a, um, *adj*, avowed
prŏfestus, a, um, *adj*, working (days)
prŏficĭo, fēci, fectum, *v.i.t.* 3, to progress; perform, help
prŏficiscor, prŏfectus, *v.i.* 3, *dep*, to set out, originate
prŏfitĕor, fessus, *v.i.* 2, *dep*, to declare, acknowledge, promise
prŏflĭgātus, a, um, *adj*, wretched, dissolute
prŏflĭgo, *v.t.* 1, to overthrow
prŏflo, *v.t.* 1, to blow out
prŏflŭo, xi, xum, *v.i.* 3, to flow out, proceed
prŏflŭens, ntis, *adj*, fluent
prŏflŭvĭum, ii, *n*, flowing out
prŏfor, *v.t.* 1, *dep*, to speak, say
prŏfŭgĭo, fūgi, *v.i.t.* 3, to escape; flee from
prŏfŭgus, a, um, *adj*, fugitive
prŏfŭgus, i, *m*, fugitive, exile
prŏfundo, fūdi, fūsum, *v.t.* 3, to pour out, utter, squander
prŏfundum, i, *n*, the deep, the sea, an abyss
prŏfundus, a, um, *adj*, deep
prŏfūsĭo, ōnis, *f*, outpouring, prodigal use
prŏfūsus, a, um, *adj*, extravagant
prŏgĕnĕro, *v.t.* 1, to beget
prŏgĕnies, ēi, *f*, family, offspring
prŏgigno, gĕnŭi, gĕnĭtum, *v.t.* 3, to produce
prŏgnātus, a, um, *adj*, born
prŏgnātus, i, *m*, descendant
prŏgrĕdĭor, gressus, *v.i.* 3, *dep*, to advance, proceed
prŏgressĭo, ōnis, *f*, growth
prŏgressus, ūs, *m*, advance
proh!, see **prō!**
prŏhibĕo, *v.t.* 2, to prevent, prohibit, defend
prŏiectus, a, um, *adj*, projecting
prŏĭcĭo, iēci, iectum, *v.t.* 3, to throw forward, extend, expel, yield, disdain
prŏin or **prŏindĕ,** *adv*, in the same way, equally, accordingly, therefore
prŏlābor, lapsus, *v.i.* 3, *dep*, to slip or slide forward, fall
prŏlātĭo, ōnis, *f*, postponement, mentioning
prŏlāto, *v.t.* 1, to postpone
prŏles, is, *f*, offspring, child
prŏlĕtārĭus, ii, *m*, citizen of lowest class
prŏlixus, a, um, *adj, adv*, **ē**, stretched out, fortunate
prŏlŏgus, i, *m*, prologue
prŏlūdo, si, sum, *v.i.* 3, to practise in advance
prŏlŭo, lŭi, lūtum, *v.t.* 3, to wash away, moisten
prŏlūsĭo, ōnis, *f*, prelude
prŏlŭvies, ēi, *f*, overflow
prŏmĕrĕo, *v.t.* 2, to deserve, merit
prŏmĕrĕor, *v.t.* 2, *dep*, to deserve, merit
prŏmĭnens, ntis, *adj*, prominent
prŏmĭnĕo, *v.i.* 2, to project
prŏmiscŭus, a, um, *adj*, common, indiscriminate
prŏmissĭo, ōnis, *f*, promise
prŏmissum, i, *n*, promise
prŏmissus, a, um, *adj*, hanging
prŏmitto, mīsi, missum, *v.t.* 3, to promise, assure
prŏmo, mpsi, mptum, *v.t.* 3, to bring out, produce, tell
prŏmontŭrĭum, ii, *n*, headland
prŏmŏvĕo, mŏvi, mŏtum, *v.t.* 2, to move forward, extend
promptus, a, um, *adj*, ready, quick
promptus, ūs, *m*, only in phrase; **in promptu**, in public; **in promptu esse**, to be at hand
prŏmulgo, *v.t.* 1, to publish
prŏmus, i, *m*, butler
prŏmŭtŭus, a, um, *adj*, loaned
prŏnĕpos, ōtis, *m*, great-grandson
prŏnōmen, ĭnis, *n*, pronoun
prŏnŭba, ae, *f*, bridesmaid
prŏnuntiātĭo, ōnis, *f*, proclamation
prŏnuntĭo, *v.t.* 1, to announce
prŏnus, a, um, *adj*, leaning or bending forward, disposed; setting, sinking (of stars, etc.)
prŏoemĭum, ii, *n*, preface
prŏpāgātĭo, ōnis, *f*, extension
prŏpāgo, *v.t.* 1, to generate, extend
prŏpāgo, ĭnis, *f*, shoot (of plant), offspring, child
prŏpālam, *adv*, openly
prŏpătŭlus, a, um, *adj*, uncovered
prŏpe, *adv. and prep. with acc*, near, nearly
prŏpĕdĭem, *adv*, soon

prōpello, pŭli, pulsum, *v.t.* 3, to push or drive forward
prōpĕmŏdum, *adv,* almost
prōpendĕo, di, sum, *v.i.* 2, to be inclined or disposed
prōpensus, a, um, *adj,* inclined, disposed
prōpĕro, *v.i.t.* 1, to hurry
prōpĕrus, a, um, *adj, adv,* **ē,** quick, hurrying
prōpexus, a, um, *adj,* combed forward
prōpīno, *v.t.* 1, to drink a toast
prōpinquĭtas, ātis, *f,* nearness, relationship
prōpinquo, *v.i.t.* 1, to approach; hasten
prŏpinquus, a, um, *adj,* near
prōpinquus, i, *m,* relative
prŏpior, ius, *comp. adj,* nearer
prōpitĭus, a, um, *adj,* kind, favourable
prŏpius, *comp. adv,* nearer
prōpōno, pŏsŭi, pŏsĭtum, *v.t.* 3, to put forward, state, display, offer
prōpŏsĭtio, ōnis, *f,* representation, theme
prōpŏsĭtum, i, *n,* plan, purpose
prŏprĭĕtas, ātis, *f,* peculiarity
prŏprĭus, a, um, *adj, adv,* **ē,** special, particular, its (his, her) own
propter, *prep. with acc,* on account of, near; *adv,* nearby
proptĕrĕā, *adv,* for that reason
prōpugnācŭlum, i, *n,* rampart
prōpugnātio, ōnis, *f,* defence
prōpugnātor, ōris, *m,* defender
prōpugno, *v.i.t.* 1, to make sorties; defend
prōpulso, *v.t.* 1, to ward off
prōra, ae, *f,* prow, ship
prōrēpo, psi, ptum, *v.i.* 3, to creep out, crawl forward
prōrĭpio, pŭi, reptum, *v.t.* 3, to drag forward; with **se,** to rush
prōrŏgātio, ōnis, *f,* prolonging
prōrŏgo, *v.t.* 1, to prolong, defer
prorsus (prorsum), *adv,* certainly, utterly
prōrumpo, rūpi, ruptum, *v.i.t.* 3, to rush forward; send forward
prōrŭo, rŭi, rŭtum, *v.i.t.* 3, to rush forward; overthrow
proscaenium, ii, *n,* stage
prōscindo, scĭdi, scissum, *v.t.* 3, to tear up, plough
prōscrĭbo, psi, ptum, *v.t.* 3, to publish, confiscate, outlaw
prōscriptio, ōnis, *f,* confiscation, outlawing
prōscriptus, i, *m,* outlaw
prōsēmĭno, *v.t.* 1, to sow
prōsĕquor, sĕcūtus, *v.t.* 3, *dep,* to accompany, follow, pursue, bestow, proceed with
prōsilio, ŭi, *v.i.* 4, to leap up
prospecto, *v.t.* 1, to look at, expect, await
prospectus, ūs, *m,* view, sight
prospĕrus, a, um, *adj, adv,* **ē,** favourable, fortunate
prospĕrĭtas, ātis, *f,* prosperity
prospĕro, *v.t.* 1, to make (something) successful
prōspĭcio, spexi, spectum, *v.i.t.* 3, to look out; discern, overlook, foresee
prōsterno, strāvi, strātum, *v.t.* 3, to overthrow, prostrate
prōsŭbigo, *v.t.* 3, to dig up
prōsum, prōdesse, prōfŭi, *v.i, irreg. with dat,* to be useful
prōtectum, i, *n,* eaves
prōtĕgo, xi, ctum, *v.t.* 3, to cover, protect
prōtēlum, i, *n,* team of oxen
prōtendo, di, sum (tum), *v.t.* 3, to stretch out, extend
prōtĕro, trīvi, trĭtum, *v.t.* 3, to trample down, crush, destroy
prōterrĕo, *v.t.* 2, to terrify
prōtervĭtas, ātis, *f,* impudence
prōtervus, a, um, *adj, adv,* **ē,** forward, impudent, violent
prōtinus, *adv,* straightforwards, continuously, immediately
prōtrăho, xi, ctum, *v.t.* 3, to drag forward, reveal
prōtrūdo, si, sum, *v.t.* 3, to push out
prōturbo, *v.t.* 1, to repel
prout, *adv,* just as
prōvectus, a, um, *adj,* advanced (of time)
prōvĕho, xi, ctum, *v.t.* 3, to carry forward, advance, promote
prōvĕnio, vēni, ventum, *v.i.* 4, to be born, thrive, occur, turn out (well or badly)
prōventus, ūs, *m,* produce, result
prōverbĭum, ii, *n,* proverb
prōvĭdens, ntis, *adj,* prudent
prōvĭdentia, ae, *f,* foresight
prōvĭdĕo, vīdi, vīsum, *v.i.t.* 2, to make preparations; foresee, provide for
prōvĭdus, a, um, *adj,* prudent
prōvincia, ae, *f,* province, duty, sphere of duty
prōvincĭālis, e, *adj,* provincial
prōvŏcātio, ōnis, *f,* appeal
prōvŏco, *v.i.t.* 1, to appeal; call out, challenge, rouse
prōvŏlo, *v.i.* 1, to fly out

prōvolvo, volvi, vŏlūtum, *v.t.* 3, to roll forward
proxĭmē, *adv*, nearest, next
proxĭmĭtas, ātis, *f*, proximity
proxĭmus, a, um, *adj*, nearest, next, previous
prūdens, ntis, *adj, adv*, **nter,** experienced, wise, sensible
prūdentĭa, ae, *f*, experience, skill, discretion
prŭīna, ae, *f*, frost, snow
prŭīnōsus, a, um, *adj*, frosty
prūna, ae, *f*, burning coal
prūnum, i, *n*, plum
prūnus, i, *f*, plum-tree
prūrĭo, *v.i.* 4, to itch
prūrĭtus, ūs, *m*, itching
psallo, i, *v.i.* 3, to play on an instrument
psalmus, i, *m*, a psalm
psittăcus, i, *m*, parrot
ptĭsăna, ae, *f*, pearl-barley
pūbens, ntis, *adj*, flourishing
pūbertas, ātis, *f*, puberty, manhood
pūbes (pūber), ĕris, *adj*, adult
pūbes, is, *f*, young men
pūbesco, bŭi, *v.i.* 3, to grow up, ripen
pūblĭcānus, i, *m*, tax-collector
pūblĭcātĭo, ōnis, *f*, confiscation
pūblĭco, *v.t.* 1, to confiscate
pūblĭcum, i, *n*, a public place
pūblĭcus, a, um, *adj, adv*, **ē,** of the state, public, general
pŭdendus, a, um, *adj*, disgraceful
pŭdens, ntis, *adj, adv*, **nter,** modest
pŭdet, *v.* 2, *impers*, it brings shame
pŭdĭbundus, a, um, *adj*, modest
pŭdĭcĭtĭa, ae, *f*, modesty, virtue
pŭdĭcus, a, um, *adj*, modest, pure
pŭdor, ōris, *m*, a sense of decency, shyness
pŭella, ae, *f*, girl, sweetheart, young wife
pŭellāris, e, *adj*, girlish
pŭer, ĕri, *m*, boy
pŭĕrĭlis, e, *adj*, youthful
pŭĕrĭtĭa (pŭertĭa), ae, *f*, childhood, youth
pŭgil, ĭlis, *m*, boxer
pŭgillāres, ĭum, *m. pl*, writing-tablets
pŭgĭo, ōnis, *m*, dagger
pugna, ae, *f*, fight, battle
pugnātor, ōris, *m*, fighter
pugnax, ācis, *adj*, warlike, quarrelsome
pugno, *v.i.* 1, to fight, disagree, struggle
pugnus, i, *m*, fist
pulcher, chra, chrum, *adj, adv*, **ē,** beautiful, handsome, glorious
pulchritūdo, ĭnis, *f*, beauty
pūlex, ĭcis, *m*, flea
pullārĭus, ii, *m*, chicken-keeper
pullŭlo, *v.i.* 1, to sprout
pullus, i. *m*, young animal, chicken
pullus, a, um, *adj*, dark, black
pulmentārium, ii, *n*, sauce
pulmentum, i, *n*, sauce
pulmo, ōnis, *m*, lung
pulpĭtum, i, *n*, platform
puls, pultis, *f*, porridge
pulsātĭo, ōnis, *f*, beating
pulso, *v.t.* 1, to beat, push, touch, disturb
pulsus, ūs, *m*, push, blow, beating
pulvĕrĕus, a, um, *adj*, dusty
pulvĕrŭlentus, a, um, *adj*, dusty
pulvīnar, āris, *n*, couch
pulvīnus, i, *m*, cushion
pulvis, ĕris, *m*, dust
pūmex, ĭcis, *m*, pumice-stone
pūmilĭo, ōnis, *m*, dwarf
punctim, *adv*, with the point
punctum, i, *n*, point, vote, moment
pungo, pŭpŭgi, punctum, *v.t.* 3, to prick, sting, vex, annoy
pūnicĕus, a, um, *adj*, red
pūnio, *v.t.* **(pūnior,** *v.t.dep.*) 4, to punish
pūpa, ae, *f*, doll
pūpilla, ae, *f*, orphan, ward
pūpillus, i, *m*, orphan, ward
puppis, is, *f*, ship's stern
pūpŭla, ae, *f*, pupil of the eye
purgāmen, ĭnis, *n*, refuse, filth
purgāmentum, i, *n*, refuse, filth
purgātĭo, ōnis, *f*, cleansing
purgo, *v.t.* 1, to clean, purify, excuse, justify, atone for
purpŭra, ae, *f*, purple, purple clothes
purpŭrĕus, a, um, *adj*, purple, clothed in purple, brilliant
pūrum, i, *n*, clear sky
pūrus, a, um, *adj, adv*, **ē,** pure, clean, plain
pūs, pūris, *n*, pus
pūsillus, a, um, *adj*, little, petty
pūsĭo, ōnis, *m*, urchin
pustŭla, ae, *f*, pimple
pūtāmen, ĭnis, *f*, peel, shell
pūtĕal, ālis, *n*, fence of a well
pūtĕo, *v.i.* 2, to stink
pūter (pūtris), tris, tre, *adj*, decaying, rotten
pūtesco, pūtŭi, *v.i.* 3, to rot
pūtĕus, i, *m*, well, pit
pūtĭdus, a, um, *adj*, rotten, disgusting
pūto, *v.t.* 1, to think, prune
pūtresco, *v.i.* 3, to decay
pūtrĭdus, a, um, *adj*, rotten
pŷra, ae, *f*, funeral pyre

For List of Abbreviations used, turn to pages 3, 4

pȳrămis, ĭdis, *f,* pyramid
pȳrum, i, *n,* pear
pȳrus, i, *f,* pear-tree
pȳthon, ōnis, *m,* python
pyxis, ĭdis, *f,* box

Q

quā, *adv,* where, in which direction, how; **qua . . . qua,** partly . . . partly
quācumque, *adv,* wheresoever
quādra, ae, *f,* square, dining-table
quādrāgēni, ae, a, *adj,* forty each
quādrāgēsimus, a, um, *adj,* fortieth
quādrāgies, *adv,* forty times
quādrāginta, *adj,* forty
quādrans, ntis, *m,* a quarter
quādrātum, i, *n,* square
quādrātus, a, um, *adj,* square
quādrīdŭum, ii, *n,* period of four days
quādrīfārĭam, *adv,* into four parts
quādrīfĭdus, a, um, *adj,* split into four
quādrīgae, ārum, *f. pl,* four-horse team or chariot
quādriiŭgis, e, *adj,* yoked in a four-horse team
quādriiŭgus, a, um, *adj,* yoked in a four-horse team
quādrilătĕrus, a, um, *adj,* quadrilateral
quādrīmus, a, um, *adj,* four years old
quādringēnārius, a, um, *adj,* of four hundred each
quādringenti, ae, a, *adj,* four hundred
quādringenties, *adv,* four hundred times
quādro, *v.i.t.* 1, to be square, agree; make square, complete
quādrum, i, *n,* square
quādrŭpēdans, ntis, *adj,* galloping
quādrŭpēs, ĕdis, *adj,* galloping, going on four feet
quādrŭplex, ĭcis, *adj,* quadruple
quādrŭplum, i, *n,* fourfold amount
quaero, sīvi, sītum, *v.t.* 3, to search for, acquire, inquire
quaesītio, ōnis, *f,* investigation
quaesītor, ōris, *m,* investigator
quaesītum, i, *n,* question
quaesītus, a, um, *adj,* far-fetched
quaeso, īvi, *v.t.* 3, to beseech, seek
quaestio, ōnis, *f,* investigation, trial, case, question, problem
quaestor, ōris, *m,* Roman magistrate in charge of public revenues
quaestōrius, a, um, *adj,* of a quaestor
quaestŭōsus, a, um, *adj,* profitable
quaestūra, ae, *f,* quaestorship
quaestus, ūs, *m,* gain, profit, employment
quālis, e, *adj,* of what kind
quāliscumque, quālĕcumque, *adj,* of whatever kind
quālĭtas, ātis, *f,* state, condition
quālum, i, *n,* basket, hamper
quam, *adv,* how; *with comparatives,* than
quamdiu, *adv,* as long as, until
quamlĭbet, *adv,* as much as you wish
quāmobrem, *adv,* why, wherefore
quamprīmum, *adv,* as soon as possible
quamquam, *conj,* although
quamvis, *conj,* although; *adv,* very
quando, *adv,* when?, some time; *conj,* since, because
quandōcumque, *adv,* whenever
quandōque, *adv,* whenever, at some time or other
quandōquĭdem, *adv,* since
quanti? at what price?
quantō, *adv,* by as much as
quantŏpĕrĕ, *adv,* how much
quantŭlus, a, um, *adj,* how small
quantŭluscumque, *adj,* however small
quantum, *adv,* as much as
quantus, a, um, *adj,* how great
quantuscumque, *adj,* however big
quantusvis, quantāvis, quantumvis, *adj,* as big as you like
quāpropter, *adv,* wherefore
quārē, *adv,* wherefore, why
quartānus, a, um, *adj,* occurring on the fourth day
quartum, *adv,* for the fourth time
quartō, *adv,* for the fourth time
quartus, a, um, *adj,* fourth
quāsi, *adv,* as if, just as
quāsillum, i, *n,* small basket
quassātio, ōnis, *f,* shaking
quasso, *v.t.* 1, to shake, shatter
quātēnus, *adv,* to what extent, how long, since
quāter, *adv,* four times
quāterni, ae, a, *pl. adj,* four each
quātio (*no perf.*), **quassum,** *v.t.* 3, to shake, shatter, excite
quattŭor, *indecl. adj,* four
quattŭordĕcim, *adj,* fourteen
quĕ *conj,* and
quĕmadmŏdum, *adv,* how
quĕo, ii, ĭtum, *v.i.* 4, to be able
quercētum, i, *n,* oak-forest
quercus, ūs, *f,* oak-tree
quĕrēla, ae, *f,* complaint

quĕrĭbundus, a, um, *adj*, complaining
quĕrĭmōnĭa, ae, *f*, complaint
quernus, a, um, *adj*, of oak
quĕror, questus, *v.i.t.* 3, *dep*, to complain
quĕrŭlus, a, um, *adj*, full of complaints, cooing, chirping
questus, ūs, *m*, complaint
qūi, quae, quod, *rel. pron*, who, which, what
quī, *adv*, how, wherewith
quiă, *conj*, because
quicquid, *pron*, whatever
quĭcumque, quaecumque, quodcumque, *pron*, whoever, whatever
quid, *interr. pron*, what? why?
quĭdam, quaedam, quoddam, *pron*, a certain somebody or something
quĭdem, *adv*, indeed; **ne . . . quidem,** not even . . .
quidni, why not?
quies, ētis, *f*, rest, quiet
quiescens, ntis, *adj*, quiescent
quiesco, ēvi, ētum, *v.i.* 3, to rest, keep quiet, sleep
quiētus, a, um, *adj*, calm
quilĭbet, quaelĭbet, quodlĭbet, *pron*, anyone or anything you like
quīn, *conj*, that not, but that, indeed, why not
quīnam, quaenam, quodnam, *pron*, who, what, which
quincunx, ncis, *m*, five-twelfths, trees planted in oblique lines
quindĕcies, *adv*, fifteen times
quindĕcim, *indecl. adj*, fifteen
quingēni, ae, a, *pl. adj*, five hundred each
quingenti, ae, a, *pl. adj*, five hundred
quingenties, *adv*, five hundred times
quīni, ae, a, *pl. adj*, five each
quinquāgēni, ae, a, *pl. adj*, fifty each
quinquāgēsĭmus, a, um, *adj*, fiftieth
quinquāginta, *indecl. adj*, fifty
quinquātrĭa, ōrum, *n.pl*, festival of Minerva (19th–23rd March)
quinquĕ, *indecl. adj*, five
quinquennālis, e, *adj*, quinquennial
quinquennis, e, *adj*, every fifth year
quinquennĭum, ii, *n*, period of five years
quinquĕrēmis, *adj*, ship with five banks of oars
quinquiens, *adv*, five times
Quintĭlis (mensis), July
quintus, a, um, *adj*, fifth
quippe, *adv*, certainly; *conj*, in as much as
quis, quid, *interr pron*, who? which? what? *indef. pron*, anyone, anything
quisnam, quaenam, quidnam, *interr. pron*, who? which?
quispĭam, quaepĭam, quodpĭam, *indef. pron*, anybody, anything
quisquam, quaequam, quicquam, *indef. pron*, anyone, anything
quisque, quaeque, quodque, *indef. pron*, each, every, everybody, everything
quisquĭlĭae, ārum, *f. pl*, rubbish
quisquis, quaeque, quodquod, *indef. pron*, whoever, whatever
quīvis, quaevis, quodvis, *indef. pron*, anyone or anything you please
quō, *adv. and conj*, wherefore, where to, whither, so that
quŏad, *adv*, as long as, until, as far as
quōcircā, *conj*, wherefore
quōcumque, *adv*, to whatever place
quod, *conj*, because
quod, *neuter of* **qui**
quōdammŏdo, in a certain manner
quōmĭnus, *conj*, that . . . not
quōmŏdŏ, *adv*, how
quondam, *adv*, once, at times
quŏnĭam, *adv*, since, because
quōquam, *adv*, to any place
quŏque, *conj*, also, too
quōquō, *adv*, to whatever place
quorsum (quorsus), *adv*, to what place, to what purpose
quŏt, *indecl. adj*, how many
quŏtannis, *adv*, every year
quŏtĭdiānus, a, um, *adj*, daily
quŏtĭdie, *adv*, daily
quŏties (quŏtiens), *adv*, how often
quŏtiescumquĕ, *adv*, however often
quotquŏt, *adv*, however many
quŏtus, a, um, *adj*, how many
quŏusquē, *adv*, how long
quum, see **cum**

R

răbĭdus, a, um, *adj*, raving, mad
răbies (em, e), *f*, madness, anger
răbiōsus, a, um, *adj*, raging
răbŭla, ae, *f*, argumentative lawyer
răcēmifer, ĕra, ĕrum, *adj*, clustering
răcēmus, i, *m*, bunch, cluster
rādĭcĭtus, *adv*, by the roots
rădĭans, ntis, *adj*, shining
rădiātĭo, ōnis, *f*, shining
rădio, *v.i.* 1, to shine
rădius, ii, *m*, rod, spoke, radius, shuttle, ray
rādix, īcis, *f*, root, radish, source
rādo, si, sum, *v.t.* 3, to scrape, shave
raeda, ae, *f*, carriage

raedārĭus, i, *m*, coachman
raia, ae, *f*, ray (fish)
rāmālĭa, ĭum, *n.pl*, brushwood
rāmōsus, a, um, *adj*, branching
rāmus, i, *m*, branch
rāna, ae, *f*, frog
rancĭdus, a, um, *adj*, rancid
rānuncŭlus, i, *m*, tadpole
răpācĭtas, ātis, *f*, rapacity
răpax, ācis, *adj*, grasping
răphănus, i, *m*, radish
răpĭdus, a, um, *adj*, *adv*, **ē,** swift, violent, tearing
răpīna, ae, *f*, robbery, plunder
răpĭo, ŭi, raptum, *v.t.* 3, to seize, snatch, drag away
raptim, *adv*, hurriedly
raptĭo, ōnis, *f*, abduction
rapto, *v.t.* 1, to snatch, drag away, plunder
raptor, ōris, *m*, robber
raptum, i, *n*, plunder
raptus, ūs, *m*, robbery, rape
răpŭlum, i, *n*, turnip
rāpum, i, *n*, turnip
rāresco, *v.i.* 3, to grow thin, open out
rārĭtas, ātis, *f*, looseness, rarity, infrequency
rārus, a, um, *adj*, *adv*, **ē, ō,** loose, loose in texture, thin, scattered, straggling, few, remarkable, rare
rāsĭlis, e, *adj*, polished
rastellus, i, *m*, hoe, rake
rastrum, i, *n*, rake, hoe
rātĭo, ōnis, *f*, account, calculation, business affairs, relationship, concern for, consideration, conduct, plan, reason, motive, reckoning, order, law, theory, system, way, manner
rātĭōcĭnor, *v.i.t.* 1, *dep*, to calculate
rātĭōnālis, e, *adj*, rational, theoretical
rātis, is, *f*, raft
rātus, a, um, *adj*, established; (*partic.*) having thought; **pro rātā,** proportionally
raucus, a, um, *adj*, hoarse
rāvus, a, um, *adj*, grey, tawny
rē, rēvērā (*adv.*), really
rēapse, *adv*, (re ipsa), in fact
rĕbellĭo, ōnis, *f*, revolt
rĕbellis, e, *adj*, rebellious
rĕbello, *v.i.* 1, to rebel, rebuff
rĕbŏo, *v.i.* 1, to re-echo
rĕcalcĭtro, *v.i.* 1, to kick back
rĕcalfăcio, fēci, *v.t.* 3, to warm
rĕcandesco, dŭi, *v.i.* 3, to grow white or hot
rĕcanto, (*no perf*) *v.t.* 1, to retract
rĕcēdo, cessi, cessum, *v.i.* 3, to retreat, withdraw
rĕcens, ntis, *adj*, fresh, new
rĕcens, *adv*, newly, recently
rĕcensĕo, ŭi, ĭtum, *v.t.* 2, to count, reckon, survey, review
rĕcensĭo, ōnis, *f*, review
rĕceptăcŭlum, i, *n*, shelter
rĕcepto, *v.t.* 1, to recover
rĕceptor, ōris, *m*, receiver
rĕceptus, ūs, *m*, retreat
rĕcessus, ūs, *m*, retreat, recess
rĕcĭdīvus, a, um, *adj*, recurring
rĕcĭdo, cĭdi, cāsum, *v.i.* 3, to fall back, recoil, return
rĕcĭdo, cīdi, cīsum, *v.t.* 3, to cut down, cut off, cut short
rĕcingo, (*no perf*,) **cinctum,** *v.t.* 3, to loosen
rĕcĭno, *v.i.* 3, to re-echo
rĕcĭpĕro (rĕcŭp-), *v.t.* 1, to regain
rĕcĭpĭo, cēpi, ceptum, *v.t.* 3, to take back, regain, receive, give an assurance; with **sē,** to retreat, recover oneself
rĕcĭprŏco, *v.i.t.* 1, to move backwards
rĕcĭprŏcus, a, um, *adj*, receding
rĕcĭtātĭo, ōnis, *f*, reading aloud
rĕcĭtātor, ōris, *m*, reader
rĕcĭto, *v.t.* 1, to read aloud
rĕclāmātĭo, ōnis, *f*, remonstrance
rĕclāmo, *v.i.t.* 1, to resound; contradict loudly, remonstrate
rĕclīno, *v.t.* 1, to lean back
rĕclūdo, si, sum, *v.t.* 3, to reveal
rĕcognĭtĭo, ōnis, *f*, review
rĕcognosco, gnōvi, gnĭtum, *v.t.* 3, to recollect, investigate
rĕcŏlo, cŏlŭi, cultum, *v.t.* 3, to cultivate again, renew
rĕconcĭlĭātĭo, ōnis, *f*, re-establishment, reconciliation
rĕconcĭlĭo, *v.t.* 1, to restore, reconcile
rĕcondĭtus, a, um, *adj*, hidden
rĕcondo, dĭdi, dĭtum, *v.t.* 3, to put away, hide
rĕcŏquo, xi, ctum, *v.t.* 3, to cook again, forge again
rĕcordātĭo, ōnis, *f*, recollection
rĕcordor, *v.i.t.* 1, *dep*, to think over, remember
rĕcrĕātĭo, ōnis, *f*, recovery
rĕcrĕo, *v.t.* 1, to revive, reproduce
rĕcresco, crēvi, crētum, *v.i.* 3, to grow again
rectā, *adv*, straightforwards
rector, ōris, *m*, master, leader, helmsman
rectum, i, *n*, virtue

rectus, a, um, *adj, adv,* **ē,** straight, upright, correct
rĕcŭbans, ntis, *adj,* recumbent
rĕcŭbo, *v.i.* 1, to lie back
rĕcumbo, cŭbŭi, *v.i.* 3, to lie down
rĕcŭpĕrātĭo, ōnis, *f,* recovery
rĕcŭpĕro, *v.t.* 1, to recover, regain
rĕcurro, curri, *v.i.* 3, to run back, return
rĕcurso, *v.i.* 1, to return
rĕcursus, ūs, *m,* return, retreat
rĕcurvo, *v.t.* 1, to bend back
rĕcurvus, a, um, *adj,* bent
rĕcūsātĭo, ōnis, *f,* refusal
rĕcūso, *v.t.* 1, to refuse
rĕcussus, a, um, *adj,* roused
rĕdargŭo, ŭi, *v.t.* 3, to contradict
reddo, dĭdi, dĭtum, *v.t.* 3, to give back, deliver, pay, produce, render, translate, recite, repeat, resemble
rĕdemptĭo, ōnis, *f,* buying back
rĕdemptor, ōris, *m,* contractor
rĕdĕo, ĭi, ĭtum, *v.i.* 4, to go back, return, be reduced to
rĕdĭgo, ēgi, actum, *v.t.* 3, to bring back, restore, collect, reduce to
rĕdĭmĭcŭlum, i, *n,* necklace
rĕdĭmio, *v.t.* 4, to encircle
rĕdĭmo, ēmi, emptum, *v.t.* 3, to repurchase, ransom, release, hire, obtain
rĕdintĕgro, *v.t.* 1, to restore
rĕditus, ūs, *m,* return
rĕdŏlĕo, *v.i.t.* 2, to smell; smell of
rĕdōno, *v.t.* 1, to restore
rĕdūco, xi, ctum, *v.t.* 3, to bring back, restore
rĕductus, a, um, *adj,* remote
rĕdundantĭa, ae, *f,* redundancy
rĕdundo, *v.i.* 1, to overflow, abound in
rĕdux, dŭcis, *adj,* brought back
rĕfello, fĕlli, *v.t.* 3, to refute
rĕfercĭo, si, tum, *v.t.* 4, to cram
rĕfĕro, fĕrre, rettŭli, rĕlātum, *v.t. irreg,* to bring back, restore, repay, report, reply, propose, record, reckon, refer, resemble; with **pedem,** to retreat
rĕfert, *v, impers,* it is of importance, it matters
rĕfertus, a, um, *adj,* filled
rĕfĭcĭo, fēci, fectum, *v.t.* 3, to re-make, repair, refresh
rĕfĭgo, xi, xum, *v.t.* 3, to unfix
rĕfingo, *v.t.* 3, to renew
rĕflecto, xi, xum, *v.i.t.* 3, to turn back; bend back
rĕflo, *v.i.* 1, to blow back
rĕflŭo, *v.i.* 3, to flow back
rĕformīdo, (*no perf,*) *v.t.* 1, to dread, avoid
rĕfrāgor, *v.i.* 1, *dep,* to resist
rĕfrēno, *v.t.* 1, to curb, check
rĕfrĭco, ŭi, *v.t.* 1, to scratch open
rĕfrĭgĕro, *v.t.* 1, to cool
rĕfrĭgesco, frixi, *v.i.* 3, to grow cool, grow stale
rĕfringo, frēgi, fractum, *v.t.* 3, to break open, break off
rĕfŭgĭo, fūgi, *v.i.t.* 3, to run away, escape; flee from, avoid
rĕfulgĕo, si, *v.i.* 2, to shine
rĕfundo, fūdi, fūsum, *v.t.* 3, to pour out, cause to overflow
rĕfūtandus, *gerundive,* see **rĕfūto**
rĕfūto, *v.t.* 1, to repress, refute
rēgālis, e, *adj,* royal, splendid
rēgĭa, ae, *f,* palace, court
rēgĭfĭcus, a, um, *adj,* royal
rēgigno, *v.t.* 3, to reproduce
rēgimen, ĭnis, *n,* guidance
rēgīna, ae, *f,* queen
rēgĭo, ōnis, *f,* district, region, direction, boundary; **ē rēgiōne,** in a straight line
rēgĭus, a, um, *adj, adv,* **ē,** royal, magnificent
regnātor, ōris, *m,* ruler
regno, *v.i.t.* 1, to reign; rule
regnum, i, *n,* kingdom, sovereignty, dominion
rĕgo, xi, ctum, *v.t.* 3, to rule, guide, direct
rĕgrĕdĭor, gressus, *v.i.* 3, *dep,* to return, retreat
rĕgressus, ūs, *m,* return, retreat
rēgŭla, ae, *f,* wooden-ruler, model, pattern
rēgŭlus, i, *m,* prince
rĕĭcĭo, iēci, iectum, *v.t.* 3, to throw back, repel, reject, postpone
rĕiectĭo, ōnis, *f,* rejection
rĕlābor, lapsus, *v.i.* 3, *dep,* to slide or sink back
rĕlanguesco, gŭi, *v.i.* 3, to grow faint, relax
rĕlātĭo, ōnis, *f,* proposition
rĕlaxo, *v.t.* 1, to loosen, ease
rĕlēgātĭo, ōnis, *f,* banishment
rĕlēgo, *v.t.* 1, to send away, banish
rĕlĕgo, lēgi, lectum, *v.t.* 3, to gather together, travel over again, read over again
rĕlĕvo, *v.t.* 1, to lift up, lighten, comfort, refresh
rĕlictĭo, ōnis, *f,* abandonment
rĕlictus, a, um, *adj,* left
rĕlĭgio, ōnis, *f,* piety, religion,

For List of Abbreviations used, turn to pages 3, 4

religious scruple, good faith, conscientiousness, sanctity
rĕlĭgiōsus, a, um, *adj*, devout, scrupulous, precise, sacred
rĕlĭgo, *v.t.* 1, to bind, fasten
rĕlĭno, lēvi, *v.t.* 3, to unseal
rĕlinquo, rĕlĭqui, lictum, *v.t.* 3, to leave, leave behind, abandon, surrender
rĕlĭquiæ, ārum, *f. pl*, remains
rĕlĭquum, i, *n*, remainder
rĕlĭquus, a, um, *adj*, remaining
rĕlūcĕo, xi, *v.i.* 2, to shine
rĕluctor, *v.i.* 1, *dep*, to resist
rĕmănĕo, nsi, *v.i.* 2, to stay behind, endure
rĕmĕdĭum, ii, *n*, cure, relief
rĕmĕo, *v.i.* 1, to return
rĕmētĭor, mensus, *v.t.* 4, *dep*, to remeasure
rēmex, ĭgis, *m*, oarsman
rēmigĭum, ii, *n*, rowing, oars, rowers
rēmigo, *v.i.* 1, to row
rĕmĭgro, *v.i.* 1, to return
rĕminiscor, *v.* 3, *dep, with genit*, to remember
rĕmiscĕo, *no perf*, **mixtum,** *v.t.* 2, to mix up
rĕmissio, ōnis, *f*, relaxation
rĕmissus, a, um, *adj, adv*, **ē,** loose, gentle, cheerful
rĕmitto, mīsi, missum, *v.i.t.* 3, to decrease; send back, send out, yield, loosen, slacken, grant, surrender, give up; *with infin*, to cease
rĕmollesco, *v.i.* 3, to grow soft
rĕmordĕo, *no perf*, **morsum,** *v.t.* 2, to torment
rĕmŏror, *v.i.t.* 1, *dep*, to loiter; obstruct
rĕmōtus, a, um, *adj*, distant
rĕmŏvĕo, mōvi, mōtum, *v.t*, 2, to remove, withdraw, set aside
rĕmūgio, *v.i.* 4, to resound
rĕmulcum, i, *n*, tow-rope
rĕmūnĕrātio, ōnis, *f*, reward
rĕmūnĕror, *v.t.* 1, *dep*, to reward
rĕmurmŭro, *v.i.t.* 1, to murmur back
rēmus, i, *m*, oar
rĕnascor, nātus, *v.i.* 3, *dep*, to be born again, spring up again
rēnes, um, *m. pl*, kidneys
rĕnīdĕo, *v.i.* 2, to glisten
rĕnŏvātio, ōnis, *f*, renewal
rĕnŏvo, *v.t.* 1, to renew, restore, refresh, repeat
rĕnuntiātio, ōnis, *f*, announcement
rĕnuntio, *v.t.* 1, to report, announce, refuse, renounce
rĕnŭo, ŭi, *v.i.t.* 3, to refuse
rĕor, rātus, *v.t.* 2, *dep*, to suppose, think, believe
rĕpāgŭla, ōrum, *n.pl*, bolts, bars
rĕpărābĭlis, e, *adj*, able to be repaired
rĕpăro, *v.t.* 1, to recover, repair, restore, refresh
rĕpello, pŭli, pulsum, *v.t.* 3, to drive back, reject
rĕpendo, di, sum, *v.t.* 3, to weigh out in return, repay
rĕpens, ntis, *adj, adv*, **ē,** sudden
rĕpentĭnus, a, um, *adj, adv*, **ō,** sudden, unexpected
rĕpercussus, ūs, *m*, reflection
rĕpercŭtio, cussi, cussum, *v.t.* 3, to drive back, reflect
rĕpĕrio, repperi, rĕpertum, *v.t.* 4, to find, discover
rĕpertor, ōris, *m*, discoverer
rĕpĕto, ii, ĭtum, *v.t.* 3, to attack again, re-visit, fetch back, resume, recollect, demand back
rĕpĕtundæ, ārum, *f.pl*, (*with* **res**), extortion
rĕplĕo, ēvi, ētum, *v.t.* 2, to fill up, complete
rĕplētus, a, um, *adj*, full
rēpo, psi, ptum, *v.i.* 3, to creep
rĕpōno, pŏsŭi, pŏsĭtum, *v.t.* 3, to replace, preserve, put away
rĕporto, *v.t.* 1, to bring back, carry back, obtain
rĕposco, *v.t.* 3, to demand back
rĕpraesentātio, ōnis, *f*, representation
rĕpraesento, *v.t.* 1, to display, do immediately
rĕprĕhendo, di, sum, *v.t.* 3, to blame, rebuke, convict
rĕprĕhensio, ōnis, *f*, blame
rĕprĭmo, pressi, ssum, *v.t.* 3, to keep back, check, restrain
rĕpŭdiātio, ōnis, *f*, refusal, renunciation
rĕpŭdio, *v.t.* 1, to divorce, reject, scorn
rĕpugnans, ntis, *adj*, contradictory, irreconcilable
rĕpugnantia, ae, *f*, opposition, inconsistency
rĕpugno, *v.i.* 1, to resist, disagree with
rĕpulsa, ae, *f*, refusal, rejection
rĕpurgo, *v.t.* 1, to clean
rĕpŭto, *v.t.* 1, to ponder, reckon
rĕquies, ētis, *f*, rest, relaxation

rĕquiesco, ēvi, ētum, *v.i.* 3, to rest
rĕquīro, sīvi, sītum, *v.t.* 3, to search for, enquire, need, notice to be missing
rēs, rĕi, *f*, thing, matter, affair, reality, fact, property, profit, advantage, business, affair, lawsuit; **rēs nŏvae, rērum nŏvārum,** *f. pl*, revolution, **respublĭca, rēĭpublicae,** *f*, the State, statesmanship
rēscindo, scĭdi, ssum, *v.t.* 3, to cut down, break down, abolish
rēscisco, īvi, ītum, *v.t.* 3, to learn, ascertain
rēscrĭbo, psi, ptum, *v.t.* 3, to write back, reply, repay
rĕsĕco, ŭi, ctum, *v.t.* 1, to cut off, curtail
rĕsĕro, *v.t.* 1, to unlock, open
rĕservo, *v.t.* 1, to save up, keep
rĕsĕs, ĭdis, *adj*, inactive
rĕsīdĕo, sēdi, *v.i.* 2, to remain, linger, sit
rĕsīdo, sēdi, *v.i.* 3, to settle
rĕsīdŭus, a, um, *adj*, remaining
rĕsigno, *v.t.* 1, to unseal, open
rĕsilĭo, ŭi, *v.i.* 4, to recoil
rĕsīna, ae, *f*, resin
rĕsipio, *v.t.* 3, to taste of
rĕsīpisco, īvi, *v.i.* 3, to revive
rĕsisto, stĭti, *v.i.* 3, to stop, remain; *with dat*, to resist
rĕsolvo, solvi, sŏlūtum, *v.t.* 3, to untie, release, open, relax, annul, abolish
rĕsŏno, *v.i.t.* 1, to resound; re-echo with
rĕsŏnus, a, um, *adj*, resounding
rĕsorbĕo, *v.t.* 2, to re-swallow
respecto, *v.t.* 1, to look at, respect
respectus, ūs, *m*, looking back, retreat, refuge, respect
rĕspergo, si, sum, *v.t.* 3, to besprinkle
rĕspĭcio, spexi, spectum, *v.i.t.* 3, to look back, give attention; look at, regard, respect
rĕspīrātio, ōnis, *f*, breathing
rĕspīro, *v.i.t.* 1, to revive; breathe out, breathe
rĕsplendĕo, *v.i.* 2, to shine
rĕspondĕo, di, sum, *v.t.* 2, to reply, give advice, agree, correspond, answer one's hopes
rĕsponso, *v.t.* 1, to reply, resist
rĕsponsum, i, *n*, answer
respublĭca, see **rēs**
rĕspŭo, ŭi, *v.t.* 3, to spit out, expel, reject
rĕstinguo, nxi, nctum, *v.t.* 3, to quench, extinguish
restis, is, *f*, rope
rĕstĭtŭo, ŭi, ūtum, *v.t.* 3, to replace, rebuild, renew, give back, restore
rĕstĭtūtio, ōnis, *f*, restoration
rĕsto, stĭti, *v.i.* 1, to remain
rĕstrictus, a, um, *adj*, bound
rĕstringo, nxi, ctum, *v.t.* 3, to bind, restrain
rĕsulto, *no perf*, *v.i.* 1, to jump back, resound
rĕsūmo, mpsi, mptum, *v.t.* 3, to resume, take back, recover
rĕsūpīnus, a, um, *adj*, lying on one's back
rĕsurgo, surrexi, surrectum, *v.i.* 3, to rise, re-appear
rĕsurrectio, ōnis, *f*, resurrection
rĕsuscito, *v.t.* 1, to revive
rĕtardo, *v.i.t.* 1, to delay
rēte, is, *n*, net, snare
rĕtĕgo, xi, ctum, *v.t.* 3, to uncover, reveal
rĕtendo, di, tum, *v.t.* 3, to slacken
rĕtento, *v.t.* 1, to keep back
rĕtento, *v.t.* 1, to try again
rĕtexo, ŭi, xtum, *v.t.* 3, to unravel, cancel
rĕticĕo, *v.i.t.* 2, to be silent; conceal
rĕticŭlātus, a, um, *adj*, net-like
rĕticŭlum, i, *n*, small net
rĕtinācŭlum, i, *n*, rope, cable
rĕtinens, ntis, *adj*, tenacious
rĕtinĕo, ŭi, tentum, *v.t.* 2, to hold back, restrain, maintain
rĕtorquĕo, si, tum, *v.t.* 2, to twist back, drive back
rĕtracto, *v.t.* 1, to handle or undertake again, reconsider, refuse
rĕtrăho, xi, ctum, *v.t.* 3, to draw back, call back, remove
rĕtrĭbŭo, ŭi, ūtum, *v.t.* 3, to repay
rĕtrō, *adv*, backwards, formerly, back, behind, on the other hand
rĕtrorsum(s), *adv*, backwards
rĕtundo, tŭdi, tūsum, *v.t.* 3, to blunt, dull, weaken
rĕtūsus, a, um, *adj*, blunt, dull
rĕus, i, *m* (**rĕa, ae,** *f*), defendant, criminal, culprit
rĕvălesco, lŭi, *v.i.* 3, to grow well again
rĕvĕho, xi, ctum, *v.t.* 3, to bring back; *in passive*, to return
rĕvello, velli, vulsum, *v.t.* 3, to pull out, tear away
rĕvĕnio, vēni, ventum, *v.i.* 4, to return
rĕvērā, *adv*, really
rĕvĕrens, ntis, *adj*, reverent
rĕvĕrentia, ae, *f*, respect
rĕvĕrĕor, *v.t.* 2, *dep*, to revere

rĕverto, ti, *v.i.* 3, to return
rĕvertor, versus, *v.i.* 3, *dep*, to return
rĕvincendus, *gerundive*, see **revinco**
rĕvincio, nxi, nctum, *v.t.* 4, to bind, fasten
rĕvinco, vīci, victum, *v.t.* 3, to conquer, convict
rĕvĭresco, rŭi, *v.i.* 3, to grow green again
rĕvīso, *v.i.t.* 3, to revisit
rĕvīvisco, vixi, *v.i.* 3, to revive
rĕvŏcābilis, e, *adj*, able to be recalled
rĕvŏcāmen, ĭnis, *n*, recall
rĕvŏcātio, ōnis, *f*, recalling
rĕvŏco, *v.t.* 1, to recall, restrain, refer
rĕvŏlo, *v.i.* 1, to fly back
rĕvolvo, volvi, vŏlūtum, *v.t.* 3, to unroll, repeat
rĕvŏmo, ŭi, *v.t.* 3, to vomit up
rex, rēgis, *m*, king
rhēda, ae, *f*, carriage
rhētor, ŏris, *m*, teacher of oratory
rhētŏrica, ae, *f*, rhetoric
rhētŏricus, a, um, *adj*, rhetorical
rhĭnŏcĕros, ōtis, *m*, rhinoceros
rhombus, i, *m*, magic circle, turbot
rhonchus, i, *m*, snore, sneer
rĭca, ae, *f*, veil
rĭcĭnium, ii, *n*, small veil
rictus, ūs, *m*, gaping mouth
rĭdĕo, si, sum, *v.i.t.* 2, to laugh, smile; laugh at, ridicule
rĭdĭcŭlum, i, *n*, joke
rĭdĭcŭlus, a, um, *adj*, *adv*, **ē,** amusing, absurd
rĭgĕo, *v.i*, 2, to be stiff
rĭgesco, gŭi, *v.i.* 3, to stiffen
rĭgĭdus, a, um, *adj*, stiff, stern
rĭgo, *v.t.* 1, to wet, water
rĭgor, ōris, *m*, stiffness, hardness, chilliness, severity
rĭgŭus, a, um, *adj*, irrigating
rīma, ae, *f*, crack, chink
rīmor, *v.t.* 1, *dep*, to tear up, explore, examine
rīmōsus, a, um, *adj*, leaky
rīpa, ae, *f*, river bank
rīsus, ūs, *m*, laughter
rĭtĕ, *adv*, rightly, properly
rĭtus, ūs, *m*, religious ceremony, custom, way; **rĭtu,** *with genit*, in the manner of
rĭvālis, is, *m*, rival
rĭvŭlus, i, *m*, brook
rīvus, i, *m*, brook, stream
rixa, ae, *f*, quarrel
rixor, *v.i.* 1, *dep*, to quarrel
rōbĭginōsus, a, um, *adj*, rusty
rōbīgo, ĭnis, *f*, rust, mould
rōbŏro, *v.t.* 1, to strengthen
rōbur, ŏris, *n*, oak, strength, power, vigour, force
rōbustus, a, um, *adj*, oaken, firm, strong, robust
rōdo, si, sum, *v.t.* 3, to gnaw, corrode, slander
rŏgātio, ōnis, *f*, proposed law or bill, request
rŏgātor, ōris, *m*, polling-clerk
rŏgo, *v.t.* 1, to ask; *with* **legem, to** propose (law), beg
rŏgus, i, *m*, funeral pile
rōro, *v.i.t.* 1, to drop, drip, trickle; wet, besprinkle
rōs, rōris, *m*, dew, moisture
rŏsa, ae, *f*, rose
rŏsārium, ii, *n*, rose-garden
roscĭdus, a, um, *adj*, dewy
rŏsētum, i, *n*, rose-bed
rŏsĕus, a, um, *adj*, of roses, rose-coloured
rostra, ōrum, *n.pl*, speaker's platform
rostrātus, a, um, *adj*, with beaks
rostrum, i, *n*, beak, snout
rŏta, ae, *f*, wheel, chariot
rŏto, *v.i.t.* 1, to revolve; swing round, whirl around
rŏtundĭtas, ātis, *f*, rotundity
rŏtundo, *v.t.* 1, to round off
rŏtundus, a, um, *adj*, round, polished
rŭbĕfăcio, fēci, factum, *v.t.* 3, to redden
rŭbens, ntis, *adj*, red
rŭbĕo, *v.i.* 2, to be red, blush
rŭber, bra, brum, *adj*, red
rŭbesco, bŭi, *v.i.* 3, to grow red
rŭbēta, ae, *f*, toad
rŭbēta, ōrum, *n.pl*, brambles
rŭbĭcundus, a, um, *adj*, red
rūbīgo . . . see **rōbīgo . . .**
rŭbor, ōris, *m*, redness, blush, bashfulness
rŭbrĭca, ae, *f*, red-chalk
rūbus, i, *m*, bramble-bush
ructo, *v.i.t.* 1, to belch
ructor, *v.* 1, *dep*, to belch
ructus, ūs, *m*, belching
rŭdens, ntis, *m*, rope, rigging
rŭdīmentum, i, *n*, first try
rŭdis, e, *adj*, rough, raw, wild, awkward, inexperienced
rŭdis, is, *f*, stick, wooden sword
rŭdo, īvi, ītum, *v.i.* 3, to bellow
rŭdus, ĕris, *n*, broken stones, rubbish
rūfus, a, um, *adj*, red
rūga, ae, *f*, wrinkle
rūgo, *v.i.t.* 1, to wrinkle
rūgōsus, a, um, *adj*, shrivelled

rŭĭna, ae, *f*, downfall, ruin
rŭĭnōsus, a, um, *adj*, in ruins
rūmĭno, *v.t.* 1, to chew over
rūmor, ōris, *m*, rumour, general opinion, reputation
rumpo, rūpi, ruptum, *v.t.* 3, to break, burst, destroy, interrupt
runcīna, ae, *f*, plane
runcĭno, *v.t.* 1, to plane
runco, *v.t.* 1, to weed
rŭo, ŭi, ŭtum, *v.i.t.* 3, to fall, rush, hurry; hurl down, throw up
rūpes, is, *f*, rock
rūrĭcŏla, ae, *adj*, rural
rursus (rursum), *adv*, again, on the contrary, backwards
rūs, rūris, *n*, countryside
rusticānus, a, um, *adj*, rustic
rusticĭtas, ātis, *f*, behaviour of country-people
rusticor, *v.i.* 1, *dep*, to live in the country
rusticus, a, um, *adj*, rural
rusticus, i, *m*, countryman
rūta, ae, *f*, bitter herb, rue
rūtĭlo, *v.i.* 1, to be red
rūtĭlus, a, um, *adj*, red

S

sabbăta, ōrum, *n.pl*, sabbath
sābīnum, i, *n*, Sabine wine
sābŭlum, i, *n*, gravel
sāburra, ae, *f*, sand, ballast
sacchăron, i, *n*, sugar
saccŭlus, i, *m*, small bag
saccus, i, *m*, bag
sācellum, i, *n*, chapel
sācer, cra, crum, *adj*, sacred, venerable, accursed
sācerdos, dōtis, *c*, priest
sācerdōtālis, e, *adj*, priestly
sācerdōtium, ii, *n*, priesthood
sācra, ōrum, *n.pl*, worship, religion
sācrāmentum, i, *n*, oath
sācrārium, ii, *n*, sanctuary
sācrātus, a, um, *adj*, sacred
sācrĭfĭcium, ii, *n*, sacrifice
sācrĭfĭco, *v.i.t.* 1, to sacrifice
sācrĭfĭcus, a, um, *adj*, sacrificial
sācrilēgus, a, um, *adj*, temple-robbing, sacrilegious
sācro, *v.t.* 1, to consecrate, condemn, doom
sācrōsanctus, a, um, *adj*, sacred, inviolable
sācrum, i, *n*, sacred thing, religious act, religion
saecŭlum, i, *n*, age, generation, century
saepe, *adv*, often
saepes, is, *f*, hedge, fence
saepīmentum, i, *n*, fencing
saepĭo, psi, ptum, *v.t.* 4, to fence in, surround
saeptum, i, *n*, fence, pen
saeta, ae, *f*, hair, bristle
saetiger, ĕra, ĕrum, *adj*, bristly
saetōsus, a, um, *adj*, bristly
saevĭo, *v.i.* 4, to rage
saevitia, ae, *f*, savageness
saevus, a, um, *adj*, savage, violent, furious, cruel
sāga, ae, *f*, fortune-teller
sāgācĭtas, ātis, *f*, shrewdness
sâgax, ācis, *adj*, *adv*, **ĭter,** keen, shrewd, acute
sāgĭno, *v.t.* 1, to fatten
sāgitta, ae, *f*, arrow
sāgittārius, ii, *m*, archer
sāgŭlum, i, *n*, military cloak
sāgum, i, *n*, military cloak
sal, sălis, *m*, salt, sea, wit, sarcasm
sălăco, ōnis, *m*, braggart
sălārium, ii, *n*, pension, salary (salt money)
sălax, ācis, *adj*, lecherous
sălĕbra, ae, *f*, roughness
sălĭāris, e, *adj*, splendid
sălictum, i, *n*, willow-grove
sălignus, a, um, *adj*, of willow
Sălii, ōrum, *m. pl*, priests of Mars
sălīnae, ārum, *f. pl*, salt-works
sălīnum, i, *n*, salt-cellar
sălĭo, ŭi, saltum, *v.i.* 4, to jump
sălīva, ae, *f*, saliva
sălix, ĭcis, *f*, willow-tree
salmo, ōnis, *m*, salmon
salsāmentum, i, *n*, brine
salsus, a, um, *adj*, *adv*, **ē,** salted, witty
saltātio, ōnis, *f*, dancing
saltātor, ōris, *m*, dancer
saltātrix, īcis, *f*, dancing-girl
saltātus, ūs, *m*, dancing
saltem, *adv*, at least
salto, *v.i.t.* 1, to dance
saltus, ūs, *m*, leap, bound
saltus, ūs, *m*, woodland, mountain-pass
sălŭbris, e, *adj*, *adv*, **ĭter,** health-giving, beneficial
sălŭbrĭtas, ātis, *f*, wholesomeness
sălum, i, *n*, sea
sălŭs, ūtis, *f*, welfare, safety
sălŭtāris, e, *adj*, *adv*, **ĭter,** beneficial, wholesome
sălŭtātio, ōnis, *f*, greeting
sălŭtātor, ōris, *m*, visitor
sălŭtĭfer, ĕra, ĕrum, *adj*, healing

For List of Abbreviations used, turn to pages 3, 4

sălūto, *v.t.* 1, to greet
salvē, salvēte, salvēto, *v, imperative* how are you? welcome!
salvĭa, ae, *f,* sage (herb)
salvus, a, um, *adj,* safe, well; *with noun in abl,* e.g. **salvā lege,** without violating the law
sambūcus, i, *f,* elder-tree
sānābĭlis, e, *adj,* curable
sānātĭo, ōnis, *f,* cure
sancĭo, xi, ctum, *v.t.* 4, to appoint, establish, ratify
sanctifĭcātĭo, ōnis, *f,* sanctification
sanctĭo, ōnis, *f,* establishing
sanctĭtas, ātis, *f,* sacredness, purity
sanctus, a, um, *adj, adv,* **ē,** sacred, inviolable, good
sandix, ĭcis, *f,* scarlet
sānē, *adv,* certainly, very
sanguĭnārĭus, a, um, *adj,* bloody, blood-thirsty
sanguĭnĕus, a, um, *adj,* bloody
sanguĭnŏlentus, a, um, *adj,* bloody
sanguis, ĭnis, *m,* blood, bloodshed, race, stock
sānĭes, em, e, *f,* bad blood
sānĭtas, ātis, *f,* health, good sense, discretion
sannĭo, ōnis, *m,* buffoon
sāno, *v.t.* 1, to cure, restore
sānus, a, um, *adj,* healthy, rational, discreet
săpĭdus, a, um, *adj,* tasty
săpĭens, ntis, *adj, adv,* **nter,** wise, sensible
săpĭens, ntis, *m,* wise man
săpĭentĭa, ae, *f,* discretion, philosophy
săpĭo, ĭvi, *v.i.t.* 3, to be wise, discreet; to taste of, savour of
sāpo, ōnis, *m,* soap
săpor, ōris, *m,* flavour, taste
sapphīrus, i, *f,* sapphire
sarcĭna, ae, *f,* pack, load
sarcĭo, si, tum, *v.t.* 4, to patch
sarcŏphăgus, i, *m,* sarcophagus
sarcŭlum, i, *n,* light hoe
sarda, ae, *f,* sardine
sarĭsa, ae, *f,* Macedonian lance
sarmentum, i, *n,* brushwood
sarrācum, i, *n,* cart
sarrānus, a, um, *adj,* Tyrian
sarrĭo, *v.t.* 4, to hoe
sartāgo, ĭnis, *f,* frying-pan
sartus, a, um, *adj,* repaired
sāta, ōrum, *n.pl,* crops
sătelles, ĭtis, *c,* attendant; *in pl,* escort
sătĭas, ātis, *f,* abundance, disgust
sătiĕtas, ātis, *f,* abundance, disgust
sătĭo, *v.t.* 1, to satisfy, glut
sātio, ōnis, *f,* sowing
sătirĭcus, a, um, *adj,* satirical
sātis (săt), *adv, or indecl. adj,* enough
sātisdătio, ōnis, *f,* giving bail
sātisfăcio, fēci, factum, *v.t.* 3, to satisfy, make amends
sătisfactĭo, ōnis, *f,* excuse, reparation
sătius, *comp. adv,* better
sātor, ōris, *m,* sower, creator
sātrăpes, is, *m,* viceroy, satrap
sātur, ŭra, ŭrum, *adj,* full, fertile
sātŭra, ae, *f,* food made of various ingredients, satire
Sāturnālĭa, ōrum, *n.pl,* festival in honour of Saturn (Dec. 17th)
sătŭro, *v.t.* 1, to fill, glut
sātus, ūs, *m,* planting
sātus, a, um, *adj,* sprung from
sătȳrus, i, *m,* forest-god
saucĭo, *v.t.* 1, to wound
saucĭus, a, um, *adj,* wounded
saxĕus, a, um, *adj,* rocky
saxĭfĭcus, a, um, *adj,* petrifying
saxōsus, a, um, *adj,* rocky
saxum, i, *n,* rock
scăbellum, i, *n,* stool
scăber, bra, brum, *adj,* rough, scabby
scăbĭes, em, e, *f,* roughness, scab, itch
scăbo, scābi, *v.t.* 3, to scratch
scaena, ae, *f,* stage, scene
scaenĭcus, a, um, *adj,* theatrical
scaenĭcus, i, *m,* actor
scāla, ae, *f,* ladder, stairs
scalmus, i, *m,* rowlock
scalpo, psi, ptum, *v.t.* 3, to carve
scalpellum, i, *n,* lancet
scalprum, i, *n,* chisel
scalptor, ōris, *m,* engraver
scalptūra, ae, *f,* engraving
scamnum, i, *n,* bench
scando, *v.i.t.* 3, to rise; climb
scăpha, ae, *f,* small boat
scăpŭlae, ārum, *f. pl,* shoulder-blades
scărăbaeus, i, *m,* beetle
scārus, i, *m,* sea-fish (scar)
scătĕbra, ae, *f,* spring water
scătĕo, *v.i.* 2, to bubble, swarm with
scaurus, a, um, *adj,* with swollen ankles
scĕlĕrātus, a, um, *adj,* wicked
scĕlĕro, *v.t.* 1, to contaminate
scĕlestus, a, um, *adj,* wicked
scĕlus, ĕris, *n,* crime, scoundrel
scēna, see **scaena**
scēnĭcus, see **scaenĭcus**

sceptrum, i, *n,* sceptre; *in pl,* dominion, authority
schĕda, ae, *f,* sheet of paper
schŏla, ae, *f,* lecture, school
scĭens, ntis, *adj, adv,* **nter,** knowing, (*i.e.* purposely), expert in
scĭentia, ae, *f,* knowledge
scĭlĭcet, *adv,* certainly, of course, namely
scilla, ae, *f,* sea-onion, prawn
scindo, scidi, scissum, *v.t.* 3, to split
scintilla, ae, *f,* spark
scintillans, ntis, *adj,* sparkling
scintillo, *v.i.* 1, to sparkle
scĭo, *v.t.* 4, to know, understand
scīpĭo, ōnis, *m,* staff
scirpĕus, a, um, *adj,* of rushes
sciscĭtor, *v.t.* 1, *dep,* to enquire
scisco, scīvi, scĭtum, *v.t.* 3, to approve, appoint, decree
scissūra, ae, *f,* tearing, rending
scĭtor, *v.t.* 1, *dep,* to inquire
scĭtum, i, *n,* decree, statute
scĭtus, a, um, *adj, adv,* **ē,** shrewd, sensible, witty
scĭūrus, i, *m,* squirrel
scŏbīna, ae, *f,* rasp, file
scŏbis, is, *f,* sawdust
scomber, bri, *m,* mackerel
scōpae, ārum, *f.pl,* broom
scōpŭlōsus, a, um, *adj,* rocky
scŏpŭlus, i, *m,* rock, cliff
scōpus, i, *m,* target
scorpĭo, ōnis, *m,* scorpion, missile-launcher
scortum, i, *n,* prostitute
scrība, ae, *m,* clerk
scrĭbo, psi, ptum, *v.t.* 3, to write, draw, compose, describe, enroll
scrīnĭum, ii, *n,* letter-case
scriptĭo, ōnis, *f,* writing
scriptor, ōris, *m,* secretary, author
scriptum, i, *n,* book, writing
scriptūra, ae, *f,* composition
scriptus, a, um, *adj,* written
scrōbis, is, *m,* ditch
scrūpĕus, a, um, *adj,* rugged
scrūpŭlus, i, *m,* anxiety, embarrassment
scrūta, ōrum, *n.pl,* frippery
scrūtātĭo, ōnis, *f,* scrutiny
scrūtor, *v.t.* 1, *dep,* to examine
sculpo, psi, ptum, *v.t.* 3, to carve
sculpōnĕae, ārum, *f. pl,* clogs
sculptor, ōris, *m,* sculptor
sculptūra, ae, *f,* sculpture
scurra, ae, *m,* clown, dandy
scurrīlis, e, *adj,* jeering
scūtātus, a, um, *adj,* armed with oblong shields
scūtella, ae, *f,* salver
scūtĭca, ae, *f,* whip
scūtŭla, ae, *f,* wooden roller
scūtum, i, *n,* oblong shield
scȳphus, i, *m,* goblet
sē, *acc. or abl. of reflexive pron,* herself, itself etc.
sēbum, i, *n,* suet
sēcāle, is, *n,* rye
sēcēdo, cessi, cessum, *v.i.* 3, to go away, withdraw
sēcerno, crēvi, crētum, *v.t.* 3, to separate, part
sēcessĭo, ōnis, *f,* withdrawal
sēcessus, ūs, *m,* solitude
sēcĭus (sēquius), *comp. adv,* differently
sēclūdo, sī, sum, *v.t.* 3, to separate, shut off
sēclūsus, a, um, *adj,* remote
sĕco, ŭi, ctum, *v.t.* 1, to cut, wound, separate
sēcrētum, i, *n,* solitude
sēcrētus, a, um, *adj, adv,* **ō,** separate, remote, secret
secta, ae, *f,* way, method, sect
sectātor, ōris, *m,* follower
sectĭo, ōnis, *f,* sale by auction
sector, ōris, *m,* cutthroat, bidder at an auction
sector, *v.t.* 1, *dep,* to pursue
sectūra, ae, *f,* mine
sēcul . . . see **saecul**
sĕcundārĭus, a, um, *adj,* secondary, second-rate
sĕcundo, *v.t.* 1, to favour
sĕcundum, *prep, with acc,* after, behind, by, next to, according to
sĕcundus, a, um, *adj,* following, second, favourable
sĕcūrĭger, ĕra, ĕrum, *adj,* armed with a battle-axe
sĕcūris, is, *f,* axe, hatchet
sēcūritas, ātis, *f,* freedom from care
sēcūrus, a, um, *adj,* carefree, tranquil
sĕcus, *adv,* differently
sĕd, *conj,* but
sēdātĭo, ōnis, *f,* a calming
sēdātus, a, um, *adj,* calm
sēdĕcim, *indecl. adj,* sixteen
sēdentārĭus, a, um, *adj,* sedentary
sēdĕo, sēdi, sessum, *v.i.* 2, to sit, remain, settle, be settled
sēdes, is, *f,* seat, residence, temple, bottom, foundation
sēdile, is, *n,* seat
sēdĭtĭo, ōnis, *f,* mutiny
sēdĭtĭōsus, a, um, *adj, adv,* **ē,** mutinous, rebellious
sēdo, *v.t.* 1, to calm, check

sēdūco, xi, ctum, *v.t.* 3, to lead aside, separate
sēdūlitas, ātis, *f,* zeal
sēdūlō, *adv,* diligently, on purpose
sēdūlus, a, um, *adj,* industrious
sēges, ētis, *f,* cornfield, crop
segmenta, ōrum, *n.pl,* trimmings
segmentum, i, *n,* piece
segnis, e, *adj, adv,* **iter** lazy
segnitia, ae, *f,* inactivity, slowness
segnities, em, e, *f,* inactivity, slowness
sēgrĕgo, *v.t.* 1, to separate
sēiungo, nxi, nctum, *v.t.* 3, to separate, divide
sēligo, lēgi, lectum, *v.t.* 3, to select
sella, ae, *f,* seat, chair
sĕmĕl, *adv,* once
sēmen, ĭnis, *n,* seed, cutting, graft, offspring, instigator
sēmentis, is, *f,* sowing
sēmestris, e, *adj,* half-yearly
sēmēsus, a, um, *adj,* half-eaten
sēmiănĭmis, e, *adj,* half-dead
sēmidĕus, a, um, *adj,* half-divine
sēmifer, ĕra, ĕrum, *adj,* half-man, half-beast
sēmihŏmo, ĭnis, *m,* half-human
sēmihōra, ae, *f,* half-hour
sēminārium, ii, *n,* nursery
sēminātor, ōris, *m,* author
sēmĭnĕcis, is, *adj,* half-dead
sēmĭno, *v.t.* 1, to produce
sēmiplēnus, a, um, *adj,* half-full
sēmirŭtus, a, um, *adj,* half-ruined
sēmis, issis, *m,* half a farthing
sēmisomnus, a, um, *adj,* half-asleep
sēmita, ae, *f,* footpath
sēmiustus, a, um, *adj,* half-burned
sēmivir, vĭri, *m,* half-man; *as adj,* effeminate
sēmivīvus, a, um, *adj,* half-alive
sēmōtus, a, um, *adj,* remote
sēmŏvĕo, mōvi, mōtum, *v.t.* 2, to remove, separate
semper, *adv,* always
sempĭternus, a, um, *adj,* everlasting
sēmustŭlo, *v.t.* 1, to half burn
sĕnātor, ōris, *m,* senator
sĕnātōrius, a, um, *adj,* senatorial
sĕnātus, ūs, *m,* the Senate
sĕnecta, ae, *f,* old age
sĕnectus, ūtis, *f,* old age
sĕnesco, nŭi, *v.i.* 3, to grow old
sĕnex, sĕnis, *m,* old man
sēni, ae, a, *pl. adj,* six each
sĕnilis, e, *adj,* old (of people)
sĕnior, ōris, *c,* elderly person
sĕnium, ii, *n,* old age, decay, trouble
sensilis, e, *adj,* sensitive
sensim, *adv,* slowly, gently
sensus, ūs, *m,* perception, disposition, good taste, sense, understanding, meaning
sententia, ae, *f,* opinion, decision, meaning, sentence, axiom; **ex mĕā sententiā,** to my liking
sententiōsus, a, um, *adj,* sententious
sentina, ae, *f,* bilge-water, dregs, ship's hold
sentio, si, sum, *v.t.* 4, to feel, perceive, endure, suppose
sentis, is, *m,* thorn, bramble
sentus, a, um, *adj,* rough
sĕorsum, *adv,* separately
sēpărātim, *adv,* separately
sēpărātio, ōnis, *f,* separation
sēpărātus, a, um, *adj,* separate
sēpăro, *v.t.* 1, to separate
sēpĕlio, livi, pultum, *v.t.* 4, to bury, overwhelm
sēpia, ae, *f,* cuttle-fish
sēpio, see **saepio**
sēpōno, pŏsŭi, pŏsĭtum, *v.t.* 3, to put aside, select
septem, *indecl. adj,* seven
September (mensis), September
septemgĕminus, a, um, *adj,* seven-fold
septemplex, ĭcis, *adj,* seven-fold
septendĕcim, *indecl. adj,* seventeen
septēni, ae, a, *pl. adj,* seven each
septentriōnālis, e, *adj,* northern
septentriōnes, um, *m. pl,* the Great Bear, the North
septies, *adv,* seven times
septĭmus, a, um, *adj,* seventh
septingenti, ae, a, *pl. adj,* seven hundred
septŭāgēsĭmus, a, um, *adj,* seventieth
septŭāginta, *indecl. adj,* seventy
septum, see **saeptum**
sĕpulcrum, i, *n,* grave, tomb
sēpultūra, ae, *f,* burial
sēquax, ācis, *adj,* pursuing
sēquens, ntis, *adj,* following
sēquester, tris, *m,* agent
sēquor, sēcūtus, *v.i.t.* 3, *dep,* to follow, attend, pursue
sĕra, ae, *f,* bolt, bar
sērēnĭtas, ātis, *f,* fair weather
sērēno, *v.t.* 1, to brighten
sērēnum, i, *n,* fair weather
sērēnus, a, um, *adj,* clear, fair, cheerful, glad
sēria, ōrum, *n.pl,* serious matters
sēricus, a, um, *adj,* silken
sĕries, em, e, *f,* row, series
sērius, a, um, *adj,* serious
sermo, ōnis, *m,* talk, conversation, common talk

sĕro, sēvi, sātum, *v.t.* 3, to sow, plant, cause
sĕro, ŭi, sertum, *v.t.* 3, to plait, join, connect, compose
sērŏ, *adv,* late
serpens, ntis, *f,* snake
serpo, psi, ptum, *v.i.* 3, to crawl
serpyllum, i, *n,* thyme
serra, ae, *f,* saw
serrŭla, ae, *f,* small saw
serta, ōrum, *n.pl,* garlands
sērum, i, *n,* whey
sērus, a, um, *adj,* late
serva, ae, *f,* maid-servant
servātor, ōris, *m,* saviour
servīlis, e, *adj, adv,* **ĭter,** of a slave, servile
servĭo, *v.i.* 4, to be a servant, to be of use to
servĭtĭum, ii, *n,* slavery, slaves
servĭtus, ūtis, *f,* slavery, slaves
servo, *v.t.* 1, to save, protect, preserve, keep, keep watch
servus, a, um, *adj,* servile
servus, i, *m,* slave, servant
sescēni, ae, a, *pl. adj,* six hundred each
sescenti, ae, a, *pl. adj,* six hundred
sescentĭes, *adv,* six hundred times
sesquipĕdālis, e, *adj,* one foot and a half long
sessio, ōnis, *f,* sitting, session
sestertĭum, 1,000 sestertii
sestertĭus, ii, *m,* small silver coin (worth about 2¼d.)
sēt . . . see **saet. . . .**
seu, *conj,* whether, or
sĕvērĭtas, ātis, *f,* sternness
sĕvērus, a, um, *adj, adv,* **ē,** stern, serious, harsh, gloomy
sĕvŏco, *v.t.* 1, to call aside
sex, *indecl adj,* six
sexāgēnārius, i, *m,* sexagenarian
sexāgēni, ae, a, *pl. adj,* sixty each
sexāgēsimus, a, um, *adj,* sixtieth
sexāgies, *adv,* sixty times
sexāginta, *indecl. adj,* sixty
sexennĭum, ii, *n,* six years
sextans, ntis, *m,* a sixth part
sextārĭus, ii, *m,* a pint
Sextīlis, (mensis), August
sextus, a, um, *adj,* sixth
sexus, ūs, *m,* sex
sī, *conj,* if
sĭbi, *dat. of reflexive pron,* to himself, herself, itself, etc.
sĭbilo, *v.i.t.* 1, to hiss; hiss at
sĭbilus, i, *m,* hissing
sĭbylla, ae, *f,* prophetess
sic, *adv,* so, in this way
sĭca, ae, *f,* dagger
sĭcārĭus, ii, *m,* assassin
siccĭtas, ātis, *f,* dryness, firmness
sicco, *v.t.* 1, to dry up, drain
siccum, i, *n,* dry land
siccus, a, um, *adj,* dry, firm, tough, thirsty, sober
sĭcŭbĭ, *adv,* if anywhere
sĭcut, (sĭcŭti), *adv,* just as
sĭdĕrĕus, a, um, *adj,* starry
sĭdo, di, *v.i.* 3, to sit down, settle, sink
sĭdus, ĕris, *n,* star, sky, constellation, season, weather
sĭgilla, ōrum, *n. pl,* little figures or images
sĭgillātus, a, um, *adj,* figured
signifer, ĕri, *m,* standard-bearer
significātio, ōnis, *f,* sign, mark
significo, *v.t.* 1, to show, notify
significans, antis, *adj,* significant
signo, *v.t.* 1, to mark out, seal, indicate
signum, i, *n,* mark, sign, military standard, watchword, statue, constellation, symptom
sĭlens, ntis, *adj,* still, quiet
silentĭum, ii, *n,* stillness, quietness
sĭlĕo, *v.i.t.* 2, to be silent; to keep quiet about
sĭlesco, *v.i.* 3, to grow quiet
sĭlex, ĭcis, *m,* flint-stone
sĭlus, a, um, *adj,* snub-nosed
silva, ae, *f,* wood, forest, grove, abundance
silvestrĭa, ĭum, *n. pl,* woodlands
silvestris, e, *adj,* woody, rural
silvĭcŏla, ae, *adj,* living in woods
sĭmia, ae, *f,* ape
sĭmilis, e, *adj, adv,* **ĭter,** similar, like
sĭmilĭtūdo, ĭnis, *f,* resemblance
sĭmius, ii, *m,* ape
simplex, ĭcis, *adj, adv,* **ĭter,** unmixed, simple, frank
simplĭcĭtas, ātis, *f,* honesty
sĭmul, *adv,* at once, together, at the same time, as soon as
sĭmŭlac, *conj,* as soon as
sĭmŭlatque, *conj.* as soon as
sĭmŭlācrum, i, *n,* portrait, statue, phantom
sĭmŭlātio, ōnis, *f,* pretence
sĭmŭlātor, ōris, *m,* pretender
sĭmŭlātus, a, um, *adj,* feigned
sĭmŭlo, *v.t.* 1, to imitate, pretend
sĭmultas, ātis, *f,* animosity
sĭmus, a, um, *adj,* snub-nosed
sĭn, *conj,* but if
sĭnāpi, is, *n,* mustard
sincēritas, ātis, *f,* cleanness, purity, entirety, sincerity
sincērus, a, um, *adj, adv,* **ē,** clean, pure, genuine, entire, sincere

For List of Abbreviations used, turn to pages 3, 4

sĭnĕ, *prep. with abl,* without
singillātim, *adv,* one by one
singŭlāris, e, *adj,* single, solitary, unique, remarkable
singŭlātim, see **singillātim**
singŭli, ae, a, *pl. adj,* one each
singultim, *adv,* with sobs
singultio, *v.i.* 4, to hiccup
singulto, (*no perf*), *v.i.* 1, to sob
singultus, ūs, *m,* sobbing
sĭnister, tra, trum, *adj,* left, awkward, wrong, unlucky, lucky
sĭnistra, ae, *f,* left hand
sĭnistrorsus, *adv,* to the left
sĭno, sīvi, sĭtum, *v.t.* 3, to allow
sĭnum, i, *n,* drinking-cup
sĭnŭo, *v.t.* 1, to bend, curve
sĭnŭōsus, a, um, *adj,* curved
sĭnus, ūs, *m,* curve, fold, bosom, lap, hiding-place, bay
sĭpho, ōnis, *m,* siphon, syringe
sĭquandō, *adv,* if ever
sĭquĭdem, *adv,* if indeed
sĭquis, *pron,* if any
sīrēn, ēnis, *f,* siren
sisto, stĭti, stātum, *v.i.t.* 3, to stand still, resist, hold out; put, place, bring, check, establish
sistrum, i, *n,* rattle
sĭtiens, ntis, *adj, adv,* **nter,** thirsty
sĭtio, *v.i.t.* 4, to thirst; long for
sĭtis, is, *f,* thirst, drought
sĭtŭla, ae, *f,* bucket
sĭtus, a, um, *adj,* situated
sĭtus, ūs, *m,* position, site, rust, mould, inactivity
sīve, *conj,* whether, or
smăragdus, i, *c,* emerald
sŏbŏles, is, *f,* sprout, twig, offspring
sŏbrĭĕtas, ātis, *f,* sobriety, temperance
sŏbrīnus, i, *m,* cousin
sŏbrĭus, a, um, *adj, adv,* **ē,** sober, moderate, sensible
soccus, i, *m,* slipper
sŏcer, ĕri, *m,* father-in-law
sŏciālis, e, *adj,* allied
sŏciĕtas, ātis, *f,* fellowship, partnership, alliance
sŏcio, *v.t.* 1, to unite
sŏcius, ii, *m,* companion, ally
sŏcius, a, um, *adj,* allied
sŏcordia, ae, *f,* laziness, folly
sŏcors, cordis, *adj,* lazy, careless, stupid
socrus, ūs, *f,* mother-in-law
sŏdālĭcium, ii, *n,* secret society
sŏdālis, is, *c,* companion
sŏdālĭtas, ātis, *f,* friendship
sŏdes, if you wish
sŏl, sŏlis, *m,* sun, sunshine
sŏlācium, ii, *n,* comfort, solace
sŏlāmen, ĭnis, *n,* consolation
sŏlārium, ii, *n,* sundial
sŏlātium, see **sŏlācium**
soldŭrii, ōrum, *m. pl,* retainers of a chieftain
sŏlĕa, ae, *f,* sandal, sole (fish)
sŏlĕātus, a, um, *adj,* wearing sandals
sŏlĕo, sŏlĭtus, *v.i.* 2, *semi-dep,* to be accustomed
sŏlĭditas, ātis, *f,* solidity
sŏlĭdo, *v.t.* 1, to strengthen
sŏlĭdum, i, *n,* a solid, solidity
sŏlĭdus, a, um, *adj,* compact, complete, genuine, real
sŏlĭtārius, a, um, *adj,* alone
sŏlĭtūdo, ĭnis, *f,* loneliness, desert
sŏlĭtus, a, um, *adj,* usual
sŏlium, ii, *n,* seat, throne
sollemnis, e, *adj,* established, appointed, usual, religious
sollemne, is, *n,* religious ceremony, sacrifice
sollers, tis, *adj,* skilled
sollertia, ae, *f,* skill, ingenuity
sollĭcitātio, ōnis, *f,* instigation
sollĭcito, *v.t.* 1, to stir up, molest, instigate
sollĭcitūdo, ĭnis, *f,* anxiety
sollĭcĭtus, a, um, *adj,* troubled
sŏlor, *v.t.* 1, *dep,* to comfort, relieve
solstĭtiālis, e, *adj,* of summer
solstĭtium, ii, *n,* summer-time
sŏlum, i, *n,* bottom, base, floor, sole, soil, ground, country, place
sŏlum, *adv,* only
sŏlus, a, um, *adj,* alone, only, lonely, deserted
sŏlūtio, ōnis, *f,* unloosing, payment, explanation
sŏlūtus, a, um, *adj, adv,* **ē,** free, loose, independent
solvendum, see **solvo**
solvo, solvi, sŏlūtum, *v.t.* 3, to set free, dissolve, release, open up, pay, perform, fulfil, acquit; with **ancŏram,** to sail
somnicŭlōsus, a, um, *adj,* drowzy
somnifer, ĕra, ĕrum, *adj,* sleep-bringing
somnĭfĭcus, a, um, *adj,* sleep-bringing
somnio, *v.t.* 1, to dream
somnium, ii, *n,* dream
somnus, i, *m,* sleep

sŏnĭpēs, pĕdis, *adj*, noisy-footed
sŏnĭtus, ūs, *m*, noise, sound
sŏno, ŭi, ĭtum, *v.i.t.* 1, to resound; call out, utter
sŏnor, ōris, *m*, noise, sound
sŏnōrus, a, um, *adj*, resounding
sons, ntis, *adj*, guilty
sŏnus, i, *m*, noise, sound
sŏphistes, ae, *m*, philosopher
sŏpio, *v.t.* 4, to lull to sleep
sŏpor, ōris, *m*, sleep
sŏpōrĭfer, ĕra, ĕrum, *adj*, sleep-bringing
sŏpōro, *v.t.* 1, to heat, stupefy
sŏpōrus, a, um, *adj*, sleep-bringing
sorbĕo, *v.t.* 2, to suck in
sordĕo, *v.i.* 2, to be dirty, to be despised
sordes, is, *f*, dirt, mourning-dress, meanness
sordĭdātus, a, um, *adj*, shabbily dressed (in mourning)
sordĭdus, a, um, *adj*, *adv*, **ē,** dirty, despicable, mean
sŏror, ōris, *f*, sister
sŏrōrĭus, a, um, *adj*, of a sister
sors, tis, *f*, chance, lot, drawing of lots, prophesy, fortune, share, destiny
sortĭor, *v.i.t.* 4, *dep*, to draw lots; to appoint by lot, obtain by lot, choose
sortĭtio, ōnis, *f*, drawing of lots
sortĭtō, *adv*, by lot
sortĭtus, a, um, *adj*, drawn by lot
sospĕs, ĭtis, *adj*, safe, lucky
spādix, īcis, *adj*, nut-brown
spargo, si, sum, *v.t.* 3, to sprinkle, scatter, spread
spărus, i, *m*, hunting-spear
spasmus, i, *m*, spasm
spătĭor, *v.i.* 1, *dep*, to walk about
spătiōsus, a, um, *adj*, spacious
spătĭum, ii, *n*, space, room, distance, walk, track, interval
spĕcĭes, ēi, *f*, sight, view, shape, appearance, pretence, display, beauty
spĕcĭmen, ĭnis, *n*, mark, sign, pattern
spĕciōsus, a, um, *adj*, handsome, plausible
spectābilis, e, *adj*, visible, remarkable
spectăcŭlum, i, *n*, show, spectacle
spectātio, ōnis, *f*, sight
spectātor, ōris, *m*, onlooker
spectātus, a, um, *adj*, tested, respected
specto, *v.t.* 1, to watch, face, examine, consider, refer
spectrum, i, *n*, image
spĕcŭla, ae, *f*, look-out point
spĕcŭla, ae, *f*, slight hope
spĕcŭlātor, ōris, *m*, spy, scout
spĕcŭlor, *v.t.* 1, *dep*, to watch, observe, explore
spĕcŭlum, i, *n*, mirror
spĕcus, ūs, *m*, cave, pit
spēlunca, ae, *f*, cave, den
sperno, sprēvi, sprētum, *v.t.* 3, to despise, scorn
spĕro, *v.t.* 1, to hope, expect
spes, spēi, *f*, hope
sphaera, ae, *f*, sphere
spīca, ae, *f*, ear (of corn)
spīcĕus, a, um, *adj*, made of ears of corn
spīcŭlum, i, *n*, point, dart
spīna, ae, *f*, thorn, spine, difficulties
spīnētum, i, *n*, thorn-hedge
spīnōsus, a, um, *adj*, thorny
spīnus, i, *f*, sloe-tree
spīra, ae, *f*, coil, twist
spīrābilis, e, *adj*, breathable
spīrăcŭlum, i, *n*, air-hole
spīrāmentum, i, *n*, air-hole
spīritus, ūs, *m*, breath, breeze, pride, arrogance, soul
spīro, *v.i.t.* 1, to breathe, blow, live; exhale
spisso, *v.t.* 1, to condense
spissus, a, um, *adj*, thick, dense
splendĕo, *v.i.* 2, to shine
splendesco, *v.i.* 3, to become bright
splendĭdus, a, um, *adj*, *adv*, **ē,** shining, magnificent, noble
splendor, ōris, *m*, brilliance, excellence
spŏlĭa, see **spŏlĭum**
spŏlĭātio, ōnis, *f*, plundering
spŏlĭo, *v.t.* 1, to plunder, rob
spŏlĭum, ii, *n*, skin (of an animal); *in pl*, booty, spoils
sponda, ae, *f*, couch, sofa
spondĕo, spŏpondi, sponsum, *v.t.* 2, to promise, pledge, betroth, warrant
spongĭa, ae, *f*, sponge
spongĭōsus, a, um, *adj*, spongy
sponsa, ae, *f*, bride
sponsālia, ĭum, *n. pl*, betrothal
sponsio, ōnis, *f*, promise, guarantee, security
sponsor, ōris, *m*, surety
sponsum, i, *n*, covenant
sponsus, a, um, *adj*, promised
sponsus, i, *m*, bridegroom
spontē, (*abl.*) *f*, *with* **mĕā, sŭā,** *etc.*, voluntarily
sportella, ae, *f*, fruit-basket
sportŭla, ae, *f*, little basket
spūma, ae, *f*, froth, foam

spūmĕus, a, um, *adj*, foaming
spūmĭfer, ĕra, ĕrum, *adj*, foaming
spūmĭger, ĕra, ĕrum, *adj*, foaming
spūmo, *v.i.* 1, to foam, froth
spūmōsus, a, um, *adj*, foaming
spŭo, ŭi, ūtum, *v.i.t.* 3, to spit
spūtum, i, *n*, spit
spurcus, a, um, *adj*, dirty
squālĕo, *v.i.* 2, to be stiff or rough, to be neglected, filthy
squālĭdus, a, um, *adj*, stiff, dirty, neglected
squālor, ōris, *m*, filthiness
squāma, ae, *f*, scale (of fish)
squāmĕus, a, um, *adj*, scaly
squāmĭger, ĕra, ĕrum, *adj*, scaly
squāmōsus, a, um, *adj*, scaly
stăbĭlio, *v.t.* 4, to fix
stăbĭlis, e, *adj*, firm, steadfast
stăbĭlitas, ātis, *f*, firmness
stăbŭlo, *v.i.* (**stăbŭlor,** *v.i. dep*,) 1, to have a home, resting-place
stăbŭlum, i, *n*, stable, hut
stădĭum, ii, *n*, stade (distance of 200 yds. approx.), racecourse
stagnans, ntis, *adj*, stagnant
stagno, *v.i.* 1, to stagnate
stagnum, i, *n*, pool, pond
stālagmĭum, i, *n*, pendant
stāmen, ĭnis, *n*, thread
stātārius, a, um, *adj*, firm, calm
stātim, *adv*, immediately
stātio, ōnis, *f*, post, station, outposts, sentries
stātīva, ōrum, *n. pl*, permanent camp
stātīvus, a, um, *adj*, stationary
stātor, ōris, *m*, messenger
stātŭa, ae, *f*, statue
stātŭo, ŭi, ūtum, *v.t.* 3, to set up, place, build, establish, settle, decide
stātūra, ae, *f*, stature
stātus, ūs, *m*, posture, position, condition, state, circumstance
stātus, a, um, *adj*, fixed
stella, ae, *f*, star
stellātus, a, um, *adj*, starry
stellĭger, ĕra, ĕrum, *adj*, starry
stellio, ōnis, *m*, newt
stemma, ătis, *n*, garland, pedigree
stercus, ŏris, *n*, manure
stĕrilis, e, *adj*, barren
stĕrilitas, ātis, *f*, sterility
sternax, ācis, *adj*, bucking (horse)
sterno, strāvi, strātum, *v.t.* 3, to scatter, extend, smooth, arrange, cover, overthrow, pave
sternūmentum, i, *n*, sneezing
sternŭo, ŭi, *v.i.t.* 3, to sneeze
sterto, ŭi, *v.i.* 3, to snore
stigma, ătis, *n*, brand
stillĭcĭdĭum, ii, *n*, dripping rain-water
stillo, *v.i.t.* 1, to drip; distil
stĭlus, i, *m*, pen, style
stĭmŭlo, *v.t.* 1, to torment, incite
stĭmŭlus, i, *m*, goad, sting, incentive
stĭpātor, ōris, *m*, attendant
stĭpendĭārius, a, um, *adj*, tribute-paying
stĭpendĭum, ii, *n*, tax, dues, pay, military service, campaign
stĭpes, ĭtis, *m*, log, post
stĭpo, *v.t.* 1, to compress, surround, accompany
stips, stĭpis, *f*, donation
stĭpŭla, ae, *f*, stalk, stem
stĭpŭlātio, ōnis, *f*, agreement
stĭpŭlor, *v.i.t.* 1, *dep*, to bargain; demand
stĭria, ae, *f*, icicle
stirps, pis, *f*, root, stem, plant, race, family
stīva, ae, *f*, plough-handle
sto, stĕti, stātum, *v.i.* 1, to stand, remain, endure, persist, cost
stōĭcus, a, um, *adj*, stoic
stōla, ae, *f*, gown, robe
stōlĭdus, a, um, *adj*, dull, stupid
stŏmăchor, *v.i.* 1, *dep*, to be angry
stŏmăchōsus, a, um, *adj*, irritable
stŏmăchus, i, *m*, gullet, stomach, taste, distaste
stŏrĕa, ae, *f*, straw-mat
străbo, ōnis, *m*, one who squints
strāges, is, *f*, destruction, massacre, slaughter
strāgŭlum, i, *n*, rug
strāgŭlus, a, um, *adj*, covering
strāmen, ĭnis, *n*, straw
strāmentum, i, *n*, straw
strāmĭnĕus, a, um, *adj*, of straw
strangŭlo, *v.t.* 1, to strangle
strătēgēma, ătis, *n*, stratagem
strātum, i, *n*, blanket, quilt, pillow, bed
strātus, a, um, *adj*, stretched out
strēnŭus, a, um, *adj*, *adv*, **ē**, brisk, quick, vigorous
strĕpito, *v.i.* 1, to rattle
strĕpitus, ūs, *m*, din
strĕpo, ŭi, *v.i.* 3, to rattle, rumble, roar
strictim, *adv*, briefly
strictūra, ae, *f*, iron bar
strictus, a, um, *adj*, tight
strīdĕo, di (**strīdo, di,** 3), *v.i.* 2, to creak, hiss, rattle
strīdor, ōris, *m*, creaking, hissing
strīdŭlus, a, um, *adj*, creaking, hissing
strigĭlis, is, *f*, scraper used by bathers for cleaning the skin

stringo, nxi, ctum, *v.t.* 3, to draw tight, graze, strip off, draw (sword)
stringor, ōris, *m*, touch, shock
strix, strĭgis, *f*, screech-owl
structor, ōris, *m*, builder
structūra, ae, *f*, construction
strŭes, is, *f*, heap, pile
strŭo, xi, ctum, *v.t.* 3, to pile up, build, contrive
strūthĭŏcămēlus, i, *m*, ostrich
stŭdĕo, *v.i.t.* 2, *with dat*, to be eager about, strive; pursue, favour
stŭdiōsus, a, um, *adj*, *adv*, **ē,** eager, anxious, friendly
stŭdĭum, ii, *n*, eagerness, endeavour, affection, devotion, study
stultĭtĭa, ae, *f*, foolishness
stultus, a, um, *adj*, *adv*, **ē,** foolish
stūpa, ae, *f*, flax, tow
stūpĕfăcio, fēci, factum, *v.t.* 3, to stun, daze
stūpĕfactus, a, um, *adj*, stunned
stūpĕo, *v.i.t.* 2, to be stunned, amazed; be astonished at
stūpĕus, a, um, *adj*, made of tow
stūpĭdus, a, um, *adj*, amazed
stūpor, ōris, *m*, astonishment, stupidity
stupp . . . see **stūp. . . .**
stŭpro, *v.t.* 1, to ravish
stŭprum, i, *n*, disgrace, lewdness
sturnus, i, *m*, starling
suādĕo, si, sum, *v.i.t.* 2, *with dat*, to urge, persuade, recommend
suāsio, ōnis, *f*, recommendation
suāsor, ōris, *m*, adviser
suāvilŏquens, ntis, *adj*, pleasant-speaking
suāvior, *v.t.* 1, *dep*, to kiss
suāvis, e, *adj*, *adv*, **ĭter,** agreeable, pleasant
suāvĭtas, ātis, *f*, pleasantness
suāvium, ii, *n*, kiss
sub, *prep. with acc. and abl*, under, beneath, near, during, towards, just after
sŭbactio, ōnis, *f*, preparation
sŭbausculto, *v.t.* 1, to eavesdrop
subcentŭrio, ōnis, *m*, subaltern
subdĭtīvus, a, um, *adj*, counterfeit
subdo, didi, ditum, *v.t.* 3, to place under, subdue
subdŏlus, a, um, *adj*, crafty
subdūco, xi, ctum, *v.t.* 3, to pull up, haul up, remove, calculate, balance (accounts)
sŭbĕo, *v.i.t.* 4, to come up to, spring up, occur; enter, submit to, suffer, incur
sūber, ĕris, *n*, cork-tree
subflāvus, a, um, *adj*, yellowish
sūbicio, iēci, iectum, *v.t.* 3, to throw or place under or near, counterfeit, subject, affix, prompt
subiectio, ōnis, *f*, placing under, forging
subiecto, *v.t.* 1, to throw up
subiectus, a, um, *adj*, lying near, subject
sŭbigo, ēgi, actum, *v.t.* 3, to bring up, plough, conquer, subdue, compel, rub down
sūbinde, *adv*, immediately, now and then
sŭbitō, *adv*, suddenly
sŭbitus, a, um, *adj*, sudden
subiungo, nxi, nctum, *v.t.* 3, to subordinate, subdue
sublābor, lapsus, *v.i.* 3, *dep*, to glide away
sublātus, a, um, *adj*, proud
sublĕgo, lēgi, lectum, *v.t.* 3, to gather up, kidnap
sublĕvo, *v.t.* 1, to lift up, support, alleviate
sublĭca, ae, *f*, stake, palisade
sublĭgo, *v.t.* 1, to tie on
sublīme, *adv*, aloft, on high
sublīmis, e, *adj*, high, eminent
sublūcĕo, *v.i.* 2, to glimmer
sublŭo, *no perf*, **lūtum,** *v.t.* 3, to flow along, wash
sublustris, e, *adj*, glimmering
subm . . . see **summ. . . .**
subnecto, xŭi, xum, *v.t.* 3, to tie on underneath
subnixus, a, um, *adj*, propped up
sŭbŏles, is, *f*, offspring, race
sŭborno, *v.t.* 1, to equip, fit out, instigate
subr . . . see **surr. . . .**
subscrĭbo, psi, ptum, *v.t.* 3, to write underneath, note down
subscriptio, ōnis, *f*, anything written underneath
subsĕco, ŭi, ctum, *v.t.* 1, to clip
subsellium, ii, *n*, seat, law-court
subsĕquor, sĕcūtus, *v.i.t.* 3, *dep*, to follow, ensue; follow closely, imitate
subsicīvus, a, um, *adj*, remaining
subsidiārius, a, um, *adj*, reserve
subsidĭum, ii, *n*, reserve-ranks, assistance, aid, protection
subsīdo, sēdi, sessum, *v.i.t.* 3, to settle down, lie in ambush; waylay
subsisto, stĭti, *v.i.* 3, to stop, halt, remain, withstand
subsortior, *v.t.* 4, *dep*, to choose as a substitute
substerno, strāvi, strātum, *v.t.* 3, to spread underneath, cover

For List of Abbreviations used, turn to pages 3, 4

substitŭo, ŭi, ūtum, *v.t.* 3, to put under, substitute
substringo, nxi, ctum, *v.t.* 3, to tie; **aurem** prick up the ear
substructio, ōnis, *f*, foundation
substrŭo, xi, ctum, *v.t.* 3, to lay foundations
subsum, esse, *v, irreg*, to be under or near, to be at hand
subtēmen, inis, *n*, texture, weft
subter, *adv. and prep. with abl*, beneath, below
subterfŭgio, fūgi, *v.t.* 3, to avoid
subterlābens, ntis, *adj*, gliding under
subterlābor, *v.i.* 3, *dep*, to glide under
subterrānĕus, a, um, *adj*, underground
subtexo, ŭi, xtum, *v.t.* 3, to veil
subtĭlis, e, *adj, adv*, **ĭter,** slender, delicate, precise
subtilĭtas, ātis, *f*, exactness, subtlety
subtrăho, xi, ctum, *v.t.* 3, to remove stealthily, carry off
sŭbŭcŭla, ae, *f*, shirt
sŭbulcus, i, *m*, pig-keeper
sŭburbānus, a, um, *adj*, suburban
sŭburbium, ii, *n*, suburb
subvectio, ōnis, *f*, conveyance
subvecto, *v.t.* 1, to convey
subvĕho, xi, ctum, *v.t.* 3, to convey
subvĕnio, vēni, ventum, *v.i.* 4, *with dat*, to help, aid, occur to the mind
subverto, ti, sum, *v.t.* 3, to overthrow
subvŏlo, *v.i.* 1, to fly up
subvolvo, *v.t.* 3, to roll up
succēdo, cessi, cessum, *v.i.t.* 3, to go under, advance, enter; ascend, follow after, succeed
succendo, di, sum, *v.t.* 3, to kindle
succensĕo, ŭi, sum, *v.i.* 2, to be angry
successio, ōnis. *f*, succession
successor, ōris, *m*, successor
successus, ūs, *m*, advance, success
succido, di, *v.i.* 3, to sink
succīdo, di, sum, *v.t.* 3, to cut down
succingo, nxi, nctum, *v.t.* 3, to surround, girdle, tuck up
succlāmo, *v.t.* 1, to shout out
succumbo, cŭbŭi, cŭbĭtum, *v.i.* 3, to surrender
succurro, curri, cursum, *v.i.* 3, *with dat*, to help, aid, occur
sūcĭnum, i, *n*, amber
sūcōsus, a, um, *adj*, juicy
suctus, ūs, *m*, sucking
sūcus, i, *m*, juice, energy, life
sūdārium, ii, *n*, handkerchief
sūdis, is, *f*, stake, pile
sūdo, *v.i.t.* 1, to sweat, toil; exude
sūdor, ōris, *m*, sweat, toil
sūdum, i, *n*, clear weather
sūdus, a, um, *adj*, clear, bright
sŭesco, sŭēvi, sŭētum, *v.i.t.* 3, to be accustomed
sŭētus, a, um, *adj*, accustomed
suffĕro, ferre, sustŭli, sublātum, *v, irreg*, to undergo, suffer
sufficio, fēci, fectum, *v.i.t.* 3, to be sufficient; impregnate, supply, substitute, elect
suffīgo, xi, xum, *v.t.* 3, to fix
suffimentum, i, *n*, incense
suffio, *v.t.* 4, to perfume
sufflāmen, inis, *n*, drag-chain
sufflātus, a, um, *adj*, puffed up
sufflo, *v.t.* 1, to inflate
suffōco, *v.t.* 1, to strangle
suffŏdio, fōdi, fossum, *v.t.* 3, to pierce underneath
suffrāgātio, ōnis, *f*, support
suffrāgātor, ōris, *m*, supporter
suffrāgium, ii, *n*, vote, ballot
suffrāgor, *v.i.* 1, *dep, with dat.* to vote for, support
suffundo, fūdi, fūsum, *v.t.* 3, to spread over, tinge
suffulcio, fulsi, fultum, *v.t.* 4, to prop up
suffūsus, a, um, *adj*, spread over
suggĕro, gessi, gestum, *v.t.* 3, to carry up, supply
suggestum, i, *n*, platform
suggestus, ūs, *m*, platform
sūgo, xi, ctum, *v.t.* 3, to suck
sŭi, *genit. of reflexive pron*, of himself, herself, itself, etc.
sulco, *v.t.* 1, to plough
sulcus, i, *m*, furrow, ditch
sulfur, ŭris, *n*, sulphur
sulfŭrāta, ōrum, *n. pl*, matches
sulfŭrĕus, a, um, *adj*, sulphurous
sum, esse, fŭi, *v, irreg*, to be, exist, happen
summa, ae, *f*, top, chief point, perfection, amount, sum
summātim, *adv*, briefly
summē, *adv*, extremely
summergo, si, sum, *v.t.* 3, to submerge, overwhelm
summĭnistro, *v.t.* 1, to supply
summissus, a, um, *adj, adv*, **ē,** gentle, soft, low, mean
summitto, mīsi, missum, *v.t.* 3, to send up, produce, rear, raise, lower, submit, supply, send
summŏvĕo, mōvi, mōtum, *v.t.* 2, to drive away, remove

summus, a, um, *adj*, highest, topmost
sūmo, mpsi, mptum, *v.t.* 3, to take hold of, assume, inflict, choose, claim, suppose, spend, use, buy
sumptĭo, ōnis, *f*, assumption
sumptŭōsus, a, um, *adj, adv,* **ē,** expensive, lavish
sumptus, ūs, *m*, expense
sŭo, sŭi, sūtum, *v.t.* 3, to sew
sŭpellex, lectĭlis, *f*, furniture
sŭper, *adv. and prep. with acc. and abl*, above, over, on, besides, concerning
sŭpĕrābĭlis, e, *adj*, able to be overcome
sŭperbĭa, ae, *f*, pride, arrogance
sŭperbĭo, *v.i.* 4, to be proud
sŭperbus, a, um, *adj, adv,* **ē,** proud, haughty, delicate, squeamish, magnificent
sŭpercĭlĭum, ii, *n*, eye-brow, ridge, summit, arrogance
sŭpercresco, crēvi, *v.i.* 3, to grow up
sŭpĕrēmĭnĕo, *v.t.* 2, to overtop
sŭperfĭcĭes, ēi, *f*, top, surface
sŭperfundo, fūdi, fūsum, *v.t.* 3, to pour over
sŭpĕri, ōrum, *m.pl*, the gods
sŭpĕrimmĭnĕo, *v.i.* 2, to overhang
sŭpĕrimpōno, *no perf*, **pŏsĭtum,** *v.t.* 3, to place upon
sŭpĕrĭnĭcĭo, *no perf*, **iectum,** *v.t.* 3, to throw over or upon
sŭperiăcĭo, iēci, iectum, *v.t.* 3, to throw over, overflow
sŭpĕrĭor, ĭus, *comp. adj*, higher, previous, former, superior
sŭperlātĭo, ōnis, *f*, exaggeration, hyperbole
sŭpernus, a, um, *adj, adv,* **ē,** upper, on high ground
sŭpĕro, *v.i.t.* 1, to have the upper hand, remain; ascend, outstrip, conquer
sŭpersĕdĕo, sēdi, sessum, *v.i.t.* 2, *with abl*, to refrain (from)
sŭperstĕs, ĭtis, *adj*, surviving
sŭperstĭtio, ōnis, *f*, excessive fear of the gods
sŭperstĭtiōsus, a, um, *adj*, superstitious
sŭpersto, *v.i.t.* 1, to stand over
sŭpersum, esse, fŭi, *v.i., irreg*, to remain, survive
sŭpĕrus, a, um, *adj*, upper, higher
sŭpervăcānĕus, a, um, *adj*, unnecessary
sŭpervăcŭus, a, um, *adj*, unnecessary
sŭpervĕnio, vēni, ventum, *v.i.t.* 4, to come up, arrive; fall upon
sŭpervŏlo, *v.i.t.* 1, to fly over
sŭpīno, *v.t.* 1, to bend backwards
sŭpīnus, a, um, *adj*, lying on the back, sloping
suppĕdĭto, *v.i.t.* 1, to be enough, plenty; to supply
suppĕto, īvi, ītum, *v.i.* 3, to be at hand, to be enough
supplanto, *v.t.* 1, to trip up
supplēmentum, i, *n*, reinforcements
supplĕo, ēvi, ētum, *v.t.* 2, to complete, fill up
supplex, ĭcis, *c*, suppliant
supplex, ĭcis, *adj*, beseeching
supplicātio, ōnis, *f*, public thanksgiving
supplĭcĭum, ii, *n*, punishment
supplico, *v.i.* 1, to implore
supplōdo, si, *v.i.t.* 3, to stamp
suppōno, pŏsŭi, pŏsĭtum, *v.t.* 3, to put under, substitute
supporto, *v.t.* 1, to convey
supprĭmo, pressi, pressum, *v.t.* 3, to sink, suppress
suppūro, *v.i.* 1, to suppurate
sŭprā, *adv. and prep. with acc*, above, over, beyond, before
sŭprēmus, a, um, *adj*, highest, last
sūra, ae, *f*, calf of the leg
surcŭlus, i, *m*, shoot, twig
surdĭtas, ātis, *f*, deafness
surdus, a, um, *adj*, deaf
surgo, surrexi, rectum, *v.i.t.* 3, to rise, stand up; raise
surrēgŭlus, i, *m*, subordinate ruler
surrēmĭgo, *v.i.* 1, to row along
surrēpo, psi, ptum, *v.i.t.* 3, to creep under
surrīdĕo, si, sum, *v.i.* 2, to smile
surrĭpio, ŭi, reptum, *v.t.* 3, to snatch away, steal
surrōgo, *v.t.* 1, to substitute
surrŭo, ŭi, ŭtum, *v.t.* 3, to undermine, overthrow
sursum, *adv*, upwards, on high
sūs, sŭis, *c*, pig
susceptio, ōnis, *f*, undertaking
suscĭpio, cēpi, ceptum, *v.t.* 3, to undertake, acknowledge, undergo
suscĭto, *v.t.* 1, to raise, arouse
suspectus, a, um, *adj*, mistrusted
suspectus, ūs, *m*, height
suspendĭum, ii, *n*, hanging
suspendo, di, sum, *v.t.* 3, to hang up, lift up, keep in suspense, interrupt
suspensus, a, um, *adj*, raised, hesitating
suspĭcio, spexi, ctum, *v.i.t.* 3, to look up; admire, suspect
suspĭcio, ōnis, *f*, suspicion

suspīciōsus, a, um, *adj, adv,* **ē,** suspicious
suspicor, *v.t.* 1, *dep,* to suspect, suppose
suspīritus, ūs, *m,* sigh
suspīrium, ii, *n,* sigh
suspīro, *v.i.t.* 1, to sigh; long for
sustento, *v.t.* 1, to support, maintain, endure
sustinĕo, ŭi, tentum, *v.t.* 2, to support, restrain, withstand, maintain
sūsurro, *v.i.t.* 1, to hum; mutter
sūsurrus, i, *m,* humming
sūsurrus, a, um, *adj,* whispering
sūta, ōrum, *n. pl,* joints
sūtilis, e, *adj,* sewed together
sūtor, ōris, *m,* cobbler
sūtōrius, a, um, *adj,* of a cobbler
sūtūra, ae, *f,* seam
sŭus, a, um, *adj,* his, hers, its, their
sȳcŏmōrus, i, *f,* sycamore
sȳcŏphanta, ae, *m,* sycophant, cheat
syllăba, ae, *f,* syllable
syllăbātim, *adv,* by syllables
symphōnia, ae, *f,* harmony
symphōniăcus, i, *m,* chorister
sȳnăgōga, ae, *f,* synagogue
syngrăpha, ae, *f,* promissory note
syngrăphus, i, *m,* passport
syntaxis, is, *f,* syntax

T

tăbānus, i, *m,* gad-fly
tăbella, ae, *f,* small board or table, writing-tablet, letter, ballot-paper, small picture
tăbellārius, ii, *m,* letter-bearer
tābĕo, *v.i.* 2, to melt away
tăberna, ae, *f,* hut, shop, inn
tăbernăcŭlum, i, *n,* tent
tăbernārius, ii, *m,* shop-keeper
tābes, is, *f,* wasting-away, disease
tābesco, bŭi, *v.i.* 3, to melt away
tābĭdus, a, um, *adj,* decaying
tăbŭla, ae, *f,* plank, writing-tablet, letter, account-book, picture, painting, map, table
tăbŭlāria, ae, *f,* record-office
tăbŭlārium, ii, *n,* archives
tăbŭlārius, ii, *m,* registrar
tăbŭlātum, i, *n,* floor, storey
tābum, i, *n,* pus, matter, infectious disease
tăcĕo, *v.i.t.* 2, to be silent; to be silent about
tăciturnĭtas, ātis, *f,* silence
tăciturnus, a, um, *adj,* silent
tăcĭtus, a, um, *adj, adv,* **ē,** secret, silent
tactus, ūs, *m,* touch, feel, influence
taeda, ae, *f,* pine-tree, torch
taedet, taedŭit, *v.* 2, *impers. with acc. of person,* it offends, disgusts, wearies
taedĭum, ii, *n,* weariness, disgust
taenia, ae, *f,* hair-ribbon
taeter, tra, trum, *adj,* hideous
taetrĭcus, a, um, *adj,* harsh
tālāris, e, *adj,* ankle-length
tālĕa, ae, *f,* stick, stake
tālentum, i, *n,* sum of money (app. £400–£500); weight (½ cwt.)
tālĭo, ōnis, *f,* similar punishment, reprisal
tālis, e, *adj,* of such a kind
talpa, ae, *f,* mole
tālus, i, *m,* ankle-bone, heel, die (marked on four sides)
tam, *adv,* so, as, equally
tamdiū, *adv,* so long
tămen, *adv,* nevertheless, however, still
tămetsi, *conj,* although
tamquam, *adv,* as much as, just as, as if, for example
tandem, *adv,* at length
tango, tĕtigi, tactum, *v.t.* 3, to touch, taste, reach, strike, affect, impress ence, mention
tanquam, see **tamquam**
tantisper, *adv,* so long, meanwhile
tantŏpĕre, *adv,* so greatly
tantŭlus, a, um, *adj,* so little
tantum, *adv,* so much, only
tantummŏdo, *adv,* only, merely
tantundem, *adv,* just as much
tantus, a, um, *adj,* so great; **tanti esse,** to be worth so much; **tantō,** by so much
tăpēte, is, *n,* tapestry
tardĭtas, ātis, *f,* slowness
tardo, *v.i.t.* 1, to delay; hinder
tardus, a, um, *adj, adv,* **ē,** slow
tăta, ae, *m,* dad, daddy
taurēus, a, um, *adj,* of a bull
taurīnus, a, um, *adj,* of a bull
taurus, i, *m,* bull, ox
taxus, i, *f,* yew-tree
tē, *acc. or abl. of* **tū**
tector, ōris, *m,* plasterer
tectōrium, ii, *n,* plaster
tectum, i, *n,* roof, house
tectus, a, um, *adj, adv,* **ō,** covered, hidden, secret
tĕges, ĕtis, *f,* mat
tēgĭmen, ĭnis, *n,* cover
tĕgo, xi, ctum, *v.t.* 3, to cover, hide, protect
tēgŭla, ae, *f,* tile
tēgŭmen, see **tēgĭmen**

tĕgŭmentum, i, *n*, cover
tēla, ae, *f*, web, warp, loom
tellūs, ūris, *f*, earth, globe, land, region
tēlum, i, *n*, weapon, javelin
tĕmĕrārius, a, um, *adj*, rash
tĕmĕrē, *adv*, by chance, rashly
tĕmĕritas, ātis, *f*, rashness
tĕmĕro, *v.t.* 1, to defile, disgrace
tēmētum, i, *n*, wine
temno, *v.t.* 3, to despise
tēmo, ōnis, *m*, pole, beam
tempĕrans, ntis, *adj*, moderate
tempĕrantia, ae, *f*, moderation
tempĕrātio, ōnis, *f*, symmetry, temperament
tempĕrātus, a, um, *adj*, moderate
tempĕries, ēi, *f*, mildness
tempĕro, *v.i.t.* 1, to abstain, be moderate, be indulgent; mix properly, regulate, govern
tempestas, ātis, *f*, time, period, weather, storm
tempestīvus, a, um, *adj*, *adv*, **ē,** suitable, timely, early
templum, i, *n*, temple, open space
tempto, see **tento**
tempus, ŏris, *n*, time, opportunity; **tempŏra,** times, temples (of the head); **ad tempus,** (*adv. phr.*) at the right time, for the time being
tēmŭlentus, a, um, *adj*, drunk
tĕnācitas, ātis, *f*, tenacity
tĕnax, ācis, *adj*, holding tight, firm, stingy
tendo, tĕtendi, tentum, *v.i.t.* 3, to aim, go, march, stretch, strive, encamp; stretch, extend
tĕnĕbrae, ārum, *f. pl*, darkness
tĕnĕbricōsus, a, um, *adj*, dark, gloomy
tĕnĕbrōsus, a, um, *adj*, dark, gloomy
tĕnĕo, ŭi, tentum, *v.i.t.* 2, to hold a position, sail, continue; hold, have, keep, restrain, uphold, maintain, control, comprehend, include
tĕner, ĕra, ĕrum, *adj*, tender
tĕnor, ōris, *m*, course, career
tensa, ae, *f*, triumphal chariot
tentāmentum, i, *n*, attempt
tentātio, ōnis, *f*, trial, attempt
tentātor, ōris, *m*, tempter
tento (tempto), *v.t.* 1, to handle, attack, attempt, tempt, excite
tentōrium, ii, *n*, tent
tentus, a, um, *adj*, extended
tĕnŭis, e, *adj*, *adv*, **ĭter,** thin, fine, meagre, poor, subtle
tĕnŭitas, ātis, *f*, slenderness, poverty
tĕnŭo, *v.t.* 1, to make thin, reduce, weaken, degrade
tĕnus, *prep. with abl*, as far as, according to
tĕpĕfăcio, fēci, factum, *v.t.* 3, to warm
tĕpĕo, *v.i.* 2, to be warm
tĕpesco, pŭi, *v.i.* 3, to grow warm
tĕpidus, a, um, *adj*, warm
tĕpor, ōris, *m*, warmth
tĕr, *adv*, three times
tĕrĕbinthus, i, *f*, terebinth tree
tĕrĕbra, ae, *f*, tool
tĕrĕbro, *v.t.* 1, to bore through
tĕrĕs, ĕtis, *adj*, rounded, smooth, polished
tergĕminus, a, um, *adj*, triple
tergĕo, si, sum, *v.t.* 2, to clean, polish
tergiversātio, ōnis, *f*, backsliding
tergiversor, *v.i.* 1, *dep*, to shuffle, refuse
tergo, si, sum, see **tergĕo**
tergum, i, *n*, back, rear, skin; **a tergo,** (*adv. phr.*) at the rear
terminālia, ium, *n. pl*, festival of Terminus (God of boundaries)
terminātio, ōnis, *f*, fixing
termino, *v.t.* 1, to limit, fix, define, determine, end
terminus, i, *m*, boundary, end
terni, ae, a, *pl. adj*, three each
tĕro, trīvi, trĭtum, *v.t.* 3, to rub, grind, smooth, polish, wear out, spend or waste time
terra, ae, *f*, earth, land, ground, region
terrēnus, a, um, *adj*, made of earth, terrestrial
terrĕo, *v.t.* 2, to frighten
terrestris, e, *adj*, of earth or land
terrĕus, a, um, *adj*, of earth or land
terribilis, e, *adj*, dreadful
terricŭla, ōrum, *n. pl*, scarecrow bugbear
terrĭfico, *v.t.* 1, to terrify
terrĭficus, a, um, *adj*, frightful
terrĭgĕna, ae, *c*, earthborn
terrĭto, *v.t.* 1, to terrify
terror, ōris, *m*, terror, dread
tertius, a, um, *adj*, *adv*, **ō,** third
tĕruncius, ii, *m*, trifling sum
tessellātus, a, um, *adj*, tesselated, mosaic
tessĕra, ae, *f*, stone or wooden cube, die, watchword, ticket
testa, ae, *f*, jug, broken piece of pottery, shell-fish
testāmentum, i, *n*, will, testament
testātor, ōris, *m*, testator
testātus, a, um, *adj*, manifest
testĭficātio, ōnis, *f*, evidence

For List of Abbreviations used, turn to pages 3, 4

testĭficor, *v.t.* 1, *dep,* to give evidence, demonstrate
testĭmōnĭum, ii, *n,* evidence
testis, is, *c,* witness
testor, *v.t.* 1, *dep,* to call a witness, prove, declare
testu(m), i, *n,* lid, earthen pot
testūdĭnĕus, a, um, *adj,* of a tortoise
testūdo, ĭnis, *f,* tortoise, lute, military shelter
tĕtănus, i, *m,* tetanus
tēter, tra, trum, *adj,* hideous
tĕtrarches, ae, *m,* petty princeling
tĕtrĭcus, a, um, *adj,* harsh
texo, ŭi, xtum, *v.t.* 3, to weave, build, devise
textile, is, *n,* fabric
textĭlis, e, *adj,* woven
textor, ōris, *m,* weaver
textum, i, *n,* web, fabric
textus, ūs, *m,* texture
thălămus, i, *m,* apartment, bedroom, marriage
thĕātrālis, e, *adj,* theatrical
thĕātrum, i, *n,* theatre
thēca, ae, *f,* envelope
thĕŏlŏgĭa, ae, *f,* theology
thĕŏlŏgus, i, *m,* theologian
thĕōrēma, ătis, *n,* theorem
thermae, ārum, *f. pl,* warm baths
thēsaurus, i, *m,* store, hoard, treasure, treasure-house
thĭăsus, i, *m,* dance in honour of Bacchus
thŏlus, i, *m,* dome
thōrax, ācis, *m,* breastplate
thunnus, i, *m,* tunny-fish
thūs, thūris, *n,* incense
thymbra, ae, *f,* savory (plant)
thȳmum, i, *n,* thyme
thyrsus, i, *m,* stem of plant, staff carried by Bacchus
tĭāra, ae, *f,* tiara
tĭbĭa, ae, *f,* flute
tĭbĭāle, is, *n,* stocking
tĭbĭcen, ĭnis, *m,* flute-player
tĭbĭcĭna, ae, *f,* flute-player
tĭbĭcĭnĭum, ii, *n,* flute-playing
tignum, i, *n,* timber, log
tĭgris, is (ĭdis), *c,* tiger
tĭlĭa, ae, *f,* linden or lime tree
tĭmĕo, *v.i.t.* 2, to fear
tĭmĭdĭtas, ātis, *f,* cowardice
tĭmĭdus, a, um, *adj, adv,* **ē,** afraid, cowardly
tĭmor, ōris, *m,* fear, alarm, object of fear
tĭnĕa, ae, *f,* moth, book-worm
tingo, nxi, nctum, *v.t.* 3, to moisten, dye
tinnĭo, *v.i.t.* 4, to ring; tinkle
tinnĭtus, ūs, *m,* ringing
tinnŭlus, a, um, *adj,* tinkling
tintinnābŭlum, i, *n,* bell
tīro, ōnis, *m,* recruit, novice
tīrōcĭnĭum, ii, *n,* first campaign, inexperience
titillātĭo, ōnis, *f,* tickling
titillo, *v.t.* 1, to tickle
titŭbo, *v.i.* 1, to stagger, hesitate, be perplexed
titŭlus, i, *m,* title, placard, notice, honour, glory
tōfus, i, *m,* tufa (rock)
tōga, ae, *f,* toga: the long outer garment of the Romans
tŏgātus, a, um, *adj,* wearing the toga
tŏlĕrābĭlis, e, *adj,* endurable
tŏlĕrantĭa, ae, *f,* tolerance
tŏlĕro, *v.t.* 1, to bear, endure
tollēno, ōnis, *m,* a swing-beam
tollo, sustŭli, sublātum, *v.t.* 3, to lift, raise, remove, destroy, educate, acknowledge
tŏnans, ntis, *m,* god of thunder
tondĕo, tŏtondi, tonsum, *v.t.* 2, to shave, crop, prune, graze
tŏnĭtrus, ūs, *m,* thunder
tŏnĭtrŭum, i, *n,* thunder
tŏno, ŭi, *v.i.t.* 1, to thunder; thunder out
tonsa, ae, *f,* oar
tonsillae, ārum, *f. pl,* tonsils
tonsor, ōris, *m,* barber
tonsōrĭus, a, um, *adj,* of shaving
tonsūra, ae, *f,* shearing
tŏpĭārius, ii, *m,* landscape-gardener
tŏreuma, ătis, *n,* embossed work
tormentum, i, *n,* missile, rope, missile-launcher, instrument of torture, rack, pain
tormĭna, um, *n. pl,* the gripes
torno, *v.t.* 1, to round off
tornus, i, *m,* lathe
tŏrōsus, a, um, *adj,* muscular
torpĕfăcio, fēci, factum, *v.t.* 3, to numb
torpens, ntis, *adj,* numb
torpĕo, *v.i.* 2, to be stiff, numb, sluggish, listless
torpesco, pŭi, *v.i.* 3, to become stiff or listless
torpor, ōris, *m,* numbness
torquātus, a, um, *adj,* wearing a collar
torquĕo, torsi, sum, *v.t.* 2, to twist, bend, wield, hurl, rack, torture

torquis (torques), is, *m, f,* collar, necklace, wreath
torrens, ntis, *adj,* burning
torrens, ntis, *m,* torrent
torrĕo, ŭi, tostum, *v.t.* 2, to dry, bake, scorch, burn
torrĭdus, a, um, *adj,* parched
torris, is, *m,* firebrand
tortĭlis, e, *adj,* twined
tortor, ōris, *m,* torturer
tortŭōsus, a, um, *adj,* winding, complicated
tortus, a, um, *adj,* twisted
tortus, ūs, *m,* twisting
tŏrus, i, *m,* muscle, knot, cushion, sofa, bed
torvus, a, um, *adj,* wild, grim
tŏt, *indecl. adj,* so many
tŏtĭdem, *indecl. adj,* just as many
tŏtĭens (tŏtĭes), *adv,* so often
tŏtum, i, *n,* whole
tŏtus, a, um, *adj,* the whole
trăbālis, e, *adj,* of a beam
trăbĕa, ae, *f,* robe of state
trabs, trăbis, *f,* beam, timber, tree, ship
tractābĭlis, e, *adj,* manageable, pliant, flexible
tractātĭo, ōnis, *f,* handling, treatment
tractātus, ūs, *m,* handling, treatment
tractim, *adv,* little by little
tracto, *v.t.* 1, to handle, manage, practise, discuss, drag
tractus, ūs, *m,* dragging, track, district, course, progress
trādĭtĭo, ōnis, *f,* surrender
trādo, dĭdi, dĭtum, *v.t.* 3, to hand over, commit, bequeath, relate
trādŭco, xi, ctum, *v.t.* 3, to bring over, degrade, spend (time)
trāductĭo, ōnis, *f,* transferring
trăgĭcus, a, um, *adj,* tragic, fearful, grand
trăgoedĭa, ae, *f,* tragedy
trăgoedus, i, *m,* tragic actor
trāgŭla, ae, *f,* javelin, dart
trăhĕa, ae, *f,* sledge
trăho, xi, ctum, *v.t.* 3, to drag, extract, inhale, quaff, drag away, plunder, spin, influence, delay, protract
trāĭcĭo, iēci, iectum, *v.t.* 3, to throw across, transport, transfix
trāiectĭo, ōnis, *f,* crossing over, passage
trāiectus, ūs, *m,* crossing
trāmēs, ĭtis, *m,* footpath, way
trāno, *v.t.* 1, to swim across
tranquillĭtas, ātis, *f,* calmness
tranquillo, *v.t.* 1, to calm
tranquillum, i, *n,* a calm
tranquillus, a, um, *adj, adv,* **ē,** calm, placid, serene
trans, *prep. with acc,* across, beyond, on the further side of
transăbĕo, *v.t.* 4, to transfix
transădĭgo, ēgi, actum, *v.t.* 3, to thrust through
transalpīnus, a, um, *adj,* beyond the Alps
transcendo, di, sum, *v.i.t.* 3, to climb over, surmount; exceed
transcrĭbo, psi, ptum, *v.t.* 3, to transcribe, forge, transfer
transcurro, curri, cursum, *v.i.t.* 3, to run across; pass through
transĕo, *v.i.t.* 4, to go over or across, pass by, surpass
transfĕro, ferre, tŭli, lātum, *v.t, irreg,* to bring across, carry along, transfer, translate
transfĭgo, xi, xum, *v.t.* 3, to pierce through
transfŏdĭo, fōdi, fossum, *v.t.* 3, to pierce through
transformo, *v.t.* 1, to transform
transfŭga, ae, *c,* deserter
transfŭgĭo, fūgi, *v.t.* 3, to desert
transfundo, fūdi, fūsum, *v.t.* 3, to transfer
transgrĕdĭor, gressus, *v.i.t.* 3, *dep,* to pass or climb over, across
transgressĭo, ōnis, *f,* passage
transĭgo, ēgi, actum, *v.t.* 3, to complete, transact, settle (a difference)
transilĭo, ŭi, *v.i.t.* 4, to leap across
transitĭo, ōnis, *f,* going over, passage
transĭtus, ūs, *m,* going over, passage
translātĭcĭus, a, um, *adj,* handed down
translātio, ōnis, *f,* transferring
translātus, a, um, *adj,* transferred, copied, figurative
translūcĕo, *v.i.* 2, to shine through
transmărīnus, a, um, *adj,* across the sea
transmĭgro, *v.i.* 1, to migrate
transmissus, ūs, *m,* transferring
transmitto, mīsi, missum, *v.i.t.* 3, to go across; send across, transfer, hand over
transmūto, *v.t.* 1, to change
transnăto, *v.i.* 1, to swim over
transpădānus, a, um, *adj,* beyond the river Po
transporto, *v.t.* 1, to carry across
transtrum, i, *n,* rowing-bench
transvĕho, xi, ctum, *v.t.* 3, to carry over
transverbĕro, *v.t.* 1, to transfix
transversārĭus, a, um, *adj,* crosswise
transversus, a, um, *adj,* crosswise

transvŏlo, *v.i.t.* 1, to fly across
trĕcēni, ae, a, *pl. adj,* three hundred each
trecentesĭmus, a, um, *adj,* three hundredth
trĕcenti, ae, a, *pl. adj,* three hundred
trĕdĕcim, *indecl. adj,* thirteen
trĕmĕbundus, a, um, *adj,* trembling
trĕmĕfăcio, fēci, factum, *v.t.* 3, to cause to tremble
trĕmendus, a, um, *adj,* dreadful
trĕmesco, *v.i.t.* 3, to tremble; tremble at
trĕmo, ŭi, *v.i.t.* 3, to tremble; tremble at
trĕmor, ōris, *m,* shuddering
trĕmŭlus, a, um, *adj,* trembling
trĕpĭdans, ntis, *adj,* trembling
trĕpĭdātio, ōnis, *f,* confusion
trĕpĭdo, *v.i.t.* 1, to be alarmed; tremble at
trĕpĭdus, a, um, *adj,* alarmed
trēs, tria, *adj,* three
triangŭlum, i, *n,* triangle
triangŭlus, a, um, *adj,* triangular
triārii, ōrum, *m. pl,* veteran soldiers who fought in the third rank
tribŭārius, a, um, *adj,* of a tribe
tribūlis, e, *adj,* of the same tribe
tribŭlum, i, *n,* threshing-platform
tribŭlus, i, *m,* thistle
tribūnal, ālis, *n,* platform, judgement-seat
tribūnātus, ūs, *m,* position of tribune
tribūnicius, a, um, *adj,* of a tribune
tribūnus, i, *m,* tribune; 1. army officer; 2. magistrate to defend the rights of the people
trĭbŭo, ŭi, ūtum, *v.t.* 3, to allot, give, attribute
trĭbus, ūs, *f,* tribe
trĭbus, see **trēs**
trĭbūtim, *adv,* by tribes
trĭbūtum, i, *n,* tribute, tax
trĭcae, ārum, *f. pl,* tricks
trĭcēni, ae, a, *pl. adj,* thirty each
trĭceps, cipĭtis, *adj,* three-headed
trĭcēsĭmus, a, um, *adj,* thirtieth
trĭcies, *adv,* thirty times
trĭclīnium, ii, *n,* dining-couch, dining-room
trĭcorpor, ŏris, *adj,* three-bodied
trĭdens, ntis, *adj,* three-pronged; *as nn,* trident
trĭdŭum, i, *n,* three days
triennium, ii, *n,* three years
triens, ntis, *m,* a third part
triĕtĕrica, ōrum, *n. pl,* festival of Bacchus
trifaux, cis, *adj,* with three throats
trĭfĭdus, a, um, *adj,* three-forked
trĭfŏlium, ii, *n,* shamrock
triformis, e, *adj,* three-fold
trigĕminus, a, um, *adj,* triple
trigēsĭmus, a, um, *adj,* thirtieth
trīginta, *indecl. adj,* thirty
trigōn, ōnis, *m,* ball
trilĭbris, e, *adj,* weighing three pounds
trilinguis, e, *adj,* three-tongued
trilix, īcis, *adj,* with three thongs
trimestris, e, *adj,* of three months
trĭmus, a, um, *adj,* three years old
trĭni, ae, a, *pl. adj,* three each
trinōdis, e, *adj,* three-knotted
triōnes, um, *m. pl,* constellation of the Great and Lesser Bear
tripartītus, a, um, *adj, adv,* **ō,** three-fold
trĭpēs, ĕdis, *adj,* three-footed
trĭplex, ĭcis, *adj,* triple
trĭplĭco, *v.t.* 1, to treble
trĭpŭdium, ii, *n,* religious dance, favourable omen
trĭpūs, ŏdis, *m,* tripod
triquĕtrus, a, um, *adj,* triangular
trirēmis, e, *adj,* with three banks of oars
tristis, e, *adj,* sad, gloomy, harsh, disagreeable
tristĭtia, ae, *f,* sadness, gloominess, harshness
trisulcus, a, um, *adj,* three-forked
trĭticĕus, a, um, *adj,* of wheat
trĭticum, i, *n,* wheat
trĭtūra, ae, *f,* threshing (of grain)
trĭtus, a, um, *adj,* beaten, common, worn, familiar
triumphālis, e, *adj,* triumphal
triumpho, *v.i.t.* 1, to celebrate a triumph; triumph over
triumphus, i, *m,* triumphal procession after a victory
triumvirātus, ūs, *m,* triumvirate
triumviri, ōrum, *m. pl,* board of three men
trĭvium, ii, *n,* cross-road
trŏchaeus, i, *m,* metrical foot
trochlĕa, ae, *f,* pulley
trŏchus, i, *m,* hoop
trōpaeum, i, *n,* trophy, victory
trōpĭcus, a, um, *adj,* tropical
trŭcīdātio, ōnis, *f,* butchery
trŭcīdo, *v.t.* 1, to slaughter
trŭcŭlentus, a, um, *adj,* harsh
trŭdis, is, *f,* pole, pike
trŭdo, si, sum, *v.t.* 3, to push, drive, put out
trulla, ae, *f,* ladle
truncātus, a, um, *adj,* maimed

trunco, *v.t.* 1, to maim, cut off
truncus, a, um, *adj*, maimed
truncus, i, *m*, trunk, stem
trūtina, ae, *f*, pair of scales
trux, ŭcis, *adj*, harsh, stern
tū, *pron*, you (singular)
tŭba, ae, *f*, trumpet
tŭber, ĕris, *n*, swelling, tumour
tŭbĭcen, ĭnis, *m*, trumpeter
tŭbŭlātus, a, um, *adj*, tubular
tŭbŭlus, i, *m*, tube
tŭĕor, *v.t.* 2, *dep*, to look at, gaze at, consider, guard, maintain, support
tŭgŭrium, ii, *n*, cottage
tŭli, see **fero**
tum, *adv, and conj*, then
tŭmĕfăcio, fēci, factum, *v.t.* 3, to cause to swell
tŭmĕo, *v.i.* 2, to swell, be puffed up
tŭmesco, mui, *v.i.* 3, to become swollen, be puffed up
tŭmĭdus, a, um, *adj*, swollen, excited, enraged
tŭmor, ōris, *m*, swelling, commotion
tŭmŭlo, *v.t.* 1, to bury
tŭmultŭārius, a, um, *adj*, hurried, hurriedly raised (troops)
tŭmultŭor, *v.i.* 1, *dep*, to be confused
tŭmultŭōsus, a, um, *adj, adv,* **ē,** restless, confused, turbulent
tŭmultus, ūs, *m*, uproar, tempest, rebellion
tŭmŭlus, i, *m*, hill, mound
tunc, *adv*, then
tundo, tŭtŭdi, tunsum (tusum), *v.t.* 3, to beat, strike, pound
tŭnĭca, ae, *f*, tunic, husk
tŭnĭcātus, a, um, *adj*, dressed in a tunic
tŭnĭcopallĭum, i, *n*, short cloak
tūrārius, ii, *m*, a dealer
turba, ae, *f*, hubbub, uproar, crowd, band, quarrel, confusion
turbātor, ōris, *m*, disturber
turbātus, a, um, *adj*, disturbed
turbĭdus, a, um, *adj, adv,* **ē,** confused, troubled, violent
turbo, *v.t.* 1, to confuse, disturb, make thick
turbo, ĭnis, *m*, hurricane, spinning-top, revolution
turbŭlentus, a, um, *adj, adv,* **ē, nter,** restless, boisterous, troublesome
turdus, i, *m*, thrush
tūrĕus, a, um, *adj*, of incense
turgĕo, rsi, *v.i.* 2, to swell
turgesco, *v.i.* 3, to swell up
turgĭdŭlus, a, um, *adj*, swollen
turgĭdus, a, um, *adj*, swollen
tūrĭbŭlum, i, *n*, incense-vessel
tūrĭcrĕmus, a, um, *adj*, for burning incense
tūrĭfer, ĕra, ĕrum, *adj*, incense-producing
turma, ae, *f*, cavalry-troop, crowd
turmālis, e, *adj*, of a squadron
turmātim, *adv*, by squadrons
turpis, e, *adj, adv,* **iter,** filthy, ugly, disgraceful, scandalous
turpitūdo, ĭnis, *f*, disgrace, baseness
turpo, *v.t.* 1, to pollute, soil
turrĭger, ĕra, ĕrum, *adj*, turreted
turris, is, *f*, tower
turrĭtus, a, um, *adj*, turreted
turtur, ŭris, *m*, turtle-dove
tūs, tūris, *n*, incense
tussĭo, *v.i.* 4, to cough
tussis, is, *f*, cough
tūtāmen, ĭnis, *n*, defence
tūtēla, ae, *f*, safeguard, defence, position of guardian, object under guardianship
tūtō, *adv*, safely
tūtor, ōris, *m*, guardian
tūtor, *v.t.* 1, *dep*, to guard, watch
tūtus, a, um, *adj*, safe, prudent
tŭus, a, um, *adj*, your(s)
tympănum, i, *n*, tambourine, door panel
tȳrannĭcus, a, um, *adj*, tyrannical
tȳrannis, ĭdis, *f*, despotic rule
tȳrannus, i, *m*, sovereign, ruler, despot

U

ūber, ĕris, *n*, teat, udder, breast
ūber, ĕris, *adj*, fertile, rich
ūbertas, ātis, *f*, fertility, richness
ŭbĭ, *adv*, where, when, as soon as
ŭbĭcumque, *adv*, wherever
ŭbique, *adv*, everywhere, anywhere
ŭbĭvis, *adv*, everywhere, anywhere
ūdus, a, um, *adj*, moist, wet
ulcĕrātio, ōnis, *f*, ulceration
ulcĕro, *v.t.* 1, to make sore
ulcĕrōsus, a, um, *adj*, ulcerous
ulciscor, ultus, *v.t.* 3, *dep*, to avenge, punish, take vengeance on
ulcus, ĕris, *n*, sore, ulcer
ulex, ĭcis, *m*, furze
ūlīginōsus, a, um, *adj*, moist, marshy
ūlīgo, ĭnis, *f*, moisture
ullus, a, um, *adj*, (*genit*, **ullĭus,** *dat*, **ullĭ**), any
ulmĕus, a, um, *adj*, of elm
ulmus, i, *f*, elm, elm-tree
ulna, ae, *f*, elbow, arm, ell
ultĕrior, ĭus, *comp. adj*, beyond, on the farther side

For List of Abbreviations used, turn to pages 3, 4

ultĕrĭus, *comp. adv,* beyond, farther
ultĭmus, a, um, *sup. adj,* farthest, extreme, last
ultĭo, ōnis, *f,* revenge
ultor, ōris, *m,* avenger
ultrā, *adv. and prep. with acc,* beyond, past, farther, besides
ultrix, īcis, *adj,* avenging
ultrō, *adv,* on the other side, moreover, spontaneously
ŭlŭla, ae, *f,* screech-owl
ŭlŭlātus, ūs, *m,* wailing
ŭlŭlo, *v.i.t.* 1, to howl; cry out to
ulva, ae, *f,* sedge
umbella, ae, *f,* parasol
umbĭlĭcus, i, *m,* navel, centre, end of rod on which Roman books were rolled
umbo, ōnis, *m,* shield, knob
umbra, ae, *f,* shadow, shade, ghost, trace, shelter
umbrācŭlum, i, *n,* shady spot, school
umbrātĭlis, e, *adj,* private, retired
umbrĭfer, ĕra, ĕrum, *adj,* shady
umbro, *v.t.* 1, to shade, cover
umbrōsus, a, um, *adj,* shady
ūmecto, *v.t.* 1, to moisten
ūmĕo, *v.i.* 2, to be damp
ūmĕrus, i, *m,* shoulder, arm
ūmesco, *v.i.* 3, to grow wet
ūmĭdus, a, um, *adj,* wet, damp
ūmor, ōris, *m,* moisture, liquid
umquam, *adv,* ever
ūnā, *adv,* at the same time, in the same place, together
ūnănĭmus, a, um, *adj,* of one mind
ūnănĭmĭtas, ātis, *f,* unanimity
uncĭa, ae, *f,* a twelfth, ounce
unctĭo, ōnis, *f,* anointing
unctus, a, um, *adj,* oiled, rich, luxurious
uncus, i, *m,* hook
uncus, a, um, *adj,* hooked
unda, ae, *f,* wave, tide
undĕ, *adv,* from where, whence
undē . . . (with number) one from. . . . e.g. **undēvīginti** (one from 20) 19
undĕcies, *adv,* eleven times
undĕcĭm, *indecl. adj,* eleven
undĕcĭmus, a, um, *adj,* eleventh
undēni, ae, a, *pl. adj,* eleven each
undĭquĕ, *adv,* from all sides, everywhere
undo, *v.i.* 1, to surge, undulate
undōsus, a, um, *adj,* billowy
ungo (unguo), unxi, unctum, *v.t.* 3, to besmear, oil
unguen, ĭnis, *n,* ointment
unguentārĭus, ii, *m,* perfume-seller
unguentum, i, *n,* ointment, perfume
unguis, is, *m,* finger or toe nail
ungŭla, ae, *f,* hoof, claw
unguo (3), see **ungo**
ūnĭcŏlor, ōris, *adj,* of one colour
ūnĭcus, a, um, *adj, adv,* **ē,** only, single, singular, unique
ūnĭo, ōnis, *m, f,* unity
ūniversitas, ātis, *f,* universe
ūniversum, i, *n,* whole world
ūniversus, a, um, *adj, adv,* **ē,** entire, all together
unquam, *adv,* ever
ūnus, a, um, *adj,* one, only
ūnusquisque, *pron,* each
ūpilĭo, ōnis, *m,* shepherd
urbānĭtas, ātis, *f,* city-life, elegance, courtesy, refinement
urbānus, a, um, *adj, adv,* **ē,** of the city, refined, elegant, courteous, humorous
urbs, urbis, *f,* city
urcĕus, i, *m,* water-jug
urgĕo, ursi, *v.t.* 2, to press, push, oppress, urge, crowd
ūrīna, ae, *f,* urine
ūrīnātor, ōris, *m,* diver
urna, ae, *f,* water-jar, urn (for voting-tablets or ashes of the dead)
ūro, ussi, ustum, *v.t.* 3, to burn, destroy by fire, scorch, nip with cold
ursa, ae, *f,* she-bear
ursus, i, *m,* bear
urtĭca, ae, *f,* nettle
ūrus, i, *m,* wild-ox
ūsĭtātus, a, um, *adj,* usual
uspĭam, *adv,* anywhere, somewhere
usquam, *adv,* anywhere
usquĕ, *adv,* all the way, all the time, as far as, until
ustor, ōris, *m,* corpse-burner
ūsūra, ae, *f,* money-lending, interest
ūsurpātio, ōnis, *f,* using, use
ūsurpo, *v.t.* 1, to use, practise, exercise, acquire
ūsus, ūs, *m,* using, use, practice, custom, habit, familiarity, advantage
ut (ŭti), *conj,* so that, that, in order to, to; *adv,* now, as, when, as soon as, where
utcumquĕ (utcunquĕ), *adv,* in whatever way, however, whenever
ūter, tris, *m,* bottle, bag
ŭter, tra, trum, *interr. pron,* which of the two

ŭtercumquĕ, utrăcumque, utrumcumque, *pron,* whichever of the two
ŭterlĭbet, utrălĭbet, utrumlĭbet, *pron,* which of the two you please
ŭterque, utrăque, utrumque, *pron,* each of the two, both
ŭtĕrus, i, *m,* womb, belly
ŭtervīs, utrăvīs, utrumvīs, *pron,* which of the two you please
ŭti, see **ut**
ūti, see **ūtor**
ūtĭlis, e, *adj, adv,* **ĭter,** useful, suitable, advantageous
ūtĭlĭtas, ātis, *f,* usefulness, advantage
ŭtĭnam, *adv,* if only! would that!
ŭtĭquĕ, *adv,* at any rate, at least, certainly
ūtor, ūsus, *v.* 3, *dep, with abl,* to use, practise, be familiar with
utpŏtĕ, *adv,* namely, as, since
ŭtrĭmquĕ, *adv,* on both sides
ŭtrŏbĭquĕ (ŭtrŭbĭquĕ), *adv,* on both sides
ŭtrōquĕ, *adv,* in both directions
ūtrum, *adv, used to form an alternative question,* is it this . . . or that?
ūva, ae, *f,* grape, cluster
ūvĭdus, a, um, *adj,* moist, damp
uxor, ōris, *f,* wife
uxōrĭus, a, um, *adj,* of a wife

V

văcans, ntis, *adj,* unoccupied
văcātĭo, ōnis, *f,* exemption
vacca, ae, *f,* cow
vaccĭnium, ii, *n,* whortleberry
văcillātĭo, ōnis, *f,* vacillation
văcillo, *v.i.* 1, to stagger, sway, hesitate
văco, *v.i.* 1, to be empty, free from, have leisure (for)
văcŭĕfăcĭo, fēci, factum, *v.t.* 3, to empty, clear
văcŭĭtas, ātis, *f,* exemption
văcŭus, a, um, *adj,* empty, free, without, unoccupied, worthless
vādĭmōnĭum, ii, *n,* bail, security
vādo, *v.i.* 3, to go, walk, rush
vădor, *v.t.* 1, *dep,* to bind over by bail
vădōsus, a, um, *adj,* shallow
vădum, i, *n,* a shallow, ford (*often in pl.*)
vae, *interj,* ah! alas!
văfer, fra, frum, *adj,* sly
văgātĭo, ōnis, *f,* wandering
vāgīna, ae, *f,* sheath, scabbard
vāgĭo, *v.i.* 4, to cry, bawl
vāgĭtus, ūs, *m,* crying, bawling
văgor, *v.i.* 1, *dep,* to wander, roam
văgus, a, um, *adj,* wandering, roaming, uncertain, vague
valdē, *adv,* energetically, very much, very
văle, *imperative,* (*pl,* **vălēte**), farewell!
vălens, ntis, *adj,* powerful, strong, healthy
vălĕo, *v.i.* 2, to be strong, vigorous or healthy, to have power or influence, to be capable or effective, be worth
vălesco, *v.i.* 3, to grow strong
vălētūdĭnārĭum, ii, *n,* hospital
vălētūdĭnārĭus, i, *m,* invalid
vălētūdo, ĭnis, *f,* health (good or bad)
vălĭdus, a, um, *adj,* strong, powerful, healthy
valles (vallis), is, *f,* valley
vallo, *v.t.* 1, to fortify with a rampart, protect
vallum, i, *n,* rampart, palisade
vallus, i, *m,* stake, palisade
valvae, ārum, *f. pl,* folding-doors
vānesco, *v.i.* 3, to disappear
vānĭtas, ātis, *f,* emptiness, uselessness, vanity
vannus, i, *f,* fan
vānus, a, um, *adj,* empty, groundless, false, deceptive
văpĭdus, a, um, *adj,* spoiled, flat
văpor, ōris, *m,* steam, vapour
văpōro, *v.t.* 1, to fumigate, warm
vappa, ae, *f,* flat wine; *m,* a good-for-nothing
vāpŭlo, *v.i.* 1, to be flogged
vārĭco, *v.i.* 1, to straddle
vărĭcōsus, a, um, *adj,* varicose
vărĭĕtas, ātis, *f,* variety
vărĭo, *v.i.t.* 1, to vary; diversify, change
vărĭus, a, um, *adj, adv,* **ē,** variegated, changing, varying
vărix, ĭcis, *m, f,* varicose vein
vārus, a, um, *adj,* knock-kneed
vās, vădis, *m,* bail, security
vās, vāsis, *n,* dish, utensil, military equipment
vāsārĭum, ii, *n,* expense-account
vascŭlārĭus, ii, *m,* metal-worker
vastātĭo, ōnis, *f,* devastation
vastātor, ōris, *m,* destroyer
vastĭtas, ātis, *f,* desert, destruction, ruin
vasto, *v.t.* 1, to devastate, destroy, leave vacant
vastus, a, um, *adj,* deserted, desolate, rough, devastated, enormous, vast
vātes, is, *c,* forecaster, poet
vātĭcĭnātĭo, ōnis, *f,* prediction
vātĭcĭnātor, ōris, *m,* prophet

vātĭcĭnor, *v.i.t.* 1, *dep,* to predict
vătĭus, a, um, *adj,* bow-legged
vĕ, *conj,* or
vēcordĭa, ae, *f,* folly, madness
vēcors, dis, *adj,* foolish, mad
vectĭgal, ālis, *n,* tax, income
vectĭgālis, e, *adj,* tax-paying
vectis, is, *m,* pole, bar, lever
vecto, *v.t.* 1, to convey
vector, ōris, *m,* carrier, traveller, passenger
vectōrĭus, a, um, *adj,* for carrying
vectūra, ae, *f,* transportation, fare
vectus, a, um, *adj,* conveyed, carried
vēgĕtus, a, um, *adj,* lively
vēgrandis, e, *adj,* small
vĕhĕmens, ntis, *adj, adv,* **nter,** violent, powerful, strong
vĕhĭcŭlum, i, *n,* vehicle
vĕho, xi, ctum, *v.t.* 3, to convey; *in passive, or with reflexive pron,* to ride, sail, go
vĕl, *conj,* either, or, indeed
vēlāmen, ĭnis, *n,* cover, garment
vēlāmentum, i, *n,* olive-branch
vēles, ĭtis, *m,* light-armed soldier
vēlĭfer, ĕra, ĕrum, *adj,* carrying sails
vēlĭfĭcātio, ōnis, *f,* sailing
vēlĭfĭcor, *v.i.* 1, *dep,* to sail, gain, procure
vēlĭvŏlus, a, um, *adj,* sail-winged; (**măre**) dotted with ships
vellĭco, *v.t.* 1, to nip, taunt
vello, vulsi, vulsum, *v.t.* 3, to tear out, pluck off
vellus, ĕris, *n,* fleece, hide
vēlo, *v.t.* 1, to cover, wrap up
vēlōcĭtas, ātis, *f,* speed
vēlox, ōcis, *adj, adv,* **ĭter,** swift, fast, fleet
vēlum, i, *n,* sail, covering
vĕlut, *adv,* just as, like
vēna, ae, *f,* vein, disposition
vēnābŭlum, i, *n,* hunting-spear
vēnālĭcĭum, ii, *n,* slave-dealing
vēnālĭcĭus, ii, *m,* slave-dealer
vēnālis, e, *adj,* for sale, able to be bribed, corrupt
vēnālis, is, *m,* slave for sale
vēnāticus, a, um, *adj,* of hunting
vēnātio, ōnis, *f,* hunting, a hunt, combat of wild beasts
vēnātor, ōris, *m,* hunter
vēnātrix, īcis, *f,* huntress
vēnātus, ūs, *m,* hunting
vendĭbĭlis, e, *adj,* saleable
venditātio, ōnis, *f,* boasting
venditio, ōnis, *f,* sale
vendito, *v.t.* 1, to try to sell
venditor, ōris, *m,* salesman
vendo, dĭdi, dĭtum, *v.t.* 3, to sell, betray, praise
vĕnēfĭca, ae, *f,* witch
vĕnēfĭcĭum, ii, *n,* poisoning, magic
vĕnēfĭcus, a, um, *adj,* poisonous, magic
vĕnēfĭcus, i, *m,* poisoner, sorcerer
vĕnēnātus, a, um, *adj,* poisonous
vĕnēnĭfer, ĕra, ĕrum, *adj,* poisonous
vĕnēno, *v.t.* 1, to poison, dye
vĕnēnum, i, *n,* poison, magic charm, drug
vēnĕo, ii, ĭtum, *v.i.* 4, to be sold
vĕnĕrābĭlis, e, *adj,* worthy of respect
vĕnĕrābundus, a, um, *adj,* devout
vĕnĕrātio, ōnis, *f,* great respect
vĕnĕrĕus, a, um, *adj,* venereal
vĕnĕror, *v.t.* 1, *dep,* to worship, revere, honour, entreat
vĕnĭa, ae, *f,* indulgence, mercy, permission, pardon
vĕnio, vēni, ventum, *v.i.* 4, to come
vēnor, *v.i.t.* 1, *dep,* to hunt
venter, tris, *m,* belly
ventĭlo, *v.t.* 1, to wave, fan
ventĭto, *v.i.* 1, to keep coming
ventōsus, a, um, *adj,* windy, swift, light, changeable, vain
ventrĭcŭlus, i, *m,* ventricle
ventūrus, *fut. partic.* from **vĕnio**
ventus, i, *m,* wind
vēnŭcŭla (uva), a preserving grape
vēnundo, dĕdi, dătum, *v.t.* 1, to sell
vēnus, ĕris, *f,* love, beauty, highest throw of the dice
vēnus, ūs, *m,* (**vēnum, i,** *n*), sale
vēnustas, ātis, *f,* charm, beauty
vēnustus, a, um, *adj, adv,* **ē,** charming, graceful, beautiful
vĕprēcŭla, ae, *f,* small thorn-bush
vĕpres, is, *m,* thorn-bush
vēr, vēris, *n,* spring
vēra, see **vērus**
vērācĭtas, ātis, *f,* veracity
vērax, ācis, *adj,* true
verbēna, ae, *f,* foliage, branches
verber, ĕris, *n,* lash, whip, flogging, blow
verbĕrātio, ōnis, *f,* punishment
verbĕro, *v.t.* 1, to whip, strike
verbōsus, a, um, *adj,* effusive
verbum, i, *n,* word, language, conversation; **verba dare** to deceive
vērē, *adv,* really, truly
vērēcundĭa, ae, *f,* shyness
vērēcundor, *v.i.* 1, *dep,* to be shy
vērēcundus, a, um, *adj, adv,* **ē,** shy, modest
vĕrendus, a, um, *adj,* venerable, terrible

vĕrĕor, *v.i.t.* 2, *dep*, to fear, respect
vergo, *v.i.* 3, to turn, bend, lie, be situated
vērĭdĭcus, a, um, *adj*, truthful
vērĭsĭmĭlis, e, *adj*, probable
vērĭtas, ātis, *f*, truth, reality
vermĭcŭlus, i, *m*, worm, grub
verminōsus, a, um, *adj*, worm-eaten
vermis, is, *m*, worm
verna, ae, *c*, slave born in his master's house
vernăcŭlus, a, um, *adj*, domestic
verniliter, *adv*, slavishly
verno, *v.i.* 1, to flourish, bloom
vernus, a, um, *adj*, of spring
vērō, *adv*, in fact, certainly, but indeed, however
verres, is, *m*, pig
verro, verri, versum, *v.t.* 3, to sweep, brush, impel, take away
verrūca, ae, *f*, wart, blemish
versātĭlis, e, *adj*, movable
versĭcŏlor, ōris, *adj*, of different colours
versĭcŭlus, i, *m*, single line of verse (or prose)
verso, *v.t.* 1, to turn, twist, whirl, consider
versor, *v.i.* 1, *dep*, to live, stay, be situated, be engaged on
versūra, ae, *f*, borrowing, loan
versus, *adv*, towards
versus, ūs, *m*, row, line, verse
versūtus, a, um, *adj*, *adv*, ē, clever, shrewd, cunning, sly
vertĕbra, ae, *f*, vertebra
vertex, ĭcis, *m*, whirlpool, whirlwind, flame, crown of the head, summit, peak
vertĭcōsus, a, um, *adj*, eddying
vertĭgĭnōsus, a, um, *adj*, suffering from giddiness
vertĭgo, ĭnis, *f*, dizziness
vĕro, see **vērus**
verto, ti, sum, *v.i.t.* 3, to turn, change; turn, change, alter, overthrow, translate
vĕru, ūs, *n*, roasting-spit, javelin
vĕrūcŭlum, i, *n*, skewer, small javelin
vērum, *adv*, but, yet, still
vērum, i, *n*, truth, reality, fact
vērumtămen, *conj*, nevertheless
vērus, a, um, *adj*, *adv*, ō, ē, true, real, proper, right
vĕrūtum, i, *n*, javelin
vĕrūtus, a, um, *adj*, armed with a javelin
vervex, ēcis, *m*, wether, sheep
vēsānia, ae, *f*, insanity
vēsānus, a, um, *adj*, mad, fierce
vescor, *v.i.t.* 3, *dep. with abl*, to feed on
vescus, a, um, *adj*, thin, weak
vēsĭca, ae, *f*, bladder
vespa, ae, *f*, wasp
vesper, ĕris (ĕri), *m*, evening, the West
vespĕra, ae, *f*, evening, the West
vespĕrasco, āvi, *v.i.* 3, to draw towards evening
vespertīnus, a, um, *adj*, of evening, western
vespillo, ōnis, *m*, undertaker
vesta, ae, *f*, fire
vestālis, e, *adj*, of Vesta, the Goddess of Fire, Hearth, Home
vestālis, is, *f*, priestess of Vesta
vester, tra, trum, *adj*, your
vestiārium, ii, *n*, wardrobe
vestibŭlum, i, *n*, entrance-hall
vestĭgium, ii, *n*, footstep, track, sole of foot, mark, moment, instant; **ē vestĭgio**, instantly
vestĭgo, *v.t.* 1, to search out, investigate
vestĭmentum, i, *n*, clothing
vestio, *v.t.* 4, to clothe, cover
vestis, is, *f*, clothing, clothes, carpet, curtain
vestĭtus, ūs, *m*, clothes, dress
vĕtĕrānus, a, um, *adj*, old, veteran
vĕtĕrānus, i, *m*, veteran soldier
vĕtĕrātor, ōris, *m*, crafty, wily or sly person
vĕtĕrātōrĭus, a, um, *adj*, sly
vĕtĕres, um, *m. pl*, ancestors
vĕtĕrĭnārius, a, um, *adj*, veterinary
vĕternus, i, *m*, sluggishness
vĕtĭtum, i, *n*, something forbidden, prohibition
vĕtĭtus, a, um, *adj*, forbidden
vĕto, ŭi, ĭtum, *v.t.* 1, to forbid
vĕtŭlus, a, um, *adj*, old
vĕtus, ĕris, *adj*, old, former
vĕtustas, ātis, *f*, old age, antiquity, posterity
vĕtustus, a, um, *adj*, old
vexātio, ōnis, *f*, distress
vexillārius, ii, *m*, standard-bearer
vexillum, ii, *n*, standard, ensign
vexo, *v.t.* 1, to shake, injure, molest, harass, torment
via, ae, *f*, road, street, way, method
viāticum, i, *n*, travelling-expenses, soldier's savings
viātor, ōris, *m*, traveller
vĭbex, ĭcis, *f*, weal
vĭbro, *v.i.t.* 1, to quiver; brandish, shake
vĭcārius, ii, *m*, deputy

For List of Abbreviations used, turn to pages 3, 4

vīcēni, ae, a, *pl. adj*, twenty each
vicēsimus (vicensimus), a, um, *adj*, twentieth
vicia, ae, *f*, vetch
vicies (viciens), *adv*, twenty times
vicīnia, ae, *f*, neighbourhood
vicīnitas, ātis, *f*, proximity, neighbourhood
vicīnus, a, um, *adj*, neighbouring, similar
vicīnus, i, *m*, neighbour
vicis (*genitive*), **vicem, vice,** change, alternation, recompense, lot, misfortune, position, duty; **in vicem, per vices,** alternately; **vicem, vice,** instead of
vicissim, *adv*, in turn
vicissitūdo, inis, *f*, change
victima, ae, *f*, victim for sacrifice
victor, ōris, *m*, conqueror
victŏria, ae, *f*, victory
victrix, īcis, *f*, female conqueror
victrix, īcis, *adj*, victorious
victus, ūs, *m*, nutriment, diet
vicus, i, *m*, street, village
vidēlicet, *adv*, obviously
vidĕo, vīdi, vīsum, *v.t.* 2, to see, perceive, understand, consider, take care, see to it
vidĕor, vīsus, *v.* 2, *dep*, to seem; *impers*, it seems right or good
vidŭa, ae, *f*, widow
vidŭitas, ātis, *f*, bereavement
vidŭlus, i, *m*, valise
vidŭo, *v.t.* 1, to deprive
vidŭus, a, um, *adj*, robbed, widowed
viētus, a, um, *adj*, withered
vigĕo, *v.i.* 2, to flourish, thrive
vigesco, gŭi, *v.i.* 3, to flourish, thrive
vigil, ilis, *adj*, alert, watching
vigil, ilis, *m*, watchman
vigilans, ntis, *adj, adv*, **nter,** watchful, careful
vigilantia, ae, *f*, watchfulness
vigilia, ae, *f*, wakefulness, vigilance, guard, watch
vigilo, *v.i.t.* 1, to keep awake, be vigilant; spend (time) in watching
viginti, *indecl. adj*, twenty
vigor, ōris, *m*, liveliness
vīlico, *v.i.t.* 1, to superintend
vīlicus (villicus), i, *m*, superintendent
vīlis, e, *adj*, cheap, mean
vīlitas, ātis, *f*, cheapness
villa, ae, *f*, country-house
villāticus, a, um, *adj*, of a villa
villicus see **vīlicus**
villōsus, a, um, *adj*, hairy, shaggy
villŭla, ae, *f*, small villa
villus, i, *m*, tuft of hair
vīmen, inis, *n*, pliant branch
Viminālis (collis), the Viminal, one of the seven hills of Rome
vīminĕus, a, um, *adj*, of wickerwork
vīnārium, ii, *n*, wine-bottle
vīnārius, a, um, *adj*, of wine
vīnārius, i, *m*, vintner
vincio, nxi, nctum, *v.t.* 4, to bind, tie, surround
vinco, vīci, victum, *v.i.t.* 3, to prevail; conquer, overcome, prove conclusively
vincŭlum (vinclum), i, *n*, cord, bond, fetter; *pl*, prison
vindēmia, ae, *f*, grape-gathering, wine
vindēmiātor, ōris, *m*, grape-gatherer
vindex, īcis, *c*, claimant, defender, liberator, avenger
vindiciae, ārum, *f. pl*, legal claim
vindico, *v.t.* 1, to claim, appropriate, set free, protect, avenge
vindicta, ae, *f*, rod used to set free a slave
vinĕa, ae, *f*, vineyard, protective shed for soldiers
vinētum, i, *n*, vineyard
vinitor, ōris, *m*, vine-pruner
vinŏlentia, ae, *f*, wine-drinking
vinŏlentus, a, um, *adj*, drunk
vinōsus, a, um, *adj*, drunken
vinum, i, *n*, wine
viŏla, ae, *f*, violet
viŏlābĭlis, e, *adj*, able to be injured or harmed
viŏlārium, ii, *n*, bed of violets
viŏlātio, ōnis, *f*, violation, profanation
viŏlātor, ōris, *m*, injurer
viŏlens, ntis, *adj, adv*, **nter,** impetuous, furious
viŏlentia, ae, *f*, ferocity
viŏlentus, a, um, *adj*, violent, impetuous
viŏlo, *v.t.* 1, to injure, outrage, break
vīpĕra, ae, *f*, viper
vīpĕrĕus, a, um, *adj*, of a viper or snake
vīpĕrīnus, a, um, *adj*, of a viper or snake
vir, viri, *m*, man, husband
virāgo, inis, *f*, female soldier, heroine
virectum, i, *n*, glade, turf
virĕo, *v.i.* 2, to be green, flourish
vīres, see **vis**
viresco, *v.i.* 3, to become green, flourish
virētum, i, *n*, glade, turf

virga, ae, *f,* twig, rod
virgātus, a, um, *adj,* striped
virgĕus, a, um, *adj,* made of rods
virgĭnālis, e, *adj,* girl-like
virgĭnĕus, a, um, *adj,* of a virgin
virgĭnĭtas, ātis, *f,* virginity
virgo, ĭnis, *f,* virgin, girl
virgŭla, ae, *f,* small twig
virgultum, i, *n,* shrubbery
virgultus, a, um, *adj,* bushy
vĭridārĭum, ii, *n,* park
vĭridis, e, *adj,* green, fresh, young, blooming
vĭrĭditas, ātis, *f,* greenness, freshness
vĭrĭdo, *v.i.t.* 1, to be green; make green
vĭrĭlis, e, *adj,* male, manly, full-grown, vigorous
vĭrĭtim, *adv,* individually
vīrōsus, a, um, *adj,* stinking
virtūs, ūtis, *f,* courage, manhood, military skill, goodness, moral perfection
vīrus, i, *n,* slime, poison, virus
vis, (*no genit*), **vim, vi,** *f,* force, power, violence, quantity, meaning; **vīres, ĭum,** *pl,* strength, power
viscātus, a, um, *adj,* sprinkled with lime
viscĕra, um, *n. pl,* inwards, flesh, bowels
viscum, i, *n,* mistletoe, birdlime
vīsĭo, ōnis, *f,* idea, notion
vīsĭto, *v.t.* 1, to visit
vīso, si, sum, *v.t.* 3, to survey, visit
vīsum, i, *n,* appearance, sight
vīsus, ūs, *m,* look, sight, appearance
vĭta, ae, *f,* life
vĭtābĭlis, e, *adj,* to be avoided
vĭtālis, e, *adj,* of life, vital
vĭtātĭo, ōnis, *f,* avoidance
vĭtellus, i, *m,* small calf, egg-yolk
vĭtĕus, a, um, *adj,* of the vine
vĭtio, *v.t.* 1, to spoil, mar, infect
vĭtiōsĭtas, ātis, *f,* vice
vĭtiōsus, a, um, *adj, adv,* **ē,** faulty, defective, wicked
vĭtis, is, *f,* vine, vine-branch
vĭtisātor, ōris, *m,* vine-planter
vĭtium, ii, *n,* fault, defect, blemish, error, crime
vĭto, *v.t.* 1, to avoid
vĭtrĕus, a, um, *adj,* made of glass, transparent, shining
vĭtrĭcus, i, *m,* step-father
vĭtrum, i, *n,* glass, woad
vitta, ae, *f,* hair-ribbon
vittātus, a, um, *adj,* bound with a hair-ribbon
vĭtŭlīnus, a, um, *adj,* of a calf
vĭtŭlus, i, *m* (**vĭtŭla, ae,** *f*), calf
vĭtŭpĕrātĭo, ōnis, *f,* blame, censure
vĭtŭpĕro, *v.t.* 1, to blame, censure
vīvārĭum, ii, *n,* fish-pond, game-reserve
vīvācĭtas, ātis, *f,* vigour or length of life
vīvax, ācis, *adj,* long-lived
vīvĭdus, a, um, *adj,* lively, animated
vīvo, xi, ctum, *v.i.* 3, to live
vīvus, a, um, *adj,* alive, fresh, natural, life-like
vix, *adv,* scarcely, barely
vixdum, *adv,* scarcely then
vōcābŭlum, i, *n,* name
vōcālis, e, *adj,* vocal
vōcātu, *abl,* at the bidding
vōcĭfĕrātĭo, ōnis, *f,* outcry
vōcĭfĕror, *v.i.t.* 1, *dep,* to cry out
vōcĭto, *v.i.t.* 1, to call out; name
vōco, *v.i.t.* 1, to call; summon, urge, challenge, arouse, name
vōcŭla, ae, *f,* feeble voice
vŏlantes, ĭum, *c, pl,* birds
vŏlātĭcus, a, um, *adj,* flighty, fleeting
vŏlātĭlis, e, *adj,* flying, swift
vŏlātus, ūs, *m,* flight
vŏlens, ntis, *adj,* willing, favourable
volg . . . see **vulg. . . .**
vŏlĭto, *v.i.* 1, to fly about, flit, flutter
vŏlo, velle, vŏlŭi, *v.i.t.* (*irreg*), to wish, mean
vŏlo, *v.i.* 1, to fly
volp . . . see **vulp. . . .**
volsella, ae, *f,* tweezers
volt, see **vult. . . .**
vŏlŭbĭlis, e, *adj,* turning, spinning, changeable
vŏlŭbĭlĭtas, ātis, *f,* whirling motion, fluency
vŏlŭcer, cris, cre, *adj,* flying, swift, transient
vŏlūmĕn, ĭnis, *n,* book, roll, fold
vŏluntārĭus, a, um, *adj,* voluntary; (of soldiers) volunteers
vŏluntas, ātis, *f,* wish, choice, will, affection, good-will
vŏluptārĭus, a, um, *adj,* sensual
vŏluptas, ātis, *f,* pleasure, delight
vŏlūto, *v.i.t.* 1, to roll, twist, writhe about; ponder, consider
volva (vulva), ae, *f,* womb
volvo, volvi, vŏlūtum, *v.t.* 3, to roll, unroll, turn, ponder, consider
vŏmer, ĕris, *m,* ploughshare
vŏmĭca, ae, *f,* abscess, boil
vŏmĭtĭo, ōnis, *f,* vomiting
vŏmo, ŭi, ĭtum, *v.i.t.* 3, to vomit; throw up, pour out
vŏrāgo, ĭnis, *f,* abyss, whirlpool

vŏrax, ācis, *adj*, greedy, destructive
vŏro, *v.t.* 1, to devour, destroy
vortex, see **vertex**
vos, *pron*, you (*plural*)
vōtīvus, a, um, *adj*, concerning a promise or vow
vōtum, i, *n*, promise, vow, offering, wish, longing
vŏvĕo, vōvi, vōtum, *v.t.* 2, to promise, vow, dedicate
vox, vōcis, *f*, voice, sound, speech, saying, proverb
vulgāris, e, *adj*, general, ordinary, common
vulgātor, ōris, *m*, a gossip
vulgātus, a, um, *adj*, ordinary, notorious
vulgo, *v.t.* 1, to divulge, spread about
vulgō, *adv*, everywhere, openly
vulgus, i, *n*, the public, crowd, rabble
vulnĕrātus, a, um, *adj*, wounded
vulnĕro, *v.t.* 1, to wound, hurt
vulnĭfĭcus, a, um, *adj*, wounding
vulnus, ĕris, *n*, wound, blow
vulpēcŭla, ae, *f*, small fox
vulpes, is, *f*, fox
vulsus, a, um, *adj*, hairless, effeminate
vultur, ŭris, *m*, vulture
vultŭrius, ii, *m*, vulture
vultus, ūs, *m*, expression, look, features, aspect, face

X

xĭphĭas, ae, *m*, sword-fish
xystus, i, *m* (**xystum, i,** *n*), open colonnade

Z

zĕphȳrus, i, *m*, west wind
zōdiăcus, i, *m*, zodiac
zōna, ae, *f*, belt, girdle, zone

A

Ăcădēmĭa, ae, *f*, the Academy, a gymnasium near Athens where Plato taught
Ăcădēmus, i, *m*, a Greek hero
Ăcestes, ae, *m*, a king of Sicily
Ăchaemēnes, is, *m*, a king of Persia
Ăchaĭa, ae, *f*, a Roman province in the northern part of the Peloponessus
Ăchātes, ae, *m*, 1, a river in Sicily; 2, a friend of Aeneas
Ăchĕron, ntis, *m*, 1, a river in Epirus; 2, a river in the Lower World
Ăchilles, is, *m*, the Greek hero, son of Peleus and Thetis
Achīvus, a, um, *adj*, Achaean, Greek
Ăcrŏcĕraunĭa, ōrum, *n.pl*, a rocky headland in Epirus
Actē, es, *f*, an old name of Attica
Actĭum, ii, *n*, a town in Epirus
Ădherbal, ălis, *m*, a Numidian prince
Ădōnis, is, *m*, a beautiful youth, beloved of Venus
Ădŭātŭci, ōrum, *m, pl*, a Gallic tribe
Aeăcus, i, *m*, a king of Aegina who became a judge in the Lower World
Aedŭi, ōrum, *m. pl*, a Gallic tribe
Aeētēs, ae, *m*, a king of Colchis, father of Medea
Aegaeum mare, *n*, the Aegean Sea
Aegātes, um, *f. pl*, three islands off the west coast of Sicily
Aegeus, i, *m*, a king of Athens, father of Theseus
Aegīna, ae, *f*, an island near Athens
Aegyptus, i, *f*, Egypt
Aemĭlius, a, um, *adj*, the name of a Roman patrician "gens"
Aenēas, ae, *m*, the hero of Vergil's Aeneid, son of Venus and Anchises
Aeŏlus, i, *m*, the god of the winds
Aequi, ōrum, *m.pl*, an Italian people
Aeschȳlus, i, *m*, the Athenian tragic poet
Aesōpus, i, *m*, the Greek writer of fables (sixth century B.C.)
Aethiŏpia, ae, *f*, Ethiopia
Aethiŏpissa, ae, *f*, Ethiopian, negress
Aethiops, ŏpis, *m*, Ethiopian, negro
Aetna, ae, *f*, Etna, the volcano in Sicily
Āfer, fra, frum, *adj*, African
Āfrĭca, ae, *f*, Africa
Āfrĭcus, i, *m*, the south-west wind
Ăgămemnon, ŏnis, *m*, a king of Mycenae
Ăgăthoclēs, is, *m*, a king of Sicily
Ăgēnor, ŏris, *m*, king of Phoenicia
Ăgēsīlāus, i, *m*, a king of Sparta
Ăglăĭa, ae, *f*, one of the Graces
Agrĭcŏla, ae, *m*, (A.D. 37–93) governor of Britain, father-in-law of Tacitus
Agrĭgentum, i, *n*, a city on the south coast of Sicily
Agrippa, ae, *m*, a Roman family name; Marcus Vipsanius A., the friend of Augustus
Agrippīna, ae, *f*, mother of Nero
Āhēnŏbarbus, i, *m*, the name of a Roman family ("red-beard")
Ăjax, ācis, *m*, the name of a Greek hero
Alba Longa, *f*, the founder city of Rome
Alcaeus, i, *m*, the Greek lyric poet (*c.* 600 B.C.)
Alcestis, is, *f*, the wife of Admetus, whose life she saved by her own death
Alceus, ĕi, *m*, grandfather of Hercules
Alcĭbiădes, is, *m*, an Athenian general
Alcmēne, es, *f*, the mother of Hercules by Juppiter
Ălecto (Allecto),us, *f*, one of the three Furies
Ălĕmanni, ōrum, *m. pl*, a German tribe
Ălexander, dri, *m* (the Great: 356–323 B.C.), king of Macedonia
Ălexandrĭa, ae, *f*, a city on the coast of Egypt
Allĭa, ae, *f*, a small river north of Rome
Allŏbrŏges, um, *m. pl*, a Gallic tribe
Alpēs, ĭum, *f. pl*, the Alps
Ămăryllis, ĭdis, *f*, a shepherdess
Āmastris, is, *f*, a town in Paphlagonia
Āmāzon, ŏnis, *f*, an Amazon; (*pl.*) a race of warlike women
Ambiŏrix, rĭgis, *m*, a chief of the Eburones

Ammōn, ōnis, *m*, a name of Juppiter
Amphiārāus, i, *m*, a famous Greek prophet
Amphiōn, ōnis, *m*, a king of Thebes
Amphĭtrŭo, ōnis, *m*, a king of Thebes
Amūlius, i, *m*, a king of Alba Longa
Ănăcrĕōn, ontis, *m*, a Greek lyric poet
Anchīses, ae, *m*, the father of Aeneas
Ancus Martĭus, i, *m*, the fourth king of Rome (640–616 B.C.)
Andrŏmăchē, es, *f*, wife of Hector
Andrŏmēda, ae, *f*, daughter of Cepheus, rescued from a sea-monster by Perseus became a star
Andrŏnĭcus, i, *m*, L. Livius A., the first Roman poet
Andros, i, *f*, one of the Cyclades Islands
Angli, ōrum, *m. pl*, a German tribe
Antĭgŏnē, es, *f*, daughter of Oedipus
Antiŏchĭa, ae, *f*, Antioch
Antiŏchus, i, *m*, a king of Syria
Antĭpăter, tri, *m*, 1, one of Alexander's generals; 2, L. Caelius A. a Roman annalist
Antŏnīnus, i, *m*, the name of two Roman emperors
Antōnius, a, um, *adj*, the name of a Roman "gens": Marcus Antonius, the triumvir, opponent of Octavianus
Ănŭbis, bis, *m*, an Egyptian god
Anxur, ŭris, *n*, an ancient Volscian town
Ăornos, i, *m*, ("birdless"), Lake Avernus
Apenninus, i, *m*, the Apennine Mts.
Ăpis, is, *m*, the ox worshipped as a god by the Egyptians
Ăpollo, ĭnis, *m*, Apollo, the sun god, also the god of archery, music and poetry
Ăpollōnius Rhŏdĭus, ii, *m*, a Greek poet
Appĭus, ii, *m*, a Roman praenomen; **Appia Via,** *f*, the Appian Way from Rome to Capua, begun by Appius Claudius, the censor (312 B.C.)
Apūlĭa, ae, *f*, a region of south Italy
Aquilēia, ae, *f*, a town of north Italy
Aquilo, ōnis, *m*, the north wind
Aquīnum, i, *n*, a town in Latium
Aquĭtānĭa, ae, *f*, a province in south-west Gaul
Ărăbĭa, ae, *f*, Arabia
Ărabs, ăbis, *adj*, Arabian
Ărar, ăris, *m*, a river in Gaul
Arcădĭa, ae, *f*, a region of the Peloponnesus
Arcas, ădis, *m*, an Arcadian
Archĭlŏchus, i, *m*, a Greek poet
Archĭmēdēs, is, *m*, a famous mathematician
Ardĕa, ae, *f*, a town in Latium
Ardŭenna, ae, *f*, the Ardennes
Ărēŏpăgus, i, *m*, Ares' hill at Athens, seat of the supreme court
Ărēs, is, *m*, the Greek war god
Argĭlētum, i, *n*, a district of Rome
Argō, us, *f*, the ship in which Jason sailed to recover the Golden Fleece
Argŏlis, ĭdis, *f*, a district of the Peloponnesus
Argos, *n*, the capital of Argolis
Ariadne, es, *f*, daughter of Minos, king of Crete, who helped Theseus to kill the Minotaur
Ărĭcĭa, ae, *f*, an old town in Latium
Ărĭminum, i, *n*, a town in Umbria
Ărion, ŏnis, *m*, a famous poet who was saved from drowning by a dolphin
Ariŏvistus, i, *m*, a German chieftain
Ăristŏphănēs, is, *m*, a Greek comic poet
Ăristŏtĕles, is, *m*, the famous Greek philosopher
Armĕnĭa, ae, *f*, a country in Asia
Arminius, i, *m*, a German prince
Armŏrĭcae, ārum, *f. pl*, states in north-west Gaul
Arnus, i, *m*, a river of Etruria
Arpīnum, i, *n*, a town in Latium
Artaxăta, ōrum, *n.pl*, capital of Armenia
Artaxerxēs, is, *m*, name of four Persian kings
Arverni, ōrum, *m. pl*, a Gallic tribe
Ascănius, i, *m*, the son of Aeneas
Ăsĭa, ae, *f*, Asia
Assărăcus, i, *m*, a king of Troy
Assŷrĭa, ae, *f*, a country of Asia
Ătălanta, ae, *f*, a Boeotian girl famous for the speed of her running
Ăthēnae, ārum, *f. pl*, Athens
Athos, *m*, a mountain in Macedonia
Ătilius, a, um, *adj*, the name of a Roman "gens"
Atlas, antis, *m*, a mountain in Africa
Atrĕbătes, um, *m. pl*, a Gallic tribe
Ătreus, ei, *m*. the son of Pelops
Attălus, i, *m*. the name of several kings of Pergamum
Attĭca, ae, *f*, the region around Athens
Attĭcus, a, um, *adj*, Athenian, Attic
Ătŷs, yos, *m*, the son of Hercules
Augustus, i, *m*, surname of Octavius, and all Roman emperors
Aulis, ĭdis, *f*, a port in Boeotia

Avārĭcum, i, *n*, a Gallic town
Āventīnus, i, *m*, one of the seven hills of Rome
Āvernus lacus, i, *m*, a lake near Cumae
Axĭus, ii, *m*, a river in Macedonia

B

Băbȳlōn, ōnis, *f*, Babylon
Baccha, ae, *f*, a female worshipper of Bacchus
Bacchus, i, *m*, the god of wine
Bāiae, ārum, *f. pl*, a town and Roman holiday-resort on the Campanian coast
Bălĕāres insulae, *f. pl*, the Balearic Islands (Majorca)
Barcas, ae, *m*, the founder of the famous Carthaginian family to which Hannibal belonged
Bătāvi, ōrum, *m. pl*, a tribe inhabiting what is now Holland
Belgae, ārum, *m. pl*, a tribe inhabiting northern Gaul
Bellĕrōphon, ontis, *m*, the rider of Pegasus who went to kill the Chimaera
Bellōna, ae, *f*, the goddess of War
Bĕnĕventum, i, *n*, a town in Samnium
Bibractĕ, is, *n*, capital of the Gallic tribe, the Aedui
Bĭthȳnĭa, ae, *f*, a country in Asia Minor
Bĭtŭrĭges, um, *m. pl*, a tribe of Aquitania
Boadicēa (or **Boudicca**), **ae,** *f*, a queen of the Iceni
Bocchus, i, *m*, a king of Mauritania
Boeōtĭa, ae, *f*, a district in northern Greece
Bōii, ōrum, *m, pl*, a Celtic people
Bōla, ae, *f*, a town of the Aequi
Bŏmilcar, ăris, *m*, a Carthaginian general
Bŏnōnĭa, ae, *f*, a town in Cisalpine Gaul
Bōōtes, ae, *m*, a constellation (from "bos", an ox)
Bŏrĕās, ae, *m*, the north wind
Bosphŏrus, i, *m*, the Straits between Thrace and Asia Minor
Brennus, i, *m*, a Gallic leader who defeated the Romans at the river Allia, 390 B.C.
Brĭăreus, i, *m*, a hundred-armed giant
Brĭgantes, um, *m. pl*, a British tribe
Brĭsēis, idis, *f*, Hippodamia, the slave of Achilles
Brĭtanni, ōrum, *m.pl*, the Britons
Brĭtannus, Brĭtannicus, a, um, British
Brundĭsĭum, ii, *n*, a town in Calabria and a Roman port
Brutĭi, ōrum, *m. pl*, a tribe in the southern tip of Italy
Brūtus, i, *m*, a Roman surname; 1, L. Junius B. the first Roman consul; 2, M. Junius B. the murderer of Caesar
Bȳzantĭum, ii, *n*, a Greek city in Thrace

C

Cācus, i, *m*, a giant, son of Vulcan, slain by Hercules
Cadmus, i, *m*, the son of Agenor
Caelĭus mons, one of the seven hills of Rome
Caerĕ, itis, *n*, an Etruscan city
Caesar, ăris, *m*, a Roman family name; Caius Julius C. general, statesman author and dictator
Caesărĕa, ae, *f*, a town in Palestine
Caius, i, *m*, a Roman "praenomen"
Cālăbrĭa, ae, *f*, the south-eastern part of Italy
Cālĕdŏnĭa, ae, *f*, the Highlands of Scotland
Cāligŭla, ae, *m*, the nickname of Gaius, the third Roman emperor, ("little-boots")
Callĭmachus, i, *m*, a Greek poet
Calliŏpē, ēs, *f*, the Muse of poetry
Cămillus, i, *m*, M. Furius C. a Roman statesman and general
Campānĭa, ae, *f*, a district of Central Italy, famous for its fertility
Camŭlŏdūnum, i, *n*, a town in Britain (now Colchester)
Cannae, ārum, *f. pl*, a village in Apulia, scene of a great defeat of the Romans by Hannibal
Cantăbrĭa, ae, *f*, a region in north-west Spain
Cantĭum, ii, *n*, a district in Britain (now Kent)
Cănŭsĭum, ii, *n*, a town in Apulia
Căpĭtōlĭum, ii, *n*, the Capitol and the Capitol Hill at Rome
Cappădŏcĭa, ae, *f*, a district of Asia Minor
Capreĕae, ārum, *f. pl*, an island off the Campanian coast (now Capri)
Căpŭa, ae, *f*, a city of Campania
Cărăcalla, ae, *m*, a Roman emperor
Caratăcus, i, *m*, a British king
Cărĭa, ae, *f*, a province of Asia Minor
Carnūtes, um, *m. pl*, a Gallic tribe
Carrhae, ārum, *f. pl*, a town in Mesopotamia

For List of Abbreviations used, turn to pages 3, 4

Carthāgo, ĭnis, *f*, Carthage, a city in North Africa
Cassander, dri, *m*, a king of Macedonia
Cassandra, ae, *f*, the daughter of Priam, gifted with prophecy
Cassĭus, a, um, *adj*, the name of a Roman "gens": C. Cassius Longinus, one of Caesar's murderers
Cassivellaunus, i, *m*, a British chief
Castor, ŏris, *m*, twin-brother of Pollux; a twin-star and a guide to sailors
Cătilīna, ae, *m*, L. Sergius C., an impoverished patrician who led a conspiracy against the state
Căto, ōnis, *m*, a Roman family name; M. Porcius C., famous for his attacks on Roman luxury and indulgence
Cătullus, i, *m*, a Roman lyric poet
Cătŭlus, i, *m*, a Roman family name
Caucăsus, i, *m*, the Caucasus Mts.
Caudĭum, ii, *n*, a city in Samnium
Caurus, i, *m*, the north-west wind
Cĕbenna, ae, *f*, a mountain range in Gaul (now the Cevennes)
Cĕcrops, ŏpis, *m*, the first king of Athens
Celtae, ārum, *m. pl*, the Celts
Celtibĕri, ōrum, *m. pl*, a people of central Spain, originally Celts
Cĕphīsus, i, *m*, a river(god)
Cerbĕrus, i, *m*, the three-headed dog guarding the entrance to Hades
Cĕrēs, ĕris, *f*, the goddess of agriculture
Chaerōnēa, ae, *f*, a town in Boeotia
Chalcēdon, ōnis, *f*, a town in Bithynia
Chalcis, ĭdis, *f*, a town of Euboea
Chaldaei, ōrum, *m. pl*, an Assyrian people
Chăŏs, i, *n*, the Lower World
Chăron, ontis, *m*, the ferryman who took the dead across the Styx
Chărybdis, is, *f*, a whirlpool off Sicily
Chatti, ōrum, *m. pl*, German tribe
Chauci, ōrum, *m. pl*, German tribe
Cherusci, ōrum, *m. pl*, German tribe
Chĭmaera, ae, *f*, a fire-breathing monster
Chĭos, ii, *f*, an island in the Aegean Sea
Chrȳsippus, i, *m*, a Stoic philosopher
Cĭcĕro, ōnis, *m*, M. Tullius C., the great Roman statesman and orator
Cĭlĭcia, ae, *f*, a province in Asia Minor
Cimbri, ōrum. *m. pl*, a German tribe who invaded Italy
Cīmon, ōnis, *m*, an Athenian statesman and general
Cincinnātus, i, *m*, a Roman family name: L. Quinctius C. dictator in 458 B.C.
Cīnēas, ae, *m*, the friend of Pyrrhus
Cingĕtŏrix, ĭgis, *m*, a chief of the Treveri
Cinna, ae, *m*, a Roman family name; L. Cornelius C., one of Marius' lieutenants
Circē, es, *f*, an enchantress, daughter of the sun
Cirta, ae, *f*, a Numidian city
Claudius, a, um, *adj*, the name of two Roman "gentes": the fourth Roman emperor
Clĕon, ōnis, *m*, an Athenian demagogue
Clĕŏpātra, ae, *f*, Queen of Egypt
Clīsthĕnes, is, *m*, an Athenian statesman
Clĭtumnus, i, *m*, a river in Umbria
Clōdĭus, P. Clodius Pulcher, tribune of the People, killed by Milo
Clūsĭum, ii, *n*, an Etruscan town
Clȳtaemnēstra, ae, *f*, the wife of Agamemnon
Cōcȳtus, i, *m*, a river in the Lower World
Cōdrus, i, *m*, an Athenian king
Colchis, ĭdis, *f*, a country on the Black Sea
Collātĭa, ae, *f*, a town in Latium
Collĭna porta, *f*, a gate of Rome
Commŏdus, i, *m*, a Roman emperor
Cōmum, i, *n*, a town of Cisalpine Gaul
Concordĭa, ae, *f*, the goddess of Concord
Cŏnōn, ōnis, *m*, an Athenian general
Constantĭnus, i, *m*, a Roman emperor
Constantĭus, i, *m*, the name of three Roman emperors
Corbŭlo, ōnis, *m*, a Roman general
Corcȳra, ae, *f*, an island in the Ionian Sea (now Corfu)
Corfĭnĭum, ii, *n*, capital of the Paeligni
Coriŏtanus, i, *m*, an early Roman hero
Cornēlĭa, ae, *f*, the daughter of P. Scipio Africanus, and mother of the Gracchi
Cornēlĭus, ii, *m*, the name of a Roman "gens", to which belonged the Scipios, and Sulla

Corsica, ae, *f*, Corsica
Cōs, Cōi, *f*, an island in the Aegean
Cotta, ae, *m*, a Roman family name
Crassus, i, *m*, a Roman family name; 1, L. Licinius C., the orator; 2, M. Licinius C., the triumvir
Crĕmōna, ae, *f*, a town in Cisalpine Gaul
Crĕon, ontis, *m*, a king of Corinth
Crēta, ae, *f*, Crete
Crĕūsa, ae, *f*, the wife of Aeneas
Croesus, i, *m*, a king of Lydia, famous for his riches
Crŏtōn, ōnis, *c*, (**Crotona, ae,** *f*), a Greek settlement in Bruttium
Cūmae, ārum, *f. pl*, an ancient city of Campania, the home of the Sibyl
Cŭpīdo, ĭnis, *m*, the god of love
Cūres, ium, *f. pl*, an ancient town of the Sabines
Cūrĭātii, ōrum, *m. pl*, an Alban family, from which came the three brothers who fought with the Roman Horatii
Cūrius, a, um, *adj*, the name of a Roman "gens"
Curtĭus, a, um, *adj*, the name of a Roman "gens"
Cybĕlē, es, *f*, a Phrygian goddess, worshipped in Rome
Cȳclădes, um, *f. pl*, a group of islands in the Aegean Sea
Cyclōpes, um, *m. pl*, a race of one-eyed giants
Cydnus, i, *m*, a river in Cilicia
Cynthia, ae, *f*, Diana
Cȳprus, i, *f*, Cyprus
Cȳrēne, es, *f*, a Greek city of north Africa
Cȳrus, i, *m*, the founder of the Persian Empire
Cȳthĕrēia, ae, *f*, Venus
Cȳtōrus, i, *m*, a mountain-range of Paphlagonia

D

Dāci, ōrum, *m. pl*, the Dacians, a tribe of Thracian origin
Daedălus, i, *m*, an Athenian craftsman and architect
Dalmătae, ārum, *m. pl*, the Dalmatians, a tribe on the east coast of the Adriatic
Dămascus, i, *f*, Damascus
Dāmŏclēs, is, *m*, a courtier of Dionysius
Dāmōn, ōnis, *m*, a Pythagorean
Dănăi, ōrum, *m. pl*, the Greeks
Dānŭbius, i, *m*, the Danube
Daphne, as, *f*, the daughter of the river-god Peneus
Dardănus, i, *m*, the ancestor of the Trojans
Dārēus (or **Darius**), **i,** *m*, a king of Persia
Dĕcius, a, um, *adj*, the name of a Roman "gens"
Dēiŏtārus, i, *m*, a king of Galatia
Dēiphŏbus, i, *m*, the son of Priam and husband of Helen
Dēlos, i, *f*, an island in the Aegean, birthplace of Apollo and Diana
Delphi, ōrum, *m. pl*, a town in Phocis, famous for its oracle
Dēmosthĕnēs, is, *m*, 1. a famous Athenian orator; 2. an Athenian general
Deucălĭōn, ōnis, *m*, he was saved from the Flood with his wife Pyrrha
Dĭāna, ae, *f*, the goddess of the moon and of hunting
Dictē, es, *f*, a mountain in Crete
Dĭdō, ūs, *f*, the founder-queen of Carthage
Dĭoclētiānus, i, *m*, a Roman emperor
Dĭŏgĕnes, is, *m*, a Greek philosopher of the fourth century B.C.
Dĭŏmēdes, is, *m*, a Greek hero of the siege of Troy
Dĭŏnȳsius, ii, *m*, a tyrant of Syracuse
Dĭŏnȳsus, i, *m*, the god of wine
Dīs, Dĭtis, *m*, Pluto, king of the Lower World
Dōdōna, ae, *f*, a city of Epirus
Dŏlābella, ae, *m*, a Roman family name
Dŏlōpes, um, *m. pl*, a people of Thessaly
Dŏmĭtiānus, i, *m*, a Roman emperor
Dŏmĭtius, a, um, *adj*, the name of a Roman "gens"
Dōres, um, *m. pl*, the Dorians, a Greek people
Drăco, ōnis, *m*, an Athenian lawgiver
Drĕpăna, ōrum, *n.pl*, a town in Sicily
Drŭĭdes, um, *m. pl*, the Druids
Drūsus, i, *m*, a Roman surname
Drȳas, ădis, *f*, a wood-nymph
Dŭillĭus, ii, *m*, a Roman consul who won a naval victory over the Carthaginians in 260 B.C.
Dyrrăchium, ii, *n*, a town in Illyria

E

Eborācum, i, *n*, York
Ebŭrōnes, um, *m. pl*, a German tribe

Ĕdessa, ae, *f*, a town in Macedonia
Ēdōni, ōrum, *m. pl*, a Thracian people
Ēlectra, ae, *f*, daughter of Agamemnon
Ĕleusis, īnis, *f*, a city of Attica where the mysteries of Ceres were held
Ēlis, ĭdis, *f*, a country in the Peloponnesus
Ēlȳsĭum, i, *n*, the dwelling-place of the Blessed in the Lower World
Ēmăthĭa, ae, *f*, a district of Macedonia
Encĕlădus, i, *m*, a giant slain by Iuppiter and buried under Etna
Ennĭus, i, *m*, the father of Roman poetry
Ēōs, *f*, the dawn
Ĕphēsus, i, *f*, an Ionian city of Asia Minor
Ĕpĭcūrus, i, *m*, an Athenian philosopher (342–270 B.C.)
Ĕpīrus, i, *f*, a region of northern Greece
Ĕrĕbus, i, *m*, a god of the Lower World
Ĕrectheus, ĕi, *m*, a king of Athens
Ĕrĕtria, ae, *f*, a town of Euboea
Ĕridănus, i, *m*, one of the names of the river Po
Ĕrīnys, ȳos, *f*, one of the Furies
Ĕrȳmanthus, i, *m*, a chain of mountains in Arcadia
Ĕrȳthēa, ae, *f*, an island near Gades
Ĕryx, ȳcis, *m*, a mountain on the N.W. coast of Sicily
Esquĭlĭae, ārum, *f. pl*, the Esquiline, the largest of the hills of Rome
Ĕtrūrĭa, ae, *f*, a district of western Italy
Euboea, ae, *f*, an island in the Aegean
Euclīdēs, is, *m*, the famous mathematician of Alexandria
Eumĕnĭdes, um, *f.pl*, a name of the Furies
Euphrātēs, is, *m*, the Euphrates
Eurĭpĭdes, is, *m*, the famous Athenian poet (480–406 B.C.)
Eurĭpus, i, *m*, the strait between Boeotia and Euboea
Eurōpa, ae, *f*, 1. the daughter of king Agenor; 2. the continent of Europe
Eurȳălus, i, *m*, friend of Nisus (in Vergil's Aeneid)
Eurȳdĭce, es, *f*, the wife of Orpheus
Eurystheus, ei, *m*, a king of Mycenae, who imposed on Hercules his Twelve Labours
Euxīnus Pontus, i, *m*, the Black Sea
Ĕvander, dri, *m*, the son of Mercury, who founded a colony on the Tiber

F

Făbĭus, a, um, *adj*, the name of a Roman "gens"; Q. Fabius Maximus Cunctator, the famous Roman general of the second Punic War
Fābrĭcĭus, a, um, *adj*, the name of a Roman "gens"
Faesŭlae, ārum, *f.pl*, an Etruscan town
Fălernus ager, *m*, the territory of Falernus in Campania, famous for its wine
Faunus, i, *m*, a forest god
Faustŭlus, i, *m*, the shepherd who found Romulus and Remus
Faustus, i, *m*, a Roman surname
Fāvōnĭus, i, *m*, the west wind
Flaccus, i, *m*, a Roman surname
Flāmĭnĭus, a, um, *adj*, the name of a Roman "gens"
Flāvĭus, a, um, *adj*, the name of a Roman "gens"
Flōra, ae, *f*, the goddess of Flowers
Flōrentĭa, ae, *f*, an Etruscan town (now Florence)
Fŏrentum, i, *n*, a town in Apulia
Formĭae, ārum, *f. pl*, a town in Latium
Frĕgellae, ārum, *f. pl*, a town in Latium
Frĭsii, ōrum, *m. pl*, the Frisians, a north German tribe
Fulvĭa ae, *f*, 1. mistress of Curius 2. wife of M. Antony.

G

Găbăli, ōrum, *m. pl*, a Gallic tribe
Găbii, ōrum, *m. pl*, a city of Latium
Găbĭnĭus, a, um, *adj*, the name of a Roman "gens"
Gādēs, ĭum, *f. pl*, a town in Spain
Gaetūli, ōrum, *m. pl*, a people of north-west Africa
Gāius (Caius), i, *m*, a Roman "praenomen"
Galba, ae, *m*, a Roman family name; Servius Sulpicius G. a Roman emperor
Galli, ōrum, *m, pl*, the Gauls
Gallĭa, ae, *f*, Gaul; **Gallia Cisalpina,** Gaul on the Roman side of the Alps; **Gallia Transalpina,** Gaul on the further side of the Alps
Gallĭcus, Gallus, a, um, *adj*, Gallic
Gangēs, is, *m*, the river Ganges
Gănȳmēdes, is, *m*, a youth who was carried off to be Juppiter's cupbearer

Gărămantes, um, *m. pl,* a people of Africa
Gărumna, ae, *m,* a river of Gaul
Gĕla, ae, *f,* a town of Sicily
Gĕlon, ōnis, *m,* a king of Syracuse
Gĕnēva, ae, *f,* Geneva
Gĕnŭa, ae, *f,* a town in Liguria (now Genoa)
Gergŏvĭa, ae, *f,* a town of the Arverni in Aquitania
Germāni, ōrum, *m. pl,* the Germans
Germānia, ae, *f,* Germany
Germānus, a, um, *adj,* German
Gērȳon, ōnis, *m,* a king of Spain slain by Hercules
Gigantes, um, *m. pl,* the Giants, who attacked Olympus and were killed by the thunder-bolts of Juppiter
Glaucus, i, *m,* 1. the son of Sisyphus; 2, the leader of the Lycians in the Trojan War
Gnossos, i, *f,* an ancient city of Crete
Gordĭum, ii, *n,* a city of Phyrgia
Gorgĭas, ae, *m,* a Greek sophist
Gorgo, ōnis, *f,* a daughter of Phorcus whose look turned people to stone
Gŏthi, ōrum, *m. pl,* the Goths
Gracchus, i, *m,* a Roman family name
Graeci, ōrum, *m. pl,* the Greeks
Grāii, ōrum, *m. pl,* the Greeks
Grampius mons, *m,* the Grampian mountains
Grātĭae, ārum, *f. pl,* the Graces
Gȳās, ae, *m,* a hundred-armed giant
Gȳgēs, is, *m,* a wealthy king of Lydia

H

Hădrĭa, ae, *f,* the Adriatic Sea
Hadrĭānus, i, *m,* a Roman emperor
Hălicarnassus, i, *f,* a town in Caria
Hămilcar, ăris, *m,* a famous Carthaginian general of the first Punic War, father of Hannibal
Hannĭbal, ălis, *m,* a famous Carthaginian general of the second Punic War, son of Hamilcar
Harpȳiae, ārum, *f. pl,* the Harpies, monsters half-vulture, half-woman
Hasdrŭbal, ălis, *m,* a Carthaginian general, brother of Hannibal
Hēbē, is, *f,* the daughter of Iuppiter, and wife of Hercules
Hĕbrus, i, *m,* a river in Thrace
Hĕcăte, es, *f,* the goddess of magic
Hector, ŏris, *m,* the son of Priam, hero of the Trojans
Hĕcŭba, ae, *f,* the wife of Priam
Hĕlĕna, ae, *f,* the wife of Menelaus; she was carried off to Troy by Paris, thus causing the Trojan War
Hĕlĭce, es, *f,* the Great Bear
Hĕlĭcon, ōnis, *m,* a mountain in Boeotia
Hellas, ădis, *f,* Greece
Hellespontus, i, *m,* the Hellespont (now the Dardanelles)
Hĕlŏtes, um, *m. pl,* the slaves of the Spartans
Helvētii, ōrum, *m. pl,* a Celtic people inhabiting the region of Switzerland
Helvii, ōrum, *m. pl,* a Gallic tribe
Henna, ae, *f,* a city in Sicily
Hēra, ae, *f,* a Greek goddess
Hēraclēa, ae, *f,* the name of several Greek towns
Hērăclēum, i, *n,* a town in Macedonia
Hercŭlānĕum, i, *n,* a town of Campania, buried in A.D. 79 by an eruption of Vesuvius
Hercŭles, is, *m,* Hercules
Hercȳnĭa silva, *f,* the Hercynian forest in Germany
Hermes, ae, *m,* a Greek god identified with the Roman Mercury
Hermiŏne, es, *f,* the daughter of Menelaus and Helen
Hernĭci, ōrum, *m. pl,* a people of Latium, Sabine in origin
Hēro, us, *f,* a priestess of Aphrodite
Hērŏdŏtus, i, *m,* the first Greek historian
Hēsiŏdus, i, *m,* a Greek poet
Hespĕrus, i, *m,* the Evening Star
Hibēri, ōrum, *m. pl,* the Spaniards
Hibēria, ae, *f,* Spain
Hibērus, a, um, *adj,* Spanish
Hibērus, i, *m,* the Ebro
Hiempsal, ălis, *m,* son of Micipsa, king of Numidia
Hiĕro, ōnis, *m,* king of Syracuse
Hippocrătes, is, *m,* a Greek physician
Hippŏdămus, i, *m,* the horse-tamer, i.e. Castor
Hippŏlȳte, es, *f,* the Queen of the Amazons, taken captive by Theseus
Hippŏlȳtus, i, *m,* the son of Theseus
Hirpĭni, ōrum, *m. pl,* a people of Central Italy
Hispāni, ōrum, *m. pl,* the Spaniards
Hispānia, ae, *f,* Spain
Hispānus, a, um, *adj,* Spanish
Hŏmērus, i, *m,* Homer
Hōrae, ārum, *f. pl,* the Hours
Hŏrātĭus, a, um, *adj,* the name of a Roman "gens"
Hortensĭus, a, um, *adj,* the name of a Roman "gens"

For List of Abbreviations used, turn to pages 3, 4

Hostĭlĭus, a, um, *adj*, the name of a Roman "gens"
Hȳădes, um, *f. pl*, a group of seven stars
Hȳdra, ae, *f*, a many-headed water snake
Hȳmen, ĕnis, *m*, the god of Marriage
Hȳpĕrĭon, ōnis, *m*, 1, the father of the sun; 2. the sun god
Hȳpermnestra, ae, *f*, the only daughter of Danaus who did not kill her husband

I

Ĭacchus, i, *m*, a name of Bacchus
Ĭăpĕtus, i, *m*, a Titan, father of Prometheus
Ĭăpix, -pygis, *m*, 1. son of Daedalus; 2. a west wind
Ĭcărus, i, *m*, son of Daedalus
Ĭcēni, ōrum, *m. pl*, a British tribe in East Anglia
Īda, ae, *f*, a mountain in Crete
Īdŏmĕneus, i, *m*, a king of Crete
Īdūmaea, ae, *f*, a region of Palestine
Īlerda, ae, *f*, a town in Spain
Īlĭa, ae, *f*, a name of Rhea Silvia
Īlĭum (or **Ilion**), **ii,** *n*, a name of Troy
Illȳrĭa, ae, *f*, a region on the Adriatic Sea
Illȳrii, ōrum, *m. pl*, a people on the Adriatic Sea
Īnăchus, i, *m*, the first king of Argos
Indus, i, *m*, a river in India
Insŭbres, ĭum, *m. pl*, a people of Cisalpine Gaul
Īo, see **Īon**
Īolcus, i, *m*, a town in Thessaly
Īon, ōnus, *f*, daughter of Inachus, beloved by Juppiter
Īōnĭa, ae, *f*, a country of Asia Minor, on the W. Coast
Īphĭgēnĭa, ae, *f*, the daughter of Agamemnon
Īris, ĭdis, *f*, the messenger of the gods
Īsis, ĭdis, *f*, an Egyptian goddess
Īsŏcrătes, is, *m*, an Athenian orator
Isthmus, i, *m*, the Isthmus of Corinth
Ĭtălĭa, ae, *f*, Italy
Ĭtăli, ōrum, *m. pl*, the Italians
Ĭtălĭcus, a, um, *adj*, Italian
Ĭtălus, a, um, *adj*, Italian
Ĭthăca, ae, *f*, an island in the Ionian Sea
Itius Portus, ūs, *m*, a port in Belgic Gaul
Ĭtȳs, ȳos, *m*, son of Tereus and Procne
Ixĭōn, ōnis, *m*, a king of the Lapithae

J

Iăcĕtāni, ōrum, *m. pl*, a people of Spain
Iānĭcŭlum, i, *n*, one of the seven hills of Rome
Iānus, i, *m*, an Italian god
Iāsōn, ōnis, *m*, leader of the Argonauts
Iūdaea, ae, *f*, the country of the Jews, Palestine
Iūdaei, ōrum, *m. pl*, the Jews
Iūgurtha, ae, *m*, a king of Numidia
Iūlĭānus, a, um, *adj*, of Julius Caesar
Iūlĭus, a, um, *adj*, the name of a famous Roman "gens"; C. Julius Caesar, statesman, soldier, author
Iūnĭus, a, um, *adj*, the name of a Roman "gens"
Iūno, ōnis, *f*, a goddess, daughter of Saturn, wife of Juppiter
Iūppĭter, Jovis, *m*, the chief god of the Romans
Iūra, ae, *m*, Mt. Jura, in Gaul
Iustĭnĭānus, i, *m*, a Roman emperor
Iūturna, ae, *f*, sister of Turnus
Iŭvĕnālis, is, *m*, D. Junius J., a Roman satirist

K

Karthāgo, ĭnis, *f*, see **Carthago**

L

Lăbĭēnus, i, *m*, a lieutenant of Julius Caesar
Lăcaena, ae, *adj*, Spartan
Lăcĕdaemon, ōnis, *f*, Sparta
Lăcĕdaemŏnĭus, a, um, *adj*, Spartan
Lacĕtāni, ōrum, *m. pl*, a people of Spain
Lăco, ōnis, *m*, a Spartan
Laelĭus, a, um, *adj*, the name of a Roman "gens"
Lāertes, ae, *m*, the father of Ulysses
Laestrȳgŏnes, um, *m. pl*, a race of giants in Sicily
Lampsăcus, i, *f*, a city on the Hellespont
Lāŏcŏōn, ontis, *m*, a Trojan priest
Lāŏmĕdōn, ontis, *m*, the father of Priam, king of Troy
Lăpithae, ārum, *m. pl*, a people of Thessaly
Lăres, um, *m. pl*, household gods

Largus, i, *m*, a Roman surname
Lārissa, ae, *f*, a city in Thessaly
Lātīnus, i, *m*, a king of the Laurentines
Lātīnus, a, um, *adj*, Latin
Lātium, ii, *n*, Latium, the country of Italy in which Rome was situated
Lātōna, ae, *f*, the mother of Apollo and Diana
Laurentum, i, *n*, a town in Latium
Lāvīnia, ae, *f*, daughter of Latinus, wife of Aeneas
Lāvīnium, ii, *n*, a city of Latium
Lēander, dri, *m*, a youth who swam the Hellespont every night to visit Hero in Sestos
Lēda, ae, *f*, mother of Castor, Pollux, Helen and Clytemnestra
Lēmannus, i, *m*, Lake Geneva
Lemnos, i, *f*, an island in the Aegean
Lēōnidās, ae, *m*, a king of Sparta
Lēpidus, i, *m*, a Roman family name; 1, M. Aemilius L. enemy of Sulla, consul 79 B.C.; 2. M. Aemilius L. triumvir 43 B.C.
Lerna, ae, *f*, a river and marsh near Argos
Lesbos, i, *f*, an island in the Aegean
Lēthē, ēs, *f*, a river in the Lower World, where departed souls drank "forgetfulness" of their past lives
Lexovii, ōrum, *m. pl*, a Gallic tribe
Lĭber, ĕri, *m*, an Italian god, identified with Bacchus
Lĭbēra, ae, *f*, Proserpina, sister of Liber, daughter of Ceres
Lĭburni, ōrum, *m. pl*, a people of N. Illyria
Lĭbŷa, ae, *f*, Libya
Licĭnius, a, um, *adj*, the name of a Roman "gens"
Lĭger, ĕris, *m*, a river in Gaul (now the Loire)
Lĭgūres, um, *m. pl*, a people of northwest Italy
Lingōnes, um, *m. pl*, a Gallic tribe
Lĭpăra, ae, *f*, an island north of Sicily
Lĭvĭus, a, um, *adj*, the name of a Roman "gens"; T. Livius Patavinus, the Roman historian
Lōcusta, ae, *f*, a Roman woman skilled in poisoning
Lollĭus, a, um, *adj*, the name of a Roman "gens"
Londīnium, ii, *n*, London
Lūcāni, ōrum, *m. pl*, a people of South Italy
Lūcānia, ae, *f*, a region of South Italy
Lūcānus, i, *m*, a Roman poet
Lŭcrētĭus, a, um, *adj*, the name of a Roman "gens"; T. Lucretius Carus, a Roman poet
Lŭcrīnus, i, *m*, a lake of Campania
Lūcullus, i, *m*, a Roman family name; Lucius Licinius L., conqueror of Mithridates
Lugdūnum, i, *n*, a city of Gaul (now Lyons)
Lūna, ae, *f*, the moon-goddess
Lŭpercālia, ōrum, *n. pl*, a Roman festival celebrated in February
Lŭpercus, i, *m*, a pastoral god who protected flocks from wolves
Lūsĭtānia, ae, *f*, the western part of Spain (now Portugal)
Lŷcēum, i, *n*, a gymnasium at Athens where Aristotle taught
Lŷcia, ae, *f*, a country of Asia Minor
Lŷcurgus, i, *m*, a Spartan lawgiver
Lŷdia, ae, *f*, a country of Asia Minor
Lynceus, i, *m*, 1. one of the Argonauts; 2. son of Aegyptus and husband of Hypermnestra
Lŷsander, dri, *m*, a Spartan general
Lŷsias, ae, *m*, a Greek orator
Lŷsimăchus, i, *m*, one of Alexander's generals

M

Măcĕdŏnes, um, *m. pl*, the Macedonians
Măcĕdŏnia, ae, *f*, Macedonia
Maecēnas, ātis, *m*, the friend of Augustus and patron of Horace and Vergil
Magnēsia, ae, *f*, a district in Thessaly
Māgo, ōnis, *m*, brother of Hannibal
Maharbal, ălis, *m*, a Carthaginian general
Maia, ae, *f*, daughter of Atlas and mother of Mercury
Māmers, ertis, *m*, a name of Mars
Māmertīni, ōrum, *m. pl* (sons of Mars), the name adopted by the mercenary troops who seized Messana in Sicily in 289 B.C.
Mandūbii, ōrum, *m. pl*, a Gallic tribe
Mānĭlius, a, um, *adj*, the name of a Roman "gens"
Mantŭa, ae, *f*, a city in north Italy
Mărăthōn, ōnis, *f*, a village in Attica, where the Athenians defeated the Persian army in 490 B.C.
Marcellus, i, *m*, a Roman family name: Marcus Claudius M. conqueror of Syracuse, Roman general against Hannibal

Marcĭus, a, um, *adj*, the name of a Roman "gens"; Ancus M. the fourth king of Rome
Marcus, i, *m*, a Roman praenomen
Mărĭus, a, um, *adj*, the name of a Roman "gens"; C. Marius, conqueror of Jugurtha and the Cimbri, leader of the Popular Party against Sulla
Măro, ōnis, *m*, the surname of Vergil
Mars, tis, *m*, the god of War
Marsi, ōrum, *m. pl*, a people of Latium
Martiālis, is, *m*, Marcus Valerius M., a Roman epigrammatic poet
Martĭus, a, um, *adj*, from Mars
Măsinissa, ae, *m*, a king of Numidia
Massĭlĭa, ae, *f*, seaport of Gaul (now Marseilles)
Mātūta, ae, *f*, the goddess of morning
Mauri, ōrum, *m. pl*, the Moors
Maurĭtānĭa, ae, *f*, a country in northwest Africa
Mausōlus, i, *m*, a king of Caria
Māvors, ortis, *m*, Mars
Mēdēa, ae, *f*, daughter of king Aeetes
Mēdi, ōrum, *m. pl*, the Medes, a people of Asia
Mĕdullĭa, ae, *f*, a town of Latium
Mĕdūsa, ae, *f*, one of the Gorgons; everything she looked at turned to stone
Mĕgălŏpŏlis, is, *f*, a town in Arcadia
Mĕgăra, ae, *f* (or **ōrum,** *n.pl*), a city of Megaris
Mĕgăris, ĭdis, *f*, a country of Greece
Mĕlĭta, ae, *f*, Malta
Mēlos, i, *f*, an island in the Aegean
Melpŏmĕnē, es, *f*, the muse of tragic poetry
Memmĭus, a, um, *adj*, the name of a Roman "gens"
Memnon, ŏnis, *m*, a king of Ethiopia, killed by Achilles in the Trojan War
Memphis, is, *f*, a city of Egypt
Mĕnander, dri, *m*, a Greek poet
Mĕnăpii, ōrum, *m. pl*, a Gallic tribe
Mĕnĕlāus, i, *m*, brother of Agamemnon and husband of Helen
Mentor, ŏris, *m*, a friend of Ulysses
Mercŭrĭus, ii, *m*, Mercury, the messenger of the gods
Mĕsŏpŏtămĭa, ae, *f*, a country of Asia
Messālĭna, ae, *f*, the wife of the emperor Claudius
Messalla, ae, *m*, a Roman family name
Messāna, ae, *f*, a Sicilian city (now Messina)
Mĕtaurus, i, *m*, a river in Umbria where Hasdrubal was defeated
Mĕtellus, i, *m*, a Roman family name; 1. Q. Metellus Macedonicus, who made Macedonia a Roman province; 2. Q. Caecilius Metellus Numidicus, who defeated Jugurtha
Mĕthymna, ae, *f*, a city of Lesbos
Mĕtiscus, i, *m*, the charioteer of Turnus
Mezentĭus, ii, *m*, a tyrant of Caere
Micipsa, ae, *m*, a king of Numidia
Mĭdās, ae, *m*, a king of Phrygia who received from Bacchus the gift of turning everything he touched to gold
Mĭlētus, i, *f*, a town in Asia Minor
Milo, ōnis, *m*, 1. famous athlete of Crotona; 2, T. Annius M. the enemy of Clodius
Miltiādes, is, *m*, the famous general of the Athenians at Marathon
Mincĭus, ii, *m*, a river in Gaul
Minerva, ae, *f*, the Roman goddess of wisdom, the arts and sciences
Mīnos, ōis, *m*, a king of Crete
Mīnōtaurus, i, *m*, a monster with a bull's head and a man's body, slain by Theseus with the help of Ariadne
Mĭsēnum, i, *n*, a promontory and town in Campania
Mĭsēnus, i, *m*, the trumpeter of Aeneas
Mĭthras, ae, *m*, the Persian sun-god
Mithrĭdātes, is, *m*, a king of Pontus who fought the Romans and was finally defeated by Pompey
Mĭtȳlēnē, es, *f*, the capital of Lesbos
Mŏlossi, ōrum, *m. pl*, a people of Epirus
Mŏlossus, i, *m*, a Molossian hound (famous for hunting)
Mŏna, ae, *f*, the Isle of Man
Mŏnēta, ae, *f*, a surname of Juno in whose temple money was minted
Mŏrĭni, ōrum, *m. pl*, a Gallic tribe
Mŏsa, ae, *m*, a river in Gaul (now the Meuse)
Mŏsella, ae, *m*, a river in Gaul (now the Moselle)
Mōses, is, *m*, Moses
Mŭcĭus, a, um, *adj*, the name of a Roman "gens"; C. Mucius Scaevola, who tried to assassinate Porsenna
Mulcĭber, bĕri, *m*, a surname of Vulcan
Mulvĭus pons, *m*, a bridge across the Tiber

Mummĭus, a, um, *adj*, the name of a Roman "gens"
Munda, ae, *f*, a city in Spain where Julius Caesar defeated Pompey's son
Mūsa, ae, *f*, a goddess of the Arts
Mūsaeus, i, *m*, a Greek poet
Mȳcēnae, ārum, *f. pl*, a famous city of Argolis where Agamemnon was king
Mȳlae, ārum, *f. pl*, a city in Sicily
Myrmĭdŏnes, um, *m. pl*, a people of Thessaly, under the rule of Achilles
Mȳsĭa, ae, *f*, a country of Asia Minor

N

Naevĭus, a, um, *adj*, the name of a Roman "gens"
Nāiăs, ădis, *f*, a water-nymph
Namnētes, um, *m. pl*, a Gallic tribe
Nantŭātes, um, *m. pl*, a Gallic tribe
Narbo, ōnis, *m*, a city of southern Gaul
Narcissus, i, *m*, son of Cephisus, who fell in love with his own reflection and was changed into a flower
Nāsĭca, ae, *m*, a Roman family name
Naxos, i, *f*, an island in the Aegean Sea
Nĕāpŏlis, is, *f*, a sea-port of Campania (now Naples)
Nĕmĕa, ae, *f*, a city in Argolis
Nĕmĕsis, is, *f*, the goddess of justice
Nĕpos, ōtis, *m*, C. Cornelius N., a Roman historian
Neptūnus, i, *m*, Neptune, god of the sea
Nēreus, ei, *m*, a sea-god
Nēro, ōnis, *m*, a Roman family name; C. Claudius N., the fifth Roman emperor
Nerva, ae, *m*, a Roman family name; M. Cocceius N., a Roman emperor
Nervii, ōrum, *m. pl*, a Gallic tribe
Nestŏr, ŏris, *m*, a king of Pylos who fought with the Greeks at Troy
Nĭcōmēdēs, is, *m*, a king of Bithynia
Nīlus, i, *m*, the river Nile
Nĭŏbē, es, *f*, daughter of Tantalus, wife of Amphion
Nīsus, i, *m*, 1. king of Megara; 2, a friend of Euryalus (in Vergil's Aeneid)
Nōla, ae, *f*, a town in Campania
Nōrĭcum, i, *n*, a country between the Danube and the Alps
Nŏtus, i, *m*, the south wind
Nŏvĭŏdūnum, i, *n*, 1, a town of the Aedui; 2. a town of the Bituriges; 3. a town of the Sessiones
Nŭma, ae, *m*, N. Pompilius, the second king of Rome
Nŭmantĭa, ae, *f*, a city in northern Spain
Nŭmĭdae, ārum, *m. pl*, the Numidians, a people of N. Africa
Nŭmĭdĭa, ae, *f*, Numidia
Nŭmĭtor, ōris, *m*, king of Alba Longa, grandfather of Romulus and Remus
Nȳsa, ae, *f*, a city in India, where Bacchus was born

O

Ocrĭcŭlum, i, *n*, a town in Umbria
Octāvĭānus, i, *m*, the surname of the Emperor Augustus
Octāvĭus, a, um, *adj*, the name of a Roman "gens"; C. Octavius, the father of the emperor Augustus
Oebălus, i, *m*, a king of Sparta
Oedĭpus, i, *m*, a king of Thebes, who killed his father and married his mother
Oenōnē, es, *f*, a Phrygian nymph, loved and then deserted by Paris
Ŏlympĭa, ae, *f*, a sacred plain in Elis where the Olympic Games were held
Ŏlympĭa, ōrum, *n. pl*, the Olympic Games
Ŏlympĭas, ădis, *f*, 1, an Olympiad, a four-year period which elapsed between Olympic Games; 2. wife of Philip of Macedon, and mother of Alexander the Great
Ŏlympĭcus, a, um, *adj*, Olympic
Ŏlympus, i, *m*, a mountain on the borders of Macedonia and Thessaly, the abode of the gods
Orbĭlĭus, i, *m*, a famous Roman grammarian and schoolmaster
Orcădes, um, *f. pl*, the Orkney Islands
Orchŏmĕnus, i, *m*, the name of two cities, one in Boeotia, one in Thessaly
Orcus, i, *m*, the Lower World
Ordovĭces, um, *m. pl*, a British tribe
Ŏrēăs, ădis, *f*, a mountain-nymph
Ŏrestēs, is, *m*, the son of Agamemnon
Ŏrĭcum, i, *n*, a seaport in Illyria
Ŏrĭon, ōnis, *m*, a hunter who was changed into a constellation
Ŏrōdēs, is, *m*, a king of Parthia
Ŏrontēs, is, *m*, a river in Syria
Orpheus, i, *m*, a famous Thracian singer

For List of Abbreviations used, turn to pages 3, 4

Osci, ōrum, *m. pl,* an ancient Italian tribe of Campania
Ŏsĭris, is, *m,* an Egyptian god
Ossa, ae, *f,* a mountain range in Thessaly
Ostĭa, ae, *f,* a seaport at the mouth of the Tiber
Ostōrĭus, i, *m,* P. Ostorius Scapula, governor of Britain
Ŏtho, ōnis, *m,* a Roman surname; M. Salvius O., a Roman emperor
Othrys, ўos, *m,* a mountain in Thessaly
Ŏvĭdius, a, um, *adj,* the name of a Roman "gens" P. Ovidius Naso, the Roman poet
Oxos, i, *m,* a river in Asia

P

Păcŏrus, i, *m,* a king of Parthia
Pācŭvĭus, i, *m,* a Roman poet
Pădus, i, *m,* the river Po
Paeligni, ōrum, *m. pl,* an Italian tribe
Pālaestĭna, ae, *f,* Palestine
Pālātĭum, ii, *n,* the Palatine, one of the seven hills of Rome
Pālĭnūrus, i, *m,* Aeneas' pilot who fell into the sea off the coast of Lucania
Pallās, ădis, *f,* a surname of Athene, the Greek goddess of Wisdom
Pallās, antis, *m,* son of Pandion
Pamphўlĭa, ae, *f,* a district of Asia Minor
Pān, Pānos, *m,* the god of woods and flocks
Panchāĭa, ae, *f,* a region of Arabia
Pandĭōn, ōnis, *m,* a king of Athens
Pandōra, ae, *f,* the first woman
Pannōnĭa, ae, *f,* a country on the Danube
Pănŏpēa, ae, *f,* a sea-nymph
Pănormus, i, *f,* a city in Sicily
Paphlăgŏnĭa, ae, *f,* a district in Asia Minor
Păpīrĭus, a, um, *adj,* the name of a Roman "gens"
Parca, ae, *f,* the goddess of fate
Păris, ĭdis, *m,* the son of Priam and Hecuba who carried away Helen from her husband Menelaus and thus caused the Trojan War
Pārĭsii, ōrum, *m. pl,* a Gallic tribe
Parma, ae, *f,* a town in Gaul
Parmĕnĭo, ōnis, *m,* one of Alexander's generals
Parnāsus, i, *m,* a mountain in Phocis, sacred to Apollo
Păros, i, *f,* an island in the Aegean
Parrhăsĭus, i, *m,* a Greek painter
Parthĕnon, ōnis, *m,* the temple of Athene at Athens
Parthĕnŏpē, es, *f,* a Siren who gave her name to Neapolis (Naples)
Parthi, ōrum, *m. pl,* the Parthians, a Scythian people, famous archers
Pāsĭphae, es, *f,* daughter of Helios, mother of the Minotaur
Pāsĭthĕa, ae, *f,* one of the three Graces
Pătăvĭum, i, *n,* a town in North Italy, birthplace of Livy
Pătrŏclus, i, *m,* friend of Achilles
Paulus, i, *m,* a Roman surname
Pausănĭas, ae, *m,* the leader of the Spartans in the battle of Plataea
Pēgăsus, i, *m,* the winged horse of the Muses
Pĕlasgi, ōrum, *m. pl,* the oldest inhabitants of Greece
Pēleus, i, *m,* a king of Thessaly
Pēligni, ōrum, *m. pl,* a people of Central Italy
Pēlĭon, ii, *n,* a mountain in Thessaly
Pella, ae, *f,* a city in Macedonia
Pēlŏpŏnnēsus, i, *f,* the southern part of Greece
Pĕlops, ŏpis, *m,* son of Tantalus, king of Phrygia
Pēlūsĭum, i, *n,* a town in Egypt
Pĕnātes, ĭum, *m. pl,* Roman guardian deities of the household
Pēnĕlŏpē, es, *f,* the wife of Ulysses
Pentheus, ĕi, *m,* a king of Thebes
Pergămum, i, *n,* a city of Asia
Pĕrĭcles, is, *m,* an Athenian statesman of the fifth century B.C.
Persae, ārum, *m. pl,* the Persians
Persĭa, ae (or **Persis, ĭdis**), *f,* Persia
Persĕphŏnē, es, *f,* Proserpine, daughter of Ceres
Persēs, ae, *m,* the last king of Macedonia
Perseus, ĕi, *m,* son of Iuppiter and Danae who killed Medusa
Phaedo, ōnis, *m,* a pupil of Socrates and friend of Plato
Phaedra, ae, *f,* daughter of Minos and wife of Theseus
Phaedrus, i, *m,* a pupil of Socrates
Phaethōn, ontis, *m,* son of Helios (the sun-god)
Phălērum, i, *n,* the oldest part of Athens
Pharsālus, i, *f,* a town of Thessaly where Pompey was defeated by Caesar

Phăros, i, *f*, an island near Alexandria with a famous light-house
Phĭdĭas, ae, *m*, a famous Athenian sculptor
Phĭlippi, ōrum, *m. pl*, a city in Macedonia
Phĭlippus, i, *m*, the name of four kings of Macedonia
Phĭloctētēs, ae, *m*, a famous archer, and a friend of Hercules
Phĭlŏmēla, ae, *f*, daughter of Pandion, she was changed into a nightingale
Phĭlōpoemen, ēnis, *m*, a famous Greek general
Phlĕgēthon, ontis, *m*, a river in the Lower World
Phōcaea, ae, *f*, a sea-port of Ionia
Phōcis, ĭdis, *f*, a country of northern Greece
Phoēbē, es, *f*, the moon-goddess
Phoebus, i, *m*, the name of Apollo
Phoenĭcē, es, *f*, Phoenicia, a country of Syria
Phorcus, i, *m*, a sea-god
Phrȳges, um, *m. pl*, the Phrygians, a people of Asia Minor
Phthĭa, ae, *f*, a region of Thessaly
Phȳlăcē, ēs, *f*, a city of Thessaly
Pĭcēnum, i, *n*, a district on the eastern side of Italy
Pĭcti, ōrum, *m. pl*, a British tribe
Pĭctŏnes, um, *m. pl*, a Gallic tribe
Pĭcus, i, *m*, son of Saturn
Pĭlumnus, i, *m*, ancestor of Turnus
Pindărus, i, *m*, Pindar, the lyric poet of Thebes
Pīraeus, i, *m*, the port of Athens
Pĭrithŏus, i, *m*, son of Ixion, friend of Theseus
Pīsa, ae, *f*. a town in Elis
Pīsae, ārum, *f. pl*, an Etruscan city
Pĭsistrătus, i, *m*, a tyrant of Athens
Plăcentĭa, ae, *f*, a city on the river Po
Plancus, i, *m*, a Roman surname
Plătaeae, ārum, *f. pl*, a town in Boeotia, where the Greeks defeated the Persians in 479 B.C.
Plăto, ōnis, *m*, the famous Greek philosopher, pupil of Socrates
Plautus, i, *m*, T. Maccius P. the famous Roman comic poet
Plĭnĭus, a, um, *adj*, the name of a Roman "gens", 1. C. Plinius Secundus (the "Elder"), author of a work on Natural History; 2. C. Plinius Caecilius (the "Younger"), author of letters
Plūto, ōnis, *m*, the king of the Lower World
Poeni, ōrum, *m. pl*, the Carthaginians
Pollĭo, ōnis, *m*, a Roman surname; C. Asinius P., a Roman orator
Pollux, ūcis, *m*, twin brother of Castor
Pŏlȳbĭus, ii, *m*, a famous Greek historian
Pŏlȳclĭtus, i, *m*, a famous Greek sculptor
Pŏlyxĕna, ae, *f*, daughter of Priam
Pompēii, ōrum, *m. pl*, a city in the south of Campania
Pompēius, a, um, *adj*, the name of a Roman "gens"; Cn. P. Magnus, the triumvir, opponent of Julius Caesar
Pompĭlĭus, a, um, *adj*, Numa Pompilius, the second king of Rome
Pomptĭnus, a, um, *adj* **(paludes),** the Pomptine Marshes, in Latium
Pontĭus, a, um, *adj*, the name of a Roman "gens"; Pontius Pilatus governor of Judaea at the time of Christ's crucifixion
Pontus, i, *m*, the Black Sea
Porcĭus, a, um, *adj*, the name of a Roman "gens"; M. Porcius Cato, the Censor
Porsenna, ae, *m*, an Etruscan king
Portūnus, i, *m*, god of harbours
Pōrus, i, *m*, a king of India
Praeneste, is, *n*, a town in Latium
Praxĭtēles, is, *m*, an Athenian sculptor
Prĭămus, i, *m*, the last king of Troy
Prŏcas, ae, *m*, a king of Alba
Procnē, es, *f*, a daughter of Pandion who was changed into a swallow
Prŏmētheus, ei, *m*, son of Iapetus, father of Deucalion; he brought fire from heaven for mankind
Prŏpertĭus, i, *m*, Sextus Aurelius P. a Roman elegiac poet
Prŏpontis, ĭdis, *f*, the Sea of Marmora
Prŏserpĭna, ae, *f*, daughter of Ceres
Prŏtăgŏras, ae, *m*, a Greek sophist
Prŏteus, ei, *m*, a sea-god
Prūsias, ae, *m*, a king of Bithynia
Ptŏlĕmaeus, i, *m*, Ptolemy, the name of a dynasty of Egyptian kings
Publius, ii, *m*, a Roman praenomen
Pŭtĕŏli, ōrum, *m. pl*, a city on the coast of Campania
Pydna, ae, *f*, a town in Macedonia
Pygmaei, ōrum, *m. pl*, a race of dwarfs
Pygmălĭon, ōnis, *m*, grandson of Agenor, who fell in love with a statue, to which Venus later gave life
Pȳlos, i, *f*, the name of three towns of the Peloponnesus
Pȳrēnē, es, *f*, the Pyrenees

Pȳrŏis, entis, *m*, the planet Mars
Pyrrha, ae, *f*, the wife of Deucalion
Pyrrhus, i, *m*, 1. son of Achilles and founder of a kingdom in Epirus; 2. a king of Epirus who invaded Italy and fought the Romans
Pȳthăgŏras, ae, *m*, the famous Greek philosopher (550 B.C.)
Pȳtho, us, *f*, the old name of Delphi

Q

Quinctĭus, a, um, *adj*, the name of a Roman "gens"; L. Quinctius Cincinnatus, who came from the plough to be dictator of Rome
Quintilĭānus, i, *m*, a Roman surname; L. Fabius Q., teacher and rhetorician
Quĭrīnus, i, *m*, a name of Romulus after he became a god

R

Raetĭa, ae, *f*, a country between the Alps and the Danube
Răvenna, ae, *f*, a Gallic town on the Adriatic
Rēgillus, i, *m*, a lake in Latium
Rēgĭum, i, *n*, a town of south Calabria
Rēgŭlus, i, *m*, a Roman family name; M. Atilius R. a famous Roman general of the first Punic War
Rēmi, ōrum, *m. pl*, a Gallic tribe
Rĕmus, i, *m*, the brother of Romulus
Rhădămanthus, i, *m*, son of Juppiter, a judge in the Lower World
Rhēa Silvia, she became, by Mars, mother of Romulus and Remus
Rhēnus, i, *m*, the Rhine
Rhōdănus, i, *m*, the Rhone
Rhŏdos, i, *f*, the island of Rhodes
Rhoetēum, i, *n*, a promontory in the Hellespont
Rōma, ae, *f*, Rome
Rōmŭlus, i, *m*. son of Mars, founder and first king of Rome
Roscĭus, a, um, *adj*, the name of a Roman "gens"
Rŭbi, ōrum, *m. pl*, a town in Apulia
Rŭbĭco, ōnis, *m*, a river which marked the boundary between Italy and Gaul
Rŭdĭae, ārum, *f. pl*, a town in Apulia
Rŭtĭlius, a, um, *adj*, the name of a Roman "gens"
Rŭtŭli, ōrum, *m. pl*, a people of Latium

S

Săbelli, ōrum, *m. pl*, a name of the Sabines
Săbīni, ōrum, *m. pl*, a people of Central Italy, the Sabines
Săgittārĭus, i, *m*, a constellation
Săguntum, i, *n*, a town on the coast of Spain
Sălămis, mĭnis, *f*, an island near Eleusis
Sălentīni, ōrum, *m. pl*, a people of southern Italy
Sălernum, i, *n*, a town of Campania (now Salerno)
Sălĭi, ōrum, *m. pl*, a Roman college of priests
Sallustĭus, a, um, *adj*, the name of a Roman "gens"; C. Sallustius Crispus, the famous Roman historian
Sămărŏbrīva, ae, *f*, a town in Gaul
Samnĭum, ii, *n*, a region of Central Italy
Sămos, i, *f*, an island in the Aegean
Santŏnes, um, *m. pl*, a Gallic tribe
Sappho, ūs, *f*, the famous Greek lyric poetess
Sardes, ĭum, *f. pl*, the capital of Lydia
Sardi, ōrum, *m. pl*, the inhabitants of Sardinia
Sarmătĭa, ae, *f*, a country in South Russia
Sāturnālĭa, ōrum, *n. pl*, the festival of Saturn, held in December
Sāturnīnus, i, *m*, a Roman surname
Sāturnus, i, *m*, father of Juppiter
Scaevŏla, ae, *m*, a Roman family name; C. Mucius Sc., opponent of Porsenna
Scămander, dri, *m*, a river at Troy
Scăpŭla, ae, *m*, a Roman family
Scīpĭo, ōnis, *m*, a Roman family name; 1. P. Cornelius Scipio Africanus; 2. P. Cornelius Scipio Aemilienus Africanus, two conquerors of the Carthaginians
Scŏpas, ae, *m*, a famous Greek sculptor
Scylla, ae, *f*, a rock in the straits between Italy and Sicily
Scythae, ārum, *m. pl*, the Scythians
Scȳthĭa, ae, *f*, a region to the north of the Black Sea
Sēgesta, ae, *f*, a city of Sicily
Sējānus, i, *m*, the prefect of the Praetorian Guard under Tiberius
Sēleucus, i, *m*, the name of several kings of Syria
Sēlīnus, untis, *f*, a port in Sicily

Sĕmĕlē, es, *f*, daughter of Cadmus, mother of Bacchus
Sempronĭus, a, um, *adj*, the name of a Roman "gens", to which belonged the brothers Tiberius and Gaius Sempronius Gracchus
Sĕnĕca, ae, *m*, a Roman family name; 1. M. Annaeus S., a famous rhetorician from Spain; 2. L. Annaeus S., his son, Stoic philosopher and tutor of Nero
Sĕnŏnes, um, *m. pl*, a Gallic tribe
Sēquăna, ae, *f*, the river Seine
Sēquăni, ōrum, *m. pl*, a Gallic tribe
Sertōrĭus, i, *m*, a general of Marius
Servĭlius, a, um, *adj*, the name of a Roman "gens"
Servĭus Tullĭus, *m*, the sixth king of Rome
Sestos, i, *f*, a city in Thrace
Sĕvērus, i, *m*, a Roman family name
Sextīlis (mensis), another name for the month of August
Sĭbylla, ae, *f*, a priestess of Apollo
Sĭcāni, ōrum, *m. pl*, a people of Italy
Sĭchaeus, i, *m*, the husband of Dido
Sĭcŭli, ōrum, *m. pl*, the Sicilians
Sĭdon, ŏnis, *f*, a Phoenician city
Sĭgēum, i, *n*, a promontory in Troas
Sīlēnus, i, *m*, the attendant of Bacchus
Sĭlĭus, a um, *adj*, the name of a Roman "gens"
Sĭlŭres, um, *m. pl*, a British tribe
Sĭlvānus, i, *m*, the god of woods
Sĭmōnĭdes, is, *m*, a famous lyric poet of Ceos
Sĭnōpē, es, *f*, a town on the Black Sea
Sīrēnes, um, *f. pl*, nymphs who lived off the coast of south Italy and lured sailors to their death
Sīsŷphus, i, *m*, son of Aeolus, king of Corinth, a robber
Smyrna, ae, *f*, a trading city of Iona
Sōcrătes, is, *m*, the famous Athenian philosopher
Sōlon, ōnis, *m*, one of the seven wise men of Greece (*c.* 600 B.C.)
Sontiātes, um, *m. pl*, a Gallic tribe
Sŏphŏcles, is, *m*, the famous Greek tragic poet
Sŏphŏnisba, ae, *f*, daughter of Hasdrubal
Sōracte, is, *n*, a mountain in Etruria
Sparta, ae, *f*, the capital of Laconia
Spartăcus, i, *m*, leader of the gladiators against Rome
Stōĭcus, i, *m*, a Stoic philosopher
Styx, ўgis, *f*, a river of the Lower World
Sŭessiōnes, um, *m. pl*, a Gallic tribe
Sŭētōnĭus, Gaius S. Tranquillus, the biographer of the Caesars
Suēvi, ōrum, *m. pl*, a German tribe
Sŭgambri, ōrum, *m. pl*, a German tribe
Sullc, ae, *m*, a Roman family name; L. Cornelius S., dictator, opponent of Marius
Sulmo, ōnis, *m*, a town of the Paeligni
Sulpĭcĭus, a, um, *adj*, the name of a Roman "gens"
Sūnĭum, i, *n*, a town of Attica
Sўbăris, is, *f*, a town of Lucania
Sychaeus, see **Sĭchaeus**
Sўphax, ācis, *m*, a king of Numidia
Sўrācūsae, ārum, *f. pl*, Syracuse
Sўrĭa, ae, *f*, Syria
Syrtes, ĭum, *f. pl*, two sandbanks on the north coast of Africa

T

Tăburnus, i, *m*, a range of mountains between Samnium and Campania
Tăcĭtus, i, *m*, Cornelius T. the famous Roman historian
Taenăros, i, *c*, a town in Laconia, near which was thought to be an entrance to the Lower World
Tăges, is, *m*, an Etruscan god
Tăgus, i, *m*, a river in Lusitania
Tāmēsis, is, *m*, the river Thames
Tănăis, is, *m*, the river Don
Tănăquil, ĭlis, *f*, the wife of Tarquinius Priscus
Tantălus, i, *m*, a son of Juppiter
Tarbelli, ōrum, *m. pl*, a tribe of Aquitania
Tărentum, i, *n*, a Greek city on the south coast of Italy
Tarpēius, a, um, *adj*, 1. the name of a Roman "gens"; Tarpeia, who betrayed the citadel to the Sabines; 2. The Tarpeian Rock at Rome from which criminals were thrown
Tarquĭnii, ōrum, *m. pl*, an Etruscan town
Tarquĭnĭus, ii, *m*, the name of two Etruscan kings of Rome
Tarsus, i, *f*. the capital of Cilicia
Tartărus, i, *m*. the Lower World
Tătĭus, i, *m*, Titus T., a king of the Sabines
Taurus, i, *m*, a mountain range in Asia Minor
Tĕgĕa, ae, *f*, a town in Arcadia
Tĕlămon, ōnis, *m*, an Argonaut
Tēlēmăchus, i, *m*, son of Ulysses and Penelope

For List of Abbreviations used, turn to pages 3, 4

Tempē, *n. pl*, a valley in Thessaly
Tenctēri, ōrum, *m. pl*, a German tribe
Tĕnĕdos, i, *f*, an island in the Aegean
Tĕrentĭus, a, um, *adj*, the name of a Roman "gens"; M. Terentius Afer a "freed man" and famous dramatist
Tēreus, i, *m*, a king of Thrace
Teucer, cri, *m*, the first king of Troy
Teutōnes, um, *m. pl*, a German people
Thapsus, i, *f*, 1. a city in Africa; 2. a city in Sicily
Thēbae, ārum, *f. pl*, the capital of Boeotia
Thĕmistŏcles, is, *m*, a famous Athenian general and statesman
Thĕŏcritus, i, *m*, the famous Greek pastoral poet
Thĕophrastus, i, *m*, a Greek philosopher
Thermŏpȳlae, ārum, *f. pl*, a famous mountain-pass on the borders of Thessaly
Thēseus, ei, *m*, king of Athens and slayer of the Minotaur
Thessălĭa, ae, *f*, Thessaly, a region of north Greece
Thessălŏnīca, ae, *f*, a town of Macedonia
Thĕtis, ĭdis, *f*, a sea-nymph
Thisbē, es, *f*, a Babylonian maiden
Thrācia, ae, *f*, Thrace, a country to the north of the Propontis
Thūcȳdĭdes, is, *m*, the famous Athenian historian
Thūlē, es, *f*, an island of northern Europe (perh. Iceland)
Thūrii, ōrum, *m. pl*, a city of Lucania
Thȳās, ădis, *f*, a female attendant of Bacchus
Thȳestes, ae, *m*, son of Pelops and brother of Atreus
Thȳni, ōrum, *m. pl*, a Thracian people who emigrated to Bithynia
Tĭbĕris, is, *m*, the river Tiber
Tibĕrius, i, *m*, a Roman praenomen; Ti. Claudius Nero Caesar, the second Roman emperor
Tĭbullus, i, *m*, a Roman poet
Tĭbur, ŭris, *n*, a town in Latium
Tĭcīnus, i, *m*, a river in Cisalpine Gaul
Tigrānes, is, *m*, a king of Armenia
Tigris, ĭdis, *m*, a river of Asia
Tīridātes, is, *m*, the name of several Armenian kings
Tīryns, ntis, *f*, a town of Argolis
Tisiphŏnē, es, *f*, one of the Furies
Tītan, ānis, *m*, ancestor of the Titans
Tīthōnus, i, *m*, the wife of Aurora who received the gift of immortality
Tĭtus, i, *m*, a Roman praenomen
Tĭtȳos, i, *m*, giant son of Juppiter, slain by Apollo
Tŏlōsa, ae, *f*, a city of southern Gaul
Tŏlumnius, i, *m*, a Rutulian soothsayer
Tŏmi, ōrum, *m. pl*, a town on the Black Sea
Torquātus, i, *m*, surname gained by T. Manlius who slew a Gaul and took his neck-chain
Trāiānus, i, *m*, a Roman emperor
Tralles, ium, *f. pl*, a town in Western Asia
Trāsĭmēnus, i, *m*, Lake Trasimene, where Hannibal gained a victory over the Romans (217 B.C.)
Trĕbĭa, ae, *m*, a river of Cisalpine Gaul, where Hannibal defeated the Romans (218 B.C.)
Trēvĕri, ōrum, *m. pl*, a Belgian tribe
Trinōbantes, um, *m. pl*, a British tribe
Triptŏlĕmus, i, *m*, the inventor of agriculture
Trĭton, ōnis, *m*, a sea-god son of Neptune
Troezēn, ēnis, *f*, a town of Argolis
Trōia, ae, *f*, Troy
Trōiānus, a, um, Trojan
Trōĭcus, a, um, Trojan
Trōius, a, um, Trojan
Trōs, ōis, *m*, a king of Phrygia, after whom Troy was named
Tullĭus, a, um, *adj*, the name of a Roman "gens"; 1. Servius T., sixth king of Rome; 2. Marcus T. Cicero, famous orator and statesman
Turnus, i, *m*, a Rutulian prince killed by Aeneas
Tusci, ōrum, *m. pl*, the Etruscans
Tuscŭlum, i, *n*, a town of Latium
Tyndăreus, ĕi, *m*, a king of Sparta
Tȳphōeus, ĕos, *m*, a giant buried beneath Mount Etna
Tȳphōn, ōnis, *m*, another name for Typhoeus
Tyrrhēni, ōrum, *m. pl*, a Pelasgian colony which came to Italy
Tȳrus, i, *f*, Tyre, a famous Phoenician city

U

Ubii, ōrum, *m. pl*, a German tribe

Ŭcălĕgōn, ontis, *m*, a Trojan, mentioned in Vergil's Aeneid
Ŭfens, ntis, *m*, a river of Latium
Ŭlysses (Ŭlixes), is, *m*, Ulysses (or Odysseus) king of Ithaca and husband of Penelope
Umbri, ōrum, *m. pl*, a people of Italy
Ŭsĭpĕtes, um, *m. pl*, a German tribe
Ŭtica, ae, *f*, a city of North Africa

V

Vălĕrĭus, a, um, *adj*, the name of a Roman "gens"
Varro, ōnis, *m*, a Roman surname; M. Terentius V., a Roman writer
Vātĭcānus mons, the Vatican hill at Rome
Vectis, is, *f*, the Isle of Wight
Vēii, ōrum, *m. pl*, an Etruscan city
Vellēius, a, um, *adj*, the name of a Roman "gens"
Vĕnĕti, ōrum, *m. pl*, 1. a people of north-east Italy; 2. a people of north-west Gaul
Vĕnus, ĕris, *f*, the goddess of love
Vĕnŭsia, ae, *f*, a town on the border of Apulia
Vercellae, ārum, *f. pl*, a town of Cisalpine Gaul
Vercingĕtŏrix, ĭgis, *m*, a Gallic chieftain
Vergĭlĭus, i, *m*, P. Vergilius Maro, the Roman poet, author of the Aeneid and the Georgics
Vergĭnĭus, a, um, *adj*, the name of a Roman "gens"
Vērōna, ae, *f*, a town of north Italy
Verres, is, *m*, C. Cornelius V., the notorious praetor of Sicily
Vertumnus, i, *m*, the god of the changing seasons
Vĕrŭlāmĭum, ii, *n*, St Albans
Vespăsĭānus, i, *m*, Ti. Flavius V., a Roman emperor
Vesta, ae, *f*, the goddess of the hearth
Virgĭlĭus, see **Vergilius**
Volcae, ārum, *m. pl*, a Gallic tribe
Volcānus, i, *m*, son of Iuppiter and Juno, god of fire
Volsci, ōrum, *m. pl*, a people of Latium
Vulcānus, see **Volcanus**
Vulturnus, i, *m*, a river in Campania

X

Xantho, ūs, *f*, a sea-nymph
Xanthus, i, *m*, a river in Lycia
Xĕno, ōnis, *m*, an Epicurean philosopher
Xĕnŏphon, ontis, *m*, the famous Athenian historian, philosopher and general
Xerxes, is, *m*, a Persian king

Z

Zăma, ae, *f*, a town in Numidia where Scipio defeated Hannibal
Zanclē, ēs, *f*, another name of Messana in Sicily
Zēno, ōnis, *m*, a Greek philosopher
Zĕphȳrus, i, *m*, the west wind

ENGLISH–LATIN

For List of Abbreviations used, turn to pages 3, 4

A

a, an, (*indefinite article*), no equivalent in Latin
abandon, *v.t*, rĕlinquo (3), dēsĕro (3)
abandoned, dērĕlictus, dēsertus; (**person**), perdĭtus
abandonment, rĕlictĭo, *f*
abase, *v.t*, dēprĭmo (3)
abasement, hŭmĭlĭtas, *f*, dēmĭssĭo, *f*
abash, *v.t*, confundo (3), perturbo (1)
abashed, pŭdōre confūsus (**perplexed with shame**)
abate, *v.t*, immĭnŭo (3), rĕmitto (3)
abatement, dēcessus, *m*, dēcessĭo, *f*, dēmĭnūtĭo, *f*
abbot, pontĭfex, *m*, (**high-priest**), săcerdos, *c*
abbreviate, *v.t*, immĭnŭo (3), contrăho (3)
abbreviation, compendĭum, *n*, contractĭo, *f*
abdicate, *v.i*, se abdĭcare (1. *reflex*)
abdication, abdĭcātĭo, *f*
abdomen, venter, *m*, abdōmen, *n*
abduction, raptus, *m*, raptĭo, *f*
abet, *v.i*, adsum (*irreg. with dat. of person*), adiŭvo (1)
abettor, mĭnister, *m*, adiūtor, *m*
abeyance (**to be in —**), *v.i*, iăcĕo (2)
abhor, ăbhorrĕo (2) (*with acc. or* ab *and abl*), ōdi. (*v. defect*)
abhorrence, ŏdĭum, *n*
abide, *v.i*, mănĕo (2), hăbĭto (1)
abide, *v.t*, (**wait for**), exspecto (1)
abiding, *adj*, (**lasting**), mansūrus
ability (**mental —**), ingĕnĭum, *n*; (**power**), pŏtestas, *f*
abject, abiectus, hŭmĭlis
abjectness, hŭmĭlĭtas, *f*
abjure, *v.t*, abiūro (1), ēiūro (1)
ablaze, *adj*, flăgrans
able, *use* possum (**be able**), pŏtens
able (**to be —**), *v.i*, possum (*irreg*)
able-bodied, vălĭdus
ablution, lăvātĭo, *f*, ablūtĭo, *f*
ably, *adv*, ingĕnĭōse
abnegation, nĕgātĭo, *f*, mŏdĕrātĭo, *f*
abnormal, abnormis, ĭnūsĭtātus
aboard, in nāve; (**to go —**), *v.i*, nāvem conscendo (3); (**to put —**), *v.t*, in nāvem impōno (3)
abode, dŏmus, *f*, dŏmĭcĭlĭum, *n*, sēdes, *f*, hăbĭtātĭo, *f*
abolish, *v.t*, tollo (3), ăbŏlĕo (2), dissolvo (3)
abolition, dissŏlūtĭo, *f*, ăbŏlĭtĭo, *f*
abominable, infandus, dētestābĭlis
abominate, *v.t*, ōdī (*defect*), ăbhorrĕo (2)
abomination (**hatred**), ŏdĭum, *n*; (**crime**), flăgĭtĭum, *n*
aborigines, indĭgĕnae, *m. pl*
abortion, ăbortus, *m*, ăbortĭo, *f*
abortive (**unsuccessful**), irrĭtus
abound (**in**), *v.i*, ăbundo (1), sŭpĕro (1), circumflŭo (3), suppĕdĭto (1)
abounding, ăbundans, afflŭens, fĕcundus
about, *prep*, circā, circum, ăd, sŭb (*with acc*), dē (*with abl*); (**of time**), circĭter (*with acc*)
about, *adv*, (**nearly**), circĭter, fermē, fĕrē
above, *prep*, sŭper, sŭprā (*with acc*); (**more than**), amplĭus
above, *adv*, sŭprā, insŭper; (**from above**), dēsŭper, sŭpernē
abrasion, attrĭtus, *m*
abreast, *adv*, părĭter
abridge, *v.t*, contrăho (3)
abridgement, ĕpĭtŏmē, *f*, ĕpĭtŏma, *f*
abroad, *adv*, (**in a foreign country**), pĕrĕgrē
abroad (**to be —**), *v.i*, pĕrĕgrīnor (1. *dep*)
abrogate, *v.t*, abrŏgo (1); rescindo (3)
abrogation, abrŏgātĭo, *f*
abrupt (**sudden**), sŭbĭtus; (**steep**), praeruptus
abruptly, *adv*, sŭbĭto, praerupte
abscess, vŏmĭca, *f*
abscond, *v.i*, lătĕo (2)
abscence, absentĭa, *f*
absent, absens
absent (**to be —**), *v.i*, absum (*irreg*)

absinth, absinthĭum, *n*
absolute, absŏlūtus
absolute power, tȳrannis, *f*, impĕrĭum, *n*, dŏmĭnātĭo, *f*
absolutely (completely), *adv*, prorsum, prorsus
absolve, *v.t*, absolvo (3), lībĕro (1)
absorb, *v.t*, bĭbo (3), haurĭo (4), absorbĕo (2)
absorbent, *adj*, bĭbŭlus
abstain, *v.i*, abstĭnĕo (2)
abstemious, tempĕrātus
abstinence, abstĭnentĭa, *f*
abstinent, abstĭnens, mŏdĕrātus
abstract, *nn*, ĕpĭtŏme, *f*
abstract, *adj*, abstractus
abstract, *v.t*, abstrăho (3)
abstruse, rĕcondĭtus, obscūrus
absurd, ĭneptus, absurdus
absurdity, ĭneptĭa, *f*, insulsĭtas, *f*
absurdly, *adv*, ĭneptē, absurdē
abundance, cōpĭa, *f*, ăbundantĭa, *f*
abundant, largus, fĕcundus
abuse, *nn*, **(insult)**, contūmēlĭa
abuse, *v.t*, **(revile)**, mălĕdĭco (3); **(misuse)**, ăbūtor (3 *dep*)
abusive, contūmēlĭōsus
abut, *v.i*, adiăcĕo (2)
abutting, adiunctus
abyss, gurges, *m*, vŏrāgo, *f*
acacia, ăcācĭa, *f*
academic, ăcădēmĭcus
academy, ăcădēmĭa, *f*
accede, *v.i*, consentĭo (4)
accelerate, *v.t*, accĕlĕro (1)
accent, vox, *f*
accentuate, *v.t*, ăcŭo (3)
accentuation, accentus, *m*
accept, *v.t*, accĭpĭo (3), rĕcĭpĭo (3)
acceptability, suāvĭtas, *f*, făcĭlĭtas, *f*
acceptable, grātus
acceptance, acceptĭo, *f*
access (approach), ădĭtus, *m*, accessus, *m*
accessible, făcĭlis; **(to be —)**, *v.i*, pătĕo (3)
accession (— to the throne), ĭnĭtĭum (*n*) regni **(beginning of reign)**; *or use phr. with* incipio **(to begin)** *and* regno **(to reign)**
accessory (of crime), *adj*, conscĭus; **(helper)**, auctor, *m*
accident, cāsus, *m*
accidental, fortŭĭtus
accidentally, *adv*, cāsū, fortē
acclaim, *v.t*, clāmo (1)
acclamation, clāmor, *m*
acclimatized, assŭētus
accommodate, *v.t*, accommŏdo (1)
accommodating, obsĕquens
accommodation (lodging), hospĭtĭum, *n*; **(loan)**, commŏdum, *n*
accompaniment (musical), cantus, *m*
accompany, *v.t*, prōsĕquor (3 *dep*), cŏmĭtor (1 *dep*); **(— in singing)**, oblŏquor (3 *dep*)
accomplice, *adj*, conscĭus, partĭceps
accomplish, *v.t*, confĭcĭo (3)
accomplished (learned), ērŭdĭtus
accomplishment (completion), confectĭo, *f*
accord (of my (your) own —), mĕā (tŭā) spontē, ultrō
accord, *v.t*, concēdo (3); *v.i*, consentĭo (4)
accordance (in — with), *prep*, ex, dē, prō (*with abl*)
according to, *as above*
accordingly, *adv*, ĭtăque
accost, *v.t*, compello (1); allŏquor (3 *dep*)
account, *nn*, rătĭo, *f*; **(statement)**, mĕmŏrĭa, *f*
on account of, *prep*, propter, ŏb (*with acc*)
to render account for, rătĭonem reddo (3)
accountant, calcŭlātor, *m*, scrĭba, *m*
account-book, tăbŭlae, *f. pl*
accoutre, *v.t*, orno (1); armo (1)
accoutrements, arma, *n. pl*
accredit, *v.t*, **(establish)**, confirmo (1)
accrue, *v.i*, accēdo (3)
accumulate, *v.t*, cŭmŭlo (1), cŏăcervo (1); *v.i*, cresco (3)
accumulation (bringing together), collātĭo, *f*
accuracy (exactness), subtĭlĭtas, *f*; **(carefulness)**, cūra, *f*
accurate (exact), subtĭlis, vērus; **(careful)**, dilĭgens
accursed, exsĕcrābĭlis
accusation, crīmen, *n*, accūsātĭo, *f*
accuse, *v.t*, accūso (1); arcesso (3), nōmen dēfĕro (*v. irreg*)
accused person, rĕus, *m*
accuser, accūsātor, *m*, dēlātor, *m*
accustom, *v.t*, assŭēfăcĭo (3)
to be accustomed, *v.i*, sŏlĕo (2)
to become accustomed, *v.i*, assŭesco (3)
accustomed, assŭētus, sŏlĭtus
ache, *v.i*, dŏlĕo (2)
ache, *nn*, dŏlor, *m*
achieve, *v.t*, confĭcĭo (3), perfĭcĭo (3)
achievement, res gesta, *f*, făcĭnus, *n*
acid, *adj*, ăcerbus, ăcĭdus
acknowledge, *v.t*. **(confess)**, confĭtĕor (2 *dep*), agnosco (3); **(accept)**, tollo (3)

acknowledgement, confessĭo, *f*
acme, summa, *f*
aconite, ăcŏnĭtum, *n*
acorn, glans, *f*
acquaint, *v.t*, certĭōrem făcĭo (3) (*with acc. of person, and* dē *with abl*)
to become acquainted with, *v.t*, nosco (3), cognosco (3)
acquaintance (knowledge of), scĭentĭa, *f*; **(with a person),** consŭētūdo, *f*; **(a person),** nōtus, *m*
acquiesce, *v.i*, acquĭesco (3)
acquire, *v.t*, acquīro (3)
acquirement (obtaining), ădeptĭo, *f*
acquit, *v.t*, absolvo (3), lĭbĕro (1)
acquittal, absŏlūtĭo, *f*, lĭbĕrātĭo, *f*
acre, iūgĕrum, *n*
acrid, asper, ācer
acrimonious, ăcerbus, asper, ămārus
acrimony, ăcerbĭtas, *f*
across, *prep*, trans (*with acc*)
act, *v.i*, ăgo (3), ĕgero (3)
act, *v.t*. **(a part in a play),** ăgo (3)
act, *nn*, factum, *n*; **(law)** lex, *f*
action (carrying out), actĭo, *f*, actus, *m*; **(at law)** līs, *f*, **(battle),** proelĭum, *n*
active, impĭger, ălăcer
actively, impĭgrē
activity (energy), industrĭa, *f*; **(agility, mobility)** ăgilĭtas, *f*
actor, actor, *m*
actual, vērus
actually, *adv*, rē vērā
actuary, actŭārĭus, *m*
actuate, *v.t*, mŏvĕo (2), impello (3)
acumen, ăcūmen, *n*
acute, ācer, ăcūtus
acuteness, ăcĭes, *f*, ăcūmen, *n*
adage, dictum, *n*
adapt, *v.t*, accommŏdo (1), compōno (3)
adapted, accommŏdātus, aptus
add, *v.t*, addo (3), adĭcĭo (3)
adder, vīpĕra, *f*
addict, *v.t*, dĕdo (3) (*with dat*)
addicted, dedĭtus
addition (numerical), *use verb* addo (3); **(increase)** accessĭo, *f*
additional (more, new, fresh), nŏvus
address, *v.t*. **(a letter),** inscrĭbo (3); **(person)** allŏquor (3 *dep*)
address, *nn*, **(letter),** inscriptĭo, *f*; **(speaking)** allŏquĭum, *n*
adduce, *v.t*, prōdūco (3), prōfĕro (*v. irreg*)
adept, pĕrĭtus
adequacy, *use* sătis **(enough)** (*with nn. in genit*)
adequate, sătis (*with genit*)
adhere, *v.i*, **(cling)** haerĕo (2)
adherent, clĭens, *m*, sectātor, *m*
adhesive, tĕnax
adjacency, vĭcĭnĭtas, *f*
adjacent, fīnĭtĭmus, vĭcĭnus, contermĭnus
adjoin, *v.i*, adiăcĕo (2)
adjoin, *v.t*, adiungo (3)
adjoining, coniunctus, contĭgŭus
adjourn, *v.t*, diffĕro (*v. irreg*)
adjournment, dīlātĭo, *f*
adjudge (adjudicate), *v.t*, adiūdĭco
adjudication, addictĭo, *f*
adjure, *v.t*, obtestor (1 *dep*), obsĕcro (1)
adjust, *v.t*, apto (1), compōno (3)
adjustment, compŏsĭtĭo, *f*
adjutant, optĭo, *m*
administer, *v.t*, admĭnistro (1)
administration, admĭnistrātĭo, *f*, prŏcūrātĭo, *f*
administrator, procūrātor, *m*
admirable, mīrābĭlis
admirably, *adv*, praeclārē
admiral, praefectus, (*m*) classis
admiration, admīrātio, *f*
admire, *v.t*, admīror (1 *dep*), mīror (1 *dep*)
admirer, laudātor, *m*
admissible, accĭpĭendus, a, um
admission, (letting in), ădĭtus, *m*; **(acknowledgement)** confessĭo, *f*
admit, *v.t*. **(let in)** admitto (3); **(grant)** dō (1), concēdo (3); **(confess)** confĭtĕor (2 *dep*)
admonish, *v.t*, mŏnĕo (2)
admonition, admŏnĭtĭo, *f*
adolescence, ădŏlescentĭa, *f*
adolescent, ădŏlescens, *c*
adopt, *v.t*, (person), ădopto (1); (custom) ascisco (3)
adoption, ădoptĭo, *f*
adorable, cŏlendus
adoration, cultus, *m*, ădōrātĭo, *f*
adore, *v.t*, cŏlo (3), ădōro (1)
adorn, *v.t*, orno (1)
adorned, ornātus
adornment (as an act), exornātĭo, *f*; **(a decoration)** ornāmentum, *n*
adrift, *adj*, in mări iactātus **(driven about on the sea)**
adroit, callĭdus, sollers
adroitness, dextĕrĭtas, *f*
adulation, ădūlātĭo, *f*
adult, *adj*, ădultus
adulterate, *v.t*, vĭtĭo (1)
adulteration, adultĕrātĭo, *f*
adulterer(-ess), ădulter, *m*, (-era, *f*)
adultery, ădultĕrĭum, *n*
advance, *nn*, prōgressus, *m*

For List of Abbreviations used, turn to pages 3, 4

advance, *v.i*, prōcēdo (3), prōgrĕdĭor (3 *dep*), incēdo (3), pĕdem infĕro (*irreg*)
advance, *v.t*, infĕro (*irreg*), prōmŏvĕo (2)
in advance, *adv*, prae, *compounded with vb: e.g.* **send in advance,** praemitto (3)
advance-guard, prīmum agmen, *n*
advantage, commŏdum, *n*
to be advantageous, *v.i*, prōsum (*irreg*), ūsui esse (*irreg*) (*with dat*)
advantageous, ūtĭlis
advantageously, *adv*, ūtĭlĭter
advent, adventus, *m*
adventure, făcĭnus, *n*
adventurous, audax
adventurously, *adv*, audacter
adversary, hostis, *c*
adverse, adversus
adversity, res adversae, *f. pl*
advert to, *v.t*, attingo (3)
advertise, *v.t*, prōscrĭbo (3), prōnuntĭo (1)
advertisement, prōscriptĭo, *f*
advice, consĭlĭum, *n*
advisable (advantageous), ūtĭlis
advise, *v.t*, mŏnĕo (2), suādĕo (2), censĕo (2)
advisedly, *adv*, consultō
adviser, suāsor, *m*, auctor, *m*
advocate, *nn*, patrōnus, *m*
advocate, *v.t*, suādĕo (2)
adze, ascĭa, *f*
aedile, aedĭlis, *m*
aedileship, aedĭlĭtas, *f*
aerial, *adj*, **(of the air),** āĕrĭus
afar, *adv*, prŏcŭl
affability, cōmĭtas, *f*
affable, cōmis
affably, *adv*, cōmĭter
affair, rēs, *f*, nĕgōtĭum, *n*
affect, *v.t*, affĭcĭo (3); **(the feelings)** mŏvĕo (2)
affectation (show), sĭmŭlātĭo, *f*
affected, pūtĭdus
affection (love), ămor, *m*
affectionate, ămans
affiance, *v.t*, spondĕo (2)
affianced, sponsus
affidavit, testĭmōnĭum, *n*
affiliate, *v.t*, cŏ-opto (1)
affinity, cognātĭo, *f*
affirm, *v.t*, affirmo (1)
affix, *v.t*, affĭgo (3)
afflict, *v.t*, affĭcĭo (3)
afflicted (with grief), mĭser
affliction (with grief etc), mĭsĕrĭa, *f*; **(a bad thing),** mălum, *n*
affluence, dīvĭtĭae, *f. pl*
affluent, dīves
afford, *v.t*. **(give),** praebĕo (2); *otherwise use phr. with* satis pecuniae habere ut . . . **(to have enough money to. . . .)**
affright, *v.t*, terrĕo (2)
affront, contŭmēlĭa, *f*
affront, *v.t*, contŭmēlĭam facio (3) (*with dat*)
afire, *adj*, flăgrans
afloat, (*use phr. with* in aquā **(on the water)**)
afoot, *adv*, pĕdĭbus
afore, *adv*, sŭprā
aforementioned, sŭprā scriptus
aforesaid, sŭprā scriptus
afraid, tĭmĭdus
afraid (to be —), *v.i. and v.t*, tĭmĕo (2), vĕrĕor (2 *dep*), mĕtŭo (3)
afresh, *adv*, rursus
aft, *nn*, puppis, *f*
after, *prep*, post (*with acc*)
after, *conj*, postquam
after, *adv*, post, postĕa
after all (nevertheless), *adv*, tămen
afternoon, *adv*, post mĕrīdĭem
afternoon, *adj*, pōmĕrīdĭānus
afterwards, *adv*, post, postĕa
again, *adv*, ĭtĕrum, rursus
again and again, *adv*, ĭdentĭdem
against, *prep*, contra, in (*with acc*)
agape, *adj*, hĭans
age, aetas, *f*, aevum, *n*, **(old —)** sĕnectus, *f*
aged (old), sĕnex
aged (three) years, nātus (tres) annos
agency (doing, action), ŏpĕra, *f*
agent, actor, *m*
aggrandize, *v.t*, amplĭfĭco (1)
aggrandizement, amplĭfĭcātĭo, *f*
aggravate, *v.t*, grăvo (1); **(annoy)** aspĕro (1); **(increase)** augĕo (2)
aggregate, *nn*, summa, *f*
aggression, incursĭo, *f*
aggressive, hostīlis
aggressor, *use phr.* suā sponte bellum infĕrre *irreg*, **(inflict war of one's own accord)**
aggrieve, *v.t*, *use* affĭcĭo (3) **(affect)**
aghast, stŭpĕfactus
agile, ăgĭlis
agility, ăgĭlĭtas, *f*
agitate, *v.t*, ăgĭto (1), commŏvĕo (2)
agitated, sollĭcĭtus
agitation (violent movement), ăgĭtātĭo, *f*; **(of the mind),** commōtĭo, *f*
agitator (political), turbātor, *m*

ago, *adv,* ăbhinc (*with acc*) e.g. **two years —,** ăbhinc duos annos
agonize, *v.t,* crŭcĭo (1)
agony, dŏlor, *m*
agrarian, ăgrārĭus
agree with, *v.i,* consentĭo (4) (*with* cum *and abl*); *v.t* compōno (3); **(it is — by all)** constat inter omnes
agreeable, grātus
agreeableness, dulcēdo, *f*
agreed upon (it is —), constat, convĕnit, *v. impers*
agreeing, congrŭens, convĕnĭens
agreement (the — itself), pactum, *n;* **(of opinions, etc)** consensĭo, *f*
agricultural, rusticus
agriculture, ăgrĭcultūra, *f*
agriculturist, agrĭcŏla, *m*
aground (to run —) *use phr.* in vădo haerĕo (2) **(stick fast in a shallow place)**
ague, horror, *m*
ah! (alas!), eheu!
ahead, *adv, use* prae, pro, *compounded with verbs, e.g.* **send ahead,** praemitto (3)
aid, auxĭlĭum, *n*, subsĭdĭum, *n*
aid, *v.t,* adiŭvo (1), subvĕnĭo (4) (*with dat*)
ail, *v.i,* aegresco (3)
ailing, aeger, aegrōtus
aim, *v.t.* **(point a weapon, etc.)** dĭrĭgo (3); **(to aim at)** pĕto (3)
aim, *nn,* **(purpose)** finis, *m*; **(throwing)** coniectus, *m*
air, āēr, *m*; **(manner)** spĕcĭes, *f*
air, *v.t,* ventĭlo (1)
air-hole, spīrācŭlum, *n*
airy, āērĭus
akin, *adj,* **(similar)** fĭnĭtĭmus
alabaster, ălăbastrites ae, *m*
alacrity, ălăcrĭtas, *f*
alarm (fear), păvor, *m*, trĕpĭdātio, *f*; **(confusion)** tŭmultus, *m*
alarm, *v.t,* perturbo (1), terrĕo (2)
alarmed, trĕpĭdus
alas!, heu!
alcove, angŭlus, *m* **(corner)**
alder, alnus, *f*
alderman, măgistrātus, *m*
ale, cerevisia, *f*
ale-house, caupona, *f*
alert, ălăcer
alertness, ălăcrĭtas, *f*
alien (*adj and nn*) **(foreign),** pĕrĕgrīnus
alienate, *v.t,* ălĭēno (1)
alienation, ălĭēnātĭo, *f*
alight, *v.i,* dēsĭlĭo (4)
alike, *adj,* sĭmĭlis
alike, *adv,* sĭmĭlĭter
alive, vīvus
alive (to be —), vīvo (3)
all, *adj,* **(every)** omnis; **(the whole)** tōtus; (*with superlative,* e.g. **all the best people)** optĭmus quisque; **(at all, in all),** *adv,* omnīno
all-powerful, omnĭpŏtens
allay, *v.t,* sēdo (1)
allegation, affirmātĭo, *f*
allege, *v.t.* **(assert),** argŭo (3), affĕro (*irreg*)
allegiance fĭdes, *f*, offĭcĭum, *n*
allegory, allēgŏrĭa, *f*
alleviate, *v.t,* lĕvo (1)
alleviation, (as an act), lĕvātĭo, *f*; **(something which brings —)** lĕvāmen, *n*
alley, angĭportus, *m*
alliance, sŏcĭĕtas, *f*, foedus, *n*; **(to make an —)** foedus făcĭo (3)
allied (states), foedĕrātus
allot, *v.t,* distrĭbŭo (3), assigno (1)
allotment (of land), ăger assignātus, *m*
allow, *v.t.* **(permit),** pătĭor (3 *dep*), sĭno (3), concēdo (3); *or use impers. vb.* lĭcet (*with dat. of person allowed*)
allowable, *use* fās, (*indecl. nn*) **(right)**
allowance (to make —), ignosco (3), rĕmitto (3)
allude to, *v.t,* signĭfĭco (1)
allure, *v.t,* allĭcĭo (3)
allurement, blandĭtĭa, *f*, illĕcĕbra,
alluring, blandus
allusion, signĭfĭcātĭo, *f*
alluvium, allŭvĭo, *f*
ally, *nn,* sŏcĭus, *m*
ally, *v.t,* **(unite),** iungo (3); **(— oneself)** se coniungere (*with dat*)
almanack, fasti, *m. pl*
almighty, omnĭpŏtens
almond, ămygdălum, *n*; **(tree),** ămygdăla, *f*
almost, *adv,* paenĕ, prŏpĕ, fĕrē, fermē
alms, stips, *f*
aloe, ălŏē, *f*
aloft, *adv,* sublīmĕ; *adj,* sublīmis
alone, *adj,* sōlus
alone, *adv,* sōlum
along, *prep,* sĕcundum, praeter (*with acc*)
aloof, *adv,* prŏcŭl; **(to stand — from),** discēdo (3)
aloud, *adv,* magnā vōcē
alphabet, *use* litterae *f. pl* **(letters)**
already, *adv,* iam
also, *adv,* ĕtiam, quŏque, ĭtem; **(likewise),** necnōn
altar, āra, *f*

alter, *v.t*, mūto (1), verto (3), corrĭgo (3)
alter, *v.i*, mūtor (1 *dep*)
alteration, mūtātĭo, *f*
altercation, rixa, *f*
alternate, *v.t*, alterno (1)
alternate, *adj*, alternus
alternately, *adv*, invĭcem
alternation, vĭcissĭtūdo, *f*
alternative, *use phr. with* ălĭus mŏdus (other way)
although, *conj*, quamquam (*indicating fact*); quamvis (*indicating a supposition*); etsi, tămetsi
altitude, altĭtūdo, *f*
altogether, *adv*, omnīno
always, *adv*, semper
amalgamate, *v.t*, iungo (3), miscĕo (2)
amalgamation, coniunctĭo, *f*
amass, *v.t*, cŏăcervo (1), cŭmŭlo (1)
amatory, ămātōrĭus
amaze, *v.t*, obstŭpĕfăcĭo (3)
amazed, stŭpĭdus, stŭpĕfactus
amazement, stŭpor, *m*
amazing, mīrus
amazingly, *adv*, mīris mŏdis
amazon, vīrāgo, *f*
ambassador, lēgātus, *m*
amber, sŭcĭnum, *n*
ambiguity, ambāges, *f. pl*
ambiguous, ambĭgŭus, anceps
ambiguously, *adv*, per ambāges
ambition, glōrĭa, *f*, ambĭtĭo, *f*
ambitious, *use phr.* cŭpĭdus glōrĭae (keen on glory)
amble, *v.i*, lēnĭter ambŭlo (1) (walk quietly)
ambrosia, ambrŏsĭa, *f*
ambrosial, ambrŏsĭus
ambush, insĭdĭae, (*f. pl*); (to ambush) insĭdĭor (1 *dep*)
ameliorate, *v.t*, mĕlĭōrem făcĭo (3)
amen! fĭat! (let it be)
amenable, obēdĭens
amend, *v.t*, ēmendo (1), corrĭgo (3)
amendment (correction), ēmendātĭo, *f*
amends, *use* expĭo (1) (to make —s)
amenity, ămoenĭtas, *f*
amethyst, ămĕthystus, *f*
amiability, suāvĭtas, *f*
amiable, suāvis
amiably, *adv*, suāvĭter
amicable, ămīcus
amid(st), *prep*, inter (*with acc*)
amiss, *adv*, māle; (to take —) aegre fĕro (*irreg*)
amity, ămīcĭtĭa, *f*
ammunition, arma, *n. pl*
amnesty, vĕnĭa, *f*
among, *prep*, inter, ăpud (*with acc*)
amorous, ămans
amount, summa, *f*, fīnis, *m*
amount to, *v.t*, *use* esse (to be)
amphitheatre, amphĭthĕātrum, *n*
ample, amplus, cōpĭōsus
amplify, *v.t*, amplĭfĭco (1), dīlāto (1)
amplitude, amplĭtūdo, *f*
amply, *adv*, amplē
amputate, *v.t*, sĕco (1), ampŭto (1)
amputation, ampŭtātĭo, *f*
amuse, *v.t*, dēlecto (1)
amusement, dēlectātĭo, *f*
amusing, făcētus
anaesthetic, *adj*, sŏpōrĭfer
analogy (comparison), compărātĭo,
analyse, *v.t*, discerpo (3), explĭco (1)
analysis, explĭcātĭo, *f*
anarchical, turbŭlentus
anarchy, lĭcentĭa, *f*
anathema, exsecrātĭo, *f* (curse)
anatomy, incĭsĭo (*f*) corporis (incision of the body)
ancestor, auctor, *m*; (*in pl*), māiōres, *m. pl*
ancestral, proăvĭtus
ancestry (descent, origin), gĕnus, *n*
anchor, ancŏra, *f*
anchor, *v.i*, *use phr.* nāvem ad ancŏras dēlĭgo (1) (fasten a ship to the anchors)
anchorage, stātĭo, *f*
ancient, antĭquus, vĕtus
and, et, atque, ac; quĕ (*joined to the second of two words*, e.g. I and you: ego tuque); (and . . . not) nĕque
anecdote, fābella, *f*
anew, *adv*, dēnŭo, dē intĕgro
anger, īra, *f*, īrācundĭa, *f*
anger, *v.t*, irrĭto (1), lăcesso (3)
angle, angŭlus, *m*
angle, *v.i* (fish), piscor (1 *dep*)
angler, piscātor, *m*
angrily, *adv*, īracundē, īrātē
angry, īrātus; (irascible) īrācundus
anguish, angor, *m*, dŏlor, *m*, ăcerbĭtas, *f*
angular, angŭlātus, angŭlāris
animal, ănĭmal, *n*, pĕcus, *f*
animal, *adj*, ănĭmālis
animate, *v.t*, ănĭmo, excĭto (1)
animated, ănĭmans; (lively) vĕgĕtus, ălăcer, vĕhĕmens
animation (liveliness), vĭgor, *m*
animosity, sĭmultas, *f*
ankle, tālus, *m*
annalist, annālĭum scriptor, *m*
annals, annāles, *m. pl*
annex, *v.t*, addo (3), iungo (3)
annihilate, *v.t*, dēlĕo (2)
annihilation, exĭtĭum, *n*, exstinctĭo, *f*

anniversary, *adj,* anniversārĭus
anniversary, *nn,* dĭes annĭversārĭus, *m*
annotate, *v.t,* annōto (1)
annotation, annōtātĭo, *f*
announce, *v.t,* nuntĭo (1)
announcement, prōnuntĭātĭo, *f*
announcer, nuntĭus, *m,* praeco, *m*
annoy, *v.t,* irrĭto (1), lăcesso (3)
annoyance, mŏlestĭa, *f,* vexātĭo, *f*
annual, anniversārĭus
annually, *adv,* quŏtannis
annuity, annŭa, *n. pl*
annul, *v.t,* abrŏgo (1), tollo (3)
annulment, ăbŏlĭtĭo, *f*
anoint, *v.t,* unguo (3)
anointing, *nn,* unctĭo, *f*
anomaly, ănōmălĭa, *f*
anon, *adv* **(immediately),** stătim; **(in a short time)** brĕvi tempŏre
anonymously, (*adv. phr*), sĭne. nōmĭne
another, ălĭus; **(the other of two),** alter; **(another's),** *adj,* ălĭēnus
answer, *nn,* responsum, *n*
answer, *v.t,* respondĕo (2); **(in writing)** rescrĭbo (3); **(to — for, be surety for),** praesto (1)
answerable, *use phr,* rătĭōnem reddo (3) **(to render an account)**
ant, formĭca, *f*
antagonism, ĭnĭmĭcĭtĭa, *f*
antagonist, adversārĭus, *m*
antagonistic, contrārĭus
antecedent, *adj,* antĕcēdens
antechamber, ātrĭŏlum, *n*
anterior, prĭor
ante-room, ātrĭŏlum, *n*
anticipate, *v.t,* occŭpo (1), antĕverto (3), praecĭpĭo (3); **(expect),** exspecto (1)
anticipation (expectation), exspectātĭo, *f*
antics, lūdi, *m, pl*
antidote, rĕmēdĭum, *n,* antĭdŏtum, *n*
antipathy rĕpugnantĭa, *f*; **(of people)** ŏdĭum, *n*
antipodes, antĭpŏdes, *m. pl*
antiquarian, *adj,* antīquitatis stŭdĭōsus **(keen on antiquity)**
antiquated, priscus
antique, *adj,* vĕtus, antīquus
antiquity, antīquĭtas, *f,* vĕtustas, *f*
antithesis (opposite), contrārĭum, *n*; **(in argument),** contentĭo, *f*
antler, rāmus, *m,* cornu, *n*
anvil, incūs, *f*
anxiety, anxiĕtas, *f,* sollĭcĭtūdo, *f,* cūra, *f*; **(alarm)** păvor, *m*
anxious, anxĭus, sollĭcĭtus; **(alarmed)** trĕpĭdus
anxiously, *adv,* anxiē
any, *adj,* ullus (*after negatives, and in questions, and comparisons*); quisquam (*pron. used like* ullus); qui, quae, quod (*after* si, nisi, ne num)
anyone, anybody, *pron,* quis (*after* si, nisi, ne, num); quisquam (*after a negative*)
anything, *use neuter of prons. given above*)
anywhere, *adv,* **(in any place),** usquam; **(to any place),** quō, quōquam; **(in any place),** ŭbĭquē
apace, *adv,* **(quickly),** cĕlĕrĭtĕr
apart, *adv,* sĕorsum; (*adj*) dĭversus
apartment, conclāve, *n*
apathetic, lentus, pĭger
apathy, ignāvĭa, *f,* lentĭtūdo, *f*
ape, simĭa, *f*
aperture, fŏrāmen, *n*
apex, căcūmen, *n,* ăpex, *m*
aphorism, sententĭa, *f*
apiary, alvĕārĭum, *n*
apiece, *use distributive numeral, e.g.* **two each,** bīni
apologize, *v.i,* excūso (1), dēfendo (3)
apology, excūsātĭo, *f*
appal, *v.t,* perterrĕo (2)
apparatus, appārātus, *m*
apparel, vestis, *f,* vestīmentum, *n*
apparent, mănĭfestus, ăpertus
apparently, *adv,* per spĕcĭem
apparition (ghost), spĕcĭes, *f,* ĭmāgo *f*
appeal, *v.i,* appello (1), prōvŏco (1), **(to — to)** *v.t,* obtestor (1 *dep*)
appeal, *nn,* appellātĭo, *f,* obsecrātĭo, *f*
appear, *v.i,* appārĕo (2), conspĭcĭor (3 *pass*); **(to seem)** vĭdĕor (2 *pass*); **(to come forward)** prōdĕo (4)
appearance (looks), spĕcĭes, *f,* aspectus, *m*; **(show),** spĕcĭes, *f*; **(image),** sĭmŭlācrum, *n*
appeasable, plācābĭlis
appease, *v.t,* **(people),** plāco (1); **(feelings),** sēdo (1)
appeasement, plācātĭo, *f*
appellant, appellātor, *m*
append, *v.t.* **(attach),** addo (3)
appendage, appendix, *f*
appertain, *v.i,* pertĭnĕo (2)
appetite, appĕtītus, *m*; **(hunger),** fāmes, *f*
applaud, *v.t,* plaudo (3), laudo (1)
applause (clapping), plausus, *m*; **(cheers),** clāmor, *m*
apple, mālum, *n*; **(— tree),** mālus, *f*
appliance (apparatus), appārātus, *m*
applicable to, commŏdus (*with dat*)
applicant, pĕtītor, *m*
application (asking), pĕtītĭo, *f*; **(mental),** stūdĭum, *n,* dĭlĭgentĭa, *f*

For List of Abbreviations used, turn to pages 3, 4

apply, *v.t,* adhĭbĕo (2), admŏvĕo (2); **(to — oneself to)** se, dēdĕre (3 *with dat*); *v.i,* **(refer to),** pertĭnĕo (2); **(— for),** flāgĭto (1)
appoint, *v.t,* constĭtŭo (3) **(people to office, etc.),** crĕo (1); **(to appoint to a command)** praefĭcĭo (3) (*acc. of person appointed, dat. of person or thing commanded*)
appointment (office), mūnus, *n*; **(creation),** crĕātĭo, *f*; **(agreed meeting),** constĭtūtum, *n*
apportion, *v.t,* dīvĭdo (3), distrĭbŭo (3)
apposite, aptus
appraise, *v.t,* **(evaluate),** aestĭmo (1)
appraisement, aestĭmātĭo, *f*
appreciate, *v.t,* **(value),** aestĭmo (1) magni
appreciation, aestĭmātĭo, *f*
apprehend, *v.t,* **(arrest),** comprĕhendo (3); **(understand),** intellĕgo (3), percĭpĭo (3)
apprehension (fear), formīdo, *f*; **(arrest)** comprĕhensĭo, *f*; **(understanding),** intellĕgentĭa, *f*
apprehensive (fearful), tĭmĭdus
apprentice, tīro, *m*
approach, *v.i,* appropinquo (1) (*with* ad *and acc. or dat*), accēdo (3)
approach, *nn,* ădĭtus, *m*, adventus, *m*, accessus, *m*
approbation, approbātĭo, *f*, laus, *f*
appropriate, *adj,* aptus, accommŏdātus (*with dat*)
appropriate, *v.t,* sūmo (3)
appropriately, *adv,* aptē
approval, approbātĭo, *f*
approve (of), *v.t,* approbo (1)
approved, spectātus, prŏbātus
approximate, proxĭmus
approximate, *v.i,* accēdo (3)
April, Aprĭlis (mensis)
apron, ŏpĕrimentum, *n*
apt, aptus, ĭdōnĕus; **(inclined),** prōnus, prōpensus
aptitude (ability), ingĕnĭum, *n*
aptly, *adv,* aptē
aptness, *use adj,* aptus **(suitable)**
aquatic, ăquātĭlis
aqueduct, ăquae ductus, *m*
aquiline, ăquĭlĭnus, ăduncus
arable land, arvum, *n*
arbiter, arbĭter, *m*
arbitrarily, *adv,* **(according to whim),** ad lĭbīdĭnem
arbitrary (capricious), lĭbīdĭnōsus
arbitrate, *v.t,* discepto (1)
arbitration, arbĭtrĭum, *n*
arbitrator, arbĭter, *m*
arbour, umbrācŭlum, *n*
arc, arcus, *m*
arcade, portĭcus, *f*
arch, fornix, *m*, arcus, *m*
arch, *adj,* **(playful),** lascīvus
archaeology, investīgātĭo, (*f*) rērum antīquārum **(search for ancient things)**
archaism, verbum obsŏlētum, *n*
archer, săgittārĭus, *m*
archipelago, *use phr,* măre, (*n*) insŭlis consĭtum **(sea set with islands)**
architect, archĭtectus, *m*, ŏpĭfex, *c*
architecture, archĭtectūra, *f*
archives, tăbŭlae, *f. pl*
arctic, septentrĭōnālis
ardent, ardens, fervĭdus
ardently, *adv,* ardenter, vĕhĕmenter
ardour, ardor, *m*, călor, *m*, fervor, *m*
arduous, ardŭus
area, spătĭum, *n*
arena, hărēna, *f*, ărēna, *f*
argue, *v.i,* discepto (1), dissĕro (3)
argument (quarrel), rixa, *f*, argūmentum, *n*; **(discussion),** dispūtātĭo, *f*
arid, ārĭdus, siccus
aridity, ārĭdĭtas, *f*, siccĭtas, *f*
aright, *adv,* rectē
arise, *v.i,* surgo (3); **(heavenly bodies),** ŏrĭor (4 *dep*)
aristocracy (aristocratic party), optĭmātes, *c. pl*; **(govt.)** optĭmātĭum dŏmĭnātus, *m*
aristocratic, patrĭcĭus
arithmetic, ărithmētĭca, *n. pl*
ark, arca, *f*
arm (fore —), brăcchĭum, *n*; **(upper —),** lăcertus, *m*; **(weapon),** telum, *n*
arms (weapons), arma, *n. pl*, tēla, *n. pl*; **(call to —),** ad arma vŏco (1); **(to take —s),** arma căpĭo (3); **(to lay down —s),** arma dēdo (3)
arm, *v.t,* armo (1); **(to take —s),** arma căpĭo (3)
armament (forces), cōpĭae, *f*, *pl*; **(weapon),** tēlum, *n*
armed, armātus
armistice, indūtĭae, *f. pl*
armour, arma, *n. pl*
armourer, făber, *m*
armour-bearer, armĭger, *m*
armoury, armāmentārĭum, *n*
army, exercĭtus, *m*; **(marching —),** agmen, *n*; **(drawn up for battle),** ăcĭes, *f*

around, *adv. and prep. with acc*, circā, circum
arouse, *v.t*, suscĭto (1), excĭto (1)
arraign, *v.t*, accūso (1)
arrange, *v.t*, compōno (3), constĭtŭo (3), collŏco (1), instrŭo (3)
arrangement (as an act), collŏcātĭo, *f* **(order)**, ordo, *m*
array, *nn*, **(clothing)**, vestis, *f*, vestĭmenta, *n. pl*; **(battle —)**, ăcĭes, *f*
array, *v.t*, compōno (3)
arrears, rĕlĭquae pĕcūnĭae, *f. pl* **(money remaining)**
arrest, *v.t*, comprĕhendo (3)
arrest, *nn*, comprĕhensĭo, *f*
arrival, adventus, *m*
arrive, *v.i*, advĕnĭo (4), pervĕnĭo (4)
arrogance, arrŏgantĭa, *f*
arrogant, arrŏgans
arrogate, *v.t*, arrŏgo (1) (*with dat*)
arrow, săgitta, *f*
arsenal, armāmentārĭum, *n*
art, ars, *f*
artery, vēna, *f*
artful, callĭdus, văfer
artfully, *adv*, callĭde
artfulness, callĭdĭtas, *f*
article (thing), rēs, *f*; **(term of a treaty, etc.)**, condĭcĭo, *f*
articulate, *adj*, clārus, distinctus
articulate, *v.t*, exprĭmo (3)
articulation, explānātĭo, *f*
artifice, ars, *f*
artificer (craftsman), artĭfex, *m*, ŏpĭfex, *c*
artificial, artĭfĭcĭōsus
artificially, *adv*, mănu, artĕ
artillery, tormenta, *n. pl*
artisan, făber, *m*, ŏpĭfex, *c*
artist, artĭfex, *m*; **(painter)**, pictor, *m*
artistic, artĭfĭcĭōsus
artless (person), simplex; **(work)**, incomptus
artlessness, simplĭcĭtas, *f*
as, *conj*, **(because)**, quod, cum, quĭa; **(*in a comparative phr, e.g.* as strong as)** tam fortis quam; **(the same as)** īdem atque; **(as . . . as possible)** quam *with the superlative, e.g.* **as quickly as possible**; quam cĕlerrime; **(as if)** tamquam, quăsĭ, vĕlut
ascend, *v.t*, ascendo (3)
ascendant (to be in the —), *v.i*, praesto (1)
ascendancy, praestantĭa, *f*
ascent, ascensus, *m*
ascertain, *v.t.* **(find out)**, cognosco (3), compĕrĭo (4)
ascetic, *adj*, abstĭnens
ascribe, *v.t*, ascrĭbo (3), assigno (1), attrĭbŭo (3)
ash (tree), fraxĭnus, *f*, (*adj*), fraxĭnĕus
ashamed (to be —), pŭdet; *impers. with acc. and genit*, (*e.g.* **I am ashamed of my brother**), pŭdet me frātris
ashes, cĭnis, *m*
ashore, *adv*, **(on shore)**, in lĭtŏre; **(to shore)**, in lĭtus
aside, *use* se, *compounded with verb*, **e.g. to put aside**, sēcerno (3)
ask, *v.t*, rŏgo (1) (*with 2 accs*) **e.g. I ask you for a sword**, tē glădĭum rŏgo
askance (to look — at), lĭmis ŏcŭlis aspĭcĭo (3) **(look with a sidelong glance)**
aslant, *adv*, oblĭque
asleep (to be —), *v.i*, dormĭo (4); **(to fall —)** obdormĭo (4)
asp, aspis, *f*
aspect (appearance), aspectus, *m*, făcĭes, *f*
asperity, ăcerbĭtas, *f*
asperse, *v.t*, aspergo (3)
aspersion, căluminĭa, *f*
asphalt, bĭtūmen, *n*
aspirate, *nn*, aspīrātĭo, *f*
aspiration (desire), affectātĭo, *f*; **(hope)** spes, *f*
aspire to, affecto (1)
ass, ăsĭnus, *m*
assail, *v.t*, appĕto (3), oppugno (1)
assailant, oppugnātor, *m*
assassin, percussor, *m*, sĭcārĭus, *m*
assassinate, *v.t*, trŭcĭdo (1)
assassination, caedes, *f*
assault, *nn*, impĕtus, *m*, oppugnātĭo, *f*
assault, *v.t*, oppugno (1), ădŏrĭor (4 *dep*)
assemble, *v.i*, convĕnĭo (4); *v.t*, cōgo (3)
assembly, coetus, *m*, conventus, *m*; **(— of the Roman people)**, cŏmĭtĭa, *n. pl*
assent, *nn*, assensĭo, *f*
assent to, *v.i*, assentĭor (4 *dep*) (*with dat*)
assert, *v.t*, affirmo (1), confirmo (1)
assertion, affirmātĭo, *f*, dēfensĭo, *f*
assess, *v.t* **(evaluate)**, aestĭmo (1)
assessment (valuation), aestĭmātĭo, *f*,
assessor, censor, *m*
assets, bŏna, *n. pl*
assiduity, assĭdŭĭtas, *f*, sēdŭlĭtas, *f*
assiduous, assĭdŭus, sēdŭlus
assiduously, *adv*, assĭdŭe, sēdŭlō
assign, *v.t*, assigno (1), trĭbŭo (3)
assignation, constĭtūtum, *n*

assimilate, *v.t*, sĭmĭlem făcĭo (3)
assist, *v.t*, iŭvo (1), auxĭlĭor (1 *dep*), subvĕnĭo (4) (*with dat*)
assistance, auxĭlĭum, *n*, ŏpem (*no nomin*), *f*
assistant, adiūtor, *m*
assize (provincial law-court), conventus, *m*
associate, *nn*, sŏcĭus, *m*
associate, *v.t* (**join**), coniungo (3); *v.i*, ūtor (3 *dep. with abl*)
association, sŏcĭĕtas, *f*, consortĭo, *f*
assort, *v.t.* (**arrange**), dīgĕro (*irreg*)
assortment (heap), ăcervus *m.*
assuage, *v.t*, lĕvo (1), mĭtĭgo (1)
assume, *v.t*, pōno (3), sūmo (3); (**take on**) suscĭpĭo (3)
assumption (hypothesis), sumptĭo, *f*
assurance (promise), fĭdes, *f*; (**confidence**) fĭdūcĭa, *f*
assure, *v.t*, confirmo (1)
assured (certain), explōrātus
assuredly, *adv*, (**certainly**), prōfecto
astern, *adv*, ā puppi
asthma, dyspnoea, *f*
astonish, *v.t*, obstŭpĕfăcĭo (3)
astonished, stŭpĕfactus; (**to be —**), *v.i*, obstŭpesco (3)
astonishing, mĭrĭfĭcus, admīrābĭlis
astonishingly, *adv. phr*, mīrum in mŏdum
astonishment, stŭpor, *m*
astound, *v.t*, obstŭpĕfăcĭo (3)
astray (to go —), *v.i*, erro (1); (**to lead —**), *v.t*, indūco (3)
astrologer, măthēmătĭcus, *m*
astrology, astrŏlŏgĭa, *f*
astronomy, astrŏlŏgĭa, *f*
astute, callĭdus
astuteness, callĭdĭtas, *f*
asylum (refuge), perfŭgĭum, *n*
at, (*of place*) in (*with abl*), ad, ăpŭd (*with acc*); *with proper names and* dŏmus *use locative case, e.g.* **at Rome,** Rōmae, **at home,** dōmi; (*of time*) *use abl. case, e.g.* **at the third hour,** tertĭa hōra; *or sometimes* ăd *with the acc. case*
atheist, ăthĕŏs, *m*
athlete, ăthlēta, *c*
athletic (strong), fortis
athwart, *prep* (**across**), trans (*with acc*)
Atlantic, Ocĕănus, *m*
atmosphere, āër, *m*
atom, ătŏmus, *f*, sēmĭna (*n.pl*) rērum (**seeds of things**)
atone for, *v.t*, expĭo (1)
atonement, expĭātĭo, *f*
atrocious, nĕfārĭus
atrociousness, fĕrĭtas, *f*
atrocity, nĕfas, *n*
atrophy, tābes, *f*
atrophy, *v.i*, tābesco (3)
attach, *v.t.* (**fasten**), affĭgo (3), applĭco (1); (**connect**) adiungo (3)
attached (fastened), fixus, aptus; (**fond**) dēvinctus, āmans
attachment (affection), stŭdĭum, *n*, ămor, *m*
attack, *nn*, impĕtus, *m*, oppugnātĭo, *f*
attack, *v.t*, oppugno (1), aggrĕdĭor (3 *dep*), ăddŏrĭor (4 *dep*), invādo (3), pĕto (3)
attacker, oppugnātor, *m*
attain, *v.i.* (**reach**), pervĕnĭo (4) (*with* ad *and acc*); *v.t.* (**obtain**), consĕquor (3 *dep*)
attainable, impĕtrābĭlis
attainment (obtaining), ădeptĭo, *f*; (**learning**) ērŭdĭtĭo, *f*
attempt *nn*, inceptum, *n*, cōnātum, *n*
attempt, *v.i*, cōnor (1 *dep*)
attend, *v.i.* (**be present at**), intersum (*irreg. with dat*); *v.t.* (**accompany**), cŏmĭtor (1 *dep*), prōsĕquor, (3 *dep*); (**pay attention**) ŏpĕram do (1), ănĭmadverto (3)
attendance (being present), *use vb.* adsum (*irreg*) (**to be present**); (**of crowds**), frĕquentĭa, *f*; (**service**), appārĭtĭo, *f*
attendant, *nn*, (**servant**) mĭnister, *m*; (**of a nobleman**) sectātor, *m*, sātellēs, *c*
attention (concentration), attentĭo (*f*) ănĭmi; (**to pay —**); ŏpĕram, (*f*) do (1)
attentive (alert), intentus, attentus; (**respectful**), observans
attentively, *adv*, sēdŭlo
attenuate, *v.t*, attĕnŭo (1)
attest, *v.t*, testor (1 *dep*)
attestation, testĭfĭcātĭo, *f*
attire, *nn*, vestis, *f*
attire, *v.t*, vestĭo (4)
attitude (of mind), ănĭmus, *m*; (**of body**), gestus *m*, hăbĭtus, *m*
attract, *v.t*, attrăho (3), allĭcĭo (3)
attraction (charms), illĕcĕbrae (*f. pl*)
attractive, blandus, iūcundus
attribute, *v.t*, attrĭbŭo (3), assigno (1)
attune, *v.t*, (**adjust**), consŏnum (aptum) reddo (3) (**make harmonious (suitable)**)
auburn, flāvus
auction, auctĭo, *f*; (**to sell by public—**), sub hastā vendo (3) (**sell under the spear**)

auctioneer, praeco, *m*
audacious, audax
audacity, audācĭa, *f*, confĭdentĭa, *f*
audibly, *use phr.* quod audīri pŏtest (**that can be heard**)
audience (**of people**), audītōres, *m,pl* (**hearing**), ădĭtus, *m*
audit, *v.t*, inspĭcĭo (3)
auditorium, auditorĭum, *n*
augment, *v.t*, augĕo (2)
augur, *nn*, augur, *c*
augur, *v.t*, vātĭcĭnor (1 *dep*)
augury, augŭrĭum, *n*, auspĭcĭum, *n*
August, Sextĭlis or Augustus (mensis)
august, *adj*, augustus
aunt (**paternal**), ămĭta, *f*; (**maternal**), mātertĕra, *f*
auspices, auspĭcĭum, *n*
auspicious, faustus, sĕcundus
auspiciously, *adv*, fēlĭcĭter
austere (**severe**), sĕvērus
austerity, sĕvērĭtas, *f*
authentic, vērus, certus
authentically, *adv*, certō
authenticate, *v.t*, rĕcognosco (3)
authenticity, auctōrĭtas, *f*
author (**writer**), scriptor, *m*; (**instigator**), auctor, *m*
authoritative, grăvis, impĕrĭosus
authority, auctōrĭtas, *f*, pŏtestas, *f*, impĕrĭum, *n*
authorize (**give permission to**), *v.i*, pŏtestātem (auctōrĭtātem), făcĭo (3) (*with dat*)
autocracy, tȳrannis, *f*
autocrat, dŏmĭnus, *m*,
autograph, mănus, *f*
autumn, auctumnus, *m*
autumnal, auctumnālis
auxiliary, *adj*, auxĭlĭāris, auxĭlĭārĭus; *nn* adiūtor, *m*; (**—forces**) auxĭlĭa, *n.pl*
avail, *v.t* (**assist**), prōsum (*irreg*) (*with dat.*); (**make use of**), ūtor (3 *dep. with abl*)
available (**ready**), expĕdĭtus, pārātus
avarice, ăvārĭtĭa, *f*
avaricious, ăvārus
avenge, *v.t*, ulciscor (3 *dep*)
avenger, ultor, *m*,
avenging, *adj*, ultrix
avenue, xystus, *m*
aver, *v.t* (**affirm**), affirmo (1)
average, *adj*, mĕdĭus (**middle**)
averse, āversus
aversion, ŏdĭum, *n*,
avert, *v.t*, āverto (3), dĕpello (3)
aviary, ăvĭārĭum, *n*
avid, ăvĭdus
avidity, ăvĭdĭtas, *f*
avoid, *v.t*, vĭto (1), fŭgĭo (3)
avoidance, vĭtātĭo, *f*, fŭga, *f*
avow, *v.t*, fātĕor (2 *dep*)
avowal, confessĭo, *f*
avowed, prŏfessus, ăpertus
await, *v.t*, exspecto (1)
awake, *adj*, vĭgĭlans; (**to be —**), *v.i*, vĭgĭlo (1); (**to awake**), *v.t*, excĭto (1)
award, *nn*, (**judicial decision**); arbĭtrĭum, *n* (**prize**), palma, *f*
award, *v.t*, trĭbŭo (3), adiūdĭco (1)
aware, gnārus; (**to be —**), sentĭo (4); (**know**), scĭo (4)
away, *use* a, ab *compounded with a verb, e.g.* (ăbĕo) **go away** (4)
awe, formĭdo, *f*, mĕtus, *m*, rĕvĕrentĭa, *f*
awe (**be in —**) vĕrĕor, (2 *dep.*)
awful, vĕrendus
awestruck, păvĭdus
awhile, *adv*, paulisper, pārumper
awkward, rŭdis, impĕrĭtus
awkwardness, inscĭtĭa, *f*
awning, vēlum, *n*
awry, *adj*, perversus; *adv*, perversē
axe, sĕcūris, *f*
axiom, sententia, *f*
axis, **axle**, axis, *m*
ay, **aye**, *adv*, ĭta, vērō; (**forever**) **in** perpĕtŭum
azure, *adj*, caerŭlĕus

B

babble, *v.i*, garrĭo (4), blătĕro (1)
babbler, **babbling**, *adj*, garrŭlus
baby, infans, *c*
babyhood, infantĭa, *f*
bacchanalian, bacchānālis
bachelor, *adj*, caelebs
back, *nn*, tergum, *n*, dorsum, *n*; (**at the —**) a tergo; (**to move something —**), rĕtro mŏvĕo (2), rēĭcĭo (3); (**to go —**) se rĕcĭpĕre (3 *reflex*)
backbite, *v.t*, obtrecto (1)
backwards, *adj*, (**dull**) pĭger
backwards, *adv*, rĕtro
bacon, lārĭdum, *n*
bad, mălus; (**of health**), aeger; (**of weather**), ādversus
badge, insigne, *n*
badger, mēles, *f*
badly, *adv*, mălĕ, prāvē, imprŏbē
badness (**worthlessness**), nēquĭtĭa, *f*
baffle, *v.t*, ēlūdo (3)
bag, saccus, *m*
baggage (**military**), impĕdĭmenta, *n.pl*; (**individual packs**), sarcĭnae, *f. pl*
bail, *nn*, (**person**), vās, *m*; (**security**) vādĭmōnĭum, *n*

For List of Abbreviations used, turn to pages 3, 4

bail (to give — for), *v.t*, spondĕo (2) prō (*with abl*)
bailiff (estate manager), villĭcus, *m*; **(official)**, appārĭtor, *m*
bait, *nn*, esca, *f*
bait, *v.t*, **(tease)**, lăcesso (3), illūdo (3)
bake, *v.t*, torrĕo (2), cŏquo (3)
baker, pistor, *m*
bakery, pistrīnum, *n*
balance, *nn*, **(scales)**, lībra, *f*; **(equilibrium)**, lībrāmentum, *n*
balance, *v.t*, lībro (1), compenso (1)
balcony, maeniāna, *n.pl*
bald, calvus, glăber; **(unadorned)**, ārĭdus
baldness, calvĭtĭum, *n*
bale out, *v.t*, **(discharge)**, ēgĕro (3)
bale (bundle), fascis, *m*
baleful, pernĭcĭōsus
balk (beam), trabs, *f*
balk, *v.t*, frustror (1 *dep*)
ball (for play), pīla, *f*; **(globe, sphere)**, glŏbus, *m*
ballad, carmen. *n*
ballad-singer, cantātor, *m*
ballast, sābura, *f*
ballet, *use vb.* salto (1) **(dance)**
ballista, ballista, *f*
ballot, suffrāgĭum, *n*
ballot-box, cista, *f*, urna, *f*
balm, balsāmum, *n*, unguentum, *n*
balmy (soothing), mollis, lēnis
balustrade (railings), cancelli, *m. pl*
bamboo, hărundo, *f* **(reed)**
ban, *v.t*, vĕto (1)
band (bond), vincŭlum, *n*; **(of people)**, mănus, *f*, grex, *m*
band together, *v.i*, coniūro (1)
bandage, fascĭa, *f*
bandage, *v.t*, lĭgo (1)
bandit, lătro, *m*
bandy (to — words), *v.i*, altercor (1 *dep*)
bandy-legged, lōrĭpes
bane (injury), pernĭcĭes, *f*; **(poison)**, vĕnēnum, *n*
baneful, pernĭcĭōsus
bang, crĕpĭtus, *m*
bang, *v.t.* (beat), tundo (3)
banish, *v.t*, *use phr.* āquā et igni interdĭco (3) (*with dat*) **(forbid one the use of fire and water)**, expello (3)
banishment, rĕlēgātĭo, *f*, exsĭlĭum, *n*
bank, *nn*, **(of earth)**, tŏrus, *m*; **(of a river)**, rīpa, *f*; **(for money)**, argentārĭa tăberna **(money shop)**
banker, argentārĭus, mensārĭus, *m*
bankrupt, *nn*, dēcoctor, *m*, **(to be —)**, *v.i*, solvendo non esse
bankruptcy (personal), rŭīna, *f* **(downfall)**
banner, vexillum, *n*
banquet, convīvĭum, *n*, ĕpŭlae, *f. pl*
banter, *nn*, căvillātĭo, *f*
banter, *v.i*, căvillor (1 *dep*)
bar (wooden), asser, *m*; **(lock)**, claustra, *n. pl*; **(bolt)**, sĕra, *f*; **(barrier)**, rĕpāgŭla, *n. pl*
bar, *v.t* **(fasten)**, obsĕro (1); **(— the way)**, obsto (1) (*with dat*)
barb (hook), uncus, *m*
barbarian, barbărus, *m*
barbaric (barbarous), barbărus, crūdēlis, immānis
barbarity, barbărĭa, *f*
barbarously, *adv*, **(cruelly)**, crūdēlĭter
barbed, hāmātus
barber, tonsor, *m*
bard (poet, etc.), poēta, *m*
bare, nūdus; **(to make —)**, *v.t*, ăpĕrĭo (4), nūdo (1)
barefaced, (shameless), impŭdens
barefoot, *adv*, nūdo pĕde
barely, *adv*, vix
bargain, *nn*, pactum, *n*
bargain, *v.i*, **(make a — with)**, paciscor (3 *dep*) (*with* cum *and abl. of person*)
barge, linter, *f*; **(— man)**, nauta, *m*
bark, *nn*, **(of trees)**, cortex, *m*; **(of dogs)**, lātrātus, *m*; **(boat)**, rătis, *f*
bark, *v.i*, lātro (1)
barley, hordĕum, *n*
barley-water, ptĭsăna, *f*
barn, horrĕum, *n*
baron, princeps, *m*
barque, rătis, *f*
barracks, castra, *n. pl*
barrel, dōlĭum, *n*
barren, stĕrĭlis
barrenness, stĕrĭlĭtas, *f*
barricade, *nn*, agger, *m*
barricade, *v.t*, obsaepĭo (4)
barrier, impĕdĭmentum, *n*, claustra, *n. pl*
barrister, pătrōnus, *m*
barrow, fercŭlum, *n*
barter, *v.t*, **(exchange)**, mūto (1);
barter, *nn*, permūtātio, (*f*,) mercĭum **(exchange of goods)**
base, *nn*, bāsis, *f*, fundāmentum, *n*
base, *adj*, **(worthless)**, turpis; **(low-born)**, hŭmĭlis
baseless, *adj*, falsus
basely, *adv*, turpĭter

basement, băsis, *f*
baseness, turpĭtūdo, *f*
bashful, vĕrēcundus
bashfulness, vĕrēcundĭa, *f*
basin, pelvis, *f*
basis, băsis, *f*, fundāmentum, *n*
bask, *v.i*, āpricor (1 *dep*)
basket, călăthus, *m*, corbis, *f*, quālum, *n*
bass, *adj*, grăvis
bastard, *adj*, nŏthus
bastion, turris, *f*
bat (animal), vespertīlĭo, *m*; **(club, stick),** clāva, *f*
bath, *nn*, balnĕum, *n*; **(public —)** balnĕae, *f. pl*
bath, bathe *v.i*, lăvor (1 *pass*); v.t, lăvo (1)
bathing, *nn*, lăvātĭo, *f*
baton, scīpĭo, *m*
battalion, cŏhors, *f*
batter, v.t, pulso (1), verbĕro (1)
battering-ram, ărĭes, *m*
battery (assault), vĭs, *f*; **(cannon),** tormenta, *n. pl*
battle, proelĭum, *n*; **(—line),** ăcĭes, *f*; **(—cry),** clāmor, *m*; **(—field),** lŏcus (*m*) pugnae
battlement, pinna, *f*, mūnĭtĭōnes, *f. pl*
bawd, lēna, *f*
bawl, *v.i*, clāmĭto (1)
bawling, *nn*, clāmor, *m*
bay (of the sea), sĭnus, *m*; **(tree)** laurus, *f*; **(at bay)** (*adj*) pārātus ad pugnam **(ready for a fight)**
bay, *v.i*, lātro (1)
bayonet, pūgĭo, *m*
be, *v.i*, sum (*irreg*)
beach, lĭtus, *n*
beacon (fire), ignis, *m*
bead, bāca, *f*
beak, rōstrum, *n*
beaker, pōcŭlum, *n*
beam (of timber), tignum, *n*, trabs, *f*; **(cross —),** transtrum, *n*; **(ray)** rādĭus, *m*
bean, fāba, *f*
bear, *nn*, ursus, *m*, ursa, *f*; **(constellation),** septentrĭōnes, *m. pl*; **(The Great —),** ursa maior; **(The Little —)** septentrio minor
bear, *v.t*, fĕro (*irreg*), gĕro (3); **(carry),** porto (1); **(produce),** părĭo (3); **(— away)** aufĕro (*irreg*)
bearable, *adj*, tŏlĕrābĭlis
beard, barba, *f*; **(bearded),** barbātus
bearer (carrier), bāiŭlus, *m*, portĭtor, *m*
bearing (posture), gestus, *m*
beast (wild), bestĭa, *f*, fĕra, *f*; **(domestic),** pĕcus, *f*
beastly (filthy), obscēnus
beat (in music, poetry), ictus, *m*
beat, *v.t*, caedo (3), fĕrĭo (4), verbĕro (1); **(conquer),** sŭpĕro (1), vinco (3); **(— back),** rĕpello (3); **(— down)** sterno (3); **(be beaten),** *v.i*, vāpŭlo (1)
beating, *nn*, verbĕra, *n. pl*
beautiful, pulcher
beautifully, *adv*, pulchre
beautify, *v.t*, orno (1)
beauty, pulchrĭtūdo, *f*, forma, *f*
beaver, castor, *m*
becalmed, vento dēstĭtūtus **(deserted by the wind)**
because, *conj*, quod, quĭa, cum; **(because of)** *prep*, propter, ŏb (*with acc*)
beckon, *v.t*, innŭo (3) (*with dat*)
become, *v.i*, fĭo (*irreg*); *v.t* **(to suit, adorn),** dĕcet (2 *impers. with acc. of person*)
becoming, *adj*, dĕcōrus
bed, lectus, *m*; **(go to —),** cŭbĭtum ĕo (4)
bedroom, cŭbĭcŭlum, *n*
bedaub, *v.t*, lĭno (3)
bedeck, *v.t*, orno (1); **(bedecked),** ornātus
bedew, *v.t*, irrōro (1)
bee, āpis, *f*
bee-hive, alvĕārĭum, *n*
beech-tree, fāgus, *f*
beef, cāro būbŭla, *f*, **(ox flesh)**
beer, cerevisia, *f*
beetle, scărăbaeus, *m*
befall, *v.i*, accĭdo (3)
befit, *v.i* **(suit),** convĕnĭo (4)
before, *prep*, **(time and place),** antĕ (*with acc*); **(place),** prae, prō (*with abl*); **(in the presence of),** cōram (*with abl*); **before,** *adv*, **(time),** antĕ, prĭus; **(space)** prae; **before,** *conj*, antĕquam, prĭusquam
befoul, *v.t*, inquĭno (1)
befriend, *v.t*, adiŭvo (1)
beg, *v.t* **(request),** pĕto (3), ōro (1); **(be a beggar),** *v.i*, mendĭco (1)
beget, *v.t*, gigno (3)
begetter, gĕnĭtor, *m*
beggar, mendĭcus, *m*
begin, *v.i*, incĭpĭo (3), coepi (3 *defect*)
beginner (originator), auctor, *m* **(learner),** tīro, *m*
beginning, *nn*, īnĭtĭum, *n*, princĭpĭum, *n*, inceptum, *n*
begone! āpăgĕ!
begrudge, *v.t* **(envy),** invĭdĕo (2) (*with dat*)

beguile, *v.t,* fallo (3), dēcĭpĭo (3)
behalf (on — of), (*prep*), prō (*with abl*)
behave oneself, *v. reflex,* se gĕrĕre (3)
behaviour (manners), mōres, *m. pl*
behead, *v.t,* sēcūri fĕrĭo (4) **(strike with an axe)**
behest (command), iussum, *n*
behind (*prep*), post (*with acc*)
behind, *adv,* post, ā tergo
behold, *v.t,* conspĭcĭo (3)
behold! (exclamation), eccĕ!
being (human —), hŏmo, *c*
belabour, *v.t,* verbĕro (1)
belated, sērus
belch, *v.i, and v.t,* ructo (1)
belch, *nn,* ructus, *m*
beleaguer, *v.t,* obsĭdĕo (2)
belfry, turris, *f*
belie, *v.t,* **(conceal),** dissĭmŭlo (1)
belief, fĭdes, *f*; **(impression),** ŏpĭnĭo, *f,* persuāsĭo, *f*
believe, *v.t,* crēdo (3) (*with dat. of person*), pūto (1), arbĭtror (1 *dep*), censĕo (2)
believer, crēdens, *c*
bell, tintinnābŭlum, *n*
belligerent, bellans, belli cŭpĭdus **(keen on war)**
bellow, *v.i,* mūgĭo (4)
bellowing, *nn,* mūgĭtus, *m*
bellows (pair of —), follis, *m*
belly, venter, *m,* abdōmen, *n*
belong to, *v.i, use* esse (*irreg*) **(to be)** *with genit. of person*
beloved, cārus, dĭlectus
below, *prep,* infrā, subter (*with acc*) sub (*with abl. or acc*)
below, *adv,* infrā, subter
belt, baltĕus, *m*
bemoan, *v.t,* gĕmo (3)
bench, scamnum, *n*; **(for rowers)** transtrum, *n*
bend, *v.t,* flecto (3), curvo (1); *v.i,* se flectĕre (3 *pass*)
bend, bending, *nn,* flexus, *m*
beneath, *see* **below**
benefactor, *phr,* qui bĕnĕfĭcĭa confert **(who confers favours)**
beneficence, bĕnĕfĭcentĭa, *f*
beneficent, bĕnĕfĭcus
beneficial, sălūtāris, ūtĭlis; **(to be —)** *v.i,* prōsum (*irreg*) (*with dat*)
benefit, *v.i,* prōsum (*irreg*) (*with dat*), adiŭvo (1)
benefit, *nn,* bĕnĕfĭcĭum, *n*
benevolence, bĕnĕfĭcentĭa, *f,* bĕnĕvŏlentĭa, *f*
benevolent, bĕnĕfĭcus, bĕnĕvŏlus
benign, bĕnignus
benignity, bĕnignĭtas, *f*
bent, *adj,* curvus; **(— on)** attentus; **(— back)** rĕsŭpīnus; **(— forward)** prōnus
benumb, *v.t, phr* torpōre affĭcĭo (3) **(affect with numbness)**
bequeath, *v.t,* lēgo (1)
bequest, lēgātum, *n*
bereave, *v.t,* orbo (1)
bereaved, orbus
bereavement, orbĭtas, *f,* damnum, *n*
berry, bāca, *f*
berth (for a ship), stātĭo, *f*
beseech, ōro (1), obsecro (1), quaeso (3)
beseem (become), dĕcet (2 *impers. with acc. of person*)
beset, *v.t,* obsĭdĕo (2), circumvĕnĭo (4)
beside, *prep,* **(near),** prŏpĕ (*with acc*); **(except),** praeter (*with acc*)
besides, *prep,* praeter (*with acc*)
besides, *adv or conj,* praeterquam
besides, *adv,* **(further),** praetĕrĕā, insŭper
besiege, *v.t,* obsĭdĕo (2), circum sĕdĕo (2)
besieger, obsessor, *m*
besmear, *v.t,* illĭno (3)
bespatter, *v.t,* aspergo (3)
bespeak, *v.t,* **(hire)** condūco (3)
besprinkle, *v.t,* aspergo (3)
best, *adj,* optĭmus; **(to the best of (one's) ability)** prō (vīrĭli) parte;
best, *adv,* optĭmē
bestial, *use phr,* bestĭārum mōre **(after the manner of beasts)**
bestir (to — oneself), *v.i,* expergiscor (3 *dep*)
bestow, *v.t,* do (1), trĭbŭo (3), confĕro (*irreg*)
bestowal, largĭtĭo, *f*
bet, *nn,* pignus, *n*
bet, *v.t,* pignŏre contendo (3)
betake, *v.t,* conferre (*irreg*)
betimes, *adv,* mātūrē
betray, *v.t,* prōdo (3)
betrayal, prōdĭtĭo, *f*
betrayer, prōdĭtor, *m*
betroth, *v.t,* spondĕo (2)
betrothal, sponsālĭa, *n. pl*
better, *adj,* mĕlĭor; **(of health),** sānus; **better,** *adv,* mĕlĭus
better, *v.t,* **(improve),** corrĭgo (3); ēmendo (1)
between, *prep,* inter (*with acc*)
beverage, pōtĭo, *f,* pōtus, *m*
bevy, căterva, *f*
bewail, *v.t,* dēplōro (1), lūgeo (2)
beware, *v.i and v.t,* căvĕo (2)
bewilder, *v.t,* perturbo (1), distrăho (3)

bewildered, turbātus, distractus
bewitch, *v.t,* fascĭno (1); **(charm),** căpĭo (3)
beyond, *prep,* ultrā, trans, sŭprā, extrā (*with acc*)
beyond, *adv,* ultrā, sŭprā
bias, inclīnātĭo, *f*
bias, *v.t,* inclīno (1)
Bible, *use phr.* scripta săcra, *n. pl* **(sacred writings)**
bicker, *v.i,* altercor (1 *dep*)
bid, *nn,* **(of a price)** lĭcĭtātĭo, *f*
bid, *v.t* **(tell, order),** iŭbĕo (2)
bide, *v.i* **(stay),** mănĕo (2)
bier, fĕrĕtrum, *n,* fercŭlum, *n*
big, magnus, vastus, ingens
bigotry, obstĭnātĭo, *f*
bile, bĭlis, *f*
bilge-water, sentīna, *f*
bilious, bĭlĭōsus
bill (written, financial), lĭbellus, *m,* rătĭo, *f,* syngrăpha, *f*; **(proposal in Parliament),** rŏgātĭo, *f*; **(a law),** lex, *f*; **(of a bird),** rōstrum, *n*
billet (of wood), lignum, *n*; **(lodging of soldiers),** hospĭtĭum, (*n*) mĭlĭtum
billet, *v.t* **(soldiers),** per hospĭtĭa dispōno (3) **(distribute through lodgings)**
billow, fluctus, *m*
billowy, fluctŭosus
bind, *v.t,* lĭgo (1), vincĭo (4); **(oblige),** oblĭgo (1); **(— together),** collĭgo (1)
biographer, scriptor rērum gestārum **(writer of exploits)**
biography, vĭta, *f*
birch (tree), betŭla, *f*
bird, ăvis, *f*; **(— cage),** căvĕa, *f*; **(— nest),** nĭdus, *m*
birth, ortus, *m,* gĕnus, *n*
birthday, (dĭes) nātālis
birth-place, sōlum, (*n*) nātāle
bishop, pontĭfex, *m*
bit (bite), offa, *f*; **(small piece of food),** frustrum, *n*; **(for a horse),** frēnum, *n*
bitch, cănis, *f*
bite, *nn,* morsus, *m*
bite, *v.t,* mordĕo (2)
biting, *adj,* mordax, asper
bitter, ămārus, ăcerbus, asper
bitterness, ăcerbĭtas, *f*
bitumen, bĭtūmen, *n*
bivouac, *nn,* excŭbĭae, *f. pl*
bivouac, *v.i,* excŭbo (1)
blab, *v.i,* blătĕro (1)
black, nĭger; **(— art),** măgĭce, *f*
blackberry, mōrum, *n,* rŭbus, *m*
blackbird, mĕrŭla, *f*
blacken, *v.t,* nigrum reddo (3)
blackguard, nĕbŭlo, *m*
Black Sea, Pontus Euxĭnus, *m*
blacksmith, făber, *m*
bladder, vēsĭca, *f*
blade (of grass), herba, *f*; **(of sword, knife),** lāmĭna, *f*
blame, *nn,* culpa, *f*
blame, *v.t,* culpo (1)
blameable, culpandus
blameless, innŏcens, intĕger
blamelessness, innocentĭa, *f*
bland, blandus
blandishment, blandĭtĭa, *f,* blandīmentum, *n*
blank, *adj,* **(empty),** văcŭus; **(paper),** pūrus
blank, *nn,* ĭnāne, *n*
blanket, lōdix, *f*
blaspheme, *v.t,* blasphēmo (1)
blast, *nn,* flāmen, *n,* flātus, *m*
blast, *v.t,* ūro (3)
blatant, *adj,* **(manifest),** ăpertus
blaze, *nn,* flamma, *f*
blaze, *v.i,* ardĕo (2), flăgro (1)
bleach, candīdum reddo (3)
bleak, algĭdus, frĭgĭdus
blear-eyed, lippus
bleat, bleating, bālātus, *m*
bleat, *v.i,* bālo (1)
bleed, *v.i,* sanguĭnem effundo (3); *v.t,* sanguĭnem mitto (3)
bleeding, *adj,* **(wound),** crūdus
bleeding, *nn, use phr* effūsĭo, (*f*), sanguĭnis **(shedding of blood)**
blemish, *nn,* **(physical),** vĭtĭum, *n,* **(moral),** măcŭla, *f*
blemish, *v.t,* măcŭlo (1)
blend, *v.t,* miscĕo (2)
bless, *v.t,* **(favour, make successful),** sĕcundo (1), bĕnĕdĭco (3)
blessed, beātus; **(of the dead),** pĭus
blessedness, bĕātĭtūdo, *f,* fēlĭcĭtas, *f*
blessing, *nn,* bĕnĕdictĭo, *f,* bŏnum, *n*
blight, *nn,* rōbīgo, *f*
blight, *v.t,* ūro (3); **(— of hopes)** frustror (1 *dep*)
blind, *adj,* caecus
blind, *v.t,* caeco (1)
blindly (rashly), *adv,* tĕmĕre
blindness, caecitas, *f*
blink, *v.i,* connĭvĕo (2)
bliss, fēlĭcĭtas, *f*
blissful, *adj,* fēlix
blister, pustŭla, *f*
blithe, hĭlāris
blizzard, imber, *m*
bloated, suffĭlātus
block, *nn,* **(of wood),** stĭpes, *m,* massa, *f*
block, *v.t,* obstrŭo (3), obsaepĭo (4)

For List of Abbreviations used, turn to pages 3, 4

blockade, *nn,* obsĭdĭo, *f*
blockade, *v.t,* obsĭdĕo (2)
blockhead, caudex, *m*
blood, sanguis, *m*; (**gore**), crŭor, *m*
blood-letting, *nn,* missĭo, (*f*) sanguĭnis
bloodshed, caedes, *f*
bloodshot, crŭōre suffusus (**spread over with blood**)
blood-stained, crŭentus
blood-thirsty, sanguĭnārĭus
bloody, crŭentus, sanguĭnĕus
bloom, *nn,* flōs, *m*
bloom, *v.i,* flōrĕo (2)
blooming, flōrens
blossom, etc., *see* **bloom**
blot, *v.t,* măcŭlo (1); (— **out, obliterate**), dēlĕo (2)
blot, *nn,* măcŭla, *f*
blow, *nn,* (**stroke**), plāga, *f*, ictus, *m*
blow, *v.i and v.t,* flo (1)
blowing, *nn,* flātus, *m*
bludgeon, fustis, *m*
blue, *adj,* caerŭlĕus
bluff, *v.t,* illūdo (3)
blunder, *nn,* mendum, *n*, error, *m*
blunder, *v.i,* offendo (3), erro (1)
blunt, *adj,* hĕbes; (**frank**), lĭber
blunt, *v.t,* hĕbĕto (1), obtundo (3)
bluntly, *adv,* lĭbērē, plāne
blush, *nn,* rŭbor, *m*
blush, *v.i,* ērŭbesco (3)
bluster, *v.i,* dēclāmo (1)
bluster, *nn,* dēclāmātĭo, *f*
blusterer, iactātor, *m*
boar, verres, *m*, āper, *m*
board, *nn,* tăbŭla, *f*; (**council**), concĭlĭum, *n*
board, *v.t* (**ship**), conscendo (3); (**to — up**), contăbŭlo (1); (**provide food**), victum praebĕo (2)
boast, *v.i,* glōrĭor (1 *dep.*), se iactare (1 *reflex*)
boasting, *nn,* glōrĭātĭo, *f*, iactātĭo, *f*
boat, scăpha, *f*, linter, *f*
boatman, nauta, *m*
bode, *v.t* (**predict**), praesāgĭo (4)
bodily, *adj,* corpŏrĕus
bodkin, ăcus, *f*
body, corpus, *n*; (— **of soldiers, etc.**), mănus, *f*, nŭmĕrus, *m*, multĭtūdo, *f*
body-guard, stĭpātōres, *m. pl*
bog, pălus, *f*
boggy, păluster
boil, *nn,* vŏmĭca, *f*
boil, *v.t,* cŏquo (3); *v.i,* fervĕo (2)
boiled, *adj,* ēlixus
boiler, caldarĭum, *n*
boisterous, prŏcellōsus, turbĭdus
bold, audax, ănĭmōsus, fortis
boldly, *adv,* audacter, anĭmōse, fortĭter
boldness, audācĭa, *f*, fĭdentĭa, *f*
bolster, cervīcal, *n*, pulvīnus, *m*
bolt, *nn* (**door, etc.**), ŏbex, *m*, rĕpāgŭla, *n.pl*
bolt, *v.t* (**door, etc.**), obsĕro (1), claudo (3); (**food**), obsorbĕo (2)
bombastic, inflātus
bond, vincŭlum, *n*, cătēna, *f*; (**legal**), syngrāpha, *f*
bondage, servĭtus, *f*
bone, ŏs, *n*
book, lĭber, *m*, lĭbellus, *m*
bookbinder, glūtĭnātor, *m*
bookcase, armārĭum, *n*
book-keeper, actŭārĭus, *m*
bookseller, biblĭŏpōla, *m*
boom, *v.i,* sŏno (1)
boon (**good thing**), bŏnum, *n*
boor, hŏmo ăgrestis
boorish, agrestis
boot, calcĕus, *m*; (**heavy —**), căllĭga, *f*
bootless (**unsuccessful**), *adj,* irrĭtus
booth, tăberna, *f*
booty, praeda, *f*, spŏlĭa, *n.pl*
booze, *v.i. and v.t,* pōto (1)
border, margo, *m*, *f*; (**of a country**), fīnis, *m*
border, *v.i,* attingo (3)
bordering, *adj,* fīnĭtĭmus
bore (**person**) use, *adj,* importūnus (**rude**)
bore, *v.t,* perfŏro (1), tĕrĕbro (1); (— **someone**), fătĭgo (1)
boredom, taedĭum, *n*
born, *adj,* nātus; (**to be —**), *v.i,* nascor (3 *dep.*)
borough, mūnĭcĭpĭum, *n*
borrow, mūtŭor (1 *dep.*)
bosom, sīnus, *m*, pectus, *n*
boss (**of a shield**), umbo, *m*
botany, ars herbārĭa, *f*
botch, *v.t,* măle sarcĭo (4), (**patch badly**)
both, ambo; (**each of two**), ŭterquĕ; (**both . . . and**), et . . . et
bother, *nn, use adj,* mŏlestus (**troublesome**)
bother, *v.t,* lăcesso (3), vexo (1)
bottle, ampulla, *f*, lăgēna, *f*
bottom, fundus, *m*, *or use adj.* īmus *in agreement with noun, e.g.* **at the bottom of the tree,** ad īmam arbŏrem
bottomless (**very deep**), prŏfundus
bough, rāmus, *m*
boulder, saxum, *n*

bounce, *v.i,* rĕsĭlĭo (4)
bound (limit), fīnis, *m,* mŏdus, *m*; **(leap),** saltus, *m*
bound, *v.i,* **(leap),** sălĭo (4); *v.t,* **(limit),** contĭnĕo (2)
boundary, fīnis, *m*
boundless, infīnītus
bountiful, largus, bĕnignus
bounty, largĭtas, *f,* bĕnignĭtas, *f*
bouquet, serta, *n.pl*
bout (contest), certāmen, *n*
bow (archery), arcus, *m*; **(of a ship),** prōra, *f*; **(of salutation),** sălūtātĭo, *f*
bow, *v.t,* inclĭno (1), dēmitto (3); *v.i,* se dēmittĕre (3 *reflex*)
bow-legged, vătĭus
bowman, săgittārĭus, *m*
bowels, viscĕra, *n.pl*
bower, umbrăcŭlum, *n*
bowl, crātēra, *f*
box, arca, *f,* cista, *f*; **(tree),** buxus, *f*; **(slap),** cŏlăphus, *m*
box, *v.i,* pugnis certo (1), **(fight with the fists)**
boxer, pŭgil, *m*
boxing, *nn,* pŭgĭlātĭo, *f*
boy, pŭer, *m*
boyhood, pŭĕrĭtĭa, *f*
boyish, pŭĕrĭlis
brace (support), fascĭa, *f*; **(in architecture),** fĭbŭla, *f*
brace, *v.t,* lĭgo (1), firmo (1)
bracelet, armilla, *f*
bracket, mūtŭlus, *m*
brackish, ămārus
brag, *v.i,* glōrĭor (1 *dep.*)
braggart, iactātor, *m*
braid, *nn,* **(of hair),** grădus, *m*
braid, *v.t,* necto (3)
brain, cĕrĕbrum, *n*
brainless (stupid), sōcors
bramble, dūmus, *m*
bran, furfur, *m*
branch, rāmus, *m*
branch, *v.i,* **(separate),** dĭvĭdor (3 *pass*)
branching, *adj,* rāmōsus
brand (fire —), fax, *f,* torris, *m*; **(burn-mark),** nŏta, *f*; **(stigma),** stigma, *n*
brand, *v.t,* ĭnūro (3), nŏto (1)
brandish, *v.t,* vibro (1)
brass, ŏrĭchalcum, *n*
brave, fortis, ănĭmōsus, ăcer
bravely, *adv,* fortĭter, ănĭmōsē
bravery, fortĭtūdo, *f*
brawl, *v.i,* rixor (1 *dep.*)
brawl, *nn,* rixa, *f*
brawny, lăcertōsus
bray, *v.i,* rŭdo (3)
brazen (made of brass), aēnĕus, aerĕus; **(impudent),** impŭdens
breach, rūĭna, *f, or use vb.* rumpo (3) **(to burst)**; **(— in a treaty, etc.)** *use* vĭŏlo (1) **(to violate)**
bread, pānis, *m*
breadth, lātĭtūdo, *f*
break, *v.t,* frango (3); **(treaty, etc.)** vĭŏlo (1); **(— promise),** fĭdem fallo (3); **(— down),** *v.t,* rēscindo (3); **(— in),** *v.t,* **(horses),** dŏmo (1); **(— into),** *v.t,* irrumpo (3); **(— loose)** ērumpo (3)
break (of day), prīma lux, *f,* **(first light)**; **(fracture),** fractūra, *f*
breakfast, ientăcŭlum, *n*
breakfast, *v.i,* iento (1)
breakwater, mōles, *f*
breast, pectus, *n,* mamma, *f*
breast-plate, lōrĭca, *f*
breath, spīrĭtus, *m,* ănĭma, *f*; **(out of —),** exănĭmātus; **(to hold one's —),** ănĭmam comprĭmo (3)
breathe, *v.i,* spīro (1); **(— out),** exspīro (1)
breathing, *nn,* aspīrātĭo, *f*
breathless, exănĭmātus
breed, *v.t,* gĕnĕro (1); *v.i,* nascor (3 *dep.*) **(to be born)**
breed, *nn,* gĕnus, *n*
breeding, *nn,* **(giving birth)** partus, *m*; **(manners),** hūmānĭtas, *f*
breeze, aura, *f*
breezy, ventōsus
brevity, brĕvĭtas, *f*
brew, *v.t,* cŏquo (3); *v.i* **(overhang)** impendĕo (2)
bribe, *nn,* praemĭum, *n*
bribe, *v.t,* corrumpo (3)
bribery, ambĭtus, *m*
brick, lăter, *m*; **(made of —),** *adj,* lătĕrĭcĭus
bricklayer, structor, *m*
bridal, nuptĭālis
bride (before marriage), sponsa, *f* **(after marriage),** nupta, *f*
bridegroom (before marriage), sponsus, *m*; **(after marriage),** nuptus, *m,* mārĭtus, *m*
bridge, pons, *m*
bridle, frēnum, *n*
brief, *adj,* brĕvis
briefly, *adv,* brĕvĭter
briar, dūmus, *m*
brigade, lĕgĭo, *f*
bright, clārus
brighten, *v.t,* illustro (1); *v.i,* clāresco (3)
brightly, *adv,* clāre
brilliance, splendor, *m,* nĭtor, *m*

brilliant, splendĭdus; (**famous**), praeclārus
brim, margo, *m*, *f*, labrum, *n*
brimstone, sulfur, *n*
brine, salsāmentum, *n*
bring, *v.t*, fĕro, affĕro (*irreg*), addūco (3) apporto (1); (— **about**), confĭcio (3); (— **back**, — **before**), rĕfĕro (*irreg*); (— **down**), dēfĕro (*irreg*); (— **forward**), prōfĕro (*irreg*); (— **in**), infĕro (*irreg*); (— **out**), ēfĕro (*irreg*); (— **over**), perdūco (3); (— **together**), cōgo (3); (— **up** (**children**), ēdūco (1)
brink (**river, etc.**), rīpa, *f*; (**of cliff, etc.**) *use adj*, summus (**highest**)
brisk, ălăcer
briskness, ălacrĭtas, *f*
bristle, saeta, *f*
bristle, *v.i*, horrĕo (2)
brittle, frăgĭlis
broach, *v.t*, ăpĕrio (4), prōfĕro (*irreg*)
broad, lātus
broadly (**widely**), *adv*, lātē
broil (**quarrel**), rixa, *f*
broil, *v.t*, torrĕo (2)
broken, fractus; (**disabled**), confectus
broker, interpres, *c* (**agent**)
bronze, aes, *n*; (*adj*), aēnĕus, aerĕus
brooch, fĭbŭla, *f*
brood, *v.i*, incŭbo (1)
brood (**of young, etc.**), fētus, *m*
brook, rīvus, *m*
brook (**no interference etc**), pătĭor (3 *dep*)
broom, scōpae, *f. pl*
broth, ius, *n*
brothel, gănĕa, *f*
brother, frāter, *m*
brotherhood sŏcĭĕtas, *f*
brow (**forehead**), frons, *f*; (**eye-brow**), sŭpercĭlĭum, *n*; (**of hill**), căcūmen, *n*
brown, fuscus
browse, *v.t* (**read**), perlĕgo (3)
bruise, *nn*, contūsum, *n*
bruise, *v.t*, contundo (3)
brunt (**bear the — of**), *use* sustĭnĕo (2) (**to bear**)
brush, *nn*, pēnĭcŭlus, *m*
brush, *v.t*, dētergĕo (2)
brushwood, sarmenta, *n.pl*
brutal, fĕrus, ătrox
brutality, immānĭtas, *f*
brutally, *adv*, immānĭter
brute, bestĭa, *f*, fĕra, *f*
bubble, bulla, *f*
bubble, *v.i*, bullo (1)
buccaneer, pīrāta, *m*
buck (**male stag**), cervus, *m*
bucket, sĭtŭla, *f*
buckle, fĭbŭla, *f*
buckle, *v.t*, fĭbŭlā necto (3) (**fasten with a buckle**)
buckler (**shield**), scūtum, *n*
bud, *nn*, gemma, *f*
bud, *v.i*, gemmo (1), germĭno (1)
budge, *v.i*, cēdo (3); *v.t*, mŏvĕo (2)
budget, rătio, *f* (**reckoning, account**)
buff, lūtĕus
buffet (**blow**), cŏlăphus, *m*
buffoon, scurra, *m*
bug, cīmex, *m*
bugbear, terrĭcŭla, *n.pl*
bugle, būcĭna, *f*
build, *v.t*, aedĭfĭco (1)
builder, aedĭfĭcātor, *m*
building (**act of —**), aedĭfĭcātio, *f*, (**structure itself**), aedĭfĭcĭum, *n*
bulb, bulbus, *m*
bulk, magnĭtūdo, *f*, mōles, *f*
bulky, ingens, grandis
bull, taurus, *m*
bullet, glans, *f*
bullion, aurum, *n*
bullock, iŭvencus, *m*
bulrush, iuncus, *m*
bulwark, mūnīmentum, *n*
bump, *nn*, tūber, *n*, tŭmor, *m*
bump, *v.i*, offendo (3)
bumpkin, rustĭcus, *m*
bunch, ūva, *f*, răcēmus, *m*
bundle, fascis, *m*
bung (**stopper**), obtūrāmentum, *n*
bungle, *v.i*, inscītē ăgo (3) (**do unskilfully**)
bungler, *adj*, impĕrītus
buoyancy, lĕvĭtas, *f*
buoyant, lĕvis
burden, ŏnus, *n*
burden, *v.t*, ŏnĕro (1)
burdensome, grăvis
bureau, scrīnĭum, *n*, armārĭum, *n*
burgess, cīvis, *c*
burglar, fūr, *m*
burglary, furtum, *n*
burgle, *v.t*, fūror (1 *dep.*) (**steal**)
burial, fūnus, *n*, sĕpultūra, *f*
burial-place, lŏcus, (*m*) sĕpultūrae
burly, lăcertōsus
burn, *v.t*, ūro (3), incendo (3); *v.i*, ardĕo (2), flagro (1)
burn, *nn*, ambustum, *n*
burning, *adj*, ardens
burnish, *v.t*, pŏlio (4)
burrow, cūnĭcŭlum, *n*
burst, *v.t*, rumpo (3); *v.i*, rumpor (3 *pass*)
burst out, *v.i*, ērumpo (3)
bursting out, *nn*, ēruptio, *f*
bury, *v.t*, sĕpĕlio (4), abdo (3)

bush, dūmus
bushel, mĕdimnum, *n*
bushy, frŭtĭcōsus
busily, *adv*, sēdŭlō
business, nēgōtĭum, *n*, res, *f*
bust (statue), īmāgo, *f*
bustle, *nn*, festĭnātĭo, *f*
bustle, *v.i*, festīno (1)
busy, occŭpātus
but, *conj*, sed, vērum, at (*first word in clause*); autem, vēro (*second word in clause*); **(except),** praeter (*with acc*)
butcher, lănĭus, *m*
butcher, *v.t* **(murder),** trŭcĭdo (1)
butchery, trŭcĭdātĭo, *f*
butler, prōmus, *m*
butt (laughing stock), lūdĭbrĭum, *n*
butt, *v.t*, cornŭ fĕrĭo (4) **(strike with the horn)**
butter, būtȳrum, *n*
butterfly, pāpĭlĭo, *m*
buttock, clūnis, *m*, *f*
buttress, antēris, *f*
buxom, vĕnustus
buy, *v.t*, ĕmo (3)
buyer, emptor, *m*
buying, *nn*, emptĭo, *f*
by, *prep*, **(of place, near),** ad, prŏpe (*with acc*); **(of time)** *often expressed by abl. of noun, e.g.* **by night,** nocte; **(— means of),** per (*with acc*) **(by an agent,** *e.g.* **by a man),** ab (*with abl*), ab hōmĭne; **(by an instrument,** *e.g.* **by a spear,** *abl. case alone*), hastā; **(— chance),** *adv*, fortĕ
by-gone, *adj*, praetĕrĭtus
by-stander, spectātor, *m*
by-way, trāmes, *m*

C

cab, raeda, *f*, cĭsĭum, *n*
cabal (faction), factĭo, *f*
cabbage, brassĭca, *f*
cabin (hut), căsa, *f*
cabinet (furniture), armārĭum, *n*; **(council),** summum consĭlĭum, *n*
cable (anchor —), ancŏrāle, *n*
cackle, cackling, *nn*, strĕpĭtus, *m*
cackle, *v.i*, strĕpo (3)
cadaverous, cădāvĕrōsus
cadence, cursus, *m*
cadet, discĭpŭlus, *m*, tīro, *m*
cage, căvĕa, *f*
cajole, *v.t*, blandĭor (4 *dep. with dat*)
cajolery, blandĭtĭae, *f. pl*
cake, *nn*, plăcenta, *f*, lĭbum, *n*
calamitous, exĭtĭōsus
calamity, clādes, *f*, mălum, *n*
calculate, *v.t*, compŭto (1), aestĭmo (1)
calculation, rătĭo, *f*
calendar, fasti, *m. pl*
calf, vĭtŭlus, *m*; **(of the leg),** sūra, *f*
call, *v.t*, **(name),** vŏco (1), appello (1); dĭco (3); **(— back),** rĕvŏco (1); **(— to, summon),** advŏco (1); **(— together),** convŏco (1); **(— up or out),** suscĭto (1)
call, *nn* **(cry),** clāmor, *m*; **(visit)** sălūtātĭo, *f*
caller, sălūtātor, *m*
calling, *nn* **(vocation),** ars, *f*, artĭfĭcĭum, *n*
callous, callōsus
callow, implūmis
calm, *adj*, plăcĭdus, tranquillus
calm, *nn*, tranquillĭtas, *f*, mălăcĭa,
calm, *v.t*, sēdo (1), plăco (1)
calmly, *adv*, tranquille, plăcĭde
calumniate, *v.t*, crīmĭnor (1 *dep.*)
calumnious, crīmĭnōsus
calumny, crīmĭnātĭo, *f*
camel, cămēlus, *m*
camp, castra, *n.pl*; **(to pitch —),** castra pōno (3); **(to move —),** castra mŏvĕo (2); **(a winter —),** hĭberna, *n.pl*
campaign, stĭpendĭum, *n*
campaign, *v.i*, stĭpendĭum mĕrĕor (2 *dep.*)
can, *nn*, urcĕus, *m*
can, *v.i* **(to be able),** possum (*irreg*)
canal, fossa, *f*
cancel, *v.t*, dēlĕo (2), abrŏgo (1)
cancer (sign of Zodiac), cancer, *m*
candid, ăpertus, lĭber
candidate, candĭdātus, *m*
candle, candēla, *f*
candlestick, candēlābrum, *n*
candour, lĭbertas, *f*
cane, hărundo, *f*, băcŭlum, *n*, virga, *f*
cane, *v.t*, verbĕro (1)
canister, arca, *f*, pyxis, *f*
canker, rōbīgo, *f*
canker, *v.t*, corrumpo (3)
cannibal, anthrōpŏphăgus, *m*
cannon, tormentum, *n*
canoe, scăpha, *f*
canon (rule), rēgŭla, *f*
canopy, vēla, *n.pl*
cant, ostentātĭo, *f*
canter, *v.i*, lēnĭter curro (3) **(run smoothly)**
canton, pāgus, *m*
canvas, vēla, *n.pl*, carbăsus, *f*
canvass, *v.i*, ambĭo (4)
canvass, *nn*, ambĭtĭo, *f*; **(illegal),** ambĭtus, *m*
cap, pillĕus, *m*

For List of Abbreviations used, turn to pages 3, 4

capability, făcultas, *f*
capable, căpax
capacious, căpax
capacity, căpăcĭtas, *f*; **(mental —),** ingĕnĭum, *n*
cape, prōmontŭrĭum, *n*
caper, *v.i*, exsulto (1), salĭo (4)
capital, *nn*, **(city),** căput, *n*
capital, *adj* **(crime, etc.),** căpĭtālis; **(chief),** princeps
capitulate, *v.t*, dēdo (3); *v.i*, se dēdĕre (3 *reflex*)
caprice, lĭbīdo, *f*
capricious, lĕvis
captain, dux, *m*, princeps, *m*; **(of a ship),** măgister, *m*, nauarchus, *m*
captivate, *v.t*, căpĭo (3), dēlēnĭo (4)
captive, *adj. and nn*, captīvus, *m*.
captivity, captīvĭtas, *f*
capture, *nn*, **(of city, camp, etc.),** expugnātĭo, *f*; **(of persons),** *use vb*, căpĭo (3) **(to capture)**
capture, *v.t*, căpĭo (3)
car, currus, *m*, plaustrum, *n*
caravan (convoy), commĕātus, *m*, **(vehicle),** raeda, *f*
carbuncle, fūrunculus, *m*
carcass, cădāver, *n*, corpus, *n*
card, charta, *f*
cardinal, *adj*, prīmus, princeps
care, cūra, *f*, sollĭcĭtūdo, *f*
care, *v.t* **(to — about or for),** cūro (1)
career, currĭculum, *n*
careful, dilĭgens; **(carefully prepared)** accūrātus; **(cautious)** cautus
carefully, *adv*, dīlĭgenter
careless, neglĕgens, indīlĭgens
carelessly, *adv*, neglegenter
carelessness, neglĕgentĭa, *f*
caress, blandīmenta, *n.pl*, complexus, *m*
caress, *v.t*, blandĭor (4 *dep.*) (*with dat.*)
caressing, *adj*, blandus
cargo, ŏnus, *n*
caricature, ĭmāgo, *f*
caricature, *v.t*, *use phr.* vultum dĕtorquĕo (2) **(distort the features)**
carnage, caedes, *f*, strāges, *f*
carnal, corpŏrĕus
carnival, fērĭae, *f.pl*
carnivorous, carnĭvŏrus
carol, cantus, *m*
carousal, cōmissātĭo, *f*
carouse, *v.i*, cōmissor (1 *dep.*)
carp at, *v.t*, carpo (3), mordĕo (2)
carpenter, făber, *m*
carpet, strāgŭlum, *n*
carriage (vehicle), raeda, *f*, carpentum, *n*; **(transportation),** vectūra, *f*; **(poise),** incessus, *m*
carrier, vector, *m*
carrion, căro, *f*, cădāver, *n*
carrot, pastĭnāca, *f*
carry, *v.t*, porto (1), fĕro (*irreg.*), vĕho (3), gĕro (3); **(— away or off),** aufĕro (*irreg.*); **(— back)** rēfĕro (*irreg.*); **(— in)** infĕro (*irreg.*); **(— on)** gĕro (3); **(— over)** transporto (1); **(— out, perform)** exsĕquor (3 *dep.*); **(— through a law, etc.),** perfĕro (*irreg.*)
cart, plaustrum, *n*
cart, *v.t*, vĕho (3)
cart-horse, iūmentum, *n*
cartilage, cartĭlāgo, *f*
carve, *v.t*, caelo (1), sĕco (1), sculpo (3)
carver, sculptor, *m*
carving, *nn*, caelātūra, *f*
case (in law), causa, *f* **(circumstances),** cāsus, *m* **(cover),** thēca, *f*
casement, fĕnestra, *f*
cash, nummus, *m*, pĕcūnĭa nŭmĕrāta, *f*
cashier, *nn*, *use phr.* qui nummos dispensat **(who dispenses the cash)**
cashier, *v.t*, **(from the army),** exauctoro (1)
cask, cūpa, *f*
casket, arcŭla, *f*
cast, *nn*, **(throw),** iactus, *m*
cast, *v.t*, iăcĭo (3), mitto (3); **(— down)** dĕĭcĭo (3); **(— off)** dēpōno (3); **(— out)** expello (3)
castaway, perdĭtus, *m*
caste, ordo, *m*
castigate, *v.t*, castīgo (1)
castle, castellum, *n*
castor-oil, cĭcĭnum ŏlĕum, *n*
castrate, *v.t*, castro (1)
casual, fortŭĭtus
casually, *adv*, neglĕgenter
casualty (accident), cāsus, *m*; **(killed)** *adj*, interfectus
cat, fēles, *f*
catalogue, index *c*
catapault, cătăpulta, *f*,
cataract (waterfall), cătăracta, *f*
catarrh, grăvēdo, *f*
catastrophe, rŭĭna, *f*
catch, căpĭo (3), comprĕhendo (3); **(a disease),** contrăho (3)
categorical (absolute), simplex, plānus
category, nŭmĕrus, *m*

cater, *v.t,* obsōno (1)
caterpillar, ērūca, *f*
catgut, chorda, *f*
cattle, pĕcus, *n*
cauldron, cortīna, *f*
cause, *nn,* causa, *f*
cause, *v.t,* făcĭo (3), effĭcĭo (3)
causeway, agger, *m*
caustic, *adj,* mordax (**biting**)
caution, cautĭo, *f*
caution, *v.t,* mŏnĕo (2)
cautious, cautus,
cavalry, ĕquĭtātus, *m,* ĕquĭtes, *m. pl*
cave, spēlunca, *f,* căverna, *f,* antrum, *n*
caw, *v.i,* crōcĭo (4)
cease, *v.i,* dēsĭno (3) (*with infin*)
ceaseless, perpĕtŭus
cedar, cedrus, *f*
ceiling, tectum, *n*
celebrate, *v.t,* căno (3), cĕlĕbro (1)
celebrated, clārus, illustris
celebration, cĕlĕbrātĭo, *f*
celebrity, fāma, *f,* glōrĭa, *f;* (**person**), vir praeclārus
celerity, cĕlĕrĭtas, *f*
celestial, caelestis
celibacy, caelĭbātus, *m*
cell, cellar, cella, *f*
cement, ferrūmen, *n*
cement, *v.t,* glūtĭno (1), ferrūmĭno (1)
cemetery, sĕpulcrētum, *n*
censor, censor, *m*
censure, vĭtŭpĕrātio, *f*
censure, *v.t,* vĭtŭpĕro (1) reprĕhendo (3)
census, census, *m*
per cent, *use nn,* centēsĭma, *f* (**one hundredth part**)
centaur, centaurus, *m*
central, mĕdĭus
centre (**of**) mĕdĭus, *in agreement with noun, e.g.* **in the centre of the line,** in mĕdĭā ăcĭe
centre on, *v.i* (**depend on**), pendĕo (2) (*with* ab *and abl*)
centurion, centŭrĭo, *m*
century, saecŭlum, *n*
ceremonial, rītus, *m,* caerĭmōnĭa, *f*
ceremonious, sollemnis
certain, certus, explōrātus; (**a — person**), *use pron,* quĭdam
certainly, *adv,* certo, certē, prŏfecto
certainty, res certa; *or use adj,* certus (**certain**)
certificate, scriptum testĭmōnĭum (**written proof**)
certify, *v.i,* rĕcognosco (3), confirmo (1)
cessation, intermissĭo, *f*
chafe, *v.t,* fŏvĕo (2), călĕfăcĭo (3); *v.i,* stŏmăchor (1 *dep.*) (**be irritated**)
chaff, pălĕa, *f*
chaffinch, fringilla,
chagrin, stŏmăchus, *m*
chain, cătēna, *f,* vincŭlum, *n*
chain, *v.t,* cătēnas īnĭcĭo (3) (*with dat*)
chair, sella, *f*
chairman, măgister, *m*
chalk, crēta, *f*
chalk out (**mark out**), *v.t,* dēsigno (1)
challenge, *nn,* prōvŏcātĭo, *f*
challenge, *v.t,* prōvŏco (1)
chamber, conclāve, *n;* (**bed —**), cŭbĭcŭlum, *n*
chamberlain, cŭbĭcŭlārĭus, *m*
chamois, căprĕŏlus, *m*
champ, *v.t,* mando (3)
champion victor *m;* (**defender**), prōpugnātor, *m*
chance, *nn,* cāsus, *m,* fors, *f,* fortūna, *f*
by chance, *adv,* (**happen**), forte, cāsu
chance, *v.i,* accĭdo (3)
chandelier, candēlābrum, *n*
change, changing, *nn,* mūtātĭo, *f,* permūtātĭo, *f*
change, *v.t,* mūto (1), converto (3); *v.i,* mūtor (1 *pass*)
changeable, mūtābĭlis
channel, cănālis, *m,* alvĕus, *m*
chant, *v.i and v.t,* canto (1)
chaos, perturbātĭo, *f*
chaotic, perturbātus
chapel, săcellum, *n*
chapter, căpŭt, *n*
char, *v.t,* ambūro (3)
character, mōres, *m. pl,* ingĕnĭum, *n;* (**reputation**), existĭmātĭo, *f,* ŏpĭnĭo, *f;* (**in a play**), persōna, *f*
characteristic, *adj,* prōprĭus
charcoal, carbo, *m*
charge, *nn,* (**attack**), impĕtus, *m;* (**accusation**), crīmen, *n;* (**price**), prĕtĭum, *n;* (**care of**), cūra, *f*
charge, *v.t,* (**attack**), impĕtum făcĭo (3); signa infĕro (*irreg*); (**accuse**), accūso (1); (**of price**), vendo (3) (**sell**) (3); (**put in—**) praefĭcĭo (3) (*with dat*); (**be in—**) praesum (*irreg.*) (*with dat*)
chariot, currus, *m,* essĕdum, *n*
charioteer, aurīga, *c*
charitable, bĕnignus, mĭtis
charity, ămor *m,* bĕnĕfĭcentĭa, *f*
charm, blandīmentum, *n,* grātĭa, *f* (**trinket**), bulla, *f*
charm, *v.t,* fascĭno (1), dēlēnĭo (4), dēlecto (1)
charming, vĕnustus, lĕpĭdus

chart, tăbŭla, *f*
charter, *v.t*, (hire), condūco (3)
chase, *nn*, (hunt), vēnātĭo, *f*, vēnātus, *m*
chase, *v.t*, sector (1 *dep.*), vēnor (1 *dep.*)
chasm, hĭātus, *m*
chaste, castus
chastise, *v.t*, castīgo (1), pūnĭo (4)
chastisement, castīgātĭo, *f*
chastity, castĭtas, *f*
chat, *v.i*, fābŭlor (1 *dep.*)
chat, *nn*, sermo, *m*
chatter, *v.i*, garrĭo (4); (of teeth), crĕpĭto (1)
chatter, *nn*, garrŭlĭtas, *f*
chattering, *adj*, garrŭlus
cheap, vīlis
cheapness, vīlĭtas, *f*
cheat, *nn*, (person), fraudātor, *m*
cheat, *v.t*, fraudo (1)
cheating, *nn*, fraudātĭo, *f*
check, *nn*, (hindrance), impedīmentum, *n*, incommŏdum, *n*; (set back), incommŏdum, *n*
check, *v.t*, cŏhĭbĕo (2), contĭnĕo (2), comprĭmo (3), cŏercĕo(2)
cheek, gĕna, *f*
cheer, *nn*, (shout), clāmor, *m*
cheer, *v.i*, (applaud), plaudo (3), clāmo (1)
cheerful, hĭlāris
cheerfulness, hĭlārĭtas, *f*
cheerless, tristis
cheese, cāsĕus, *m*
cheque, perscriptĭo, *f*, (written entry)
chequered, vărĭus
cherish, *v.t*, fŏvĕo (2), cŏlo (3)
cherry, cherry-tree, cĕrăsus, *f*
chess, latruncŭli, *m. pl*
chest (box), amārĭum, *n*, cista, *f*; (body), pectus, *n*, thorax, *m*
chestnut, glans, *f*; (— tree), castănĕa, *f*
chew, mando (3)
chicken, pullus, *m*
chide, *v.t*, obiurgo (1), incrĕpĭto (1), rĕprĕhendo (3)
chiding, rĕprĕhensĭo, *f*
chief, *nn*, princeps, *m*, prōcer, *m*
chief, *adj*, prīmus, princeps
chieftain, *see* **chief**
child, pŭer, *m*, infans, *c*; (*pl.*) lĭbĕri, *m. pl*
childbirth, partus, *m*
childhood, pŭĕrĭtĭa, *f*
childish, pŭĕrīlis
childless, orbus
chill, chilly, *adj*, frīgĭdus
chill, *v.t*, rĕfrīgĕro (1)
chime, *nn*, concentus, *m*
chime, *v.i*, (sound), cănо (3)
chimney, cămīnus, *m*
chin, mentum, *n*
chine, tergum, *n*
chink, rīma, *f*
chip, assŭla, *f*
chirp, chirping, *nn*, pīpātus, *m*
chirp, *v.i*, pīpĭo (4)
chisel, scalprum, *n*
chisel, *v.t*, sculpo (3)
chivalrous, magnănĭmus
chivalry, magnănĭmĭtas, *f*
choice, *nn*, dēlectus, *m*; (— between), optĭo, *f*
choice, *adj*, ēlectus
choir, chŏrus, *m*
choke, *v.t*, suffōco (1); *v.i*, suffōcor (1 *pass*)
choose, *v.t*, lĕgo (3), ēlĭgo (3)
chop, *v.t*, caedo (3); (cut off), abscīdo (3)
chord, *use* nervus, *m*, (string)
chorus, chŏrus, *m*
Christ, Christus, *m*
Christian, Christĭānus
chronic (long-lasting), dĭūturnus
chronicle, annāles, *m. pl*
chuckle, *v.i*, căchinno (1)
church, templum, *n*
church-yard, ārĕa, *f*
churl, hŏmo rustĭcus
churlish, rustĭcus
churn, *v.t*, (stir), ăgĭto (1)
cinder, cĭnis, *m*, fāvilla, *f*
cipher (a nonentity), nŭmĕrus, *m*; (secret writing), nŏta, *f*
circle, orbis, *m*
circuit, circŭĭtus, *m*
circuitous (route, etc.), flexŭōsus
circular, rŏtundus
circulate, *v.t*, spargo (3), dīvulgo (1); *v.i*, diffundor (3 *pass*), percrēbresco (3)
circulation, (to be in —) (of books etc.) in mānibus esse (*irreg*)
circumcise, *v.t*, circumcīdo (3)
circumference, ambĭtus, *m*
circumscribe, *v.t*, circumscrĭbo (3)
circumstance, res, *f*; *or use neuter of an adj, e.g.* adversa (adverse circumstances)
circumstantial evidence, coniectūra, *f*
circumvent, *v.t*, circumvĕnĭo (4)
circus, circus, *m*
cistern, cisterna, *f*
citadel, arx, *f*
cite, *v.t*, (quote), prōfĕro (*irreg*)
citizen, cīvis, *c*
citizenship, cīvĭtas, *f*

city, urbs, *f*
civic, cīvīlis
civil (polite), urbānus; **(civic)** cīvīlis; (— **war),** bellum dŏmestĭcum
civilian (opp. military), tŏgātus, *m*
civilization, cultus, *m*, hūmānĭtas, *f*
civilize, *v.t*, excŏlo (3), expŏlio (4)
civilized, hūmānus, cultus
claim, *v.t*, postŭlo (1), rĕposco (3)
claim, *nn*, postŭlātĭo, *f*
claimant, pĕtītor, *m*
clammy, lentus
clamorous, clāmans
clamour, *nn*, clāmor, *m*, strĕpĭtus, *m*
clamour, *v.i*, vōcĭfĕror (1 *dep*)
clandestine, clandestīnus
clang, *nn*, clangor, *m*
clang, *v.i. and v.t*, strĕpo (3)
clank, crĕpĭtus, *m*
clank, *v.i*, crĕpo (1)
clap, *nn*, **(hands),** plausus, *m*; **(thunder),** frăgor, *m*
clap, *v.i. and v.t*, plaudo (3)
clash, *v.i.*, concrĕpo (1), crĕpĭto (1); **(opinions)** rĕpugno (1); **(fight),** conflīgo (3)
clash, *nn*, **(noise),** crĕpĭtus, *m*; **(collision),** concursus, *m*
clasp, *nn*, **(embrace),** complexus, *m*; **(fastener),** fĭbŭla, *f*
clasp, *v.t.* **(fasten),** fĭbŭlo (1); **(embrace),** complector (3 *dep.*)
class, classis, *f*, gĕnus, *n*
classic, classical (well-established), prŏbus
classify, *v.t*, dēscrĭbo (3) ordĭne
clatter, *nn*, strĕpĭtus, *m*
clatter, *v.i*, incrĕpo (1)
clause, membrum, *n*, căpŭt, *n*
claw, unguis, *m*
clay, argilla, *f*, lŭtum, *n*
clean, *adj*, mundus, pūrus
clean, *v.t*, purgo (1), mundo (1)
cleanliness, mundĭtĭa, *f*
cleanse, *v.t*, purgo (1)
clear, clārus; **(weather),** sĕrēnus; **(matter),** mănĭfestus
clear, *v.t*, **(open up),** expĕdĭo (4); (— **oneself),** sē purgāre (1 *reflex*); *v.i*, **(of the weather),** dissĕrēnat (1 *impers*)
clearing, *nn*, **(open space),** lŏcus ăpertus
clearly, *adv*, clārē, ăpertē, plānē
clearness, clārĭtas, *f*
cleave, *v.t*, **(split),** findo (3); *v.i* **(stick to),** adhaerĕo (2)
cleft, hĭātus, *m*, rīma, *f*
clemency, clēmentĭa, *f*
clement, clēmens, lēnis
clench (the fist), *v.t*, comprĭmo (3)
clerk, scrĭba, *m*
clever, callĭdus, astūtus
cleverness, *f*, callĭdĭtas, *f*
client, clĭens, *m*, consultor, *m*
cliff, cautes, *f*, scŏpŭlus, *m*, rūpes,
climate, caelum, *n*
climax, grădātĭo, *f*
climb, *v.i. and v.t*, ascendo (3), scando (3)
climb, *nn*, ascensus, *m*
cling to, *v.i*, ădhaerĕo (2) (*with dat*)
clip, *v.t*, tondĕo (2)
cloak, pallĭum, *n*, lăcerna, *f*
cloak, *v.t*, **(hide),** dissĭmŭlo (1)
clock, hŏrŏlŏgĭum, *n*
clod, glaeba, *f*
clog (hindrance), impĕdĭmentum, *n*; **(shoe),** sculpōnĕa, *f*
clog, *v.t*, **(impede),** impĕdĭo (4)
close, *adj*, **(near),** vĭcīnus; **(packed together)** confertus, densus; **(at close quarters),** commĭnus, *adv*
close, *nn*, **(end),** fīnis, *m*, termĭnus, *m*
close, *adv*, prŏpe, iuxta
close, *v.t*, claudo (3); *v.i*, claudor (3 *pass*)
close in on, *v.t*, prĕmo (3) **(press)**
closely, *adv*, prŏpe; **(accurately),** exacte
closeness, prŏpinquĭtas, *f*,
closet, cella, *f*
clot (of blood), crŭor, *m*
cloth, textum, *n*
clothe, *v.t*, vestĭo (4), indŭo (3)
clothes, vestis, *f*, vestīmenta, *n.pl*
cloud, nūbes, *f*
cloudy, nūbĭlus
cloven, bĭsulcus
clown, scurra, *m*
club (cudgel), clāva, *f*; **(association),** sŏdālĭtas, *f*
cluck, *v.i*, singultĭo (4)
clump, massa, *f*
clumsy, ĭnhăbĭlis, rustĭcus
cluster, *nn*, răcēmus, *m*; **(people),** glŏbus, *m*
clutch, *v.t*, arrĭpĭo (3)
coach, carpentum, *n*, raeda, *f*
coachman, raedārĭus, *m*
coagulate, *v.i*, concresco (3)
coal, carbo, *m*
coalition, coniunctĭo, *f*, conspīrātĭo, *f*
coarse, crassus; **(manners),** incultus
coarseness, crassĭtūdo, *f*, ĭnhūmānĭtas, *f*
coast, ōra, *f*, lĭtus, *n*
coast, *v.i*, praetervĕhor (3 *pass*)
coat, tŭnĭca, *f*, ămictus, *m*; **(animal's),** pellis, *f*

For List of Abbreviations used, turn to pages 3, 4

coat, *v.t*, illĭno (3)
coax, *v.t*, mulcĕo (2), blandĭor (4 *dep*)
cobble, *v.t*, sarcĭo (4)
cobbler, sūtor, *m*
cock, gallus, *m*
code, (**method, system**), rătĭo, *f*
coerce, *v.t*, cōgo (3), cŏercĕo (2)
coercion, cŏercĭtĭo, *f*
coffin, arca, *f*
cog, dens, *m*
cogent, vălĭdus
cogitate, *v.i*, cōgĭto (1)
cognizance, cognĭtĭo, *f*
cohabit, *v.i*, consŭesco (3)
cohere, *v.i*, cŏhaerĕo (2)
coherent, cŏhaerens
cohesion, cŏhaerentĭa, *f*
cohort, cŏhors, *f*
coil, *nn*, spīra, *f*
coil, *v.t*, glŏmĕro (1)
coin, *nn*, nummus, *m*
coin, *v.t*, cūdo (3)
coinage, nummi, *m. pl*
coincide, *v.i*, compĕto (3), concurro (3)
coincidence, concursātĭo, *f*, concursus, *m*
cold, *adj*, frīgĭdus, gĕlĭdus
cold (**to be** —), *v.i*, algĕo (2)
coldness, frīgus, *n*
collapse, *v.i*, collābor (3 *dep.*)
collar, torques, *m and f*
collation (**comparison**), collātĭo, *f*
colleague, collēga, *m*
collect, *v.t*, collīgo (3), cōgo (3)
collection (**act of** —), collātĭo, *f*; (**heap, etc.**), congĕrĭes, *f*
collector (**of taxes, etc.**), exactor, *m*
college, collēgĭum, *n*
collide, *v.i*, conflīgo (3), concurro (3)
collision, concursus, *m*
colloquial (**speech**), *use* sermo, *m*
collusion, collūsĭo, *f*
colon, cōlon, *n*
colonel, praefectus, *m*
colonist, cŏlōnus, *m*
colony, cŏlōnĭa, *f*
colonnade, portĭcus, *f*
colossal, ingens
colour, cŏlor, *m*; (**flag**), vexillum, *n*; (— **bearer**), signĭfer, *m*
colour, *v.t*, cŏlōro (1)
coloured, pictus
colourful, fūcātus
colt, equŭlĕus, *m*
column (**pillar**), columna, *f*; (**military**), agmen, *n*
comb, *nn*, pecten, *m*
comb, *v.t*, pecto (3)
combat, *nn*, proelĭum, *n*
combat, *v.i*, pugno (1), luctor (1 *dep*)
combat, *v.t*, (**oppose**), obsto (1)
combatant, pugnātor, *m*
combination, coniunctĭo, *f*
combine, *v.t*, coniungo (3)
come, *v.i*, vĕnĭo (4); (— **about, happen**), ēvĕnĭo (4); (— **across, find**), *v.t*, invĕnĭo (4); (— **back**), *v.i*, rĕvĕnĭo (4); (— **by, obtain**), *v.t*, ădĭpiscor (3 *dep*); (— **down**), *v.i*, dēscendo (3); (— **in**) incēdo (3); (— **near**) appropinquo (1); (— **on, advance**), prōgrĕdĭor (3 *dep*); (— **out**) exĕo (4); (— **to**) advĕnĭo (4) (**regain consciousness**) ad se rĕdire (4); (— **together**) convĕnĭo (4); (— **upon**), *v.t*, sŭpervĕnĭo (4) (**attack**) incĭdo (3)
comedian, cōmoedus, *m*
comedy, cōmoedĭa, *f*
comely, pulcher
comet, cŏmētes, *m*
comfort, sōlācĭum, *n*, consōlātĭo, *f*
comfort, *v.t*, consōlor (1 *dep.*)
comfortable, commŏdus
comforter, consōlātor, *m*
comic, comical, cōmĭcus
coming, *adj*, ventūrus
coming, *nn*, adventus, *m*
command, *nn*, (**power**), impĕrĭum, *n*; (**an order**), iussum, *n*, mandātus, *m*; (**to be in** —) *v.i*, praesum (*with dat*)
command, *v.t.* impĕro (1) (*with dat.*), iŭbĕo (2)
commander, dux, *m*, impĕrātor, *m*
commemorate, *v.t*, cĕlĕbro (1)
commemoration, cĕlĕbrātĭo, *f*
commence, *v.i*, incĭpĭo (3)
commencement, ĭnĭtĭum, *n*
commend, *v.t*, commendo (1); (**praise**), laudo (1)
commendable, laudābĭlis
comment, *v.i*, dĭco (3), sententĭas dĭco (3) (**declare one's opinion**)
comment, *nn*, dicta, *n.pl*
commentary, commentārĭi, *m. pl*
commerce, commercĭum, *n*
commercial traveller, instĭtor, *m*
commiserate, *v.i. and v.t*, mĭsĕror (1 *dep.*)
commisariat, praefecti (*m. pl.*) rĕi frūmentārĭae (**superintendents of corn supply**); (**provisions**), commĕātus, *m*

commissary, prōcūrātor, *m*, lēgātus, *m*
commission (task), mandātum, *n*
commission, *v.t*, **(give a task to),** mando (1) (*dat. of person*)
commit, *v.t*, **(crime, etc.),** admitto (3); **(entrust),** committo (3), mando (1)
committee, dēlecti, *m. pl*, **(selected ones)**
commodious (opportune), commŏdus; **(capacious),** amplus
commodity (thing), res, *f*
common, *adj*, commūnis; **(belonging to the public),** pūblĭcus; **(ordinary),** vulgāris; **(common land),** ăger pūblĭcus, *m*, **(usual),** ūsĭtātus
commonplace, *adj*, vulgāris, trĭtus
commonly, *adv*, **(mostly),** plērumque
commonwealth, respublĭca, *f*
commotion, mōtus, *m*, tŭmultus, *m*, commōtĭo, *f*
communicate, *v.t*, commūnĭco (1); **(report),** dēfĕro (*irreg*)
communication, commūnĭcātĭo, *f*; **(reporting),** nuntĭus, *m*
communicative, lĭber, lŏquax
communion, sŏcĭētas, *f*
community, cĭvĭtas, *f*, sŏcĭētas, *f*
commute, *v.t*, mūto (1)
compact, *adj*, confertus, pressus
compact, *nn*, pactum, *n*, foedus, *n*
companion, sŏcĭus, *m*, cŏmes, *c*
companionable, făcĭlis
companionship, sŏdālĭtas, *f*
company, coetus, *m*, sŏcĭētas, *f*; **(military body),** mănĭpŭlus, *m*
comparable, conferendus
comparative, compărātīvus
compare, *v.t*, compăro (1), confĕro (*irreg*)
comparison, compărātĭo, *f*
compartment, lŏcŭlus, *m*
compass (range), fĭnes, *m. pl*; **(pair of compasses),** circĭnus, *m*
compass, *v.t*, complector (3 *dep*)
compassion, mĭsĕrĭcordĭa, *f*
compassionate, mĭsĕrĭcors
compatability, congrŭentĭa, *f*
compatible, congrŭens
compatriot, cĭvis, *c*
compel, *v.t*, cōgo (3), compello (3)
compensate for, *v.t*, compenso (1)
compensation, compensātĭo, *f*
compete, *v.i*, certo (1) **(struggle)**
competent, căpax; **(to be — to),** *v.i*, suffĭcĭo (3)
competition, certāmen, *n*
competitor, compĕtĭtor, *m*
complacent, sĭbi plăcens **(pleasing to oneself)**
complain, *v.i*, gĕmo (3); *v.t*, quĕror (3 *dep.*)
complaint, questus, *m*, quĕrēla, *f*; (disease), morbus, *m*
complement, complēmentum, *n*
complete, plēnus, perfectus
complete, *v.t*, complĕo (2), confĭcĭo (3)
completely, *adv*, omnĭno
completion, perfectĭo, *f*, confectĭo, *f*
complex, multĭplex
complexion, cŏlor, *m*
compliance, obsĕquĭum, *n*
compliant, obsĕquens
complicated, invŏlūtus
complication, implĭcātĭo, *f*
compliment, *nn*, **(esteem),** hŏnor, *m*; (praise) laus, *f*; **(greeting),** sălūtātĭo, *f*
compliment, *v.t*, **(praise),** laudo (1)
complimentary, hŏnōrĭfĭcus
comply with, *v.i*, concĕdo (3) (*with dat*)
component, *nn*, **(part),** ĕlĕmentum, *n*
compose, *v.t*, compōno (3)
composed (calm), sēdātus
composer, scriptor, *m*
composition (act of —), compŏsĭtĭo, *f*; **(a literary —),** ŏpus scriptum, *n*
composure, tranquillĭtas, *f*
compound, *adj*, compŏsĭtus
compound, *v.t*, compōno (3), miscĕo (2)
comprehend, *v.t*, **(understand),** intellĕgo (3)
comprehension, comprĕhensĭo, *f*
comprehensive, *use phr*, ad omnĭa pertĭnens **(extending to everything)**
compress, *v.t*, comprĭmo (3)
comprise, *v.t*, contĭnĕo (2)
compromise, *nn*, **(agreement),** compŏsĭtĭo, *f*
compromise, *v.t*, compōno (3); **(implicate),** implĭco (1)
compulsion, nĕcessĭtas, *f*
compunction, paenĭtentĭa, *f*
compute, *v.t*, compŭto (1)
comrade, sŏcĭus, *m*, cŏmes, *c*
concave, căvus
conceal, *v.t*, cēlo (1), abdo (3)
concede, *v.t*, cēdo (3)
conceit, arrŏgantia, *f*
conceited, arrŏgans
conceive, *v.t*, concĭpĭo (3)
concentrate (mentally), *v.i*, ănĭmum intendo (3); **(bring together),** *v.t*, contrăho (3), cōgo (3)
conception (mental), nōtĭo, *f*; **(physical),** conceptĭo, *f*

concern, *nn,* (**affair, circumstance**), rēs, *f*; (**worry**), sollĭcĭtūdo, *f*
concern, *v.t,* pertĭnĕo (2); (**it concerns**), rēfert (*irreg. impers*)
concerned (to be —), *v.i,* sollĭcĭtus esse
concerning, *prep,* dē (*with abl. of nn. etc*)
concert, *v.t,* (**plans, etc.**), confero (*irreg*), compōno (3)
concession, concessĭo, *f*
conciliate, *v.t,* concĭlĭo (1)
conciliation, concĭlĭātĭo, *f*
conciliatory, pācĭfĭcus
concise, brĕvis
conciseness, brĕvĭtas, *f*
conclude, *v.t,* (**decide**), stātŭo (3); (**end**), perfĭcĭo (3)
conclusion (**end**), exĭtus, *m*, fīnis, *m*; (**decision**), decrētum, *n*
conclusive, certus
concord, concordĭa, *f*
concourse, concursus, *m*
concubine, pellex, *f*
concupiscence, lĭbĭdo, *f*
concur, *v.i,* consentĭo (4)
concurrence, consensus, *m*
concurrent, *use adv,* sĭmŭl (**at the same time**)
concurrently, *adv,* sĭmŭl
condemn, *v.t,* damno (1) (*with acc. of person and genit. of crime or punishment*)
condemnation, damnātĭo, *f*
condense, *v.t,* denso (1), comprĭmo (3)
condensed, densus
condescend, *v.i,* dēscendo (3)
condescension, cōmĭtas, *f*, (**friendliness**)
condition, condĭcĭo, *f*, stātus, *m*
condole, *v.i,* dŏlĕo (2) cum (*with abl*)
condone, *v.t,* condōno (1)
conduce, *v.t,* condūco (3)
conducive, ūtĭlis (**advantageous**)
conduct, *nn,* (**personal, etc.**), mōres, *m. pl*; (**administration**), administrātĭo, *f*
conduct, *v.t* (**lead**), dūco (3); (**administer**), admĭnistro (1); (**— oneself**), sē gĕrĕre (3 *reflex*)
conductor, dux, *m*
conduit, cănālis, *m*
cone, cōnus, *m*
confectionery, crustum, *n*
confederacy, sŏcĭĕtas, *f*
confederate, foedĕrātus
confer, *v.t,* confero (*irreg*); (**— with**), collŏquor (3 *dep*); (**— about**), ăgo (3) dē
conference, collŏquĭum, *n*
confess, *v.t,* confĭtĕor (2 *dep*)
confession, confessĭo, *f*
confide, *v.t,* confĭdo (3), fĭdo (3) (*with dat*)
confidence, fĭdes, *f*, fĭdūcĭa, *f*
confident, fĭdens
confidential (**trusty**), fĭdus; (**one's own, special**), prŏprĭus; (**secret**), arcānus
confine, *v.t,* inclūdo (3), contĭnĕo (2)
confinement, inclūsĭo, *f*, custōdĭa, *f*; (**childbirth**), partus, *m*; pŭerpĕrĭum, *n*
confirm, *v.t,* confirmo (1)
confiscate, *v.t,* pūblĭco (1), ădĭmo (3)
confiscation, pūblĭcātĭo, *f*
conflagration, incendĭum, *n*
conflict, *nn,* certāmen, *n*
conflict, *v.i,* certo (1); dissentĭo (4)
confluence, conflŭens, *m*
conform to, *v.i,* obtempĕro (1) (*with dat*); *v.t,* accommŏdo (1)
conformity, convĕnĭentĭa, *f*
confound, *v.t,* (**disturb**), turbo (1); (**amaze**), obstŭpĕfăcĭo (3); (**bring to nothing, thwart**), frustor (1 *dep.*)
confront, *v.i,* obvĭam ĕo (*irreg.*) (*with dat*)
confuse, *v.t,* turbo (1)
confused, perturbātus
confusion, perturbātĭo, *f*
congeal, *v.i, and v.t,* congĕlo (1)
congenial, concors
congested, frĕquens
congratulate, *v.t,* grātŭlor (1 *dep*)
congratulation, grātŭlātĭo, *f*
congregate, *v.i,* sē congrĕgare (1 *reflex.*)
congress, concĭlĭum, *n*, conventus, *m*
congruous, congrŭens
conjecture, *nn,* coniectūra, *f*
conjecture, *v.i,* cōnĭcĭo (3)
conjugate, *v.t,* dēclĭno (1)
conjunction (**grammar**), coniunctĭo, *f*
conjure, *v.i* (**perform tricks**), praestigĭis ūtor (3 *dep.*); (**image**) cōgĭto (1)
conjurer, măgus, *m*
connect, *v.t,* coniungo (3)
connected, coniunctus
connection, coniunctĭo, *f*; (**by marriage**), affĭnĭtas, *f*
connive at, *v.i,* connīvĕo (2) in (*with abl*)
connoisseur, *use vb,* stŭdĕo (2) (**to be keen on**)
conquer, *v.t,* vinco (3), sŭpĕro (1)
conqueror, victor, *m*
conquest, victōrĭa, *f*

conscience, conscĭentĭa, *f*
conscientious, rēlĭgĭōsus
conscientiousness, fĭdes, *f*
conscious, conscĭus
consciously, *adv, use adj,* scĭens (knowing)
consciousness, conscĭentĭa, *f*, sensus, *m*
conscript (recruit), tīro, *m*
consecrate, *v.t,* conscĕro (1)
consecrated, săcer
consecutive, contĭnŭus
consent, *nn,* consensus, *m*; **(by the — of),** consensu;
consent to, *v.i,* assentĭo (4)
consequence (result), exĭtus, *m*; **(importance),** mōmentum, *n*; **(in — of),** *prep,* propter (*with acc*)
consequent, sĕquens
consequently, *adv,* ĭgĭtur, ĭtăque
conserve, *v.t,* conservo (1)
consider, *v.t,* cōgĭto (1), dēlĭbĕro (1), existĭmo (1);(— **with respect),** respĭcĭo (3)
considerable, ălĭquantus
considerate, hūmānus
consideratenesss, hūmānĭtas, *f*
consideration, consīdĕrātĭo, *f*; **(regard),** rătĭo, *f*
considering, *conj,* ut
consign, *v.t,* mando (1), committo (3)
consignment (of goods), merces, *f.pl*
consist of, *v.i,* consisto (3) **in** (*with abl*)
consistency, constantĭa, *f*
consistent (constant), constans; **(consistent with),** consentānĕus
console, *v.t,* consōlor (1 *dep.*)
consolidate, *v.t,* firmo (1), sŏlĭdo (1)
consonant, consŏnans littĕra
consort (husband), mărĭtus, *m*; **(wife),** mărĭta, *f*
consort with, *v.i,* ūtor (3 *dep*) (*with abl*)
conspicuous, mănĭfestus, insignis
conspiracy, coniūrātĭo, *f*
conspirator, coniūrātus, *m*
conspire, *v.i,* coniūro (1)
constable, dĕcŭrĭo, *m*, lictor, *m*
constancy, fĭdes, *f*; **(steadiness),** constantĭa, *f*, fĭdēlĭtas, *f*
constant, fĭdēlis, constans
constellation, sīdus, *n*
consternation, păvor, *m*
constituent parts, ĕlĕmenta, *n.pl*
constitute, *v.t,* constĭtŭo (3), compōno (3), crĕo (1)
constitution (of a state), respūblĭca, *f*; **(of a body),** hăbĭtus, *m*
constitutional, lēgĭtĭmus
constrain, *v.t,* cōgo 3), compello (3)
construct, *v.t,* făbrĭcor (1 *dep.*), exstrŭo (3)
construction (act of —), făbrĭcātĭo, *f*; **(method),** fīgūra, *f*, structūra, *f*
construe, *v.t,* interprĕtor (1 *dep*)
consul, consul, *m*
consulship, consŭlātus, *m*
consult, *v.t,* consŭlo (3); *v.i,* dēlĭbĕro (1); **(— someone's interests),** consŭlo (3) (*with dat*)
consultation, collŏquĭum, *n*
consume, *v.t,* consumo (3), confĭcĭo (3)
consummate, *v.t,* consummo (1), perfĭcĭo (3)
consummate, *adj,* summus
consummation, consummātĭo, *f*
consumption, consumptĭo, *f*
contact, tactus, *m*
contagion, contāgĭo, *f*
contain, *v.t,* contĭnĕo (2)
contaminate, *v.t,* contāmĭno (1)
contamination, contāgĭo, *f*, măcŭla, *f*
contemplate, *v.t,* contemplor (1 *dep.*)
contemplation (study), mĕdĭtātĭo, *f*
contempory, aequālis
contempt, contemptus, *m*
contemptible, contemnendus
contend, *v.i,* contendo (3), certo (1), pugno (1); **(argue),** *v.t,* affirmo (1)
content, contentus
content, *v.t,* sătisfăcĭo (3) (*with dat.*); *v.i,* **(be content),** sătis hăbĕo (2)
contentment, aequus ănĭmus, *m*
contest, *nn,* certāmen, *n*, pugna, *f*
contest, *v.t,* certo (1), contendo (3)
contestant, pugnātor, *m*, pĕtĭtor, *m*
contiguous, contĭgŭus, confĭnis
continent, *adj,* contĭnens
continent, *nn,* contĭnens, *f*
contingency, cāsus, *m*
continual, perpĕtuus, contĭnens
continually, *adv,* perpĕtuo, contĭnenter
continuation, perpĕtŭĭtas, *f*
continue, *v.t,* prōdūco (3), prōrŏgo (1); *v.i,* mănĕo (2)
continuity, perpĕtŭĭtas, *f*
continuous, contĭnens
contort, *v.t,* torquĕo (2)
contour, fīgūra, *f*
contraband, *adj,* vĕtĭtus
contract, *nn,* pactum, *n*
contract, *v.i,* **(grow smaller),** sē contrăhĕre (3 *reflex*); *v.t,* contrăho (3)
contraction, contractĭo, *f*
contractor, conductor, *m*
contradict, *v.t,* contrādĭco (3) (*with dat*)

For List of Abbreviations used, turn to pages 3, 4

contradiction, contrādictĭo, *f*; **(inconsistency),** rĕpugnantĭa, *f*
contradictory, rĕpugnans
contrary, *adj*, adversus, contrārĭus; **(— to),** *prep*, contrā (*with acc*); **the contrary,** *nn*, contrārĭum, *n*; **(on the —),** *adv*, contrā
contrast, *v.t*, confĕro (*irreg*); *v.i*, discrĕpo (1)
contravene, *v.t*, vĭŏlo (1)
contribute, *v.t*, confĕro (*irreg*)
contribution, collātĭo, *f*, trĭbūtum, *n*
contrivance (gadget), māchĭna, *f*
contrive, *v.t*, **(think out),** excōgĭto (1)
control, *v.t*, mŏdĕror (1 *dep*) (*with dat*); **(guide),** rĕgo (3)
control, *nn*, pŏtestas, *f*, tempĕrantĭa, *f*
controversy, contrōversĭa, *f*
contumacious, pertĭnax
contumacy, pertĭnācĭa, *f*
contumely, contŭmēlĭa, *f*
convalescent, convălescens
convenience, commŏdĭtas, *f*, opportūnĭtas, *f*
convenient, commŏdus, opportūnus
convention (meeting), conventus, *m*; **(agreement),** conventĭo, *f*
converge, *v.i*, ĕŏdem vergo (3)
conversation, sermo, *m*, collŏquĭum, *n*
converse, *v.i*, collŏquor (3 *dep*)
conversion, commūtātĭo, *f*
convert, *v.t*, mūto (1), converto (3)
convex, convexus
convey, *v.t*, vĕho (3), porto (1)
conveyance (act of —), vectūra, *f*; **(vehicle),** vĕhĭcŭlum, *n*
convict, *v.t*, damno (1)
conviction (belief), *use phr*, persuāsum est (*with dat. of person*), e.g. persuāsum est mĭhi **(it is my conviction); (convicting),** damnātĭo, *f*
convince, *v.t*, persuādĕo (2) (*with dat.*)
conviviality, hĭlārĭtas, *f*
convoke, *v.t*, convŏco (1)
convoy, *nn*, commĕātus, *m*; **(escort),** praesĭdĭum, *n*
convulse, *v.t*, concŭtĭo (3), ăgĭto (1)
convulsion, tŭmultus, *m*, mōtus, *m*; **(medical),** convulsĭo, *f*
cook, *nn*, cŏquus, *m*
cook, *v.t*, cŏquo (3)
cool, frīgĭdus; **(of mind),** lentus
cool, *v.t*, rĕfrīgĕro (1); *v.i*, rĕfrīgĕror (1 *pass*)
coolly, *adv*, frīgĭde, lentē
coolness, frīgus, *n*
co-operate with, *v.t*, adiŭvo (1)
co-operation, auxĭlĭum, *n*, **(help)**
cope with, *v.i*, congrĕdĭor (3 *dep.*)
copious, largus, cōpĭōsus
copper, aes, *n*
copper, *adj*, aēnĕus
coppice, dūmētum, *n*
copy, exemplum, *n*
copy, *v.t*, ĭmĭtor (1 *dep*), dēscrĭbo (3)
coral, cŏrălĭum, *n*
cord, fūnis, *m*
cordial, *adj*, bĕnignus
cordiality, bĕnignĭtas, *f*
cordon, cŏrōna, *f*
core, nucleus, *m*
cork, *nn*, cortex, *m*, *f*
corn, frūmentum, *n*; **(-crop),** sĕges, *f*; **(on the foot),** clāvus, *m*
corner, angŭlus, *m*
cornice, cŏrōna, *f*
coronation, *use* crĕo (1) **(elect to office)**
coroner, quaesĭtor, *m*
corporal, *adj*, corpŏrĕus
corporal, *nn*, dĕcŭrĭo, *m*
corps (company), mānus, *f*
corpse, cădāver, *n*, corpus, *n*
corpulence, ŏbēsĭtas, *f*
corpulent, ŏbēsus
correct, rectus, pūrus
correct, *v.t*, corrĭgo (3), ēmendo (1)
correction, ēmendātĭo, *f*; **(chastisement),** castĭgātĭo, *f*
correctly, *adv*, rectē
correctness, vērĭtas, *f*
correspond, *v.i*, **(agree with),** convĕnĭo (4) (*with dat*); **(write),** littĕras mitto (3) et accĭpĭo (3) **(send and receive letters)**
correspondence, missĭo et acceptĭo ĕpistŏlārum **(sending and receiving of letters)**
corresponding, par, gĕmellus
corroborate, *v.t*, confirmo (1)
corrode, *v.t*, rōdo (3), ĕdo (3)
corrosive, mordax
corrupt, *v.t*, corrumpo (3)
corrupt, *adj*, corruptus
corruption, dĕprāvātĭo, *f*
corselet, lōrīca, *f*
cost, *nn*, prĕtĭum, *n*, sumptus, *m*
cost, *v.i*, sto (1) (*with dat. of person and abl. or genit. of price*) e.g. **the victory cost the Carthaginians much bloodshed:** victōrĭa stĕtit Poenis multo sanguĭne
costly, *adj*, prĕtĭōsus
costume, hăbĭtus, *m*

cot, lectŭlus, *m*
cottage, căsa, *f*
cotton, gossypĭum, *n*
couch, lectus, *m*
couch, *v.i*, subsīdo (3); *v.t* (— **a weapon**), intendo (3)
cough, *nn*, tussis, *f*
cough, *v.i*, tussĭo (4)
council, concĭlĭum, *n*
counsel (advice), consĭlĭum, *n*; **(lawyer)**, pătrōnus, *m*
count, *v.t*, nūmĕro (1); (— **upon, trust**), confīdo (3) (*with dat*)
countenance, *nn*, vultus, *m*
countenance, *v.t*, permitto (3), făvĕo (2), indulgĕo (2)
counter (in shop), mensa, *f*; **(for counting)**, calcŭlus, *m*
counter, *adv*, contra
counteract, *v.t*, obsisto (3) (*with dat.*)
counter-balance, *v.t*, exaequo (1)
counterfeit, *adj*, ădultĕrīnus, fictus
counterfeit, *v.t*, sĭmŭlo (1), fingo (3)
counterpart, res gĕmella **(paired, twin thing)**
countless, innŭmĕrābĭlis
country (fatherland), pătriă, *f*; **(countryside)**, rūs, *n*; **(region)**, rĕgĭo, *f*
country-house, villa, *f*
countryman (of the same country), cīvis, *c*; **(living in the countryside)**, rustĭcus, *m*
couple, *nn*, **(pair)**, pār *n*
couple, *v.t*, coniungo (3)
courage, virtus, *f*, ănĭmus, *m*
courageous, fortis, ācer, fĕrox
courier (messenger), nuntĭus, *m*
course (motion), cursus, *m*; **(route)**, vĭa, *f*, ĭter *n*; **(plan)**, rătĭo, *f*; **(race —)**, circus, *m*; **(of —)**, *adv*, nīmīrum, certē
court (— of justice), iūdĭcĭum, *n*; **(judges themselves)**, iūdĭces, *m. pl*; **(palace)**, aula, *f*, dŏmus, (*f*) rēgis **(the house of the king)**; **(courtyard)**, ārĕa, *f*
court, *v.t*, cŏlo (3)
court-martial, *use phr.* in castris iudĭcare (1) **(to try in camp)**
courteous, cōmis, hūmānus
courtesy, cōmĭtas, *f*, hūmānĭtas, *f*
courtier, aulĭcus, *m*
courtship, ămor, *m*
cousin, consōrbrīnus, *m* (. . . a), *f*
covenant, pactum, *n*
cover, *v.t*, tĕgo (3); **(conceal)** occulto (1)
cover, covering, *nn*, tĕgŭmen, *n*; **(lid)**, ŏpĕrīmentum, *n*
coverlet, strāgŭlum, *n*
covert, *nn*, dūmētum, *n*
covet, *v.t*, cŭpĭo (3)
covetous, ăvārus, ăvĭdus, cŭpĭdus
covetousness, ăvārĭtĭa, *f*, cŭpĭdĭtas, *f*
cow, vacca, *f*
cow, *v.t*, terrĕo (2), dŏmo (1) **(tame)**
coward, ignāvus, *m*
cowardice, ignāvĭa, *f*
cowardly, *adj*, ignāvus
cowl, cŭcullus, *m*
coy (bashful), vĕrēcundus
crab, cancer, *m*
crabbed, mōrōsus
crack, *nn*, **(noise)**, crĕpĭtus, *m*; **(chink)**, rīma, *f*
crack, *v.t*, findo (3), frango (3); *v.i*, **(open up)**, dĕhisco (3); **(sound)**, crĕpo (1)
cradle, cūnae, *f. pl.*
craft (deceit), dŏlus, *m*; **(skill)**, artĭfĭcĭum, *n*; **(boat)**, rătis, *f*, nāvis, *f*
craftsman, ŏpĭfex, *m*
crafty, callĭdus
crag, scŏpŭlus, *m*
cram, *v.t*, confercĭo (4)
cramp, *v.t*, comprĭmo (3)
crane (bird), grus, *m*, *f*; **(machine)**, tollĕno, *f*
crank, uncus, *m*
cranny, rīma, *f*
crash, *nn*, frăgor, *m*
crash, *v.i*, (noise), strĕpo (3); **(bring into collision)**, *v.t*, collĭdo (3)
crate, corbis, *m*
crater, crāter, *m*
crave for, *v.t*, ōro (1), appĕto (3)
craving, *nn*, dēsīdĕrĭum, *n*
crawl, *v.i*, rĕpo (3)
crayon, crēta, *f*
crazy, cerrĭtus, dēmens
creak, *v.i*, crĕpo (1)
creaking, *nn*, strĭdor, *m*, crĕpĭtus, *m*
crease, *nn*, rūga, *f*
crease, *v.t*, rūgo (1)
create, *v.t*, crĕo (1)
creation (act of —), crĕātĭo, *f*; **(making)**, făbrīcātĭo, *f*; **(universe)**, mundus, *m*
creator, auctor, *m*, crĕātor, *m*
creature, ănĭmal, *n*
credence (belief), fĭdes, *f*
credible, crēdĭbĭlis
credit (belief or commercial credit), fĭdes, *f*; **(reputation)**, existīmātĭo, *f*
credit, *v.t*, **(believe)**, crēdo (3); (— **an account, person, etc.**), acceptum rĕfĕro (*irreg*) (*with dat. of person*)
creditable (honourable), hŏnestus

creditor, crēdĭtor, *m*
credulous, crēdŭlus, *m*
creek, sĭnus, *m*
creep, *v.i*, serpo (3), rēpo (3)
crescent, lūna, *f*, **(crescent moon)**
crescent-shaped, lūnātus
crest, crista, *f*
crested, cristātus
crest-fallen, dēmissus
crevice, rīma, *f*
crew, nautae, *m*, *pl*, rēmĭges, *m*, *pl*
crib (child's bed), lectŭlus, *m*
cricket (insect), cĭcāda, *f*
crime, făcĭnus, *n*, scĕlus, *n*
criminal, *nn*, hŏmo sons, hŏmo nŏcens
criminal, *adj*, nĕfārĭus, scĕlestus
crimson, *adj*, coccĭnĕus
cringe to, *v.i*, ădŭlor (1 *dep*)
cripple, *nn*, hŏmo claudus
cripple, *v.t*, dēbīlĭto (1); **(— a person),** claudum reddo (3)
crippled, dēbĭlis, claudus
crisis, discrĭmen, *n*
crisp, frăgĭlis
critic, existĭmātor, *m*, censor, *m*
critical, ēlĕgans; **(of a crisis, etc.),** *use* discrĭmen, *n* **(crisis)**
criticise, *v.t*, **(find fault)** rĕprĕhendo (3), iŭdĭco (1)
croak, *nn*, quĕrēla, *f*, clāmor, *m*
croak, *v.i*, căno (3), crŏcĭo (4)
crockery, fictĭlĭa, *n.pl*
crocodile, crŏcŏdīlus, *m*
crocus, crŏcus, *m*
crook (shepherd's —), pĕdum, *n*
crooked, curvus; **(bad, etc.),** prāvus
crop (of corn), sĕges, *f*, frūges, *f*, *pl*; **(of a bird),** inglŭvĭes, *f*
crop, *v.t*, tondĕo (2)
cross, *nn*, crux, *f*
cross, *adj*, transversus; **(annoyed),** īrātus
cross, *v.i. and v.t*, transĕo (4 *irreg*)
cross-examine, *v.t*, interrŏgo (1)
crossing (act of —), transĭtus, *m*; **(cross-road),** compĭtum, *n*
crouch, *v.i*, sē dēmittĕre (3 *reflex*)
crow (bird), cornix, *f*
crow, *v.i*, **(of a cock),** căno (3); **(boast),** sē iactare (1 *reflex*)
crowd, turba, *f*
crowd together, *v.i*, congrĕgor (1 *dep*); *v.t*, stīpo (1), frĕquento (1)
crowded, confertus, cĕlĕber
crown, cŏrōna, *f*; **(royal),** dĭādēma, *n*; **(of head, etc.),** vertex, *m*
crown, *v.t*, cŏrōno (1)
crucifixion, *use phr. with* crux, *f*, **(cross)**
crucify, *v.t*, crŭce affĭcĭo (3)
crude, rŭdis
cruel, crūdēlis, atrox
cruelty, crūdēlĭtas, *f*
cruet, gutus, *m*
cruise, *nn*, nāvĭgātĭo, *f*
cruise, *v.i*, nāvĭgo (1)
crumb, mīca, *f*
crumble, *v.t*, tĕro (3); *v.i*, corrŭo (3)
crumple, *v.t*, rūgo (1)
crush, *v.t*, contundo (3), opprĭmo (3)
crust, crusta, *f*
crutch, băcŭlum, *n*
cry, *nn*, clāmor, *m*, vox, *f*
cry, *v.i*, clāmo (1); **(weep),** lacrĭmo (1)
crystal, *nn*, crystallum, *n*
cub, cătŭlus, *m*
cube, tessĕra, *f*
cubic, cŭbĭcus
cuckoo, cŭcŭlus, *m*, coccyx, *m*
cucumber, cŭcŭmis, *m*
cudgel, fustis, *m*
cudgel, *v.t*, verbĕro (1), mulco (1)
cue, signum, *n*
cuff, *nn*, **(blow),** cŏlăphus, *m*, ălăpa,
cuff, *v.t*, incŭtĭo (3)
cuirass, lōrĭca, *f*, thōrax, *m*
culminate, *use adj*, summus **(topmost)**
culpable, culpandus, nŏcens
culprit, hŏmo nŏcens
cultivate, *v.t*, cŏlo (3)
cultivation, cultus, *m*, cultūra, *f*
cultivator, cultor, *m*
culture, cultus, *m*, cultūra, *f*
cumbersome, inhăbĭlis
cunning, *adj*, callĭdus, dŏlōsus
cunning, *nn*, callĭdĭtas, *f*, dŏlus, *m*
cup, pōcŭlum, *n*
cupboard, armārĭum, *n*
cupidity, cŭpĭdĭtas, *f*
cupola, thŏlus, *m*
curate, săcerdos, *c*, **(priest)**
curator, cūrātor, *m*
curb, *v.t*, frēno (1), cŏhĭbĕo (2)
curdle, *v.t*, cōgo (3), cŏăgŭlo (1); *v.i*, concresco (3)
cure, *nn*, sānātĭo, *f*
cure, *v.t*, mĕdĕor (2 *dep*) (*with dat.*)
curiosity, stŭdĭum, *n*
curious (inquisitive), cūrĭōsus; **(rare),** rārus
curl, *v.t*, crispo (1)
curl, *nn*, cincinnus, *m*
curly, cincinnātus
currant, ăcĭnus, *m*
currency, mŏnēta, *f*, nummi, *m. pl*
current, *nn*, **(of river),** flūmen, *n*
current, *adj*, **(present),** hic; **(general),** ūsĭtātus

curse, *nn,* imprĕcātĭo, *f,* dīrae, *f. pl*
curse, *v.t,* exsĕcror (1 *dep.*)
cursed, exsĕcrābĭlis
cursorily, *adv,* summātim, brĕvĭter
curt, brĕvis
curtail, *v.t,* arto (1)
curtain, aulaeum, *n*
curve, *nn,* flexus, *m*
curve, *v.t,* flecto (3), curvo (1)
curved, curvātus
cushion, pulvīnar, *n*
custodian, cūrātor, *m*
custody (keeping), custōdĭa, *f*; **(imprisonment),** vincŭla, *n.pl*
custom, mos, *m,* consŭētūdo, *f*; **(— duty),** portōrĭum, *n*
customary, ūsĭtātus, sŏlĭtus
customer, emptor, *m*
cut, *nn,* **(incision),** incīsĭo, *f*; **(blow),** ictus, *m,* plāga, *f*
cut, *v.t,* sĕco (1), caedo (3); **(— away),** abscīdo (3); **(— down),** succīdo (3); **(— off),** praecīdo (3); **(— off from communications, supplies, etc.)** interclūdo (3); **(— out),** excīdo (3); **(— short),** praecīdo (3); **(— to pieces),** concīdo (3), trŭcĭdo (1)
cutaneous, *use genit. of* cūtis **(skin)**
cutlass, glădĭus, *m*
cutlery, cultri, *m. pl* **(knives)**
cutter (boat), phăsēlus, *m,* cĕlox, *f*
cutting, *adj,* **(biting),** mordax
cuttle-fish, sēpĭa, *f*
cycle (circle), orbĭs, *m*
cygnet, pullus, *m*
cylinder, cȳlindrus, *m*
cymbal, cymbălum, *n*
cynic, cȳnĭcus, *m*
cynical, mordax, diffĭcĭlis
cynicism, dūrĭtĭa, *f*
cypress, cupressus, *f*

D

dab, *v.t,* illĭdo (3)
dabble in, *v.t,* attingo (3)
daffodil, narcissus, *m*
dagger, pūgĭo, *m*
daily *adj,* quŏtĭdĭānus
daily, *adv,* quŏtĭdĭē
daintiness (of manners), fastĭdĭum, *n*
dainty (things), dēlĭcātus; **(people),** fastĭdĭōsus
daisy, bellis, *f*
dale, valles, *f*
dalliance, lūsus, *m*
dally, *v.i,* **(delay),** mŏror (1 *dep*)
dam (breakwater), mōles, *f*
dam, *v.t,* obstrŭo (3)
damage, *nn,* dētrīmentum, *n,* damnum, *n*
damage, *v.t,* laedo (3), affīgo (3)
dame, dŏmĭna, *f,* mātrōna, *f*
damn, *v.t,* damno (1)
damp, *adj,* hūmĭdus
damp, *v.t,* hūmecto (1); **(enthusiasm, etc.),** immĭnŭo (3) **(lessen)**
damp, *nn,* hūmor, *m*
dance, *v.i,* salto (1)
dance, *nn,* saltātus, *m*
dancer, saltātor, *m* (. . . trix, *f*)
dandy, hŏmo lĕpĭdus, ēlĕgans, bellus
danger, pĕrĭcŭlum, *n*
dangerous, pĕrĭcŭlōsus
dangle, *v.i,* pendĕo (2)
dank, hūmĭdus, ūvĭdus
dapper (spruce), nĭtĭdus
dappled, măcŭlōsus
dare, *v.i,* audĕo (2 *semi-dep*) mŏllĭor (4 *dep*)
daring, *adj,* audax
daring, *nn,* audācĭa, *f*
dark, *adj,* obscūrus tĕnĕbrōsus; **(in colour),** fuscus
dark, darkness, *nn,* tĕnĕbrae, *f. pl*
darken, *v.t,* obscūro (1), occaeco (1)
darling, *nn,* dēlĭcĭae, *f. pl*; *adj,* mellĭtus
darn, *v.t,* sarcĭo (4)
dart, *nn,* tēlum, *n,* iăcŭlum, *n*
dart, *v.i,* **(rush),** *use compound of* vŏlo (1) **(to fly)**
dash, *nn,* **(rush),** *use vb,* vŏlo (1) **(to fly)**
dash, *v.i,* prōvŏlo (1), rŭo (3); *v.t,* affīgo (3), impingo (3)
dashing, *adj,* ălăcer
dastardly, *adj,* ignāvus
date (fruit), palmŭla, *f*; **(time),** dĭes, *f*
date, *v.t,* **(something),** dĭem ascrĭbo (3) in (*with abl.*)
daub, *v.t,* oblĭno (3)
daughter, fīlĭa, *f*; **(— in-law),** nŭrus,
daunt, *v.t,* percello (3)
dauntless, impăvĭdus
dawdle, *v.i,* cesso (1)
dawn, prĭma lux, aurōra, *f*
dawn, *v.i,* dīlŭcesco (3)
day, dĭes, *m, f*; **(at — break),** *adv. phr,* prĭmā lūce; **(by —),** *adv,* interdĭu; **(every —),** *adv,* quŏtĭdĭe; **(late in the —),** multo dĭe; **(on the — before),** prĭdĭe; **(on the next —),** postrĭdĭe; **(— time),** tempus dĭurnum, *n*
daze, *v.t,* stŭpĕfăcĭo (3)
dazzle, *v.t,* perstringo (3)

For List of Abbreviations used, turn to pages 3, 4

dazzling, splendĭdus
dead, *adj*, mortŭus; (**the dead or departed**), mānes, *m. pl*; (**a — body**), corpus, *n*
deaden, *v.t*, (**senses, etc.**), hĕbĕto (1)
deadly, *adj*, mortĭfer, pernĭcĭōsus, fūnestus
deaf, surdus
deafen, *v.t*, exsurdo (1), obtundo (3)
deafness, surdĭtas, *f*
deal (**a good-,**), ălĭquantum, (**business**) nĕgōtĭum, *n*
deal, *v.t*, (**distribute**), distrĭbŭo (3); mētĭor (4 *dep.*); *v.i*, (**deal with**), ăgo (3) cum (*with abl*)
dealer, mercātor, *m*
dealings, *nn*, ūsus, *m*, commercĭum, *n*
dear, cārus; (**of price**), prĕtĭōsus
dearly, *adv*, (**at a high price**), magni
death, mors, *f*
death-bed (**on his —**), *use adj*, mŏrĭens (**dying**)
deathless, immortālis
debar, *v.t*, exclūdo (3)
debase, *v.t*, dēmitto (3), vĭtĭo (1)
debate, contrōversĭa, *f*
debate, *v.t*, dispūto (1), discepto (1)
debater, dispūtātor, *m*
debauch, *v.t*, corrumpo (3)
debauchery, stŭprum, *n*
debit, *nn*, expensum, *n*
debit, *v.t*, expensum fĕro (*irreg*) (*with dat*)
debt, aes ălĭēnum, *n*
debtor, dēbĭtor, *m*
debut, ĭnĭtĭum, *n*
decamp, *v.i*, castra mŏvĕo (2); discēdo (3)
decant, *v.t*, diffundo (3)
decanter, lăgēna, *f*
decapitate, *v.t*, sĕcūri fĕrĭo (4)
decay, *nn*, tābes, *f*, dēmĭnūtĭo, *f*
decay, *v.i*, dīlābor (3 *dep*), tābesco (3)
decease, dēcessus, *m*
deceased, *adj*, mortŭus
deceit, fraus, *f*, dŏlus, *m*
deceitful, fallax
deceive, *v.t*, dēcĭpĭo (3), fallo (3)
December, Dĕcember (mensis)
decency, dĕcōrum, *n*, hŏnestas, *f*
decent, dĕcōrus, hŏnestus
deception, fraus, *f*, dŏlus, *m*
deceptive, fallax
decide, *v.t*, constĭtŭo (3), stătŭo (3), dēcerno (3)
decided (**persons**), firmus; (**things**), certus
decidedly, *adv*, (**assuredly**), plānē, vēro
decimate, *v.t*, dĕcĭmo (1)
decision, arbitrĭum, *n*, dēcrētum *n*
deck, pons, *m*
deck, *v.t*, orno (1)
declaim, *v.t*, dēclāmo (1)
declaration, prŏfessĭo, *f* (**— of war**), dēnuntĭātĭo, *f* (belli)
declare, *v.i*, prŏfĭtĕor (2 *dep*), affirmo (1); *v.t*, dēclāro (1); (**— war**), dēnuntĭo (1) (bellum)
decline, *nn*, dēmĭnūtĭo, *f* (**diminution**)
decline, *v.t*, (**refuse**), rĕcūso (1); *v.i*, inclīno (1), dēcresco (3)
declivity, clīvus, *m*
decompose, *v.t*, solvo (3); *v.i*, solvor (3 *pass*)
decomposition, sŏlūtĭo, *f*
decorate, *v.t*, orno (1), dĕcŏro (1)
decoration (**ornament**), ornāmentum, *n*, dĕcus, *n*; (**badge**), insigne, *n*
decorous, dĕcōrus
decorum, dĕcōrum, *n*, pŭdor, *m*
decoy, illex, *m*; (**bait**), esca, *f*
decrease, *nn*, dēmĭnūtĭo, *f*
decrease, *v.i*, dēcresco (3); *v.t*, mĭnŭo (3)
decree, *nn*, dēcrētum, *n*; (**— of the Senate**), consultum, *n*
decree, *v.t*, dēcerno (3), censĕo (2)
decrepit, dēcrĕpĭtus, dēbĭlis
decry, *v.t*, vĭtŭpĕro (1), obtrecto (1)
dedicate, *v.t*, consĕcro (1)
deduce, *v.t*, conclūdo (3)
deduct, *v.t*, dēdūco (3)
deduction (**taking away**), dēductĭo, *f*
deed, factum, *n*, făcĭnus, *n*; (**legal**), tăbŭla, *f*
deem, *v.t*, pŭto (1)
deep, *nn*, (**the sea**), altum, *n*
deep, altus; (**of sound**), grăvis
deepen, *v.t*, altĭōrem reddo (3)
deeply, *adv*, altē, pĕnĭtus (**deep within**)
deer, cervus, *m* cerva, *f*
deface, *v.t*, dēformo (1)
defame, *v.t*, mălĕdĭco (3) (*with dat*)
default, *v.i*, dēfĭcĭo (3) (**fail to answer bail**), vădĭmōnĭum dēsĕro (3)
defeat, *nn*, clādes, *f*
defeat, *v.t*, vinco (3), sŭpĕro (1)
defect, vĭtĭum, *n*
defective, vĭtĭōsus
defence (**protection**), praesĭdĭum, *n*; (**legal**), dēfensĭo, *f*
defenceless, ĭnermis

defend, *v.t,* dēfendo (3)
defendant (in a trial), rĕus, *m*
defender, dēfensor, *m*; **(in court),** pătrōnus, *m*
defer, *v.t,* **(put off),** differo (*irreg*); *v.i,* **(show deference to),** cēdo (3)
deference, observantĭa, *f*
defiance, prōvŏcātĭo, *f*
defiant, fĕrox
deficiency, dēfectĭo, *f*
deficient, inops, mancus
deficit, lăcūna, *f*
defile, *v.t,* contāmĭno (1)
defile, *nn,* angustĭae, *f, pl*
define, *v.t,* circumscrĭbo (3)
definite, constĭtūtus, certus
definition, dēfīnĭtĭo, *f*
deflect, *v.t,* dēflecto (3)
deform, *v.t,* dēformo (1)
deformity, dēformĭtas, *f*
defraud, *v.t,* fraudo (1)
defray, *v.t,* suppēdĭto (1) **(supply)**
deft, doctus **(skilled)**
defy, *v.t* obsto (1), prōvŏco (1)
degenerate, *v.i,* dēgĕnĕro (1)
degenerate, *adj,* dēgĕner
degradation, ignōmĭnĭa, *f*
degrade, *v.t,* mŏvĕo (2), dē *or* ex (*with abl*), **(move down from);** dĕhŏnesto (1)
degree (interval, stage, rank), grĕdus, *m*; **(to such a degree),** *adv,* ădĕo; **(by degrees),** *adv,* **(gradually),** grădātim
deify, *v.t,* consĕcro (1)
deign, *v.t,* dignor (1 *dep*)
deity, dĕus, *m*
deject, *v.t,* afflīgo (3)
dejected, dēmissus, afflictus
dejection, maestĭtĭa, *f*
delay, *nn,* mŏra, *f*
delay, *v.i,* mŏror (1 *dep*), cunctor (1 *dep*); *v.t,* mŏror (1 *dep*), tardo (1)
delegate, *nn,* lēgātus, *m*
delegate, *v.t* **(depute),** lēgo (1), mando (1) (*with acc. of thing and dat. of person*)
delegation, lēgātĭo, *f*
deliberate, *adj,* consĭdĕrātus
deliberate, *v.t,* consŭlo (3), dēlĭbĕro (1)
deliberately, *adv,* consultō
deliberation, dēlĭbĕrātĭo, *f*
delicacy, subtīlĭtas, *f,* suāvĭtas, *f*; **(food),** cūpēdĭa, *n.pl*
delicate, subtīlis, tĕner; **(of health),** infirmus
delicious, suāvis
delight, *nn,* **(pleasure),** vŏluptas, *f*
delight, *v.t,* dēlecto (1); *v.i,* gaudĕo (2)
delightful, iūcundus, āmoenus
delineate, *v.t,* dēscrĭbo (3)
delinquency, dēlictum, *n*
delinquent, *nn,* peccātor, *m*
delirious, dēlīrus
delirium, dēlīrĭum, *n*
deliver, *v.t,* **(set free),** lĭbĕro (1); **(hand over),** do (1), trādo (3), dēdo (3); **(— a speech),** hăbĕo (2), ōrātĭonem
deliverance (freeing), lĭbĕrātĭo, *f*
deliverer, lĭbĕrātor, *m*
delivery (freeing), lĭbĕrātĭo, *f*; **(childbirth),** partus, *m*; **(of a speech),** ēlŏcūtĭo, *f*
delude, *v.t,* dēcĭpĭo (3)
deluge, dĭlŭvĭum, *n,* inundātĭo, *f*
delusion, error, *m*; **(trick),** fallācĭa, *f,* fraus, *f*
delusive (deceitful), fallax; **(empty),** vānus
demagogue, plēbĭcŏla, *c*
demand, *nn,* postŭlātĭo, *f*
demand, *v.t,* posco (3), postŭlo (1)
demean oneself, dēmittor (3 pass), sē dēmittĕre (3 *reflex*)
demeanour, mōres, *m. pl,* hăbĭtus, *m*
demented, dēmens
demise, *nn,* **(death),** dēcessus, *m,* mors, *f*
democracy, cīvĭtas pŏpŭlāris, *f*
democrat, plēbĭcŏla, *c*
demolish, *v.t,* dīrŭo (3), dēlĕo (2), dēmōlĭor (4 *dep.*)
demolition, ēversĭo, *f,* rŭīna, *f*
demon, daemŏnĭum, *n*
demonstrate, *v.t,* dēmonstro (1)
demonstration, dēmonstrātĭo, *f*
demur, *v.i,* haesĭto (1)
demure, *adj,* vĕrēcundus
den, lătĭbŭlum, *n*
denial, nĕgātĭo, *f*
denominate, *v.t,* nōmĭno (1)
denote, *v.t,* indĭco (1), signĭfĭco (1), nŏto (1)
denounce, *v.t,* (nōmen) dēfĕro (*irreg*)
dense, densus, confertus
density, crassĭtūdo, *f*
dent, nŏta, *f*
dentist, dentĭum mĕdĭcus, *m*
denude, *v.t,* nūdo (1)
deny, *v.t,* nĕgo (1), abnŭo (3)
depart, *v.i,* ăbĕo (4), discēdo (3)
departed (dead), mortŭus
department (of administration, etc.), prōvĭncĭa, *f*; **(part),** pars, *f*
departure, discessus, *m*
depend on, *v.i,* pendĕo (2) ex *or* in (*with abl*); **(rely on),** confīdo (3 *semi-dep*) (*with dat*)
dependant, *nn,* clĭens, *c*
dependence on, clĭentēla, *f*; **(reliance),** fĭdes, *f*

dependency (subject state), prōvincĭa, *f*
depict, *v.t*, dēscrĭbo (3), effingo (3)
deplorable, mĭsĕrābĭlis
deplore, *v.t*, dēplōro (1)
deploy, *v.t*, explĭco (1)
depopulate, *v.t*, pŏpŭlor (1 *dep*); vasto (1)
deport, *v.t*, dēporto (1); **(behave oneself)**, se gĕrĕre (3 *reflex*)
deportment, hăbĭtus, *m*
depose, *v.t*, mŏvĕo (2) (*with abl*)
deposit, *v.t*, dēpōno (3)
deposit, *nn*, dēpŏsĭtum, *n*
deprave, *v.t*, dēprāvo (1), corrumpo (3)
depravity, prāvĭtas, *f*
deprecate, *v.t*, dēprĕcor (1 *dep*)
depreciate, *v.t*, dētrăho (3); *v.i*, mĭnŭor (3 *pass*) **(grow less)**
depreciation (decrease), dēmĭnūtĭo, *f*; **(disparagement)**, obtrectātĭo, *f*
depredation, expĭlātĭo, *f*, praedātĭo, *f*
depress, *v.t*, dēprĭmo (3); **(spirits, etc.)**, infringo (3)
depression (sadness), tristĭtĭa, *f*
deprive, *v.t*, privo (1) (*with acc. of person deprived, and abl. of thing*)
depth, altĭtūdo, *f*
deputation, lēgātĭo, *f*
depute, *v.t*, lēgo (1), mando (1) (*with dat*)
deputy, lēgātus, *m*
deputy-governor, prōcūrātor, *m*
derange, *v.t*, perturbo (1)
deride, *v.t*, dērīdĕo (2)
derision, irrĭsĭo, *f*, rĭsus, *m*
derive (from), *v.t*, **(deduce)**, dūco (3), ab (*and abl*)
derogate from, *v.i*, dērŏgo (1) dē (*with abl*)
derogatory (remark), noxĭus
descend, *v.i*, dēscendo (3)
descendant, prōgĕnĭes, *f*
descent (lineage), prōgĕnĭes, *f*; **(movement)**, dēscensus, *m*; **(slope)**, dēclīve, *n*
describe, *v.t*, dēscrĭbo (3), expōno (3)
description, dēscriptĭo, *f*, narrātĭo, *f*
descry, *v.t*, conspĭcor (1 *dep*)
desecrate, *v.t*, prŏfāno (1)
desert (wilderness), sōlĭtūdo, *f*
desert, *v.t*, dēsĕro (3), rēlinquo (3)
deserted, dēsertus
deserter, perfŭga, *m*, transfŭga, *m*
deserve, *v.t*, mĕrĕor (2 *dep*); dignus esse (*irreg*) (*with abl*)
deservedly, *adv*, mĕrĭto
design, dēscriptĭo, *f*; **(plan)**, consĭlĭum, *n*
design, *v.t*, dēscrĭbo (3); **(intend)**, in ănĭmo hăbĕo (2)
designate, *v.t*, dēsigno (1)
designing, *adj*, callĭdus, dŏlōsus
desirable, optābĭlis
desire, *nn*, dēsīdĕrĭum, *n*, cŭpĭditas,
desire, *v.t*, cŭpĭo (3), opto (1)
desirous, cŭpĭdus
desist, *v.i*, dēsisto (3), dēsĭno (3)
desk, scrĭnĭum, *n*
desolate, dēsertus, sōlus
despair, *nn*, dēspērātĭo, *f*
despair, *v.i*, dēspēro (1)
despatch, *v.t* mitto (3); **(kill)**, interfĭcĭo (3)
despatch, *nn*, **(sending)**, dĭmissĭo, *f*; **(letter)**, littĕrae, *f. pl*; **(speed)**, cĕlĕrĭtas, *f*
desperate, dēspērātus; **(situation)**, extrēmus
desperation, dēspērātĭo, *f*
despicable, contemptus
despise, *v.t*, dēspĭcĭo (3), sperno (3)
despite, *prep*, contrā (*with acc*)
despoil, *v.t*, spŏlĭo (1)
despond, *v.i*, ănĭmum dēmitto (3)
despondent, *use adv. phr*, ănĭmo dēmisso
despot, dŏmĭnus, *m*
despotic, tȳrannĭcus, *m*
despotism, dŏmĭnātus, *m*
dessert, mensa sĕcunda **(second table)**
destination, *often* quo? **(whither)**, *or* ĕo **(to that place)**
destine, *v.t*, dēstĭno (1), dēsigno (1)
destiny, fātum, *n*
destitute, ĭnops
destroy, *v.t*, perdo (3), dēlĕo (2), ēverto (3)
destroyer, vastātor, *m*
destruction, pernĭcĭes, *f*, ēversĭo, *f*, exĭtĭum, *n*
destructive, pernĭcĭōsus
desultory, inconstans
detach, *v.t*, sēiungo (3), sēpăro (1)
detached, sēpărātus
detachment (of troops, etc.), mănus,
details, singŭla, *n.pl*
detail, *v.t*, explĭco (1)
detain, *v.t*, rĕtĭnĕo (2)
detect, *v.t*, dēprĕhendo (3), compĕrĭo (4)
deter, *v.t*, dēterrĕo (2), dēpello (3)
deteriorate, *v.i*, corrumpor (3 *pass*)
determinate, *adj*, certus
determination (resolution), constantĭa, *f*; **(intention)**, consĭlĭum, *n*
determine, *v.i and v.t*, constĭtŭo (3)
determined (resolute), firmus; **(fixed)**, certus

detest, *v.t,* ōdī (*v. defect*)
detestable, ŏdĭōsus
dethrone, *v.t,* regno pello (3) (**expel from sovereignty**)
detour, circŭĭtus, *m*
detract from, *v.t,* dētrăho (3) dē (*with abl*)
detriment, dētrīmentum, *n*
detrimental (to be —), *v.i,* esse (*irreg*) dētrīmento (*with dat*)
devastate, *v.t,* vasto (1)
devastation, vastātĭo, *f*
develop, *v.t,* explĭco (1), ēdŭco (1); *v.i,* cresco (3) (**grow**)
development, prōlātĭo, *f*; (**unfolding**), explĭcātĭo, *f*
deviate, *v.i,* dēclīno (1), discēdo (3)
deviation, dēclīnātĭo, *f*
device (contrivance), artĭfĭcium, *n*; (**emblem**), insigne, *n*; (**plan**), dŏlus, *m*
devil, daemŏnĭum, *n*
devilish, nĕfandus
devious, dēvĭus
devise, *v.t,* excōgĭto (1), fingo (3)
devoid, expers, văcŭus
devolve, *v.i,* obvĕnĭo (4); *v.t,* dēfĕro (*irreg*)
devote, *v.t,* dēdĭco (1), dēdo (3); (**consecrate**), dēvŏvĕo (2)
devoted, dēdĭtus, dēvōtus
devotion, stŭdĭum, *n*; (**love**), ămor, *m*
devour, *v.t,* dēvŏro (1), consūmo (3)
devouring, ĕdax
devout, pĭus, vĕnĕrābundus, rēlĭgĭōsus
dew, rōs, *m*
dexterity, sollertĭa, *f*, callĭdĭtas, *f*
dexterous, sollers, callĭdus
diadem, dĭădēma, *n*
diagonal, *adj,* dĭăgōnālis
diagram, forma, *f*
dial, sōlārĭum, *n*
dialect, dĭălectus, *f*
dialectics, dĭălectĭca, *n.pl*
dialogue, sermo, *m*; (**written**), dĭălŏgus, *m*
diameter, crassĭtūdo, *f*
diamond, ădāmas, *m*
diaphragm, praecordĭa, *n.pl*
diarrhoea, prōflŭvĭum, *n*
diary, commentārii dĭurni, *m. pl*
dice, tāli, *m. pl*; (**the game**), ălea, *f*
dictate, *v.t,* dicto (1); *v.i,* impĕro (1) (*with dat*)
dictation, dictātĭo, *f*
dictator, dictātor, *m*
dictatorial, impĕrĭōsus
dictatorship, dictātūra, *f*
dictionary, glossārĭum, *n*
die, *v.i,* mŏrĭor (3 *dep*), cădo (3)
diet, victus, *m*
differ, *v.i,* discrĕpo (1), diffĕro (*irreg*)
difference, discrīmen, *n*, dĭversĭtas, *f*; (**— of opinion**), discrĕpantĭa, *f*
different, ălĭus, dĭversus
difficult, diffĭcĭlis
difficulty, diffĭcultas, *f*; (**to be in —**), lăbōro (1); (**with —**), *adv,* aegrē
diffidence, diffĭdentĭa, *f*
diffident, diffīdens
diffuse, *v.t,* diffundo (3)
dig, *v.t,* fŏdĭo (3)
digest, *v.t,* concŏquo (3)
digestion, concoctĭo, *f*
dignified, grăvis
dignify, *v.t,* hŏnesto (1)
dignity (of character), grăvĭtas, *f*, dignĭtas, *f*
digress, *v.i,* dīgrĕdĭor (3 *dep*)
digression, dīgressĭo, *f*
dike (ditch), fossa, *f*; (**mound**), agger, *m*
dilapidated, rŭīnōsus
dilate, *v.t,* sē dīlātāre (1 *reflex*); *v.i* (**— upon**), dīlāto (1)
dilatory, ignāvus, lentus
dilemma (difficulty), angustĭae, *f. pl*
diligence, dīlīgentĭa, *f*
dilute, *v.t,* dīlŭo (3), miscĕo (2)
dim, *adj,* (**light, etc.**), obscūrus; (**dull, stupid**), hĕbes
dim, *v.t,* obscūro (1)
dimension, mŏdus, *m*
diminish, *v.t,* mīnŭo (3); *v.i,* mĭnŭor (3 *pass*)
diminution, dēmĭnūtĭo, *f*
diminutive, parvus, exĭgŭus
dimness, obscūrĭtas, *f*
dimple, lăcūna, *f*
din, strĕpĭtus, *m*
dine, *v.i,* cēno (1)
dingy, sordĭdus
dining-room, trīclīnĭum, *n*, cēnātĭo, *f*
dinner, cēna, *f*
by dint of, *prep,* per (*with acc*)
dip, *v.t,* mergo (3); *v.i,* mergor (3 *pass*)
diploma, dĭplōma, *n*
diplomacy (by —), per lĕgātos (**by means of diplomats**)
diplomat(ist), lēgātus, *m*
direct, *adj,* rectus
direct, *v.t,* dīrĭgo (3); (**order**), praecĭpĭo (3) (*with dat. of person*); (**show**), monstro (1)
direction (of motion), cursus, *m*; (**pointing out**), monstrātĭo, *f*; (**affairs**), admĭnĭstrātĭo, *f*; (**in different —s**), (*pl. adj*), dĭversi
director, cūrātor, *m*
dirt, sordes, *f*

For List of Abbreviations used, turn to pages 3, 4

dirty, sordĭdus, spurcus
dirty, *v.t*, inquĭno (1), foedo (1)
disable, *v.t*, dēbĭlĭto (1)
disabled, inhăbĭlis, confectus
disadvantage, incommŏdum, *n*
disadvantageous, incommŏdus
disaffected, ălĭēnātus
disaffection, ănĭmus āversus, *m*
disagree, *v.i*, discrĕpo (1), dissentĭo (4)
disagreeable (unpleasant), iniūcundus
disagreement, discrĕpantĭa, *f*, dissensĭo, *f*
disappear, *v.i*, ēvānesco (3), diffŭgĭo (3)
disappearance, exĭtus, *m*
disappoint, *v.t*, frustror (1 *dep*)
disappointment, incommŏdum, *n*
disapproval, rĕprĕhensĭo, *f*
disapprove, *v.t*, imprŏbo (1)
disarm, *v.t*, armis exŭo (3) **(strip of arms)**
disaster, clādes, *f*
disastrous, pernĭcĭōsus
disavow, *v.t*, diffĭtĕor (2 *dep*)
disavowal, infĭtĭātĭo, *f*
disband, *v.t*, dĭmitto (3)
disbelieve, *v.t*, non crēdo (3), diffĭdo (3) (*with dat*)
disburse, *v.t*, expendo (3)
disc, orbis, *m*
discard, *v.t*, rĕpŭdĭo (1)
discern, *v.t*, cerno (3)
discerning, *adj*, perspĭcax
discernment, intellĕgentĭa, *f*
discharge, *v.t*, **(missiles, etc.)**, ēmitto (3), iăcŭlor (1 *dep*); **(soldiers, etc.)**, dĭmitto (3); **(duties, etc.)**, fungor (3 *dep*) (*with abl*)
discharge, *nn*, ēmissĭo, *f*, dĭmissĭo, *f*
disciple, discĭpŭlus, *m*
discipline, disciplīna, *f*
discipline, *v.t*, instĭtŭo (3)
disclaim, *v.t*, nĕgo (1), rĕpŭdĭo (1)
disclose, *v.t*, āpĕrĭo (4)
disclosure, indĭcĭum, *n*
discolour, *v.t*, dēcŏlōro (1)
discomfiture, clādes, *f*
discomfort, incommŏdum, *n*
disconcert, *v.t*, perturbo (1)
disconnect, *v.t*, sēiungo (3)
disconsolate, maestus
discontented, mălĕ contentus
discontinue, *v.t*, intermitto (3)
discord (strife), discordĭa, *f*, dissensĭo, *f*
discount, *nn*, dēcessĭo, *f* **(decrease)**
discourage, *v.t*, ănĭmum dēmitto (3)
discouragement, ănĭmi infractĭo, *f*, *or* dēmissĭo, *f*
discourse, *v.i*, dissĕro (3)
discourse, *nn*, sermo, *m*, contĭo, *f*
discover, *v.t*, invĕnĭo (4), rĕpĕrio (4), cognosco (3)
discovery inventĭo, *f*; **(thing discovered)**, inventum, *n*
discredit, *v.t*, fĭdem abrŏgo (1)
discreditable, ĭnhŏnestus
discreet, consīdĕrātus, prūdens
discretion, prūdentĭa, *f*
discriminate, *v.t*, discerno (3)
discuss, *v.t*, discepto (1), dispŭto (1)
discussion, dispŭtātĭo, *f*
disdain, *v.t*, sperno (3), dēspĭcĭo (3)
disdain, *nn*, fastīdĭum, *n*
disdainful, fastīdĭōsus
disease, morbus, *m*
diseased, aeger
disembark, *v.t*, expōno (3); *v.i*, ēgrĕdĭor (3 *dep*)
disengage, *v.t*, **(release)**, solvo (3)
disengaged (at leisure), ōtĭōsus; **(free, loose)**, sŏlūtus
disentangle, *v.t*, explĭco (1)
disfigure, *v.t*, dēformo (1)
disgrace, *nn*, dēdĕcus, *n*, ignōmĭnĭa, *f*
disgrace, *v.t*, dēdĕcŏro (1)
disgraceful, turpis, flāgĭtĭōsus
disguise, *nn*, persōna, *f*, intĕgŭmentum, *n*
disguise, *v.t*, vestem mūto (1) **(change the clothes)**; dissĭmŭlo (1) **(pretend, hide)**
disgust, *nn*, fastīdĭum, *n*, taedĭum, *n*
disgust, *v.t*, taedĭum mŏvĕo (2) (*with dat*)
disgusted (to be —), *use impersonal vb*, pĭget (2) **(it disgusts)**
disgusting, foedus
dish, *nn*, pătĭna, *f*
dishearten, *v.t*, exănĭmo (1), percello (3)
dishonest, imprŏbus, perfĭdus
dishonesty, *f*, imprŏbĭtas, *f*
dishonour, *nn*, dēdĕcus, *n*
dishonour, *v.t*, dēdĕcŏro (1)
dishonourable, ĭnhŏnestus
disinclination, dēclīnātĭo, *f*
disinherit, *v.t*, exhērēdo (1)
disintegrate, *v.t*, solvo (3); *v.i*, solvor (3 *pass*)
disinterested, neutri făvens **(favouring neither side)**
disjointed, ĭnordĭnātus
disk, orbis, *m*
dislike, *nn*, ŏdĭum, *n*

dislike, *v.t,* ăbhorrĕo (2) ab (*with abl*); displĭcĕo (2)
dislocate, *v.t,* extorquĕo (2)
dislodge, *v.t,* dĕĭcĭo (3), pello (3)
disloyal, infĭdēlis
dismal, āter, maestus
dismantle, *v.t,* dīrĭpĭo (3)
dismay, *nn,* pāvor, *m*
dismay, *v.t,* consterno (1), perturbo (1)
dismiss, *v.t,* dĭmitto (3)
dismissal, dĭmissĭo, *f*
dismount, *v.i,* ex ĕquo dēscendo (3)
disobedience, *use phr. with vb,* pārĕo (obey)
disobedient, mălĕ pārens
disobey, *v.t,* mălĕ pārĕo (*with dat*)
disoblige, *v.t,* offendo (3)
disorder, *nn,* perturbātĭo, *f*
disorderly, *adv,* turbātus; **(crowd),** turbŭlentus
disown, *v.t,* infĭtĭor (1 *dep*)
disparage, *v.t,* dētrăho (3), obtrecto (1)
dispatch, *v.t,* (see **despatch**)
dispel, *v.t* dēpello (3), discŭtĭo (3)
dispense, *v.t* dispertĭor (4 *dep*) distrĭbŭo (3); **(— with),** dĭmitto (3)
dispersal, dissĭpātĭo, *f*
disperse, *v.t,* dispergo (3), dissĭpo (1), *v.i,* diffŭgĭo (3)
dispirited, *use adv. phr,* dēmisso ănĭmo
display, *nn,* ostentātĭo, *f*
display, *v.t,* ostento (1)
displease, *v.t,* displĭcĕo (2) (*with dat*)
displeasing, ŏdĭōsus
displeasure, offensĭo, *f*
disposal, ēmissĭo, *f*; **(power),** arbĭtrĭum, *n*
dispose, *v.t,* **(arrange),** constĭtŭo (3), dispōno (3); **(induce),** inclīno (1); **(get rid of),** ēlŭo (3)
disposed, inclīnātus
disposition (arrangement), dispŏsĭtĭo, *f*; **(of mind, etc.),** nātūra, *f*, ingĕnĭum, *n*
dispossess, *v.t,* dēturbo (1), dētrūdo (3)
disproportion, dissĭmĭlĭtūdo, *f*; **(of parts, etc.),** inconcinnĭtas, *f*
disprove, *v.t,* rĕfello (3), rĕfūto (1)
dispute, *nn,* contrōversĭa, *f*
dispute, *v.t,* dispŭto (1)
disqualify, *v.t,* **(prevent),** prŏhĭbĕo (2)
disregard, *nn,* neglĕgentĭa, *f*
disregard, *v.t,* neglĕgo (3)
disreputable, infāmis
disrespectful, contŭmax, insŏlens
dissatisfaction, mŏlestĭa, *f*
dissatisfied (to be —), *use impers. vb,* paenĭtet (*with acc. of subject and genit. of object*)
dissect, *v.t,* insĕco (1), persĕco (1)
dissemble, *v.i,* dissĭmŭlo (1)
dissension, discordĭa, *f*, dissensĭo, *f*
dissent, *v.i,* dissentĭo (4)
dissimilar, dissĭmĭlis
dissipate, *v.t,* dissĭpo (1)
dissipated, dissŏlūtus, lĭbĭdĭnōsus
dissipation, lĭcentĭa, *f*
dissolute, dissŏlūtus, lĭbĭdĭnōsus
dissolve, *v.t,* solvo (3), lĭquĕfăcĭo (3), *v.i,* solvor (3 *pass*), lĭquesco (3)
dissuade, *v.t,* dissuādĕo (2) (*with dat*)
distaff, cŏlus, *f*
distance, spătĭum, *n*; **(remoteness),** longinquĭtas, *f*; **(at a —),** *adv,* longē, prŏcul
distant, rĕmōtus, distans; **(to be —),** absum (*irreg*)
distaste, fastīdĭum, *n*
distasteful, iniūcundus
distemper (malady), morbus, *m*
distend, *v.t,* tendo (3)
distil, *v.t,* stillo (1)
distinct (separate), sēpărātus; **(clear),** clārus, mănĭfestus
distinction (difference), discrīmen, *n*; **(mark of honour),** hŏnor, *m*, dĕcus, *n*
distinctive, prŏprĭus
distinguish, *v.t,* distinguo (3); *v.i,* **(— oneself),** clāresco (3), ēmĭnĕo (2)
distinguished, insignis, clārus
distort, *v.t,* dētorquĕo (2)
distortion, distortĭo, *f*
distract, *v.t,* distrăho (3)
distracted (mentally), āmens, turbātus
distraction (mental), āmentĭa, *f*
distress, mĭsĕrĭa, *f*, dŏlor, *m*
distress, *v.t,* sollĭcĭto (1)
distressed, sollĭcĭtus
distribute, *v.t,* distrĭbŭo (3), partĭor (4 *dep*)
distribution, partītĭo, *f*
district, rĕgĭo, *f*
distrust, *nn,* diffĭdentĭa, *f*
distrust, *v.t,* diffĭdo (3) (*with dat*)
distrustful, diffĭdens
disturb, *v.t,* turbo (1)
disturbance, mōtus, *m*, tŭmultus, *m*
disunion, discordĭa, *f*
disunite, *v.t,* sēiungo (3), dissŏcĭo (1)
disused, dēsŭētus
ditch, fossa, *f*
ditty, carmen, *n*
divan, lectŭlus, *m*
dive, *v.i,* sē mergĕre (3 *reflex*)
diver, ūrīnātor, *m*
diverge, *v.i,* discēdo (3)
divergence, dēclīnātĭo, *f*

diverse, ălĭus, dĭversus
diversion, dērīvātĭo, *f*; **(of thought,** etc.), āvŏcātĭo, *f*
divert, *v.t*, āverto (3), āvŏco (1); **(amuse),** oblecto (1), prōlecto (1)
divide, *v.t*, dīvĭdo (3); **(share out),** partĭor (4 *dep*); *v.i*, sē dīvĭdĕre (3 *reflex*)
divine, dīvīnus
divine, *v.t*, dīvīno (1), augŭror (1 *dep*)
diviner, augur, *m*
divinity, dīvīnĭtas, *f*
divisible, dīvĭdŭus
division (act of —), dīvīsĭo, *f*; **(a section),** pars, *f*; **(discord),** discĭdĭum, *n*
divorce, dīvortĭum, *n*
divorce, *v.i*, dīvortĭum făcĭo (3), cum (*and abl*)
divulge, *v.t*, pătĕfăcĭo (3), ăpĕrĭo (4)
dizziness, vertīgo, *f*
dizzy, vertīgĭnōsus
do, *v.t*, făcĭo (3), ăgo (3); **(to be satisfactory),** *v.i*, sātis esse; **(— away with),** abŏlĕo (2); **(— without),** cărĕo (2) (*with abl*)
docile, făcĭlis, dŏcĭlis
dock, nāvālĭa, *n.pl*
doctor, mĕdĭcus, *m*
doctor, *v.t*, cūro (1)
doctrine, dogma, *n*, rătĭo, *f*
document, tăbŭla, *f*, littĕrae, *f. pl*
dodge, dŏlus, *m*
dodge, *v.t*, **(elude),** ēlūdo (3)
doe, cerva, *f*
dog, cănis, *c*
dog, *v.t*, insĕquor (3 *dep.*)
dogged (stubborn), pertĭnax, pervĭcax
dogged (by ill-luck, etc.), ăgĭtātus
dogma, dogma, *n*
dogmatic, arrŏgans
dole (small allowance), dĭurna, *n.pl*
dole out, *v.t*, dīvĭdo (3)
doleful, tristis, maestus
dolefulness, tristĭtĭa, *f*
doll, pūpa, *f*
dolphin, delphīnus, *m*
dolt, caudex, *m*
dome, thŏlus, *m*
domestic, dŏmestĭcus, fămĭlĭāris; **(animals)** villātĭcus
domestic, *nn*, **(servant),** fămŭlus, *m*
domicile, dŏmĭcĭlĭum, *n*
dominant, pŏtens
dominate, *v.t*, dŏmĭnor (1 *dep*)
domination, dŏmĭnātus, *m*
domineering, impĕrĭōsus
dominion, impĕrĭum, *n*, regnum, *n*
donation, dōnum, *n*
donkey, ăsĭnus, *m*
doom, fātum, *n*
doom, *v.t*, damno (1)
door, iānŭa, *f*; **(out of -s),** *adv*, fŏrīs
doorkeeper, iānĭtor, *m*
doorpost, postis, *f*
dormitory, cŭbĭcŭlum, *n*
dormouse, glīs, *m*
dot, *nn*, punctum, *n*
dotage, sĕnĭum, *n*
dotard, sĕnex, *m*
dote upon, *v.i*, dēpĕrĕo (4)
double, *adj*, dŭplex, gĕmĭnus
double, *v.t*, dŭplĭco (1); *v.i*, dŭplex fĭo (*irreg*), ingĕmĭno (1)
double-dealing, *nn*, fraus, *f*
double-faced fallax
doubt, *v.i*, dŭbĭto (1)
doubt, *nn*, dŭbĭum, *n*, dŭbĭtātĭo,
doubtful, dŭbĭus, incertus
doubtless, *adv*, sĭne dŭbĭo, nīmīrum
dough, fārīna, *f*
dove, cŏlumba, *f*
dove-coloured, cŏlumbīnus
dove-cot, cŏlumbārĭum, *n*
dowager, vĭdŭa, *f*
down, *prep*, dē (*with abl*); *adv*, *use* dē *in a compound verb, e.g.* **run down,** dēcurro (3)
down, *nn* **(feathers, etc.),** plūma, *f*;
down, *v.t*, **(put down),** dēpōno (3)
downcast, dēiectus, dēmissus
downfall, occāsus, *m*, rŭĭna, *f*
down-hearted, *adv*, dēmisso ănĭmo
downpour, imber, *m*
downright, dīrectus; **(sheer),** mĕrus
downward, *adj*, dēclīvis
downwards, *adv*, dĕorsum
downy, *adj*, plūmĕus
dowry, dos, *f*
doze, *v.i*, dormĭto (1)
dozen (twelve), dŭŏdĕcim
dozing, *adj*, somnĭcŭlōsus
drab, cĭnĕrĕus **(ash-coloured)**
drag, *v.t*, trăho (3)
dragon, drăco, *m*
drain, *nn*, clŏāca, *f*, fossa, *f*
drain, *v.t*, **(land),** sicco (1); **(a drink),** haurĭo (4)
dram, cŷăthus, *m*
drama, fābŭla, *f*, scēna, *f*
dramatic (theatrical), scēnĭcus
dramatist, pŏēta, *m*
drapery, vēlāmen, *n*
draught (of air), spīrĭtus, *m*; **(water, etc.)** haustus, *m*; **(game of -s),** lătruncŭli, *m, pl*
draw, *v.t* **(pull),** trăho (3); **(portray),** dēscribo (3); **(— a sword),** glădĭum stringo (3); **(— aside),** sēdŭco (3); **(— water, etc.),** haurĭo (4); *v.i* (—

back), pĕdem rĕfĕro (*irreg*); (— **lots**), sortes dūco (3); (— **up troops, etc.**), *v.t*, instrŭo (3)
drawback, *nn*, incommŏdum, *n*
drawbridge, pontĭcŭlus, *m*
drawing (**picture**), pictūra, *f*
drawl, *v.i*, lentē prōnuntĭo (1) (**pronounce slowly**)
dray, plaustrum, *n*
dread, *nn*, formīdo, *f*, păvor, *m*
dread, *v.t*, tĭmĕo (2), formīdo (1)
dreadful, terrĭbĭlis, ātrox
dream, *nn*, somnĭum, *n*
dream, *v.t*, somnĭo (1)
dreamy, somnĭcŭlōsus
dreary, tristis
dregs, faex, *f*
drench, *v.t*, măděfăcĭo (3)
dress, *nn*, vestis, *f*, hăbĭtus, *m*
dress, *v.t*, (**clothe**); vestĭo (4); (— **a wound**), cūro (1) (**care for**)
dressing, *nn*, (**of wound**), fōmentum, *n*
drift, *nn*, (**heap**), agger, *m*; (**tendency**), *use phr. with* quōrsus (**to what end?**)
drift, *v.i*, dĕfĕror (*irreg. pass*)
drill (**military**), exercĭtātĭo, *f*; (**tool**), tĕrĕbra, *f*
drill, *v.t* (**pierce**), tĕrĕbro (1); (**train**), exercĕo (2)
drink, *v.t*, bĭbo (3), pōto (1)
drink, *nn*, pōtĭo, *f*
drinker, pōtātor, *m*
drinking, pōtĭo, *f*; (— **party**), cōmissātĭo, *f*
drip, *v.i*, stillo (1)
dripping, *adj*, mādĭdus
drive, *nn* gestātĭo, *f*
drive, *v.t*, ăgo (3); (— **away**), fŭgo (1) pello (3); (— **back**), rĕpello (3); (— **out**), expello (3)
drive, *v.i*, (**on horse-back, etc.**), vĕhor (3 *pass*)
drivel ĭneptĭae, *f*, *pl*
drivel, *v.i*, dēlīro (1)
driver, aurīga, *c*
drizzle, *v.i*, rōro (1)
droll, rĭdĭcŭlus, lĕpĭdus
drollery, făcētĭae, *f*. *pl*
dromedary, drŏmas, *m*
drone, *nn*, (**bee**), fūcus, *m*; (**sound**), murmur, *n*
drone, *v.i*, murmŭro (1)
droop, *v.i*, pendĕo (2), languesco (3)
drooping, *adj*, pendŭlus; (**of spirits, etc.**), dēmissus
drop, *nn*, gutta, *f*
drop, *v.t*, dēmitto (3); (**leave off**), omitto (3); *v.i*, cădo (3)
dropsy, hydrops, *m*
drought, siccĭtas, *f*
drove (**flock**), grex, *m*
drown, *v.t*, submergo (3); (**of noise**) obstrĕpo (3)
drowsy, somnĭcŭlōsus
drudge, *nn*, servus, *m*
drudge, *v.i*, servĭo (4); (**weary oneself**), *v.i*, sē fātīgāre (1 *reflex*)
drudgery, lăbor servĭlis (**servile labour**)
drug, *nn*, mĕdĭcāmentum, *n*
drug, *v.t*, mĕdĭco (1)
drum, tympănum, *n*
drunk, *adj*, ēbrĭus
drunkenness, ēbrĭĕtas, *f*
dry, siccus, ārĭdus; (**thirsty**), sĭtĭens
dry (**up**), *v.t*, sicco (1); *v.i*, āresco (3)
dryness, sĭccĭtas, *f*, ārĭdĭtas, *f*
dubious, dŭbĭus
duck, *nn*, ănas, *f*
duck, *v.t*, mergo (3)
duckling, ănătĭcŭla, *f*
duct, fōrāmen, *n*
due, *adj*, (**owed**), dēbĭtus; (**just**), iustus; (**suitable**), ĭdōnĕus, aptus
due, *nn*, (**a right**), ius, *n*; (**taxes**), vectīgal, *n*, portōrĭum, *n*
duel, certāmen, *n*
dull (**person**), hĕbes, obtūsus; (**colour**), obscūrus; (**blunt**), hĕbes; (**weather**), subnūbĭlus
dullness (**of mind**), tardĭtas, *f*
duly, *adv*, (**established by precedent**), rītĕ
dumb, mūtus
dumbfound, *v.t*, obstŭpĕfăcĭo (3)
dump, *v.t*, cŏăcervo (1)
dun, fuscus
dunce, hŏmo stŭpĭdus
dung, stercus, *n*
dungeon, carcer, *m*
dupe, *nn*, hŏmo crēdŭlus
dupe, *v.t*, dēcĭpĭo (3)
duplicate, exemplum, *n*
duplicity, fallācĭa, *f*
durability, firmĭtas, *f*
durable, firmus
duration, spătĭum, *n*; (**long —**), dĭŭturnĭtas, *f*
during, *prep*, per (*with acc*)
dusk, crĕpuscŭlum, *n*
dusky, fuscus, nĭger
dust, *nn*, pulvis, *m*
dust, *v.t*, dētergĕo (2)
duster, pēnĭcŭlus, *m*
dusty, pulvĕrŭlentus
dutiful, pĭus
dutifulness, pĭĕtas, *f*
duty (**moral**), offĭcĭum, *n*; (**given**), mūnus, *n*; (**tax**), vectīgal, *n*; (**it is my —**), *use vb.* dēbĕo (2) (**ought**)

For List of Abbreviations used, turn to pages 3, 4

dwarf, pŭmĭlĭo, *c*
dwarfish, pŭsillus
dwell, *v.i,* hăbĭto (1), incŏlo (3); (— **on a theme**), commŏror (1 *dep*), haerĕo (2) in (*with abl*)
dweller, incŏla, *c*
dwelling (place), dŏmĭcĭlĭum, *n*
dwindle, *v.i,* dēcresco (3)
dye, *nn,* fūcus, *m*
dye, *v.t,* tingo (3), infĭcĭo (3)
dyer, infector, *m*
dying, *adj,* mŏrĭens
dynasty, dŏmus, *f*
dysentery, dȳsentĕrĭa, *f*
dyspeptic, crūdus

E

each, ūnusquisque; (— **of two**), ŭterque; (**one** —), *use distributive num,* singŭli, bīni
eager, cŭpĭdus, ăvĭdus (*with genit*)
eagerness, cŭpĭdĭtas, *f,* ăvĭdĭtas, *f*
eagle, āquĭla, *f*
ear, auris, *f*; (— **of corn**), spĭca, *f*
early, *adj,* (**in the morning**), mātūtĭnus; (**of time, etc.**), mātūrus
early, *adv,* (**in the morning**), māne; (**in time, etc.**), mātūrē
earn, *v.t,* mĕrĕo (2), mĕrĕor (2 *dep*)
earnest, intentus, ācer
earnestly, *adv* intentē
earth (land), terra, *f*; (**ground**), sŏlum, *n*; (**globe**), orbis, (*m*) terrārum
earthenware, fictĭlĭa, *n.pl*
earthly, *adj,* (**terrestrial**) terrestris
earthquake, terrae mōtus, *m,* (**movement of the earth**)
earth-work, agger, *m*
ease, quĭes, *f,* ōtĭum, *n*
ease, *v.t,* (**lighten**), lĕvo (1), exŏnĕro (1)
easily, *adv,* făcĭlĕ
easiness, făcĭlĭtas, *f*
east, *nn,* ŏrĭens, *m*
eastern, *use genit. of* ŏrĭens (**east**)
eastward, *adv. phr,* ăd ŏrĭentem
easy, făcĭlis
eat, *v.t,* ĕdo (3); (— **away**), rōdo (3)
eatable, escŭlentus
eating-house, pŏpīna, *f*
eaves, prōtectum, *n*
eaves-dropper, auceps, *c*
ebb, *v.i,* rĕcĕdo (3)
ebb-tide, rĕcessus aestus (**receding of the tide**)
ebony, ĕbĕnus, *f*
eccentric (of persons), nŏvus
echo, *nn,* īmāgo, *f,* ĕcho, *f*
echo, *v.t,* rĕfĕro (*irreg*), rĕsŏno (1)
echoing, *adj,* rĕsŏnus
eclipse, *nn,* dēfectĭo, *f*
eclipse, *v.t,* obscūro (1)
economical, parcus, dilĭgens
economy, parsĭmōnĭa, *f,* (**frugality**)
ecstasy, fūror, *m*
ecstatic, fūrens
eddy, vertex, *m*
edge (of knife, etc.), ăcĭes, *f*; (**margin**), margo, *c,* ōra, *f*
edible, escŭlentus
edict, ēdictum, *n*
edifice, aedĭfĭcĭum, *n*
edify, *v.t,* instĭtŭo (3)
edit, *v.t,* ēdo (3)
edition, ēdĭtĭo, *f*
educate, *v.t,* ēdŭco (1)
education, ēdŭcātĭo, *f,* doctrīna, *f*
eel, anguilla, *f*
efface, *v.t,* dēlĕo (2)
effect, *v.t,* effĭcĭo (3)
effect, *nn,* (**influence, impression**), vīs, *f*; (**result**), effectus, *m*; (**consequence**), ēventus, *m*; (**without** —), (*adv*), nēquĭquem
effective (impressive), grăvis; *or use phr. with* confĭcĭo (3) (**to bring to a conclusion**)
effectual, effĭcax
effeminate, effēmĭnātus
effervescence (of spirit, etc.), fervor, *m*
efficacy, vīs, *f*
efficiency, vīs, *f*
efficient, hăbĭlis, effĭcĭens
effigy, īmāgo, *f*
effort, ŏpĕra, *f*
effrontery, ōs, *n*
effulgent, fulgens
effusion, effūsĭo, *f*
egg, ōvum, *n*
egg on, *v.t,* incĭto (1)
egoism, ămor, (*m*) sŭi (**fondness of oneself**)
egoist, ămātor, (*m*) sŭi
egregious, insignis
egress, exĭtus, *m*
eight, octo; (— **each**), octōni; (— **times**), *adv.* octĭens; (— **hundred**) octingenti
eighteen, dŭŏdēvīginti
eighteenth, dŭŏdēvĭcensimus
eighth, octāvus
eightieth, octōgēsĭmus
eighty, octōginta
either, *pron,* altĕrŭter; *conj,* aut
either . . . or, aut . . . aut, vel . . . vel

ejaculate, *v.t,* ēmitto (3)
ejaculation (cry), vox, *f,* clāmor, *m*
eject, *v.t,* ēĭcĭo (3)
eke out, *v.t,* parco (3) (*with dat*)
elaborate, *adj,* ēlābōrātus
elaborate, *v.t,* ēlābōro (1)
elapse, *v.i,* (of time), intercēdo (3)
elate, *v.t,* effĕro (*irreg*)
elated (joyful), laetus
elbow, cŭbĭtum, *n*
elder, *adj,* māior nātu (**greater by birth**)
elder-tree, sambūcus, *f*
elderly, *adj,* prōvectus aetāte (**advanced in age**)
elect, *v.t,* crĕo (1), dēlĭgo (3)
elect, *adj,* dēsignātus
election, ēlectĭo, *f,* cŏmĭtĭa, *n.pl*
elector, suffrāgātor, *m*
elegance, ēlĕgantĭa, *f,* vĕnustas, *f*
elegant, ēlĕgans, vĕnustus
elegy, ēlĕgĭa, *f*
element, ēlĕmentum, *n,* prĭncĭpĭa, *n.pl*
elementary, prīmus, simplex
elephant, ēlĕphantus, *m*
elevate, *v.t,* tollo (3)
elevated, ĕdĭtus; (**mind**) ēlātus
elevation, altĭtūdo, *f,* ēlātĭo, *f*
eleven, undĕcim; (— **each**), undēni
eleventh, undĕcĭmus
elicit, *v.t,* ēlĭcĭo (3)
eligible, ĭdōnĕus, opportūnus
elk, alces, *f*
ell, ulna, *f*
elm, ulmus, *f*
elocution, prōnuntĭātĭo, *f*
elope, *v.i,* aufŭgĭo (3) (**run away**
eloquence, ēlŏquentĭa, *f*
eloquent, ēlŏquens, dĭsertus
else, *adj,* ălĭus
else, *adv,* ălĭter
elsewhere, *adv,* ălĭbī
elude, *v.t,* ēlūdo (3)
emaciate, *v.t,* attĕnŭo (1)
emaciated, măcer
emaciation, măcĭes, *f*
emanate, *v.i,* ēmāno (1)
emancipate, *v.t,* lībĕro (1), mănūmitto (3)
embalm, *v.t,* condĭo (4)
embankment, mōles, *f*
embark, *v.t,* in nāvem impōno (3); *v.i,* nāvem conscendo (3)
embarrass, *v.t,* (**entangle**), impĕdĭo (4); (**confuse**), turbo (1)
embarrassment, scrūpŭlus, *m*; (**difficulty**), dĭfficultas, *f*
embassy (delegation), lēgāti, *m. pl,* (**ambassadors**)
embedded, sĭtus
embellish, *v.t,* orno (1)
embellishment, ornāmentum, *n*
embers, cĭnis, *m*
embezzle, *v.t,* āverto (3), pĕcŭlor (1 *dep*)
embezzlement, pĕcŭlātus, *m*
embezzler, āversor, (*m*) pĕcūnĭae
embitter, *v.t,* exăcerbo (1)
emblem, insigne, *n,* indĭcĭum, *n*
embody, *v.t,* inclūdo (3)
embolden, *v.t,* confirmo (1)
embrace, *nn,* amplexus, *m,* complexus, *m*
embrace, *v.t,* amplector (3 *dep*), complector (3 *dep*); (— **an opportunity**), arrĭpĭo (3)
embroidered (clothing, etc.), pictus
embroil, *v.t,* (**entangle**), implĭco (1)
emerald, smăragdus, *c*
emerge, *v.i,* ēmergo (3), prōdĕo (4)
emergency, discrīmen, *n,* tempus, *n*
emigrate, *v.i,* mĭgro (1)
emigration, mĭgrātĭo, *f*
eminence (high ground), tŭmŭlus, *m*; (**of rank, etc.**), lŏcus amplissĭmus
eminent, ēgrĕgĭus, insignis
emissary, lēgātus, *m*
emit, *v.t,* ēmitto (3)
emolument, lŭcrum, *n*
emotion, mōtus, (*m,*) ănĭmi (**movement of the mind**)
emperor, impĕrātor, *m,* princeps, *m*
emphasize, *v.t,* prĕmo (3)
emphatic, grăvis
empire, impĕrĭum, *n*
empirical, empīrĭcus
employ, *v.t,* ūtor (3 *dep*) (*with abl*)
employed (of persons), occŭpātus
employer, conductor, *m*
employment (occupation), quaestus, *m*; (**business**), nĕgōtĭum, *n*; (**using**) ūsurpātĭo, *f*
emporium, empŏrĭum, *n*
empower (someone to do . . .), *v.i,* pōtestātem făcĭo (3) (*with dat. of person and genit. of gerund(ive)*)
empty, *adj,* văcŭus, ĭnānis
empty, *v.t,* exĭnānĭo (4)
emulate, *v.t,* aemŭlor (1 *dep*)
emulous, aemŭlus
enable, *v.t,* făcultātem do (1) (*with dat*)
enact, *v.t,* (**law**), sancĭo (4), constĭtŭo (3)
enactment lex, *f*
enamoured (to be — of somone), *v.t,* ămo (1)
encamp, *v.i,* castra pōno (3)
enchant, *v.t.* fascĭno (1), dēlecto (1)

enchantment (allurement), blandīmentum, *n*
encircle, *v.t*, circumdo (1)
enclose, *v.t*, inclūdo (3), saepĭo (4)
enclosure, saeptum, *n*
encounter, *v.t*, incīdo (3) **in** (*with acc*); concurro (3), obviam ĕo (4) (*irreg*) (*with dat*)
encounter, *nn*, congressus, *m*
encourage, *v.t*, hortor (1 *dep*)
encouragement, hortātus, *m*; confirmātĭo, *f*, hortātĭo, *f*
encroach upon, *v.t*, occŭpo (1)
encumber, *v.t*, ŏnĕro (1), impĕdĭo (4)
encumbrance, impĕdimentum, *n*
end, fīnis, *m*; *or use* extrēmus, *adj*, *agreeing with a noun*; *e.g.* **at the end of the bridge**, in extrēmo ponte
end, *v.t*, confĭcĭo (3), fīnĭo (4); *v.i*, *use phr. with* extrēmum, *n*, **(end)**; **(turn out, result)**, cēdo (3), ēvĕnĭo (4)
endanger, *v.t*, in pĕrĭcŭlum addūco (3)
endear, *v.t*, dēvincĭo (4)
endeavour, *nn*, cōnātus, *m*
endeavour, *v.t*, cōnor (1 *dep*)
endless, infīnītus, perpĕtŭus
endorse, *v.t*, confirmo (1)
endow, *v.t*, dōno (1)
endowed, praedītus
endurable, tŏlĕrābĭlis
endurance, pătĭentĭa, *f*
endure, *v.t*, pătĭor (3 *dep*), fĕro (*irreg*); *v.i*, dūro (1)
enemy (public), hostis, *c*; **(private)**, inimīcus, *m*
energetic, ācer, strēnŭus, impĭger
energy, vīs, *f*, vĭgor, *m*
enervate, *v.t*, ēnervo (1)
enervation, dēbĭlĭtātĭo, *f*
enfeeble, *v.t*, dēbĭlĭto (1)
enforce, *v.t*, **(carry out)**, exsĕquor (3 *dep*)
enfranchise, *v.t*, **(give the right of voting)**, suffrāgĭum do (1) (*with dat*)
enfranchisement, cīvĭtātis dōnātĭo, *f*, **(granting of citizenship)**
engage, *v.t*, **(join)** iungo (3); **(hire)**, condūco (3); **(— in battle)**; signa conferre (*irreg*); **(enter into)**, ingrĕdĭor (3 *dep*)
engaged, occŭpātus; **(betrothed)**, sponsus
engagement (battle), proelĭum, *n*; **(agreement)**, pactum, *n*; **(promise)**, sponsĭo, *f*
engender, *v.t*, gigno (3), părĭo (3)
engine, māchĭna, *f*; **(military —)**, tormentum, *n*
engineer, făber, *m*
England, Brĭtannĭa, *f*
English, Brĭtannus, Brĭtannĭcus
engrave, *v.t*, scalpo (3)
engraver, scalptor, *m*
engraving, *nn*, scalptūra, *f*
engross, *v.t*, occŭpo (1)
enhance, *v.t*, augĕo (2), orno (1)
enigma, aenigma, *n*, ambāges, *f*, *pl*
enigmatic, ambĭgŭus
enjoin, *v.t*, iŭbĕo (2), mando (1)
enjoy, *v.t*, frŭor (3 *dep*) (*with abl*); **(possess)**, ūtor (3 *dep*) (*with abl*)
enjoyment (pleasure), gaudĭum, *n*, lībĭdo, *f*
enlarge, *v.t*, augĕo (2), amplĭfĭco (1)
enlargement, prōlātĭo, *f*
enlighten, *v.t*, **(instruct)**, dŏcĕo (2)
enlist, *v.t*, **(troops)**, conscrĭbo (3); **(bring over)**, concĭlĭo (1); *v.i*, nōmen do (1) **(give one's name)**
enliven, *v.t*, excĭto (1)
enmity, inĭmīcĭtĭa, *f*
ennoble, *v.t*, **(make honourable)**, hŏnesto (1)
enormity, immānĭtas, *f*; **(crime)**, scĕlus, *n*
enormous, ingens
enough, *nn. and adv*, sătis; (*foll. by genit*), *e.g.* **enough water**, sătis āquae
enquire, *v.t*, quaero (3) ab (*with abl*)
enrage, *v.t*, irrĭto (1), inflammo (1)
enrapture, *v.t*, oblecto (1)
enrich, *v.t*, lŏcŭplēto (1)
enroll, *v.t*, scrĭbo (3)
ensign, signum, *n*; **(— bearer)**, signĭfer, *m*
enslave, *v.t*, servĭtūtem iniungo (3) (*with dat*)
ensue, *v.i*, sĕquor (3 *dep*)
entail, *v.t*, affĕro (*irreg*)
entangle, *v.t*, impĕdĭo (4)
enter, *v.i*, *and v.t*, intro (1), ingrĕdĭor (3 *dep*), īnĕo (4 *irreg*); *v.t*, **(— write in)**, inscrĭbo (3)
enterprise (undertaking), inceptum, *n*
enterprising, promptus, strēnŭus
entertain, *v.t*, **(people)**, excĭpĭo (3) **(receive)**; **(amuse)**, oblecto (1); **(an idea, etc.)** hăbĕo (2)
entertainment (of guests), hospĭtĭum, *n*
enthusiasm, stŭdĭum, *n*, fervor, *m*
enthusiastic, fānātĭcus, stŭdĭōsus
entice, *v.t*, illĭcĭo (3)
entire, tōtus, intĕger
entirely, *adv*, omnīno
entitle, *v.t*, **(give the right to)**, ius do (1) (*with dat*); **(name)**, inscrĭbo (3)

entitled (to be — to), *v.i*, ius hăbĕo (2)
entrails, viscĕra, *n.pl*
entrance (act of —), ingressĭo, *f*; **(door, etc)**, ădĭtus, *m*, ostĭum, *n*
entreat, *v.t*, obsĕcro (1), ōro (1)
entreaty, obsĕcrātĭo, *f*
entrust, *v.t*, crēdo (3) (*with dat*) committo (3) (*with dat*)
enumerate, *v.t*, nŭmĕro (1)
envelop, *v.t*, involvo (3)
envelope, *nn*, invŏlūcrum, *n*
enviable, fortūnātus
envious, invĭdus
envoy, lēgātus, *m*
envy, invĭdĭa, *f*
envy, *v.t*, invĭdĕo (2) (*with dat*)
ephemeral, brĕvis
epic, *adj*, ĕpĭcus
epidemic, pestĭlentĭa, *f*
epigram, ĕpĭgramma, *n*
epigrammatic, ĕpĭgrammătĭcus, a, um, *adj*
epilepsy, morbus cŏmĭtĭālis, *m*
episode (digression), excursus, *m*; res, *f*
epitaph, ĕlŏgĭum, *n*
epoch, aetas, *f*
equable. aequus
equal, *adj*, aequus, pār
equal, *nn*, *use adj*, pār
equal, *v.i and v.t*, aequo (1)
equality, aequālĭtas, *f*
equanimity, aequus ănĭmus, *m*
equator, aequĭnoctĭālis circŭlus, *m*
equestrian, ĕquester
equilibrium, aequĭlĭbrĭum, *n*
equinox, aequĭnoctĭum, *n*
equip, *v.t*, orno (1), armo (1)
equipment, arma, *n.pl*, armāmenta, *n.pl*
equitable, aequus
equity, aequĭtas, *f*; **(justice)**, iustĭtĭa, *f*
equivalent, *adj*, **(equal)**, pār; **(to be —)**, *v.i*, *use* vălĕo (2) **(to be worth)** tanti
equivocal, ambĭgŭus
era, tempus, *n*, aetas, *f*
eradicate, *v.t*, ĕvello (3), exstirpo (1)
erase, *v.t*, dēlĕo (2)
ere (before), *conj*, prĭusquam
erect, *v.t*, ērĭgo (3); **(build)**, exstrŭo (3)
erect, *adj*, rectus
erection (act of —), aedĭfĭcātĭo, *f*; **(a building)**, aedĭfĭcĭum, *n*
err, *v.i*, erro (1), pecco (1)
errand, mandātum, *n*
erratic, vāgus
erroneous, falsus
error, error, *m*
erudite, doctus
eruption, ēruptĭo, *f*
escape, *nn*, fŭga, *f*
escape, *v.i*, *and v.t*, effŭgĭo (3), ēlābor (3 *dep*)
escarpment, praeruptus lŏcus, *m*
escort, *nn*, comĭtātus, *m*; **(protective)**, praesĭdĭum, *n*
escort, *v.t*, cŏmĭtor (1 *dep*)
especial, praecĭpŭus
especially, *adv*, praecĭpŭē
espouse, *v.t*, **(betroth)**, spondĕo (2); **(marry)**, dūco (3), nūbo (3)
essay (attempt), cōnātus, *m*; **(composition)**, lĭbellus, *m*
essence (nature), nātūra, *f*, vīs, *f*
essential (necessary), nēcessārĭus
establish, *v.t*, constĭtŭo (3), confirmo (1)
establishment, constĭtūtĭo, *f*
estate (property), rēs, *f*, fundus, *m*
esteem, *nn*, existĭmātĭo, *f*
esteem, *v.t*, **(think)**, aestĭmo (1), pŭto (1); **(think highly of)**, magni aestĭmo (1)
estimable, laudātus
estimate, *nn*, aestĭmātĭo, *f*
estimate, *v.t*, aestĭmo (1)
estimation (opinion), ŏpĭnĭo, *f*
estrange, *v.t*, ălĭēno (1)
estrangement, ălĭēnātĭo, *f*
estuary, aestŭārĭum, *n*
eternal, aeternus
eternally, *adv. phr*, **in aeternum**
eternity, aeternĭtas, *f*
ether, aether, *m*
ethereal, aethĕrĭus
ethical (moral), mōrālis
eulogy, laudātĭo, *f*
evacuate, *v.t*, **(— troops from a place)**, dēdūco (3); *v.i*, **(depart from)**, excēdo (3), ex (*with abl*)
evade, *v.t*, ēlūdo (3)
evaporate, *v.i*, discŭtĭor (3 *pass*)
evasion, lătĕbra, *f*
evasive, ambĭgŭus
eve (evening), vesper, *m*
even, *adv*, ĕtĭam, *often use emphatic pron*, *e.g.* **even Caesar**, Caesar ipse; **(not —)**, nĕ . . . quĭdem
even, *adj*, **(level, equable)**, aequus; **(— number)**, pār
even if, *conj*, etsi
evening, vesper, *m*, **(in the —)**, sub vespĕrum
event (occurrence), rēs, *f*; **(outcome)**, exĭtus, *m*
eventually, *adv*, ălĭquando
ever, *adv*, **(at any time)**, umquam; **(always)**, semper; **(if —)**, si quando
evergreen, *adj*, semper vīrĭdis
everlasting, aeternus

For List of Abbreviations used, turn to pages 3, 4

every (all), omnis; (each), quisque; (— day), *adv*, cottĭdiē; (— one), omnes, *m.pl*; (— thing), omnĭa, *n.pl*; (— where), *adv*, ŭbĭque
evict, *v.t*, expello (3)
evidence, testĭmōnĭum, *n*; (factual), argūmentum, *n*
evident, mănĭfestus, perspĭcŭus; (it is —), appāret (2 *impers*)
evil, *adj*, mălus, prāvus
evil, *nn*, mălum, *n*
evil-doer, hŏmo nĕfārĭus
evoke, *v.t*, ēvŏco (1)
evolve, *v.t*, ēvolvo (3)
ewe, ŏvis, *f*
exact, *adj*, (number, etc.), exactus; (persons), dīlĭgens
exact, *v.t*, exĭgo (3)
exactness, subtīlĭtas, *f*
exaggerate, *v.t*, augĕo (2)
exaggeration, sŭperlātĭo, *f*
exalt, *v.t*, tollo (3), augĕo (2)
exalted, celsus
examination (test, etc.), prŏbātĭo, *f*; (enquiry), investīgātĭo, *f*
examine, *v.t*, investīgo (1), interrŏgo (1); (test), prŏbo (1)
example, exemplum, *n*; (for —), verbi causā
exasperate, *v.t*, exăcerbo (1)
excavate, *v.t*, căvo (1)
excavation (cavity), căvum, *n*
exceed, *v.t*, sŭpĕro (1), excēdo (3)
exceedingly, *adv*, admŏdum; *or use superlative of adj, e.g.* (— large), maxĭmus
excel, *v.t*, praesto (1) (*with dat*)
excellence, praestantĭa, *f*
excellent, praestans, ēgrĕgĭus
except, *prep*, praeter (*with acc*)
except, *v.t*, excĭpĭo (3)
exception (everyone, without —), omnes ad ūnum; (take — to) aegre fĕro (*irreg*)
exceptional, rārus, insignis
excess (over-indulgence), intempĕrantĭa, *f*
excessive, nĭmĭus
exchange, *nn*, permūtātĭo, *f*
exchange, *v.t*, permūto (1)
exchequer, aerārĭum, *n*
excitable, fervĭdus, fĕrox
excite, *v.t*, excĭto (1), incendo (3)
excited, commōtus, incensus
excitement, commōtĭo, *f*
exclaim, *v.i*, clāmo (1), conclāmo (1)
exclamation, exclāmātĭo, *f*
exclude, *v.t*, exclūdo (3)
exclusion, exclūsĭo, *f*
exclusive (one's own), prŏprĭus
excrescence, tūber, *n*
excruciating (pain, etc.), ācer
excursion, ĭter, *n*
excusable, excūsābĭlis
excuse, *nn*, excūsātĭo, *f*
excuse, *v.t*, excūso (1); (pardon), ignosco (3) (*with dat*)
execrable, nĕfārĭus
execrate, *v.t*, dētestor (1 *dep*)
execute, *v.t*, (carry out), exsĕquor (3 *dep*); (inflict capital punishment), nĕco (1)
execution (carrying out), *use vb* exsĕquor; (capital punishment), supplĭcĭum, *n*
executioner, carnĭfex, *m*
exemplary, ēgrĕgĭus
exempt, *v.t*, excĭpĭo (3)
exempt, *adj*, immūnis
exemption, immūnĭtas, *f*
exercise, exercĭtātĭo, *f*; (set task), ŏpus, *n*
exercise, *v.t*, exercĕo (2)
exert, *v.t*, contendo (3), ūtor (3 *dep*) (*with abl*); (to — oneself), *v.i*, nĭtor (3 *dep*)
exertion, contentĭo, *f*, lăbor, *m*
exhale, *v.t*, exhālo (1)
exhaust, *v.t*, exhaurĭo (4); (weary), confĭcĭo (3), dēfătīgo (1)
exhausted (tired out), confectus
exhaustion, vīrĭum dēfectĭo, *f*, (failing of strength)
exhibit, *v.t*, expōno (3)
exhibition (spectacle), spectăcŭlum, *n*
exhilarate, *v.t*, hĭlăro (1)
exhilaration, hĭlārĭtas, *f*
exhort, *v.t*, hortor (1 *dep*)
exhume, *v.t*, ērŭo (3)
exile, *nn*, (person), exsul, *c*; (banishment), exsĭlĭum, *n*; (to be in —), *v.i*, exsŭlo (1)
exile, *v.t*, in exsĭlĭum pello (3) (drive into exile)
exist, *v.i*, sum (*irreg*), exsisto (3)
existence (life), vīta, *f*
exit, exĭtus, *m*
exonerate, *v.t*, lĭbĕro (1)
exorbitant, nĭmĭus
exotic, externus
expand, *v.t*, extendo (3); *v.i*, extendor (3 *pass*)
expanse, spătĭum, *n*
expatiate (on a theme, etc.), *v.*, permulta dissĕro (3) dē (*with abl.*)

expatriate, *v.t,* ĕĭcĭo (3)
expect, *v.t,* exspecto (1)
expectation, exspectātĭo, *f*
expediency, ūtĭlĭtas, *f*
expedient, *adj,* ūtĭlis
expedient, *nn,* rătĭo, *f*
expedite, *v.t,* expĕdĭo (4)
expedition (military, etc.), expĕdĭtĭo, *f*
expeditious, cĕler
expel, *v.t,* expello (3)
expend, *v.t,* expendo (3)
expenditure, ērŏgātĭo, *f*
expense, impensa, *f,* sumptus, *m*
expensive, sumptŭōsus, prĕtĭōsus
experience, ūsus, *m,* pĕrĭtĭa, *f*
experience, *v.t,* expĕrĭor (4 *dep*), pătĭor (3 *dep*)
experienced, pĕrĭtus
experiment, expĕrĭmentum, *n*
expert, *adj,* sciens
expiate, *v.t,* expĭo (1)
expiation, expĭātĭo, *f*
expiatory, pĭăcŭlāris
expiration (breathing out), exspīrātĭo, *f*; **(time),** *use partic.* confectus **(completed)**
expire, *v.i,* **(persons),** exspīro (1); **(time),** exĕo (4), confĭcĭo (3)
explain, *v.t,* explĭco (1), expōno (3)
explanation, explĭcātĭo, *f*
explicit, ăpertus
explode, *v.i* , dīrumpor (3 *pass*)
explore, *v.t,* explōro (1)
export, *v.t,* exporto (1)
exports, merces, *f, pl*
expose, *v.t,* expōno (3), dētĕgo (3), nūdo (1); **(— to danger, etc.),** offĕro (*irreg*)
exposition (statement), expŏsĭtĭo, *f*
expostulate, *v.i,* expostŭlo (1)
expound, *v.t,* explĭco (1), expōno (3)
express, *v.t,* exprĭmo (3); **(— in-writing),** dēscrĭbo (3)
expression (verbal), vox, *f,* verba, *n.pl*; **(facial),** vultus, *m*
expressive, *use phr,* multam vim hăbens **(having much significance)**
expulsion, exactĭo, *f*
expunge, *v.t,* dēlĕo (2)
exquisite, conquīsĭtus
extant (to be —), *v.i,* exsto (1)
extemporary, extempŏrālis
extemporize, *v.i,* sŭbĭta dĭco (3)
extend, *v.t,* extendo (3), distendo (3); *v.i,* pătĕo (2); **(— to),** pertĭnĕo (2) ad (*with acc*)
extension (act of), porrectĭo, *f*; **(of boundaries, etc.),** prŏpāgātĭo, *f*
extensive, amplus
extent, spătĭum, *n*
extenuate, *v.t,* lĕvo (1), mītĭgo (1)
exterior, *adj,* externus
exterior, *nn,* spĕcĭes, *f*
exterminate, *v.t,* interfĭcĭo (3), dēlĕo (2)
extermination, internĕcĭo, *f*
external, externus
extinct, exstinctus
extinguish, *v.t,* exstinguo (3)
extirpate, *v.t,* exstirpo (1), excīdo (3)
extol, *v.t,* laudo (1)
extort, *v.t,* **(by force),** extorquĕo (2)
extortion, res rĕpĕtundae, *f. pl*
extra, *adv,* praetĕrĕā
extract, *nn,* **(from a book, etc.),** exceptĭo, *f*
extract, *v.t,* extrăho (3), ēvello (3)
extraction (pulling out), ēvulsĭo, *f*
extraordinary, extraordĭnārĭus, insŏlĭtus
extravagance, sumptus, *m,* luxŭrĭa, *f,* intempĕrantĭa, *f*
extravagant, immŏdĭcus, sumptŭōsus
extreme, *adj,* extrēmus, ultĭmus
extremity, extrēmum, *n*; **(top),** căcūmen, *n,* vertex, *m*; *or use adj,* extrēmus **(extreme)**
extricate, *v.t,* expĕdĭo (4), solvo (3)
exuberance, luxŭrĭa, *f*
exuberant, luxŭrĭōsus, effūsus
exude, *v.i,* māno (1)
exult, *v.i,* exsulto (1), laetor (1 *dep*)
exultant, laetus, ēlātus
eye, ŏcŭlus, *m*; **(— lash),** palpĕbrae pĭlus, *m*; **(— lid),** palpĕbra, *f*; **(— sight),** ăcies, *f*; **(— witness),** arbĭter, *m*

F

fable, fābŭla, *f*
fabric (woven), textum, *n*; **(building),** aedĭfĭcĭum, *n*
fabricate, *v.t,* fabrĭcor (1 *dep*)
fabrication mendācĭum, *n*
fabulous, fictus, falsus
face, făcies, *f,* vultus, *m,* ōs, *n*
face, *v.t* **(confront),** obvĭam ĕo (4) (*with dat*); **(look towards),** specto (1) ad (*with acc*)
facetious, făcētus
facilitate, *v.t,* făcĭlĭorem reddo (3) **(make easier)**
facility (possibility), făcultas, *f*; **(dexterity),** făcĭlĭtas, *f*
facing, *prep,* adversus (*with acc*)
fact, rēs, *f*; **(in —, truly),** *conj,* ĕnim; *adv,* vērō
faction, factĭo, *f*
factious, factĭōsus

factory, offĭcīna, *f*
faculty, făcultas, *f*, vīs, *f*
fade, *v.i*, pallesco (3)
faggot, sarmenta, *n.pl*
fail, *v.i*, cădo (3), dēfĭcĭo (3), dēsum (*irreg*) (*with dat*)
failing, *nn* (**defect**), vĭtĭum, *n*
failure (**of supplies, strength, etc.**), dēfectĭo, *f*, *otherwise use* irrĭtus (**vain, unsuccessful**)
faint, *v.i*, collābor (3 *dep*), languesco (3)
faint, *adj*, (**exhausted**), dēfessus
faint-hearted, tĭmĭdus, imbellis
faintness (**of body**), languor, *m*
fair, *nn*, (**market**), nundĭnae, *f*, *pl* (**ninth day**)
fair, *adj*, (**beautiful**), pulcher; (**just**), aequus; (**colour**), candĭdus; (**weather**), sērēnus; (**wind, etc.**), sĕcundus; (**fairly good**), mēdĭŏcris
fairly, *adv*, (**justly**), iustē; (**moderately**), mēdĭŏcrĭter
fairness (**justice**), aequĭtas, *f*; (**of complexion, etc.**), candor, *m*
faith, fĭdes, *f*; (**to keep —**), *v.i*, fĭdem servo (1)
faithful, fĭdēlis, fĭdus
faithfulness, fĭdēlĭtas, *f*
faithless, infĭdus, perfĭdus
faithlessness, perfĭdĭa, *f*
falcon, falco, *m*
fall, *nn*, cāsus, *m*, rŭīna, *f*
fall, *v.i*, cădo (3); (**— back**) rĕcĭdo (3); (**retreat**), pēdem rĕfĕro (*irreg*); (**— headlong**), praecĭpĭto (1); (**— in love with**), ădămo (1); (**— off**), dēlābor (3 *dep*); (**— out, happen**), cădo (3); (**— upon, attack**), *v.t*, invādo (3)
fallacious, fallax, falsus
fallacy, vĭtĭum, *n*
falling off, *nn*, (**revolt**), dēfectĭo, *f*
fallow, nŏvālis, ĭnārātus
false, falsus; (**not genuine**), fictus; (**person**), perfĭdus
falsehood, mendācĭum, *n*
falsify, *v.t*, vĭtĭo (1)
falter, *v.i*, haerĕo (2), haesĭto (1)
faltering, *adj*, haesĭtans
fame, glōrĭa, *f*, fāma, *f*
familiar, nōtus, fămĭlĭāris; (**usual**), consŭētus, *f*
familiarity, fămĭlĭārĭtas, *f*
familiarize, *v.t*, consŭesco (3)
family, *nn*, fămĭlĭa, *f*, dŏmus, *f*, gens, *f*
family, *adj*, fămĭlĭāris, gentīlis
famine, fămes, *f*
famished, fāme confectus (**exhausted from hunger**)
famous, clārus
fan, flābellum, *n*
fan, *v.t*, ventĭlo (1)
fanatical, fānātĭcus
fanaticism, sŭperstĭtĭo, *f*
fancied (**imaginary**), fictus
fancy, *nn*, (**notion**), ŏpĭnĭo, *f*; (**liking for**), lĭbīdo, *f*
fancy, *v.t*, (**imagine**), fingo (3); (**think**), ŏpinor (1 *dep*); (**want**) cŭpĭo (3)
fang, dens, *m*
far, *adv*, (**of distance**), prŏcul, longē; (**as — as**), *prep*, tēnus; *with comparatives*, multō, *e.g.* **far bigger**, multō māior; (**how —**), quātēnus; (**— and wide**), longē lātēque
far-fetched, quaesītus
farce, mīmus, *m*
farcical, mīmĭcus
fare (**food**), cĭbus, *m*; (**charge**), vectūra, *f*
farewell!, ăvē; (*pl*) ăvete; vălē, vălete; (**to bid —**), vălēre iŭbĕo (2)
farm, *nn*, fundus, *m*
farm, *v.t*, cŏlo (3)
farmer, agrĭcŏla, *m*, cŏlōnus, *m*
farming, agrĭcultūra, *f*
farther, *adj*, ultĕrĭor
farther, *adv*, longĭus
farthest, *adj*, ultĭmus
farthest, *adv*, longissĭme
fascinate, *v.t*, fascĭno (1)
fascination, fascĭnātĭo, *f*
fashion, *nn*, mōs, *m*
fashion, *v.t*, fingo (3)
fashionable, ēlēgans
fast, *nn*, iēiūnĭum, *n*
fast, *v.i*, iēiūnus sum (*irreg*) (**be hungry**)
fast, *adj*, (**quick**), cĕler; (**firm**), firmus; (**make —**), *v.t*, firmo (1), dēlīgo (1)
fast, *adv*, (**quickly**), cĕlĕrĭter; (**firmly**), firme
fasten, *v.t*, fīgo (3), dēlīgo (1); (**doors, etc.**), obtūro (1)
fastening, *nn*, vincŭlum, *n*
fastidious, dēlĭcātus
fat, *adj*, pinguis
fat, *nn*, ădeps, *c*
fatal (**deadly**), pernĭcĭōsus
fatality, cāsus, *m*
fate, fātum, *n*
fated, fātālis
father, păter, *m*; (**-in-law**), sŏcer, *m*
fatherland, pătrĭa, *f*
fatherless, orbus
fathom, *nn*, ulna, *f*
fatigue, *nn*, dēfātīgātĭo, *f*
fatigue, *v.t*, fātīgo (1)
fatigued, fātīgātus

fatten, *v.t*, săgĭno (1)
fault, culpa, *f*, vĭtĭum, *n*
faultless, intĕger, perfectus
faulty, mendōsus, vĭtĭōsus
favour, *nn*, grātĭa, *f*, făvor, *m*, stŭdĭum, *n*; (**a benefit**), grātĭa, *f*, bĕnĕfĭcĭum, *n*
favour, *v.t*, făvĕo (2) (*with dat*)
favourable, commŏdus; (**of wind**), sĕcundus
favourite, *nn*, dēlĭcĭae, *f. pl*
favourite, *adj*, grātus
fawn, *nn*, hinnŭlēus, *m*
fawn upon, *v.t*, ădūlor (1 *dep*)
fear, *nn*, tĭmor, *m*, mĕtus, *m*
fear, *v.t*, tĭmĕo (2), mĕtŭo (3), vĕrĕor (2 *dep*)
fearful, *adj*, (**afraid**), tĭmĭdus; (**terrible**), terrĭbĭlis
fearless, intrĕpĭdus
fearlessness, audācĭa, *f*
feasible, *use phr. with vbs*, posse (**to be able**) *and* effĭcĕre (**to bring about**)
feast, *nn*, daps, *f*, ĕpŭlae, *f. pl*; (— **day**), dĭes festus, *m*
feast, *v.i*, ĕpŭlor (1 *dep*); *v.t*, pasco (3)
feat, făcĭnus, *n*
feather, penna, *f*, plūma, *f*
feature (**of face, etc.**), lĭnĕāmentum, *n*; (**peculiarity**) *use adj*, prŏprĭus, (**one's own**)
February, Fĕbrŭārĭus (mensis)
fecundity, fēcundĭtas, *f*
federal, foedĕrātus
fee, merces, *f*, hŏnor, *m*
feeble, infirmus, imbēcillus
feebleness, infirmĭtas, *f*
feed, *v.t*, pasco (3), ălo (3); *v.i*, vescor (3 *dep*), pascor (3 *dep*)
feel, *v.t*, sentĭo (4); (**with the hands**), tempto (1)
feeler, cornĭcŭlum, *n*
feeling, *nn*, (**sensation or emotion**), sensus, *m*, tactus, *m*; (**spirit, etc.**), ănĭmus, *m*
feign, *v.t*, sĭmŭlo (1)
feigned, sĭmŭlātus
feint, sĭmŭlātĭo, *f*
felicitous, fēlĭx
felicity, fēlĭcĭtas, *f*
fell, *v.t*, excīdo (3), sterno (3)
fellow (**companion**), cŏmĕs, *c*; (— **citizen**), cīvis, *c*; (— **feeling**), consensĭo, *f*; (— **soldier**), commĭlĭto, *m*; (**worthless** —), nĕbŭlo, *m*
fellowship (**companionship**), sŏcĭĕtas, *f*
felt, *nn*, cŏactum, *n*
female, *nn*, fēmĭna, *f*
female, *adj*, mŭlĭĕbris
fen, pălus, *f*
fence, *nn*, saeptum, *n*, cancelli, *m*, *pl*
fence, *v.t*, saepĭo (4); (**with swords**), *v.i*, băttŭo (3)
fencing (**art of** —), ars, (*f*) glădĭi
ferment, *nn*, (**excitement**), aestus, *m*
ferment, *v.i*, fervĕo (2)
fern, fĭlix, *f*
ferocious, saevus, fĕrus
ferocity, saevĭtĭa, *f*
ferry, *nn*, trāiectus, *m*; (— **boat**), cymba, *f*
ferry, *v.t*, trāĭcĭo (3)
fertile, fēcundus, fertĭlis
fertility, fēcundĭtas, *f*
fervent, ardens, fervĭdus
fervour, ardor, *m*, fervor, *m*
festival (**holidays**), fērĭae, *f. pl*; (**religious** —, **etc.**), sollemne, *n*
festive (**gay**), hĭlāris
festivity (**gaiety**), hĭlārĭtas, *f*
fetch, *v.t*, pĕto (3), affĕro (*irreg*)
fetter, *nn*, vincŭlum, *n*
fetter, *v.t*, vincŭla ĭnĭcĭo (3) (*with dat*)
feud (**quarrel**), sĭmultas, *f*
fever, fĕbris, *f*
feverish, fĕbrĭcŭlōsus; (**excited**) commōtus
few, *adj*, pauci (*pl*)
fewness, paucĭtas, *f*
fib, mendācĭum, *n*
fibre, fibra, *f*
fickle, inconstans
fickleness, inconstantĭa, *f*
fiction, commentum, *n*, fābŭla, *f*
fictitious, commentĭcĭus
fiddle (**instrument**), fĭdes, *f. pl*
fidelity, fĭdēlĭtas, *f*
fidgety, inquiĕtus
field, ăger, *m*; (**plain**), campus, *m*; (— **of battle**), lŏcus, (*m*) pugnae; (**scope**), lŏcus, *m*
fiendish, nĕfandus
fierce, fĕrox, fĕrus
fierceness, fĕrōcĭtas,
fiery (**of temper, etc.**), ardens
fifteen, quindĕcim; (— **times**), *adv*, quindĕcĭes
fifteenth, quintus dĕcĭmus
fifth, quintus
fiftieth, quinquāgēsĭmus
fifty, quinquāginta
fig, **fig-tree**, fĭcus, *f*
fight, *nn*, pugna, *f*
fight, *v.i*, pugno (1)
fighter, pugnātor, *m*
figurative, translātus
figure, fĭgūra, *f*, forma, *f*

For List of Abbreviations used, turn to pages 3, 4

figure, *v.t*, (**imagine**), fingo (3)
figured, sĭgillātus
filch, *v.t*, surrĭpĭo (3)
file (**tool**), scŏbīna, *f*; (**rank**), ordo, *m*
file, *v.t*, (**wood, metal**), līmo (1)
filial (**dutiful, respectful**), pĭus
fill, *v.t*, implĕo (2), complĕo (2); (**a post, etc.**), fungor (3 *dep*) (*with abl*)
fillet (**for the hair**), vitta, *f*
film, membrāna, *f*
filter, *v.t*, cōlo (1)
filth, caenum, *n*
filthy, sordĭdus, foedus
fin, pinna, *f*
final, ultĭmus
finally, *adv*, postrēmo, dēnĭque, tandem
finance (**of the state**), aerārĭum, *n*
find, *v.t*, invĕnĭo (4), rĕpĕrĭo (4); (— **out**); cognosco (3), compĕrĭo (4); (— **fault with**), culpo (1); accūso (1)
fine, *v.t*, multo (1)
fine, *nn*, multa, *f*
fine, *adj*, (**of texture**), subtīlis; (**handsome, etc.**), praeclārus; (**weather**), sĕrēnus
finery, mundĭtĭa, *f*
finger, dĭgĭtus, *m*; (**fore —**), index dĭgĭtus
finger, *v.t*, tango (3)
finish, *nn*, (**perfection**), perfectĭo, *f*
finish, *v.t*, confĭcĭo (3); (**limit**), fĭnĭo (4)
finished (**complete, perfect**), perfectus
fir, fir-tree, ăbĭes, *f*
fire, ignis, *m*; (**ardour**), vīs, *f*, ardor, *m*; (**to be on —**), *v.i*, ardĕo (2); (**to set on —**), *v.t*, incendo (3)
fire, *v.t*, incendo (3); (**missiles**), cōnĭcĭo (3)
fire-brand, fax, *f*
fire-place, fŏcus, *m*
fire-wood, lignum, *n*
firm, firmus; (**constant**), constans; (**to make —**), *v.t*, confirmo (1)
first, *adj*, prīmus
first, *adv*, prīmum, prīmō
fish, *nn*, piscis, *m*
fish, *v.i*, piscor (1 *dep*)
fisherman, piscātor, *m*
fishing, *nn*, piscātus, *m*
fishing-boat, hŏrĭŏla, *f*
fishing-net, rēte, *n*
fishmonger, cētārĭus, *m*
fishpond, piscīna, *f*
fissure, rīma, *f*
fist, pugnus, *m*
fit (**violent seizure**), accessĭo, *f*, impĕtus, *m*
fit, fitted, aptus, ĭdōnĕus, accommŏdātus
fit, *v.t*, accommŏdo (1), apto (1); (— **out**), exorno (1)
five, quinque; (— **each**), quīni; (— **times**), *adv*, quinquĭes
five hundred, quingenti
fix, *v.t*, fīgo (3); (**determine**), stātŭo (3), constĭtŭo (3)
fixed, certus
flabby, flaccĭdus
flag, vexillum, *n*
flag, *v.i*, (**become weak**), languesco (3)
flagrant (**clear**), mănĭfestus; (**heinous**), nĕfandus
flail, pertĭca, *f*
flame, *nn*, flamma, *f*
flame, *v.i*, flagro (1)
flame-coloured, flamměus
flank (**of army, etc.**), lătus, *n*; (**of animal**), ilĭa, *n. pl*
flap (**of dress, etc.**), lăcĭnĭa, *f*
flare, *v.i*, flăgro (1)
flash, *nn*, fulgor, *m*
flash, *v.i*, fulgĕo (2)
flask, ampulla, *f*
flat, aequus, plānus
flatness, plānĭtĭes, *f*
flatter, *v.t*, ădūlor (1 *dep*)
flatterer, ădūlātor, *m*
flattering, ădūlans
flattery, ădūlātĭo, *f*
flaunt, *v.t*, iacto (1)
flavour, săpor, *m*
flaw, vĭtĭum, *n*
flawless, ēmendātus
flax, līnum, *n*
flaxen, *adj*, līnĕus
flea, pūlex, *m*
flee, *v.i*, (**flee from**, *v.t.*), fŭgĭo (3)
fleece, *nn*, vellus, *n*
fleece, *v.t*, (**rob**), spŏlĭo (1)
fleecy, lānĭger
fleet, *nn*, classis, *f*
fleet, *adj*, cĕler
fleeting, fŭgax
flesh, căro, *f*
flesh-coloured, fleshy, carnōsus
flexibility, făcĭlĭtas, *f*
flexible, flexĭbĭlis
flicker, *v.i*, trĕpĭdo (1), cŏrusco (1)
flickering, trĕpĭdans, trĕmŭlus
flight (**flying**), vŏlātus, *m*; (**escape**) fŭga, *f*
flighty, mōbĭlis, lĕvis

fling, *v.t*, cōnĭcĭo (3)
flint, sĭlex, *m*
flippant, făcētus
flirt, *v.i*, blandĭor (4 *dep*)
flit, *v.i*, vŏlĭto (1); (— **in, or upon**), inno (1) (*with dat*)
float, *v.i*, nāto (1); (**in the air**), vŏlĭto (1)
flock, grex, *m*, pĕcus, *n*
flock, *v.i*, conflŭo (3), concurro (3)
flog, *v.t*, verbĕro (1)
flogging, verbĕra, *n. pl*
flood, dĭlŭvĭes, *f*, *n*
flood, *v.t*, inundo (1)
floor, sŏlum, *n*; (**upper** —) contăbŭlātĭo, *f*
florid, flōrĭdus
flotilla, classis, *f*
flounder, *v.i*, vŏlūtor (1 *pass*)
flour, fărīna, *f*
flourish, *v.i*, flōrĕo (2); *v.t*, vĭbro (1)
flourishes (**of style**), călămistri, *m*, *pl*
flow, *nn*, cursus, *m*, fluxĭo, *f*; (**of the tide**), accessus, *m*
flow, *v.i*, flŭo (3); (— **past**), praeterflŭo (3); (— **together**), conflŭo (3); (**trickle**), mano (1)
flower, *nn*, flos, *m*
flower, *v.i*, flōrĕo (2)
flowing, flŭens; (**hair**), fūsus
fluctuate, *v.i*, iactor (1 *pass*); aestŭo (1)
fluctuation, mūtātĭo, *f*
fluency, vŏlūbĭlĭtas, *f*
fluent, vŏlūbĭlis
fluid, *nn*, hūmor, *m*, lĭquor, *m*
fluid, *adj*, lĭquĭdus
flurry concĭtātĭo, *f*
flush, *nn*, rŭbor, *m*
flush, *v.i*, ērŭbēsco (3)
fluster, *v.i*, ăgĭto (1)
flute, tĭbĭa, *f*; (— **player**), tĭbĭcen, *m*
flutter, *nn*, trĕpĭdātĭo, *f*
flutter, *v.i*, vŏlĭto (1), (**in fear**), trĕpĭdo (1)
flux (**flow**), fluctus, *m*, fluxus, *m*
fly, *nn*, musca, *f*
fly, *v.i*, vŏlo (1)
flying, *adj*, vŏlātĭlis, vŏlŭcer
flying, *nn*, vŏlātus, *m*
foal, ĕquŭlĕus, *m*, pullus, *m*
foam, *nn*, spūma, *f*
foam, *v.i*, spūmo (1)
foaming, **foamy**, spūmōsus
fodder, pābŭlum, *n*
foe, hostis, *c*
fog, cālīgo, *f*
foggy, cālīgĭnōsus
foil (**sword**), rŭdis, *f*; (**metal leaf**), lāmĭna, *f*
foil, *v.t*, (**parry a blow, delude**), ēlūdo (3)
fold, *nn*, (**of garment, etc.**), sĭnus, *m*
fold, *v.t*, plĭco (1)
folding-doors, valvae, *f. pl*
foliage, frons, *f*
folk (**people**), hŏmĭnes, *c. pl*
follow, *v.i. and v.t*, sĕquor (3 *dep*); sector (1 *dep*); (**succeed**), succēdo (3) (*with dat*)
follower (**attendant**), assectātor, *m*; or use *adj*, *e.g.* (—**of Caesar**) Caesărĭānus
following, sĕquens, proxĭmus, sĕcundus
folly, stultĭtĭa, *f*
foment, *v.t*, fŏvĕo (2); (— **trouble, etc.**), sollĭcĭto (1)
fond, ămans (*with genit*)
fondle, *v.t*, mulcĕo (2)
food, cĭbus, *m*; (**fodder**), pābŭlum, *n*
fool, hŏmo stultus; (**to act the** —), *v.i*, dēsĭpĭo (3)
fool, *v.t*, lūdo (3)
foolhardy, tĕmĕrārĭus
foolish, stultus
foot, pes, *m*; (**on** —), *adj*, pĕdester; (— **in length**), *adj*, pĕdālis; (**bottom of**), *use adj*, īmus, *in agreement with noun*, *e.g.* īma quercus (**foot of an oak**)
footing, stātus, *m*, *or use vb*, consisto (3), (**to stand**)
footman, pĕdĭsĕquus, *m*
footpath, sēmĭta, *f*
footprint, vestĭgĭum, *n*
footsoldier, pĕdes, *m*
for, *prep*, (**on behalf of**), prō (*with abl*); (**on account of**), propter, ŏb (*with acc*); (**during a certain time**), *use acc*, *e.g.* **for two hours**, dŭas hōras, *or* per (*with acc*); (**expressing purpose**), *use* ad (*with acc.*)
for, *conj*, nam, namque; ĕnim (*second word in clause*); (**because**), quippe, quod
forage, *nn*, pābŭlum, *n*
forage, *v.i. and v.t*, pābŭlor (1 *dep*)
forbear, *v.i. and v.t*, parco (3)
forbearance, contĭnentĭa, *f*
forbid, *v.t*, vĕto (1)
force, *nn*, vīs, *f*; (**military forces**), cōpĭae, *f*, *pl*
force, *v.t*, (**compel**), cōgo (3); (**break through**), perrumpo (3)
forced (**unnatural**), quaesītus; (**a** — **march**), magnum ĭter *n*
forcible, **forcibly**, *use adv. phr*, per vim
ford, *nn*, vădum, *n*
ford, *v.i. and v.t*, vădo transĕo (4) (**cross by a ford**)

forearm, bracchĭum, *n*
forebode, *v.t*, praesāgĭo (4), portendo (3)
foreboding, *nn*, praesensĭo, *f*
forecast, *v.t*, praevĭdĕo (2)
forefather, prŏăvus, *m*; (*pl*) māiōres *m. pl*
forehead, frons, *f*
foreign, externus, pĕrĕgrīnus
foreigner, pĕrĕgrīnus, *m*
foreman, qui (servis) praeest (**who is in charge of (slaves)**)
foremost, prīmus
forensic, fŏrensis
forerunner, praenuntĭus, *m*
foresee, *v.t*, prōvĭdĕo (2)
foresight, prōvĭdentĭa, *f*
forest, silva, *f*
foretell, *v.t*, praedĭco (3)
forethought, prōvĭdentĭa, *f*
forewarn, *v.t*, praemŏnĕo (2)
forefeit, *nn*, poena, *f*
forefeit, *v.t*, āmitto (3)
forge, *nn*, fornax, *f*
forge, *v.t*, făbrĭcor (1 *dep*), excūdo (3); (**strike counterfeit coins**), nummos ădultĕrīnos cūdo (3); (**documents**), suppōno (3)
forgery *use phr.* subiectĭo falsārum littĕrārum (**substitution of counterfeit letters**)
forget, *v.t*, oblĭviscor (3 *dep*) (*with genit*)
forgetful, immĕmor
forgetfulness, oblĭvĭo, *f*
forgive, *v.t*, ignosco (3) (*with dat of person*)
forgiveness, vĕnĭa,
fork, furca, *f*
forked, bĭfurcus
forlorn, destĭtūtus, perdĭtus
form, forma, *f*, fĭgūra, *f*
form, *v.t*, (**shape**), formo (1), fingo (3); (— **a plan**), ĭnĕo (4), căpĭo (3); (**troops, etc.**), instrŭo (3)
formality, rĭtus, *m*
formally, *adv*, rĭtĕ
formation, conformātĭo, *f*
former, prĭor, sŭpĕrĭor; (**the — and the latter**), ille . . . hic
formerly, *adv*, antĕā, ōlim
formidable, grāvis, mĕtŭendus
formula, formŭla, *f*
forsake, *v.t*, rĕlinquo (3), dēsĕro (3)
forswear, *v.t*, (**renounce**), abiūro (1); (**swear falsely**), periūro (1)
fort, castellum, *n*
forth, *adv*, *use compound vb. with* e *or* ex, e.g. exĕo, **go forth**; (**of time**), inde
forthwith, *adv*, stātim, extemplo
fortification, mūnĭtĭo, *f*
fortify, *v.t*, mūnĭo (4)
fortitude, fortĭtūdo, *f*
fortuitous, fortŭĭtus
fortunate, fēlix, fortūnātus
fortune, fortūna, *f*, (**property, etc.**), rēs, *f*, ŏpes, *f. pl*
fortune-teller, hărĭolŭs, *m*
forty, quădrāginta
forum, fŏrum, *n*
forward, forwards, *adv*, porro, prorsum, ante; *or use compound verb with* pro, e.g. prōdūco, (**lead forward**)
forward, *adj*, praecox
forward, *v.t*, (**send on**), perfĕro (*irreg*)
foster, *v.t*, nūtrĭo (4)
foster-brother, collactĕus, *m*; (— **child**), ălumnus, *m*; (— **father**), altor, *m*; (— **mother**), nūtrix, *f*; (— **sister**), collactĕa, *f*
foul, *adj*, foedus
found, *v.t*, condo (3); (**metal**), fundo (3)
foundation, fundāmenta, *n*, *pl*
founder, condĭtor, *m*
founder, *v.i*, submergor (3 *pass*)
fountain, fons, *m*
four, quattŭor; (— **times**), *adv*, quătĕr; (— **each**), quăterni
fourteen, quattŭordĕcim; (**-teenth**), quartus dĕcĭmus
fourth, quartus; (— **part, quarter**), quădrans, *m*
fowl, ăvis, *f* gallīna, *f*
fowler, auceps, *c*
fox, vulpes, *f*
fraction (part) pars, *f*
fractious, difficĭlis
fracture, *nn*, fractūra, *f*
fracture, *v.t*, frango (3)
fragile, frăgĭlis
fragment, fragmentum, *n*
fragrance, dulcis ŏdōr, *m*, (**pleasant smell**)
fragrant, dulcis, suāvis
frail, frăgĭlis, dēbĭlis
frailty, frăgĭlĭtas, *f*, dēbĭlĭtas
frame, forma, *f*, compāges, *f*; (— **of mind**), ănĭmus, *m*, affectĭo, *f*
frame, *v.t*, (**shape**), făbrĭcor (1 *dep*), fingo (3); (**form**), compōno (3)
franchise (citizenship), cīvĭtas, *f*; (**right of voting**), suffrāgĭum, *n*
frank, lĭber, ăpertus
frantic, āmens
fraternal, frāternus
fraternity (association of men), sŏdālĭtas, *f*
fratricide (the person), frātrĭcīda, *m*; (**the crime**), fraternum parrĭcīdĭum, *n*

fraud, fraus, *f*, dŏlus, *m*
fraudulent, fraudŭlentus, dŏlōsus
fraught, opplētus (**filled**)
fray, certāmen, *n*, pugna, *f*
freak, (**prodigy**), prōdĭgĭum, *n*
freckle, lentīgo, *f*
free, lĭber; (**generous**), lĭbĕrālis; (**of one's will**), sua sponte
free, *v.t*, lĭbĕro (1), solvo (3)
free-born, ingĕnŭus
freedman, lĭbertus, *m*
freedom, lĭbertas, *f*; (— **from a burden, tax, etc.**), immūnĭtas, *f*
freehold, *nn*, praedĭum lĭbĕrum, *n*, (**free estate**)
freely, *adv*, lĭbĕrē; (**generously**), mūnĭfĭcē, largē; (**of one's own free will**), sŭā sponte
free-will, vŏluntas, *f*
freeze, *v.t*, glăcĭo (1); *v.i*, congĕlo (1)
freight, *nn*, ŏnus, *n*
freight, *adj*, ŏnustus
French, *adj*, Gallĭcus; (**The French**), Galli, *pl*
frenzied, fŭrens, āmens
frenzy, fŭror, *m*, āmentĭa, *f*
frequent, *adj*, crēber, frĕquens
frequent, *v.t*, cĕlĕbro (1)
frequently, *adv*, saepe
fresh (**new**), rĕcens, nŏvus; (**wind**), vĕhĕmens
freshen, *v.t*, rĕcrĕo (1); *v.i*, (**of wind**), incrēbresco (3)
freshness, vĭrĭdĭtas, *f*
fret, *v.i*, dŏlĕo (2)
fretful, mōrōsus
fretfulness, mōrōsĭtas, *f*
friction, trĭtus, *m*
friend, ămĭcus, *m*
friendless, ĭnops, ămĭcōrŭm (**destitute of friends**)
friendliness, cōmĭtas, *f*
friendly, ămĭcus, cōmis
friendship, ămĭcĭtĭa, *f*
fright, terror, *m*, păvor, *m*; (**to take —**), *v.i*, păvesco (3)
frighten, *v.t*, terrĕo (2)
frightful, terrĭbĭlis, horrĭbĭlis
frigid, frīgĭdus
frill, segmenta, *n.pl*
fringe, fimbrĭae, *f. pl*
frippery, nūgae, *f. pl*
frisk, *v.i*, lascĭvĭo (4)
fritter away, *v.t*, dissĭpo (1)
frivolity, lĕvĭtas, *f*
frivolous, lĕvis; (**opinion, etc.**), fūtĭlis
fro (**to and —**), *adv. phr*, hūc et illūc
frock, stŏla, *f*
frog, rāna, *f*
frolic, *nn*, lūdus, *m*
frolic, *v.i*, lūdo (3)
from, ā, ab, dē, ē, ex (*all with abl*) (*with expressions of place, time and cause*)
front, *nn*, frons, *f*, prĭor pars; (**in —**) ā fronte, *or use adj*, adversus; (**in — of**) *prep*, prō (*with abl*)
front, *adj*, prĭor
frontage, frons, *f*
frontier, fīnis, *m*
frost, gĕlu, *n*; (**— bitten**), *adj*, ambustus
frosty, gĕlĭdus
froth, *nn*, spūma, *f*
froth, *v.i*, spūmo (1)
frown, *nn*, contractĭo, (*f*) frontis (**contraction of the forehead**)
frown, *v.i*, frontem contrăho (3)
frowsy, incultus
frozen, rĭgĭdus, glăcĭālis
fructify, *v.t*, fĕcundo (1)
frugal, frūgi, *indecl*
frugality, parsĭmōnĭa, *f*
fruit, fructus, *m*, pōmum, *n*
fruitful, fēcundus
fruitfulness, fēcundĭtas, *f*
fruition, fructus, *m*
fruitless (**without result**), irrĭtus
fruit-tree, pōmum, *n*, pōmus, *f*
frustrate, *v.t*, (**an undertaking, etc.**), ad vānum rĕdĭgo (3)
frustrated (**to be —**), *v.i*, frustrā esse
frustration, frustrātĭo, *f*
fry, *v.t*, frīgo (3)
frying-pan, sartāgo, *f*
fuel, ligna, *n. pl*
fugitive, *nn*, prŏfŭgus, *m*, fŭgĭtīvus, *m*
fugitive, *adj*, fŭgĭtīvus
fulfil, *v.t*, explĕo (2), exsĕquor (3 *dep*), fungor (3 *dep*) (*with abl*)
full, plēnus, replētus; (**with people**), frĕquens, crēber
full-grown, ădultus
fulminate, *v.i*, fulmĭno (1), intŏno (1)
fulness (**abundance**), ūbertas, *f*
fulsome, pūtĭdus
fumble, *v.t*, (**handle**), tento (1)
fume, *nn*, hālĭtus, *m*
fume, *v.i*, (**with anger, etc.**), fŭro (3)
fumigate, *v.t*, suffĭo (4)
fun, iŏcus, *m*, lūdus, *m*
function, offĭcĭum, *n*, mūnus, *n*
fund (**of knowledge, etc.**), cōpĭa, *f*, *with nn. in genit.*
fundamental, prīmus
funeral, fūnus, *n*, exsĕquĭae, *f*, *pl*
funeral, funereal, *adj*, fūnĕbris
fungus, fungus, *m*
funnel, infundĭbŭlum, *n*
funny, rīdĭcŭlus

For List of Abbreviations used, turn to pages 3, 4

fur, pĭlus, *m*
furbish, *v.t*, interpŏlo (1)
furious, fŭrens, saevus; **(to be —),** *v.i*, saevĭo (4), fŭro (3)
furl, *v.t*, contrăho (3), lĕgo (3), subdūco (3)
furlough, commĕātus, *m*
furnace, fornax, *f*
furnish, *v.t*, suppĕdĭto (1), orno (1)
furniture, sŭpellex, *f*
furrow, *nn*, sulcus, *m*
furrow, *v.t*, sulco (1)
further, *adj*, ultĕrĭor; *adv*, ultĕrĭus
further, *v.t*, **(help),** adiŭvo (1)
furthermore, *adv*, porro, praetĕrĕa
furthest, *adj*, ultĭmus
furtive, furtīvus
fury, fŭror, *m*
fuse, *v.t*, **(melt),** lĭquĕfăcĭo (3); **(— together),** miscĕo (2)
fuss, *nn*, perturbātĭo, *f*
fussy, nĭmis stŭdĭōsus
fusty, mūcĭdus
futile, vānus, fūtĭlis
futility, fūtĭlĭtas, *f*
future, *adj*, fūtūrus
future, *nn*, fūtūra, *n.pl*; **(in —),** *adv*, in rĕlĭquum tempus
futurity, tempus fūtūrum, *n*

G

gabble, *v.i*, blătĕro (1)
gabbler, blătĕro, *m*
gable, fastīgĭum, *n*
gad about, *v.i*, văgor (1 *dep*)
gadfly, tăbānus, *m*
gag, *v.t*, ōs obvolvo (3) (*with dat*) **(muffle the mouth)**
gage, pignus, *n*
gaiety, hĭlārĭtas, *f*
gaily, *adv*, hĭlāre
gain, *nn*, lŭcrum, *n*, quaestus, *m*
gain, *v.t*, **(profit, etc.),** lŭcror (1 *dep*); **(obtain),** consĕquor (3 *dep*), pŏtĭor (4 *dep*) (*with abl*); **(— a victory),** victōrĭam rĕporto (1) *or* părĭo (3)
gainsay, *v.t*, contrā dĭco (3)
gait, incessus, *m*
gaiters, ŏcrĕae, *f. pl*
galaxy, *use* vĭa lactĕa, *f*. **(milky way)**
gale, ventus, *m*, prŏcella, *f*
gall, *nn*, fel, *n*
gall, *v.t*, **(chafe),** ūro (3); **(annoy),** sollĭcĭto (1); *or* pĭget (2 *impers*) **(it irks)**
gallant, fortis
gallant, *nn*, **(lover),** ămātor, *m*
gallantry, virtus, *f*
gallery, portĭcus, *f*
galley (ship), nāvis, *f*
galling, mordax
gallon, congĭus, *m*
gallop, *v.i*, ĕquo cĭtāto vĕhi (3 *pass*) **(to be carried by a swift horse)**
gallows, furca, *f*, crux, *f*
gamble, *v.i*, ālĕa lūdo (3) **(play with dice)**
gambler, ālĕātor, *m*
gambling, *nn*, ālĕa, *f*
gambol, *v.i*, lascĭvĭo (4),
game, lūdus, *m*; **(wild beasts),** fĕrae, *f. pl*
gamester, ālĕātor, *m*
gammon, perna, *f*
gander, anser, *m*
gang, grex, *m*, căterva, *f*
gangrene, gangraena, *f*
gangway, fŏrus, *m*
gaol, carcer, *m*
gaoler, custos, *m*
gap, lăcūna, *f*, hĭātus, *m*
gape, *v.i*, hĭo (1)
gaping, *adj*, hĭans
garb, vestĭtus, *m*
garbage, quisquĭlĭae, *f, pl*
garden, hortus, *m*
gardening, cūra, (*f*) hortōrum **(care of gardens)**
gargle, *v.i*, gargărĭzo (1)
garland, serta, *n.pl*
garlic, ālĭum, *n*
garment, vestĭmentum, *n*
garner, *v.t*, **(store),** condo (3)
garnish, *v.t*, dĕcŏro (1)
garret, cēnăcŭlum, *n*
garrison, praesĭdĭum, *n*
garrison, *v.t*, praesĭdĭum collŏco (1) **in** (*with abl*)
garrulity, lŏquācĭtas, *f*
garrulous, lŏquax
gas, spīrĭtus, *m*
gash, *nn*, plāga, *f*
gash, *v.t*, percŭtĭo (3)
gasp, *nn*, ănhēlĭtus, *m*
gasp, *v.i*, ănhēlo (1)
gastric, *use genitive* stŏmăchi **(of the stomach)**
gate, porta, *f*, iānŭa, *f*; **(-keeper),** iānĭtor, *m*
gather, *v.t*, lĕgo (3), collĭgo (3); **(pluck),** carpo (3); *v.i*, convĕnĭo (4), congrĕgor (1 *dep*)
gathering, coetus, *m*
gaudy, fūcātus
gauge, *v.t*, mĕtĭor (4 *dep*)

gauge, *nn*, mŏdŭlus, *m*
gaunt, măcer
gay, hĭlāris
gaze at, *v.t*, tŭĕor (2 *dep*)
gaze, *nn*, obtūtus, *m*
gazelle, dorcas, *f*
gazette, acta dĭurna, *n. pl*, (**daily events**)
gear, appărātus, *m*
geld, *v.t*, castro (1)
gelding, cantērĭus, *m*
gem, gemma, *f*
gender, gĕnus, *n*
geneology (**lineage**), ŏrīgo, *f*, gĕnus, *n*
general, *adj*, (**opp. to particular**), gĕnĕrālis; (**common, wide-spread**), vulgāris, commūnis
general, *nn*, dux, *m*, impĕrator, *m*
generality (**majority**), plērĭque
generally (**for the most part**), *adv*, plērumque
generalship, ductus, *m*
generate, *v.t*, gĕnĕro (1), gigno (3)
generation, saecŭlum, *n*
generosity, bĕnignĭtas, *f*
generous (**with money, etc.**), lībĕrālis
genial, cōmis
geniality, cōmĭtas, *f*
genius (**ability**), ingĕnĭum, *n*; (**guardian spirit**), gĕnĭus, *m*
genteel, urbānus.
gentle (**mild**), mītis; (**of birth**), gĕnĕrōsus
gentleman, hŏmo ingĕnŭus
gentlemanly, *adj*, lībĕrālis, hŏnestus
gentleness, lēnĭtas, *f*
gently, *adv*, lēnĭter
gentry, nōbĭles, *m. pl*
genuine, sincērus
geography, gēōgraphĭa, *f*
geometry, gēōmĕtrĭa, *f*
germ, germen, *n*
German, Germānus
germane, affīnis
germinate, *v.i*, germĭno (1)
gesticulate, *v.i*, sē iactāre (1 *reflex*)
gesture, gestus, *m*
get, *v.t*, (**obtain**), ădĭpiscor (3 *dep*), nanciscor (3 *dep*); (**a request**), impĕtro (1); (**become**), *v.i*, fīo (*irreg*); (**— about, or spread, etc.**), percrēbesco (3); (**— away**), effŭgĭo (3); (**— back**), *v.t*, rĕcĭpĭo (3); (**— the better of**), sŭpĕro (1); (**— down**), *v.i*, dēscendo (3); (**— out**), exĕo (4); (**— ready**), *v.t*, păro (1); (**— rid of**), āmŏvĕo (2) in *or* ad (*with acc*); (**— up, rise**), surgo (3)
ghastly, exsanguis,
ghost, mānes, *m. pl*
giant, vir ingenti stătūra (**man of huge stature**)
gibbet, crux, *f*
giddy, vertīgĭnōsus
gift, dōnum, *n*
gifted (**mentally, etc.**), ingĕnĭōsus
gigantic, ingens
giggle, *v.i*, *use* rīdĕo (2), (**to laugh**)
gild, *v.t*, ĭnauro (1)
gills (**of fish**), branchĭae, *f. pl*
gimlet, tĕrĕbra, *f*
gin, pĕdĭca, *f*
giraffe, cămēlŏpardālis, *f*
gird, *v.t*, cingo (3); (**— oneself**), sē accingĕre (3 *reflex*)
girder, trabs, *f*
girdle, cingŭlum, *n*
girl, pŭella, *f*, virgo, *f*
girlhood, aetas, (*f*) pŭellāris
girth, ambĭtus, *m*
give, *v.t*, do (1), dōno (1); (**render**), reddo (3); (**— an opportunity**), făcultātem do (1); (**— back**), reddo (3); (**— in,**), *v.i*, cēdo (3); (**— up, deliver**), trādo (3); (**abandon**), dīmitto (3); (**— up hope**), *v.i*, dēspēro (1); (**— orders**), iŭbĕo (2)
glad, laetus, hĭlāris
gladden, *v.t*, hĭlāro (1)
glade, nĕmus, *n*, saltus, *m*
gladiator, glădĭātor, *m*
gladness, laetĭtĭa, *f*
glance at, *v.t*, aspĭcĭo (3); (**graze**) stringo (3)
glance, *nn*, aspectus, *m*
gland, glans, *f*
glare, *nn*, fulgor, *m*
glare, *v.i*, fulgĕo (2); (**look with stern glance**), torvis ŏcŭlis tŭĕor (2 *dep*)
glaring (**conspicuous**), mănĭfestus
glass, *nn*, vĭtrum, *n*; (**drinking —**), pōcŭlum, *n*
glass, *adj*, vĭtrĕus
gleam, *nn*, fulgor, *m*
gleam, *v.i*, fulgĕo (2)
glean, *v.t*, spīcas collĭgo (3) (**collect ears of corn**)
glee, laetĭtĭa, *f*
glen, valles, *f*
glib (**of tongue**), vŏlūbĭlis
glide, lābor (3 *dep*)
glimmer, *v.i*, sublūcĕo (2)
glimmering, *adj*, sublustris
glimpse (**get a — of**), *v.t*, dispĭcĭo (3)
glitter, *v.i*, fulgĕo (2)
glittering, *adj*, fulgĭdus, cŏruscus
gloat over, *v.t*, gaudens aspĭcĭo (3)
globe, glŏbus, *m*; (**the earth**), orbis, *m*
gloom, tĕnebrae, *f. pl*, tristĭtĭa, *f*
gloomy, tĕnebrōsus, tristis

glorify, *v.t,* laudo (1), extollo (3)
glorious, praeclārus, illustris
glory, glōrĭa, *f,* dĕcus, *n,* laus, *f*
gloss, *nn,* nĭtor, *m*
gloss over, *v.t,* praetĕrĕo (4)
glossy, nĭtĭdus
gloves, mănĭcae, *f. pl*
glow, *nn,* ardor, *m*
glow, *v.i,* ardĕo (2), candĕo (2)
glue, *nn,* glūten, *n*
glut, *nn,* sătĭĕtas, *f*
glut, *v.t,* explĕo (2), sătĭo (1)
glutton, hellŭo, *m*
gluttonous, ĕdax
gluttony, ĕdācĭtas, *f*
gnarled, nōdōsus
gnash (the teeth), *v.t,* frendĕo (2), (dentibus)
gnat, cŭlex, *m*
gnaw, *v.t,* rōdo (3)
gnawing, *adj,* mordax
go, *v.i,* ĕo (*irreg*), vādo (3); **(depart),** ăbĕo (4), prŏfĭciscor (3 *dep*); **(— abroad),** pĕrĕgre exĕo (4 *irreg*); **(— away),** ăbĕo (4 *irreg*); **(— back),** rĕdĕo (4 *irreg*); **(— by, past),** praetĕrĕo (4 *irreg*); **(— down),** dēscendo (3); **(— in),** ĭnĕo (4 *irreg*); **(— over),** transĕo (4 *irreg*); **(— round),** circumĕo (4 *irreg*) **(— through),** ŏbĕo (4 *irreg*); **(— up),** ascendo (3); **(— without),** cărĕo (2) (*with abl*)
goad, *v.t,* stĭmŭlo (1)
goal, mēta, *f*
goat, căper, *m*
go-between, *nn,* interpres, *c*
goblet, pōcŭlum, *n*
god, dĕus, *m*
goddess, dĕa, *f*
godless, impĭus
godlike, dīvīnus
godly, *adj,* pĭus
gold, aurum, *n*
golden, aurĕus
goldsmith, aurĭfex, *m*
good, *adj,* bŏnus, prŏbus, hŏnestus, aptus, commŏdus
good, *nn,* bŏnum, *n*; **(advantage),** commŏdum, *n*; **(goods, possessions),** bŏna, *n.pl*; **(— for nothing),** *adj,* nēquam; **(to do —),** prōdesse (*irreg*) (*with dat*)
good-bye! vălē! (*pl,* vălete!)
good-humour, cōmĭtas, *f*
good-humoured, cōmis
good-looking, spĕcĭōsus
good-nature, cōmĭtas, *f*
good-natured, cōmis
goodness (virtue), virtus, *f,* prŏbĭtas, *f*; **(excellence),** bŏnĭtas, *f*
good-tempered, mītis
goose, anser, *m*
gore, *nn,* crŭor, *m*
gorge (throat), guttur, *n,* fauces, *f. pl*; **(mountain pass),** angustĭae, *f. pl*
gorge oneself, *v.i,* sē ingurgĭtāre (1 *reflex*)
gorgeous, spĕcĭōsus, splendĭdus
gorgeousness, magnĭfĭcentĭa, *f*
gory, crŭentus
gossip, *v.i,* garrĭo (4)
gossip, *nn,* **(talk),** rūmor, *m*; **(person),** garrŭlus, *m*
gouge, *v.t,* **(— out eyes),** ŏcŭlos ērŭo (3)
gourd, cŭcurbĭta, *f*
gout, morbus, (*m*) artĭcŭlōrum **(disease of the joints)**
gouty, arthrĭtĭcus
govern, *v.t,* gŭberno (1), impĕro (1), tempĕro (1), mŏdĕror (1 *dep*)
government (act of —), admĭnĭstrātĭo, *f,* cūra, *f*; **(persons),** *use phr,* ii qui summum impĕrĭum hăbent **(those who hold supreme authority)**
governor (supreme), gŭbernātor, *m*; **(subordinate),** prōcūrātor, *m,* lēgātus, *m*
gown (woman's), stŏla, *f*; **(man's),** tŏga, *f*
grace, grātĭa, *f*; **(pardon),** vĕnĭa, *f*; **(charm),** vĕnustas, *f*; **(to say —),** grātĭas ăgo (3)
grace, *v.t,* **(adorn),** dĕcŏro (1)
graceful, vĕnustus, lĕpĭdus
gracious, prŏpĭtĭus, bĕnignus
grade, grădus, *m*
gradient, clīvus, *m*
gradually, *adv,* paulātim
graft, *v.t,* insĕro (3)
grain, frumentum, *n*
grammar, grammătĭca, *f*
granary, horrĕum, *n*
grand, magnĭfĭcus, grandis
grandchild, nĕpos, *m, f*
granddaughter, neptis, *f*
grandeur, magnĭfĭcentĭa, *f*
grandfather, ăvus, *m*
grandiloquent, grandĭlŏquus
grandmother, ăvĭa, *f*
grandson, nĕpos, *m*
granite, (hard rock), *use* sĭlex, *m,* **(flint stone)**
grant, granting, *nn,* concessĭo, *f*
grant, *v.t,* concēdo (3), do (1)
grape, ăcĭnus, *m,* ūva, *f*
graphic, expressus
grapple, *v.i,* luctor (1 *dep*)
grappling-iron, harpăgo, *m*
grasp, *nn,* mănus, *f*; **(of the mind),** captus, *m*

grasp, *v.t,* prĕhendo (3); **(mentally),** intellĕgo (3); **(snatch at, aim at),** capto (1)
grass, grāmen, *n,* herba, *f*
grasshopper, gryllus, *m*
grassy, grāmĭnĕus
grate, crātĭcŭla, *f*
grate, *v.t,* tĕro (3); *v.i,* strīdĕo (2)
grateful, grātus
gratification, explētĭo, *f,* vŏluptas, *f*
gratify, *v.t,* grātĭfĭcor (1 *dep*) (*with dat*)
grating, *nn,* **(noise),** strīdor, *m*
gratitude, grātĭa, *f,* grātus ănĭmus, *m*
gratuitous, grātŭĭtus
gratuity, congiārĭum, *n*
grave, *nn,* sĕpulcrum, *n*
grave, *adj,* grăvis,
gravel, glārĕa, *f*
gravity, grăvĭtas, *f*
gravy, iūs, *n*
gray, *see* **grey**
grayness, *see* **grey, greyness**
graze, *v.t,* **(animals),** pasco (3); *v.i,* pascor (3 *dep*); **(touch lightly),** *v.t,* stringo (3)
grease, *nn,* ădeps, *c*
grease, *v.t,* ungo (3)
greasy, unctus
great, magnus, grandis, amplus; **(distinguished),** illustris
greatcoat, lăcerna, *f*
great-grandfather, prŏăvus, *m*
great-grandson, prŏnēpos, *m*
greatness, magnĭtūdo, *f*
greaves, ŏcrĕae, *f. pl*
Greece, Graecĭa, *f*
greed, ăvārĭtĭa, *f*
greedy, ăvārus
Greek, Graecus
green, *adj,* vīrĭdis; **(unripe),** crūdus; **(to become —),** *v.i,* vīresco (3)
greet, *v.t,* sālūto (1)
greeting, sālūtātĭo, *f*
gregarious, grĕgālis
grey, caesĭus, rāvus; **(of hair),** cānus
greyness (of hair), cānĭtĭes, *f*
gridiron, crātĭcŭla, *f*
grief, dŏlor, *m,* luctus, *m*
grievance, quĕrĭmōnĭa, *f*
grieve, *v.i. and v.t,* dŏlĕo (2)
grievous, grăvis, ăcerbus
grim, trux
grin, *v.i,* rīdĕo (2)
grind, *v.t,* contĕro (3); mŏlo (3) **(— down, oppress),** opprĭmo (3);
grindstone, cōs, *f*
grip, *nn, use* mănus, *f,* **(hand)**
grip, *v.t,* arrĭpĭo (3)
gripes, tormĭna, *n.pl*
grisly, horrendus
grist, fārĭna, *f*
gristle, cartĭlāgo, *f*
grit, glārĕa, *f*
groan, *nn,* gĕmĭtus, *m*
groan, *v.i,* gĕmo (3)
grocer, tūrārĭus, *m*
groin, inguen, *n*
groom, *nn,* ăgāso, *m*
groom, *v.t,* **(look after),** cūro (1)
groove, cănālis, *m*
grope, *v.i,* praetento (1)
gross, *adj,* crassus; **(unseemly),** indĕcōrus
grotto, antrum, *n*
grotesque, monstrŭōsus
ground (earth), hŭmus, *f,* sŏlum, *n,* terra, *f*; **(cause, reason),** causa, *f*; **(to give —),** pĕdem rĕfĕro (*irreg*)
ground, *v.i,* **(of ships),** sīdo (3)
groundless, vānus
groundwork (basis), fundāmentum, *n*
group, glŏbus, *m*
group, *v.t,* dispōno (3)
grouse, lăgōpūs, *f*
grove, lūcus, *m*
grovel, *v.i,* serpo (3)
grow, *v.i,* cresco (3), augesco (3); **(— up),** ădŏlesco (3); **(become),** fĭo (*irreg*); *v.t,* cŏlo (3)
growl, *nn,* frĕmĭtus, *m*
growl, *v.i,* frĕmo (3)
growth, incrēmentum, *n*
grub, *nn,* vermĭcŭlus, *m*
grudge, *nn,* sĭmultas, *f*
grudge, *v.t,* invīdĕo (2) (*with dat*)
grudgingly, *adv, use adj,* invĭtus
gruel, ptĭsăna, *f*
gruff, asper
grumble, *v.i,* frĕmo (3)
grunt, *nn,* grunnĭtus, *m*
grunt, *v.i,* grunnĭo (4)
guarantee, *nn,* fĭdes, *f*
guarantee, *v.i,* fĭdem do (1) (*with dat*)
guarantor, vas, *m*
guard (person), custos, *c*; **(defence),** custōdĭa, *f,* praesīdĭum, *n*: **(to keep —),** *v.i,* custōdĭam ăgo (3)
guard, *v.t,* custōdĭo (4)
guarded (cautious), cautus
guardian, custos, *c*; **(of child),** tūtor, *m*
guardianship, custōdĭa, *f*; **(of child),** tūtēla, *f*
guess, *nn,* coniectūra, *f*
guess, *v.t,* cōnĭcĭo (3), dīvīno (1)
guest, hospes, *m,* hospĭta, *f*; **(at a party, etc.),** convīva, *c*
guidance (advice), consĭlĭum, *n*

For List of Abbreviations used, turn to pages 3, 4

guide, *nn,* dux, *c*
guide, *v.t,* dūco (3)
guild, collēgĭum, *n*
guile, dŏlus, *m*
guileful, dŏlōsus
guileless, simplex
guilt, culpa, *f*
guiltless, innŏcens, insons
guilty, sons, nŏcens
guise, hăbĭtus, *m,* spĕcĭes, *f*
gulf (bay), sĭnus, *m*; **(abyss),** gurges, *m,* vŏrāgo, *f*
gullet, guttur, *n*
gullible, crēdŭlus
gully (channel), cănālis, *m,* fossa, *f*
gulp, *v.t,* haurĭo (4)
gum (of the mouth), gingīva, *f*; **(of plants, etc.),** gummi, *n*
gurgle, *v.i,* singulto (1)
gush, *v.i,* prŏfundor (3 *pass*)
gust, flātus, *m*
gut, intestīna, *n.pl*
gutter, fossa, *f,* clŏāca, *f*
guttural, grăvis
gymnasium, gymnăsĭum, *n*
gymnastics, pălaestra, *f*

H

haberdasher, lintĕo, *m*
habit, consŭētūdo, *f,* mōs, *m*
habitable, hăbĭtābĭlis
habitation, dŏmĭcĭlĭum, *n*
habitual, ūsĭtātus
habituate, *v.t,* consŭēfăcĭo (3)
hack, căballus, *m*
hack, *v.t,* concĭdo (3)
hackneyed, trĭtus
haft, mănūbrĭum, *n*
hag, ănus, *f*
haggard, măcĭe corruptus **(marred by leanness)**
haggle, *v.i,* dē prĕtĭo căvillor (1 *dep*) **(to quibble about price)**
hail, *nn,* grando, *f*
hail, *v.i,* **(weather),** grandĭnat (*impers.*); *v.t,* **(greet),** sălūto (1)
hair, căpillus, *m,* crīnis, *m,* caesărĭes, *f*
hair-dresser, tonsor, *m*
hairless (bald), calvus
hairy, pĭlōsus
halcyon, *adj,* alcyŏnēus
hale (healthy), vălĭdus
half, *nn,* dīmĭdĭum, *n*; *adj,* dīmĭdĭus; *adv, use prefix* sēmi-, *e.g.* **half-asleep,** sēmĭsomnus; **(half-dead),** sēmĭănĭmis, mŏrĭbundus; **(— hour),** sēmĭhōra, *f*; **(— moon),** lūna dīmĭdĭāta, *f*; **(— yearly),** sēmestris
hall (of house), ātrĭum, *n*; **(public),** concĭlĭābŭlum, *n*
hallo! heus!
hallow, *v.t,* consĕcro (1)
hallucination, somnĭa, *n.pl*
halo, cŏrōna, *f*
halt, *nn, use vb,* consisto (3)
halt, *v.i,* consisto (3)
halter (horse), căpistrum, *n*; **(noose),** lăqŭeus, *m*
halve, *v.t.* ex aequo dīvĭdo (3)
ham, perna, *f*
hamlet, vīcus, *m*
hammer, *nn,* mallĕus, *m*
hammer, *v.t,* contundo (3)
hamper, quălum, *n*
hamper, *v.t,* impĕdĭo (4)
hamstring, *v.t,* poplĭtem succĭdo (3) (*with dat*)
hand, mănus, *f*; **(left) —),** mănus sĭnistra; **(right —),** dextra mănus; **(to shake —s),** dextras coniungĕre (3); **(— cuffs),** mănĭcae, *f, pl*; **(— writing),** chīrŏgrăphum, *n*; **(on the one —, on the other —),** et . . . et, *or* quĭdem (*second word in clause*) . . . autem (*second word in clause*); **(— to— fighting, etc.),** commĭnus, *adv*; **(at hand),** praesto, *adv*
hand, *v.t,* do (1), trādo (3); **(—down or over),** trādo (3)
handful (few), *use adj,* pauci
handicraft, artĭfĭcĭum, *n*
handiwork, ŏpus, *n*
handkerchief, sūdārĭum, *n*
handle, mănūbrĭum, *n*
handle, *v.t,* tracto (1)
handling (treatment), tractātĭo, *f*
handsome, spĕcĭōsus, pulcher
handy (manageable), hăbĭlis
hang, *v.t,* suspendo (3); **(— the head),** dēmitto (3); *v.i,* pendĕo (2); **(— back, hesitate),** dŭbĭto (1); **(overhang),** impendĕo (2)
hanger-on, assecla, *c*
hanging (death by —), suspendĭum, *n*
hangman, carnĭfex, *m*
hanker after, *v.t,* opto (1)
haphazard, *use adv. phr.* nullo ordĭne **(in no order)**
happen, *v.i,* accĭdo (3), ēvĕnĭo (4)
happiness, fēlĭcĭtas, *f*
happy, fēlix, bĕātus
harangue, *nn,* contĭo, *f*
harangue, *v.t,* contĭōnor (1 *dep.*)

harass, *v.t,* sollĭcĭto (1)
harbour, portus, *m*; (— **dues**), portōrĭum, *n*
harbour, *v.t,* (**shelter**), excĭpĭo (3)
hard, dūrus; (**difficult**), difficĭlis
hard, *adv,* (**strenuously**), strēnŭē
harden, *v.t,* dūro (1); *v.i,* dūresco (3)
hard-hearted, dūrus
hardiness, rōbur, *n*
hardly, *adv,* vix; (**harshly**), crūdēlĭter
hardness, dūrĭtĭa, *f*
hardship, lăbor, *m*
hardware, ferrāmenta, *n.pl*
hardy, dūrus
hare, lĕpus, *m*
hark! heus!
harlot, mĕrĕtrix, *f*
harm, *nn,* damnum, *n*
harm, *v.t,* nŏcĕo (2) (*with dat*)
harmful, noxĭus
harmless, innŏcŭus, innŏcens
harmonious, concors
harmonize, *v.i,* concĭno (3)
harmony, concentus, *m*, consensus, *m*
harness, *nn,* ĕquestrĭa arma, *n.pl*, (**horse equipment**), frēnum, *n*
harness, *v.t,* iungo (3)
harp, fĭdes, *f. pl*; (**harpist**), fĭdĭcen, *m*
harrow, *nn,* irpex, *m*
harrow, *v.t,* occo (1)
harrowing, *adj,* horrendus, terrĭbĭlis
harsh, asper, ăcerbus
harshness, aspĕrĭtas, *f*
hart, cervus, *m*
harvest, messis, *f*
hasp, fĭbŭla, *f*
haste, *nn,* festĭnātĭo, *f*
hasten, *v.i,* prŏpĕro (1), festĭno(1); *v.t,* mātūro (1), accĕlĕro (1)
hastily, *adv,* prŏpĕrē
hastiness (**of temper**), īrācundĭa, *f*
hasty, prŏpĕrus; (**of temper**), īrācundus
hat, pĕtăsus, *m*
hatch, *v.t,* (**eggs**), exclūdo (3); (**plans etc.**), ĭnĕo (4)
hatchet, sĕcūris, *f*
hate, *nn,* ŏdĭum, *n*
hate, *v.t,* ōdi (*v.defect*)
hateful, ŏdĭōsus
haughtiness, sŭperbĭa, *f*
haughty, sŭperbus, arrŏgans
haul, *v.t,* trăho (3)
haunt, *nn,* lătĕbrae, *f. pl*
haunt, *v.t,* (**visit frequently**), cĕlĕbro (1); (**trouble**), sollĭcĭto (1)
have, *v.t,* hăbĕo (2); *or use* esse (*irreg*) *with dat. of possessor, e.g.* **I have a brother,** est mĭhĭ frāter
haven, portus, *m*
haversack, saccus, *m*
havoc, strāges, *f*, vastātĭo,
hawk, *nn,* accĭpĭter, *m,f*
hay, faenum, *n*
hazard, *nn,* pĕrĭcŭlum, *n*
hazardous, pĕrĭcŭlōsus
haze, nĕbŭla, *f*
hazel, *nn,* cŏrўlus, *f*
hazy, nĕbŭlōsus
he, *pron, If not emphatic, use* 3*rd pers. of verb; otherwise,* ille, hic, is
head, căput, *n*, vertex, *m*; (**chief**), princeps, *m*; (**to be at the — of**) praesum (*irreg*) (*with dat*)
head, *adj,* (**of wind**), adversus
head, *v.t,* (**be in charge**), praesum (*irreg*) (*with dat*)
head-ache, căpĭtĭs dŏlor, *m*; (— **band**), vitta, *f*; (— **land**), prōmontōrĭum, *n*; (— **long**), *adj,* praeceps; (— **quarters**), praetōrĭum, *n*; (— **strong**), *adj,* pervĭcax
heal, *v.t,* sāno (1), mĕdĕor (2 *dep*) (*with dat*); *v.i,* consānesco (3)
healing, *nn,* sānātĭo, *f*
healing, *adj,* sālūtāris
health, vălētūdo, *f*
healthy, sānus, vălĭdus; (**of place or climate**), sălūbris
heap, *nn,* ăcervus, *m*
heap, *v.t,* cŭmŭlo (1), congĕro (3)
hear, *v.t,* audĭo (4); (**learn**), cognosco (3)
hearer, audĭtor, *m*
hearing, *nn,* (**sense of —**), audĭtus, *m*
hearsay, rūmor, *m*
heart, cor, *n*; (**interior**), *use adj,* intĭmus (**inmost**); (**feelings, etc.**), pectus, *n*, mens, *f*; (**courage**), ănĭmus, *m*; (— **ache**), sollĭcĭtūdo, *f*; (— **break**), dŏlor, *m*; (— **broken**) *adj. phr,* ănĭmo afflictus
hearth, fŏcus, *m*
heartiness, stŭdĭum, *n*
heartless, dūrus
heartlessness, crūdēlĭtas, *f*
hearty, ălăcer
heat, *nn,* călor, *m*, ardor, *m*, aestus, *m*, fervor, *m*
heat, *v.t,* călĕfăcĭo (3); (**excite**), incendo (3)
heath, lŏca obsĭta, *n.pl*, lŏca inculta, *n.pl*
heave, *v.t,* tollo (3); *v.i,* tŭmesco (3)
heaven, caelum, *n*; (— **dwelling**) *adj,* caelĭcōla
heavenly, *adj,* dīvīnus
heaviness, grăvĭtas, *f*; (— **of mind**), tristĭtĭa, *f*

heavy, grăvis; (**sad**), tristis; (**air, etc.**), crassus
hectic (**agitated, confused**), turbŭlentus
hedge, saepes, *f*
hedge in, *v.t*, saepĭo (4)
hedgehog, ĕchīnus, *m*
heed, *v.t*, (**obey**), pārĕo (2) (*with dat*); (**to take —**), *v.i*, căvĕo (2)
heedless, incautus
heedlessness, neglĕgentĭa, *f*
heel, calx, *f*; (**take to one's —s**), fŭgĭo (3)
heifer, iŭvenca, *f*
height, altĭtūdo, *f*; (**high ground**) sŭpĕrĭor lŏcus, *m*
heighten, *v.t*, *use* augĕo (2) (**increase**)
heinous, ătrox
heir, heiress, hēres, *c*
hell, inferi, *m. pl*, Orcus, *m*
hellish, infernus
helm, gŭbernācŭlum, *n*
helmet, cassis, *f*, găléa, *f*
helmsman, gŭbernātor, *m*
help, *nn*, auxĭlĭum, *n*
help, *v.t*, iŭvo (1), subvĕnĭo (4) (*with dat*); (**I cannot help coming**), non possum făcĕre quīn vĕnĭam
helper, adiūtor, *m*
helpful, ūtĭlis
helpless, īnops
helplessness, īnŏpĭa, *f*
helpmate, consors, *m, f*
hem, *nn*, limbus, *m*
hem in, *v.t*, circumsĕdĕo (2), saepĭo (4)
hemisphere, hēmisphaerĭum, *n*
hemp, cannābis, *f*
hen, gallĭna, *f*; (**— house**), gallīnārĭum, *n*
hence, *adv*, (**place or cause**), hinc; (**time**), posthāc
henceforth, *adv*, posthāc
her, *pron, adj*, eius; (*if it refers to the subject of the sentence*), sŭus, a, um
herald, praeco, *m*
herb, herba, *f*, hŏlus, *n*
herd, grex, *m*
herd together, *v.i*, congrĕgor (1 *pass*)
herdsman, pastor, *m*
here, hīc; (**hither**), hūc; (**to be —**), *v.i*, adsum (*irreg*)
hereafter, *adv*, posthāc
hereby, *adv*, ex hōc
hereditary, hērēdĭtārĭus
heredity, gĕnus, *n*
heretical, prāvus
hereupon, *adv*, hīc
heritage, hērēdĭtas, *f*
hermit, hŏmo sōlĭtārĭus
hernia, hernĭa, *f*
hero, vir fortissĭmus
heroic (**brave**), fortis
heroine, fēmĭna fortis, *f*
heroism, virtus, *f*
heron, arděa, *f*
hers, *see* **her**
herself, *pron. reflexive*, sē; (*pron. emphatic*), ipsa
hesitancy, hesitation, haesĭtātĭo, *f*
hesitate, *v.i*, dŭbĭto (1), haesĭto (1)
hew, *v.t*, caedo (3)
hey-day (**youth**), iŭventus, *f*
hibernate, *v.i*, condor (3 *pass*)
hiccough, singultus, *m*
hidden, occultus
hide, *nn*, (**skin**), cŏrĭum, *n*, pellis, *f*
hide, *v.t*, abdo (3), cēlo (1)
hideous, foedus
hideousness, foedĭtas, *f*
hiding-place, lătĕbrae, *f. pl*
high, altus, celsus; (**of rank**), amplus; (**of price**), magnus, magni; (**— born**), gĕnĕrōsus; (**— handed**), impĕrĭōsus; (**— lands**), montes, *m. pl*; (**— landers**), montāni, *m. pl*; (**— spirited**), ănĭmōsus; (**— treason**), măiestas, *f*; (**— way**), vĭa, *f*; (**— wayman**), lătro, *m*
hilarity, hĭlārĭtas, *f*
hill, collis, *m*
hillock, tŭmŭlus, *m*
hilly, montŭōsus
hilt, căpŭlus, *m*
himself, *pron. reflexive*, sē; *pron. emphatic*, ipse
hind, *adj*, postĕrĭor
hinder, *v.t*, impĕdĭo (4), obsto (1) (*with dat*)
hindrance, impĕdīmentum, *n*
hinge, *nn*, cardo, *m*
hinge on, *v.i*, vertor (3 *dep*), versor (1 *dep*) in (*with abl*)
hint, *nn*, significātĭo, *f*
hint at, *v.t*, significo (1)
hip, coxendix, *f*
hippopotamus, hippŏpŏtămus, *m*
hire (**wages**), merces, *f*
hire, *v.t*, condūco (3)
hired, conductus
his, *pron*, ēius, hūius, illĭus; *or* sŭus (*referring to the subject of the sentence*)
hiss, *nn*, sībĭlus, *m*
hiss, *v.i. and v.t*, sībĭlo (1)
historian, scriptor, (*m*) rērum
historic(al) *use nn*, histŏrĭa, *f*, (**history**)
history, histŏrĭa, *f*, rēs gestae, *f. pl*
hit, *nn*, (**blow**), plāga, *f*
hit, *v.t*, (**strike**), fĕrĭo (4); (**— upon**), incĭdo (3)

hitch, impĕdīmentum, *n*
hitch, *v.t*, necto (3)
hither, *adv*, hūc; (**— and thither**), hūc illūc
hitherto, *adv*, ădhūc
hive, alvĕārĭum, *n*
hoard, *nn*, ăcervus, *m*
hoard, *v.t*, collĭgo (3), condo (3)
hoar-frost, prūĭna, *f*
hoarse, raucus
hoary, cānus
hoax, *nn*, lūdus, *m*
hoax, *v.t*, lūdĭfĭcor (1 *dep*), lūdo (3)
hobble, *v.i*, claudĭco (1)
hobby, stūdĭum, *n*
hob-nail, clāvus, *m*
hoe, *nn*, sarcŭlum, *n*
hoe, *v.t*, sarrĭo (4)
hog, porcus, *m*
hogshead, dōlĭum, *n*
hoist, *v.t*, tollo (3)
hold, *nn*, (**grasp**), *use* comprĕhendo (3), *or* mănus, *f*
hold, *v.t*, tĕnĕo (2), obtĭnĕo (2), hăbĕo (2); (**— an office**), obtĭnĕo (2), fungor (3 *dep*); (**— elections, etc.**), hăbĕo (2); (**— back**), *v.i*, cunctor (1 *dep*), *v.t*, rĕtĭnĕo (2); (**— fast**), rĕtĭnĕo (2); (**— out**), *v.t*, porrĭgo (3); (**endure**), sustĭnĕo (2), perfĕro (*irreg*); (**— up, lift**), tollo (3)
hold-fast, *nn*, fĭbŭla, *f*
hole, fŏrāmen, *n*, căvum, *n*
holiday, fērĭae, *f. pl*
holiness, sanctĭtas, *f*
hollow, *nn*, căvum, *n*, lăcūna, *f*; (**— of the hand**), căva mănus, *f*
hollow, *adj*, căvus; (**false**), vānus
hollow, *v.t*, căvo (1)
holm-oak, īlex, *f*
holy, săcer
homage (**respect**), observantĭa, *f*
home, *adj*, dŏmestĭcus; (**homely**), rustĭcus
home, dŏmus, *f*; (**at —**), dŏmi; (**homewards**), dŏmum; (**from —**), dŏmo; (**— less**), cārens tecto (**lacking shelter**)
homicide (**deed**), caedes, *f*; (**person**), hŏmĭcīda, *c*
honest, prŏbus
honesty, prŏbĭtas, *f*, intĕgrĭtas, *f*
honey, mel, *n*
honeycomb, făvus, *m*
honorary, hŏnōrārĭus
honour, hŏnos, *m*; (**glory**), dĕcus, *n*; (**integrity**), hŏnestas, *f*, intĕgrĭtas, *f*; (**repute**), fāma, *f*
honour, *v.t*, cŏlo (3), hŏnesto (1)
honourable, hŏnōrātus, hŏnestus
hood, cŭcullus, *m*
hoof, ungŭla, *f*
hook, hāmus, *m*
hook, *v.t*, hāmo căpĭo (3), (**catch by a hook**)
hooked, hāmātus
hoop, circŭlus, *m*
hoot, *nn*, cantus, *m*
hoot, *v.i*, cano (3); *v.t*, (**hoot at**), explōdo (3)
hop, *v.i*, sălĭo (4)
hope, *nn*, spes, *f*
hope, *v.i. and v.t*, spēro (1)
hopeful (**promising**), *use genit. phr*, bŏnae spĕi
hopefully, *adj*, *phr*, multa spĕrans
hopeless (**desperate**), dēspērātus
hopelessness, dēspērātĭo, *f*
horizon, orbis, (*m*) fīniens (**limiting circle**)
horizontal, lĭbrātus
horn, cornu, *n*; (**made of —**), *adj*, corněus
hornet, crābro, *m*
horrible, horrĭbĭlis, horrendus, ătrox, foedus
horrid, horrĭbĭlis, horrendus, ătrox, foedus
horrify, *v.t*, (**dismay**), perceello (3), terrĕo (2)
horror, horror, *m*
horse, ĕquus, *m*
horseback (**to ride on —**), in ĕquo vĕhor (3 *pass*); (**to fight on —**), ex ĕquo pugno (1)
horse-fly, tăbānus, *m*
horse-race, certāmen ĕquestre, *n*
horse-shoe, sŏlĕa, *f*
horse-whip, flăgellum, *n*
horticulture, hortōrum cultus, *m*
hospitable, hospĭtālis
hospital, vălētūdĭnārĭum, *n*
hospitality, hospĭtĭum, *n*
host (**one who entertains**), hospes, *m*; (**innkeeper**), caupo, *m*; (**large number**), multĭtūdo, *f*
hostage, obses, *c*
hostess, hospĭta, *f*
hostile, hostĭlis, infestus
hostility, ĭnĭmĭcĭtĭa, *f*; (**hostilities, war**), bellum, *n*
hot, călĭdus, fervens; (**of temper**), ācer; (**to be —**), *v.i*, călĕo (2), fervĕo (2); (**to become —**), *v.i*, călesco (3); (**— headed**), *adj*, fervĭdus, fervens; (**hotly**), *adv*, ardenter
hotel, hospĭtĭum, *n*
hound, cānis, *m*, *f*
hound on, *v.t*, (**goad on**), instīgo (1), ăgĭto (1)

For List of Abbreviations used, turn to pages 3, 4

hour, hōra, *f*
hourly, *adv,* in hōras
hour-glass, hōrārĭum, *n*
house, dŏmus, *f,* aedes, *f, pl*; (**family**), gens, *f*; (— **hold**), dŏmus, *f,* fămĭlĭa, *f*; (— **keeper**), prōmus, *m*; (— **maid**), ancĭlla, *f*; (— **wife**), mātĕrfămĭlĭas, *f*
house, *v.t,*(**store**), condo (3), rĕpōno, (3)
hovel, tŭgŭrĭum, *n,* căsa, *f*
hover, *v.i,* vŏlĭto (1), impendĕo (2)
how (**in what way?**), quōmŏdŏ?; *with adj. or adv,* quam?; (— **many**), quot?; (— **often**), qŭotĭes?; (— **great or big**), quantus?
however, *conj,* tămen; *adv,* quamvis; (**how big or great**), quantumvis
howl, *nn,* ŭlŭlātus, *m*
howl, *v.i,* ŭlŭlo (1)
hubbub, tŭmultus, *m*
huddle, *v.i,* (— **together**), congrĕgor (1 *dep*), conflĕror (*irreg. pass*)
hue (**colour**), cŏlor, *m*
huff (**to be in a — about**), *v.t,* aegrē fĕro (*irreg*)
hug, *nn,* complexus, *m*
hug, *v.t,* amplector (3 *dep*)
huge, ingens, immānis
hull (**of a ship**), alvĕus, *m*
hum, *nn,* frĕmĭtus, *m*
hum, *v.i,* frĕmo (3), strĕpo (3)
human, *adj,* hūmānus; (— **being**), hŏmo, *c*
humane (**compassionate**), mĭsĕrĭcors
humanity, hūmānĭtas, *f*; (**human race**), hŏmĭnes, *c. pl;* (**compassion**), mĭsĕrĭcordĭa, *f*
humble, hŭmĭlis, vĕrēcundus
humble, *v.t,* dēprĭmo (3); (— **in war**), dēbello (1); (— **oneself**), sē summittĕre (3 *reflex*)
humdrum, *adj,* mĕdĭŏcris, tardus
humid, hūmĭdus
humidity, hūmor, *m*
humiliate, *v.t,* dēprĭmo (3)
humility, mŏdestĭa, *f*
humorous, rĭdĭcŭlus
humour, făcētĭae, *f. pl*; (**disposition**), ingĕnĭum, *n.* lĭbĭdo, *f*; (**to be in the — to**), *use* lĭbet (*v. 2 impers*) (*with dat. of person*)
humour, *v.t,* obsĕquor (3 *dep*) (*with dat. of person*)
hump, gibber, *m*
humpbacked, *adj,* gibber
hunch, hunchbacked, *see* **humpbacked**
hundred, *adj,* centum; (— **times**), *adv,* centies; (— **fold**), *adj,* centŭplex
hundredth, centēsĭmus
hundredweight, centumpondĭum, *n*
hunger, fāmes, *f*
hunger, *v.i,* ēsŭrĭo (4)
hungry, ēsŭrĭens, ăvĭdus (cĭbi)
hunt, *v.t,* vĕnor (1 *dep*)
hunt, hunting, *nn,* vĕnātĭo, *f*
hunter, vĕnātor, *m*
huntress, vĕnātrix, *f*
hurdle, crātes, *f. pl*
hurl, *v.t,* iăcŭlor (1 *dep*), cōnĭcĭo (3)
hurricane, tempestas, *f,* prŏcella, *f*
hurried, praeceps
hurriedly, *adv,* raptim
hurry, *v.i,* festīno (1), prŏpĕro (1); *v.t,* răpĭo (3); (**an action, etc.**), mātūro (1)
hurt, *nn,* (**wound**), vulnus, *n*
hurt, *v.t,* laedo (3), nŏcĕo (2) (*with dat*)
hurt, *adj,* (**wounded**), saucĭus
hurtful, nŏcens, noxĭus
husband, vir, *m,* mărĭtus, *m*
husbandry, agrĭcultūra, *f*
hush! tăcē; *pl,* tăcētĕ (*from* tăcĕo)
hush up, *v.t* (**conceal**), tĕgo (3), cēlo (1)
husk, follĭcŭlus, *m*
husky, fuscus, raucus
hustle, *v.t,* pulso (1), trūdo (3)
hut, căsa, *f,* tūgūrĭum, *n*
hutch, căvĕa, *f*
hyacinth, hŷăcinthus, *m*
hybrid, hybrĭda, ae, *c*
hymn, carmen, *n*
hyperbole, hŷperbŏlē, *f*
hyperchondriac, mĕlanchŏlĭcus
hypocrisy, sĭmŭlātĭo, *f*
hypocrite, sĭmŭlātor, *m*
hypocritical, sĭmŭlātus
hypothesis, coniectūra, *f,* condĭcĭo, *f*
hysteria, āmentĭa, *f,* perturbātĭo, *f*

I

I, *pron,* (**emphatic**), ĕgo; *otherwise use* 1*st pers. sing. of verb, e.g.* **I love,** ămo
iambic, *adj,* ĭambĕus
ice, glăcĭes, *f*
icicle, stīrĭa, *f*
icy, gĕlĭdus, glăcĭālis
idea, nōtĭo, *f,* īmāgo, *f,* sententĭa, *f*; (**to form an —**) *v.i,* cōgĭtātĭōne fingo (3)
ideal, *adj,* (**perfect**), perfectus, summus, optĭmus
ideal, *nn,* exemplar, *n*
identical, īdem (**the same**)
identify, *v.t,* agnosco (3)

identity (to find the — of), cognosco (3) quis sit . . .
ides, īdūs, *f. pl*
idiocy, fătŭĭtas, *f*
idiom, prŏprĭĕtas, *f.* (linguae) **(peculiarity of language)**
idiot, fătŭus, *m*
idiotic, fătŭus
idle (unemployed), ōtĭōsus; **(lazy)**, ignāvus; **(useless)**, vānus; **(to be —)**, *v.i*, cesso (1)
idleness, ignāvĭa, *f*, cessātĭo, *f*
idler, cessātor, *m*, cessātrix, *f*
idol (statue), sĭmŭlācrum, *n*; **(something loved)**, dēlĭcĭae, *f. pl*
idolatry, vĕnērātĭo, (*f*) sĭmŭlācrōrum **(worship of images)**
idolize, *v.t*, cŏlo (3)
idyl, īdyllĭum, *n*
if, *conj*, sī; **(— not)**, sīn; (*after a vb. of asking* — **whether)**, num, ŭtrum; **(whether . . . or if)**, sīve . . . sīve; **(— only)**, dummŏdo
ignite, *v.i*, ardesco (3); *v.t*, accendo (3)
ignoble (of birth), ignōbĭlis; **(dishonourable)**, turpis
ignominious, turpis
ignominy, ignōmĭnĭa, *f*, infāmĭa, *f*
ignorance, inscĭentĭa, *f*
ignorant, ignārus, inscĭus
ignore, *v.t*, praetĕrĕo (4)
ill, *adj*, aeger; **(evil)**, mālus; **(to be —)**, *v.i*, aegrōto (1); **(to fall —)**, *v.i*, in morbum incĭdo (3)
ill, *adv*, mālĕ
ill, *nn*, **(evil)**, mālum, *n*
ill-advised (reckless), tĕmĕrārĭus
ill-bred, inhūmānus
ill-disposed, mālĕvŏlus
illegal, illĭcĭtus
illegitimate, non lēgĭtĭmus
ill-favoured, dēformis, turpis
ill-health, vălētūdo, *f*
illicit, illĭcĭtus
illiterate, illittĕrātus
ill-natured, mālĕvŏlus
ill-omened, dīrus
ill-starred, infēlix
ill-temper, īrācundĭa,
illness, morbus, *m*
illogical, absurdus, rĕpugnans
illuminate, *v.t*, illustro (1)
illusion, error, *m*
illusive, vānus
illustrate, *v.t*, illustro (1)
illustration, exemplum, *n*
illustrious, clārus, illustris
image, īmāgo, *f*, effĭgies, *f*
imaginable, *use phr*, quod concĭpi pōtest **(that can be imagined)**
imaginary, commentĭcĭus
imagination, cōgĭtātĭo, *f*
imagine, *v.t*, ănĭmo concĭpĭo (3) *or* fingo (3)
imbecile, fătŭus
imbecility, imbēcillĭtas, (*f*) ănĭmi
imbibe, *v.t*, bĭbo (3), haurĭo (4)
imbue, *v.t*, infĭcĭo (3)
imitate, *v.t*, īmĭtor (1 *dep*)
imitation, īmĭtātĭo, *f*; **(likeness)**, effĭgies, *f*
imitator, īmĭtātor, *m*
immaculate, intĕger
immaterial (unimportant), *use phr*, nullo mōmento
immature, immātūrus
immeasurable, immensus
immediate, praesens, proxĭmus
immediately, *adv*, stātim, confestim
immemorial (from time —), ex hŏmĭnum mĕmōrĭa
immense, immensus, ingens
immensity, immensĭtas, *f*
immerse, *v.t*, immergo (3)
immigrant, advĕna, *m. f*
immigrate, *v.i*, immĭgro (1)
imminent, praesens; **(to be —)**, *v.i*, imminĕo (2)
immobility, immōbĭlĭtas, *f*
immoderate, immŏdĕrātus, immŏdĭcus
immodest, impŭdĭcus
immodesty, impŭdĭcĭtĭa, *f*
immolate, *v.t*, immŏlo (1)
immoral, prāvus, turpis
immorality, mōres māli, *m. pl*
immortal, immortālis, aeternus
immortality, immortālĭtas, *f*
immovable, immōbĭlis
immunity, immūnĭtas, *f*, văcātĭo, *f*
immutable, immūtābĭlis
impair, *v.t*, mĭnŭo (3)
impale, *v.t*, transfĭgo (3)
impart, *v.t*, impertĭo (4)
impartial, aequus, iustus
impartiality, aequĭtas, *f*
impassable, insŭpĕrābĭlis
impassioned, concĭtātus, fervens
impassive, pătĭens
impatience (haste), impătĭentĭa, *f*, festīnātĭo *f*
impatient, ăvĭdus
impeach, *v.t*, accūso (1)
impeachment, accūsātĭo, *f*
impeccable, impeccābĭlis
impede, *v.t*, impĕdĭo (4)
impediment, impĕdīmentum, *n*; **(of speech)**, haesĭtantĭa, *f*
impel, *v.t*, impello (3), incĭto (1)
impend, *v.i*, impendĕo (2), imminĕo (2)

impending, fŭtūrus
impenetrable, impĕnĕtrābĭlis
imperfect, imperfectus
imperfection (defect), vĭtĭum, *n*
imperial (kingly), rēgĭus *or use genit. of* impĕrĭum, *n*, **(empire),** *or* impērātor, *m*, **(emperor)**
imperil, *v.t*, in pĕrīcŭlum addūco (3)
imperious impĕrĭōsus
impermeable, impervĭus
impersonate, *v.t*, partes sustĭnĕo (2) **(keep up a part)**
impertinence, insŏlentĭa, *f*
impertinent, insŏlens
imperturbable, immōtus, immōbĭlis
impetuosity, vīs, *f*
impetuous, vĕhĕmens
impetus, vīs, *f*, impĕtus, *m*
impious, impĭus
implacable, implācābĭlis
implant, *v.t*, insĕro (3)
implement, instrūmentum, *n*
implicate, *v.t*, implĭco (1)
implicit, *adj*, tăcĭtus; **(absolute),** omnis, tōtus
implore, *v.t*, implōro (1), ōro (1)
imply, *v.t*, signĭfĭco (1); **(involve),** hăbĕo (2)
impolite, ĭnurbānus
import, *nn*, **(meaning),** signĭfĭcātĭo, *f*
import, *v.t*, importo (1)
importance, mōmentum, *n*; **(of position),** amplĭtūdo, *f*
important, grăvis; **(people),** amplus
importunate, mŏlestus
importune, *v.t*, flāgĭto (1)
impose, *v.t*, impōno (3)
imposition (fraud), fraus, *f*
impossible, *use phr*, quod fĭĕri nōn pŏtest **(which cannot be done)**
imposter, fraudātor, *m*
impotence, imbĕcillĭtas, *f*
impotent, imbĕcillus, infirmus
impoverish, *v.t*, in paupertātem rĕdĭgo (3)
impoverishment, paupertas, *f*
imprecation, exsĕcrātĭo, *f*
impregnable, ĭnexpugnābĭlis
impregnate, *v.t*, ĭnĭcĭo (3)
impress, *v.t*, imprĭmo (3); **(the mind),** mŏvĕo (2)
impression (mental), mōtus, (*m*) ănĭmi; **(idea, thought),** ŏpĭnĭo, *f*, ŏpĭnātĭo, *f*; **(mark),** vestīgĭum, *n*
impressive, grăvis
imprint, *nn*, signum, *n*; **(of a foot),** vestīgĭum, *n*
imprison, *v.t*, in vincŭla cōnĭcĭo (3) **(throw into chains)**
imprisonment, vincŭla, *n.pl*
improbable, nōn vērĭsĭmĭlis **(not likely)**
improper, indĕcōrus
improve, *v.t*, mĕlĭōrem făcĭo (3) *or* reddo; *v.i*, mĕlĭor fĭo (*irreg*)
improvement, ēmendātĭo, *f*
improvident, neglĕgens, imprōvĭdus
imprudence imprūdentĭa, *f*
imprudent, inconsultus, imprūdens
impudence, impŭdentĭa, *f*
impudent, impŭdens
impulse, impĕtus, *m*, impulsus, *m*
impulsive, vĕhĕmens
impunity (with —), *adv*, impūnĕ
impure, impūrus, foedus
impurity, impūrĭtas, *f*, incestus, *m*
impute, *v.t*, attrĭbŭo (3)
in, *prep*, **(place),** in (*with abl.*) *or use locative case if available, e.g.* Londīnĭi, **in London; (time),** *use abl. or* in (*with abl.*)
inability (weakness), imbĕcillĭtas, *f*
inaccessible, ĭnaccessus
inaccuracy (fault), error, *m*
inaccurate, (things), falsus
inactive, ĭners
inactivity, cessātĭo, *f*, ĭnertĭa, *f*
inadequate, impar
inadmissible, *use phr*, quod nōn lĭcet **(which is not allowed)**
inadvertent, imprūdens
inane, ĭnānis
inanimate, ĭnănĭmus
inappropriate, nōn aptus **(not suitable)**
inasmuch as, *conj*, quŏnĭam, quandōquĭdem
inattention, neglĕgentĭa, *f*
inattentive, neglĕgens
inaudible, *use phr*, quod audīri nōn pŏtest **(which cannot be heard)**
inaugurate, *v.t*, ĭnaugūro (1)
inauguration, consĕcrātĭo, *f*
inauspicious, infēlix
inborn, insĭtus
incalculable, *use phr*, quod aestĭmāri nōn pŏtest **(which cannot be estimated)**
incapable, inhăbĭlis
incarcerate, *v.t*, in vincŭla cōnĭcĭo (3) **(throw into chains)**
incarnate, spĕcĭe hūmānā indūtus **(clothed with human form)**
incautious, incautus
incendiary, incendĭārĭus, *m*
incense, *nn*, tūs, *n*
incense, *v.t*, ad īram mŏvĕo (2) **(arouse to anger)**
incentive, stĭmŭlus, *m*
incessant, perpĕtŭus, assĭdŭus
incest, incestum, *n*

inch, uncĭa, *f*
incident, rēs, *f*
incidental (casual), fortŭĭtus
incipient, *use vb*, incĭpĭo (**begin**)
incision, incĭsūra, *f*
incisive, mordax, ācer
incite, *v.t*, incĭto (1)
inclemency, aspĕrĭtas, *f*, sĕvērĭtas, *f*
inclement, asper, sĕvērus
inclination (desire), stŭdĭum, *n*, vŏluntas, *f*; **(leaning, bias),** inclīnātĭo, *f*
incline, *v.t*, inclīno (1); *v.i*, inclīnor (1 *pass*)
incline, *nn*, **(slope),** acclīvĭtas, *f*
inclined (disposed), prōpensus
include, *v.t*, rĕfĕro (*irreg*), comprĕhendo (3)
including (together with), cum (*with abl*)
incoherent; *use vb. phr. with* nōn *and* cōhaerĕo (2) **(to hold together)**
income, fructus, *m*, stĭpendĭum, *n*
incomparable, singŭlāris
incompatibility, rĕpugnantĭa, *f*
incompatible. rĕpugnans
incompetent, ĭnhăbĭlis
incomplete, imperfectus
incomprehensible, *use phr*, quod intellĕgi nōn pŏtest
inconceivable, *use phr*, quod ănĭmo fingi nōn pŏtest **(that cannot be conceived)**
inconclusive (weak), infirmus
incongruous, rĕpugnans
inconsiderable, parvus
inconsiderate, inconsīdĕrātus
inconsistency, inconstantĭa, *f*
inconsistent, inconstans; **(to be —),** *v.i*, rĕpugno (1)
inconsolable, inconsōlābĭlis
inconspicuous, obscūrus
inconstancy, inconstantĭa, *f*
inconstant, inconstans
inconvenience, incommŏdum, *n*
inconvenient, incommŏdus
incorporate, *v.t*, constĭtŭo (3), iungo (3)
incorrect, falsus
incorrigible, perdĭtus
incorruptible, incorruptus
increase, *nn*, incrēmentum, *n*
increase, *v.t*, augĕo (2), *v.i*, cresco (1)
incredible, incrēdĭbĭlis
incredulous, incrēdŭlus
incriminate, *v.t*, implĭco (1)
inculcate, *v.t*, inculco (1)
incumbent upon (it is —), ŏportet (*v. 2 impers. with acc. of person*)
incur, *v.t*, sŭbĕo (4)
incurable, insānābĭlis
indebted, obnoxĭus
indecency, turpĭtūdo, *f*
indecent, turpis, obscēnus
indecisive, dŭbĭus, anceps
indeed, *adv*, *emphatic*, prŏfecto; **(yes —),** vēro; *concessive*; quĭdem
indefatigible, assĭdŭus
indefensible, *use phr*, quod nōn pŏtest făcĭlĕ dēfendi **(that cannot be defended easily)**
indefinite, incertus
indemnify, *v.t*, damnum rēstĭtŭo (3) **(restore a loss)**
indentation, lăcūna, *f*
independence, lībertas, *f*
independent, lĭber
indescribable, īnēnarrābĭlis
indestructible (unfailing), pĕrennis
indeterminate, incertus
index, index, *m*
indicate, *v.t*, indĭco (1), signĭfĭco (1)
indication, indĭcĭum, *n*
indict, *v.t*, accūso (1)
indictment, accūsātĭo, *f*
indifference, lentĭtūdo, *f*
indifferent, neglĕgens; **(middling),** mĕdĭŏcris
indifferently, *adv* **(moderately),** mĕdĭŏcrĭter
indigenous, *adj*, indĭgĕna
indigestible, *adj*, grăvis
indigestion, crūdĭtas, *f*
indignant, īrātus; **(to be —),** *v.i*, indignor (1 *dep*), īrātus esse
indignation, indignātĭo, *f*, īra, *f*
indignity, contŭmēlĭa, *f*
indirect, oblīquus, **(path, etc.),** dēvĭus
indiscreet, inconsultus
indiscriminate, prōmiscŭus
indispensable, nĕcessārĭus
indispose, *v.t*, ălĭēno (1)
indisposed (not inclined), āversus; **(ill),** aegrōtus
indisposition (unwillingness), ănĭmus āversus; **(sickness),** vălētūdo, *f*
indisputable, certus
indistinct, obscūrus
individual, *nn*, hŏmo, *c*
individual, *adj*, prŏprĭus
indivisible, indīvĭdŭus
indolence, ignāvĭa, *f*
indolent, ignāvus
indomitable, indŏmĭtus
indoor, *adj*, umbrātĭlis **(in the shade)**
indoors (motion), in tectum
indubitable, certus
induce, *v.t*, addūco (3)
inducement, praemĭum, *n*
indulge, *v.i. and v.t*, indulgĕo (2)
indulgence, indulgentĭa, *f*

For List of Abbreviations used, turn to pages 3, 4

indulgent, indulgens
industrious, industrĭus, dīlĭgens
industry (diligence), industrĭa, *f*, dilĭgentĭa, *f*
inebriated, ēbrĭus
ineffective, īnūtĭlis
inefficient, *use phr*, qui rem cĕlĕrĭter confĭcĕre nōn pŏtest (**who cannot complete a matter quickly**)
inelegant, īnēlĕgans
inept, īneptus
inequality, dissĭmĭlĭtūdo, *f*
inert, īners, segnis
inertly, *adv*, segnĭter
inestimable, īnaestĭmābĭlis
inevitable, nĕcessārĭus
inexcusable, *use phr*, quod praetermittī nōn pŏtest (**that cannot be overlooked**)
inexhaustible, infīnītus, sĭne fĭne
inexorable, īnexōrābĭlis
inexperience, impĕrĭtĭa, *f*, inscĭentĭa, *f*
inexperienced, impĕrĭtus
inexplicable, īnexplĭcābĭlis
inexpressible, īnēnarrābĭlis, *or phr*, quod exprĭmi nōn pŏtest (**that cannot be expressed**)
infallible, qui falli nōn pŏtest (**who cannot be mistaken**)
infamous, infāmis
infamy, infāmĭa, *f*
infancy, infantĭa, *f*
infant, *adj. and nn*, infans
infantry, pĕdĭtātus, *m*
infatuate, *v.t*, infātŭo (1)
infatuated, dēmens
infect, *v.t*, infĭcĭo (3)
infection, contāgĭo, *f*
infer, *v.t*, collĭgo (3)
inference, coniectūra, *f*
inferior, *adj*, infĕrĭor, dētĕrĭor
infernal, infernus
infested, infestus
infidelity, perfĭdĭa, *f*
infinite, infīnītus
infinity, infīnītas, *f*
infirm, invălĭdus, infirmus
infirmity, infirmĭtas, *f*
inflame, *v.t*, accendo (3)
inflammable, *use phr*, quod făcĭlĕ incendi pŏtest (**that can be set on fire easily**)
inflammation, inflammātĭo, *f*
inflate, *v.t*, inflo (1)
inflexible, rīgĭdus
inflict, *v.t*, infligo (3); (**war, etc.**), infĕro (*irreg*) (*with dat of person*)
infliction, mălum, *n* (**trouble**)
influence, *nn*, vīs, *f*, mōmentum, *n*; (**authority**), auctōrĭtas, *f*; (**to have —**), *v.i*, vălĕo (2)
influence, *v.t*, mŏvĕo (2)
influential, grăvis
inform, *v.t*, certĭōrem făcĭo (3); (**— against someone**), nōmen dēfĕro (*irreg*) (*with genit*)
information (news), nuntĭus, *m*
informer, dēlātor, *m*
infrequency, rārĭtas, *f*
infrequent, rārus
infringe, *v.t*, vĭŏlo (1)
infringement, vĭŏlātĭo, *f*
infuriate, *v.t*, effĕro (1)
infuriated, īrā incensus
infuse, *v.t*, infundo (3), īnĭcĭo (3)
ingenious, subtīlis
ingenuity, *f*, ars, *f*, callĭdĭtas, *f*
ingenuous, ingĕnŭus
inglorious, inglōrĭus
ingot, lăter, *m*
ingrained, insĭtus
ingratiate oneself with, *v.t*, concĭlĭo (1), sē grātum reddere (*with dat*)
ingratitude, ănĭmus ingrātus, *m*
ingredient, pars, *f*
inhabit, *v.t*, incŏlo (3), hăbĭto (1)
inhabitant, incŏla, *c*
inhale, *v.t*, (spīrĭtum) haurĭo (4)
inherent, insĭtus
inherit, *v.t*, *use phr. with*, hēres (**heir**), *and* accĭpĭo (**to receive**)
inheritance, hērēdĭtas, *f*
inherited, hērēdĭtārĭus
inhibit, *v.t*, interdĭco (3)
inhospitable, īnhospĭtālis
inhuman, immānis, crūdēlis
inhumanity, immānĭtas, *f*, crūdēlĭtas, *f*
inimitable, nōn ĭmĭtābĭlis
iniquitous, īnīquus, imprŏbus
iniquity, imprŏbĭtas, *f*
initial, *adj*, prīmus
initiate, *v.t*, īnĭtĭo (1)
initiative (take the —), *v.i*, occŭpo (1)
inject, *v.t*, īnĭcĭo (3)
injudicious, inconsultus
injure, *v.t*, nŏcĕo (2) (*with dat*)
injurious, noxĭus, nŏcens
injury (of the body), vulnus, *n*; (**disadvantage**), dētrīmentum, *n*, iniūrĭa, *f*
injustice, īnīquĭtas, *f*, iniūrĭa, *f*
ink, ātrāmentum, *n*
inland, mĕdĭterrānĕus
inlay, *v.t*, insĕro (3)
inlet, aestŭārĭum, *n*

inn, dēversōrĭum, *n*, caupōna, *f*; (**keeper**), caupo, *m*
innate, insĭtus, innātus
inner, intĕrĭor
innocence, innŏcentĭa, *f*
innocent, innŏcens, insons
innocuous, innŏcŭus
innovate, *v.t*, nŏvo (1)
innumerable, innŭmĕrābĭlis
inobservant, nōn perspĭcax
inoffensive, innŏcens
inopportune, inopportūnus
inordinate, immŏdĕrātus
inquest, quaestĭo, *f*
inquire, *v.i*, quaero (3) ab (*with abl*) *or* dē (*with abl*)
inquiry, interrŏgātĭo, *f*; (**official**), quaestĭo, *f*
inquisitive, cūrĭōsus
inquisitor, quaesĭtor, *m*
inroad, incursĭo, *f*
insane, insānus, dēmens
insanity, insānĭa, *f*, dēmentĭa, *f*
insatiable, insătĭābĭlis
inscribe, *v.t*, inscrĭbo (3) in (*with abl*)
inscription, inscriptĭo, *f*
inscrutable, obscūrus
insect, bestĭŏla, *f*
insecure, intūtus (**unsafe**)
insecurity, *use adj*, intūtus
insensible (**unfeeling**), dūrus
inseparable, *use phr*, quod sēpărāri nōn pŏtest (**that cannot be separated**)
insert, *v.t*, insĕro (3)
inside, *prep*, intrā (*with acc*)
inside, *adv*, intus
inside, *nn*, intĕrĭor pars, *f*
insidious, insĭdĭōsus
insight (**understanding**), intellĕgentĭa, *f*
insignia, insignĭa, *n.pl*
insignificant, exĭgŭus, nullĭus mōmenti
insincere, sĭmŭlātus
insincerity, fallācĭa, *f*, sĭmŭlātĭo, *f*
insinuate, *v.t*, insĭnŭo (1); (**hint**), signĭfico (1)
insinuating (**smooth**), blandus
insipid, insulsus
insist, *v.i*, insto (1); *v.t*, (— **on, demand**), posco (3), flāgĭto (1)
insolence, contŭmācĭa, *f*, insŏlentĭa, *f*
insolent, contŭmax, insŏlens
insoluble, *use phr*, quod explĭcāri nōn pŏtest (**that cannot be explained**)
insolvent (**to be —**), *v.i*, nōn esse solvendo
inspect, *v.t*, inspĭcĭo (3)
inspection, *use vb*, inspĭcĭo (3), *or* lustro (1)
inspector (**superintendent**), cūrātor, *m*
inspiration (**divine, poetic,** etc), instinctus, *m*, afflātus, *m*
inspire, *v.t*, inĭcĭo (3) (*with acc. of thing inspired and dat. of person*); (**rouse**), accendo (3)
inspired (**of persons**), incensus
instal, *v.t*, ĭnaugŭro (1)
instalment, pensĭo, *f*
instance (**example**), exemplum, *n*; (**for —**), verbi grātĭā
instant, *adj*, praesens
instant, *nn*, mōmentum, *n*
instantly (**at once**), *adv*, stătim
instantaneous, praesens
instead, *adv*, māgis (**rather**)
instead of, *prep*, prō (*with abl*); *with a clause, use* tantum ăbĕrat (ābest) ut . . . ut
instigate, *v.t*, instīgo (1)
instill, *v.t*, instillo (1), inĭtĭo (3)
instinct, nātūra, *f*
instinctive, nātūrālis
institute, *v.t*, instĭtŭo (3)
institute, institution, collēgĭum *n*; instĭtūtum, *n*
instruct, *v.t*, dŏcĕo (2), ērŭdĭo (4); (**order**), praecĭpĭo (3)
instruction, dĭscĭplīna, *f*, institutio, *f*; (**command**), mandātum, *n*
instructor, măgister, *m*
instrument, instrūmentum, *n*
instrumental (**in doing something**), ūtĭlis
insubordinate, sēdĭtĭōsus
insufferable, intŏlĕrābĭlis
insufficiency, ĭnŏpĭa, *f*
insufficient, haud sătis (*with genit*) (**not enough . . .**)
insult, *nn*, contŭmēlĭa, *f*
insult, *v.t*, contŭmēlĭam impōno (3) (*with dat*)
insulting, contŭmēlĭōsus
insuperable, *use phr*, quod sŭpĕrāri nōn pŏtest (**that cannot be overcome**)
insure against, *v.t*, praecăvĕo (2)
insurgent, rĕbellis, *m*
insurrection, mōtus, *m*
intact, intĕger
integral, nĕcessārĭus (**necessary**)
integrity, intĕgrĭtas, *f*
intellect, mens, *f*, ingĕnĭum, *n*
intellectual, ingĕnĭōsus
intelligence, ingĕnĭum, *n*; (**news**), nuntĭus, *m*
intelligent, săpĭens, intellĕgens

intelligible, perspĭcŭus
intemperate, intēmpĕrans
intend, *v.t,* in ănĭmo hăbĕo (2) (*with infinitive*)
intense, ācer
intensify, *v.t,* augĕo (2), incendo (3) (**inflame, rouse**)
intensity, vīs, *f*
intent, *adj,* intentus; (**to be — on**), ănĭmum intendo (3) in (*with acc*)
intention, consĭlĭum, *n,* prōpŏsĭtum, *n*
intentionally, *adv,* consultō
inter, *v.t,* sĕpĕlĭo (4)
intercede (**on behalf of**), dēprĕcor (1 *dep*) pro (*with abl*)
intercept, *v.t,* (**catch**), excĭpĭo (3); (**cut off**), interclūdo (3)
intercession, dēprĕcātĭo, *f*
interchange, *nn,* permūtātĭo, *f*
interchange, *v.t,* permūto (1)
intercourse, commercĭum, *n,* ūsus, *m*
interest, *nn,* (**zeal**), stŭdĭum, *n*; (**advantage**), commŏdum, *n*; (**it is in the — of**), intĕrest (*v. impers. with genit*); (**financial**), fēnus, *n,* ūsūra, *f*
interest, *v.t,* tĕnĕo (2), plăcĕo (2); (**— oneself in**), stŭdĕo (2) (*with dat*)
interested, attentus
interesting, *use vb.* **to interest**
interfere, *v.i,* sē interpōnĕre (3 *reflex*)
interim, *adv,* (**in the —**), intĕrim
interior, *adj,* intĕrĭor; *nn,* pars intĕrĭor, *f*
interject, *v.t,* intericĭo (3)
interlude, embŏlĭum, *n*
intermarriage, connŭbĭum, *n*
intermediate, mĕdĭus
interminable, infīnītus
intermingle, *v.t,* miscĕo (2); *v.i,* sē miscēre (2 *reflex*)
intermission, intermissĭo, *f*
internal, intestīnus
international, *use genit,* gentĭum (**of nations**)
internecine, internĕcīnus
interpose, *v.t,* interpōno (3)
interpret, *v.t,* interprĕtor (1 *dep*)
interpretation, interprĕtātĭo, *f*
interpreter, interpres, *c*
interregnum, interregnum, *n*
interrogate, *v.t,* interrŏgo (1)
interrupt, *v.t,* interpello (1), interrumpo (3)
interruption, interpellātĭo, *f*
intersect, *v.t,* sĕco (1) (**cut**)
interval, intervallum, *n,* spătĭum, *n*
intervene, *v.i,* intercēdo (3), sē interpōnĕre (3 *reflex*) (*both with dat*)
intervention, intercessĭo, *f*
interview, collŏquĭum, *n*
interview, *v.t,* collŏquor (3 *dep*) cum (*with abl*) (**speak with**)
interweave, *v.t,* intertexo (3), implĭco (1)
intestines, intestīna, *n.pl*
intimacy, consŭētūdo, *f,* fămĭlĭārĭtas, *f*
intimate, *adj,* fămĭlĭāris
intimate, *v.t,* signĭfĭco (1)
intimidate, *v.t,* dēterrĕo (2)
intimidation, terror, *m,* mĭnae, *f. pl*
into, *prep,* in (*with acc*)
intolerable, intŏlĕrābĭlis
intolerance, sŭperbĭa, *f*
intolerant, sŭperbus
intone, *v.t,* cănо (3)
intoxicate, *v.t,* ēbrĭum reddo (3) (**make drunk**)
intoxicated, ēbrĭus
intoxication, ēbrĭĕtas, *f*
intractable, diffĭcĭlis
intrepid, intrĕpĭdus
intricacy (**difficulty**), diffĭcultas,
intricate, diffĭcĭlis
intrigue, dŏlus, *m*
intrigue, *v.i,* dŏlis ūtor (3 *dep*)
introduce, *v.t,* intrōdūco (3)
introduction, intrōductĭo, *f*; (**letter of —**) littĕrae commendātĭcĭae, *f. pl*
intrude, *v.i,* sē inculcāre (1 *reflex*)
intrusive *use phr,* qui interpellāre sŏlet (**who usually disturbs**)
intuition, cognĭtĭo, *f*
inundate, *v.t,* ĭnundo (1)
inundation, ĭnundātĭo, *f*
inure, *v.t,* assŭēfăcĭo (3)
invade, *v.t,* bellum infĕro (*irreg*) (*with dat*), invādo (3) in (*with acc*)
invader, hostis, *c*
invalid, *nn,* aeger, *m*
invalid, *adj,* (**of no avail**), irrĭtus, infirmus
invalidate, *v.t,* infirmo (1)
invariable, constans
invasion, incursĭo, *f*
invective, convĭcĭum, *n*
inveigh against, *v.i,* invĕhor (3 *dep*) in (*with acc.*)
inveigle, *v.t,* illĭcĭo (3)
invent, *v.t,* invĕnĭo (4)
invention (**faculty**), inventĭo, *f*; (**thing invented**), inventum, *n*
inventor, inventor, *m*
inverse, inversus
invert, *v.t,* inverto (3)
invest, *v.t,* (**money**), collŏco (1); (**besiege**), obsĭdĕo (2); (**— someone with an office**), măgistrātum committo (3) (*with dat*)

investigate, *v.t,* exquīro (3), cognosco (3)
investigation, investīgātĭo, *f,* cognĭtĭo, *f*
investiture, consĕcrātĭo, *f*
inveterate, invĕtĕrātus
invidious (envious, hateful), invĭdĭōsus
invigorate, *v.t,* vīres rĕfĭcĭo (3)
invincible, invictus
inviolability, sanctĭtas, *f* **(sacredness)**
inviolable, invĭŏlātus
invisible, caecus
invitation, invĭtātĭo, *f*; **(at your —),** tŭo invĭtātu
invite, *v.t,* invĭto (1)
inviting, blandus
invoke, *v.t,* invŏco (1)
involuntary, nōn vŏluntārĭus,
involve, *v.t,* involvo (3), illĭgo (1), hăbĕo (2)
invulnerable, *use phr,* quod vulnĕrāri nōn pŏtest **(that cannot be wounded)**
inward, *adj,* intĕrĭor
inwardly, inwards, *adv,* intus
irascibility, īrācundĭa, *f*
irascible, īrācundus
iris, īris, *f*
irk (it —s), pĭget (*v. 2 impers.*) (*with acc. of person*)
irksome, grăvis, mŏlestus
iron, *nn,* ferrum, *n*
iron, *adj,* ferrĕus
ironical, *use nn,* īrōnĭa, *f* **(irony)**
ironmongery, ferrāmenta, *n.pl*
irony, īrōnĭa, *f,* dissĭmŭlātĭo, *f*
irradiate, *v.t,* illustro (1)
irrational, rātĭōnis expers **(devoid of reason)**
irreconcilable, rĕpugnans
irrefutable, firmus
irregular (out of the ordinary), īnūsĭtātus, extrăordĭnārĭus; **(not well regulated),** nōn ordĭnātus
irregularity, vĭtĭum, *n*; *otherwise use adjs. above*
irrelevant, ălĭēnus
irreligious, ĭmpĭus
irremediable, īnsānābĭlis
irreparable, *use phr,* quod rĕfĭci nōn pŏtest **(that cannot be repaired)**
irreproachable, intĕger, invictus
irresistible, invictus
irresolute, dŭbĭus
irretrievable, irrĕpĕrābĭlis
irreverance,, impĭĕtas, *f*
irreverent, impĭus
irrevocable, irrĕvŏcābĭlis
irrigate, *v.t,* irrĭgo (1)
irrigation, irrĭgātĭo, *f*
irritable, stŏmăchōsus
irritate, *v.t,* irrĭto (1); **(make worse),** pēius reddo (3)
irruption, (attack), incursĭo, *f*
island, insŭla, *f*
islander, insŭlānus, *m*
isolate, *v.t,* sēpăro (1)
isolation, sōlĭtūdo, *f*
issue, *nn,* **(result),** ēventus, *m*; **(topic),** rēs, *f*; **(offspring),** prŏgĕnies, *f*
issue, *v.i,* **(proceed),** ēgrĕdĭor (3 *dep*); **(turn out),** ēvĕnio (4); *v.t* **(give out),** ēdo (3); **(edicts, etc.)** ēdĭco (3)
isthmus, isthmus, *m*
it, *pron,* id, hoc, illud; *often expressed by 3rd person sing. of verb, e.g.* **it is,** est
itch, *nn,* prūrĭtus, *m*; **(disease),** scăbies, *f*
itch, *v.i,* prūrĭo (4)
item, rēs, *f*
itinerant, circumfŏrānĕus
itinerary, ĭter, *n* **(route)**
itself, *see* **himself**
ivory, *nn,* ĕbur, *n*; *adj,* ĕburnĕus.
ivy, hĕdĕra, *f*

J

jab, *v.t,* fŏdĭo (3)
jabber, *v.i,* blăterro (1)
jackass, ăsĭnus, *m*
jacket, tŭnĭca, *f*
jaded, dēfessus
jagged, asper
jail, carcer, *m*
jailer, custos, *c*
janitor, iānĭtor, *m*
January, Iānŭārĭus (mensis)
jar, olla, *f,* amphŏra, *f,* dōlĭum, *n*
jarring, dissŏnus
jaunt, excursĭo, *f*
javelin, pīlum, *n*
jaws, faucēs, *f. pl*
jealous, invĭdus
jealousy, invĭdĭa, *f*
jeer at, *v.t,* dērīdĕo (2)
jeering, *nn,* irrīsĭo, *f*
jejune, iĕiūnus
jeopardize, *v.t,* pĕrĭclĭtor (1 *dep*)
jeopardy, pĕrĭcŭlum, *n*
jerk, *v.t,* quătĭo (3)
jerkin, tŭnĭca, *f*
jest, *nn,* iŏcus, *m*
jest, *v.i,* iŏcor (1 *dep*)
jester, scurra, *m*
jetty, mōles, *f*
Jew, *nn,* Jūdaeus, *m*
jewel, gemma, *f*

For List of Abbreviations used, turn to pages 3, 4

jeweller, gemmārĭus, *m*
jibe, convĭcĭum, *n*
jilt, *v.t,* rĕpŭdĭo (1)
jingle, *nn,* tinnĭtus *m*
jingle, *v.i,* tinnĭo (4)
job, ŏpus, *n*
jockey, ăgāso, *m*
jocose, iŏcōsus
jocular, iŏcŭlāris
jocund, hĭlāris, iūcundus
jog, *v.t,* fŏdĭco (1) **(nudge)**
join, *v.t,* iungo (3); *v.i,* sē coniungĕre (3 *reflex*); (— **battle**) committo (3)
joiner, lignārĭus, *m*
joint, commissūra, *f*
joist, tignum transversum, *n*
joke, *nn,* iŏcus, *m*
joke, *v.i,* iŏcor (1 *dep*)
joker, iŏcŭlātor, *m*
jollity, hĭlārĭtas, *f*
jolly, hĭlāris
jolt, *v.t,* concŭtĭo (3)
jostle, *v.t,* pulso (1)
jot, *v.t,* adnŏto (1)
journal, commentārĭi dĭurni, *m. pl*
journey, *nn,* ĭter, *n*
journey, *v.i,* ĭter făcĭo (3)
journey-man, ŏpĭfex, *c*
jovial, hĭlāris
jowl, gĕnae, *f. pl*
joy (outward), laetĭtĭa, *f*; **(inner),** gaudĭum, *n*
joyful, laetus
joyless, tristis
jubilant, gaudĭo (*or* laetĭtĭā) exsultans **(exultant with joy)**
judge, *nn,* iūdex, *m*
judge, *v.t,* iūdĭco (1), aestĭmo (1)
judgement, iūdĭcĭum, *n*
judicature, iūdĭces, *m. pl*
judicial, iūdĭcĭālis
judicious, săpĭens
judiciously, săpĭenter
judiciousness, prūdentĭa, *f*
jug, urcĕus, *m*
juggling-tricks, praestĭgĭae, *f. pl*
juice, sūcus, *m*
juicy, sūcōsus
July (before Caesar), Quintĭlis (mensis); **(after Caesar),** Iūlĭus (mensis)
jumble, *nn,* congĕrĭes, *f*
jumble, *v.t,* confundo (3)
jump, *nn,* saltus *m*
jump, *v.i,* sălĭo (4)
junction, coniunctĭo, *f*
juncture, tempus, *n*
June, Iūnĭus (mensis)
junior, mĭnor nātu, iūnĭor
juniper, iūnĭpĕrus, *f*
jurisconsult, iūrisconsultus, *m*
jurisdiction, iūrisdictĭo, *f*
juror, iūdex, *m*
jury, iūdĭces, *m. pl*
just, iustus
justice, iustĭtĭa, *f*
justification, sătisfactĭo, *f*
justify, *v.t,* purgo (1), excūso (1)
justly, *adv,* iustē
jut, *v.i,* exsto (1)
juvenile, iūvĕnīlis

K

keel, cărīna *f*
keen, ācer; **(mentally),** perspĭcax
keenness (eagerness), stŭdĭum, *n*; **(sagacity),** săgācĭtas, *f*; **(sharpness, etc.),** ăcerbĭtas, *f*
keep, *nn,* arx, *f*
keep, *v.t,* **(hold),** tĕnĕo (2), hăbĕo (2); **(preserve),** servo (1); **(store),** condo (3); **(support, rear),** ălo (3); (— **apart**), distĭnĕo (2); (— **back**), rĕtĭnĕo (2), dētĭnĕo (2); (— **off**), arcĕo (2); *v.i,* **(remain),** mănĕo (2)
keeper, custos, *c*
keeping (protection), tūtēla, *f*, custōdĭa, *f*
keg, dōlĭum, *n*, amphŏra, *f*
kennel, stăbŭlum, *n*
kerb (stone), crĕpĭdo, *f*
kernel, nŭclĕus, *m*
kettle, lĕbes, *m*
key, clāvis, *f*
kick, *nn,* calcĭtrātus, *m*
kick, *v.i,* calcĭtro (1)
kid, haedus, *m*
kidnap, *v.t,* surrĭpĭo (3)
kidney, rēn, *m*
kidney-bean, phăsēlus, *m*, *f*
kill, *v.t,* nĕco (1), interfĭcĭo (3)
kiln, fornax, *f*
kind, *nn,* gĕnus, *n*; **(of such a —),** *adj,* tālis
kind, *adj,* bĕnignus
kindle, *v.t,* accendo (3), excĭto (1)
kindliness, bĕnignĭtas, *f*
kindness, bĕnĕfĭcĭum, *n*; **(of disposition),** bĕnignĭtas, *f*
kindred (relatives), consanguĭnĕi, *m. pl*; cognāti, *m. pl*
king, rex, *m*
kingdom, regnum, *n*
kingfisher, alcēdo, *f*
kinsman, nĕcessārĭus, *m*
kiss, *nn,* oscŭlum, *n*

kiss, *v.t*, oscŭlor (1 *dep*)
kitchen, cŭlīna, *f*
kitten, fēlis cătŭlus, *m* **(the young of a cat)**
knapsack, sarcĭna, *f*
knave, scĕlestus, *m*
knavery, nēquĭtĭa, *f*, imprŏbĭtas, *f*
knavish, nēquam (*indeclinable*); imprŏbus
knead, *v.t*, sŭbĭgo (3)
knee, gĕnu, *n*; **(knock-kneed),** *adj*, vārus
knee-cap, pătella, *f*
kneel, gĕnu (gĕnĭbus) nītor (3 *dep*) **(rest on the knee(s))**
knife, culter, *m*
knight, ĕques, *m*
knighthood, dignĭtas ĕquestris, *f*
knit, *v.t*, texo (3); **(— the forehead)** frontem contrăho (3)
knob, bulla, *f*, nōdus, *m*
knock, *v.t*, pulso (1); **(— against),** offendo (3); **(— down),** dēpello (3), dēĭcĭo (3)
knock, knocking pulsus, *m*, pulsātĭo, *f*
knoll, tŭmŭlus, *m*
knot, *nn*, nōdus, *m*
knot, *v.t*, nōdo (1)
knotty, nōdōsus
know, *v.t*, scĭo (4); **(get to —),** cognosco (3); **(person, acquaintance)** nosco (3); **(not to —),** nescĭo (4)
knowing, *adj*, **(wise),** prūdens
knowingly, *adv*, consultō
knowledge, scĭentĭa, *f*
known, nōtus; **(to make —),** dēclāro (1)
knuckle, artĭcŭlus, *m*

L

label, tĭtŭlus, *m*, pittăcĭum, *n*
laborious, lăbōrĭōsus
labour, lăbor, *m*, ŏpus, *n*; **(to be in —),** *v.i*, partŭrĭo (4)
labour, *v.i*, lăbōro (1), ēnĭtor (3 *dep*)
labourer, ŏpĕrārĭus, *m*
labyrinth, lăbȳrinthus, *m*
lace, rētĭcŭlāta texta, *n.pl* **(net-like fabric)**
lacerate, *v.t*, lăcĕro (1)
laceration, lăcĕrātĭo, *f*
lack, *nn*, ĭnŏpĭa, *f*
lack, *v.i*, ĕgĕo (2), cărĕo (*both with abl*)
lackey, pĕdĭsĕquus, *m*
laconic, brĕvis
lad, pŭer, *m*
ladder, scālae, *f. pl*
ladle, trulla, *f*
lady, mātrōna, *f*, dŏmĭna, *f*
lady-like, lībĕrālis **(gracious)**
lag, *v.i*, cesso (1)
laggard, cessātor, *m*
lagoon, lăcus, *m*
lair, lătĭbŭlum, *n*
lake, lăcus, *m*
lamb, agnus, *m*; (agna, *f*)
lame, claudus; **(argument, etc.),** lĕvis; **(to be —),** *v.i*, claudĭco (1)
lameness, claudĭcātĭo, *f*
lament, lāmentātĭo, *f*, complōrātĭo, *f*, ŭlŭlātus, *m*
lament, *v.i, and v.t*, lāmentor (1 *dep*), dēplōro (1), lūgĕo (2)
lamentable, lāmentābĭlis
lamented, dēplōrātus, flēbĭlis
lamp, lŭcerna, *f*
lampoon, carmen rīdĭcŭlum et fāmōsum **(facetious defamatory verse)**
lance, lancĕa, *f*, hasta, *f*
lancet, scalpellum, *n*
land (earth, etc.), terra, *f*; **(region or country),** rĕgĭo, *f*, fĭnes, *m. pl*; **(native —),** pătrĭa, *f*
land, *v.t*, expōno (3); *v.i*, ēgrĕdĭor (3 *dep*)
landing, *nn*, ēgressus, *m*
landlord (innkeeper), caupo, *m*; **(owner),** dŏmĭnus, *m*
landmark, lăpis, *m*
landslide, lapsus, (*m*) terrae
lane, sēmĭta, *f*,
language, lingua, *f*; **(speech, style),** ōrātĭo, *f*
languid, languĭdus, rĕmissus
languish, *v.i*, languĕo (2), tābesco (3)
languor, languor, *m*
lank, (hair), prōmissus; **(persons),** prōcerus
lantern, lanterna, *f*
lap, grĕmĭum, *n*, sĭnus, *m*
lap up, *v.t*, lambo (3)
lapse, *nn*, **(mistake),** peccātum, *n*; **(of time),** fŭga, *f*
lapse, *v.i*, **(err),** pecco (1); **(time),** praetĕrĕo (4)
larceny, furtum, *n*
larch, lărix, *f*
lard, ădeps, *c*, lārĭdum, *n*
larder, use cella, *f*, **(store-room),** *or* armārĭum, *n*, **(food cupboard)**
large, magnus
largeness, magnĭtūdo, *f*
largess, largītĭo, *f*
lark, ălauda, *f*
larynx, *use* guttur, *n*, **(throat)**
lascivious, lĭbĭdĭnōsus
lash (whip), lōrum, *n*, flăgellum, *n*; **(eye —),** pĭlus, *m*

lash, *v.t,* **(whip),** verbĕro (1); **(bind),** allĭgo (1)
lass, pŭella, *f*
last, *adj,* ultĭmus, postrēmus, extrēmus; **(most recent),** nŏvissĭmus, proxĭmus; **(at —),** *adv,* tandem
last, *v.i,* dūro (1), mănĕo (2)
lasting, *adj,* dĭūturnus
lastly, *adv,* postrēmo, dēnĭque
latch, pessŭlus, *m*
late, sērus, tardus; **(dead),** mortŭus; *adv,* sēro; **(— at night)** (*adv. phr.*), multā nocte
lately, *adv,* nūper
latent, occultus
lathe, tornus, *m*
Latin, Lātīnus; **(— language),** lingua Lātīna, *f*
latitude (freedom, scope), lībertas, *f*
latter (the —), hic
lattice, cancelli, *m. pl*
laud, *v.t,* laudo (1)
laudable, laudābĭlis
laugh, *nn,* rīsus, *m*; **(loud —),** căchinnus, *m*
laugh, *v.i,* cachinno (1)
laughing-stock, lūdĭbrĭum, *n*
launch, *v.t,* **(a ship),** dēdūco (3); *v.i,* **(launch out),** insĕquor (3 *dep*)
laurel, laurus, *f*; *adj,* laurĕus
lava, massa lĭquĕfacta, *f,* **(molten mass)**
lavish, *adj,* prōdĭgus, prŏfūsus
lavish, *v.t,* prŏfundo (3)
law (a law), lex, *f*; **(the law),** iūs, *n*
lawful, lēgĭtĭmus
lawless, nĕfārĭus
lawn, prātum, *n*
lawsuit, lis, *f*
lawyer, iūrisconsultus, *m*
lax, dissŏlūtus
laxness, rĕmissĭo, *f,* neglĕgentĭa, *f*
laxity, rĕmissĭo, *f,* neglĕgentĭa, *f*
lay, *v.t,* pōno (3); **(— aside),** pōno (3); **(— foundations),** iăcĭo (3); **(— an ambush),** insĭdĭas collŏco (1); **(— down arms),** ab armis discēdo (3); **(— eggs),** ōva părĭo (3)
layer, cŏrĭum, *n,* tăbŭlātum, *n*
laziness, ignāvĭa, *f*
lazy, ignāvus, pĭger
lead, *nn,* plumbum, *n*; *adj,* plumbĕus
lead, *v.t,* dūco (3); **(— a life, etc.),** ăgo (3); **(— on, persuade),** addūco (3)
leader, dux, *c*
leadership, ductus, *m*; *or use phr. in abl, e.g.* **under the — of Brutus,** Brūto dūce **(with Brutus leader)**
leading, *adj,* princeps
leaf, frons, *f,* fŏlĭum, *n*; **(paper)** schĕda, *f*
leafy, frondōsus
league, foedus, *n,* sŏcĭĕtas, *f*
league together, *v.i,* coniūro (1)
leak, *nn,* rīma, *f*
leak (let in water), ăquam per rīmas accĭpĭo (3)
leaky, rīmōsus
lean, *adj,* măcer, exĭlis
lean, *v.i,* innĭtor (3 *dep*); *v.t,* inclīno (1)
leanness, măcĭes, *f*
leap, *nn,* saltus, *m*
leap, *v.i,* sălĭo (4); **(— down)** dēsĭlĭo (4)
leap-year, bĭsextĭlis annus, *m*
learn, *v.t,* disco (3); **(ascertain)** cognosco (3)
learned, doctus
learning, doctrīna, *f,* ērŭdĭtĭo, *f*
lease, *nn,* conductĭo, *f*
lease, *v.t,* condūco (3)
leash, cōpŭla, *f*
least, *adj,* mĭnĭmus; *adv,* mĭnĭmē; **(at —),** *adv,* saltem
leather, cŏrĭum, *n*
leave, *nn,* **(permission),** pŏtestas, *f,* permissĭo, *f*; **(— of absence)** commĕātus, *m*
leave, *v.i,* discēdo (3); *v.t,* rĕlinquo (3), dēsĕro (3)
leave off, *v.i. and v.t,* dēsĭno (3)
leavings, *nn,* rĕlĭquĭae, *f. pl*
lecture, *nn,* audĭtĭo, *f,* **(hearing)**
lecture, *v.i,* schŏlas hăbĕo (2)
lecture-room, schŏla, *f*
ledge, *use adj,* ēmĭnens **(projecting)** *in agreement with a noun*
ledger, cōdex, *m*
leech, hĭrūdo, *f*
leek, porrum, *n*
leering, *adj,* lĭmus
left, *adj,* **(opp. to right),** sĭnister, laevus; **(remaining),** rĕlĭquus
leg, crus, *n*
legacy, lēgātum, *n*
legal, lēgĭtĭmus
legalize, *v.t,* sancĭo (4)
legate, lēgātus, *m*
legation, lēgātĭo, *f*
legend, fābŭla, *f*
legendary, fābŭlōsus
leggings, ŏcrĕae, *f. pl*
legible, *use phr,* făcĭlis ad lēgendum **(easy for reading)**
legion, lēgĭo, *f*
legislate, *v.i,* lēges făcĭo (3) **(make laws)**
legislator, lātor, (*m*) lēgum **(proposer of laws)**
legitimate, lēgĭtĭmus

leisure, ōtĭum, *n*; (**to be at —**), *v.i*, ōtĭor (1 *dep*)
leisurely, *adj*, lentus
lend, *v.t*, mūtŭum do (1) (**give a loan**), commŏdo (1)
length, longĭtūdo, *f*; (**of time**), dĭūturnĭtas, *f*; (**at —**), *adv*, tandem
lengthen, *v.t*, prōdūco (3), longĭōrem reddo (3)
leniency, clēmentĭa, *f*
lenient, mītis, clēmens
lentil, lens, *f*
leper, hŏmo lĕprōsus, *m*
leprosy, lĕprae, *f. pl*
less, *adj*, mĭnor; *adv*, mĭnus
lessen, *v.i. and v.t*, mĭnŭo (3)
lesson, dŏcŭmentum, *n*
lest, *conj*, nē
let, *v.t*, sĭno (3), permitto (3) (*with dat of person*); (**lease**), lŏco (1);(**— go**), dĭmitto (3); (**— in**), admitto (3); (**— out**), ēmitto (3)
lethal, mortĭfer
lethargic, lentus
letter (of the alphabet), littĕra, *f*; (**epistle**), littĕrae, *f. pl*, ĕpistŏla, *f*
lettering, *nn*, littĕrae, *f.pl*
letters (learning), littĕrae, *f. pl*
lettuce, lactūca, *f*
level, *adj*, plānus; (**— place**), *nn*, plānĭtĭes, *f*
level, *v.t*, aequo (1);(**— to the ground**), sterno (3)
lever, vectis, *m*
levity, lĕvĭtas, *f*
levy, *nn*, dēlectus, *m*
levy, *v.t*, (**troops**), scrĭbo (3); (**taxes, etc.**), impĕro (1), ĕxĭgo (3)
lewd, incestus, impŭdĭcus
lewdness, incestum, *n*
liable, obnoxĭus
liar, hŏmo mendax
libellous, fāmōsus
liberal, lĭbĕrālis, largus
liberality, lĭbĕrālĭtas, *f*, largĭtas, *f*
liberate, *v.t*, lĭbĕro (1)
liberation, lĭbĕrātĭo, *f*
liberty, lĭbertas, *f*
librarian, bibliŏthēcārĭus, *m*
library, bibliŏthēca, *f*
licence, lĭcentĭa, *f*; (**permission**), pŏtestas, *f*
licentious, dissŏlūtus
lick, *v.t*, lambo (3)
lid, ŏpercŭlum, *n*
lie, *nn*, mendācĭum, *n*
lie, *v.i*, (**tell a —**), mentĭor (4 *dep*)
lie, *v.i*, iăcĕo (2); (**rest**), cŭbo (1); (**— ill**), iăcĕo (2); (**— in wait**), insĭdĭor (1 *dep*)
lieutenant, lēgātus, *m*
life, vīta, *f*, ănĭma, *f*; (**vivacity**) vĭgor, *m*; (**— blood**), sanguis, *m*
lifeless, exănĭmis, exsanguis
lifelike, *use* sĭmĭlis (**similar**)
lifetime, aetas, *f*
lift, *v.t*, tollo (3)
ligament, lĭgāmentum, *n*
light, *nn*, lux, *f*, lūmen, *n*; (**to bring to —**), in mĕdĭum prōfĕro (*irreg*)
light, *adj* (**not dark**), illustris; (**in weight**), lĕvis; (**— armed**), expĕdĭtus; (**trivial, of opinions, etc.**), lĕvis
light, *v.t*, (**illuminate**), illustro (1); (**kindle**), accendo (3)
lighten, *v.t*, (**burden, etc.**), lĕvo (1); *v.i*, (**of lightning**), fulgĕo (2)
lighthouse, phārus, *f*
lightly, *adv*, lĕvĭter
lightning, fulmen, *n*
like, *v.t*, ămo (1)
like, *adj*, sĭmĭlis (*with genit. or dat*), par (*with dat*)
like, *adv*, sĭmĭlĭter; (**just as**), sĭcut
likelihood, sĭmĭlĭtūdo, (*f*) vĕri
likely, sĭmĭlis vĕri; *often use future participle, e.g.* **likely to come,** venturus
liken, *v.t*, compăro (1)
likeness, sĭmĭlĭtūdo, *f*
likewise, *adv*, ĭtem
liking, *nn*, ămor, *m*, lĭbĭdo, *f*
lily, lilĭum, *n*
limb, membrum, *n*, artus, *m. p*
lime, calx, *f*; (**tree**), tĭlĭa, *f*
limit, *nn*, fīnis, *m*, terminus, *m*
limit, *v.t*, fīnĭo (4)
limitation, fīnis, *m*
limited (small), parvus
limitless, infīnĭtus
limp, *adj*, (**slack**), rĕmissus
limp, *v.i*, claudĭco (1)
limping, *adj*, claudus
limpid, limpĭdus
linden-tree, tĭlĭa, *f*
line, lĭnĕa, *f*; (**boundary —**), fīnis, *m*; (**of poetry**), versus, *m*; (**of battle**), ăcĭes, *f*; (**front —**), prima ăcĭes, *f*; (**second —**), princĭpes, *m.pl*; (**third —**), trĭārĭi, *m.pl*; (**— of march**), agmen, *n*
line, *v.t*, (**put in —**), instrŭo (3)
lineage, stirps, *f*, gĕnus, *n*
linen, *nn*, lintĕum, *n*; *adj*, lintĕus
linger, *v.i*, mŏror (1 *dep*); cunctor (1 *dep*)
lingering, *nn*, mŏra, *f*
link, *nn*, (**of chain**), ănŭlus, *m*
link, *v.t*, coniungo (3)

For List of Abbreviations used, turn to pages 3, 4

lint, lĭnāmentum, *n*
lintel, limen sŭpĕrum, *n*
lion, lĕo, *m*; **(lioness)**, lĕaena,,
lip, lābrum, *n*
liquefy, *v.t*, lĭquĕfăcĭo (3)
liquid, *nn*, lĭquor, *m*
liquid, *adj*, lĭquĭdus
liquidate, *v.t*, solvo (3)
liquor, lĭquor, *m*
lisping, *adj*, blaesus
list, tăbŭla, *f*
listen (to), *v.t*, audĭo (4)
listener, auscultātor, *m*
listless, languĭdus
listlessness, languor, *m*
literal, *use*, prŏprĭus **(its own)**
literally, *adv. phr*, ad verbum
literary (person), littĕrātus
literature, littĕrae, *f. pl*
lithe, flexĭbĭlis, ăgĭlis
litigation, lĭs, *f*
litter (of straw, etc.), strāmentum, *n*; **(sedan)**, lectĭca, *f*; **(of young)**, fētus, *m*
little, *adj*, parvus, exĭgŭus; **(for a —while)**, *adv*, pārumper, paulisper
little, *adv*, paulum
little, *nn*, paulum, *n*, nonnĭhil, *n*; **(too little)**, pārum, *n*; *with comparatives*, paulo; *e.g.* **a little bigger**, paulo māior
littleness, exĭgŭĭtas, *f*
live, *v.i*, vivo (3); **(— in or at)**, hăbĭto (1), incŏlo (3); **(— on)**, vescor (3 *dep*) (*with abl*); **(— one's life, etc.)**, vītam ăgo (3)
live, *adj*, vīvus
livelihood, victus, *m*
liveliness, ălăcrĭtas, *f*
lively, *adj*, ălăcer
liver, iĕcur, *n*
livery, vestĭtus, *m*
livid, lĭvĭdus
living, *adj*, vīvus
lizard, lăcerta, *f*
load, ŏnus, *n*
load, *v.t*, ŏnĕro (1)
loaded, ŏnustus
loaf, pānis, *m*
loam, lŭtum, *n*
loan, mūtŭum, *n*, *or use adj*, mūtuus **(borrowed, lent)**
loathe, *v.t*, ōdi (*defect*)
loathing, *nn*, ŏdĭum, *n*
loathesome, tēter
lobby, vestĭbŭlum, *n*
local, *use genit. of* lŏcus **(place)**
locality, lŏcus, *m*
lock (bolt), claustra, *n.pl*; **(hair)**, crīnis, *m*
lock, *v.t*, obsĕro (1)
locker, capsa, *f*, armārĭum, *n*
locust, lŏcusta, *f*
lodge, *v.i*, dĕversor (1 *dep*); **(stick fast)**, adhaerĕo (2) fixus; *v.t* **(accommodate temporarily)**, excĭpĭo (3)
lodger, inquĭlīnus, *m*
lodgings, dĕversōrĭum, *n*
loft, cēnăcŭlum, *n*
loftiness, altĭtūdo, *f*
lofty, celsus, altus
log, tignum, *n*
logic, dĭălectĭca, *f*
logical, dĭălectĭcus
loin, lumbus, *m*
loiter, *v.i*, cesso (1), cunctor (1 *dep*)
loiterer, cessātor, *m*
loneliness, sōlĭtūdo, *f*
lonely, *adj*, sōlus
long, *adj*, longus (*with acc. of extent of length*), *e.g.* **three feet long**, longus tres pĕdes; **(a — way)**, *adv*, prŏcul, longē; **(of time)**, dĭŭtĭnus, dĭŭturnus; **(how —?)**, quam diŭ? **(for a -time)**, *adv*, dĭŭ
long, *adv*, **(time)**, dĭŭ
long for, *v.t*, dēsīdĕro (1), cŭpĭo (3)
longevity, vīvācĭtas, *f*
longing, *nn*, dēsīdĕrĭum, *n*
long-suffering, *adj*, pătĭens
look at, *v.t*, aspĭcĭo (3); **(— back)**, rĕspĭcĭo (3); **(— down (upon))**, dēspĭcĭo (3); **(— for)**, quaero (3); **(— round)**, circumspĭcĭo (3); *v.i* **(— towards)**, specto (1); **(seem)**, vĭdĕor (2 *pass*)
look, *nn*, aspectus, *m*; **(appearance)**, spĕcĭes, *f*; **(expression)**, vultus, *m*
looking-glass, spĕcŭlum, *n*
loom, tēla, *f*
loop (winding), flexus, *m*
loop-hole, fĕnestra, *f*
loose, *adj*, laxus; **(at liberty)**, sŏlūtus; **(hair)**, passus, prōmissus; **(dissolute)**, dissŏlūtus
loose, *v.t*, laxo (1), solvo (3)
loosely, *adv*, sŏlūtē
loot, *nn*, praeda, *f*
loot, *v.t*, praedor (1 *dep*)
lop off, *v.t*, ampŭto (1)
loquacious, lŏquax
loquacity, lŏquăcĭtas, *f*
lord, dŏmĭnus, *m*
lordly, *adv*, rēgālis, sŭperbus
lordship (supreme power), impĕrĭum, *n*

lore, doctrīna, *f*
lose, *v.t,* āmitto (3), perdo (3); (— **heart),** ănĭmo dēfĭcĭo (3)
loss (act of losing), āmissĭo, *f*; (**the loss itself),** damnum, *n,* dētrīmentum, *n*; (**to be at a —),** *v.i,* haerĕo (2)
lost (*adj*) āmissus, perdĭtus
lot (chance), sors, *f*; (**to draw —s),** sortĭor (4 *dep*); (**much),** multum, *n*
loth (unwilling), invītus
lottery, sortĭtĭo, *f*
loud, clārus, magnus
loudness, magnĭtūdo, *f*
lounge, *v.i,* (**recline),** rĕcŭbo (1)
louse, pĕdĭcŭlus, *m*
lousy, pĕdĭcŭlōsus
lout, hŏmo agrestis
love, *nn,* ămor, *m*
love, *v.t,* ămo (1), dĭlĭgo (3)
loveliness, vĕnustas, *f*
lovely, vĕnustus
lover, ămātor, *m,* ămans, *c*
loving, *adj,* ămans
low, hŭmĭlis; (**sounds),** grăvis; (— **born),** hŭmĭli lŏco nātus; (**price),** vīlis; (**conduct, etc.),** sordĭdus; (**in spirits),** *adv. phr,* ănĭmo dēmisso
low, *v.i,* mūgĭo (4)
lower, *comp. adj,* infĕrĭor
lower, *v.t,* dēmitto (3); (— **oneself),** sē ăbĭcĕre (3 *reflex*)
lowering, mĭnax
lowest, infĭmus
lowing, mūgĭtus, *m*
lowlands, lŏca, plāna, *n.pl*
lowness, lowliness, hŭmĭlĭtas, *f*
lowly, hŭmĭlis, obscūrus
loyal, fĭdēlis
loyalty, fĭdes, *f*
lozenge, pastillus, *m*
lubricate, *v.t,* ungo (3)
lucid, lūcĭdus
lucidity, perspĭcŭĭtas, *f*
luck, fortūna, *f,* fors, *f*; (**good —),** fēlĭcĭtas, *f*; (**bad —),** infēlĭcĭtas,
luckily, *adv,* fēlĭcĭter
luckless, infēlix
lucky, fēlix, fortūnātus
lucrative, quaestŭōsus
ludicrous, rīdĭcŭlus
lug, *v.t,* trăho (3)
luggage, impĕdīmenta, *n.pl*
lugubrious, lūgŭbris
lukewarm, tĕpĭdus
lull, *v.t,* sēdo (1); *v.i,* (**of wind),** sēdor (1 *pass*)
lull, *nn, use vb.* intermitto (3)
lumber, scrūta, *n.pl*
luminary, lūmen, *n*
luminous, illustris, lūcĭdus
lump, massa, *f*
lunacy, insānĭa, *f,* ălĭēnātĭo, *f*
lunar, lūnāris
lunatic, hŏmo insānus
lunch, *nn,* prandĭum, *n*
lunch, *v.i,* prandĕo (2)
lung, pulmo, *m*
lurch, *v.i,* ăgĭtor (1 *pass*) (**leave in the —),** rĕlinquo (3)
lure, *nn,* illex, *c,* illĕcĕbrae, *f. pl*
lure, *v.t,* allĭcĭo (3)
lurid, lūrĭdus
lurk, *v.i,* lătĕo (2)
lurking in wait, *use* insĭdĭor (1 *dep*) (**lie in ambush)**
luscious, dulcis
lust, *nn,* lĭbīdo, *f*
lust after, *v.t,* concŭpisco (3)
lustful, lĭbīdĭnōsus
lustiness, vĭgor, *m*
lustre, splendor, *m*
lusty, vălĭdus
lute, cĭthăra, *f*
luxuriance, luxŭrĭa, *f*
luxuriant, luxŭrĭōsus
luxurious, luxŭrĭōsus, lautus
luxury, luxus, *m,* luxŭrĭa, *f*
lying, *adj,* (**telling lies),** mendax
lynx, lynx, *c*
lyre, cĭthăra, *f,* fĭdes, *f, pl*
lyrical, lyrĭcus

M

mace-bearer, lictor, *m*
macerate, *v.t,* măcĕro (1)
machination, dŏlus, *m*
machine, măchĭna, *f*
machinery, măchĭnātĭo, *f*
mackerel, scomber, *m*
mad, insānus, vĕcors, fŭrĭōsus; (**to be —),** *v.i.,* fŭro (3)
madden, *v.t,* mentem ălĭēno (1) (*with dat*); (**excite),** accendo (3)
maddening, *adj,* fŭrĭōsus
madman, hŏmo vĕcors
madness, insānĭa, *f*
magazine, horrĕum, *n*; (**arsenal),** armāmentārĭum, *n*
maggot, vermĭcŭlus, *m*
magic, *adj,* măgĭcus
magic, *nn,* ars măgĭca, *f*
magician, măgus, *m*
magistracy, măgistrātus, *m*
magistrate, măgistrātus, *m*
magnanimity, magnănĭmĭtas, *f*
magnanimous, magnănĭmus
magnet, lăpis magnes, *m*

magnetic, magnētĭcus
magnificence, magnĭfĭcentĭa, *f*
magnificent, magnĭfĭcus, splendĭdus
magnify, *v.t,* amplĭfĭco (1), exaggĕro (1)
magnitude, magnĭtūdo, *f*
magpie, pĭca, *f*
maid, maiden, virgo, *f*; **(servant),** ancilla, *f*
maiden, *adj,* virgĭnālis
mail (letters), littĕrae, *f. pl,* ĕpistŏlae, *f. pl*; **(armour),** lōrĭca, *f*
maim, *v.t,* mūtĭlo (1)
main, *adj,* prĭmus, praecĭpŭus
mainland, contĭnens terra, *f*
maintain, *v.t,* servo (1), sustĭnĕo (2); **(with food, etc.),** ălo (3); **(by argument),** affirmo (1)
maintenance, *use vb.* servo (1) **(to maintain)**
majestic, augustus
majesty, māiestas, *f*
major, *nn,* **(officer),** praefectus, *m*
major, *adj,* māior
majority, māior pars, *f*
make, *v.t,* făcĭo (3), effĭcĭo (3), fingo (3), reddo (3); **(compel),** cōgo (3); **(appoint),** crĕo (1); **(— for, seek),** pĕto (3); **(— haste),** *v.i,* festīno (1), accĕlĕro (1); **(—good),** *v.t,* rĕpăro (1), sarcĭo (1); **(— ready),** praepăro (1); **(— up, a total, etc.),** explĕo (2); **(— use of),** ūtor (3 *dep*) (*with abl*)
maker, făbrĭcātor, *m*
maladministration, măla admĭnistrātĭo, *f*
malady, morbus, *m*
malcontent, cŭpĭdus nŏvārum rērum **(eager for innovations)**
male, *adj,* mascŭlus, mās
male, *nn,* mās, *m*
malediction, dīrae, *f.pl,* **(curses)**
malefactor, hŏmo mălĕfĭcus, nŏcens
malevolence, mălĕvŏlentĭa, *f*
malevolent, mălĕvŏlus
malice, mălĕvŏlentĭa, *f*; **(envy),** invĭdĭa, *f*
malicious, mălĕvŏlus
malignant, mălĕvŏlus
maligner, obtrectātor, *m*
malignity, mălĕvŏlentĭa, *f*
malleable, ductĭlis
mallet, mallĕus, *m*
maltreat, *v.t,* vĕxo (1)
maltreatment, vexātĭo, *f*
man (human being), hŏmo, *c*; **(opp. to woman, child),** vīr, *m*; **(mankind),** hŏmĭnes, *c.pl*; **(chess, etc.),** latrunculus, *m*; **(fighting —),** mīles, *c*
man, *v.t,* **(ships, etc.),** complĕo (2)
man-of-war(ship), nāvis longa, *f*
manacle, *nn,* mănĭcae, *f.pl,* vincŭla *n.pl*
manage, *v.t,* admĭnistro (1), cūro (1), gĕro (3)
manageable, tractābĭlis, hăbĭlis
management, cūra, *f,* admĭnistrātĭo, *f*
manager, prōcūrātor, *m,* admĭnistrātor, *m*
mandate, impĕrātum, *n,* mandātum, *n*
mane (of horse), iūba, *f*
manful, vīrĭlis
manger, praesēpe, *n*
mangle, *v.t,* lăcĕro (1), lănĭo (1)
mangled, truncus
mangy, scăber
manhood, pūbertas, *f,* tŏga vīrĭlis, *f* **(manly dress)**
mania, insānĭa, *f*
maniac, hŏmo vēcors, āmens
manifest, *v.t,* ostendo (3), ăpĕrĭo (4)
manifest, *adj,* mănĭfestus, ăpertus
manifestation, ostentātĭo, *f, or use vbs. above*
manifold, multĭplex
maniple (of a legion), mănĭpŭlus, *m*
manipulate, *v.t,* tracto (1)
mankind, hŏmĭnes, *c.pl*
manliness, virtus, *f*
manly, vīrĭlis
manner (way), mŏdus, *m,* rātĭo, *f*; **(custom),** mos, *m*; **(type),** gĕnus, *n*; **(good manners),** dĕcōrum, *n*
mannerism, gestus prŏprĭus
manoeuvre (military), dēcursus, *m*; **(trick),** dŏlus, *m*
manoeuvre, *v.i,* dēcurro (3)
manor, praedĭum, *n*
manservant, servus, *m*
mansion, dŏmus magna, *f*
manslaughter, hŏmĭcīdĭum, *n*
mantle, palla, *f,* lăcerna, *f*
manual, *adj, use* mănus **(hand)**
manual, *nn,* **(book),** lĭbellus, *m*
manufacture, *nn,* făbrĭca, *f*
manufacture, *v.t,* făbrĭcor (1 *dep*)
manufacturer, făbrĭcātor, *m*
manumission, mănūmissĭo, *f*
manure, stercus, *n*
manuscript, lĭber, *m*
many, *adj,* multi (*pl*); **(very —),** plūrĭmi; **(a good —),** plērĭque, complūres; **(as — as),** tŏt . . . quŏt; **(how —?),** quŏt?; **(so —),** tŏt; **(— times),** *adv,* saepĕ
map, tăbŭla, *f*
map (to — out), *v.t,* dēsigno (1)
maple, ăcer, *n*; *adj,* ăcernus
mar, *v.t,* dēformo (1)
marauder, praedātor, *m*

marble, marmor, *n*; *adj*, marmŏrĕus
March, Martĭus (mensis)
march, *nn*, ĭter, *n*; (**forced —**), magnum ĭter; (**on the —**), *adv. phr*, in ĭtĭnĕre
march, *v.i*, ĭter făcĭo (3); (**— quickly**), contendo (3); (**advance**), prōgrĕdĭor (3 *dep*)
mare, ĕqua, *f*
margin, margo, *m,f*
marine, *nn*, mĭles classĭcus, *m*
marine, *adj*, mārīnus
mariner, nauta, *m*
maritime, mārĭtĭmus
mark, nŏta, *f*, signum, *n*, vestĭgĭum, *n*; (**characteristic**), *use genit. case of nn. with* esse; *e.g.* **it is the — of a wise man,** est sāpĭentis. . . .
mark, *v.t*, nŏto (1); (**indicate**), dēsigno (1); (**notice, observe**), ănĭmādverto (3)
market, fŏrum, *n*, măcellum, *n*; (**cattle —**), fŏrum bŏārĭum, *n*
market, *v.t*, nundĭnor (1 *dep*)
market-day, nundĭnae, *f. pl*, (**ninth day**)
marketing, *nn*, *use vb.* vendo (3) (**sell**)
market-place, fŏrum, *n*
marriage, coniŭgĭum, *n*, connūbĭum, *n*, mātrĭmōnĭum, *n*; (**— feast**), nuptĭae, *f.pl*; (**— contract**), pactĭo nuptĭālis, *f*
marriageable, nūbĭlis
marrow, mĕdulla, *f*
marry, *v.t*, (**— a woman**), dūco (3); (**— a man**), nūbo (3) (*with dat*)
marsh, pălus, *f*
marshal, appārĭtor, *m*
marshal, *v.t*, (**troops, etc.**), dispōno (3)
marshy, păluster
martial, bellĭcōsus; (**court —**), castrense iūdĭcĭum, *n*
martyr, martyr, *c*
martyrdom, martȳrĭum, *n*
marvel (miracle, etc.), mīrācŭlum, *n*
marvel at, *v.t*, mīror (1 *dep*)
marvellous, mīrus, mīrābĭlis
masculine, vīrĭlis
mash, *nn*, farrāgo, *f*
mash, *v.t*, contundo (3)
mask, *nn*, persōna, *f*; (**disguise**), intĕgŭmentum, *n*
mask, *v.t*, (**oneself**), persōnam indŭo (3); (**disguise**), dissĭmŭlo (1)
mason, structor, *m*
masonry, structūra, *f*
mass, mŏles, *f*; (**of people**), multĭtūdo, *f*
mass, *v.t*, cŭmŭlo (1), ăcervo (1)
massacre, *nn*, caedes, *f*
massacre, *v.t*, trŭcĭdo (1), caedo (3)
massive, sŏlĭdus; (**huge**), ingens
mast, mālus, *m*
master, dŏmĭnus, *m*; (**— of the household**), păterfămĭlĭas, *m*; (**school —**), măgister, *m*; (**skilled in . . .**), *use adj.* pĕrĭtus
master, *v.t*, (**subdue**), dŏmo (1); (**knowledge, etc.**), bĕne scĭo (4), disco (3)
masterful, impĕrĭōsus
masterly, *adj*, bŏnus; (**plan, etc.**), callĭdus
masterpiece, ŏpus summā laude dignum (**work worthy of the highest praise**)
mastery (rule), dŏmĭnātus, *m*
masticate, *v.t*, mandūco (1)
mastiff, cănis Mŏlossus (**Molossian hound**)
mat, stŏrĕa, *f*
mat, *v.t*, implĭco (1)
match (contest), certāmen, *n*; (**equal**), *adj*, pār; (**marriage —**), nuptĭae, *f. pl*
match, *v.t*, (**equal**), aequo (1)
matchless, ēgrĕgĭus
matching, *adj*, (**equal**) pār
mate, sŏcĭus, *m*; (**— in marriage**), coniunx, *m,f*.
mate, *v.i*, coniungor (3 *pass*)
material, *nn*, mātĕrĭa, *f*
material, *adj*, corpŏrĕus
materially, *adv*, (**much**), multum
maternal, maternus
maternity, māter, *f*, (**mother**)
mathematician, măthēmătĭcus, *m*
mathematics, măthēmătĭca, *f*
matter (substance), corpus, *n*, mātĕrĭa, *f*; (**affair**), res, *f*; (**what is the —?**), quid est?; (**it matters, it is important**), rēfert (*v. impers*)
mattress, culcĭta, *f*
mature, *adj*, mātūrus, ădultus
mature, *v.t*, mātūro (1); *v.i*, mātūresco (3)
maturity, mātūrĭtas, *f*
maudlin, ĭneptus
maul, *v.t*, mulco (1), lănĭo (1)
maw, inglŭvĭes, *f*
maxim, praeceptum, *n*
maximum, *use adj*, maxĭmus (**bigges**
May, Māius (mensis)
may, *v. auxiliary*, (**having permission to**), lĭcet (2 *impers. with dat. of person allowed*), *e.g.* **you may go,** lĭcet tĭbĭ īre; (**having ability to**), possum (*irreg*); *often expressed by subjunctive mood of verb*
maybe (perhaps), *adv*, fortassĕ

For List of Abbreviations used, turn to pages 3, 4

may-day, Kălendae Māiae **(first day of May)**
mayor, praefectus, *m*
maze, *nn*, lăbȳrinthus, *m*
meadow, prātum, *n*
meagre, mācer, iēiūnus
meagreness, iēiūnĭtas, *f*
meal (flour), fārīna, *f*; **(food),** cĭbus, *m*
mean, *nn*, mŏdus, *m*
mean, *adj*, **(middle, average),** mĕdĭus; **(of low rank),** hūmĭlis; **(miserly),** sordĭdus
mean, *v.t*, signĭfĭco (1); **(intend),** in ănĭmo hăbĕo (2)
meander, *v.i*, **(of a river),** sĭnŭōso cursu flŭo (3) **(flow on a winding course)**
meaning, *nn*, signĭfĭcātĭo, *f*
meanness, hŭmĭlĭtas, *f*; **(of disposition),** sordes, *f. pl*
means (method), mŏdus, *m*; **(opportunity),** făcultas, *f*; **(resources),** ŏpes, *f. pl*; **(by no —),** *adv*, haudquāquam, nullo mŏdo
meantime, meanwhile (in the —), *adv*, intĕrĕā, intĕrim
measure, mensūra, *f*, mŏdus, *m*; **(plan),** consĭlĭum, *n*; **(music),** mŏdi, *m, pl*
measure, *v.t*, mētĭor (4 *dep*)
measureless, immensus
meat, căro, *f*
mechanic, făber, *m*, ŏpĭfex, *c*
mechanical, măchĭnālis
mechanism, măchĭnātĭo, *f*
medal, medallion, phălĕrae, ārum, *f. pl*
meddle, *v.i*, sē interpōnĕre (3 *reflex*)
mediate, *v.i*, sē interpōnĕre (3 *reflex*) intervĕnĭo (4)
mediator, dēprĕcātor, *m*
medical, mĕdĭcus
medicine (art of —), ars mĕdĭcīna, *f*; **(the remedy itself),** mĕdĭcāmentum, *n*
mediocre, mĕdĭŏcris
mediocrity, mĕdĭŏcrĭtas, *f*
meditate, *v.t*, cōgĭto (1)
Mediterranean Sea, mărĕ nostrum, *n*, **(our sea)**
medium, *use adj*, mĕdĭus **(middle); (through the — of)** per
medley, farrāgo, *f*
meek, mītis
meekness, ănĭmus summissus, *m*
meet, *v.t*, obvĭam fĭo (*irreg*) (*with dat*); **(go to —, encounter),** obvĭam ĕo (*irreg*) (*with dat*); *v.i*, convĕnĭo (4); concurro (3)
meeting, *nn*, conventus, *m*
melancholy, *nn*, tristĭtĭa, *f*
melancholy, *adj*, tristis
mellow, mītis
mellow, *v.i*, mātūresco (3)
melodious, cănōrus
melody, mĕlos, *n*
melon, mēlo, *m*
melt, *v.t*, lĭquĕfăcĭo (3); **(people, etc.),** mŏvĕo (2); *v.i*, lĭquesco (3)
member (of a society), sŏcĭus, *m*; **(of the body),** membrum, *n*
membrane, membrāna, *f*
memoirs, commentārii, *m. pl*
memorable, mĕmŏrābĭlis
memorandum, lĭbellus mĕmŏrĭālis
memorial, mŏnŭmentum, *n*
memory, mĕmŏrĭa, *f*
menace mĭnae, *f. pl*
menace, *v.t* mĭnor (1 *dep*)
menacing, *adj*, mĭnax
mend, *v.t*, rĕfĭcĭo (3), sarcĭo (4); *v.i*, **(in health),** mĕlĭor fĭo (*irreg*) **(get better)**
mendacious, mendax
mendicant, mendīcus, *m*
menial, *adj*, servĭlis
mensuration, rătĭo, (*f*) mētĭendi; **(system of measuring)**
mental, *use genitive of* mens, *or* ănĭmus **(mind)**
mention, *nn*, mentĭo, *f*
mention, *v.t*, mĕmŏro (1), dĭco (3)
mercantile, mercātōrum, **(of merchants)**
mercenary, *adj*, mercēnārĭus
merchandise, merx, *f*
merchant, mercātor, *m*
merchant-ship, nāvis ŏnĕrārĭa, *f*
merciful, mĭsĕrĭcors
merciless, crūdēlis, inclĕmens
mercury (quick silver), argentum vīvum, *n*; **(god),** Mercŭrĭus
mercy, mĭsĕrĭcordĭa, *f*
mere, *adj*, sōlus, *or use emphatic pron*, ipse
merely, *adv*, tantummŏdo
merge, *v.i*, miscĕor (2 *pass*)
meridian, circŭlus mĕrĭdĭānus, *m*
meridian, *adj*, mĕrĭdĭānus
merit, *nn*, mĕrĭtum, *n*
merit, *v.t*, mĕrĕor (2 *dep*)
meritorious, dignus laude **(worthy of praise)**
merriment, hĭlărĭtas, *f*
merry, hĭlăris
mesh, măcŭla, *f*
mess (confused state), turba, *f*; **(dirt),** squālor, *m*
message, nuntĭus, *m*

messenger, nuntĭus, *m*
metal, mĕtallum, *n*
metallic, mĕtallĭcus
metamorphosis, *use vb*, **transformo** (1) **(to change in shape)**
metaphor, translātĭo, *f*
metaphorical, translātus
meteor, fax, *f*
method, rātĭo, *f*
methodically, ex ordĭne, *or use adv phr*, rātĭōne et vĭā **(by reckoning and method)**
metre, nūmĕrus, *m*
metrical, mĕtrĭcus
metropolis, căpŭt, *n*
mettle, fĕrōcĭtas, *f*
mettlesome, ănĭmōsus, fĕrox
mew, *v.i*, **(cat)**, quĕror (3 *dep*)
mica, phengītes, *m*
mid, *adj*, mĕdĭus
midday, *nn*, mĕrīdĭes, *m*
midday, *adj*, mĕrīdĭānus
middle, *adj*, mĕdĭus
middle, *nn*, *use* mĕdĭus *in agreement with noun*, *e.g.* **the middle of the river**, mĕdĭus flŭvĭus
middling, *adj*, mĕdĭŏcris
midnight, mĕdĭa nox, *f*
midst, *nn*, *use adj*, mĕdĭus
midsummer, mĕdĭa aestas, *f*
midwife, obstĕtrix, *f*
might (power), vīs, *f*
mighty, fortis, vălĭdus, magnus
migrate, *v.t*, ăbĕo (4)
migratory bird, advĕna ăvis, *f*
mild, mītis, clēmens, lĕvis
mildew, rōbīgo, *f*
mildness, lēnĭtas, *f*,
mile, mille passus (*or* passŭum) **(a thousand paces)**
milestone, mĭlĭārĭum, *n*
military, *adj*, mĭlĭtāris; **(— service)**, stĭpendĭa, *n.pl.*
militate against, *v.t*, făcĭo (3) contrā (*with acc*)
milk, lac, *n*
milk, *v.t*, mulgĕo (2)
milky, lactĕus
mill, mŏla, *f*, pistrīnum, *n*
miller, mŏlĭtor, *m*
million, dĕcĭēs centēna mĭlĭa
mill-stone, mŏla, *f*
mimic, *v.t*, ĭmĭtor (1 *dep*)
mince, *v.t*, concĭdo (3)
mincemeat, mĭnūtal, *n*
mind, ănĭmus, *m*, mens, *f*; **(intellect)**, ingēnĭum, *n*; **(to make up one's —)** constĭtŭo (3)
mind, *v.t*, **(I — my own business)**, nĕgōtĭum mĕum ăgo (3)
mindful, mĕmor (*with genit*)
mine, *adj*, mĕus
mine, *nn*, mĕtallum, *n*, cŭnĭcŭlus, *m*
mine, *v.i*, fŏdĭo (3)
miner, fŏdĭens, *m*
mineral, *nn*, mĕtallum, *n*
mineral, *adj*, mĕtallĭcus
mingle, *v.i*, sē miscēre (2 *reflex*)
miniature, *nn*, parva tăbella, *f*
minimum, *adj*, mĭnĭmus **(smallest)**
minister mĭnister, *m*, admĭnĭster, *m*
ministry (office), mĭnĭstĕrĭum, *n*
minor, *nn*, pūpillus, *m*
minority, mĭnor pars, *f*
minstrel, tĭbĭcen văgus **(wandering —)**
mint (plant), menta, *f*; **(coinage)**, mŏnēta, *f*
mint, *v.t*, cūdo (3)
minute, *adj*, exĭgŭus, mĭnūtus
minute, *nn*, **(of time)**, mōmentum, **(*n*)** tempŏris
miracle, mīrăcŭlum, *n*
miraculous, mīrus
mire, lŭtum, *n*
mirror, spĕcŭlum, *n*
mirth, hĭlārĭtas, *f*
mirthful, hĭlāris
misadventure, cāsus, *m*
misanthropy, *use phr.* ŏdĭum, (*n*) ergā hŏmĭnes **(hatred towards mankind)**
misapply, *v.t*, ăbūtor (3 *dep with abl*)
misbehave, *v.i*, mălĕ sē gĕrĕre (3 *reflex*)
miscalculate, *v.i*, fallor (3 *pass*), erro (1)
miscalculation, error, *m*
miscarriage (childbirth), ăbortus, *m*; (— **of justice**) error, (*m*) iūdĭcum
miscarry, *v.i*, **(child)**, ăbortum făcĭo (3); **(fail)** frustrā *or* irrĭtum ēvĕnĭo (4)
miscellaneous, vărĭus
mischief (injury, wrong) mălĕfĭcĭum, *n*
mischievous, mălĕfĭcus; **(playful)**, lascīvus
misconduct, *nn*, dĕlictum, *n*
miscreant, hŏmŏ scĕlestus
misdeed, dĕlictum, *n*
misdemeanour, dĕlictum, *n*, peccātum, *n*
miser, hŏmŏ ăvārus
miserable, mĭser, infēlix
miserliness, ăvārĭtĭa, *f*
miserly, *adj*, ăvārus, sordĭdus
misery, mĭsĕrĭa, *f*, angor, *m*
misfortune, rēs adversae, *f*, *pl*
misgiving, praesāgĭum, *n*
misgovern, *v.t*, mălĕ rĕgo (3)
misguided (deceived), dĕceptus

misinterpret, *v.t,* mălĕ ĭnterprĕtor (1 *dep*)
misjudge, *v.t,* mălĕ iūdĭco (1)
mislay, *v.t,* āmitto (3)
mislead, *v.t,* dēcĭpĭo (3)
misplace, *v.t,* ălĭēno lŏco pōno (3) (**put in an unsuitable place**)
misprint, *nn,* mendum, *n*
misrepresent, *v.t,* verto (3); (**disparage**), obtrecto (1)
misrule, *v.t,* mălĕ rĕgo (3)
miss, *v.i,* (**fail to hit or meet**), ăberro (1), frustrā mittor (3 *pass*); *v.t,* (**want**), dēsīdĕro (1)
misshapen, dēformis
missile, tēlum, *n*
mission (embassy), lēgātĭo, *f*; (**task**), ŏpus, *n*
misspend, *v.t,* perdo (3)
mist, nĕbŭla, *f*
mistake, error, *m*; (**make a —**), *v.i,* erro (1)
mistake, *v.t,* (**for someone else**), crēdĕre ălĭum esse
mistaken, falsus; (**to be —**), *v.i,* erro (1)
mistletoe, viscum, *n*
mistress (of the house, etc.), dŏmĭna, *f*; (**sweetheart**), pŭella, *f*, concŭbĭna, *f*
mistrust, *v.t,* diffĭdo (3 *semi-dep. with dat*)
misty, nĕbŭlōsus
misunderstand, *v.t,* haud rectē, *or* mălĕ, intellĕgo (3)
misunderstanding, error, *m*
misuse, *v.t,* ăbūtor (3 *dep. with abl*)
mitigate, *v.t,* mītĭgo (1), lēnĭo (4)
mitigation, mītĭgātĭo, *f*
mittens, mănĭcae, *f. pl*
mix, *v.t,* miscĕo (2); (**— up together**), confundo (3); *v.i,* miscĕor (2 *pass*)
mixed, *adj,* mixtus; (**indiscriminate**), prōmiscŭus
mixture, mixtūra, *f*
moan, *nn,* gĕmĭtus, *m*
moan, *v.i,* gĕmo (3)
moat, fossa, *f*
mob, turba, *f*, vulgus, *n*
mobile, mōbĭlis
mock, *v.t,* illūdo (3) (*with dat*); dērīdĕo (2)
mockery, irrīsus, *m*, lūdĭbrĭum, *n*
mode, mŏdus, *m*, rātĭo, *f*
model, exemplum, *n*, exemplar, *n*
model, *v.t,* fingo (3)
moderate, mŏdĕrātus, mŏdĭcus
moderate, *v.t,* tempĕro (1)
moderation, mŏdus, *m*, mŏdĕrātĭo, *f*
modern, rĕcens, nŏvus
modest, vĕrēcundus
modesty, vĕrēcundĭa, *f*, pŭdor, *m*
modify, *v.t,* immūto (1)
modulate, *v.t,* flecto (3)
moist, hūmĭdus
moisten, *v.t,* hūmecto (1)
moisture, hūmor, *m*
molar, dens gĕnŭīnus
mole (animal), talpa, *f*; (**dam, etc.**), mōles, *f*; (**on the body**), naevus, *m*
molest, *v.t,* vexo (1), sollĭcĭto (1)
mollify, *v.t,* mollĭo (4)
molten, lĭquĕfactus
moment, punctum, (*n*) tempŏris; (**in a —**), *adv,* stātim; (**importance**), mōmentum, *n*
momentary, brĕvis
momentous, magni mōmenti (**of great importance**)
momentum, impĕtus, *m*
monarch, rex, *m*
monarchy, regnum, *n*
monastery, mŏnastĕrĭum, *n*
money, pĕcūnĭa, *f*; (**coin**), nummus, *m*; (**profit**), quaestus, *m*
money-bag, fiscus, *m*
money-lender, faenĕrātor, *m*
money-making, quaestus, *m*
moneyed, pĕcūnĭōsus
mongrel, *nn,* hibrĭda, *c*
monkey, sīmĭa, *f*
monopolize, *v.i, use phr. with* sōlus (**alone**), *and* hăbĕo (2)
monopoly, mŏnŏpōlĭum, *n*
monotonous, *use phr. with* mŏlestus (**laboured**), *or* sĭmĭlis (**similar**)
monster, monstrum, *n*
monstrous (huge), immānis; (**shocking**), infandus
month, mensis, *m*
monthly, *adj,* menstrŭus
monument, mŏnŭmentum, *n*
mood, affectĭo, (*f*) ănĭmi
moody, mōrōsus
moon, lūna, *f*
moonlight, lūmen, (*n*) lūnae; (**by —**), ad lūnam
moonlit, *adj,* illustris lūnā (**lighted up by the moon**)
moor, lŏca dēserta, *n.pl,* (**a lonely place**)
moor, *v.t,* (**ship, etc.**), rĕlĭgo (1)
moorhen, fŭlĭca, *f*
moot (it is a — point), nondum convĕnit . . . (**it is not yet decided . . .**)
mop, *nn,* pēnĭcŭlus, *m*
mop, *v.t,* dētergĕo (2)
moral, *adj,* mōrālis; (**of good character**), hŏnestus
moral, *nn,* (**of a story**), *use phr. with*

signĭfĭco (1) (to indicate), *e.g.* haec fābŭla signĭfĭcat ... (this story indicates ...)
morale, ănĭmus, *m*
morals, morality, mōres, *m. pl*
moralize, *v.i,* dē mōrĭbus dissĕro (3) (discuss conduct)
morbid, aeger, aegrōtus
more, *nn,* plus, *n,* (*with genit*), *e.g.* more corn, plus frūmenti; (*adv. before adjs. or advs*) *use comparative of adj. or adv, e.g.* more quickly, cĕlĕrĭus; *otherwise use* măgis (to a higher degree) *or* pŏtĭus; (in addition), amplĭus
moreover, *adv,* praetĕrĕā
moribund, mŏrĭbundus
morning, *nn,* tempus mātūtīnum, *n*; (in the —), *adv,* mānĕ
morning, *adj,* mātūtīnus
morose, tristis
morrow (following day), postĕrus dĭes, *m*
morsel, offa, *f*
mortal, *adj,* mortālis; (causing death), mortĭfer
mortality, mortālĭtas, *f*
mortar, mortārĭum, *n*
mortgage, pignus, *n*
mortgage, *v.t,* oblĭgo (1)
mortification, offensĭo, *f*
mortify, *v.t,* (vex) offendo (3)
mosaic, *adj,* tessellātus
mosquito, cŭlex, *m*
moss, muscus, *m*
mossy, muscōsus
most, *adj,* plūrĭmus *or* plūrĭmum, *n, with genit, of noun, e.g.* most importance, plūrĭmum grăvĭtātis; (for the — part), *adv,* plērumque
most, *adv, with adjs. and advs. use superlative*; e.g. most quickly, cĕlerrĭmē; *with vbs,* maxĭmē
mostly (usually), *adv,* plērumque
moth, blatta, *f*
mother, māter, *f*; (-in-law), socrus, *f*
motherly, *adj,* māternus
motion (movement), mōtus, *m*; (proposal), rŏgātĭo, *f*
motion, *v.t,* gestu indĭco (1) (indicate by a gesture)
motionless, immōtus
motive, causa, *f*
mottled, măcŭlōsus
motto, sententĭa, *f*
mould (soil), sŏlum, *n*; (shape), forma, *f*
mould, *v.t,* formo (1)
mouldiness, sĭtus, *m*
mouldy, mūcĭdus
moult, *v.i,* plūmas exŭo (3) (lay down feathers)
mound, tŭmŭlus, *m*
mount, *v.t* (horse, ship, etc.), conscendo (3); *otherwise,* scando (3)
mounted (on horseback), *adj,* ĕquo vectus
mountain, mons, *m,* iŭgum, *n*
mountaineer, hŏmŏ montānus
mountainous, montŭōsus
mourn, *v.t. and v.i,* lūgĕo (2)
mournful luctŭōsus; (of sounds, etc.), lūgŭbris
mourning, luctus, *m,* maeror, *m*
mouse, mūs, *c*
mouse-trap, muscĭpŭlum, *n*
mouth, ōs, *n*; (of river), ostĭum, *n*
mouthful, bucca, *f,* (filled out cheek)
mouth-piece interpres, *c,* ōrātor, *m*
movable, mōbĭlis
move, *v.t,* mŏvĕo (2); *v.i,* sē mŏvēre (2 *reflex*)
movement, mōtus, *m*
moving, *adj,* (of pity, etc.), mĭsĕrābĭlis
mow, *v.t,* sĕco (1)
much, *adj,* multus; (too —), nĭmĭus
much, *adv,* multum; *with comparative adj. or adv,* multo, *e.g.* much bigger, multo māior
muck, stercus, *n*
mucous, *adj,* mūcōsus
mud, muddiness, lūtum, *n*
muddle, *v.t,* confundo (3)
muddle, *nn,* turba, *f*
muddy, lūtĕus
muffle, *v.t,* obvolvo (3)
mug, pōcŭlum, *n*
muggy, ūmĭdus
mulberry (tree), mōrus, *f*; (fruit), mōrum, *n*
mule, mūlus, *m*
mullet, mullus, *m*
multifarious, vărĭus
multiplication, multĭplĭcātĭo,
multiply, *v.t,* multĭplĭco (1)
multitude, multĭtūdo, *f*
multitudinous, plūrĭmus, crēber
mumble, *v.i. and v.t,* murmŭro (1)
munch, *v.t,* mandūco (1)
mundane, *use genit. of* mundus (world)
municipal, mūnĭcĭpālis
municipality, mūnĭcĭpĭum, *n*
munificence, mūnĭfĭcentĭa, *f*
munificent, mūnĭfĭcus
munition, appārātus (*m*) belli (war-equipment), arma, *n. pl*
murder, *nn,* caedes, *f*
murder, *v.t,* nĕco (1), interfĭcĭo (3)
murderer, hŏmĭcīda, *c,* sĭcārĭus, *m*
murky, cālĭgĭnōsus

For List of Abbreviations used, turn to pages 3, 4

murmur, *nn,* murmur, *n,*
murmur, *v.i,* murmŭro (1)
muscle, tŏrus, *m,* lăcertus, *m*
muscular, lăcertōsus
muse, *nm,* mūsa, *f*
muse, *v.i,* mĕdĭtor (1 *dep*)
museum, mūsēum, *n*
mushroom, fungus, *m*
music, mūsĭca, *f,* cantus, *m*
musical, mūsĭcus; (**person**), stŭdĭōsus mūsĭcōrum (**keen on music**)
musician, mūsĭcus, *m*
muslin, byssus, *f*
must, *v.i,* (**obligation**), *use gerundive: e.g.* **Carthage must be destroyed,** Carthāgo dēlenda est; (**duty**), ŏportet (2 *impers*) *with acc. of person and infinitive, e.g.* **we must go,** nōs ŏportet īre
mustard, sĭnāpi, *n*
muster, *nn,* dēlectus, *m*
muster, *v.t,* convŏco (1), rĕcensĕo (2); *v.i,* convĕnio (4)
musty, mūcĭdus
mutable, mūtābĭlis
mute, *adj,* mūtus, tăcĭtus
mutilate, *v.t,* mūtĭlo (1), trunco (1)
mutilated, mūtĭlus, truncātus
mutiny, sēdĭtio, *f*
mutiny, *v.i,* sēdĭtiōnem făcio (3)
mutter, *v.i. and v.t,* musso (1)
muttering, *nn,* murmur *n*
mutton, ŏvilla căro, *f,* (**sheep's flesh**)
mutual, mūtŭus
muzzle (**for the mouth**), fiscella, *f*
my, mĕus
myriad (10,000), dĕcem mĭlĭa (*with genit*)
myrrh, murra, *f*
myrtle, myrtus, *f*
myself (*emphatic*), ipse; (*reflexive*) mē
mysterious, occultus
mystery, rēs abdĭta, *f*; (**religious, etc.**), mystĕrĭa, *n.pl*
mystic, mystĭcus
mystification, ambāges, *f, pl*
mystify, *use adv. phr,* per ambāges (**in an obscure way**)
myth, fābŭla, *f*
mythology, fābŭlae, *f, pl*

N

nab, *v.t,* (**catch**), apprĕhendo (3)
nag, *nn,* căballus, *m*
nag, *v.t,* incrĕpĭto (1), obiurgo (1)
nail (**finger, toe**), unguis, *m*; (**of metal**), clāvus, *m*
nail, *v.t,* clāvīs affīgo (3) (**fix on with nails**)
naive, simplex
naked, nūdus
nakedness, *use adj,* nūdus (**naked**)
name, nōmen, *n*; (**personal —, equivalent to our Christian name**), praenōmen, *n*; (**— of a class of things**), vŏcābŭlum, *n*; (**reputation**), existimātĭo, *f*
name, *v.t,* nōmĭno (1), appello (1)
nameless, nōmĭnis expers (**without a name**)
namely (**I mean to say**), dĭco (3)
namesake, *use phr,* cui est ĭdem nōmen (**who has the same name**)
nap, *v.i,* (**sleep**), paulisper dormĭo (4)
napkin, mappa, *f*
narcissus, narcissus, *m*
narcotic, mĕdĭcāmentum somnĭfĕrum, *n,* (**sleep-bringing drug**)
narrate, narro (1)
narrative, narrātĭo, *f*; *adj, use vb,* narro (1) (**narrate**)
narrator, narrātor, *m*
narrow, angustus
narrow, *v.t,* cŏarto (1); *v.i,* sē cŏartāre (1 *reflex*)
narrowly (**nearly, scarcely**), *adj,* vix
narrow-minded, anĭmi angusti (**of narrow mind**)
narrowness, angustĭae, *f, pl*
nasal, nārĭum (**of the nose**)
nastiness, foedĭtas, *f*
nasty, foedus
natal, nātālis
nation, gens, *f*
national, dŏmestĭcus *or use genit. of* gens
nationality, pŏpŭlus, *m,* cīvĭtas, *f*
native, *adj,* indĭgĕna; (**— land**), pătrĭa, *f*
native, *nn,* indĭgĕna, *c*
nativity (**birth**), gĕnus, *n,* ortus, *m*
natural, nātūrālis; (**inborn**), nātīvus, innātus; (**genuine**), sincērus
naturalize, *v.t,* cīvĭtātem do (1) (*with dat*) (**grant citizenship**)
naturally, sĕcundum nātūram (**according to nature**)
nature, nātūra, *f*; (**character of persons**), ingĕnĭum, *n*
naught, nĭhil, *n*
naughty, imprŏbus, lascīvus
nausea, nausĕa, *f*
nauseate, *v.t,* fastīdĭo (4)
nautical, nāvālis, nautĭcus
navel, umbĭlĭcus, *m*
navigable, nāvĭgābĭlis

navigate, *v.i,* nāvĭgo (1)
navigation, nāvĭgātĭo, *f*
navy, classis, *f*
nay (no), nōn
neap-tide, mĭnĭmus aestus, *m*
near, *adv,* prŏpĕ, iuxtā
near, *prep, adv,* prŏpĕ
nearly, *adv,* prŏpĕ, fermē
nearness, prŏpinquĭtas, *f,* vĭcĭnĭtas, *f*
neat, nĭtĭdus, mundus
neatly, *adv,* mundē
neatness, mundĭtĭa, *f*
nebulous, nĕbŭlōsus
necessarily, *adv,* nĕcessārĭo
necessary, nĕcessārĭus, nĕcesse
necessitate, *v.t,* (compel), cōgo (3)
necessity (inevitableness), nĕcessĭtas, *f;* (something indispensable), rēs nĕcessārĭa, *f*
neck, collum, *n,* cervix, *f*
necklace, mŏnĭle, *n*
need, *nn,* ŏpus, *n,* (*with abl. of thing needed or infinitive*); (lack), ĭnŏpĭa, *f*
need, *v.t,* ĕgĕo (2) (*with abl*)
needful, nĕcessārĭus, *or use nn,* ŏpus, *n,* (necessity)
needle, ăcus, *f*
needless, nōn nĕcessārĭus
needy, ĕgens
nefarious, nĕfārĭus
negation, nĕgātĭo, *f*
negative, *adj, use* nōn (not), *or* nĕgo (1) (to deny)
neglect, *v.t,* neglĕgo (3), praetermitto (3)
neglect, *nn,* neglĕgentĭa, *f*
negligent, neglĕgens
negotiate, *v.t,* ăgo (3) dē (*with abl. of thing*) cum (*with abl. of person*)
negotiation, *use vb,* ăgo (3), (to negotiate)
negress, Aethĭŏpissa, *f*
negro, Aethĭops, *m*
neigh, *v.i,* hinnĭo (4)
neigh, neighing, hinnĭtus, *m*
neighbour, vĭcĭnus, *m;* (of nations), *adj,* fĭnĭtĭmus
neither, *pron,* neuter
neither, *conj,* nĕque, nĕc; **neither . . . nor,** neque . . . neque, *or* nec . . . nec
nephew, fĭlĭus, (*m*) frātris (*or* sŏrōris)
nerve, nervi, *m. pl*
nervous (afraid), tĭmĭdus
nervousness, tĭmĭdĭtas, *f,* formīdo, *f*
nest, nĭdus, *m*
nestle, *v.i,* haerĕo (2), ĭacĕo (2)
nestlings, nĭdi, *m, pl*
net, rētĕ, *n*
net, *v.t,* plăgĭs căpĭo (3) (catch with a net)
nettle, urtĭca, *f*
net-work, rētĭcŭlum, *n*
neuter, neuter
neutral, mĕdĭus; (to be or remain —), neutri parti fāvĕo (2) (to favour neither side)
neutralize, *v.t,* aequo (1), compenso (1)
never, *adv,* numquam
nevertheless, nĭhĭlōmĭnus, tămen
new, nŏvus; (fresh), rĕcens
new-comer, advĕna, *c*
newly, *adv,* nūper, mŏdo
newness, nŏvĭtas, *f*
news, nuntĭus, *m*
newspaper, acta dĭurna, *n.pl*
newt, lăcertus, *m*
next, *adj,* proxĭmus; (on the — day), *adv,* postrĭdiē
next, *adv,* (of time), dĕinceps, dĕinde; (of place), iuxtā, proxĭmē
nibble, *v.t,* rōdo (3)
nice (pleasant), dulcis; (particular), fastĭdiōsus; (precise), subtĭlis
nicety (subtlety), subtĭlĭtas, *f*
niche, aedĭcŭla, *f*
in the nick of time, in ipso artĭcŭlo tempŏris
nickname, agnōmen, *n,* (an additional name)
niece, fĭlĭa, (*f*) frātris (*or* sŏrōris)
niggardly, ăvārus, parcus
night, nox, *f;* (by, at —), *adv,* noctu, nocte; (at mid —), mĕdĭā nocte; (at the fall of —), prīmis tĕnĕbris
nightingale, luscĭnĭa, *f*
nimble, ăgĭlis
nine, nŏvem; (— times), *adv,* nŏvĭens; (— each), nŏvēni; (— hundred), nongenti
nineteen, undēvīginti
ninety, nōnāginta
ninth, nōnus
nip, *v.t,* vellĭco (1); (with frost), ūro (3)
nipple, păpilla, *f*
no, *adj,* nullus. nĭhil (*foll. by genit*)
no, *adv,* nōn, mĭnĭmē; (to say —), *v.i,* nĕgo (1)
nobility, (of birth), nōbĭlĭtas, *f;* (people of noble birth), nōbĭles, *m. pl*
noble (of birth), nōbĭlis; (of birth or character), gĕnĕrōsus
nobody, nēmo, *m, f*
nocturnal, nocturnus
nod, *v.i,* nūto (1); (assent), annŭo (3)
nod, *nn,* nūtus, *m*
noise, strĕpĭtus, *m,* sŏnĭtus, *m;* (of shouting), clāmor, *m;* (to make a —), *v.i,* strĕpo (3)

noiseless, tăcĭtus
noisily, *adv,* cum strĕpĭtu
noisy, *use a phr. with* strĕpo (**to make a noise**)
nomadic, văgus
nominal, *use* nōmen (**name**)
nominally, *adv,* nōmĭne
nominate, *v.t,* nōmĭno (1)
nomination, nōmĭnātĭo, *f*
nominee, *use vb.* nōmĭno, (**name**)
nonchalant, aequo ănĭmo (**with unruffled mind**)
nondescript, nōn insignis
none, nullus
nonentity, nĭhil, *n*
nonsense, nūgae, *f. pl,* ĭneptĭae, *f. pl*
nonsensical, ĭneptus, absurdus
nook, angŭlus, *m*
noon, mĕrīdĭes, *m*; (**at —**), *adv,* mĕrīdĭe; *adj,* mĕrīdĭanus
noose, lăquĕus, *m*
nor, *conj,* nĕc, nĕque
normal (usual), ūsĭtātus
north, *nn,* septentrĭōnes, *m. pl*
north, northern, northerly, *adj,* septentrĭōnālis
north-east wind, ăquĭlo, *m*
north-pole, arctos, *f*
northwards, versus ad septentrĭōnes
north wind, ăquĭlo, *m*
nose, nāsus, *m,* nāres, *f. pl* (**nostrils**)
not, nōn, haud; (**— at all**), *adv,* haudquāquam; (**not even . . .**), nĕ . . . quĭdem; (**and not**), nĕc, nĕque; (**in commands, e.g. do not go,** nōli īre
notable, insignis, mĕmŏrābĭlis
notary, scrĭba, *m*
notch, *nn,* incīsūra, *f*
notch, *v.t,* incīdo (3)
note (explanatory, etc.), adnŏtātĭo, *f*; (**mark**), nŏta, *f*; (**letter**), littĕrae, *f. pl*
note, *v.t,* (**notice**), ănĭmadverto (3); (**jot down**), ēnŏto (1)
note-book, commentārĭi, *m. pl*
noted (well-known), insignis
nothing, nĭhil, *n*; (**good for —**), nēquam
nothingness, nĭhĭlum, *n*
notice, *v.t,* ănĭmadverto (3)
notice, *nn,* (**act of noticing**), ănĭmadversĭo, *f*; (**written —**), prōscriptĭo, *f*
noticeable, insignis
notification, dēnuntĭātĭo, *f*
notify, *v.t,* dēnuntĭo (1)
notion, nŏtĭo, *f*
notoriety, infāmĭa, *f*
notorious, nōtus, fāmōsus
notwithstanding, *adv,* nĭhĭlōmĭnus, tămen
nought, nĭhil
noun, nōmen, *n,* (**name**)
nourish, *v.t,* ălo (3)
nourishment, ălĭmentum, *n*
novel, *nn,* (**story**), fābŭla, *f*
novel, *adj,* (**new**), nŏvus
novelist, fābŭlārum scriptor, *m,* (**writer of stories**)
novelty (strangeness), nŏvĭtas, *f*
November, Nŏvember (mensis)
novice, tīro, *m*
now (at the present time), *adv,* nunc; (**at the time of the action**), iam; (**just —**), mŏdŏ; (**now . . . now**), mŏdŏ . . . mŏdŏ; (**— and then**), ălĭquandŏ
nowadays, *adv,* nunc
nowhere, *adv,* nusquam
noxious, nŏcens
nozzle, nāsus, *m*
nude, nūdus
nudge, *v.t,* fŏdĭco (1)
nuisance, incŏmmŏdum, *n, or use adj,* mŏlestus (**troublesome**)
null, irrĭtus, vānus
nullify, *v.t,* irrĭtum făcĭo (3)
numb, torpens; (**to be —**), *v.i,* torpĕo (2)
numb, *v.t,* torpĕfăcĭo (3)
number, *nn,* nŭmĕrus, *m*; (**what —, how many?**), quot?; (**a large —**), multĭtūdo, *f*
number, *v.t,* nŭmĕro (1)
numbering (in number), ad (*with acc*)
numberless, innŭmĕrābĭlis
numbness, torpor, *m*
numerically, *adv,* nŭmĕro
numerous, plūrĭmi, crēber
nun, mŏnăcha, *f*
nuptial, nuptĭālis, iŭgālis
nuptials, nuptĭae, *f. pl*
nurse, nūtrix, *f*
nurse, *v.t,* (**the sick**), cūro (1); (**cherish**), fŏvĕo (2)
nursery (for plants), sēmĭnārĭum, *n*
nurture, ēdŭcātĭo, *f*
nut, nut-tree, nux, *f*
nutriment, ălĭmentum, *n*
nutrition, ălĭmentum, *n*
nutritious, vălens
nutshell, pŭtāmen, *n*
nymph, nympha, *f*

O

o! oh! o! oh!; (**Oh that . . .**) ŭtĭnam . . .
oak, quercus, *f*; (**holm —**), ĭlex, *f*; (**oak-wood**), rōbur, *n*

oak, oaken, *adj*, quernus
oakum, stuppa, *f*
oar, rēmus, *m*
oarsmen, rēmĭges, *m. pl*
oats, ăvēna, *f*
oath, iusiūrandum, *n*; **(to take an—),** *v.i*, iusiūrandum accĭpĭo (3); **(military —),** săcrāmentum, *n*
oatmeal, fārīna ăvēnācĕa, *f*
obdurate, obstīnātus, dūrus
obedience, ŏbēdĭentĭa, *f*; *or use vb*, pārĕo (2) **(to obey,** *with dat*)
obeisance (to make an —), ădōro (1) (reverence)
obelisk, ŏbĕliscus, *m*
obese, ŏbēsus
obey, *v.i. and v.t*, pārĕo (2) (*with dat*), ŏbēdĭo (4) (*with dat*)
object, *nn*, (thing), rēs, *f*; **(aim),** consĭlĭum, *n*. fĭnis, *m*; **(to be an — of hatred),** ŏdĭo esse (*irreg*)
object, *v.t*, rĕcūso (1), nōlo (*irreg*)
objection, *use vb*, rĕcūso (1) **(object to)**
objectionable, ingrātus, *m*
objective *nn*, quod petitur **(that is sought)**
obligation (moral), offĭcĭum, *n*; **(legal),** oblĭgātĭo, *f*; **(religious —, conscientiousness),** rĕlĭgĭo, *f*; **(to put someone under an —),** *v.t*, obstringo (3); **(to be under an —),** *v.i*, dēbĕo (2)
obligatory (it is —), ŏportet (2 *impers*) *or use gerundive of vb*
oblige, *v.t*, obstringo (3); **(compel),** cōgo (3)
obliging, cōmis
oblique (slanting), oblīquus
obliterate, *v.t*, dēlĕo (2)
oblivion, oblivĭo, *f*
oblivious, immĕmor
oblong, *adj*, oblongus
obloquy, vĭtŭpĕrātĭo, *f*
obnoxious, invīsus, noxĭus
obscene, obscēnus
obscenity, obscēnĭtas, *f*
obscure, obscūrus, caecus, rĕcondĭtus; **(of birth, etc.),** hŭmĭlis
obscure, *v.t*, obscūro (1)
obscurity, obscūrĭtas, *f*
obsequies, exsĕquĭae, *f. pl*
obsequious, obsĕquens, offĭcĭōsus
observance, observantĭa, *f*, conservātĭo *f*; **(practice),** rĭtus, *m*
observant, attentus, dĭlĭgens
observation, observātĭo, *f*; **(attention),** ănĭmadversĭo, *f*; **(remark),** dictum, *n*
observatory, spĕcŭla, *f*
observe, *v.t*, observo (1), ănĭmadverto (3); **(remark),** dĭco (3); **(maintain),** conservo (1)
observer, spectātor, *m*
obsolete, obsŏlētus; **(to become —),** *v.i*, obsŏlesco (3), sĕnesco (3)
obstacle, impĕdĭmentum, *n*
obstinacy, pertĭnācĭa, *f*
obstinate, pertĭnax
obstreperous, (noisy), vŏcĭfĕrans
obstruct, *v.t*, obstrŭo (3), obsto (1) (*with dat*)
obstruction, impĕdĭmentum, *n*
obtain, *v.t*, ădĭpiscor (3 *dep*), nanciscor (3 *dep*), conseĕquor (3 *dep*), (— **possession of),** pŏtĭor (4 *dep. with abl*)
obtrude, *v.t*, inculco (1)
obtrusive, mŏlestus
obtuse, hĕbes
obviate, *v.t*, **(meet),** obvĭam ĕo (4 *irreg*) (*with dat*)
obvious, ăpertus, mănĭfestus
occasion (opportunity), occāsĭo, *f*; **(cause),** causa, *f*; **(on that —),** illo tempŏre
occasion, *v.t* mŏvĕo (2), fĕro (*irreg*)
occasionally, *adv*, interdum, rāro
occult, occultus, arcānus
occupancy, possessĭo, *f*
occupant, possessor, *m*
occupation (act of —), *use vb*, occŭpo (1); **(employment),** quaestus, *m*; nĕgōtĭum, *n*
occupy, *v.t*, occŭpo (1), obtĭnĕo (2); **(to be occupied with something),** *v.i*, tĕnĕor (2 *pass*)
occur, *v.i*. **(take place),** accĭdo (3); **(come into the mind),** in mentem vĕnĭo (4), sŭbĕo (4) (*with dat*)
occurrence, rēs, *f*
ocean, ŏcĕănus, *m*
ochre, ōchra, *f*
octagon, octŏgōnum, *n*
October, Octōber (mensis)
oculist, ŏcŭlārĭus mĕdĭcus, *m*
odd (numbers, etc.), impar; **(strange),** nŏvus
odds (to be at — with), *v.i*, dissĭdĕo (2) ab (*with abl*)
odious, ŏdĭōsus, invīsus
odium, invĭdĭa, *f*, ŏdĭum, *n*
odorous, ŏdōrātus
odour, ŏdor, *m*
of, *usually the genit. of the noun, e.g.* **the head of the boy,** căput pŭĕri; **(made —),** ex (*with abl*); **(about, concerning),** dē (*with abl*)
off, *adv, often expressed by prefix* **ab-** *with vb, e.g.* **to cut off,** abscĭdo (3); **(far —),** *adv*, prŏcul; **(a little way —),** *prep and adv*, prŏpe
offal (waste), quisquĭlĭae, *f. pl*

For List of Abbreviations used, turn to pages 3, 4

offence, offensĭo, *f*; (**crime, etc.**), dēlictum, *n*; (**to take — at**), aegrē fĕro (*irreg.*)
offend, *v.t*, offendo (3), laedo (3); (**to be offended**), aegrē fĕro (*irreg*) (**tolerate with displeasure**)
offensive, *adj*, ŏdĭōsus, grăvis
offensive, *nn*, (**military**), *use phr*, bellum infĕro (*irreg*) (**to inflict war**)
offer, *nn*, condĭcĭo, *f*
offer, *v.t*, offĕro (*irreg*); (**stretch out**), porrĭgo (3); (**give**), do (1)
offering (**gift**), dōnum, *n*
office (**political power**), măgistrātus, *m*; (**duty**), offĭcĭum, *n*; (**place of business**), fŏrum, *n*
officer (**military**), praefectus, *m*
official, *nn*, măgistrātus, *m*, mĭnister, *m*
official, *adj*, (**state**), pūblĭcus
officiate, *v.i*, (**perform**), fungor (3 *dep*)
officious, mŏlestus
offing, (**in the —**), *use* longē (**far off**), *or* prŏpĕ (**near**), *acc. to sense*
offshoot, surcŭlus, *m*
offspring, prōgĕnĭes, *f* lĭbĕri, *m, pl*
often, *adv*, saepĕ; (**how —?**), quŏtĭes?; (**so —**), *adv*, tŏtĭes
ogle, *v.t*, ŏcŭlis lĭmis intŭĕor (2 *dep*) (**look at with sidelong glances**)
oil, ŏlĕum, *n*
oily, ŏlĕăcĕus
ointment, unguentum, *n*
old, vĕtus; (**of persons**), sĕnex; (**so many years —, of persons**), nātus (*with acc. of extent of time*), *e.g.* **three years old,** tres annos nātus; (**— age**), sĕnectus, *f*; (**— man**), sĕnex, *m*; (**— woman**), ănus, *f*
olden, prĭscus
oldness, vĕtustas, *f*
oligarchy, dŏmĭnātĭo, (*f*) paucōrum (**rule of a few**)
olive (**tree**), ŏlĕa, *f*
Olympic, *adj*, Ŏlympĭcus; (**— Games**), Ŏlympĭa, *n.pl*
omelet, lăgănum, *n*
omen, ōmen, *n*
ominous, infaustus
omission, praetermissĭo, *f*
omit, *v.t*, ŏmitto (3), praetermitto (3)
omnipotent, omnĭpŏtens
on, *prep*, in (*with abl*); (**in the direction of**, *e.g.* **on the right**), ā, āb (*with abl*); (**— everyside**), *adv*, undĭque; (**of time**), *abl case, e.g.* **on the Ides of March,** Īdĭbus Martĭis; (**about a subject**), dē (*with abl*)
once, *num. adv*, sĕmel; (**— upon a time**), ŏlim, ălĭquandŏ; (**at —, immediately**), stătim; (**at the same time**), sĭmul
one, *num. adj*, ūnus; (**in —s, singly**), *adv*, singillātim, *adj*, singŭli; (**at — time**), *adv*, ălĭquandŏ; (**one ... another**), ălĭus ... ălĭus; (**one ... the other**), alter ... alter; (**a certain**), quĭdam; (**indefinite**), *use 2nd pers sing. of the vb*
onerous, grăvis
oneself (*emphatic*) ipse; (*reflexive*), sē
one-sided, īnaequālis
onion, caepa, *f*
onlooker, circumstans, *m*
only, *adj*, ūnus, sōlus, ūnĭcus
only, *adv*, sōlum, tantum, mŏdŏ; (**not only ...**), non mŏdŏ ...
onset, impĕtus, *m*
onwards, *adv*, porro, *often use compound vb. with* pro, *e.g.* prŏcēdĕre (3) (**to go onwards**)
ooze, *nn*, ūlĭgo, *f*
ooze, *v.i*, mano (1)
oozy, ūlĭgĭnōsus
opal, ŏpălus, *m*
opaque, caecus
open, *v.t*, ăpĕrĭo (4), pătĕfăcĭo (3), pando (3); (**inaugurate**), consĕcro (1); *v.i*, sē ăpĕrīre (4 *reflex*); (**gape open**), hisco (3)
open, *adj*, ăpertus; (**wide —**), pătens, hĭans; (**to lie, stand or be —**), pătĕo (2); (**— handed**), *adj*, lĭbĕrālis
opening (**dedication**), consĕcrātĭo, *f*; (**hole**), fŏrāmen, *n*; (**opportunity**), occāsĭo, *f*
openly, *adv*, pălam
operate, *v.t*, (**set in motion**), mŏvĕo (2); *v.i*, (**in war**), rem gĕro (3)
operation (**task**), ŏpus, *n*; (**military —**), rēs bellĭca, *f*; (**naval —**), rēs mărĭtĭma, *f*
operative, *adj*, effĭcax
opiate, mĕdĭcāmentum somnĭfĕrum, *n*, (**sleep-bringing drug**)
opinion, sententĭa, *f*, ŏpĭnĭo, *f*, existĭmātĭo, *f*
opium, ŏpĭum, *n*
opponent, adversārĭus, *m*
opportune, opportūnus
opportunity, occāsĭo, *f*, cŏpĭa, *f*, făcultas, *f*
oppose, *v.t*, oppōno (3); (**resist**), rĕsisto (3 *with dat*), adversor (1 *dep*)
opposite, *adj*, adversus, contrārĭus, dĭversus

opposite (to), *prep*, contrā (*with acc*)
opposition (from people), *use partic*, adversans *or* rĕsistens; **(from a party)**, *use* factĭo, *f*, **(party)**
oppress, *v.t*, opprĭmo (3)
oppression (tyranny), iniūrĭa, *f*
oppressive, grăvis, mŏlestus
oppressor, tȳrannus, *m*
opprobrious, turpis
optical, *adj*, *use genit. case of* ŏcŭlus, *m*, (eye)
option, optĭo, *f*
opulence, ŏpŭlentĭa, *f*, ŏpes, *f*, *pl*
opulent, dīves, lŏcŭples
or, aut, vel; **(either . . . or)**, aut . . . aut, vel . . . vel; **(whether . . . or)** (*questions*), ŭtrum . . . an; **(or not)** (*direct questions*), annon, (*indirect questions*), necne
oracle, ōrācŭlum, *n*
oral, *use* vox **(voice)**
oration, ōrātĭo, *f*
orator, ōrātor, *m*
oratory, ars ōrātōrĭa, *f*
orb, orbit, orbis, *m*
orchard, pōmārĭum, *n*
orchid, orchis, *f*
ordain, *v.t*, ēdico (3), stătŭo (3)
ordeal, discrīmen, *n*
order, *nn*, **(arrangement)**, ordo, *m*; **(in —)**, *adv*, ordīne; **(command, direction)**, iussum, *n*; **(class, rank)**, ordo, *m*; **(in — to)**, ut
order, *v.t*, **(command)**, iŭbĕo (2); **(arrange)**, dispōno (3)
orderly, *adj*, **(behaviour)**, mŏdestus; **(arrangement)**, ordīnātus dispŏsĭtus
orderly, *nn*, stător, *m*
ordinary, ūsĭtātus, mĕdĭŏcris
ordnance, tormenta, *n.pl*
ore, aes, *n*
organ (of the body), membrum, *n*
organization, dispŏsĭtĭo, *f*
organize, *v.t*, ordĭno (1)
orgies, orgĭa, *n.pl*; **(revelry)**, cōmissātĭo, *f*
orient, ŏrĭens, *m*
oriental, *use genit. of* ŏrĭens **(orient)**
orifice, fŏrāmen, *n*, os, *n*
origin, ŏrīgo, *f*, princĭpĭum, *n*
original, princĭpālis, antīquus, **(one's own)**, prŏprĭus
originally, *adv*, princĭpĭo, ĭnĭtĭo
originate, *v.i*, ŏrĭor (4 *dep*)
originator, auctor, *m*
ornament, *nn*, ornāmentum, *n*
ornament, *v.t*, orno (1)
ornate, *adj*, ornātus, pictus
orphan, orbus, *m*
oscillate, *v.i*, quătĭor (3 *pass*)
oscillation, *nse vb.* quătĭor (*above*) (3 *pass*)
osier, *nn*, vīmen, *n*
osier, *adj*, vīmĭnĕus
osprey, ossĭfrăgus, *m*
ostensible, *use adv. below*
ostensibly, *adv*, per spĕcĭem
ostentation, ostentātĭo, *f*
ostentatious, glōrĭōsus
ostler, ăgāso, *m*
ostracise, *v.t*, vĭto (1) **(avoid)**
ostrich, strūthĭŏcămēlus, *m*
other, *adj*, ălĭus; **(the — of two)**, alter; **(the others, the rest)**, cētĕri
others, *adj*, **(belonging to —)**, ălĭēnus
otherwise, *adv*, **(differently)**, ălĭter; **(in other respects also)**, ălĭōqui
otter, lūtra, *f*
ought, *v.auxil*, dēbĕo (2), ŏportet (2 *impers*, *with acc. of person*), *e.g.* **I ought**, ŏportet mē
ounce, uncĭa, *f*
our, ours, noster
ourselves (*in apposition to subject*), ipsi; (*reflexive*), nos
out, *adv*, **(being out)**, fŏris; **(going out)**, fŏras
out of, *prep*, ē, ex, dē (*with abl*); extrā (*with acc*); **(on account of)**, propter (*with acc*)
outbid, *v.t*, *use phr*, plūs offĕro quam . . . **(offer more than . . .)**
outbreak, use *vb.* ŏrĭor (4 *dep*) **(to arise)**; **(beginning)**, ĭnĭtĭum, *n*
outcast, prŏfŭgus, *m*
outcome (result), exĭtus, *m*
outcry, clāmor, *m*
outdo, *v.t*, sŭpĕro (1)
outdoors, *adv*, fŏras
outer, *adj*, extĕrĭor
outfit (equipment), appărātus, *m*
outflank, *v.i*, circŭmĕo (4)
outgrow, *v.t*, *use phr*, magnĭtūdĭne sŭpĕro (1) **(surpass in size)**
outhouse, tŭgŭrĭum, *n*
outlast, *v.t*, dĭūturnĭtāte sŭpĕro **(surpass in duration)**
outlaw, *nn*, prōscrĭptus, *m*
outlaw, *v.t*, prōscrĭbo (3)
outlay, *nn*, sumptus, *m*
outlet, exĭtus, *m*
outline, fīnis, *m*, ădumbrātĭo, *f*
outlive, *v.i*, sŭperstĕs sum (*irreg*) **(to be a survivor)**
outlook (future), fŭtūra, *n.pl*
outnumber, *v.t*, plūres nūmĕro esse quam . . . **(to be more in number than . . .)**
outpost, stătĭo, *f*
outrage, *nn*, iniūrĭa, *f*

outrage, *v.t,* vĭŏlo (1)
outrageous, indignus
outright, *adv,* prorsus; **(immediately),** stātim
outset, ĭnĭtĭum, *n*
outside, *nn,* extĕrna pars, *f*; **(on the —),** *adv,* extrinsĕcus; **(appearance),** spĕcĭes, *f,* frons, *f*
outside, *adj,* externus
outside, *adv,* extrā
outside of, *prep,* extrā (*with acc*)
outskirts, *use adj.* sŭburbānus **(near the city)**
outspoken (frank), lĭber
outstretched, porrectus
outstrip, *v.t,* sŭpĕro (1)
outward, *adj,* externus
outwardly, *adv,* extrā
outweigh, *v.t,* grăvĭtāte sŭpĕro (1) **(surpass in weight)**
outwit, *v.t,* dēcĭpĭo (3)
oval, *adj,* ōvātus
oven, furnus, *m*
over, *prep,* **(above, across, more than),** sŭper (*with acc*)
over, *adv,* **(above),** sŭper, suprā; **(left —),** *adj,* rĕlĭquus; **(it is —, all up with),** actum est; **(— and — again),** *adv,* ĭdentĭdem
overawe, *v.t,* percello (3)
overbearing, sŭperbus
overboard, *adv,* ex nāvi
overcast (sky), nūbĭlus
overcoat, lăcerna, *f*
overcome, *v.t,* vinco (3), sŭpĕro (1)
overdone, *use adv,* nĭmis **(too much)**
overdue, *use adv,* diūtĭus **(too long),** *and* differo (*irreg*), **(to put off)**
overflow, *v.i,* effundor (3 *pass*); *v.t,* ĭnundo (1)
overgrown, obsĭtus
overhang, *v.i,* immĭnĕo (2), impendĕo (2) (*both with dat*)
overhanging, impendens
overhasty, praeceps
overhaul, *v.t,* **(repair),** rĕsarcĭo (4)
overhead, *adv,* insŭper
overhear, *v.t,* excĭpĭo (3)
overjoyed, laetĭtĭā ēlātus **(elated with joy)**
overland, *adv,* terrā, per terram
overlap, *v.t,* **(overtake),** sŭpervĕnĭo (4)
overlay, *v.t,* indūco (3)
overload, *v.t,* grăvo (1)
overlook, *v.t,* prōspĭcĭo (3); **(forgive),** ignosco (3) (*with dat*); **(neglect),** praetermitto (3)
overmuch, *adv,* nĭmis
overpower, *v.t,* opprĭmo (3)
overrate, *v.t,* plūris aestĭmo (1) **(value too highly)**
override, *v.t,* praeverto (3)
overrule, *v.t,* vinco (3)
overrun, *v.t,* pervăgor (1 *dep*)
oversee, *v.t,* cūro (1), inspĭcĭo (3)
overseer, cūrātor, *m*
overshadow, *v.t,* offĭcĭo (3) (*with dat*)
oversight (omission), error, *m,* neglĕgentĭa, *f, or use vb,* praetermitto (3) **(overlook)**
overspread, *v.t,* obdūco (3)
overt, ăpertus, plānus
overtake, *v.t,* consĕquor (3 *dep*)
overtax (strength, etc.), *v.t,* nĭmis ūtor (3 *dep*) (*with abl*)
overthrow, *nn,* rŭīna, *f*
overthrow, *v.t,* ĕverto (3), opprĭmo (3)
overtop, *v.t,* sŭpĕro (1)
overture (to make —s), *use vb.* instĭtŭo (3) **(to begin)**
overweening, sŭperbus
overwhelm, *v.t,* opprĭmo (3), obrŭo (3)
overwork, *v.i,* nĭmis lăbōro (1)
overwrought (exhausted), confectus
owe, *v.t,* dĕbĕo (2)
owing to, *prep,* **(on account of),** propter, ob (*both with acc*)
owl, būbo, *m,* strix, *f*
own, *adj,* prŏprĭus; *often expressed by possessive pron, e.g.* **my own,** mĕus
own, *v.t,* **(possess),** tĕnĕo (2), possĭdĕo (2); **(confess),** fătĕor (2 *dep*)
owner, possessor *m,* dŏmĭnus, *m*
ox, bōs, *c*
oxherd, armentārĭus, *m*
oyster, ostrĕa, *f*

P

pace, *nn,* passus, *m*
pace (step), spătĭor (1 *dep*), grădĭor (3 *dep*)
pacific, pācĭfĭcus
pacification, pācĭfĭcātĭo, *f*
pacify, *v.t,* plāco (1), sēdo (1)
pack (bundle), sarcĭna, *f*; **(— of people),** turba, *f*
pack, *v.t,* **(gather together),** collĭgo (3); **(— close together),** stīpo (1)
package, sarcĭna, *f*
packet, fascĭcŭlus, *m*
pack-horse, iūmentum, *n*
pact, pactum, *n,* foedus, *n*
padding, *nn,* fartūra, *f*
paddle, *nn,* **(oar),** rēmus, *m*
paddle, *v.t,* rēmĭgo (1), **(to row)**
paddock, saeptum, *n*

padlock, sĕra, *f*
pagan, pāgānus
page (book), pāgĭna, *f*; **(boy),** pŭer, *m*
pageant, spectācŭlum, *n*, pompa, *f*
pageantry, spĕcĭes, (*f*) atque pompa, *f* **(display and public procession)**
pail, sĭtŭla, *f*
pain, dŏlor, *m*; **(to be in —),** *v.i*, dŏlĕo (2)
pain, *v.t*, dŏlōre affĭcĭo (3) **(inflict pain)**
painful, ăcerbus
painless, *use adv. phr*, sĭne dŏlōre **(without pain)**
pains (endeavour), ŏpĕra, *f*; **(to take — over),** ŏpĕram do (1) (*with dat*)
painstaking, ŏpĕrōsus
paint, *v.t*, pingo (3); **(colour),** fūco (1)
paint, *nn*, pigmentum, *n*
paint-brush, pēnĭcullus, *m*
painter, pictor, *m*
painting, pictūra, *f*
pair, pār, *m*
pair, *v.t*, iungo (3); *v.i*, iungor (3 *pass*)
palace, rēgĭa, *f*
palatable, iūcundus
palate, pălātum, *n*
palatial, rēgĭus
pale, *adj*, pallĭdus; **(to be —),** *v.i*, pallĕo (2); **(to become —),** *v.i*, pallesco (3)
pale, *nn*, **(stake),** pālus, *m*
paleness, pallor, *m*
palisade, vallum, *n*
pall, *nn*, pallĭum, *n*
pall, *v.i*, **(it —s),** taedet (2 *impers*)
pallet lectŭlus, *m*
palliate, *v.t*, extĕnŭo (1)
palliation, *use vb*, extĕnŭo (1) **(palliate)**
palliative, lēnĭmentum, *n*
pallid, *adj* pallĭdus
pallor, pallor, *m*
palm (of hand, tree), palma, *f*
palm (to — off), *v.t*, suppōno (3)
palpable (obvious), mănĭfestus
palpitate, *v.t*, palpĭto (1)
palpitation, palpĭtātĭo, *f*
palsy, părălȳsis, *f*
paltry, vĭlis
pamper, *v.t*, nĭmĭum indulgĕo (2) (*with dat*) **(to be too kind to . . .)**
pamphlet, lĭbellus, *m*
pamphleteer, scriptor, (*m*) lĭbellorum
pan, pătĭna, *f*; **(frying —),** sartāgo, *f*
panacea, pănăcēa, *f*
pancake, lăgănum, *n*
pander, *v.i*, lēnōcĭnor (1 *dep*)
panegyric, laudātĭo, *f*
panel (of door, etc.), tympānum, *n*
panelled, lăquēātus
pang, dŏlor, *m*
panic, păvor, *m*
panic-stricken, păvĭdus
pannier, clĭtellae, *f*, *pl*
panorama, prŏspectus, *m*
pant, *v.i*, ănhēlo (1)
panther, panthēra, *f*
panting, *nn*, ănhēlĭtus, *m*
pantomime, mīmus, *m*
pantry, cella pĕnarĭa, *f*
pap (nipple), păpilla, *f*
paper, charta, *f*; **(sheet of —),** schēda, *f*; **(newspaper),** acta dĭurna, *n.pl*
papyrus, păpȳrus, *m*, *f*
par (on a — with), *adj*, pār
parable, părăbŏla, *f*
parade (military), dēcursus, *m*; **(show),** appărātus, *m*, pompa, *f*
parade, *v.i*, **(of troops),** dēcurro (3); *v.t* **(display),** ostento (1)
paradise, Ēlȳsĭum, ĭi, *n*
paragon, spĕcĭmen, *n*
paragraph, căput, *n*
parallel, *adj*, părallēlus; **(like),** sĭmĭlis
paralyse, *v.t*, dēbĭlĭto (1)
paralysed, dēbĭlis
paralysis, părălȳsis, *f*, dēbĭlĭtas, *f*
paramount summus
paramour ădulter, *m*, ămātor, *m*
parapet, lōrĭca, *f*, mūnĭtĭo, *f*
paraphernalia, appărātus, *m*
parasite, assecla, *c*
parasol, umbella, *f*
parcel, fascĭcŭlus, *m*
parcel out, *v.t*, partĭor (4 *dep*)
parch, *v.t*, torrĕo (2)
parched (dry), ărĭdus; **(scorched),** torrĭdus
parchment, membrāna, *f*
pardon, *nn*, vĕnĭa, *f*
pardon, *v.t*, ignosco (3) (*with dat*)
pardonable, *use phr*, cui ignoscendum est **(who should be pardoned)**
pare, *v.t*, (circum)sĕco (1) **(cut around))**
parent, pārens, *m*, *f*
parentage, gĕnus, *n*
parental, pătrĭus, *or use genit pl*, pārentum **(of parents)**
parenthesis, interpŏsĭtĭo, *f*
parish, pāroecĭa, *f*
park, horti, *m. pl*
parley, collŏquĭum, *n*
parley, *v.i*, collŏquor (3 *dep*)
parliament, sĕnātus, *m*
parliamentary, *use genit. case of* sĕnātus
parlour, conclāve, *n*

For List of Abbreviations used, turn to pages 3, 4

parody, versus rīdĭcŭli, *m, pl*
parole, fĭdes, *f* **(promise)**
paroxysm, *use* accessus, *m*, **(approach)**
parricide (person), parrĭcīda, *c*; **(act),** parrĭcīdĭum, *n*
parrot, psittăcus, *m*
parry, *v.t*, prōpulso (1)
parse, *v.t*, *use phr*, verba singŭlātim percĭpĭo **(understand the words one by one)**
parsimonious, parcus
parsimony, parsĭmōnĭa, *f*
parsley, ăpĭum, *n*
parson (priest), săcerdos, *c*
part, pars, *f*; **(in a play),** persōna, *f*, partes, *f, pl*; **(side, faction),** partes, *f, pl*; **(duty),** offĭcĭum, *n*; **(region),** lŏca, *n.pl*; **(from all —s),** *adv*, undĭque; **(for the most —),** *adv*, plērumque; **(to take — in),** intersum (*irreg*) (*with dat*)
part, *v.t*, dīvĭdo (3), sēpăro (1); *v.i*, discēdo (3)
partake of, *v.t*, partĭceps sum (*irreg*) (*with genit*); **(food),** gusto (1)
partaker, partĭceps, *adj*
partial (affecting only a part), *use adv. phr*, ex ălĭquā parte; **(unfair),** ĭnīquus
partiality, stŭdĭum, *n*
participate, *v.i*, partĭceps sum (*irreg*) (*with genit*)
participation, sŏcĭĕtas, *f*
particle, partĭcŭla, *f*
particular (characteristic), prŏprĭus; **(special),** singŭlāris; **(exacting),** dēlĭcātus
particularly (especially), *adv*, praecĭpŭē
parting, *nn*, dīgressus, *m*
partisan, fautor, *m*
partition (act of —), partĭtĭo, *f*; **(wall),** păries, *m*
partly, *adv*, partim
partner, sŏcĭus, *m* (sŏcĭa, *f*)
partnership, sŏcĭĕtas, *f*
partridge, perdix, *c*
party (political, etc.), factĭo, *f*; **(of soldiers),** mănus, *f*; **(for pleasure),** convīvĭum, *n*
pasha, sătrăpes, *m*
pass, *nn* **(mountain),** angustĭae, *f. pl*
pass, *v.t.* **(go beyond),** praetergrĕdĭor (3 *dep*); **(surpass),** excēdo (3); **(— on, — down),** trādo (3); **(of time),** ăgo (3), tĕro (3); **(— over, omit),** praetĕrĕo (4); **(— a law),** sancĭo (4); **(approve),** prŏbo (1); *v.i*, praetĕrĕo (4); **(of time),** transĕo (4); **(give satisfaction),** sătisfăcĭo (3); **(— over, cross over),** transĕo (4); **(come to —, happen),** fĭo (*irreg*)
passable (road, etc.), pervĭus
passage (crossing), transĭtus, *m*, trăiectĭo, *f*; **(route, way),** ĭter, *n*, vĭa, *f*; **(in a book),** lŏcus, *m*
passenger, vector, *m*
passion, mōtus, (*m*) ănĭmi **(impulse of the mind)**; **(love),** ămor, *m*
passionate, fervĭdus, ardens, īrācundus
passive, pătĭens
passivity, pătĭentĭa, *f*
passport, dĭplōma, *n*
password, tessĕra, *f*
past, *adj*, praetĕrĭtus; **(just —),** proxĭmus
past, *nn*, praetĕrĭtum tempus, *n*
past, *prep*, praeter (*with acc*); **(on the far side of),** ultrā (*with acc*)
past, *adv*, *use compound vb. with* praeter, *e.g.* praetĕrĕo (4) **(go past)**
paste, fărīna, *f*
paste, *v.t*, glūtĭno (1)
pastime, oblectāmentum, *n*
pastor, pastor, *m*
pastoral pastōrālis
pastry, crustum, *n*
pastry-cook, crustŭlārĭus, *m*
pasture, pascŭum, *n*
pasture, *v.t*, pasco (3)
pat, *v.t*, (caress), permulcĕo (2)
patch, *nn*, pannus, *m*
patch, *v.t*, sarcĭo (4)
patent, *adj*, ăpertus
paternal, păternus
path, sēmĭta, *f*, vĭa, *f*
pathetic, mĭsĕrandus
pathless, invĭus
pathos, *f*; affectĭo, (*f*) ănĭmi
pathway, sēmĭta, *f*
patience, pătĭentĭa, *f*
patient, *adj*, pătĭens
patient, *nn*, *use* aeger **(ill)**
patiently, *adv*, pătĭenter
patrician, *nn. and adj*, pătrĭcĭus
patrimony, pătrĭmōnĭum, *n*
patriot, *use phr*, qui pătrĭam ămat **(who loves his country)**
patriotic, ămans pătrĭae
patriotism, ămor (*m*) pătrĭae
patrol, *nn*, *use* custōdes, *m. pl*, **(guards)**
patrol, *v.t*, circŭmĕo (4)

patron, pătrōnus, *m*
patronage, pătrōcĭnĭum, *n*
patronize, *v.t*, făvĕo (2) (*with dat*)
patter, *nn*, crĕpĭtus, *m*
patter, *v.i*, crĕpo (1)
pattern, exemplum, *n*, exemplar, *n*
paucity, paucĭtas, *f*
pauper, pauper *c*, ĕgens (**needy**)
pause, *nn*, mŏra, *f*
pause, *v.i*, intermitto (3)
pave, *v.t*, sterno (3)
pavement, păvīmentum, *n*
pavilion, *use* praetōrĭum, *n*, (**general's tent**), *or* tăbernācŭlum, *n*, (**tent**)
paw, *nn*, pes, *m*
paw, *v.t*, pĕdĭbus calco (1) (**tread with the feet**)
pawn (chess), lătruncŭlus, *m*; (**security**), pignus, *n*
pawn, *v.t*, pignĕro (1)
pay, *nn*, stĭpendĭum, *n*
pay, *v.t*, solvo (3), pendo (3), nŭmĕro (1); *v.i* (— **attention**), ŏpĕram do (1); (— **the penalty**), poenas do (1)
pay-master (in army), trĭbūnus aerārĭus, *m*
payment, sŏlūtĭo, *f*
pea, pĭsum, *n*, cĭcer, *n*
peace, pax, *f*, ōtĭum, *n*
peaceable, plăcĭdus
peaceful, plăcĭdus, pācātus
peacefulness, tranquillĭtas, *f*
peace-offering, pĭăcŭlum, *n*
peacock, pāvo, *m*
peak, ăpex, *m*; (**mountain**), căcūmen, *n*
peal (thunder), frăgor, *m*; *otherwise use* sŏnus, *m*, (**sound**)
peal, *v.i*, sŏno (1)
pear, pȳrum, *n*; (— **tree**), pȳrus, *f*
pearl, margărĭta, *f*
peasant, rustĭcus, *m*, ăgrestis, *m*
peasantry, ăgrestes, *m. pl*
pebble, lăpillus, *m*
peck (measure), mŏdĭus, *m*
peck, *v.t*, vellĭco (1)
peculation, pĕcŭlātus, *m*
peculiar (to one person, etc.), prŏprĭus; (**remarkable**), singŭlāris
peculiarity, prŏprĭĕtas, *f*
pecuniary, pĕcŭnĭārĭus
pedagogue, măgister, *m*
pedant, hŏmo īneptus
pedantic (affected — of style, etc.), pūtĭdus
peddle, *v.t*, vendĭto (1)
pedestal, băsis, *f*
pedestrian, *nn*, pĕdes, *m*
pedestrian, *adj*, pĕdester
pedigree, stemma, *n*
pedlar, instĭtor, *m*
peel, *nn*, cŭtis, *f*
peel, *v.i*, cŭtem rĕsĕco (1)
peep, *nn*, aspectus, *m*
peep at, *v.t*, inspĭcio (3); *v.i*, sē prōferre (*irreg*)
peer (equal), par, *m*
peer at, *v.t*, rīmor (1 *dep*)
peerless, ūnĭcus
peevish, stŏmăchōsus
peevishness, stŏmăchus, *m*
peg, clāvus, *m*
pelt, *v.t*, *use* intorquĕo (2) (**hurl at**); *v.i*, (**of rain, etc.**), *use* plŭit (**it rains**)
pen, căllămus, *m*; (**for cattle**), saeptum, *n*
pen, *v.t*, (**write**), scrĭbo (3)
penal, poenālis
penalty, poena, *f*, damnum, *n*; (**to pay the —**), poenas do (1)
penance (do —), *use vb.* expĭo (1) (**to make amends**)
pencil, pēnĭcillum, *n*
pending, *prep*, inter, per (*with acc*)
pendulous, pendŭlus
penetrate, *v.i*, *and v.t*, pĕnĕtro (1) pervādo (3)
penetrating, *adj*, ăcūtus, ācer (**mentally**), săgax
penetration, ăcūmen, *n*
peninsula, paeninsŭla, *f*
penitence, paenĭtentĭa, *f*
penitent, *use vb*, paenĭtet (2 *impers*) (*with acc. of person*), *e.g.* **I am penitent,** mē paenĭtet
pennant, vexillum, *n*
penny, as, *m*
pension, annŭa, *n.pl*
pensive, multa pŭtans (**thinking many things**)
penthouse, vīnĕa, *f*
penultimate, paenultĭmus
penurious, parcus
penury, ĕgestas, *f*, īnŏpĭa, *f*
people (community), pŏpŭlus, *m*; (**persons**), hŏmĭnes, *c. pl*; (**the common —**), plebs, *f*, vulgus, *n*
people, *v.t*; frĕquento (1); (**inhabit**), incŏlo (3)
pepper, pĭper, *n*
perambulate, *v.t*, pĕrambŭlo (1)
perceive, *v.t*, sentĭo (4), percĭpĭo (3), ănĭmadverto (3), intellĕgo (3)
percentage, pars, *f*
perception, perspĭcācĭtas, *f*, *or use adj*, perspĭcax (**sharp-sighted**)
perceptive, perspĭcax
perch, *nn*, pertĭca, *f*; (**fish**), perca, *f*
perch, *v.i*, insīdo (3)

perchance, *adv,* fortĕ
percolate, *v.i,* permāno (1)
percussion, ictus, *m*
perdition, exĭtĭum, *n*
peremptory, *use vb.* obstringo (3) (**to put under obligation**)
perennial, pĕrennis
perfect, perfectus, absŏlūtus
perfect, *v.t,* perfĭcĭo (3), absolvo (3)
perfection, perfectĭo, *f*, absŏlūtĭo, *f*
perfidious, perfĭdus
perfidy, perfĭdĭa, *f*
perforate, *v.t,* perfŏro (1)
perform, *v.t,* fungor (3 *dep. with abl*); perāgo (3), praesto (1), exsĕquor (3 *dep*)
performance, functĭo, *f*
performer, actor, *m*
perfume, ŏdor, *m*
perfume, *v.t,* ŏdōro (1)
perfunctory, neglĕgens
perhaps, *adv,* fortĕ, fortassĕ, forsĭtan
peril, pĕrīcŭlum, *n*
perilous, pĕrīcŭlōsus
period, spătĭum, *n*
periodical, *adj,* stătus
perish, *v.i,* pĕrĕo (4)
perishable, frăgĭlis
perjure, *v.t,* periūro (1)
perjured, periūrus
perjury, periūrĭum, *n*
permanence, stăbĭlĭtas, *f*
permanent, stăbĭlis
permanently, *adv,* perpĕtŭo
permeate, *v.i,* permāno (1)
permissible (**it is —**), lĭcet (2 *impers*)
permission (**to give —**), permitto (3) (*with dat*); (**without your —**), tē invīto
permit, *v.t,* sĭno (3), permitto (3)
pernicious, pernĭcĭōsus
perpendicular, *adj,* directus
perpetrate, *v.t,* admitto (3)
perpetual, sempĭternus
perpetuate, *v.t,* contĭnŭo (1)
perplex, *v.t,* distrăho (3), sollĭcĭto (1)
perplexed, dŭbĭus
perquisite, pĕcŭlĭum, *n*
persecute, *v.t,* insector (1 *dep*)
persecution, insectātĭo, *f*
persecutor, insectātor, *m*
perseverance, persĕvĕrantĭa, *f*
persevere, *v.i,* persĕvĕro (1)
persist, *v.i,* persto (1)
persistence pertĭnācĭa, *f*
person, hŏmo, *c*; (**body**), corpus, *n*; (**in person**), *use pron,* ipse (**self**)
personal (**opp. to public**), prīvātus
personality, ingĕnĭum, *n*
perspicacious, perspĭcax
perspicacity, perspĭcācĭtas, *f*
perspiration, sūdor, *m*
perspire, *v.i,* sūdo (1)
persuade, *v.t,* persuādĕo (2) (*with dat of person*)
persuasion, persuāsĭo, *f*
persuasive, suāvĭlŏquens
pert, prŏcax
pertain, *v.i,* attĭnĕo (2)
pertinacious, pertĭnax
pertinacity, pertĭnācĭa, *f*
perturb, *v.t,* turbo (1)
perusal, perlectĭo, *f*
peruse, *v.t,* perlĕgo (3)
pervade, *v.t,* permāno (1), perfundo (3)
perverse, perversus
perversion, dĕprāvātĭo, *f*
pervert, *v.t,* dĕprāvo (1)
pervious, pervĭus
pest, pestis, *f*
pester, *v.t,* sollĭcĭto (1)
pestilence, pestĭlentĭa, *f*
pestilential, pestĭlens
pestle, pistillum, *n*
pet, *nn,* dēlĭcĭae, *f. pl*
pet, *v.t,* in dēlĭcĭis hăbĕo (2) (**regard among one's favourites**), indulgĕo (2)
petition, *use vb.* pĕto (3) (**seek**)
petition, *v.t,* rŏgo (1)
petitioners, pĕtentes, *c.pl*
petrify, *v.t,* (**with fear, etc.**), terrōrem īnĭcĭo (3), (*with dat*)
pettifogging, vĭlis
petty, mĭnūtus
petulance, pĕtŭlantĭa, *f*
petulant, pĕtŭlans
phantom, sĭmŭlācrum, *n*, ĭmāgo, *f*
phases (**alternations**), vĭces, *f. pl*
pheasant, āles, (*c*) Phāsĭdis (**bird of Phasis**)
phenomenon, rēs, *f*; (**remarkable occurrence**), rēs mīrābĭlis
phial, lăguncŭla, *f*
philanthropic, hŭmānus
philanthropy, hŭmānĭtas, *f*
philologist, phĭlŏlŏgus, *m*
philology, phĭlŏlŏgĭa, *f*
philosopher, phĭlŏsŏphus, *m*
philosophical, phĭlŏsŏphus
philosophy, phĭlŏsŏphĭa, *f*
philtre, philtrum, *n*
phlegm, pĭtŭĭta, *f*; (**of temperament**), aequus ănĭmus, *m*
phoenix, phoenix, *m*
phrase, *nn,* lŏcūtĭo, *f*
phraseology, *use* verba, *n.pl,* (**words**)
phthisis, phthĭsis, *f*
physic, mĕdĭcāmentum, *n*

physical (relating to the body), *use nn*, corpus, *n*, (body); (natural), *use* nātūra, *f*, (nature)
physician, mĕdĭcus, *m*
physics, phȳsĭca, *n.pl*
physiology, phȳsĭŏlŏgĭa, *f*
pick (axe), dŏlābra, *f*; (choice), *use adj*, dēlectus (chosen)
pick, *v.t*, (pluck), lĕgo (3), carpo (3); (choose), ēlĭgo (3); (— up, seize), rāpĭo (3)
picked (chosen), dēlectus
picket, stātĭo, *f*
pickle, mŭrĭa, *f*
pickle, *v.t*, condĭo (4)
pickpocket, fūr, *c*
picnic, *use phr*, fŏrīs ĕpŭlor (1 *dep*) (to eat out of doors)
picture, tăbŭla, *f*
picture, *v.t*, expingo (3)
picturesque, ămoenus
pie, crustum, *n*
piebald, bĭcŏlor
piece (part), pars, *f*; (of food), frustrum, *n*; (to pull or tear to —s), discerpo (3), dīvello (3); (to fall to —s), dīlābor (3 *pass*)
piecemeal, *adv*, membrātim
piece together, *v.t*, compōno (3)
pier, mōles, *f*
pierce, *v.t*, perfŏdĭo (3)
piercing, *adj*, ăcūtus
piety, pĭĕtas, *f*
pig, porcus, *m*, sūs, *c*
pigeon, cŏlumba, *f*
pigheaded, obstĭnātus, difficĭlis
pigsty, hăra, *f*
pike, hasta, *f*
pile (heap), ăcervus, *m*; (building), mōles, *f*; (supporting timber), sublĭca, *f*
pile, *v.t*, ăcervo (1), congĕro (3)
pilfer, *v.t*, surrĭpĭo (3)
pilfering, *nn*, furtum, *n*
pilgrim, pĕrĕgrīnātor, *m*
pilgrimage, pĕrĕgrīnātĭo, *f*
pill, pĭlŭla, *f*
pillage, *nn*, rāpīna, *f*, dīreptĭo, *f*
pillage, *v.t*, praedor (1 *dep*), dīrĭpĭo (3)
pillar, cŏlumna, *f*
pillory, vincŭla, *n.pl*
pillow, pulvīnus, *m*
pillow, *v.t*, suffulcĭo (4)
pilot, gŭbernātor, *m*
pilot, *v.t*, gŭberno (1)
pimp, lēno, *m*
pimple, pustŭla, *f*
pin, ăcus, *f*
pin, *v.t*, ăcu fīgo (3) (fix with a pin)
pincers, forceps, *m*, *f*
pinch, *nn*, (bite), morsus, *m*
pinch, *v.t*, ūro (3), vellĭco (1); (squeeze), cŏarto (1)
pine, *nn*, pīnus, *f*; *adj*, pīnĕus
pine, *v.i*, tābesco (3); *v.t*, (—for), dēsīdĕro (1)
pinion (nail), clāvus, *m*; (bond), vincŭla, *n.pl*
pinion, *v.t*, rĕvincĭo (4)
pink, rŭbor, *m*
pinnace, lembus, *m*
pinnacle, fastīgĭum, *n*
pint, sextārĭus, *m*
pioneer, explōrātor, *m*
pious, pĭus
pip (seed), sēmen, *n*, grānum, *n*
pipe, cănālis, *m*; (musical), fistŭla, *f*
pipe, *v.i*, cano (3)
piper, tĭbĭcen, *m*
piquant, ăcerbus
pique, *nn*, offensĭo, *f*
pique, *v.t*, laedo (3)
piracy, lătrōcĭnĭum, *n*
pirate, praedo, *m*, pīrāta, *m*
pit, fŏvĕa, *f*; (arm —), āla, *f*; (theatre), cāvĕa, *f*
pit (— one's wits, etc.), *use* ūtor (3 *dep*) (to use)
pitch, *nn*, pix, *f*; (in music), sŏnus, *m*
pitch, *v.t*, (camp, tent, etc.), pōno (3); (throw), cōnĭcĭo (3); (ships), *use* ăgĭtor (1 *pass*) (to be tossed about)
pitcher, urcĕus, *m*
pitchfork, furca, *f*
piteous, pitiable, mĭsĕrābĭlis
pitfall, fŏvĕa, *f*
pith, mĕdulla, *f*
pitiful mĭser, mĭsĕrĭcors
pitifulness, mĭsĕrĭa, *f*
pitiless, immĭsĕrĭcors
pittance (small pay) tips, *f*
pity, *v.t*, mĭsĕret (2 *impers*) (*with acc. of subject and genit. of object, e.g.* I pity you; mē mĭsĕret tŭi
pity, *nn*, mĭsĕrĭcordĭa, *f*
pivot, cardo, *m*
placard, inscriptum, *n*
placate, *v.t*, plăco (1)
place, lŏcus, *m*; (in this —), *adv*, hīc; (in that —), illīc, ĭbĭ; (in what —?) ŭbĭ?; (in the same —), ĭbĭdem; (to this —) hūc; (to that —), illūc; (to the same —), ĕōdem; (to what —?), quō; (from this —), hinc; (from that —), inde; (from the same —), indĭdem; (from what —?), unde?; (in the first —), prīmum; (to take —, happen), *v.i*, accĭdo (3)
place, *v.t*, pōno (3), lŏco (1); (— in

For List of Abbreviations used, turn to pages 3, 4

command), praefĭcĭo (3); (— **upon)**, impōno (3)
placid, plăcĭdus, tranquillus
plague, *nn*, pestĭlentĭa, *f*, pestis, *f*
plague, *v.t*, **(trouble)**, sollĭcĭto (1)
plain, *nn*, campus, *m*, plānĭtĭes, *f*
plain, *adj*, **(clear)**, clārus, plānus; **(unadorned)**, subtĭlis, simplex; **(frank, candid)**, sincērus
plainness, perspĭcŭĭtas, *f*, simplĭcĭtas, *f*, sincērĭtas, *f*
plaintiff, pĕtĭtor, *m*
plaintive, *adj*, mĭsĕrābĭlis
plait, *v.t*, intexo (3)
plan, *nn*, consĭlĭum, *n*; **(drawing)**, dēscriptĭo, *f*; **(to make a —)**, consĭlĭum căpĭo (3)
plan, *v.i*, **(intend)**, in ănĭmo hăbĕo (2); *v.t*, **(design)**, dēscrĭbo (3)
plane, *nn*, **(tool)**, runcīna, *f*; **(tree)**, plătănus, *f*
plane, *v.t*, runcīno (1)
planet, sīdus, (*n*) errans **(moving constellation)**
plank, tăbŭla, *f*
plant, *nn*, herba, *f*
plant (seeds, etc.), sĕro (3); **(otherwise)**, pōno (3), stătŭo (3)
plantation, plantārĭum, *n*, arbustum, *n*
planter, sātor, *m*
planting, *nn*, sātus, *m*
plaster, *nn*, tectōrĭum, *n*; **(medical)**, emplastrum, *n*
plaster, *v.t*, gypso (1)
plasterer, tector, *m*
plate (dish), cătĭllus, *m*; **(thin layer of metal)**, lāmĭna, *f*; **(silver, gold)**, argentum, *n*
plate, *v.t*, indūco (3)
platform, suggestus, *m*
Platonic, Plătōnĭcus
platoon, dĕcŭrĭa, *f*
plausible, spĕcĭōsus
play, *nn*, lūdus, *m*, lūsus, *m*; **(theatre)**, fābŭla, *f*; **(scope)**, campus, *m*
play, *v.i*, lūdo (3) (*with abl. of game played*); **(musical)**, căno (3); **(a part in a play)**, partes ăgo (3); **(a trick)**, lūdĭfĭco (1)
player (stage), histrĭo, *m*; **(flute —)**, tĭbĭcen, *m*; **(strings —)**, fĭdĭcen, *m*; **(lute, guitar —)**, cĭthărista, *m*
playful (frolicsome), lascīvĭa, *f*
playfulness, lascīvĭa, *f*
playground, ārĕa, *f*
playwright, fābŭlārum scriptor, *m*
plea (asking), obsĕcrātĭo, *f*; **(excuse)**, excūsātĭo, *f*
plead, *v.t*, ōro (1), ăgo (3); **(as an excuse)**, excūso (1); **(beg earnestly)**, obsĕcro (1); **(law)**, dīco (3)
pleader (in law), ōrātor, *m*
pleasing, pleasant, iūcundus
pleasantness, iūcundĭtas, *f*
please, *v.t*, plăcĕo (2) (*with dat*); **(if you —)**, si vis
pleasurable, iūcundus
pleasure, vŏluptas, *f*; **(will)**, arbĭtrĭum, *n*; **(— gardens)**, horti, *m. pl*
plebian, plēbēius
pledge, *nn*, pignus, *n*; **(to make a —, promise)**, sē obstringĕre (3 *reflex*)
pledge, *v.t*, oblĭgo (1), prōmitto (3)
plenipotentiary, lēgātus, *m*
plenitude, plēnĭtūdo, *f*
plentiful, largus, cōpĭōsus
plenty, cōpĭa, *f*; **(enough)**, sătis (*with genit*)
pleurisy, pleurĭtis, *f*
pliable, flexĭbĭlis, lentus
plight, angustĭae, *f. pl* **(difficulties)**
plight, *v.t*, spondēō (2), oblĭgo (1)
plinth, plinthus, *m*, *f*
plod, *v.i*, lentē prōcēdo (3)
plot (of ground), ăgellus, *m*; **(conspiracy)**, coniūrātĭo, *f*; **(story)**, argūmentum, *n*
plot, *v.i*, coniūro (1)
plough, *nn*, ărātrum, *n*; **(— share)**, vōmer, *m*
plough, *v.t*, ăro (1)
ploughman, ărātor, *m*, bŭbulcus, *m*
pluck, *nn*, fortĭtūdo, *f*, ănĭmus, *m*
pluck, *v.t*, carpo (3); **(— up courage)**, ănĭmum rĕvŏco (1)
plug, *nn*, obtūrāmentum, *n*
plum, prūnum, *n*
plum-tree, prūnus, *f*
plumage, plūmae, *f*, *pl*
plume, penna, *f*
plumb-line, lĭnĕa, *f*
plump, pinguis
plumpness, nĭtor, *m*, pinguĭtūdo, *f*
plunder, *nn*, praeda, *f*; **(act of plundering)**, răpĭna, *f*, dīreptĭo, *f*
plunder, *v.t*, praedor (1 *dep*), dīrĭpĭo (3)
plunderer, praedātor, *m*
plunge, *v.i*, sē mergĕre (3 *reflex*); *v.t*, mergo (3)
plural, *adj*, plūrālis
plurality, multĭtūdo, *f*
ply, *v.t*, exercĕo (2)
poach, *v.t*, *use* răpĭo (3), **(to seize)**; **(cook)**, cŏquo (3)
poacher, fur, *c*, raptor *m*.
pocket, sĭnus, *m*

pocket, *v.t,* (money), āverto (3)
pocket-book, pŭgillāres, *m, pl*
pocket-money, pĕcŭlĭum, *n*
pod, sĭlĭqua, *f*
poem, pŏ̄ēma, *n,* carmen, *n*
poet, pŏ̄ēta, *m*
poetical, pŏ̄ētĭcus
poetry, pŏ̄ēsis, *f,* carmĭna, *n.pl*
poignant, ăcerbus
point, ăcūmen, *n*; (**of a sword**), mūcro, *m*; (**spear**), cuspis, *f*; (**place**), lŏcus, *m*; (**issue**), res, *f*; (**on the — of**), *use fut. participle of vb, e.g.* **on the point of coming;** ventūrus
point, *v.t* (**make pointed**), praeăcŭo (3); (**direct**), dīrĭgo (3)
point out *or* **at,** *v.t,* monstro (1)
pointed, praeăcūtus; (**witty**) salsus
pointer, index, *m, f*
pointless, insulsus
poison, vĕnēnum, *n,* vīrus, *n*
poison, *v.t,* vĕnēno nĕco (1) (**kill by poison**)
poisoning, *nn,* vĕnēfĭcĭum, *n*
poisonous, vĕnēnātus
poke, *v.t,* fŏdĭco (1)
polar, septentrĭōnālis
pole (**rod, staff**), contus, *m,* longŭrĭus, *m*; (**earth**), pŏlus, *m*
polemics, contrōversĭae, *f. pl*
police (**men**), vĭgĭles, *m, pl*
policy, rătĭo, *f*
polish, *nn,* (**brightness**), nĭtor, *m*
polish, *v.t,* pŏlĭo (4)
polished, pŏlītus
polite, cōmis, urbānus
politeness, cōmĭtas, *f,* urbānĭtas, *f*
politic, *adj,* prūdens
political, cīvĭlis, pūblĭcus
politician, qui reīpūblĭcae stŭdet (**who pursues state affairs**)
politics, rēs pūblĭca, *f*
poll (**vote**), suffrāgĭum, *n*
pollute, *v.t,* inquĭno (1)
pollution, collŭvĭo, *f*
polytheism, *use phr,* crēdĕre multos esse dĕos (**believe that there are many gods**)
pomade, căpillāre, *n*
pomegranate, mālum grānātum, *n*
pommel, *v.t,* verbĕro (1)
pomp, appărātus, *m*
pompous, magnĭfĭcus
pompousness, magnĭfĭcentĭa, *f*
pond, stagnum, *n*; (**fish —**), piscīna, *f*
ponder, *v.t,* rĕpŭto (1)
ponderous, grăvis
poniard, pŭgĭo, *m*
pontiff, pontĭfex, *m*
pontoon, pons, *m*
pony, mannus, *m*
pool, lăcūna, *f*
poop, puppis, *f*
poor, pauper, ĭnops; (**worthless**), vīlis; (**wretched**), mĭser
poorly, *adj,* (**sick, ill**), aeger
poorly, *adv,* tĕnŭĭter, mālĕ
pop, *v.i,* crĕpo (1)
pope, Pontĭfex Maxĭmus, *m*
poplar, pōpŭlus, *f*
poppy, păpāver, *n*
populace, vulgus, *n,* plebs, *f*
popular, grātĭōsus; (**of the people**), pŏpŭlāris
popularity, făvor, (*m*) pŏpŭli (**goodwill of the people**)
population, cīves, *c. pl*
populous, frĕquens
porch, vestĭbŭlum, *n*
porcupine, hystrix, *f*
pore, fŏrāmen, *n*
pore over, *v.i,* ănĭmum intendo (3) (**direct the mind**)
pork, porcīna, *f*
porker, porcus, *m*
porous, rārus
porpoise, porcŭlus mărīnus, *m*
porridge, puls, *f*
port, portus, *m*
portable, quod portāri pŏtest (**that can be carried**)
portal, porta, *f,* iānŭa, *f*
portcullis, cătăracta, *f*
portend, *v.t,* portendo (3)
portent, portentum, *n*
portentous, monstrŭōsus
porter (**doorkeeper**), iānĭtor, *m*; (**baggage carrier**), băiŭlus, *m*
portfolio, lĭbellus, *m*
portico, portĭcus, *f*
portion, pars, *f*
portion out, *v.t,* partĭor (4 *dep*)
portrait, ĭmāgo, *f*
portray, *v.t,* dĕpingo (3)
pose, *nn,* stătus, *m*
position, lŏcus, *m*; (**site**), sĭtus, *m*
positive, certus
possess, *v.t,* hăbĕo (2), possĭdĕo (2)
possession, possessĭo, *f*; (**to take — of**), pŏtĭor (4 *dep. with abl*); (**property**), *often use possessive pron. e.g.* mĕa (**my —s**), *or* bŏna *n.pl*
possessor, possessor, *m,* dŏmĭnus, *m*
possibility, *use phr. with* posse; (**to be possible**)
possible, *use vb,* posse (*irreg*) (**to be possible**); (**as . . . as possible**), *use* quam *with superlative, e.g.* **as large as possible,** quam maxĭmus; (**as soon as —**), quam prĭmum

post, cippus, *m*, pālus, *m*; (**military**), stātĭo, *f*, lŏcus, *m*; (**letter**), tăbellārĭi pūblĭci, *m. pl* (**state couriers**)
post, *v.t*, (**in position**), lŏco (1); (**letter**), tăbellārĭo do (1) (**give to a courier**)
posterior, *nn*, nātes, *f. pl*
posterity, postĕri, *m. pl*
postern, postĭcum, *n*
posthumous, *use phr*, post mortem (*with genit*) (**after the death of . . .**)
postman, tăbellārĭus, *m*
postpone, *v.t*, diffĕro (*irreg*)
postscript, verba subiecta, *n.pl*, (**words appended**)
posture, stātus, *m*
pot, olla, *f*
potent, pŏtens, effĭcax
potentate, tȳrannus, *m*
potion, pōtĭo, *f*
potsherd, testa, *f*
potter, fĭgŭlus, *m*
pottery (articles), fictĭlĭa, *n.pl*
pouch, saccŭlus, *m*
poultice, mălagma, *n*
poultry, āves cŏhortāles, *f. pl*
pounce upon, *v.t*, invŏlo (1)
pound, *nn*, (**weight**), lĭbra, *f*
pound, *v.t*, tundo (3), tĕro (3)
pour, *v.t*, fundo (3); *v.i*, fundor (3 *pass*)
pouring, *adj*, effūsus
pout, *v.i*, lăbellum extendo (3) (**stretch a lip**)
poverty, paupertas, *f*, ĕgestas, *f*, ĭnŏpĭa, *f*; (— **stricken**), *adj*, ĭnops
powder, *nn*, pulvis, *m*
power, vīres, *f. pl*; (**dominion**), pŏtestas, *f*; (**authority**), ius, *n*, impĕrĭum, *n*; (**unconstitutional —**), pŏtentĭa, *f*
powerful, pŏtens; (**of body**), vălĭdus
powerless, invălĭdus; (**to be —**), *v.i*, mĭnĭmum posse (*irreg*)
practicable, *use phr*, quod fĭĕri pŏtest (**that can be done**)
practical (person), făbrĭcae pĕrĭtus (**skilled in practical work**)
practically (almost), *adv.*, paene
practice, ūsus, *m*; (**custom**), mos, *m*, consŭētūdo, *f*
practise, *v.t*, exercĕo (2), factĭto (1)
practitioner (medical), mĕdĭcus, *m*
praetor, praetor, *m*
praetorship, praetūra, *f*
praise, *nn*, laus, *f*
praise, *v.t*, laudo (1)
praiseworthy, laudābĭlis
prance, *v.i*, exsulto (1)
prank, *use* lūdĭfĭcor (1 *dep*) (**to make fun of**)
prattle, *v.i*, garrĭo (4)
pray, *v.i. and v.t*, ōro (1), prĕcor (1 *dep*)
prayer, prĕces, *f. pl*
preach, *v.t*, contĭōnor (1 *dep*)
preamble, exordĭum, *n*
precarious, incertus
precaution (to take —s (against)), *v.i. and v.t*, praecăvĕo (2)
precede, *v.t*, antĕcĕdo (3), antĕĕo (4)
precedence (to give —), *use vb*, cĕdo (3); (**to take —**), prĭor esse (*irreg*)
precedent, exemplum, *n*
preceding, *adj*, prĭor, proxĭmus
precept, praeceptum, *n*
precious (of great price), magni prĕtĭi; (**dear**), dilectus
precipice, lŏcus praeceps, *m*
precipitate, *adj*, praeceps
precipitate, *v.t*, praecĭpĭto (1)
precipitous, praeceps
precise, subtĭlis
precision, subtĭlĭtas, *f*
preclude, *v.t*, prŏhĭbĕo (2)
precocious, praecox
preconceived, praeiūdĭcātus
precursor, praenuntĭus, *m*
predatory, praedātōrĭus
predecessor (my —), *use phr*, qui ante me . . . (**who before me . . .**)
predicament, angustĭae, *f. pl*
predict, *v.t*, praedĭco (3)
prediction, praedictĭo, *f*
predilection, stŭdĭum, *n*
predisposed, inclīnātus
predominant, pŏtens
predominate, *v.i*, *use phr*, qui in pŏtentĭā sunt (**who are in authority**)
preeminent, praestans
preface, praefātĭo, *f*
preface, *v.t*, praefor (1 *dep*)
prefer, *v.t*, *with infinitive*, mālo (*irreg*); (**put one thing before another**), antĕpōno (3); (— **a charge**), dĕfĕro (*irreg*)
preferable, pŏtĭor
preference, (**desire**), vŏluntas, *f*; (**in —**), *adv*, pŏtĭus
preferment, hŏnor, *m*
pregnant, praegnans, grăvĭda
prejudge, *v.t*, praeiūdĭco (1)
prejudice, praeiūdĭcāta ŏpĭnĭo, *f*
prejudice, *v.t*, (**impair**), immĭnŭo (3)
prejudicial, noxĭus; (**to be — to**), obsum (*irreg*) (*with dat*)
prelate, săcerdos, *c*
preliminary, *use compound word with* prae, *e.g.* **to make a — announcement**, praenuntĭo (1)

prelude, prŏoemĭum, *n*
premature, immātūrus
premeditate, *v.t,* praemĕdĭtor (1 *dep*)
premeditation, praemĕdĭtātĭo, *f*
premier, princeps, *m*
premise, prōpŏsĭtĭo, *f*
premises (buildings), aedĭfĭcĭa, *n.pl*
premium, praemĭum, *n*
premonition, mŏnĭtĭo, *f*
preoccupy (to be — with), stŭdĕo (2) (*with dat*)
preparation, compārātĭo, *f,* appārātus, *m*; **(to make —s),** compāro (1)
prepare, *v.t,* pāro (1), compāro (1)
prepossess, *v.t,* commendo (1)
prepossessing, *adj,* suāvis, blandus
preposterous, praepostĕrus
prerogative, iūs, *n*
presage, praesāgĭum, *n*
presage, *v.t,* portendo (3)
prescribe, *v.t,* praescrĭbo (3)
presence, praesentĭa, *f*; **(in the — of),** *prep,* cōram (*with abl*)
present, *nn* **(gift),** dōnum, *n*; **(time),** praesentĭa, *n.pl*
present, *adj,* praesens; **(to be —),** *v.i,* adsum (*irreg*)
present, *v.t,* offĕro (*irreg*); **(give),** dōno (1) (*with acc. of person and abl. of gift*)
presentation, dōnātĭo, *f*
presentiment, augŭrĭum, *n*
presently, *adv,* **(soon),** mox
preservation, conservātĭo, *f*
preserve, *v.t,* servo (1)
preserver, servātor, *m*
preside, *v.i,* praesĭdĕo (*with dat*)
presidency, praefectūra, *f*
president, praefectus, *m*
press, *nn,* **(machine),** prēlum, *n*
press, *v.t,* prĕmo (3); **(urge),** urgĕo (2)
pressure, nĭsus, *m*
prestige, fāma, *f,* ŏpĭnĭo, *f*
presume, *v.t,* **(assume),** crēdo (3); **(dare),** *v.i,* audĕo (2)
presumption (conjecture), coniectūra, *f*; **(conceitedness),** arrŏgantĭa, *f*
presumptuous, arrŏgans
pretence, sĭmŭlātĭo, *f*; **(under — of),** per sĭmŭlātĭōnem
pretend, *v.t,* sĭmŭlo (1)
pretended, *adj,* sĭmŭlātus
pretender (claimant), *use vb,* pĕto (3) **(aspire to)**
pretension postŭlātĭo, *f*
pretext, spĕcĭes, *f*; **(on the — of),** use *vb.* sĭmŭlo (1) **(to pretend)**
prettily, *adv,* bellē, vĕnustē
prettiness, concinnĭtas, *f,* vĕnustas, *f*
pretty, *adj,* pulcher
pretty, *adv,* sătis **(enough)**
prevail, *v.i,* obtĭnĕo (2), sŭpĕrĭor esse (*irreg*); **(to — upon),** *v.t,* persuādĕo (2) (*with dat*)
prevalent, vulgātus
prevaricate, *v.t,* tergĭversor (1 *dep*)
prevent, *v.t,* prŏhĭbĕo (2)
prevention, *use vb,* prŏhĭbĕo **(prevent)**
previous, prŏxĭmus
previously, *adv,* antĕā
prey, *nn,* praeda, *f*
prey, *v.t,* praedor (1 *dep*)
price, *nn,* prĕtĭum, *n*; **(— of corn),** annōna, *f*
price, *v.t,* prĕtĭum constĭtŭo (3) **(fix the price)**
priceless, inaestĭmābĭlis
prick, *nn,* punctum, *n*
prick, *v.t,* pungo (3); **(spur),** stĭmŭlo (1)
prickly, *adj,* ăcŭlĕātus
pride, sŭperbĭa, *f*; **(honourable —),** spīrĭtus, *m*
priest, săcerdos, *c*
priesthood, săcerdōtĭum, *n*
prim, mōrōsĭor
primarily, *adv,* princĭpĭō
primary, prīmus
prime, *nn,* **(of life, etc.),** *use vb,* flōrĕo (2) **(flourish); (best part),** flōs, *m*
prime, *adj,* ēgrĕgĭus
primeval, prīmĭgĕnĭus
primitive, prīmĭgĕnĭus
prince (king), rēgŭlus, *m*; **(king's son),** filĭus, (*m*) rēgis
princess (king's daughter), fĭlĭa, (*f*) rēgis
principal, *adj,* princĭpālis, praecĭpŭus
principal, *nn,* măgister, *m*
principality, regnum, *n*
principle, princĭpĭum, *n*; **(element),** ĕlĕmentum, *n,* prīmordĭa, *n.pl*; **(rule, maxim),** praeceptum, *n*
print, *nn,* **(mark),** nŏta, *f*
print, *v.t,* imprĭmo (3)
prior, *adj,* prĭor
priority, *use adj,* prĭor
prism, prisma, *n*
prison, carcer, *m*
prisoner, captĭvus, *m*
privacy, sōlĭtūdo, *f*
private, prīvātus, sēcrētus
private soldier, mīles grĕgārĭus, *m*
privately, *adv,* prīvātim, clam
privation, ĭnŏpĭa, *f*
privet, lĭgustrum, *n*
privilege, iūs, *n*
privy, *adj,* **(acquainted with),** conscĭus; **(secret),** prīvātus

For List of Abbreviations used, turn to pages 3, 4

privy, *nn,* fŏrĭca, *f*
privy-council, consĭlĭum, *n*
privy-purse, fiscus, *m*
prize, praemĭum, *n*; **(booty),** praeda, *f*
prize, *v.t,* **(value),** magni aestĭmo (1)
probability, sĭmĭlĭtūdo, (*f*) vēri
probable, sĭmĭlis vēri
probation, prŏbātĭo, *f*
probe, *v.t,* tento (1)
problem, quaestĭo, *f*
problematical (doubtful), dŭbĭus
procedure, rătĭo, *f*
proceed, *v.i,* **(move on),** pergo (3); **(originate)** prŏfĭciscor (3 *dep*); **(take legal action against)** lĭtem intendo (3) (*with dat*)
proceedings (legal), actĭo, *f*; **(doings),** acta, *n.pl*
proceeds, fructus, *m*
process, rătĭo, *f*; **(in the — of time),** *adv, use phr,* tempŏre praetĕrĕunte **(with time going by)**
procession, pompa, *f*
proclaim, *v.t,* praedĭco (1), prōnuntĭo (1)
proclamation, prōnuntĭātĭo, *f,* ēdictum, *n*
proconsul, prōconsul, *m*
procrastinate, *v.t,* diffĕro (*irreg*)
procrastination, tardĭtas, *f,* mŏra, *f*
procreate, *v.t,* prōcrĕo (1)
procreation, prōcrĕātĭo, *f,* partus, *m*
procure, *v.t,* compăro (1)
procurer, lēno, *m*
prodigal, *adj,* prōdĭgus
prodigality, effūsĭo, *f*
prodigious, immānis
prodigy, prōdĭgĭum, *n*
produce, *nn,* fructus, *m*
produce, *v.t.* **(into view)** prōfĕro (*irreg*); **(create),** părĭo (3); **(— an effect),** mŏvĕo (2)
product, production, ŏpus, *n*
productive, fĕrax
profanation, vĭŏlātĭo, *f*
profane, impĭus, prŏfānus
profane, *v.t,* vĭŏlo (1)
profanity, impĭĕtas, *f*
profess, *v.t,* prŏfĭtĕor (2 *dep*)
profession (occupation), mūnus, *n,* officĭum, *n*; **(avowal),** prŏfessĭo, *f*
professor, prŏfessor, *m*
proffer, *v.t,* pollĭcĕor (2 *dep*)
proficient (skilled), pĕrĭtus
profile, oblĭqua făcĭes, *f*
profit, *nn,* ēmŏlŭmentum, *n,* lŭcrum, *n,* quaestus, *m*
profit, *v.t,* **(benefit),** prōsum (*irreg. with dat*)
profitable, fructŭōsus
profitless, ĭnūtĭlis
profligacy, nēquĭtĭa, *f*
profligate, perdĭtus
profound, altus
profuse, effūsus
profusion, effūsĭo, *f*
progeny, prōgĕnĭes, *f*
prognostic, signum, *n*
programme, lĭbellus, *m*
progress (improvement, etc.), prōgressus, *m*; **(to make —),** prōfĭcĭo (3), prōgrĕdĭor (3 *dep*)
progress, *v.i,* prōgrĕdĭor (3 *dep*)
prohibit, *v.t,* vĕto (1)
prohibition, interdictum, *n*
project, *nn,* **(plan),** consĭlĭum, *n*
project, *v.t,* prōĭcĭo (3); *v.i,* ēmĭnĕo (2)
projectile, tēlum *n,*
projecting, ēmĭnens
proleteriat, vulgus, *n*
prolific, fĕcundus
prolix, verbōsus
prologue, prŏlŏgus, *m*
prolong, *v.t,* prōdūco (3); **(— a command),** prōrŏgo (1)
prolongation, prōpāgātĭo, *f*
promenade, ambŭlātĭo, *f*
prominence, ēmĭnentĭa, *f*
prominent, ēmĭnens; **(person),** praeclārus
promiscuous, prōmiscŭus
promise, *nn,* prōmissum, *n,* fĭdes, *f*
promise, *v.i,* prōmitto (3), pollĭcĕor (2 *dep*)
promising, *adj, use adv. phr,* bŏnā spe **(of good hope)**
promissory note, chĭrŏgrăphum, *n*
promontory, prōmontōrĭum, *n*
promote, *v.t,* prōmŏvĕo (2); **(favour, assist),** iŭvo (1), prōsum (*irreg*) (*with dat*)
promoter, auctor, *m*
promotion (act of —), *use vb.* prōmŏvĕo (2); **(honour),** hŏnor, *m*
prompt, *adj,* promptus
prompt, *v.t,* **(assist in speaking),** sŭbĭcĭo (3) (*with dat. of person*); **(incite),** incĭto (1)
promptitude, promptness, cĕlĕrĭtas, *f*
promulgate, *v.t,* prōmulgo (1)
prone, prōnus; **(inclined to),** prōpensus
prong, dens, *m*
pronoun, prōnōmen, *n*
pronounce, *v.t,* prōnuntĭo (1)

pronunciation, appellātĭo, *f*
proof, argūmentum, *n*, dŏcūmentum *n*, prŏbātĭo, *f*
prop, *nn*, admĭnĭcŭlum, *n*
prop, *v.t*, fulcĭo (4)
propagate, *v.t*, prōpāgo (1)
propel, *v.t*, prōpello (3)
propensity, ănĭmus inclīnātus, *m*
proper, dĕcōrus, vērus, aptus
properly, *adv*, (**correctly**), rectē
property (possessions), bŏna, *n.pl*, rēs, *f*; (**characteristic quality**), prŏprĭētas, *f*
prophecy, praedictĭo, *f*, praedictum, *n*
prophesy, *v.t*, praedīco (3), vātĭcĭnor (1 *dep*)
prophet, vātes, *c*
prophetic, dīvīnus
propitiate, *v.t*, plāco (1)
propitious, prŏpĭtĭus, praesens
proportion, portĭo, *f*; (**in —**), prō portĭōne
proportional, *use adv. phr*, prō portĭōne
proposal, condĭcĭo, *f*
propose, *v.t*, fĕro (*irreg*), rŏgo (1)
proposer, lātor, *m*
proposition, condĭcĭo, *f*
proprietor, dŏmĭnus, *m*
propriety (**decorum**), dĕcōrum, *n*
prorogation, prōrŏgātĭo, *f*
prosaic (**flat**), ĭēiūnus
proscribe, *v.t*, prōscrĭbo (3)
proscription, prōscriptĭo, *f*
prose, ōrātĭo sōlūta, *f*
prosecute, *v.t*, (**carry through**), exsĕquor (3 *dep*); (**take legal proceedings**), lĭtem intendo (3)
prosecution, exsĕcūtĭo, *f*; (**legal**), accūsātĭo, *f*
prosecutor, accūsātor, *m*
prospect (**anticipation**), spes fūtūra, *f*; (**view**), prospectus, *m*
prospective, fūtūrus
prosper, *v.i*, flŏrĕo (2)
prosperity, res sĕcundae, *f. pl*
prosperous, sĕcundus
prostitute, *nn*, mĕrĕtrix, *f*
prostitute, *v.t*, vulgo (1)
prostitution, mĕrĕtrĭcĭus quaestus, *m*
prostrate (**in spirit, etc.**), fractus; (**lying on the back**), sūpīnus; (**lying on the face**), prōnus
prostrate, *v.t*, sterno (3), dĕĭcĭo (3)
protect, *v.t*, tĕgo (3), tŭĕor (2 *dep*), dēfendo (3)
protection, tūtēla, *f*, praesĭdĭum, *n*
protector, dēfensor, *m*
protest against, *v.t*, intercēdo (3)
prototype, exemplar, *n*
protract, *v.t*, dūco (3)
protrude, *v.t*, prōtrūdo (3); *v.i*, ēmĭnĕo (2)
protuberance, tūber, *n*
proud, sūperbus
prove, *v.t*, prŏbo (1); (**to — oneself**) sē praestāre (1 *reflex*); (**test**), pĕrĭclĭtor (1 *dep*); *v.i*, (**turn out—of things**), fĭo (*irreg*), ĕvĕnĭo (4)
proverb, prōverbĭum, *n*
proverbial, *use nn*, prōverbĭum, *n*, (**proverb**)
provide, *v.t*, (**supply**), păro (1), praebĕo (2); *v.i*, (**make provision for**), prōvĭdĕo (2); (**— against**), căvĕo (2) ne (*with vb. in subjunctive*)
provided that, *conj*, dum, dummŏdo
providence, prōvĭdentĭa, *f*
provident, prōvĭdus
province, prōvĭncĭa, *f*
provincial, prōvĭncĭālis
provision (**to make —**), prōvĭdĕo (2)
provisional, *use adv. phr*, ad tempus (**for the time being**)
provisions, cĭbus, *m*
provocation, use, *vb*, irrĭto (1) (**to provoke**)
provoke, *v.t*, irrĭto (1); (**stir up**), incĭto (1)
prow, prōra, *f*
prowess, virtus, *f*
prowl, *v.i*, văgor (1 *dep*)
proximity, prŏpĭnquĭtas, *f*
proxy, prōcūrātor, *m*
prudence, prūdentĭa, *f*
prudent, prūdens
prune, *nn*, prūnum, *n*, (**plum**)
prune, *v.t*, ampŭto (1)
prurient, lĭbĭdĭnōsus
pry, *v.t*, rīmor (1 *dep*)
psalm, carmen, *n*
psychological, *use genit. of* mens, (**mind**)
puberty, pūbertas, *f*
public, *adj*, pūblĭcus; (**of the state**), *use nn*, respublĭca, *f*, (**state**), *or* pŏpŭlus, *m*, (**people**)
public, *nn*, hŏmĭnes, *c. pl*
publican (**innkeeper**), caupo, *m*
publication, *use* ēdo (3), (**publish**)
publicity, cĕlĕbrĭtas, *f*
publicly, *adv*, pălam
publish, *v.t*, effĕro (*irreg*), prōfĕro (*irreg*); (**book**), ēdo (3)
pucker, *v.t*, corrūgo (1)
puddle, lăcūna, *f*
puerile (**silly**), ĭneptus

puff, *v.i*, (**pant**), ănhēlo (1); *v.t*, (**inflate**), inflo (1); (**puffed up**), inflātus
pugilist, pūgil, *m*
pull, *v.t*, trăho (3); (— **down, demolish**), dēstrŭo (3)
pulley, trochlĕa, *f*
pulp, căro, *f*
pulpit, suggestus, *m*
pulsate, *v.i*, palpĭto (1)
pulse, vēnae, *f. pl.* (**veins**)
pulverize, *v.t*, in pulvĕrem contĕro (3) (**pound into dust**)
pumice, pūmex, *m*
pump, *nn*, antlĭa, *f*
pump, *v.t*, haurĭo (4)
pumpkin, pĕpo, *m*
pun, făcētĭae, *f. pl*
punch, ictus, *m*, pugnus, *m*
punch, *v.t*, percŭtĭo (3)
punctilious, mōrōsus
punctual, punctuality, *use adv. phr*, ad tempus (**at the right time**)
punctuate, *v.t*, distinguo (3)
punctuation, interpunctĭo, *f*
puncture, *nn*, punctum, *n*
puncture, *v.t*, pungo (3)
pungency, morsus, *m*, ăcerbĭtas, *f*
pungent, ăcer
punish, *v.t*, pūnĭo (4), ănĭmadverto (3) in (*with acc*), poenas sūmo (3); (**to be —ed**), poenas do (1)
punishment, poena, *f*, supplĭcĭum, *n*; (**to undergo —**), poenam sŭbĕo (4)
punitive; *use vb*, pūnĭo (**punish**)
puny, pūsillus
pup, puppy, cătŭlus, *m*
pupil (**scholar**), discĭpŭlus, *m*; (**of the eye**), pūpilla, *f*
puppet, pūpa, *f*
purchase, *nn*, emptĭo, *f*
purchase, *v.t*, ĕmo (3)
pure, pūrus, mĕrus; (**morally**), intĕger
purgative, *use phr. with* mĕdĭcāmentum, *n*, (**medicine**)
purge, *nn*, *use vb*, purgo (1)
purge, *v.t*, purgo (1)
purification, purgātĭo, *f*
purify, *v.t*, purgo (1), lustro (1)
purity, castĭtas, *f*, intĕgrĭtas, *f*
purloin, *v.t*, surrĭpĭo (3)
purple, *nn*, purpŭra, *f*
purple, *adj*, purpŭrĕus
purport, *nn*, (**meaning**), signĭfĭcātĭo, *f*
purport, *v.t*, (**mean**), signĭfĭco (1)
purpose, *nn*, prōpŏsĭtum, *n*, consĭlĭum, *n*; (**for the — of doing something**), ĕo consĭlĭo ut (*with vb in subjunctive*); (**on —**), *adv*, consulto; (**to no —, in vain**), *adv*, frustrā; (**for what —?**), quārē
purpose, *v.t*, (**intend**), in ănĭmo hăbĕo (2)
purr, *v.i*, murmŭro (1)
purse, saccŭlus, *m*
in pursuance of, ex (*with abl*)
pursue, *v.t*, sĕquor (3 *dep*)
pursuit (**chase**), *use vb*, sĕquor (**to pursue**); (**desire for**), stŭdĭum, *n*
purvey, *v.t*, obsōno (1)
purveyor, obsōnātor, *m*
pus, pūs, *n*
push, pushing, *nn*, impulsus, *m*, impĕtus, *m*
push, *v.t*, pello (3), trūdo (3); (— **back**), rĕpello (3); (— **forward**), prōmŏvĕo (2)
pushing, *adj*, mŏlestus
pusillanimity, ănĭmus hŭmĭlis, *m*
pusillanimous, hŭmĭlis
pustule, pustŭla, *f*
put, *v.t*, (**place**), pōno (3), do (1), impōno (3); (— **aside**), sēpōno (3); (— **away**), abdo (3), condo (3); (— **back**), rĕpōno (3); (— **down**), dēpōno (3); (**suppress**), exstinguo (3); (— **forward**), praepōno (3), prōfĕro (*irreg*); (— **in**), immitto (3); (— **into land, port, etc.**), *v.i*, portum căpĭo (3); (— **off**), *v.t*, pōno (3); (**delay**), differo (*irreg*); (— **on**), impōno (3); (—**clothes**), indŭo (3); (— **out**), ēĭcĭo (3); (**quench**), exstinguo (3); (— **to, drive to**), impello (3); (— **together**), collĭgo (3), confĕro (*irreg*); (— **under**), sŭbĭcĭo (3); (— **up, erect**), stătŭo (3); (**offer**), prōpōno (3); (**put up with, bear**), fĕro (*irreg*); (— **upon**), impōno (3); (— **to flight**) fŭgo (1)
putrefy, *v.i*, pūtesco (3)
putrid, pŭtrĭdus
putty, glūten, *m or n*
puzzle, *nn*, (**riddle**), nōdus, *m*; (**difficulty**), difficultas, *f*, angustĭae, *f*, *pl*
puzzling, *adj*, perplexus; (**in a — way**), *adv. phr*, per ambāges
pygmy, nānus, *m*
pyramid, pȳrămis, *f*
pyre, rŏgus, *m*
Pyrenees, Montes Pȳrēnaei, *m. pl*
python, pȳthon, *m*

Q

quack, *nn*, (**medicine**), pharmăcŏpōla, *m*
quadrangle, ārĕa, *f*
quadrant, quădrans, *m*
quadrilateral, quădrĭlătĕrus

quadruped, quădrŭpes
quadruple, *adj,* quădruplex
quaff, *v.t,* haurĭo (4)
quagmire, pălus, *f*
quail, *nn,* cŏturnix, *f*
quail, *v.i,* trĕpĭdo (1)
quaint, nŏvus
quake, *nn,* trĕmor, *m*
quake, *v.i,* trĕmo (3)
qualification, iūs, *n*; **(condition),** condĭcĭo, *f*
qualified (suitable), aptus, ĭdōnĕus
qualify, *v.t,* **(fit someone for something),** aptum reddo (3); **(restrict),** circumscrĭbo (3), mītĭgo (1)
quality, nātūra, *f*
qualm (doubt), dŭbĭtātĭo, *f*
quantity, nŭmĕrus, *m,* magnĭtūdo, *f*; **(a certain —),** ălĭquantum, *n* (*nn*); **(a large —)** cōpĭa, *f,* multum, *n*; **(what —?),** *use adj,* quantus **(how great)**
quarrel, iurgĭum, *n,* rixa, *f*
quarrel, *v.i,* iurgo (1), rixor (1 *dep*)
quarrelsome, lĭtĭgĭōsus
quarry (stone), lăpĭcĭdĭnae, *f. pl*; **(prey),** praeda, *f*
quarry, *v.t,* caedo (3)
quart (measure), dŭo sextārĭi, *m. pl*
quarter, quarta pars, *f,* quădrans, *m*; **(district),** rĕgĭo, *f*; **(surrender),** dēdĭtĭo, *f*
quarter, *v.t,* quădrĭfārĭam dīvĭdo (3), **(divide into four parts)**
quarter-deck, puppis, *f*
quartermaster, quaestor mĭlĭtāris, *m*
quarterly, *adj,* trĭmestris
quarters (lodging), hospĭtĭum, *n*; **(at close —),** *adv,* comminus; **(to come to close —),** signa confĕro (*irreg*)
quash, *v.t,* opprĭmo (3); **(sentence, verdict),** rēscindo (3)
quaver, *v.i,* trĕpĭdo (1)
quay, crĕpĭdo, *f*
queen, rēgĭna, *f*
queer, rīdĭcŭlus
queerness, insŏlentĭa, *f*
quell, *v.t,* opprĭmo (3)
quench, *v.t,* exstinguo (3)
quenchless, ĭnexstinctus
querulous, quĕrŭlus
query, quaestĭo, *f*
query, *v.t,* quaero (3)
quest, inquĭsĭtĭo, *f*
question, *nn,* rŏgātĭo, *f,* interrŏgātum, *n,* quaestĭo, *f*; *or use vb,* rŏgo (1) **(to ask —s); (doubt),** dŭbĭum, *n*
question, *v.t,* rŏgo (1), quaero (3); **(doubt),** dŭbĭto (1)
questionable, incertus
questioner, interrŏgātor, *m*
quibble, *nn,* captĭo, *f*
quibble, *v.i,* căvillor (1 *dep*)
quick, *adj,* cĕler; **(sprightly),** ăgĭlis; **(— witted),** săgax
quickly, *adv,* cĕlĕrĭter, cĭto
quicken, *v.t,* accĕlĕro (1), stĭmŭlo (1); *v.i,* **(move quicker),** sē incĭtāre (1 *reflex*)
quickness, vēlōcĭtas, *f*; **(— of wit),** săgācĭtas, *f*
quicksilver, argentum vīvum, *n*
quick-tempered, īrācundus
quiescent, quĭescens
quiet, *nn,* quĭes, *f*
quiet, *adj,* quĭētus, tranquillus
quiet, quieten, *v.t,* sēdo (1)
quietly, *adv,* quĭētē, tranquillē
quill, penna, *f*; **(for writing),** *use* stĭlus, *m,* **(pen)**
quilt, *nn,* strāgŭlum, *n*
quinquennial, quinquennālis
quinsy, angĭna, *f*
quintessence, vīs, *f,* flōs, *m*
quip, *nn,* rēsponsum (salsum) **((witty) reply)**
quirk, căvillātĭo, *f*
quit, *v.t,* rĕlinquo (3)
quite, *adv,* admŏdum, prorsus; **(— enough),** sātis
quiver, *nn,* phărĕtra, *f*
quiver, *v.i,* trĕmo (3)
quoit, discus, *m*
quota, rāta pars, *f*
quotation, prōlātĭo, *f*
quote, *v.t,* prōfĕro (*irreg*)
quotidian, cottĭdĭānus

R

rabbit, cŭnĭcŭlus, *m*
rabble, turba, *f*
rabid, răbĭdus
race (family), gĕnus, *n,* prōgĕnĭes, *f*; **(running),** cursus, *m,* certāmen, *n*
race, *v.i,* cursu certo (1) **(contend by running)**
race-course, stădĭum, *n,* currĭcŭlum, *n*
race-horse, ĕquus cursor, *m*
rack (for torture), ĕquŭlĕus, *m*
rack, *v.t,* **(torture),** torquĕo (2)
racket (bat), rētĭcŭlum, *n*; **(noise),** strĕpĭtus, *m*
racy (smart), salsus
radiance, fulgor, *m*
radiant, clārus, fulgens
radiate, *v.i,* fulgĕo (2)
radiation, rădĭātĭo, *f*

For List of Abbreviations used, turn to pages 3, 4

radical (fundamental), tōtus; **(original)**, innātus; **(keen on change)**, cŭpĭdus rērum nŏvārum
radically, *adv*, pēnĭtus, fundĭtus
radish, rādix
radius, rădĭus, *m*
raffle, ālĕa, *f*
raft, rătis, *f*
rafter, cantērĭus, *m*
rag, pannus, *m*
rage, fŭror, *m*
rage, *v.i*, fŭro (3)
ragged, pannōsus
raging, *adj*, fŭrens
raid, incursĭo, *f*; **(to make a —)**, invādo (3) in (*with acc.*)
rail, longŭrĭus, *m*
rail at (abuse), mălĕdĭco (3) (*with dat.*)
railing, cancelli, *m. pl*
raillery, căvillātĭo, *f*
raiment, vestĭmenta, *n.pl*
rain, *nn*, plŭvĭa, *f*, imber, *m*
rain, *v.i*, **(it rains)**, plŭit (3 *impers.*)
rainbow, arcus, *m*
rainy, plŭvĭus
raise, *v.t*, **(lift)**, tollo (3); **(forces)**, compăro (1); **(rouse)**, ērĭgo (3); **(—a seige)**, obsĭdĭōnem solvo (3)
raisin, ăcĭnus passus, *m*, **(dried berry)**
rake, *nn*, **(tool)**, rastellus, *m*; **(person)**, nĕpos, *c*
rake, *v.t*, rādo (3)
rally, *v.t*, **(troops)**, mīlĭtes in ordĭnes rĕvŏco (1), **(call back the soldiers to their ranks)**; *v.i*, se collĭgĕre (3 *reflex.*)
ram (or battering —), ărĭes *m*; **(beak of a ship)**, rostrum, *n*
ram, *v.t*, fistūco (1); **(ship)** rostro laedo (3)
ramble, *v.i*, erro (1)
rambler, erro, *m*
rammer, fistūca, *f*
rampart, agger, *m*, vallum, *n*
rancid, rancĭdus
rancorous, infestus
rancour, ŏdĭum, *n*
random, *adj*, fortŭĭtus; **(at —)**, *adv*, fortŭĭto
range, ordo, *m*; **(— of mountains)**, iŭga, *n.pl*; **(of a missile)**, iactus, *m*; **(scope)**, campus, *m*
rank, *nn*, ordo, *m*
rank, *v.i*, sē hăbĕre (2 *reflex.*)
rank, *adj*, **(smell, etc.)**, fētĭdus
rankle, *v.t*, exulcĕro (1), mordĕo (2)
ransack, *v.t*, dīrĭpĭo (3)
ransom, *nn*, rĕdemptĭo, *f*; **(— money)**, prĕtĭum, *n*
ransom, *v.t*, rĕdĭmo (3)
rant, *v.t*, dēclāmo (1)
ranting, *nn*, sermo tŭmĭdus, *m*, **(bombastic speech)**
rap, *nn*, pulsātĭo, *f*
rap, *v.t*, pulso (1)
rapacious, răpax
rapacity, răpācĭtas, *f*
rape, *nn*, raptus, *m*
rapid, răpĭdus, cĕler
rapidity, cĕlĕrĭtas, *f*
rapier, glădĭus, *m*
rapine, răpīna, *f*
rapture, laetĭtĭa, *f*
rapturous, laetus
rare, rārus
rarefy, *v.t*, extĕnŭo (1)
rareness, rarity, rārĭtas, *f*
rascal, scĕlestus, *m*
rascality, scĕlĕra, *n.pl*
rase (to the ground), *v.t*, sŏlo aequo (1)
rash, *adj*, tĕmĕrārĭus
rash, *nn*, ēruptĭo, *f*
rashness, tĕmĕrĭtas, *f*
rasp, *nn*, **(file)**, scŏbĭna, *f*
rasp, *v.t*, rādo (3)
rat, mūs, *c*
rate (price), prĕtĭum, *n*; **(tax)**, vectīgal, *n*; **(speed)**, cĕlĕrĭtas, *f*; **(at any —)**, *adv*, ūtĭque
rate, *v.t*, **(value)**, aestĭmo (1); **(chide)**, increpo (1); **(tax)**, censĕo (2)
rather, *adv*, **(preferably)**, pŏtĭus; **(somewhat)**, ălĭquantum; **(a little)**, *with comparatives, e.g.* **rather (more quickly)**, paulo (cĕlĕrĭus)
ratification, sanctĭo, *f*
ratify, *v.t*, rātum făcĭo (3)
ratio, portĭo, *f*
ration, *nn*, dēmensum, *n*, cĭbārĭa, *n.pl*
rational (a — being), partĭceps rātĭonis **(participant in reason)**
rationally, *adv*, rātĭōne
rattle, *nn*, crĕpĭtus, *m*; **(toy)**, crĕpĭtăcŭlum, *n*
rattle, *v.i*, crĕpo (1)
ravage, *v.t*, pŏpŭlor (1 *dep.*)
ravaging, *nn*, pŏpŭlātĭo, *f*
rave, *v.i*, fŭro (3)
raven, corvus, *m*
ravening, ravenous, răpax
ravine, fauces, *f.pl*
raving, *adj*, fŭrens, insānus
raving, *nn*, fŭror, *m*
ravish, *v.t*, răpĭo (3), stŭpro (1)
ravishing, suāvis

raw, crūdus; **(inexperienced, unworked),** rŭdis
ray, rădĭus, *m*
razor, nŏvăcŭla, *f*
reach, *nn*, **(range),** iactus, *m*; **(space),** spătĭum, *n*
reach, *v.i*, **(extend),** pertĭnĕo (2), attingo (3); *v.t*, **(come to),** pervĕnĭo (4) ad (*with acc.*)
react, *v.t*, **(be influenced),** affĭcĭor (3 *pass.*)
reaction (of feeling), *use vb*, commŏvĕo (2) **(to make an impression on)**
read, *v.t*, lĕgo (3); **(— aloud),** rĕcĭto (1)
readable, făcĭlis lectu
reader, lector, *m*
readily, *adv*, **(willingly),** lĭbenter
readiness (preparedness), *use adj*, părātus **(ready); (willingness),** ănĭmus lĭbens, *m*
reading, *nn*, lectĭo, *f*, rĕcĭtātĭo, *f*
reading-room, bibliŏthēca, *f*
ready, părātus, promptus; **(to be —),** pārātus, praesto esse (*irreg.*); **(to make, get —),** păro (1)
real, *adj*, vērus
realism, vērĭtas, *f*
reality, rēs, *f*
realization (getting to know), cognĭtĭo, *f*; **(completion),** confectĭo, *f*
realise, *v.t*, intellĕgo (3); **(a project),** perfĭcĭo 3), perdūco (3)
really, *adv*, rēvērā; **(is it so?),** ĭtăne est?
realm, regnum, *n*
reap, *v.t*, mĕto (3); **(gain),** compăro (1)
reaper, messor, *m*
reaping-hook, falx, *f*
reappear, *v.i*, rĕdĕo (irreg.)
rear, *nn*, **(of a marching column),** agmen nŏvissĭmum, *n*; **(of an army),** ăcĭes nŏvissĭma, *f*; **(in the —),** *adv*, ā tergo
rear, *v.t*, **(bring up),** ēdŭco (1), ălo (3); *v.i*, **(of horses),** sē ērĭgĕre (3 *reflex.*)
reason (faculty of thinking), mens, *f*; **(cause),** causa, *f*; **(for this —),** *adv*, ĭdĕo, idcirco; **(for what —, why?),** cur, quārē; **(without —, heedlessly),** *adv*, tĕmĕrē
reason, *v.t*, rātĭōcĭnor (1 *dep.*); **(— with),** dissĕro (3), cum (*with abl.*)
reasonable (fair), aequus, iustus; **(in size),** mŏdĭcus
reasonableness (fairness), aequĭtas, *f*
reasoning, *nn*, rātĭo, *f*
reassemble, *v.t*, cōgo (3), in ūnum lŏcum collĭgo (3), **(collect into one place);** *v.i*, rĕdĕo (4)
reassert, *v.t*, rēstĭtŭo (3)
reassure, *v.t*, confirmo (1)
rebel, *nn*, sēdĭtĭōsus, *m*
rebel, *v.i*, rĕbello (1), dēfĭcĭo (3)
rebellion, sēdĭtĭo, *f*
rebellious, sēdĭtĭōsus
rebound, *v.i*, rĕsĭlĭo (4)
rebuff, *v.t*, rĕpello (3)
rebuff, *nn*, rĕpulsa, *f*
rebuke, *nn*, rĕprĕhensĭo, *f*
rebuke, *v.t*, rĕprĕhendo (3)
recall, *nn*, rĕvŏcātĭo, *f*
recall, *v.t*, rĕvŏco (1); **(— to mind),** rĕpĕto (3)
recapitulate, *v.t*, ēnŭmĕro (1)
recapitulation, ēnŭmĕrātĭo, *f*
recapture, *v.t*, rĕcĭpĭo (3)
recede, *v.i*, rĕcēdo (3)
receipt (act of receiving), acceptĭo, *f*; **(document),** ăpocha, *f*
receipts (proceeds), rĕdĭtus, *m*
receive, *v.t*, accĭpĭo (3), excĭpĭo (3)
receiver (of stolen goods), rĕceptor, *m*
recent, rĕcens
recently, *adv*, nūper
receptacle, rĕceptāculum, *n*
reception, ădĭtus, *m*
receptive, dŏcĭlis
recess, rĕcessus, *m*; **(holidays),** fĕrĭae, *f. pl*
reciprocal, mūtŭus
reciprocate, *v.t*, rĕfĕro (*irreg.*)
recital, narrātĭo, *f*
recite, *v.t*, rĕcĭto (1), prōnuntĭo (1)
reckless, tĕmĕrārĭus
recklessness, tĕmĕrĭtas, *f*
reckon, *v.t*, **(count),** nŭmĕro (1); **(— on, rely on),** confĭdo (3) (*with dat.*); **(consider),** dūco (3)
reckoning, rātĭo, *f*
reclaim, *v.t*, rĕpĕto (3)
recline, *v.i*, rĕcŭbo (1)
recluse, hŏmo sōlĭtārĭus
recognizable, *use phr*, quod agnosci pŏtest **(that can be recognized)**
recognize, *v.t*, agnosco (3), cognosco (3); **(acknowledge),** confĭtĕor (2 *dep.*)
recognition, cognĭtĭo, *f*
recoil, *v.i*, rĕsĭlĭo (4)
recollect, *v.t*, rĕmĭniscor (3 *dep. with genit*)
recollection, mĕmŏrĭa, *f*
recommence, *v.t*, rĕdintĕgro (1)
recommend, *v.t*, commendo (1)
recommendation, commendātĭo, *f*
recompense, *v.t*, rĕmūnĕror (1 *dep*)
reconcile, *v.t*, rĕconcĭlĭo (1)
reconciliation, rĕconcĭlĭātĭo, *f*
reconnoitre, *v.t*, explōro (1)
reconsider, *v.t*, rĕpŭto (1)

record, *v.t,* in tăbŭlas rĕfĕro (*irreg*)
records, tăbŭlae, *f. pl,* fasti, *m. pl*
recount, *v.t.* (**expound**), ēnarro (1)
recourse (**to have — to**), *v.i,* confŭgĭo (3) ad (*with acc*)
recover, *v.t,* rĕcŭpĕro (1), rĕcĭpĭo (3); *v.i,* (**from illness, etc.**), rĕvălesco (3), rĕfĭcĭor (3 *pass*), sē collĭgĕre (3 *reflex*)
recovery, rĕcŭpĕrātĭo, *f*; (**from illness**), sălus, *f*
recreate, *v.t,* rĕcrĕo (1)
recreation, rĕmissĭo, *f*
recruit, *nn,* tĭro, *m*
recruit, *v.t,* (**enrol**), conscrĭbo (3)
recruiting, *nn,* dēlectus, *m*
rectify, *v.t,* corrĭgo (3)
rectitude, prŏbĭtas, *f*
recumbent, rĕcŭbans
recur, *v.i,* rĕdĕo (4)
red, rŭber, rūfus; (**redhanded**), *adj,* mănĭfestus
redden, *v.t,* rŭbĕfăcĭo (3); *v.i,* rŭbesco (3)
redeem, *v.t,* rĕdĭmo (3)
redeemer, lĭbĕrātor, *m*
redemption, rĕdemptĭo, *f*
red-lead, mĭnĭum, *n*
redness, rŭbor, *m*
redouble, *v.t,* ingĕmĭno (1)
redound, rĕdundo (1)
redress, *v.t,* rēstĭtŭo (3)
reduce, *v.t,* rĕdĭgo (3)
reduction, dēmĭnūtĭo, *f*; (**taking by storm**), expugnātĭo, *f*
redundancy, rĕdundantĭa, *f*
redundant, sŭpervăcŭus
re-echo, *v.i,* rĕsŏno (1)
reed, ărundo, *f*
reef, saxa, *n.pl*
reek, *v.i,* fūmo (1)
reel, *v.i,* (**totter**), văcillo (1)
re-elect, *v.t,* rĕcrĕo (1)
re-establish, *v.t,* rēstĭtŭo (3)
refectory, cēnăcŭlum, *n*
refer, *v.t,* rĕfĕro *or* dĕfĕro (*irreg*) ad (*with acc*); (**to — to**), perstringo (3), specto (1) ad (*with acc*)
referee, arbĭter, *m*
reference, rătĭo, *f*
refill, *v.t,* rĕplĕo (2)
refine, *v.t,* (**polish**), expŏlĭo (4)
refined, pŏlītus, hūmānus
refinement, hūmānĭtas, *f*
refinery, offĭcĭna, *f*
reflect, *v.t,* rĕpercŭtĭo (3), rĕdĕo (3); *v.i,* (**ponder**), rĕpŭto (1) (ănĭmo) (**in the mind**)
reflection (**image**), ĭmāgo, *f*; (**thought**), cōgĭtātĭo, *f*
reform, ēmendātĭo, *f*
reform, *v.t,* rēstĭtŭo (3); (**correct**), corrĭgo (3); *v.i,* sē corrĭgĕre (3 *reflex*)
reformer, ēmendātor, *m*
refract, *v.t,* infringo (3)
refractory, contŭmax
refrain from, *v.i,* sē contĭnēre (2 *reflex*) ab (*with abl*)
refresh, *v.t,* rĕcrĕo (1), rĕfĭcĭo (3)
refreshment (**food**), cĭbus, *m*
refuge, perfŭgĭum, *n*; (**to take —**), *v.i,* confŭgĭo (3) ad (*with acc*)
refugee, *adj,* prŏfŭgus
refulgent, splendĭdus
refund, *v.t,* reddo (3)
refusal, rĕcūsātĭo, *f*
refuse, *nn,* purgāmentum, *n*
refuse, *v.t,* rĕcūso (1); (**to — to do**) nōlo (*irreg*) (*with infin*); (**say no**), nĕgo (1)
refute, *v.t,* rĕfello (3)
regain, *v.t,* rĕcĭpĭo (3)
regal, rēgālis
regale, *v.t,* excĭpĭo (3)
regalia, insignĭa, *n.pl*
regard, *nn,* (**esteem**), studĭum, *n*, hŏnor, *m*; (**consideration**), rēspectus, *m*
regard, *v.t,* (**look at**), intŭĕor (2 *dep*); (**consider**), hăbĕo (2); (**esteem**), aestĭmo (1)
regardless, neglĕgens
regency, interregnum, *n*
regent, interrex, *m*
regicide, caedes, (*f*) rēgis (**killing of a king**)
regiment, lĕgĭo, *f*
region, rĕgĭo, *f*, tractus, *m*
register, tăbŭlae, *f.pl*
register, *v.t,* perscrĭbo (3)
registrar, tăbŭlārĭus, *m*
regret, *nn,* dŏlor, *m*
regret, *v.t,* (**repent of**), *use* paenĭtet (2 *impers*) (*with acc. of subject*), *e.g.* **I repent of,** mē paenĭtet (*with genit*)
regular (**correctly arranged**), ordĭnātus, compŏsĭtus; (**customary**), sollĕmnis
regularity, ordo, *m*
regularly, *adv,* (**in order**), ordĭne; (**customarily**), sollemnĭter
regulate, *v.t,* ordĭno (1)
regulation (**order**), iussum, *n*; (**rule**), praeceptum, *n*
rehabilitate, *v.t,* rēstĭtŭo (3)
rehearsal (**practice**), exercĭtātĭo, *f*
rehearse, *v.t,* (**premeditate**), praemĕdĭtor (1 *dep*)
reign, *nn,* regnum, *n*
reign, *v.i,* regno (1)

reimburse, *v.t*, rĕpendo (3)
rein, *nn*, hăbēna, *f*
rein, *v.t*, (curb), frēno (1)
reinforce, *v.t*, confirmo (1)
reinforcement (help), auxĭlĭum, *n*
reinstate, *v.t*, rēstĭtŭo (3)
reiterate, *v.t*, ĭtĕro (1)
reject, *v.t*, rēĭcĭo (3)
rejection, rēiectĭo, *f*
rejoice, *v.i*, gaudĕo (2)
rejoicing, *nn*, laetĭtĭa, *f*
rejoin, *v.i*, rĕdĕo (4)
relapse, *v.i*, rĕcĭdo (3)
relate, *v.t*, (tell), narro (1), expōno (3); *v.i*, pertĭnĕo (2)
related (by birth), cognātus; (by marriage), affīnis; (by blood), consanguĭnĕus; (near), prŏpinquus
relation (relative), cognātus *m*, affīnis *m*; (connection), rătĭo, *f*
relationship, cognātĭo, *f*, affīnĭtas, *f*
relative, *nn*, cognātus, *m*, affīnis, *m*
relative, *adj*, compārātus (compared)
relax, *v.t*, rĕmitto (3); *v.i*, rēlanguesco (3)
relaxation, rĕmissĭo, *f*
relay, *v.t*, (send), mitto (3)
relays of horses, ĕqui dispŏsĭti, *m.pl* (horses methodically arranged)
release, *nn*, lĭbĕrātĭo *f*
release, *v.t*, exsolvo (3) lĭbĕro (1)
relent, *v.t*, rĕmitto (3)
relentless, immĭsĕrĭcors
relevant, *use vb*, pertĭnĕo (2) (to concern)
reliance, fĭdūcĭa, *f*
relic, rēlĭquĭae, *f,pl*
relief (alleviation), lĕvātĭo, *f*; (help), auxĭlĭum, *n*
relieve, *v.t*, lĕvo (1), rĕmitto (3); (help), subvĕnĭo (4) (*with dat*); (of command, etc.), succĕdo (3) (*followed by in with acc. or by dat*)
religion, rēlĭgĭo, *f*, săcra, *n.pl*
religious, rēlĭgĭōsus, pĭus
relinquish, *v.t*, rēlinquo (3)
relish, *nn*, stŭdĭum, *n*, săpor, *m*
relish, *v.t*, frŭor (3 *dep. with abl*)
reluctance, *use adj*, invītus (unwilling)
reluctant, invītus
rely on, *v.t*, confīdo (3) (*with dat. of person or abl. of thing*)
relying on, *adj*, frētus (*with abl*)
remain, *v.i*, mănĕo (2); (be left over), sŭpersum (*irreg*)
remainder, rēlĭquum, *n*
remaining, *adj*, rēlĭquus
remains, rēlĭquĭae, *f*, *pl*
remand, *v.t*, amplĭo (1)
remark, *nn*, dictum, *n*
remark, *v.t*, (say), dĭco (3); (observe), observo (1)
remarkable, insignis
remedy, rĕmĕdĭum, *n*, mĕdĭcāmentum, *n*
remedy, *v.t*, sāno (1); (correct), corrĭgo (3)
remember, *v.i*, mĕmĭni (*v.defect. with genit*), rĕcordor (1 *dep. with acc*)
remembrance, rĕcordātĭo, *f*, mĕmŏrĭa, *f*
remind, *v.t*, mŏnĕo (2)
reminiscence, rĕcordātĭo, *f*
remiss, neglĕgens
remission (forgiveness), vĕnĭa, *f*; (release), sŏlūtĭo, *f*
remit, *v.t*, rĕmitto (3)
remittance, pĕcūnĭa, *f*
remnant, rēlĭquĭae, *f. pl*
remonstrate, *v.i*, rĕclāmo (1) (*with dat*)
remorse, conscĭentĭa, *f*
remorseless, immĭsĕrĭcors, dŭrus
remote, rĕmōtus
remoteness, longinquĭtas, *f*
removal (driving away), āmōtĭo, *f*; (sending away), rēlēgātĭo, *f*; (— by force), raptus, *m*
remove, *v.t*, rĕmŏvĕo (2); (send away), rēlēgo (1); *v.i*, migro (1)
remunerate, *v.t*, rĕmūnĕror (1 *dep*)
remuneration, rĕmūnĕrātĭo, *f*
rend, *v.t*, scindo (3)
render, *v.t*, reddo (3)
rendezvous (to fix a —), lŏcum (et dĭem) constĭtŭo (3), (place and day)
rending (severing), discĭdĭum, *n*
renegade (deserter), transfŭga, *c*
renew, *v.t*, rĕnŏvo (1), rĕdintĕgro (1)
renewal, rĕnŏvātĭo, *f*
renounce, *v.t*, rĕnuntĭo (1), rĕmitto (3)
renovate, *v.t*, rĕnŏvo (1)
renovation, rēstĭtūtĭo, *f*
renown, fāma, *f*, glōrĭa, *f*
renowned, clārus
rent, *nn*, scissūra, *f*; (of houses, etc.), merces, *f*
rent, *v.t*, (let), lŏco (1); (hire), condūco (3)
renunciation, rĕpŭdĭātĭo, *f*
repair, *v.t*, rĕfĭcĭo (3), sarcĭo (4)
repaired, sartus
reparation, sātisfactĭo, *f*
repast, cĭbus, *m*
repay, *v.t*, (grātĭam) rĕfĕro (*irreg*)
repayment, sŏlūtĭo, *f*
repeal, *nn*, abrŏgātĭo, *f*
repeal, *v.t*, abrŏgo (1), rēscindo (3)
repeat, *v.t*, ĭtĕro (1), reddo (3)

For List of Abbreviations used, turn to pages 3, 4

repeatedly, *adv,* ĭdentĭdem
repel, *v.t,* rĕpello (3)
repent, *v.i,* paenĭtet (2 *impers*) (*with acc. of person and genit. of cause*), *e.g.* **I repent of this deed,** mē paenĭtet huius facti
repentance, paenĭtentĭa, *f*
repentant, paenĭtens
repetition, ĭtĕrātĭo, *f*
replace, *v.t,* rĕpōno (3); **(substitute),** substĭtŭo (3)
replenish, *v.t,* rĕplĕo (2)
replete, rĕplētus
reply, *nn,* rēsponsum, *n*
reply, *v.i,* rēspondĕo (2)
report, *nn,* nuntĭus, *m*; **(rumour),** fāma, *f*; **(bang),** crĕpĭtus, *m*
report, *v.t,* rĕfĕro (*irreg*), nuntĭo (1)
repose, *nn,* quĭes, *f*
repose, *v.i,* **(rest),** quĭesco (3)
repository, rĕceptācŭlum, *n*
reprehend, *v.t,* rĕprĕhendo (3)
reprehensible, culpandus
represent, *v.t,* exprĭmo (3), fingo (3); **(take the place of),** persōnam gĕro (3)
representation, ĭmāgo, *f*
representative (deputy), prōcūrātor, *m*
repress, *v.t,* cŏhĭbĕo (2)
reprieve, *nn,* **(respite),** mŏra, *f*
reprieve, *v.t,* **(put off),** diffĕro (*irreg*)
reprimand, *nn,* rĕprĕhensĭo, *f*
reprimand, *v.t,* rĕprĕhendo (3)
reprisal, *use* poena, *f,* **(punishment)**
reproach, *nn,* exprŏbrātĭo, *f,* opprŏbrĭum, *n*
reproach, *v.t,* exprŏbro (1), ōbĭcĭo (3) (*both with acc. of thing and dat. of person*)
reproachful, obiurgātōrĭus
reprobate, *nn,* perdĭtus, *m,* nĕbŭlo, *m*
reproduce, *v.t,* rĕcrĕo (1)
reproof, rĕprĕhensĭo, *f,* obiurgātĭo, *f,* vĭtŭpĕrātĭo, *f*
reprove, *v.t,* rĕprĕhendo (3), obiurgo (1), vĭtŭpĕro (1)
reptile, serpens, *f*
republic, respublĭca, *f*
republican, *adj,* pŏpŭlāris
repudiate, *v.t,* rĕpŭdĭo (1)
repudiation, rĕpŭdĭātĭo, *f*
repugnance, ŏdĭum, *n*
repugnant, āversus; **(it is — to me, I hate it),** *use phr,* ŏdĭo esse **(to be hateful),** *with dat. of person*
repulse, *v.t,* rĕpello (3)
repulsive, foedus, ŏdĭōsus
reputable, hŏnestus
reputation, repute, fāma, *f*; **(good —),** existĭmātĭo, *f*; **(bad —),** infāmĭa, *f*
request, *nn,* rŏgātĭo, *f*
request, *v.t,* rŏgo (1), prĕcor (1 *dep*)
require, *v.t,* **(demand),** postŭlo (1); **(need),** ĕgĕo (2) (*with abl*)
requirement (demand), postŭlātĭo, *f*; *or use adj,* nĕcessārĭus
requisite, *adj,* nĕcessārĭus
requisition, postŭlātĭo, *f*
requite, *v.t,* rĕpōno (3)
rescind, *v.t,* rēscindo (3)
rescue, *v.t,* ērĭpĭo (3)
rescue, *nn,* lĭbĕrātĭo, *f*
research, investīgātĭo, *f*
resemblance, sĭmĭlĭtūdo, *f*
resemble, *v.t,* rĕfĕro (*irreg*), sĭmĭlis esse (*irreg*) (*with genit. or dat*)
resembling, *adj,* sĭmĭlis
resent, *v.t,* aegrē fĕro (*irreg*) **(tolerate with displeasure)**
resentful, īrācundus
resentment, īra, *f*
reservation (restriction), exceptĭo, *f*
reserve, *nn,* **(military),** subsĭdĭum, *n*; **(of disposition),** grăvĭtas, *f*
reserve, *v.t,* servo (1); **(put aside),** sēpōno (3)
reserved (of disposition), grăvis
reservoir, lăcus, *m*
reside, *v.i,* hăbĭto (1)
residence, sēdes, *f. pl,* dŏmĭcĭlĭum, *n*
resident, incŏla, *c*
resign, *v.i, and v.t,* concēdo (3); **(to — oneself to),** sē committĕre (3 *reflex. with* in *and acc*)
resignation (of office, etc.), abdĭcātĭo, *f*; **(of mind)** aequus ănĭmus, *m*
resin, rēsīna, *f*
resist, *v.t,* rĕsisto (3) (*with dat*)
resistance, rĕpugnantĭa, *f, or use vb,* rĕsisto (3) **(to resist)**
resolute, fĭrmus, fortis
resolution, obstĭnātĭo, *f,* constantĭa, *f*; **(decision),** *use vb,* plăcet **(it is resolved)**
resolve, *v.t,* **(determine),** stătŭo (3); **(solve),** dissolvo (3)
resort to, *v.t* **(a place),** cĕlĕbro (1); **(have recourse to),** confŭgĭo (3) ad (*with acc*)
resort, *nn,* **(plan),** consĭlĭum, *n*; **(last —),** extrēma, *n.pl*
resound, *v.i,* rĕsŏno (1)
resource (help), auxĭlĭum, *n*; **(wealth, means),** ŏpes, *f, pl*
respect, *nn,* **(esteem),** observantĭa, *f*; **(in all —s),** omnĭbus partĭbus; **(in**

— of), *use abl. case, e.g.* **stronger in respect of number**, sŭpĕrĭor nŭmĕro
respect, *v.t*, (**esteem**), observo (1); (**reverence**), suspĭcĭo (3)
respectability, hŏnestas, *f*
respectable, hŏnestus
respectful, observans
respecting, *prep*, dē (*with abl*)
respective, *use* quisque (**each**) *with* sŭus (**his own**)
respiration, respīrātĭo, *f*
respite (**delay**), mŏra, *f*
resplendent, splendĭdus
respond, *v.i*, rēspondĕo (2)
response, rēsponsum, *n*
responsibility (**duty, function**), offĭcĭum, *n*; *or use imp. vb*, ŏportet (**it behoves**)
responsible, (**to be — for**), praesto (1)
rest, *nn*, (**repose**), quĭes, *f*, ōtĭum, *n*; (**remainder**), *use adj*, rĕlĭquus, *e.g.* **the — of one's life**, rĕlĭqua vīta, *f*
rest, *v.i*, quĭesco (3); (**— on, depend on**), nĭtor (3 *dep*)
resting-place, cŭbĭle, *n*
restitution (**to make —**), *v.t*, rēstĭtŭo (3)
restive, *use phr*, qui nōn făcĭle dŏmāri pŏtest (**that cannot easily be subdued**)
restless, inquĭētus
restlessness, inquĭes, *f*
restoration, rēstĭtūtĭo, *f*
restore, *v.t*, rēstĭtŭo (3)
restrain, *v.t*, cŏercĕo (2), rĕprĭmo (3), cŏhĭbĕo (2)
restraint, mŏdĕrātĭo, *f*
restrict, *v.t*, circumscrĭbo (3)
restriction (**bound**), mŏdus, *m*
result, *nn*, ēventus, *m*
result, *v.i*, ēvĕnĭo (4)
resume, *v.t*, rĕpĕto (3)
resurrection, rēsurrectĭo, *f*
resuscitate, *v.t*, rēsuscĭto (1)
retail, *v.t*, dĭvendo (3)
retailer, caupo, *m*
retain, *v.t*, rĕtĭnĕo (2)
retainer, sătelles, *c*; (*pl*) soldūrĭi, *m. pl*
retake, *v.t*, rĕcĭpĭo (3)
retaliate, *v.t*, ulciscor (3 *dep*)
retaliation, ultĭo, *f*
retard, *v.t*, mŏror (1 *dep*)
reticent, tăcĭturnus
retinue (**companions**), cŏmĭtes, *c.pl*
retire, *v.i*, (**go away**), rĕcēdo (3), ăbĕo (4); (**from a post, etc.**), dēcēdo (3); (**retreat**), sē rĕcĭpĕre (3 *reflex*)
retired, rĕmōtus
retirement (**act of —**), rĕcessus, *m*; (**leisure**), ōtĭum, *n*
retiring, *adj*, vĕrĕcundus
retort, *v.t*, rĕfĕro (*irreg*)
retrace, *v.t*, rĕpĕto (3)
retract, *v.t*, rĕnuntĭo (1)
retreat, *nn*, rĕceptus, *m*; (**place of refuge**), rĕfŭgĭum, *n*
retreat, *v.i*, sē rĕcĭpĕre (3 *reflex*)
retrench, *v.t*, mĭnŭo (3)
retribution, poena, *f*
retrieve, *v.t*, rĕcŭpĕro (1)
retrograde, *adj*, *use comp. adj*, pĕior (**worse**)
retrogression, rĕgressus, *m*
retrospect, *use vb*, rĕspĭcĭo (3) (**to look back**)
return, *nn*, (**coming back**), rĕdĭtus, *m*; (**giving back**), rēstĭtūtĭo, *f*; (**profit**), quaestus, *m*
return, *v.t*, (**give back**), reddo (3), rĕfĕro (*irreg*); *v.i*, (**go back**), rĕdĕo (4)
reunite, *v.t*, rĕconcĭlĭo (1)
reveal, *v.t*, pătĕfăcĭo (3)
revel, *nn*, cŏmissātĭo, *f*
revel, *v.i*, cŏmissor (1 *dep*)
revelation, pătĕfactĭo, *f*
revenge, *nn*, ultĭo, *f*
revenge oneself on, *v.t*, ulciscor (3 *dep*)
revengeful, cŭpĭdus ulciscendi (**keen on revenge**)
revenue, vectīgal, *n*
reverberate, *v.i*, rĕsŏno (1)
revere, reverence, *v.t*, vĕnĕror (1 *dep*)
reverence, vĕnĕrātĭo, *f*
revered, vĕnĕrābĭlis
reverend, vĕnĕrābĭlis
reverent, rĕvĕrens
reverse (**contrary**), *adj*, contrārĭus (**opposite**); (**defeat**), clādes,
reverse, *v.t*, inverto (3)
revert, *v.i*, rĕdĕo (4)
review, *nn*, rĕcognĭtĭo, *f*, rĕcensĭo, *f*
review, *v.t*, rĕcensĕo (2)
revile, *v.t*, mălĕdĭco (3) (*with dat*)
reviling, *nn*, mălĕdĭctĭo, *f*
revise, *v.t*, ēmendo (1)
revision, ēmendātĭo, *f*
revisit, *v.t*, rĕvīso (3)
revival, rĕnŏvātĭo, *f*
revive, *v.t*, rĕcrĕo (1), excĭto (1); *v.i*, rĕvīvisco (3)
revocable, rĕvŏcābĭlis
revoke, *v.t*, abrŏgo (1)
revolt, *nn*, dēfectĭo, *f*, sēdĭtĭo, *f*
revolt, *v.i*, dēfĭcĭo (3)
revolting, *adj*, (**disgusting**), foedus
revolution (**turning round**), conversĭo, *f*; (**political**), nŏvae res, *f. pl*
revolutionize, *v.t*, nŏvo (1)
revolutionary, sēdĭtĭōsus

revolve, *v.i,* sē volvĕre (3 *reflex*)
reward, *nn,* praemĭum, *n*
reward, *v.t,* rēmunĕror (1 *dep*)
rewrite, *v.t,* rēscrĭbo (3)
rhetoric, rhētŏrĭca, *f*
rhetorical, rhētŏrĭcus
Rhine, Rhēnus, *m*
rhinoceros, rhīnŏcĕros, *m*
rhubarb, rādix Pontĭca, *f* **(Black Sea root)**
rhyme (verse), versus, *m*
rhythm, nŭmĕrus, *m*
rhythmical, nŭmĕrōsus
rib, costa, *f*
ribald, obscēnus
ribbon, taenĭa, *f*
rice, ŏrȳza, *f*
rich, dīves, lŏcŭples; **(fertile),** pinguis
riches, dīvĭtĭae, *f. pl*
richness, ūbertas, *f*
rick (heap), ăcervus, *m*
rid, *v.t* lĭbĕro (1); **(to get — of),** dēpōno (3), dēpello (3)
riddle, aenigma, *n*; **(in —s),** per ambāges
riddle, *v.t,* **(sift),** cerno (3); **(— with holes),** confŏdĭo (3)
ride, *v.i,* vĕhor (3 *dep*); **(— at anchor),** consisto (3)
rider (horseman), ĕquĕs, *m*
ridge (mountain —), iŭgum, *n*
ridicule, *nn,* rīdĭcŭlum, *n*
ridicule, *v.t,* irrīdĕo (2)
ridiculous, rīdĭcŭlus
riding, *nn,* ĕquĭtātĭo, *f*
rife, frĕquens, crēber
rifle, *v.t,* praedor (1 *dep.*)
rift, rīma, *f*
rig, *v.t,* armo (1)
rigging, armāmentum, *n.pl*
right, *adj,* **(direction),** dexter; **(true),** rectus, vērus; **(correct),** rectus; **(fit),** ĭdōnĕus; **(—hand),** dextra (manus)
right, *nn,* **(moral),** fas, *n*; **(legal),** iūs, *n*
rightly, *adv,* rectē, vērē
right, *v.t,* rēstĭtŭo (3)
righteous, iustus
righteousness, prŏbĭtas, *f*
rightful, iustus
rigid, rĭgĭdus, dūrus
rigorous, dūrus
rigour, dūrĭtĭa, *f*
rill, rīvŭlus, *m*
rim, ōra, *f,* lābrum, *n*
rime, prŭīna, *f*
rind, crusta, *f*
ring (finger, etc.), ānŭlus, *m*; **(circle),** orbis, *m*
ring, *v.i,* tinnĭo (4); **(surround)** circŭmĕo (4)
ringing, *nn,* tinnĭtus, *m*
ringing, *adj,* tinnŭlus
ringleader, auctor, *m*
ringlet, cincinnus, *m*
rinse, *v.t,* collŭo (3)
riot, turba, *f,* tŭmultus, *m*; **(to make a —),** tŭmultum făcĭo (3)
riotous, turbŭlentus; **(extravagent),** luxŭrĭōsus
rip, *v.t,* scindo (3)
ripe, mātūrus
ripen, *v.i,* mātūresco (3); *v.t,* mātūro (1)
ripeness, mātūrĭtas, *f*
ripple, *v.i.* **(tremble),** trĕpĭdo (1)
rise, *nn,* **(of sun, etc.,** *or* **origin),** ortus, *m,*
rise, *v.i,* surgo (3); **(of sun, etc.),** ŏrĭor (4 *dep*); **(in rank),** cresco (3); **(in rebellion),** consurgo (3)
rising, *nn,* ortus, *m*; **(in rebellion),** mōtus, *m*
rising (ground), *nn,* clīvus, *m*
risk, *nn,* pĕrĭcŭlum, *n*
risk, *v.t,* pĕrĭclĭtor (1 *dep*)
ritual, rītus, *m*
rival, *nn,* aemŭlus, *m,* rīvālis, *c*
rival, *v.t,* aemŭlor (1 *dep*)
rivalry, aemŭlātĭo, *f*
river, *nn,* flūmen, *n,* flŭvĭus, *m*
river-bank, rīpa, *f*
river-bed, alvĕus, *m*
rivet, clāvus, *m*
rivulet, rīvŭlus, *m*
road, vĭa, *f,* ĭter, *n*; **(to make a —),** vĭam mūnĭo (4)
road-making, mūnĭtĭo, (*f*) vĭārum
roadstead (for ships), stātĭo, *f*
roam, *v.i,* văgor (1 *dep*), erro (1)
roaming, *adj,* văgus
roar, *nn,* frĕmĭtus, *m*
roar, *v.i,* frĕmo (3)
roast, *v.t,* torrĕo (2)
roasted, assus
rob, *v.t,* spŏlĭo (1) (*with acc. of person robbed, abl. of thing taken*)
robber, lătro, *m*
robbery, lătrōcĭnĭum, *n*
robe, vestis, *f,* vestīmentum, *n*; **(woman's —),** stŏla, *f*; **(— of state),** trăbĕa, *f*; **(— of kings),** purpŭra, *f*
robe, *v.t,* vestĭo (4), indŭo (3)
robust, rōbustus
rock, rūpes, *f*
rock, *v.t,* ăgĭto (1)
rocky, scŏpŭlōsus
rod, virga, *f*; **(fishing —),** ărundo, *f*
roe, căprĕa, *f*; **(of fish),** ōva, *n.pl* **(eggs)**

rogue, scĕlestus, *m*
roguery, nēquĭtĭa, *f*
roll, *nn*, (**something rolled up**), vŏlūmen, *n*; (**names**), album, *n*
roll, *v.t*, volvo (3); *v.i*, volvor (3 *pass*)
roller, cȳlindrus, *m*
rolling, *adj*, vŏlūbĭlis
Roman, Rōmānus
romance (**story**), fābŭla, *f*
romance, *v.i*, fābŭlor (1 *dep*)
romantic (**fabulous**), commentĭcĭus
Rome, Rōma, *f*
romp, *v.i*, lūdo (3)
romp, *nn*, lūsus, *m*
roof, *v.t*, tĕgo (3)
roof, *nn*, tectum, *n*
rook (**raven**), corvus, *m*
room, conclāve, *n*; (**space**), spătĭum, *n*; (**bed —**), cŭbĭcŭlum, *n*; (**dining —**), trĭclīnĭum, *n*
roomy, căpax
roost, *nn*, pertĭca, *f*
root, rādix, *f*; (**to strike —s, become rooted**), rādīces ăgo (3); (**—ed to the spot**), dēfixus
rope, fūnis, *m*, restis, *f*, rŭdens, *m*
rosary (**garden**), rŏsārĭum, *n*
rose, rŏsa, *f*
rosemary, ros mărīnus, *m*
rostrum, rostra, *n.pl*
rosy, rŏsĕus
rot, *nn*, tābes, *f*
rot, *v.i*, pūtesco (3)
rotate, *v.i*, sē volvĕre (3 *reflex*)
rotation, turbo, *m*
rotten, pŭtrĭdus
rotundity, rŏtundĭtas, *f*
rouge, *nn*, fūcus, *m*
rouge, *v.t*, fūco (1)
rough, asper; (**weather**), ătrox; (**of sea**), turbĭdus; (**of manner**), incultus
roughness, aspĕrĭtas, *f*
round, *adj*, rŏtundus
round, *adv*, circum
round, *prep*, circum (*with acc*)
round, *v.t*, (**to make —**), rŏtundo (1), curvo (1); (**to — off**), conclūdo (3); *v.i*, (**to go —**), circumăgor (3 *pass*)
roundabout, *adj*, dēvĭus
rouse, *v.t*, excĭto (1)
rout, *nn*, (**flight, defeat**), fŭga, *f*
rout, *v.t*, fŭgo (1)
route, ĭter, *n*
routine, ūsus, *m*
rove, *v.i*, văgor (1 *dep*)
roving, *nn*, văgātĭo, *f*
row (**line**), ordo, *m*; (**quarrel**), rixa, *f*; (**noise**), strĕpĭtus, *m*
row, *v.i*, rēmĭgo (1)
rowing, *nn*, rēmĭgĭum, *n*
royal, rēgĭus
royalty, regnum, *n*
rub, *v.t*, tĕro (3), frĭco (1); (**— out**), dēlĕo (2)
rubbish, quisquĭlĭae, *f. pl*
rubicund, rŭbĭcundus
ruby, *nn*, carbuncŭlus, *m*
ruby, *adj*, purpŭrĕus
rudder, gŭbernācŭlum, *n*
ruddy, rŭbĭcundus
rude (**person**), asper, ĭnurbānus
rudeness, ĭnhūmānĭtas, *f*
rudimentary, incŏhātus (**incomplete**)
rudiments, ĕlĕmenta, *n.pl*
rue, *nn*, rūta, *f*
rueful, maestus
ruff, torquis, *m. or f*
ruffian, perdĭtus, *m*, lătro, *m*
ruffianly, *adj*, scĕlestus
ruffle, *v.t*, ăgĭto (1)
rug, strāgŭlum, *n*
rugged, asper
ruin, exĭtĭum, *n*, rŭīna, *f*; (**building**), părĭĕtĭnae, *f. pl*
ruin, *v.t*, perdo (3)
ruinous, exĭtĭōsus, damnōsus
rule, *nn*, (**law**), lex, *f*; (**precept**), praeceptum, *n*; (**pattern**), norma, *f*; (**for measuring**), rēgŭla, *f*; (**government**), impĕrĭum, *n*
rule, *v.t*, rĕgo (3); *v.i*, regno (1)
ruler (**person**), dŏmĭnus, *m*; (**measurement**), rēgŭla, *f*
rumble, *nn*, murmur, *n*
rumble, *v.i*, murmŭro (1), mūgĭo (4)
ruminate, *v.t*, cōgĭto (1)
rummage, *v.t*, rĭmor (1 *dep*)
rumour, *nn*, rūmor, *m*, fāma, *f*
rump, clūnes, *f. pl*
rumple, *v.t*, corrŭgo (1)
run, *v.i*, curro (3); (**— about**), hūc illūc curro (3); (**— after**), persĕquor (3 *dep*); (**— away**), fŭgio (3); (**— aground**), impingor (3 *pass*), inflĭgor (3 pass); (**— back**), rĕcurro (3); (**— down**), dē curro (3); (**— forward**), prōcurro (3); (**— into**), incurro (3); (**— out**), excurro (3); (**— over, with vehicle etc.**), obtĕro (3); (**— through**), percurro (3)
runaway, *adj*, fŭgĭtīvus
runner, cursor, *m*
running, *nn*, cursus, *m*
running, *adj*, (**water**), vīvus
rupture (**disease**), hernĭa, *f*
rupture, *v.t*, rumpo (3)
rural, rustĭcus
rush, *nn*, (**plant**), iuncus, *m*; (**rushing, running**), impĕtus, *m*

For List of Abbreviations used, turn to pages 3, 4

rush, *v.i,* rŭo (3); (— **forward**), sē prōrĭpĕre (3 *reflex*); (— **into**), irrŭo (3); (— **out**), sē effundĕre (3 reflex)
rusk, crustum, *n*
russet, rūfus
rust, *nn,* rōbīgo, *f*
rustic, *adj,* rusticus
rusticate, *v.i,* rustĭcor (1 *dep*); *v.t,* rĕlĕgo (1)
rusticity, rustĭcĭtas, *f*
rustle, *v.i,* crĕpo (1)
rustle, rustling, *nn,* sŭsurrus, *m*
rusty, rōbīgĭnōsus
rut, orbĭta, *f*
ruthless, immītis, sĕvērus
rye, sĕcāle, *n*

S

Sabbath, sabbăta, *n.pl*
sable, *adj,* (**black**), āter
sabre, glădĭus, *m*
sack (**bag**), saccus, *m*; (**pillage**), dīreptĭo, *f*
sack, *v.t,* (**pillage**), dīrĭpĭo (3)
sackcloth, saccus, *m*
sacrament, săcrāmentum, *n*
sacred, săcer, sanctus
sacredness, sanctĭtas, *f*
sacrifice, săcrĭfĭcĭum, *n*; (**the victim**), hostĭa, *f*
sacrifice, *v.i,* săcrĭfĭco (1); *v.t,* immŏlo (1)
sacrificial, săcrĭfĭcus
sacrilege, săcrĭlĕgĭum, *n*; *or use vb,* dīrĭpĭo (3) (**to plunder**)
sad, tristis
sadden, *v.t,* tristĭtĭā affĭcĭo (3) (**affect with sadness**)
saddle, *nn,* ĕphippĭum, *n*
saddle, *v.t,* sterno (3); (**impose**), impōno (3)
sadness, tristĭtĭa, *f*
safe (**free from danger**), tūtus; (**having escaped from danger**), incŏlŭmis
safe-conduct, fĭdes, *f*
safeguard (**act of —**), cautĭo, *f*; (**defence**), prōpugnācŭlum, *n*
safely, *adv,* tūtō
safety, sălus, *f*
saffron, *nn,* crŏcus, *m*
saffron, *adj,* crŏcĕus
sagacious, prūdens, săgax
sagacity, prūdentĭa, *f,* săgācĭtas, *f*
sage (**wise man**), săpĭens, *m*; (**plant**), salvĭa, *f*
sail, *nn,* vēlum, *n*; (**to set —**), vēla do (1)
sail, *v.i,* nāvĭgo (1), vĕhor (3 *pass*); (**to go by means of sails**), vēla făcĭo (3)
sailing, *nn,* nāvĭgātĭo, *f*
sailor, nauta, *m*
saint, sanctus, *m*
saintly, sanctus
sake (**for the — of**), *prep,* causā (*with genit*); (**on behalf of**), prō (*with abl*), ŏb, propter (*with acc*)
salad, ăcētārĭa, *n.pl*
salary, merces, *f*
sale, vendĭtĭo, *f*; (**auction**), hasta, *f*
salient, *adj,* prīmus (**first**)
saline, salsus
saliva, sălīva, *f*
sallow, pallĭdus
sally, *nn,* ēruptĭo, *f*
sally, *v.i,* ēruptĭōnem făcĭo (3)
salmon, salmo, *m*
saloon, ātrĭum, *n*
salt, *nn,* sal, *m*
salt, *adj,* salsus
salt, *v.t,* sāle condĭo (4) (**season with salt**)
salt-cellar, sălīnum, *n*
salt-mines, sălīnae, *f. pl*
salubrious, sălūbris
salutary, sălūtāris; (**useful**), ūtĭlis
salutation, sălūtātĭo, *f*
salute, *v.t,* sălūto (1)
salvation, sălus, *f*
salve, unguentum, *n*
salver, scŭtella, *f,* păterra, *f*
same, *prep,* īdem; (**the same as**), īdem qui, īdem atque; (**in the — place**), *adv,* ĭbīdem (**at the — time**), sĭmŭl; (**fixed, constant**), constans
sample, exemplum, *n*
sanctification, sanctĭfĭcātĭo, *f*
sanctify, *v.t,* consĕcro (1)
sanction, auctōrĭtas, *f*; (**penalty**) poena, *f*
sanction, *v.t,* rătum făcĭo (3)
sanctity, sanctĭtas, *f*
sanctuary, fānum, *n,* templum, *n*: (**refuge**), rĕfŭgĭum, *n*
sand, hărēna, *f*
sandal, sŏlĕa, *f*
sandstone, tōfus, *m*
sandy, hărēnōsus
sane, sānus
sanguinary, crŭentus, sanguĭnārĭus
sanguine, *use* spēs, *f,* (**hope**)
sanity, mens sāna, *f*

sap, *nn*, sūcus, *m*
sap, *v.t*, subrūo (3)
sapient, *adj*, sāpiens
sapless, ārĭdus
sapling, arbor nŏvella,
sappers (military), mūnītōres, *m. pl*
sapphire, sapphīrus, *f*
sarcasm, cāvillātĭo, *f*, **(scoffing)**
sarcastic, ăcerbus
sarcophagus, sarcŏphăgus, *m*
sash, cingŭlum, *n*
satanic, nĕfandus
satchel, lŏcŭlus, *m*
satellite (star), stella, *f*; **(attendant)**, sātelles, *c*
satiate, *v.t*, sātĭo (1)
satiety, sātiĕtas, *f*
satire, sātŭra, *f*
satirical (bitter), ăcerbus
satirize, *v.t*, perstringo (3)
satirist; scriptor sātīrĭcus, *m*
satisfaction (inner), vŏluptas, *f*; **(compensation, punishment)**, poena, *f*
satisfactorily, *adv*, ex sententĭā
satisfactory, idōnĕus, *or* sātis **(enough)**
satisfied, contentus
satisfy, *v.t*, **(a need)**, explĕo (2), (*with dat*); **(convince)**, persuādĕo (2)
satrap, sātrăpes, *m*
saturate, *v.t*, sātŭro (1)
satyr, sātŷrus, *m*
sauce, condīmentum, *n*
saucepan, cācābus, *m*, cortīna, *f*
saucer, pātella, *f*
saucy, pĕtŭlans
saunter, *v.i*, vāgor (1 *dep*)
sausage, farcĭmen, *n*
savage, *adj*, fĕrus, ātrox, effĕrātus
savageness, savagery fĕrĭtas, *f*, saevĭtĭa, *f*
save, *v.t*, servo (1); **(defend)**, tŭĕor (2 *dep*); **(lay by)**, rĕservo (1)
save, *prep*, praeter (*with acc*)
saving, *nn*, conservātĭo, *f*
savings, pĕcŭlĭum, *n*
saviour, servātor, *m*
savour, *nn*, săpor, *m*
savour, *v.t*, săpĭo (3)
savoury, *adj*, conditus
saw serra, *f*
saw, *v.t*, serrā sĕco (1) **(cut with a saw)**
sawdust, scŏbis, *f*
say, *v.t*, dĭco (3), lŏquor (3 *dep*); **(to — that something will** *not* . . .), *use* nĕgo (1) **(to deny)**; **(it is said)**, fertur
saying, *nn*, dictum, *n*
scab, crusta, *f*
scabbard, vāgĭna, *f*
scabby, scăber
scaffold (frame), māchĭna, *f*; **(execution)**, supplĭcĭum, *n*
scald, *nn*, ădusta, *n.pl*
scale (pair of —s), lĭbra, *f*; **(of fish)**, squāma, *f*; **(gradation)**, grădus, *m*
scale, *v.t*, **(climb with ladders)**, scālis ascendo (3)
scaling-ladders, scālae, *f. pl*
scallop, pecten, *m*
scalp, cūtis, *f*, **(skin)**
scalpel, scalpellum, *n*
scamp, scĕlestus, *m*
scamper, *v.i*, fŭgĭo (3)
scan, *v.t*, contemplor (1 *dep*)
scandal, opprŏbrĭum, *n*; **(disparagement)** obtrectātĭo, *f*
scandalous, infāmis
scanty, exĭgŭus
scantiness, exĭgŭĭtas, *f*
scapegrace, nĕbŭlo, *m*
scar, cĭcātrix, *f*
scarce, rārus
scarcely, *adv*, vix, aegrē
scarcity, (of supplies, etc.), ĭnŏpĭa, *f*
scare, *v.t*, terrĕo (2)
scarecrow, formīdo, *f*
scarf, chlămys, *f*
scarlet, *nn*, coccum, *n*
scarlet, *adj*, coccĭnĕus
scathing, ăcerbus
scatter, *v.t*, spargo (3); *v.i*, sē spargĕre (3 *reflex*)
scene (of play), scēna, *f*; **(spectacle)**, spectăcŭlum, *n*
scenery (natural —), *use* rĕgĭo, *f*, (region)
scent (sense of smell), ŏdōrātus, *m*; **(the smell itself)**, ŏdor, *m*
scent, *v.t*, **(discern by smell)**, ŏdōror (1 *dep*);
scented, ŏdōrātus
sceptical, dŭbĭtans
sceptre, sceptrum, *n*
schedule, tăbŭla, *f*
scheme, *nn*, consĭlĭum, *n*
scheme, *v.t*, consĭlĭum căpĭo (3) **(make a plan)**
scholar (pupil), discĭpŭlus, *m*; **(learned man)**, doctus, *m*
scholarly, doctus
scholarship, littĕrae, *f. pl*
school, lūdus, *m*, schŏla,
school, *v.t*, ērŭdĭo (4)
school-master, măgister, *m*
school-mistress, măgistra, *f*
schooner, phăsēlus, *m*
sciatica, ischĭas, *f*
science, scĭentĭa, *f*, discĭplĭna, *f*, rātĭo, *f*

scientific, *use genit. of nouns above*
scimitar, ăcināces, *m*
scintillate, *v.i,* scintillo (1)
scion, prōles, *f*
scissors, forfĭces, *f. pl*
scoff at, *v.t,* irrīdĕo (2)
scoffer, irrīsor, *m*
scoffing, *nn,* irrīsĭo, *f*
scold, *v.t,* obiurgo (1), increpo (1)
scoop out, *v.t,* cāvo (1)
scoop, *nn,* trulla, *f*
scope (room), campus, *m*
scorch, *v.t,* ambūro (3)
scorched, torrĭdus
scorching, torrĭdus
score (total), summa, *f*; **(account, reckoning),** rātĭo, *f*; **(mark),** nŏta, *f*
score, *v.t,* **(note, mark),** nŏto (1); **(— a victory),** victōrĭam rĕporto (1)
scorn, *nn,* contemptus, *m*
scorn, *v.t,* sperno (3), contemno (3)
scornful, sūperbus
scorpion, scorpĭo, *m*
scoundrel, nĕbŭlo, *m*
scour, *v.t,* **(clean),** tergĕo (2); **(run over)** percurro (3)
scourge, *nn,* **(whip),** flăgellum, *n*; **(pest),** pestis, *f*, pernĭcĭes, *f*
scourge, *v.t,* verbĕro (1)
scourging, *nn,* verbĕra, *n.pl*
scout, explōrātor, *m*
scout, *v.t,* **(spy out),** spĕcŭlor (1 *dep*)
scowl, *nn,* frontis contractĭo, *f*
scowl, *v.i,* frontem contrăho (3), **(contract the brow)**
scramble for, *v.t, use phr,* inter sē certāre **(struggle among themselves)**
scrap, frustrum, *n*
scrape, *v.t,* rādo (3)
scraper, strĭgĭlis, *f*
scratch, *v.t,* rādo (3), scalpo (3)
scream, *nn,* vōcĭfĕrātĭo, *f*
scream, *v.i,* vōcĭfĕror (1 *dep*)
screech-owl, ŭlŭla, *f*
screen, tĕgĭmen, *n*
screen, *v.t,* tĕgo (3)
screw, *nn,* clāvus, *m*
scribble, *v.t,* scrĭbo (3)
scribe, scrĭba, *m*
Scripture, Scriptūra, *f*
scroll, vŏlūmen, *n*
scrub, *v.t,* tergĕo (2)
scruple (religious, etc.), rĕlĭgĭo, *f*
scrupulous, rĕlĭgĭōsus, dĭlĭgens
scrutinize, *v.t,* scrūtor (1 *dep*)
scrutiny, scrūtātĭo, *f*
scuffle, *nn,* rixa, *f*
scull (oar), rēmus, *m*; (*v.i,* rēmĭgo (1)
sculptor, sculptor, *m*
sculpture (art of —), sculptūra, *f*; **(the work itself),** ŏpus, *n*
scum, spūma, *f*
scurf, furfur, *m*
scurrility, prŏcăcĭtas, *f*
scurrilous, scurrĭlis, prŏcax
scurvy, foedus
scuttle, *v.t,* **(a ship),** *use phr,* nāvem ultro dēprĭmo (3) **(sink the ship of their own accord)**
scythe, falx, *f*
sea, măre, *n*, **(to be at —),** nāvĭgo (1)
sea, *adj,* mărĭtĭmus, mărĭnus
sea-coast, ōra mărĭtĭma, *f*
sea-faring, *adj,* mărĭtĭmus
sea-fight, pugna nāvālis, *f*
sea-gull, lārus, *m*
seal, *nn,* **(of letter),** signum, *n*; **(animal),** phōca, *f*
seal, *v.t,* **(letter),** signo (1); **(close up),** comprĭmo (3)
sealing-wax, cēra, *f*
seam, sūtūra, *f*
seaman, nauta, *m*
sear, *v.t,* ădūro (3)
search for, *v.t,* quaero (3); **(explore),** rĭmor (1 dep)
search, *nn,* investĭgātĭo, *f*
seasick, *adj,* nausēăbundus; **(to be —),** *v.i,* nausĕo (1)
seasickness, nausĕa, *f*
season, tempus, *n*, tempestas, *f*; **(right time),** tempus, *n*
season, *v.t,* condĭo (4)
seasonable, tempestīvus
seasoned (flavoured), condĭtus; **(hardened),** dūrātus
seasoning, *nn,* condĭmentum, *n*
seat, sēdes, *f*, sĕdile, *n*, sella, *f*; **(home),** dŏmĭcĭlĭum, *n*: *v.t.* collŏco (1)
sea-weed, alga, *f*
secede, *v.i,* dēcēdo (3)
secession, dēfectĭo, *f*
secluded, sēcrētus
seclusion, sōlĭtūdo, *f*
second, *adj,* sĕcundus; **(— of two),** alter; **(for the — time),** *adv,* ĭtĕrum; **(—ly),** *adv,* de inde
second, *nn,* **(time),** mōmentum, *n*
second, *v.t,* adiŭvo (1)
secondary, infĕrĭor
second-hand, ūsu trītus **(worn with usage)**
secrecy, sēcrētum, *n*
secret, arcāna, *n.pl*
secret, *adj,* occultus, arcānus; **(hidden),** clandestīnus; **(to keep something —),** *v.t,* cēlo (1)
secretary, scrĭba, *m*

secrete, *v.t*, cēlo (1), abdo (3)
secretly, *adv*, clam
sect, secta, *f*
section, pars, *f*
secular (not sacred), prŏfānus
secure, *v.t*, mūnĭo (4), firmo (1), lĭgo (1) **(tie up)**
secure, *adj*, tūtus
security, sălus, *f*; **(guarantee),** pignus, *n*; **(to give —),** căvĕo (2)
sedate, grăvis
sedative, mĕdĭcāmentum sŏpōrĭfĕrum
sedentary, sĕdentārĭus
sedge, ulva, *f*
sediment, faex, *f*
sedition, sēdĭtĭo, *f*
seditious, sēdĭtĭōsus
seduce, *v.t*, tento (1), sollĭcĭto (1)
seducer, corruptor, *m*
seduction, corruptēla, *f*
sedulous, assĭdŭus
see, *v.t*, vĭdĕo (2), cerno (3), aspĭcĭo (3); **(to — to it that . . .),** cūro (1) ad (*with gerund phr*); **(understand),** intellĕgo (3)
seed, sēmen, *n* **(literal and metaphorical)**
seedling, arbor nŏvella, *f*
seedy, grānōsus
seeing that, *conj*, cum
seek, *v.t*, quaero (3), pĕto (3), affecto (1)
seem, *v.i*, vĭdĕor (2 *pass.*)
seeming, *nn*, spĕcĭes, *f*
seemly, *adj*, dĕcōrus, **(it is —),** dĕcet (2 *impers*)
seer, vātes, *c*
seethe, *v.i*, fervĕo (2)
segment, segmentum, *n*
segregate, *v.t*, sēcerno (3)
seize, *v.t*, răpĭo (3), corrĭpĭo (3), prendo (3), occŭpo (1); **(of illness, passion, etc.),** affĭcĭo (3)
seizure, comprĕhensĭo, *f*
seldom, *adv*, rārō
select, *v.t*, lĕgo (3)
select, *adj*, lectus
selection, dēlectus, *m*
self, *pron*, **(emphatic),** ipse; **(reflexive),** sē
self-confident, confīdens
self-satisfied, contentus
selfish, selfishness, (to be —), sē ămāre (1 *reflex*)
sell, *v.t*, vendo (3)
seller, vendĭtor, *m*
semblance, ĭmāgo, *f*
semicircle, hēmĭcyclĭum, *n*
senate, sĕnātus, *m*
senate-house, cūrĭa, *f*
senator, sĕnātor, *m*
send, *v.t*, mitto (3); **(— away),** dĭmitto (3); **(— back),** rĕmitto (3); **(— for),** arcesso (3); **(— forward),** praemitto (3); **(— in),** immitto (3)
senile, sĕnīlis
senior, (in age) nātu maior
sensation (feeling), sensus, *m*; mōtus (*m*) ănĭmi **(impulse)**
sensational, nŏtābĭlis
sense (feeling), sensus, *m*; **(understanding),** prūdentĭa, *f*; **(meaning),** sententĭa, *f*
senseless (unconscious), *use adv. phr*, sensu ablāto **(with feeling withdrawn); (stupid),** sōcors
sensible, prūdens
sensitive, sensīlis
sensitiveness, mollĭtĭa,
sensual, lĭbīdĭnōsus
sensuality, lĭbīdo, *f*
sentence (criminal), iūdĭcĭum, *n*; **(writing, etc.),** sententĭa, *f*
sentence, *v.t*, damno (1)
sententious, sententĭōsus
sentiment (feeling), sensus, *m*; **(opinion),** ŏpīnĭo, *f*
sentimental, mollis
sentimentality, mollĭtĭa, *f*
sentinel, vīgil, *m*; **(to be on — duty),** in stătĭōne esse (*irreg*)
separable, dīvĭdŭus
separate, *v.t*, sēpăro (1), dīvĭdo(3), sēiungo (3), sēcerno (3)
separate, *adj*, sēpărātus, sēcrētus
separately, *adv*, sēpărātim
separation, sēpărātĭo, *f*
September, September (mensis)
sepulchre, sĕpulcrum, *n*
sequel (outcome), exĭtus, *m*
sequence, ordo, *m*
serene, tranquillus
serf, servus, *m*
series, sĕrĭes, *f*
serious, grăvis
seriousness, grăvĭtas,
sermon, ōrātĭo, *f*
serpent, serpens, *f*
serried, confertus
servant, mĭnister, *m*, fămŭlus, *m*, servus, *m*
serve, *v.t*, servĭo (4), (*with dat*); **(at table, etc.),** mĭnistro (1); **(in the army),** stīpendĭa mĕrĕor (2 *dep*); **(to — as),** esse (*irreg*) (*with* prō *and abl*)
service, mĭnistĕrĭum, *n*, ŏpĕra, **(military),** mĭlĭtĭa, *f*
serviceable, ūtĭlis
servile, servīlis

For List of Abbreviations used, turn to pages 3, 4

servitude, servĭtus, *f*
session (assembly), conventus, *m*
set, *nn*, **(of people)**, glŏbus, *m*
set, *adj*, stătus
set, *v.i*, **(place)**, stătŭo (3), pōno (3); *v.i*, **(of the sun)**, occĭdo (3); **(— about, begin)**, incĭpĭo (3); **(— aside)**, *v.t*, sēpōno (3); **(— down in writing)**, nŏto (1); **(— free)**, lĭbĕro (1); **(set off or out)**, *v.i*, prŏfĭciscor (3 *dep*); **(— up)**, *v.t*, stătŭo (3)
settee, lectŭlus, *m*
setting (of sun), occāsus, *m*
settle, *v.t*, constĭtŭo (3); **(a dispute)**, compōno (3); **(debt)**, solvo (3); *v.i* **(in a home, etc.)**, consīdo (3)
settled, certus
settlement (colony), cŏlōnĭa, *f*; **(— of an affair)**, compōsĭtĭo, *f*
settler, cŏlōnus, *m*
seven, septem; **(— hundred)**, septingenti; **(— times)**, *adv*, septĭies
seventeen, septendĕcim
seventeenth, septĭmus dĕcĭmus
seventh, septĭmus
seventieth, septŭāgēsĭmus
seventy, septŭāginta
sever, *v.t*, sēpăro (1); sēiungo (3)
several, complūres, ălĭquot
severe, sĕvērus, dūrus
severity, sĕvērĭtas, *f*, ăcerbĭtas, *f*
sew, *v.t*, sŭo (3)
sewer (drain), clŏāca, *f*
sex, sexus, *m*
sexagenarian, sexāgēnārĭus, *m*
sexual, *use nn.* sexus, *m*, **(sex)**
shabbiness, sordes, *f. pl*
shabby, sordĭdus
shackle, *v.t*, vincŭlis constringo (3) **(bind with chains)**
shackle(s), *nn*, vincŭla, *n.pl*
shade, *nn*, umbra, *f*; **(the —s of the dead)**, mānes, *m. pl*
shade, *v.t*, ŏpāco (1)
shadow, umbra, *f*
shadowy, ŏpācus, ĭnānis
shady, ŏpācus
shaft (of a weapon), hastĭle, *n*; **(an arrow)**, săgitta, *f*; **(of a mine)**, pŭtĕus, *m*
shaggy, hirtus, hirsūtus
shake, *v.t*, quătĭo (3), ăgĭto (1) lăbĕfăcio (3); *v.i*, trĕmo (3), trĕpĭdo (1); **(— hands)**, dextras iungo (3) **(join right hands)**
shaking, *nn*, quassātĭo, *f*
shallow, *adj*, **(sea)**, vădōsus, brĕvis
shallows, *nn*, vāda, *n.pl*
sham, *adj*, sĭmŭlātus
sham, *nn*, sĭmŭlātĭo, *f* **(pretence)**
sham, *v.t*, sĭmŭlo (1)
shambles, *use* turba, *f*
shame, *nn*, **(feeling)**, pŭdor, *m*; **(disgrace)**, dĕdĕcus, *n*
shame, *v.t*, rŭbōrem incŭtĭo (3) (*with dat*)
shamefaced, vĕrēcundus
shameful, turpis
shamefulness, turpĭtūdo, *f*
shameless, impŭdens
shamelessness, impŭdentĭa, *f*
shamrock, trĭfŏlĭum, *n*
shank, crus, *n*
shape, *nn*, forma, *f*
shape, *v.t*, formo (1)
shapeless, informis
shapely, formōsus
share (part), pars, *f*; **(plough —)**, vōmer, *m*
share, *v.t*, partĭor (4 *dep*)
sharer, partĭceps, *c*
shark, pistrix, *f*
sharp, ăcūtus, ăcer
sharp-sighted, perspĭcax
sharp-witted, ăcūtus
sharpen, *v.t*, ăcŭo (3)
sharply, *adv*, ăcūte, ăcrĭter
sharpness (of tongue), aspĕrĭtas, *f*; **(mental)**, ăcūmen, *n*
shatter, *v.t*, frango (3)
shave, *v.t*, rādo (3)
shawl, ămĭcŭlum, *n*
she, *pron*, illa, ĕa, haec, ista
sheaf, mănĭpŭlus, *m*
shear, *v.t*, tondĕo (2)
shearing, *nn*, tonsūra, *f*
shears, forfex, *f*
sheath, vāgīna, *f*
sheathe, *v.t*, in vāgīnam rĕcondo (3) **(put back into the sheath)**
shed, *nn*, tūgŭrĭum, *n*
shed, *v.t*, fundo (3)
sheen, fulgor, *m*
sheep, ŏvis, *f*
sheep-fold, saeptum, *n*
sheep-skin, pellis ŏvilla, *f*
sheepish, sōcors, *or use adv. phr*, dēmisso vultu **(with downcast face)**
sheer (steep), abruptus; **(pure, absolute)**, mĕrus
sheet (cloth), lintĕum, *n*; **(paper)**, schĕda, *f*; **(— of a sail)**, pes, *m*
shelf, plŭtĕus, *m*
shell, concha, *f*, crusta, *f*
shell-fish, conchÿlĭum, *n*

shelter, *nn,* perfŭgĭum, *n,* tectum, *n*
shelter, *v.t,* tĕgo (3); *v.i, use phr,* ad perfŭgĭum sē conferre (*irreg*) (**betake oneself to shelter**)
shelving, *adj,* dēclīvis
shepherd, pastor, *m*
shield, *nn,* scūtum, *n*
shield, *v.t,* tĕgo (3), dēfendo (3)
shift (change), vĭcissĭtūdo, *F.*
shift, *v.t,* mūto (1); *v.i,* mūtor (1 *pass*)
shifty, versūtus
shin, crūs, *n*
shine, *v.i,* lūcĕo (2), fulgĕo (2)
ship, *nn,* nāvis, *f*; (**war —**), nāvis longa, *f*; (**transport —**), nāvis ŏnĕrārĭa, *f*
ship, *v.t,* (**put on board**), **in** nāvem impōno (3); (**transport**), nāve transporto (1)
ship-owner, nāvĭcŭlārĭus, *m*
shipping, nāvĭgĭa, *n.pl*
shipwreck, naufrăgĭum, *n*
shipwrecked, naufrăgus
shirt, sŭbūcŭla, *f*
shiver, *v.i,* horrĕo (2)
shivering, *nn,* horror, *m*
shoal (water), vădum, *n*; (**fish**), exāmen, *n*
shock, offensĭo, *f,* ictus, m; (**of battle**), concursus, *m*
shock, *v.t,* offendo (3), percŭtĭo (3)
shocking, *adj,* ătrox
shoe, *nn,* calcĕus, *m*
shoe, *v.t,* calcĕo (1)
shoe-maker, sūtor, *m*
shoot, *nn,* (**sprout**), surcŭlus, *m*
shoot, *v.t,* (**a missile**), mitto (3); *v.i,* (**— along, across**), vŏlo (1)
shooting-star, fax caelestis, *f*
shop, tăberna, *f*
shop-keeper, tăbernārĭus, *m* (*pl. only*)
shore, lĭtus, *n,* ōra, *f*
shore-up, *v.t,* fulcĭo (4)
short, brĕvis, ĕxĭgŭus; (**— cut**), vĭa compendĭārĭa, *f*; (**in —**), *adv,* dēnĭque
shortage, ĭnŏpĭa, *f* (**lack**)
shortcoming, dēlictum, *n*
shorten, *v.t,* contrăho (3)
shortly, *adv,* (**of time**), brĕvi; (**briefly**), brĕvĭter
shortness, brĕvĭtas, *f*
shot (firing), ictus, *m*
shoulder, hŭmĕrus, *m*; (**— blade**), scăpŭlae, *f. pl*
shoulder, *v.t,* fĕro (*irreg*) (**to bear**)
shout, *nn,* clāmor, *m*
shout, *v.i,* clāmo (1)
shove, *v.t,* trūdo (3)
shovel, pāla, *f*
show, *nn,* (**appearance**), spĕcĭes, *f*; (**spectacle**), spectācŭlum, *n*; (**procession, etc.**), pompa, *f*
show, *v.t,* monstro (1), praebĕo (2), ostendo (3); (**— off**), *v.t,* ostento (1); *v.i,* sē ostentare (1 *reflex*)
shower, imber, *m*
shower, *v.t,* fundo (3)
showery, plŭvĭus
showy, spĕcĭōsus
shred, pannus, *m*
shrew, fēmĭna prŏcax
shrewd, ăcūtus, săgax
shrewdness, săgācĭtas, *f*
shriek, *nn,* ŭlŭlātus, *m*
shriek, *v.i,* ŭlŭlo (1)
shrill, ăcūtus, ăcer
shrine, dēlūbrum, *n*
shrink, *v.t,* contrăho (3); *v.i,* (**—from**), ăbhorrĕo (2)
shrinking, *nn,* contractĭo, *f*
shrivel, *v.t,* corrūgo (1)
shrivelled, rūgōsus
shroud, *use* lintĕum, *n,* (**cloth**)
shroud, *v.t,* involvo (3)
shrub, frŭtex, *m*
shrubbery, frŭtĭcētum
shudder, *v.i,* horrĕo (2)
shudder, *nn,* horror, *m*
shuffle, *v.t,* miscĕo (2); *v.i, use phr,* lentē ambŭlo (1) (**walk slowly**)
shun, *v.t,* fŭgĭo (3), vĭto (1)
shut, *v.t,* claudo (3); (**— in or up**), inclūdo (3); (**— out**), exclūdo (3)
shutters, fŏrĭcŭlae, *f. pl*
shuttle, rădĭus, *m*
shy, vĕrēcundus
shy, *v.i,* (**of horses**), consternor (1 *pass*)
shyness, vĕrēcundĭa, *f*
sick, aeger; (**to be —**), *v.i,* aegrōto (1); (**vomit**), *v.i, and v.t,* vŏmo (3)
sicken, *v.t,* fastĭdĭum mŏvĕo (2); *v.i,* aeger fĭo (*irreg*)
sickle, falx, *f*
sickly, infirmus
sickness morbus, *m*
side (of the body), lătus, *n*; (**part, region**), pars, *f*; (**party, faction**), pars, *f*; (**from (or on) all —s**), *adv,* undĭque; (**on both —s**), ŭtrimque; (**on this —**), hinc; (**on that —**), illinc; (**on this — of**), *prep,* citra (*with acc*); (**on that — of**), ŭltra
side, *adj,* (**sidelong**), oblīquus
sideboard, ăbăcus, *m*
sideways, *adv,* oblīquē
siege, *nn,* obsĭdĭo, *f*
siege-works, ŏpĕra, *n.pl*
sieve, crĭbrum, *n*

sift, *v.t*, crĭbro (1); (— **evidence, etc.**), scrūtor (1 *dep*)
sigh, *nn*, suspĭrĭum, *n*
sigh, *v.i*, suspīro (1)
sight (sense or act), vīsus, *m*; (**view**), conspectus, *m*; (**spectacle**), spectăcŭlum, *n*
sight, *v.t*, conspĭcor (1 *dep*)
sightly, formōsus, vĕnustus
sign, *nn*, signum, *n*; (**mark**), nŏta, *f*; (**trace, footprint**), vestĭgĭum, *n*; (**portent**), portentum, *n*
sign, *v.t*, subscrĭbo (3); (**give a —**), *v.i*, signum do (1)
signal, signum, *n*
signal, *v.i*, signum do (1)
signature, nōmen, *n*
signet, signum, *n*
significance, signĭfĭcātĭo, *f*
significant, signĭfĭcans
signify, *v.t*, signĭfĭco (1)
silence, sĭlentĭum, *n*
silent, tăcĭtus, (**to be —**), *v.i*, tăcĕo (2), sĭlĕo (2)
silk, *nn*, bombyx, *m*
silk, silken, *adj*, sērĭcus
silk-worm, bombyx, *m*
silky, mollis
sill, lĭmen, *n*
silliness, stultĭtĭa, *f*
silly, stultus
silt, *nn*, lĭmus, *m*, sentĭna, *f*
silver, *nn*, argentum, *n*
silver, *adj*, argentĕus
silver-mine, argentārium metallum
similar, sĭmĭlis (*with genit. or dat*)
similarity, sĭmĭlĭtūdo, *f*
similarly, *adv*, sĭmĭlĭter
simmer, *v.i*, lentē fervĕo (3) (**boil slowly**)
simper, *v.i*, subrīdĕo (2)
simple, simplex; (**weak-minded**), ĭneptus
simpleton, stultus, *m*
simplicity, simplĭcĭtas, *f*
simplify, *v.t*, făcĭlem reddo (3)
simulation, sĭmŭlātĭo, *f*
simultaneous, *use adv*, sĭmul (**at the same time**)
sin, *nn*, peccātum, *n*
sin, *v.i*, pecco (1)
since, *conj*, cum (*foll. by vb. in subjunctive*); (**temporal**) postquam
since, *adv*, ăbhinc
since, *prep*, ē, ex, ā, ăb (*with ăbl*)
sincere, sincērus, simplex
sincerity, sincērĭtas, *f*, simplĭcĭtas, *f*
sinew, nervus, *m*
sinful, impĭus,
sinfulness, impĭĕtas, *f*
sing, *v.i. and v.t*, căno (3)
singe, *v.t*, ădūro (3)
singer, cantātor, *m*
singing, *nn*, cantus, *m*
single, *adj*, (**one, sole**), ūnus, sōlus; (**unmarried**), caelebs
single out, *v.t*, ēlĭgo (3)
singly, *adv*, singŭlātim
singular, (**one**), singŭlāris; (**strange**), nŏvus
singularly, *adv*, ūnĭcē
sinister, sĭnister
sink, *v.t*, mergo (3); *v.i*, sīdo (3), consīdo (3)
sinner, peccātor, *m*
sinuous, sĭnŭōsus
sip, *v.t*, dēgusto (1), lĭbo (1)
sir (respectful address), bŏne vir
sire, păter, *m*
siren, sīrēn, *f*
sister, sŏror, *f*
sit, *v.i*, sĕdĕo (2); (— **down**), consīdo (3); (— **up, stay awake**), vĭgĭlo (1)
site, sĭtus, *m*
sitting, *nn*, sessĭo, *f*
situated, sĭtus
situation sĭtus, *m*
six, sex; (— **each**), sēni; (— **times**), *adv*, sexĭens
sixteen, sēdĕcim
sixteenth, sextus dĕcĭmus
sixth, sextus
sixtieth, sexāgēsĭmus
sixty, sexāginta
size, magnĭtūdo, *f*; (**of great —**), *adj*, magnus; (**of small —**), parvus; (**of what —?**), quantus?
skeleton, ossa, *n.pl*, (**bones**)
sketch, *nn*, ădumbrātĭo, *f*
sketch, *v.t*, ădumbro (1)
skewer, vĕrūcŭlum, *n*
skiff, scăpha, *f*
skilful, skilled, pĕrĭtus
skilfulness, skill, pĕrĭtĭa, *f*
skim, *v.t*, (— **off**), dēspūmo (1); (— **over**), percurro (3)
skin, cūtis, *f*, pellis, *f*
skin, *v.t*, pellem dīrĭpĭo (3) (**tear away the skin**)
skip, *v. i*, exsulto (1); (— **over**), *v.i. and v.t*, praetĕrĕo (4)
skipper, nauarchus, *m*
skirmish, *nn*, lĕve certāmen, *n*
skirmish, *v.i*, parvŭlis proelĭis contendo (3) (**fight in small engagements**)
skirmisher, vĕlĕs, *m*
skirt, *nn*, limbus, *m*
skirt, *v.t*, (**scrape past**), rādo (3)
skittish, lascīvus

skulk, *v.i,* lătĕo (2)
skull, calvārĭa, *f*
sky, caelum, *n*
sky-blue, caerŭlĕus
sky-lark, ălauda, *f*
slab (of stone), ăbăcus, *m*
slack, rĕmissus
slacken, *v.t,* rĕmitto (3); *v.i,* rĕmittor (3 *pass*)
slackness, rĕmissĭo, *f*; **(idleness),** pĭgrĭtĭa, *f*
slake (thirst), *v.t,* (sĭtim) exstinguo (3)
slander, *nn,* călumnĭa, *f*
slander, *v.t,* călumnĭor (1 *dep*)
slanderer, obtrectātor, *m*
slanderous, fāmōsus
slanting, *adj,* obliquus
slap, *nn,* ălăpa, *f*
slap, *v.t,* fĕrĭo (4)
slash, *nn,* **(blow),** ictus, *m*
slash, *v.t,* caedo (3)
slate (roofing), tēgŭlae, *f. pl.*
slate, *v.t,* rĕprehendo (3)
slaughter, *nn,* caedes, *f,* strāges, *f*
slaughter, *v.t,* caedo (3)
slaughter-house, *use* lānĭēna, *f* **(butcher's stall)**
slave, servus, *m*
slave-dealer, vēnālĭcĭus, *m*
slavery, servĭtus, *f*
slave-trade, vēnālĭcĭum, *n*
slavish, servĭlis
slay, *v.t,* interfĭcĭo (3)
slayer, interfector, *m*
slaying, *nn,* trŭcĭdātĭo, *f*
sledge, trăhĕa, *f*
sleek, nĭtĭdus
sleep, *nn,* somnus, *m*
sleep, *v.i,* dormĭo (4), quĭesco (3); **(to go to —),** obdormisco (3)
sleepless, insomnis
sleeplessness, insomnĭa, *f*
sleepy, somnĭcŭlōsus
sleeve, mănĭcae, *f. pl*
sleigh, trăhĕa, *f*
sleight-of-hand, praestĭgĭae, *f. pl*
slender, grăcĭlis
slenderness, grăcĭlĭtas, *f*
slice, segmentum, *n,* frustum, *n*
slice, *v.t,* concĭdo (3)
slide, *v.i,* lābor (3 *dep*)
slight, *adj,* lĕvis, exĭgŭus
slight, *v.t,* neglĕgo (3)
slim, grăcĭlis
slime, lĭmus, *m*
slimy, lĭmōsus
sling, *nn,* **(for throwing),** funda, *f*; **(bandage),** mĭtella, *f*
sling, *v.t,* mitto (3)
slinger, fundĭtor, *m*
slip, *v.i,* lābor (3 *dep*); **(— away),** sē subdŭcĕre (3 *reflex*); **(— out from),** ēlābor (3 *dep*)
slip, *nn,* lapsus, *m*; **(mistake),** error, *m*
slipper, sŏlĕa, *f*
slippery, lūbrĭcus
slipshod, neglĕgens
slit, *nn,* scissūra, *f*
slit, *v.t,* incĭdo (3)
sloop, nāvis longa, *f*
slope, *nn,* clīvus, *m*
slope, *v.i,* sē dēmittĕre (3 *reflex*), vergo (3)
sloping, *adj,* **(down),** dēclīvis; **(up),** acclīvis
sloth, segnĭtĭa, *f,* ignāvĭa, *f*
slothful, segnis
slough (mire), pălus, *f*
slovenliness, cultus neglectus **(neglected dress)**
slow, tardus, lentus
slowly, *adv,* tardē, lentē
slowness, tardĭtas, *f*
slug, lĭmax, *f*
sluggish, pĭger, segnis
sluggishness, pigrĭtĭa, *f*
sluice, ductus, (*m*) ăquārum **(bringing of water)**
slumber, *nn,* somnus, *m*
slumber, *v.i,* dormĭo (4)
slur, *nn,* măcŭla, *f*
sly, astūtus, callĭdus
smack *nn,* **(blow),** ălăpa, *f*; **(taste),** săpor, *m*
smack, *v.t,* **(slap),** verbĕro (1)
small, parvus, exĭgŭus
smallness, exĭgŭĭtas, *f*
smart, *adj,* ācer; **(clothes, etc.),** nĭtĭdus; **(witty),** făcētus
smart, *nn,* dŏlor, *m*
smart, *v.i,* dŏlĕo (2), ūror (3 *pass*)
smartness (alertness), ălăcrĭtas, *f*
smash, *nn,* fractūra, *f*
smash, *v.t,* confringo (3)
smattering, lĕvis cognĭtĭo, *f,* **(slight knowledge)**
smear, *v.t,* lĭno (3)
smell, *nn,* **(sense of —),** ŏdōrātus, *m*; **(scent),** ŏdor, *m*
smell, *v.t,* olfăcĭo (3); *v.i,* ŏlĕo (2)
smelt, *v.t,* cŏquo (3)
smile, *nn,* rīsus, *m*
smile, *v.i,* subrīdĕo (2)
smirk, *nn,* rīsus, *m*
smite, *v.t,* fĕrĭo (4)
smith, făber, *m*
smithy, făbrĭca, *f*
smock, indūsĭum, *n*
smoke, *nn,* fūmus, *m*

For List of Abbreviations used, turn to pages 3, 4

smoke, *v.i,* fūmo (1)
smoky, fūmōsus
smooth, lĕvis, (**of the sea**), plăcĭdus; (**of temper**), aequus
smooth, *v.t,* lēvo (1)
smoothness, lēvĭtas, *f,* lēnĭtas, *f*
smother, *v.t,* suffŏco (1), opprĭmo (3)
smoulder, *v.i,* fūmo (1)
smudge, *nn,* lābes, *f*
smuggle, *v.t,* furtim importo (1) (**bring in secretly**)
snack, cēnŭla, *f*
snail, cochlĕa, *f*
snake, anguis, *m, f*
snaky, vīpĕrĕus
snap, *v.t,* rumpo (3); (— **the fingers**), *v.i,* concrĕpo (1); (— **up**), *v.t,* corrĭpĭo (3)
snare, lăquĕus, *m*
snarl, *nn,* gannĭtus, *m*
snarl, *v.i,* gannĭo (4)
snatch, *v.t,* răpĭo (3)
sneak, *v.i* corrĕpo (3)
sneer, *nn,* obtrectātĭo, *f*
sneer at, *v.t,* dĕrīdĕo (2)
sneeze, *v.i,* sternŭo (3)
sneezing, sternūmentum, *n*
sniff at (**smell at**), *v.t,* ŏdōror (1 *dep*)
snip, *v.t,* (**cut off**), ampūto (1)
snob, nŏvus hŏmo (**upstart**)
snore, *v.i,* sterto (3)
snore, snoring, *nn,* rhonchus, *m*
snort, *v.i,* frĕmo (3)
snorting, *nn,* frĕmĭtus, *m*
snout, rostrum, *n*
snow, *nn,* nix, *f*
snow (**it —s**), ningit (*v. impers*)
snowy, nīvĕus
snub, *v.t,* rĕprĕhendo (3)
snub-nosed, sīlus
snuff, *v.t,* (**extinguish**), exstinguo (3)
snug, commŏdus
so, *adv,* (**in such a way**), sīc, ĭtă; (**to such an extent**), ădĕo; (*with adj and adv*) tam, *e.g.* **so quickly,** tam cĕlĕrĭter; (*with a purpose or consecutive clause,* **so that . . .**) ut; (— **big,** — **great**), tāntus; (— **many**), tot; (— **much**), tantum; (— **often**), tŏties
soak, *v.t,* mădĕfăcĭo (3)
soaking, mădens; (**of rain**), largus
soap, *nn,* sāpo, *m*
soar, *v.i,* sublīme fĕror (*irreg pass*) (**be borne aloft**)
sob, *nn,* singultus, *m*
sob, *v.i,* singulto (1)
sober, sōbrĭus
sobriety, sōbrĭĕtas, *f,* mŏdĕrātĭo, *f*
sociability, făcĭlĭtas, *f*
sociable, făcĭlis
social, commūnis
society (**in general**), sŏcĭĕtas, *f*; (**companionship**), sŏdālĭtas, *f*
sock, tĭbĭāle, *n*
sod, caespes, *m*
soda, nĭtrum, *n*
sodden, mădĭdus
sofa, lectŭlus, *m*
soft, mollis
soften, *v.t,* mollĭo (4); *v.i,* mollĭor (4 *pass*)
softness, mollĭtĭa, *f*
soil, sŏlum, *n*
soil, *v.t,* inquĭno (1)
sojourn, *nn,* commŏrātĭo, *f*
sojourn, *v.i,* commŏror (1 *dep*)
solace, *nn,* sōlātĭum, *n*
solace, *v.t,* consōlor (1 *dep*)
solar, *use genit. case of* sōl, *m,* (**sun**)
solder, *nn,* ferrūmen, *n*
solder, *v.t,* ferrūmĭno (1)
soldier, mīles, *c*; (**foot** —), pĕdes, *m*; (**cavalry** —), ĕques, *m*; *v.i,* (**serve as a** —), stĭpendĭa mĕrĕor (2 *dep*)
soldierly, *adj,* mīlĭtāris
sole, *adj,* sōlus
sole, *nn,* sŏlum, *n*; (**fish**), sŏlĕa, *f*
solely, *adv,* sōlum
solemn (**serious**), grăvis; (**festivals, etc.**), sollemnis
solemnity, grăvĭtas, *f*; (**religious** —), sollemne, *n*
solemnize, *v.t,* cĕlēbro (1)
solicit, *v.t,* pĕto (3), obsĕcro (1), sollĭcĭto (1)
solicitation, flāgĭtātĭo, *f*
solicitor, advŏcātus, *m*
solicitude, anxĭĕtas, *f*
solid, *adj* sŏlĭdus
solid, *nn,* sŏlĭdum, *n*
solidity, sŏlĭdĭtas, *f*
soliloquize, *v.i,* sēcum lŏquor (3 *dep*) (**speak with oneself**)
solitary, sōlus, sōlĭtārĭus; (**places**), dēsertus
solitude, sōlĭtūdo, *f*
solstice (**summer** —), solstĭtĭum, *n*; (**winter** —), brūma, *f*
solution, *use vb.* solvo (3) (**to solve**), *or nn,* explĭcātĭo, *f*
solve, *v.t,* explĭco (1)
solvent (**to be** —), solvendo esse(*irreg*)
sombre, obscūrus
some, *adj,* ălĭquis, nonnullus; (**a certain**), quīdam

somebody, someone, *pron,* ălĭquis, nonnullus; **(a certain one),** quĭdam; **(— or other),** nescĭo quis; **(some . . . others),** ălĭi . . . ălĭi
somehow, *adv,* nescĭŏ quŏmŏdŏ
something, *pron,* ălĭquid
sometime, *adv,* ălĭquandŏ
sometimes *adv,* ălĭquandŏ, interdum; **(occasionally),** sŭbinde; **(sometimes . . . sometimes . . .),** mŏdŏ . . . mŏdŏ . . .
somewhat, *adv,* ălĭquantum
somewhere, *adv,* ălĭcŭbi; **(to —),** ălĭquo
somnolent, sēmĭsomnus
son, fĭlĭus, *m*; **(— in-law),** gĕner, *m*
song, carmen, *n*
sonorous, sŏnōrus,
soon, *adv,* mox; **(as — as),** sĭmul ac, sĭmŭl atque, cum prĭmum; **(as— as possible),** quam prĭmum
sooner (earlier), mātūrĭus; **(rather),** pŏtĭus
soot, fūlīgo, *f*
soothe, *v.t,* mulcĕo (2), lēnĭo (4)
soothing, *adj,* lēnis
soothsayer, auspex, *c,* hăruspex, *m*
sooty, fūlīgĭnōsus
sop, offa, *f*
sophist, sŏphistes, *m*
soporific, sŏpōrĭfer
sorcerer, vĕnēfĭcus, *m*
sorcery, vĕnēfĭcĭa, *n.pl*
sordid, sordĭdus
sore, ăcerbus
sore, *nn,* ulcus, *n*
sorrel, lăpăthus, *f*
sorrow, *nn,* dŏlor, *m,* maeror, *m*
sorrow, *v.i,* dŏlĕo (2)
sorrowful, maestus, tristis
sorry (to be —), mĭsĕret (2 *impers*) (*with acc. of subject and genit. of object*), *e,g.* **I am sorry for you,** me mĭsĕret tŭi
sort, gĕnus, *n*; **(what — of?),** quālis?
sort, *v.t,* dīgĕro (3)
sot, pōtātor, *m*
soul, ănĭma, *f,* ănĭmus, *m,* spīrĭtus, *m*
sound, *nn,* sŏnus, *m,* sŏnĭtus, *m*
sound, *adj,* sānus; **(of sleep),** artus; **(of arguments),** firmus
sound, *v.i,* sŏno (1); *v.t,* inflo (1); **(— the trumpet),** būcĭnam inflo (1), căno (3)
soundness, sānĭtas, *f,* intgĕrĭtas, *f*
soup, iūs, *n*
sour, ăcerbus, ăcer, ămārus
source, fons, *m,* căput, *n*
sourness, ăcerbĭtas, *f*
south, *nn,* mĕrīdĭes, *m*
south, southern, *adj,* mĕrīdĭānus
southwards, *adv. phr,* in mĕrīdĭem
sovereign, *nn,* princeps, *m,* rex, *m* tȳrannus, *m*
sovereign (independent), *adj, use phr* sŭi iūris **(of one's own authority)**
sovereignty, impĕrĭum, *n*
sow, *nn,* sūs, *f*
sow, *v.t,* sĕro (3)
sower, sātor, *m*
space, spătĭum, *n*; **(— of time),** spătĭum, (*n*) tempŏris
spacious, amplus
spaciousness, amplĭtūdo, *f*
spade, pāla, *f*
span palmus, *m*
span, *v.t,* **(river, etc.),** *use vb,* iungo (3) **(join)**
spangled, distinctus
Spanish, Hispānus
spar (of timber), asser, *m*
spare, *adj,* exĭlis **(thin)**
spare, *v.t,* parco (3) (*with dat*)
sparing, *adj,* **(frugal),** parcus
spark, *nn,* scintilla, *f*
sparkle, *v.i,* scintillo (1)
sparkling, *adj,* scintillans
sparrow, passer, *m*
sparse, rārus
spasm, spasmus, *m*
spatter, *v.t,* aspergo (3)
spawn, *nn,* ōva, *n.pl*
spawn, *v.i,* ōva gigno (3) **(produce eggs)**
speak, *v.t,* lŏquor (3 *dep*), dĭco (3); **(— out),** ēlŏquor (3 *dep*); **(— to),** allŏquor (3 *dep*)
speaker, ōrātor, *m*
spear, hasta, *f*
special (one in particular), pĕcŭlĭāris; **(one's own),** prŏprĭus; **(outstanding),** praecĭpŭus
speciality, *use adj,* prŏprĭus **(one's own)**
specially, *adv,* praecĭpŭē, praesertim .
species, gĕnus, *n*
specific, dĭsertus; *or use emphatic pron,* ipse
specify, *v.t,* ēnŭmĕro (1)
specimen, exemplum, *n*
specious, prŏbābĭlis
speck, măcŭla, *f*
spectacle, spectăcŭlum, *n*
spectator, spectātor, *m*
spectre, īmāgo, *f*
spectrum, spectrum, *n*
speculate, *v.i,* cōgĭto (1); **(guess),** cōnĭcĭo (3)
speculation, cōgĭtātĭo, *f*; **(guess),** coniectūra, *f*

speech, ōrātĭo, *f*
speechless (**literally so**), mūtus; (**struck with fear, etc.**), stŭpĕfactus
speed, cĕlĕrĭtas, *f*
speed, *v.t*, mātūro (1); *v.i*, festīno (1)
speedy, cĕler, cĭtus
spell (**charm**), carmen, *n*
spell, *v.t*, *use phr. with* littĕra, *f*, (**letter**)
spellbound, obstŭpĕfactus
spend, *v.t*, (**money**), impendo (3), insūmo (3); (**time**), ăgo (3)
spendthrift, nĕpos, *m*, *f*
spew, *v.t*, vŏmo (3)
sphere, glŏbus, *m*; (— **of responsibility, etc.**), prōvincĭa, *f*
spherical, glŏbōsus
sphinx, sphinx, *f*
spice, condīmentum, *n*
spice, *v.t*, condĭo (4)
spicy, condĭtus
spider, ărāněa, *f*
spider's web, ărāněa, *f*
spike, clāvus, *m*
spill, *v.t*, effundo (3)
spin, *v.t*, (**thread, etc.**), nĕo (2); (**turn rapidly**), verso (1); *v.i*, versor (1 *pass*)
spinster, virgo, *f*
spiral, *nn*, cochlĕa, *f*
spiral, *adj*, invŏlūtus
spire, turris, *f*
spirit (**breath of life**), ănĭma, *f*; (**mind, soul**), ănĭmus, *m*; (**disposition**), ingĕnĭum, *n*; (**character**), mōres, *m. pl*; (**courage**), ănĭmus, *m*; (**departed** —), mānes, *m. pl*
spirited, ănĭmōsus
spiritual (**of the mind**), *use* ănĭmus, *m*
spit, *nn*, (**for roasting**), vĕru, *n*
spit, *v.t*, spŭo (3)
spite, mălĕvŏlentĭa, *f*; (**in — of**), *often use abl. phr. with* obstans (**standing in the way**)
spiteful, mălignus
spittle, spūtum, *n*
splash, *v.t*, aspergo (3)
spleen, lĭĕn, *m*; (**vexation**), stŏmăchus, *m*
splendid, splendĭdus
splendour, splendor, *m*
splint, fĕrŭlae, *f. pl*
splinter, fragmentum, *n*
split, *v.t*, findo (3); *v.i*, findor (3 *pass*)
split, *nn*, fissūra, *f*
splutter, *v.i*, balbūtĭo (4)
spoil, *nn*, praeda, *f*, spŏlĭa, *n.pl*
spoil, *v.t*, corrumpo (3), vĭtĭo (1)
spokesman, ōrātor, *m*
sponge, *nn*, spongĭa, *f*
spongy, spongĭōsus
sponsor auctor, *c*
spontaneous, *use adv. phr*, sŭā (mĕā), sponte (**of his (my) own accord**)
spoon, cocl̆ĕar, *n*
sporadic, rārus
sport, *nn*, lūdus, *m*, lūsus, *m*; (**ridicule**), lūdĭbrĭum, *n*
sport, *v.i*, lūdo (3)
sportive (**playful**), lascīvus
sportsman, vēnātor, *m*
spot, *nn*, (**stain**), măcŭla, *f*; (**place**), lŏcus, *m*
spot, *v.t*, (**look at**), aspĭcĭo (3); (**stain**), măcŭlo (1)
spotless (**of character, etc.**), intĕger, pūrus
spotted, măcŭlōsus
spouse, coniunx, *c*
spout, *nn*, ōs, *n*
spout, *v.i*, ēmĭco (1); *v.t*, (**pour out**), effundo (3)
sprain, *v.t*, intorquĕo (2)
sprawl, *v.i*, fundor (3 *pass*)
spray, *nn*, aspergo, *f*
spread, *v.t*, extendo (3), pando (3), diffundo (3); (— **about, publish**), diffĕro (*irreg*) dīvulgo (1); *v.i*, diffundor (3 *pass*), incrēbresco (3)
sprightly, ălăcer
spring, *nn*, (**season**), vēr, *n*; (**leap**), saltus, *m*; (**fountain**), fons, *m*
spring, *adj*, vernus
spring, *v.i*, (**leap**), sălĭo (4); (— **from, proceed from**), ŏrĭor (4 *dep*) (— **upon, assault**), ădŏrĭor (4 *dep*)
sprinkle, *v.t*, spargo (3)
sprout, *nn*, surcŭlus, *m*
sprout, *v.i*, pullŭlo (1)
spruce, *adj*, nĭtĭdus
spruce, *nn*, (**fir**), pīnus, *f*
spur, *nn*, calcar, *n*
spur, *v.t*, concĭto (1)
spurious, ădultĕrīnus
spurn, *v.t*, aspernor (1 *dep*)
spurt, *v.i*, ēmĭco (1)
spy, *nn*, explōrātor, *m*, dēlātor, *m*
spy, *v.t*, spĕcŭlor (1 *dep*)
squabble, *nn*, rixa, *f*
squabble, *v.i*, rixor (1 *dep*)
squadron (**of cavalry**), turma, *f*; (**of ships**), classis, *f*
squalid, sordĭdus
squall (**storm**), prŏcella, *f*
squall, *v.i*, (**cry**), vāgĭo (4)
squalor, sordes, *f. pl*
squander, effundo (3)
squanderer, nĕpos, *m*, *f*
square, *adj*, quădrātus; *nn*, quădrātum, *n*

square, *v.t,* quădro (1); **(accounts, etc.),** subdūco (3), constĭtŭo (3)
squash, *v.t,* contĕro (3)
squat, *v.i,* subsīdo (3)
squat, *adj,* **(of figure),** brĕvis
squeak, *nn,* strīdor, *m*
squeak, *v.i,* strīdĕo (2)
squeamish, fastīdĭōsus
squeeze, *v.t,* prĕmo (3)
squint, *v.i,* strābō esse (*irreg*)
squirrel, sciūrus, *m*
squirt, *v.t,* ēĭcĭo (3); *v.i,* ēmĭco (1)
stab, *v.t,* fŏdĭo (3)
stab, *nn,* ictus, *m*
stability, stăbĭlĭtas, *f*
stable, *adj,* stăbĭlis
stable, *nn,* stăbŭlum, *n*
stack, *nn,* ăcervus, *m*
stack, *v.t,* cŏăcervo (1)
staff, băcŭlum, *n*; **(advisers),** consĭlĭārĭi, *m. pl*
stag, cervus, *m*
stage (theatre), proscaenĭum, *n*; **(step),** grădus, *m*
stagger, *v.i,* văcillo (1); *v.t,* concŭtĭo (3), commŏvĕo (2)
stagnant, stagnans
stagnate, *v.i,* stagno (1)
staid, grăvis
stain, *nn,* măcŭla, *f*
stain, *v.t,* măcŭlo (1)
stainless, pūrus, intĕger
stairs, scālae, *f. pl*
stake (post, etc), pālus, *m,* sŭdis, *f,* stīpes, *m*; **(pledge, wager),** pignus, *n*
stake, *v.t,* **(wager),** dēpōno (3)
stale, vĕtus
stalk, stirps, *f*
stalk, *v.i,* incēdo (3); **(game, etc),** *use phr,* cautē sĕquor (3 *dep*) **(follow cautiously)**
stall (cattle), stăbŭlum, *n*; **(shop, etc.),** tăberna, *f*
stallion, admissārĭus, *m*
stalwart, *adj,* fortis
stamina, vīres, *f. pl*
stammer, *nn,* haesĭtantĭa (*f*) linguae **(hesitation of speech)**
stammer, *v.i,* balbūtĭo (4)
stamp (mark), nŏta, *f*; **(with a ring, etc.),** signum, *n*
stamp, *v.t,* **(mark),** signo (1); **(— with the foot),** supplōdo (3)
stand, *nn* **(halt),** mŏra, *f*; **(to make a —)** consisto (3) rĕsisto (3), (*with dat.*); **(platform),** suggestus, *m*; **(stall),** mensa, *f*
stand, *v.i,* sto (1), consisto (3); **(— back),** rĕcēdo (3), **(— by, help),** adsum (*irreg with dat*); **(— for, seek a position),** *v.t,* pĕto (3); **(endure),** pătĭor (3 *dep*); **(— out, project)** exsto (1); **(— up),** surgo (3)
standard, signum, *n*; **(of the legion),** ăquĭla, *f*; **(measure),** norma, *f*; **(— bearer),** signĭfer, *m*
standing, *nn,* **(position),** stătus, *m*
staple products, merces, *f, pl*
star, stella, *f,* sīdus, *n*
starboard, *use adj,* dexter **(right)**
starch, *nn,* ămŷlum, *n*
stare, *nn,* obtūtus, *m*
stare, *v.t,* **(— at),** intŭĕor (2 *dep*)
stark (stiff), rĭgĭdus; **(— naked),** nūdus; (—mad) āmens
starling, sturnus, *m*
start, *nn,* **(movement),** trĕmor, *m*; **(beginning),** ĭnĭtĭum, *n*; **(setting out),** prŏfectĭo, *f*; **(starting point),** carcĕres, *m. pl*
start, *v.i,* **(make a sudden movement),** trĕmo (3), horrĕo (2); **(— out),** prŏfĭcĭscor (3 *dep*); *v.t* **(establish),** instĭtŭo (3)
startle, *v.t,* terrĕo (2)
startling, *adj,* terrĭbĭlis
starvation, fāmes, *f*
starve, *v.t,* fāme nĕco (1) **(kill by starvation)**; *v.i,* fāme nĕcor (1 *pass*)
state (condition), stătus, *m,* condĭcĭo, *f*; **(the —),** respublĭca, *f,* cĭvĭtas, *f*
state, *v.t,* prŏfĭtĕor (2 *dep*)
stately, magnĭfĭcus, cĕlĕber
statement, dictum, *n*
statesman, *use phr. with* respublĭca **(state),** *and* admĭnistro (1), **(to manage)**
station (standing), stătus, *m*; **(occupied place),** stătĭo, *f*
station, *v.t,* lŏco (1)
stationary, *adj,* immōtus
stationer, bibliŏpōla, *m*
statistics, census, *m*
statue, stătŭa, *f*
stature, stătūra, *f*
status, stătus, *m*
statute, lex, *f*
staunch, *adj,* firmus
stave off, *v.t,* arcĕo (2)
stay, *nn,* **(prop),** firmāmentum, *n*; **(rest, etc),** mansĭo, *f,* commŏrātĭo, *f*
stay, *v.i,* mănĕo (2), mŏror (1 *dep*); *v.t,* **(obstruct, stop),** mŏror (1 *dep*)
steadfast, firmus, stăbĭlis
steady, firmus, stăbĭlis
steadfastness, stăbĭlĭtas, *f*
steadiness, stăbĭlĭtas, *f*
steak, offa, *f*

For List of Abbreviations used, turn to pages 3, 4

steal, *v.t,* fūror (1 *dep*); *v.i,* **(— upon),** surrēpo (3)(*with dat*)
stealing, *nn,* **(theft),** furtum, *n*
stealth, (by —), (*adv*) furtim
stealthy, furtīvus
steam, văpor, *m*
steam, *v.i,* exhālo (1)
steed, ĕquus, *m*
steel, chălybs, *m*; **(iron, sword, etc.),** ferrum, *n*
steel, *v.t,* **(strengthen),** confirmo (1)
steep, praeruptus
steep, *v.t,* **(soak),** mădĕfăcĭo (3)
steeple, turris, *f*
steer, *nn,* iŭvencus, *m*
steer, *v.t,* gŭberno (1)
steersman, gŭbernātor, *m*
stem, stirps, *f,* (— *literal and metaphorical*)
stem, *v.t,* **(check),** sisto (3), rĕsisto (3) (*with dat*)
stench, fētor, *m*
step, *nn,* grādus, *m,* passus, *m*; **(foot —),** vestīgĭum, *n*; **(— by —),** pĕdĕtentim; **(steps, stairs),** scālae, *f.pl*
step, *v.i,* grădĭor (3 *dep*); **(— forward);** prōgrĕdĭor (3 *dep*)
step-brother (father's side), fīlĭus vĭtrĭci; **(mother's side),** fīlĭus nŏvercae; **(— daughter),** prīvigna, *f*; **(— father)** vĭtrĭcus, *m*; **(— mother),** nŏverca, *f*; **(— sister),** fīlĭa vĭtrĭci *or* nŏvercae; **(— son),** prīvignus, *m*
sterile, stĕrĭlis
sterility, stĕrĭlĭtas, *f*
sterling, *adj,* **(genuine),** vērus
stern, *nn,* puppis, *f*
stern, *adj,* dūrus
sternness, sĕvērĭtas, *f*
stew, *v.t,* cŏquo (3)
steward, vĭlĭcus, *m*
stick, *nn,* băcŭlum, *n*
stick, *v.t,* **(fix),** fīgo (3); *v.i,* haerĕo (2)
sticky, *adj,* tĕnax
stiff, rĭgĭdus; **(to be —),** *v.i,* rĭgĕo (2)
stiffen, *v.i,* rĭgĕo (2); *v.t,* rĭgĭdum făcĭo (3)
stiffness, rĭgor, *m*
stifle, *v.t,* suffōco (1); **(suppress),** opprĭmo (3)
stigma, stigma, *n*
stigmatize, *v.t,* nŏto (1)
still, *adj,* immōtus, tranquillus
still, *adv,* **(nevertheless),** tămen; **(up to this time),** ădhuc; **(even),** ĕtĭam
still, *v.t,* sēdo (1)
stillness, quĭes, *f*
stilts, grallae, *f. pl*
stimulant (incentive), stĭmŭlus, *m*
stimulus (incentive), stĭmŭlus, *m*
stimulate, *v.t,* stĭmŭlo (1)
sting, *nn,* ăcŭlĕus, *m*
sting, *v.t,* pungo (3)
stinging, *adj,* mordax
stingy, sordĭdus
stink, *nn,* fētor, *m*
stink, *v.i,* fētĕo (2)
stipend, merces, *f*
stipulate, *v.i,* stĭpŭlor (1 *dep*)
stir, *nn,* mōtus, *m*
stir, *v.t,* mŏvĕo (2); *v.i,* mŏvĕor (2 *pass*)
stitch, *v.t,* sŭo (3)
stock (of tree, family, etc.), stirps, *f*; **(amount),** vīs, *f*
stock, *v.t,* complĕo (2)
stockbroker, argentārĭus, *m*
stocking, tĭbĭāle, *n*
stoic, *nn. and adj,* stōĭcus
stoical, dūrus
stoicism, rătĭo Stōĭca, *f*
stolen, furtīvus
stomach, stŏmăchus, *m*
stomach, *v.t,* **(put up with),** perfĕro (*irreg*)
stone, lăpis, *m*; **(precious —),** gemma, *f*; **(fruit —),** nūclĕus, *m*
stone, *adj,* lăpĭdĕus
stone, *v.t,* **(— to death),** lăpĭdĭbus cŏŏpĕrĭo (4) **(overwhelm with stones)**
stone-quarry, lăpĭcīdĭnae, *f. pl*
stony, lăpĭdōsus; **(of heart),** asper
stool, scăbellum, *n*
stoop, *v.i,* sē dēmittĕre (3 *reflex*); **(condescend),** dēscendo (3)
stop, *nn,* intermissĭo, *f*
stop, *v.t,* sisto (3); **(— up a hole, etc.),** obtūro (1); *v.i,* **(pause),** sisto (3); **(desist),** dēsĭno (3); **(remain),** mănĕo (2)
stoppage (hindrance), impĕdīmentum, *n*
stopper, obtūrāmentum, *n*
store (supply), cōpĭa, *f*; **(place),** rĕceptăcŭlum, *n*
store, *v.t,* condo (3)
storey, tăbŭlātum, *n*
stork, cĭcōnĭa, *f*
storm, *nn,* tempestas, *f*
storm, *v.t,* **(attack),** expugno (1)
storming, *nn,* expugnātĭo, *f*
stormy (weather), turbĭdus
story, fābŭla, *f*
story-teller, narrātor, *m*

stout, (fat), pinguis; (strong), vălĭdus; (— hearted), fortis
stove, fŏcus, *m*
stow, *v.t*, rĕpōno (3)
straddle, *v.i*, vārĭco (1)
straggle, *v.i*, văgor (1 *dep*)
straight, *adj*, rectus
straight, *adv*, rectā
straight away, *adv*, stătim
straighten, *v.t*, corrĭgo (3)
straightforward, simplex
strain, *nn*, contentĭo, *f*
strain, *v.t*, (stretch), tendo (3); (liquids, etc.), cōlo (3); *v.i*, (strive), nĭtor (3 *dep*)
strait, *adj*, angustus
strait, *nn*, (a narrow place or a difficulty), angustĭae, *f. pl* (sea) frĕtum *n*.
strand (shore), lĭtus, *n*
stranded, rĕlictus
strange, insŏlĭtus, nŏvus
strangeness, insŏlentĭa, *f*
stranger, hospes, *m*
strangle, *v.t*, strangŭlo (1)
strap, *nn*, lōrum, *n*
stratagem, dŏlus, *m*
strategist, *use phr. with* pĕrĭtus (skilled in), *with phr. below*
strategy, ars, (*f*) bellandi (the art of making war)
straw, strāmentum, *n*
strawberry, frāgum, *n*
stray, *v.i*, erro (1)
stray, *adj*, errābundus
streak, *nn*, lĭnea, *f*
streak, *v.t*, lĭneis vărĭo (1), (variegate with streaks)
streaky, virgātus
stream, *nn*, flūmen, *n*
stream, *v.i*, effundor (3 *pass*)
street, vĭa, *f*
strength, vĭres, *f. pl*, rōbur, *n*
strengthen, *v.t*, firmo (1)
strenuous, impĭger
stress (importance), mōmentum, *n*
stretch, *nn*, (extent), spătĭum, *n*
stretch, *v.t*, tendo (3); (— out), extendo (3); *v.i*, sē tendĕre (3 *reflex*)
stretcher, lectĭca, *f*
strew, *v.t*, sterno (3)
strict (severe), dūrus; (careful), dĭlĭgens
strictness, sĕvērĭtas, *f*
stricture, rĕprĕhensĭo, *f*
stride, *nn*, passus, *m*
strife, certāmen, *n*, discordĭa, *f*
strike, *v.t*, fĕrĭo (4), percŭtĭo (3), pulso (1); (— the mind, occur to), subvĕnĭo (4)
striking, *adj*, insignis
string, lĭnea, *f*; (of bow or instrument), nervus, *m*
stringent, sĕvērus
strip, *v.t*, spŏlĭo (1), nūdo (1)
strip, *nn*, (flap, edge), lăcĭnĭa, *f*
stripe, lĭmes, *m*; (blow), verber, *n*
stripling, ădŏlescentŭlus, *m*
strive, *v.i*, nĭtor (3 *dep*), contendo (3)
striving, *nn*, contentĭo, *f*
stroke, *nn*, verber, *n*, ictus, *m*; (line), lĭnea, *f*
stroke, *v.t*, mulcĕo (2)
stroll, *nn*, ambŭlātĭo, *f*
stroll, *v.i*, ambŭlo (1)
strong, vălĭdus, firmus; (powerful), fortis; (to be —), *v.i*, vălĕo (2)
stronghold, arx, *f*
structure (building), aedĭfĭcĭum, *n*
struggle, *nn*, certāmen, *n*
struggle, *v.i*, luctor (1 *dep*), nĭtor (3 *dep*)
strumpet, mĕrĕtrix, *f*
strut, *v.i*, incēdo (3)
stubble, stĭpŭla, *f*
stubborn, pertĭnax
stucco, tectōrĭum, *n*
stud, clāvus, *m*; (horses), ĕquārĭa, *f*
stud, *v.t*, insĕro (3)
student, *use adj*, stŭdĭōsus (devoted to), *with a suitable noun*
studied, mĕdĭtātus
studious, stŭdĭosus
study, *nn*, stŭdĭum, *n*; (room, library), bĭblĭŏthēca, *f*
study, *v.t*, stŭdĕo (2) (*with dat*)
stuff (material), mātĕrĭa, *f*; (woven-), textĭle, *n*
stuff, *v.t*, farcĭo (4)
stuffing, *nn*, fartum, *n*
stumble, *nn*, (fall), lapsus, *m*
stumble, *v.i*, offendo (3)
stumbling-block, impĕdĭmentum, *n*.
stump (post), stĭpes, *m*
stun, *v.t*, obstŭpĕfăcĭo (3)
stupefaction, stŭpor, *m*
stupefy, *v.t*, obstŭpĕfăcĭo (3)
stupendous, mīrābĭlis
stupid, stŏlĭdus, stultus
stupidity, stultĭtĭa, *f*
stupor, stŭpor, *m*
sturdiness, firmĭtas, *f*
sturdy, firmus, vălĭdus
sturgeon, ăcĭpenser, *m*
stutter, *v.i*, balbūtĭo (4)
sty, hăra, *f*; (in the eye), hordĕŏlus, *m*
style, gĕnus, *n*
style, *v.t* (name), appello (1)
stylish, spĕcĭōsus
suave, suāvis

subaltern, subcentŭrĭo, *m*
subdivide, *v.t,* dīvĭdo (3)
subdue, *v.t,* sŭbĭcĭo (3)
subject, *adj,* subiectus
subject, *nn,* (**of a state, etc**), cīvis, *c*; (**matter**), rēs, *f*
subject, *v.t,* sŭbĭcĭo (3)
subjection (**slavery**), servĭtus, *f*
subjoin, *v.t,* subiungo (3)
subjugate, *v.t,* sŭbĭgo (3)
sublime, ēlātus
sublimity, ēlātĭo, *f*
submerge, *v.t,* submergo (3)
submission (**compliance**), obsĕquĭum, *n*
submissive, ŏbēdĭens
submit, *v.t,* sŭbĭcĭo (3); (**present**), rĕfĕro (*irreg*); *v.i,* (**yield**), cēdo (3)
subordinate, *adj,* subiectus
subordination (**obedience**), obsĕquĭum, *n*
subscribe, *v.t,* (**give money, etc.**), confĕro (*irreg*); (**signature**), subscrĭbo (3)
subscription (**of money, etc.**), collātĭo, *f*
subsequent, sēquens
subsequently, *adv,* postēā
subservient, obsēquens
subside, *v.i,* rĕsīdo (3)
subsidize, *v.t,* pĕcūnĭam suppĕdĭto (1), (**furnish with money**)
subsidy, subsīdĭum, *n*
subsist, *v.i,* consto (1)
subsistence, victus, *m*
substance (**essence**), nātūra, *f*; (**being**), rēs, *f*; (**goods**), bŏna, *n.pl*
substantial (**real**), vērus; (**important**), grăvis
substitute, *nn,* vĭcārĭus, *m*
substitute, *v.t,* suppōno (3)
subterfuge, lātēbra, *f*
subterranean, subterrānĕus
subtle (**crafty**), astūtus; (**refined**), subtĭlis
subtlety (**craftiness**), astūtĭa, *f*; (**fineness**), subtĭlĭtas, *f*
subtract, *v.t,* dēdūco (3)
subtraction, dētractĭo, *f*
suburb, sŭburbĭum, *n*
suburban, sŭburbānus
subvert, *v.t,* ēverto (3)
succeed, *v.t,* (**in, do well**), bĕnĕ effĭcĭo (3); (**of things**), *v.i,* prospĕrē ēvĕnĭo (4); *v.t,* (**follow**), sēquor (3 *dep*); (**to an office**), succēdo (3)
success, res sēcundae, *f.pl*
successful (**persons**), fēlix; (**things**), prospĕrus
succession (**to an office, etc.**), successĭo, *f*; (**series**), continŭātĭo, *f*
successive, contĭnŭus
successor, successor, *m*
succinct, brĕvis
succour, *nn,* auxĭlĭum, *n*
succour, *v.t,* succurro (3) (*with dat*)
succulent, sūcōsus
succumb, *v.i,* cēdo (3)
such, *adj,* tālis, hūius mŏdi (**of this kind**)
suck, *v.t,* sūgo (3)
sucker, planta, *f*
suckle, *v.t,* ūbĕra do (1) (*with dat*)
suction, suctus, *m*
sudden, sŭbĭtus
suddenly, *adv,* sŭbĭto, rĕpentē
sue, *v.t,* (**in law**), in ius vŏco (1); (**— for, beg for**), rŏgo (1)
suet, sēbum, *n*
suffer, *v.t,* pătĭor (3 *dep*), fĕro (*irreg*); (**permit**), permitto (3) (*with dat*); *v.i,* affĭcĭor (3 pass)
sufferance, pătĭentĭa, *f*
sufferer (**of illness**), aeger, *m*
suffering, *nn,* dŏlor, *m*
suffice, *v.i,* sātis esse (*irreg*)
sufficiency, *use adv,* sātis (**enough**)
sufficient, *use* sātis, *adv,* (*with genit. of noun*)
suffocate, *v.t,* suffōco (1)
suffrage, suffrāgĭum, *n*
sugar, sacchăron, *n*
suggest, *v.t,* sŭbĭcĭo (3) (*with acc. of thing and dat. of person*)
suggestion, admŏnĭtus, *m*
suicide, mors vŏluntārĭa, *f*; (**to commit —**), sĭbĭ mortem conscisco (3) (**inflict death upon oneself**)
suit (**law —**), līs, *f*; (**clothes**), vestīmenta, *n.pl*
suit, *v.i,* convĕnĭo (4); *or use impers. vb,* dĕcet (**it —s**)
suitable, aptus, īdōnĕus
suite (**retinue**), cŏmĭtes, *c, pl*
suitor, prŏcus, *m*
sulky, mōrōsus
sullen, torvus
sully, *v.t,* inquĭno (1)
sulphur, sulfur, *n*
sultry, aestŭōsus
sum (**total**), summa, *f*; (**— of money**), pĕcūnĭa, *f*
sum up, *v.t,* compŭto (1); (**speak briefly**), summātim dĭco (3)
summarily, *adv,* (**immediately**), sīne mŏrā
summary, *nn,* ĕpĭtŏme, *f*
summary, *adj,* (**hasty**), sŭbĭtus
summer, *nn,* aestas, *f*; *adj,* aestīvus
summit, căcūmen, *n, or use adj,* summus (**top of**)

summon, *v.t,* arcesso (3)
summon up, *v.t,* excĭto (1)
summons, vŏcātĭo, *f,* accĭtu (*abl. case only:* **at the — of**)
sumptuous, sumptŭōsus
sumptuousness, appărātus, *m*
sun, sōl, *m*
sun, *v.i,* (— **oneself**), ăprĭcor (1 *dep*)
sunbeam, rădĭus, (*m*) sōlis
sunburnt, ădustus
sundial, sōlārĭum, *n*
sunny, aprĭcus
sunrise, ortus, (*m*) sōlis
sunset, occāsus, (*m*) sōlis
sunshine, sōl, *m*
sup, *v.i,* cēno (1)
superabound, *v.i,* sŭpersum (*irreg*)
superb, magnĭfĭcus
supercilious, sŭperbus
superficial, lĕvis
superfluous, sŭpervăcāněus
superhuman, divīnus
superintend, *v.t,* prōcūro (1)
superintendent, cūrātor, *m,* praefectus, *m*
superior, sŭpĕrĭor; (**to be —**), *v.i,* sŭpĕro (1)
superiority, *use adj,* sŭpĕrĭor
superlative, exĭmĭus
supernatural, dīvīnus
supernumerary, ascriptīvus
superscription, tĭtŭlus, *m*
supersede, *v.t,* succēdo (3) (*with dat*)
superstition, sŭperstĭtĭo, *f*
superstitious, sŭperstĭtĭōsus
supervise, *v.t,* prōcūro (1)
supper, cēna, *f*
supplant, *v.t.* (**surpass**), praeverto (3)
supple, flexĭbĭlis
supplement, supplēmentum, *n*
suppliant, supplex, *c*
supplication, obsēcrātĭo, *f*
supply, *nn,* cōpĭa, *f*; (**supplies, esp. military**), commĕātus, *m*
supply, *v.t,* suppĕdĭto (1); affĕro (*irreg*)
support, *nn,* (**bearing**), firmāmentum, *n*; (**military**), subsĭdĭa, *n.pl*; (**sustenance**), ălĭmentum, *n*
support, *v.t,* sustĭněo (2); (**aid**), adiūvo (1); (**nourish**), ălo (3)
supportable, tŏlĕrābĭlis
supporter, adiūtor, *m*
suppose, *v.t,* pŭto (1), ŏpĭnor (1 *pass*)
supposition, ŏpĭnĭo, *f*
suppress, *v.t,* opprĭmo (3)
suppurate, *v.i,* suppūro (1)
supremacy, impĕrĭum, *n*
supreme, sŭprēmus
sure, certus; (**reliable**), fĭdēlis; (**I am —**), compertum hăbĕo (2)
surely, *adv,* prŏfecto; (**no doubt**), nĭmīrum; (*in questions; if an affirmative answer is expected*) nonne; (*if a negative answer*), num
surety, vas, *m,* sponsor, *m*
surf, fluctus, *m*
surface, sŭperfĭcĭes, *f*
surge, *v.i,* surgo (3)
surgeon, chīrurgus, *m*
surgery, chīrurgĭa, *f*
surly, mōrōsus
surmise, *nn,* coniectūra, *f*
surmise, *v.t,* suspĭcor (1 *dep*)
surmount, *v.t,* sŭpĕro (1)
surname, cognōmen, *n*
surpass, *v.t,* sŭpĕro (1)
surplus, rĕlĭquum, *n*
surprise, *nn,* mīrātĭo, *f*
surprise, *v.t,* admīrātĭōnem mŏvĕo (2) (*with dat*); (**to attack**), ădŏrĭor (4 *dep*)
surrender, *nn,* dēdĭtĭo, *f*
surrender, *v.t,* dēdo (3), trādo (3); *v.i,* sē dēdĕre (3 *reflex*)
surround, *v.t,* cingo (3), circumdo (1)
survey, *v.t,* contemplor (1 *dep*); (**land**), mētĭor (4 *dep*)
surveyor, fīnītor, *m*
survive, *v.i,* sŭpersum (*irreg*)
survivor, sŭperstes, *m, f*
susceptibility, mollĭtĭa, *f*
susceptible, mollis
suspect, *v.t,* suspĭcor (1 *dep*)
suspend, *v.t,* suspendo (3); (**interrupt**), intermitto (3); (**— from office**), dēmŏvĕo (2)
suspense, dŭbĭtātĭo, *f*
suspension (**interruption**), intermissĭo, *f*
suspicion, suspĭcĭo, *f*
suspicious, suspĭcĭōsus
sustain, *v.t,* sustĭněo (2)
sustenance, ălĭmentum, *n*
swaddling-clothes, incūnābŭla, *n.pl*
swagger, *v.i,* sē iactāre (1 *reflex*)
swallow, *nn,* hĭrundo, *f*
swallow, *v.t,* gluttĭo (4), sorbĕo (2)
swamp, *nn,* pălus, *f*
swamp, *v.t,* opprĭmo (3)
swampy, pălŭdōsus
swan, cycnus, *m*
swarm (**people**), turba, *f*; (**bees**), exāmen, *n*
swarm, *v.i,* glŏmĕror (1 *pass*)
swarthy, fuscus
swathe, *v.t,* collĭgo (1)
sway, *nn,* impĕrĭum, *n*
sway, *v.t,* (**rule**), rĕgo (3); *v.i* (**— to and fro**), văcillo (1)

For List of Abbreviations used, turn to pages 3, 4

swear, *v.i,* iūro (1); (— **allegiance to),** iūro in nōmen (*with genit. of person*)
sweat, *nn,* sūdor, *m*
sweat, *v.i,* sūdo (1)
sweep, *v.t,* verro (3)
sweet, dulcis
sweeten, *v.t,* dulcem reddo (3) **(make sweet)**
sweetheart, dēlĭcĭae, *f. pl*
sweetness, dulcĭtūdo, *f*
swell, *nn,* **(wave),** fluctus, *m*
swell, *v.i,* tŭmĕo (2); *v.t,* augĕo (2)
swelling, tŭmor, *m*
swerve, *v.i,* dēclīno (1)
swift, *adj,* cĕler
swiftness, cĕlĕrĭtas, *f*
swill, *v.t,* **(drink),** pōto (1)
swim, *v.i,* nāto (1)
swimmer, nātātor, *m*
swimming, *nn,* nātātĭo, *f*
swindle, *nn,* fraus, *f*
swindle, *v.t,* fraudo (1)
swindler, fraudātor, *m*
swine, sūs, *m, f*
swineherd, sŭbulcus, *m*
swing, *nn,* oscillātĭo, *f*
swing, *v.t,* ăgĭto (1); *v.i,* pendĕo (2)
switch, (cane), virga, *f*
switch, *v.t,* mūto (1)
swollen, tŭmĭdus
swoon, *v.i, use phr,* ănĭmus rĕlinquit . . . **(sensibility leaves . . .)**
swoop, *nn, use vb.* advŏlo (1)
swoop on, *v.i,* advŏlo (1)
sword, glădĭus, *m*
sword-edge, ăcies, *f*
swordfish, xĭphĭas, *m*
sworn (treaty, etc.), confirmātus iūrĕiūrando **(confirmed by swearing)**
sycamore, sȳcămōrus, *f*
sycophant, sȳcŏphanta, *m*
syllable, syllăba, *f*
symbol, signum, *n*
symmetrical, congrŭens
symmetry, convĕnĭentĭa, *f*
sympathetic, mĭsĕrĭcors
sympathize, *v.t,* consentĭo (4)
sympathy, consensus, *m*
symphony, symphōnĭa, *f*
symptom, signum, *n*
synagogue, sȳnăgōga, *f*
syndicate, sŏcĭĕtas, *f*
synonym, verbum īdem signĭfĭcans **(word expressing the same thing)**
synopsis, ĕpĭtŏma, *f*
syntax, syntaxis, *f*
syringe, sīpho, *m*
syringe, *v.t,* aspergo (3) **(sprinkle)**
system, formŭla, *f,* rătĭo, *f*
systematic, ordĭnātus

T

table, mensa, *f,* tăbŭla, *f;* **(list),** index, *m*
tablecloth, mantēle, *n*
tablet, tăbŭla, *f*
tacit, tăcĭtus
taciturn, tăcĭturnus
tack, clāvŭlus, *m*
tack, *v.t,* **(fix),** fīgo (3); *v.i,*(**ships),** rĕcĭprŏcor (1 *pass*)
tackle (fittings), armāmenta, *n.pl*
tact, dextĕrĭtas, *f,* urbānĭtas, *f*
tactician, pĕrĭtus, (*m*) rĕi mĭlĭtāris
tactics (military), rătĭo, (*f*) bellandi **(method of making war)**
tadpole, rānuncŭlus, *m*
tag, *v.t, use* fīgo (3) **(fix)**
tail, cauda, *f*
tailor, vestĭtor, *m*
taint, *nn,* contāgĭo, *f*
taint, *v.t,* infĭcĭo (3)
take, *v.t,* căpĭo (3); **(grasp),** prĕhendo (3); **(receive),** accĭpĭo (3); **(seize),** răpĭo (3); **(take possession of),** occŭpo (1); (— **by storm),** expugno (1); (— **away),** aufĕro (*irreg*) ădĭmo (3); (— **in),** excĭpĭc (3); (— **off),** dēmo (3); (— **on),** suscĭpĭo (3); (— **up),** sūmo (3)
taking (capture of a city), expugnātĭo, *f*
tale, fābŭla, *f*
talent (ability), ingĕnĭum, *n;* **(money),** tălentum, *n*
talk, *nn,* sermo, *m*
talk, *v.i,* lŏquor (3 *dep*)
talkative, lŏquax
tall, prōcērus
tallness, prōcērĭtas, *f*
tallow, sēbum, *n*
tally, *v.i,* convĕnĭo (4)
talon, unguis, *m*
tamable, dŏmābĭlis
tame, *v.t,* dŏmo (1), mansŭēfăcĭo (3)
tame, *adj,* mansŭēfactus, dŏmĭtus
tameness, mansŭētūdo, *f*
tamer, dŏmĭtor, *m*
tamper with, *v.t,* tempto (1)
tan, *v.t,* **(leather, etc.),** confĭcĭo (3)
tangent, *use* lĭnĕa, *f,* **(line)**
tangible, tractābĭlis
tangle, *nn,* implĭcātĭo, *f*

tangle, *v.t,* implĭco (1)
tank, lăcus, *m*
tanner, cŏrĭărĭus, *m*
tantalize, *v.t,* **(torment),** fătīgo (1)
tap, *nn,* (blow), ictus, *m*
tap, *v.t,* (hit), fĕrĭo (4), pulso (1); *with* lĕvĭter **(lightly)**
tape, taenĭa, *f*
taper, cērĕus, *m*
taper, *v.i,* fastīgor (1 *pass*)
tapestry, *use* vēlum, *n,* **(curtain)**
tar, pix lĭquĭda, *f*
tardiness, tardĭtas, *f*
tardy, tardus
tare, lŏlĭum, *n*
target, scŏpus, *m*
tarnish, *v.i,* hĕbesco (3); *v.t,* inquĭno (1)
tarry, *v.i,* mŏror (1 *dep*)
tart, *nn,* crustŭlum, *n*
tart, *adj,* ăcĭdus
task, ŏpus, *n*
taste, *nn,* **(sense of —),** gustātus, *m*; **(flavour),** săpor, *m*; **(judgement),** iŭdĭcĭum, *n*
taste, *v.t,* gusto (1); *v.i* **(have a flavour),** săpĭo (3)
tasteful (elegant), ēlĕgans
tasteless, insulsus
tasty, săpĭdus
tattered, pannōsus
tatters, pannus, *m*
tattle, *v.i,* garrĭo (4)
taunt, *nn,* convĭcĭum, *n*
taunt, *v.t,* ŏbĭcĭo (3) (*dat. of person and acc. of thing*)
taunting, *adj,* contŭmēlĭōsus
tavern, caupōna, *f*
tavern-keeper, caupo, *m*
tawdry, fūcōsus
tawny, fulvus
tax, *nn,* vectīgal, *n*
tax, *v.t,* **(impose —),** vectīgal impōno (3) (*with dat*)
taxable, vectīgālis
tax-collector, exactor, *m,* pūblĭcānus, *m*
teach, *v.t,* dŏcĕo (2) (*with acc. of person and acc. of thing*)
teacher, doctor, *m,* măgister, *m*
teaching, *nn,* doctrīna, *f*
team (— of horses), iŭgum, *n*
tear, *nn,* lăcrĭma, *f*; **(to shed —s),** lăcrĭmas fundo (3); **(rent),** scissūra, *f*
tear, *v.t,* scindo (3); **(— away),** abscindo (3); **(— down, open),** rēscindo (3); **(— up, in pieces),** distrăho (3)
tearful, flēbĭlis
tease, *v.t,* obtundo (3)
teat, mamma, *f*
technical, *use phr,* prŏprĭus artis **(particular to a skill)**
tedious, lentus
teem with, *v.i,* scătĕo (2)
teethe, *v.i,* dentĭo (4)
teething, *nn,* dentĭtĭo, *f*
tell, *v.t,* **(give information),** dĭco (3); narro (1) (*with acc. of thing said and dat. of person told*), certiŏrem făcĭo (3) (*acc. of person told, foll. by* dē *with abl. of thing said*); **(order),** iŭbĕo (2)
teller (counter), nŭmĕrātor, *m*
temerity, tĕmĕrĭtas, *f*
temper (of mind), ănĭmus, *m*; **(bad —),** īrācundĭa, *f*
temper, *v.t,* tempĕro (1)
temperament, nātūra, *f,* ingĕnĭum, *n*
temperance, tempĕrantĭa, *f*
temperate, tempĕrātus
temperate climate, tĕmpĕrĭes, *f*
temperateness, mŏdĕrātĭo, *f*
tempest, tempestas, *f*
tempestuous, prŏcellōsus
temple, templum, *n,* aedes, *f*; **(of the head),** tempus, *n*
temporal, hūmānus
temporary, *use adv. phr,* ad tempus **(for the time being)**.
tempt, *v.t,* tento (1)
temptation (allurement), illĕcĕbra, *f*
tempter, tentātor, *m*
tempting, *adj,* illĕcĕbrōsus
ten, dĕcem; (— **each),** dēni; (— **times),** *adv,* dĕcies
tenacious, tĕnax
tenacity, tĕnācĭtas, *f*
tenant, inquĭlīnus, *m*
tend, *v.t,* **(care for),** cŏlo (3); *v.i,* **(go, direct oneself),** tendo (3); **(incline to),** inclĭno (1); **(be accustomed),** consŭesco (3)
tendency, inclĭnātĭo, *f*
tender, *adj,* tĕner, mollis
tender, *v.t,* **(offer),** dĕfĕro (*irreg*)
tenderness, mollĭtĭa, *f,* indulgentĭa, *f*
tenement, conductum, *n*
tenour (course), tĕnor, *m,* cursus, *m*
tense, *adj,* tentus, intentus
tense, *nn,* tempus, *n*
tension, intentĭo, *f*
tent, tăbernācŭlum, *n*; **(general's —),** praetōrĭum, *n*
tentacle, cornĭcŭlum, *n*
tenth, dĕcĭmus
tepid, ēgĕlĭdus, tĕpĭdus; **(to be —),** *v.i,* tĕpĕo (2)

term (period of time), spătĭum, *n*; **(limit)**, fĭnis, *m*; **(word)**, verbum, *n*; **(condition)**, condĭcĭo, *f*
term, *v.t*, vŏco (1)
terminate, *v.t*, termĭno (1)
termination, fĭnis, *m*
terrace, sōlārĭum, *n*
terrestrial, terrestris
terrible, terrĭbĭlis
terrify, *v.t*, terrĕo (2)
territory, fĭnes, *m. pl*, ăger, *m*
terror, terror, *m*, păvor, *m*
terse, brĕvis
terseness, brĕvĭtas, *f*
test, *nn*, expĕrĭmentum, *n*
test, *v.t*, expĕrĭor (4 *dep*)
testament, testāmentum, *n*
testator, testātor, *m*
testify, *v.t*, testĭfĭcor (1 *dep*)
testimony, testĭmōnĭum, *n*
testy, stŏmăchōsus
text, scriptum, *n*
textile, textĭle, *n*
texture, textus, *m*
than, *conj*, quam
thank, *v.t*, grātĭas ăgo (3) (*with dat. of person*)
thankfulness, grātus ănĭmus, *m*
thankless, ingrātus
thanks, grātĭae, *f. pl*
thanksgiving, actĭo, (*f*) grātĭārum
that, *demonstrative pron*, ille, is, iste
that, *relative pron*, qui, quae, quod
that, *conj*, (*with purpose or consecutive clauses*) ut (ne *if negative*); (*after vbs introducing statements*) *no separate word, but rendered by the expression itself: e.g.* **he said that the king was coming**, rēgem vĕnīre dixit
thatch, strāmentum, *n*
thaw, *v.t*, solvo (3); *v.i*, sē rĕsolvĕre (3 *reflex*)
the, *no equivalent in Latin*
theatre, thĕātrum, *n*
theatrical, thĕātrālis
theft, furtum, *n*
their, *reflexive*, sŭus; *otherwise* ĕōrum, (*f*, ĕārum)
them, *use appropriate case of pron*, is, ille, iste
theme, prōpŏsĭtĭo, *f*
themselves, *reflexive pron*, sē; **(emphatic)**, ipsi, ae, a
then, *adv. of* **(time)**, tum **(therefore)**, ĭgĭtur
thence, *adv*, inde, illinc
theologian, thĕŏlŏgus, *m*
theology, thĕŏlŏgĭa, *f*
theorem, thĕōrēma, *n*
theoretical, rătĭōnālis
theory, rătĭo, *f*
there (in *or* at that place), ĭbĭ; **(to that place)**, ĕō; **(— is)**, est; **(— are)**, sunt (*from* esse)
thereabouts, *adv*, circā
thereafter, *adv*, dĕinde
therefore, *adv*, ĭgĭtur, ergo
thereupon, *adv*, sŭbinde
thesis, prōpŏsĭtum, *n*
they, *as subject of vb. usually not rendered*; *otherwise use* ĭi, illi, isti.
thick, crassus, densus, confertus
thicken, *v.t*, denso (1); *v.i*, concresco (3)
thicket, dūmētum, *n*
thick-headed, crassus
thickness, crassĭtūdo, *f*
thick-set (of body), compactus
thick-skinned, (indifferent), neglĕgens
thief, fur, *c*
thieve, *v.t*, fūror (1 *dep*)
thieving, *nn*, **(theft)**, furtum, *n*
thigh, fĕmur, *n*
thin, tĕnŭis, grăcĭlis
thin, *v.t*, tĕnŭo (1)
thing, rēs, *f*
think, *v.t*, cōgĭto (1); **(believe, suppose)**, crēdo (3), arbĭtror (1 *dep*), pŭto (1), existĭmo (1)
thinker, phĭlŏsŏphus, *m*
thinness, tĕnŭĭtas, *f*
third, *adj*, tertĭus; **(a — part)**, tertĭa pars, *f*; **(thirdly)**, *adv*, tertĭo
thirst, *v.i*, sĭtĭo (4)
thirst, *nn*, sĭtis, *f*
thirsty, sĭtĭens
thirteen, trĕdĕcim
thirteenth, tertĭus dĕcĭmus
thirtieth, trīgēsĭmus
thirty, trīginta
this, *demonstrative pron*, hīc, haec, hōc
thistle, cardŭus, *m*
thither, *adv*, ĕō, illūc; **(hither and —)**, hūc atque illūc
thong, lōrum, *n*
thorn, sentis, *m*, spīna, *f*
thorn-bush, vĕpres, *m*
thorny, spīnōsus
thorough, perfectus; **(exact)**, subtĭlis
thoroughbred, gĕnĕrōsus
thoroughfare, pervĭum, *n*
those, *demonstrative pron*, illi
though, *conj*, etsi
thought (act or faculty of thinking), cōgĭtātĭo, *f*; **(opinion)**, cōgĭtātum, *n*; **(plan, intention)**, consĭlĭum, *n*
thoughtful (careful), prōvĭdus; **(deep in thought)**, multa pŭtans

thoughtfulness, cūra, *f*, cōgĭtātĭo, *f*
thoughtless, tĕmĕrārĭus, inconsultus
thoughtlessness, nĕglegentĭa, *f*, tĕmĕrĭtas, *f*
thousand, mille (*indeclinable adj*); *in pl*, mīlĭa (*n.pl, nn*)
thrash, *v.t*, tundo (3); **(corn),** tĕro (3)
thrashing, *nn*, trĭtūra, *f*; **(chastisement),** verbĕrātĭo, *f*
thrashing-floor, ārĕa, *f*
thread, fīlum, *n*
thread, *v.t*, **(— one's way),** sē insĭnŭāre (1 *reflex*)
threadbare, obsŏlētus
threat, mĭnae, *f. pl*
threaten, *v.t*, mĭnor (1 *dep*) (*with acc. of thing and dat. of person*); *v.i*, **(impend),** immĭnĕo (2)
threatening, *adj*, mĭnax
three, tres; **(— each),** terni; **(— times),** *adv*, ter
threefold (triple), trĭplex
threehundred, trĕcenti
threehundredth, trĕcentensĭmus
thresh, *v.t*, tĕro (3)
threshold, līmen, *n*
thrice, *adj*, ter
thrift, frūgālĭtas, *f*
thrifty, parcus
thrill, *v.t, use* affĭcĭo (3) **(affect)**
thrill (of pleasure), hĭlārĭtas, *f*; **(a shock),** stringor, *m*
thrilling, *adj, use vb*, affĭcĭo (3) **(to affect)**
thrive, *v.i*, vĭgĕo (2)
throat, fauces, *f. pl*
throb, *v.i*, palpĭto (1)
throbbing, *nn*, palpĭtātĭo, *f*
throne, sŏlĭum, *n*; **(regal, imperial power),** regnum, *n*
throng, *nn*, multĭtūdo, *f*
throng, *v.t*, cĕlĕbro (1)
throttle, *v.t*, strangŭlo (1)
through, *prep*, per (*with acc*); **(on account of),** propter (*with acc*)
through, *adv, often expressed by a compound vb, with* per: **e.g.** perfĕro **(carry through)**
throughout, *prep*, per; *adv*, pĕnĭtus **(entirely, wholly)**
throw, *nn*, iactus, *m*
throw, *v.t*, iăcio **(3),** cōnĭcĭo (3) **(— away),** ăbĭcĭo (3); **(— back),** rĕĭcĭo (3); **(— down),** dĕĭcĭo (3); **(— oneself at the feet of),** se prōĭcĕre ad pĕdes (*with genit. of person*); **(— out),** ēĭcĭo (3)
thrush, turdus, *m*
thrust, *nn*, pĕtĭtĭo, *f*
thrust, *v.t*, trūdo (3); **(— forward),** prōtrūdo (3)
thumb, pollex, *m*
thump, *nn*, cŏlăphus, *m*
thump, *v.t*, tundo (3)
thunder, *nn*, tŏnĭtrus, *m*; **(— bolt),** fulmen, *n*
thunder, *v.i*, tŏno (1)
thunderstruck, attŏnĭtus
thus, *adv*, ĭta, sīc
thwart, *nn*, **(seat),** transtrum, *n*
thwart, *v.t*, obsto (1) (*with dat. of person*), impĕdĭo (4)
tiara, tĭāra, *f*
ticket, tessĕra, *f*
tickle, *v.t*, tĭtillo (1)
tickling, *nn*, tĭtillātĭo, *f*
ticklish, lūbrĭcus
tide, aestus, *m*
tidiness, mundĭtĭa, *f*
tidings, nuntĭus, *m*
tidy, mundus
tie, *nn*, vincŭlum, *n*
tie, *v.t*, lĭgo (1), nōdo (1)
tier, ordo, *m*
tiger, tigris, *c*
tight, strictus
tighten, *v.t*, stringo (3)
tile, tĕgŭla, *f*
till, *prep*, usque ad (*with acc*)
till, *conj*, dum, dōnĕc
till, *nn*, arca, *f*
till, *v.t*, cŏlo (3)
tillage, tilling, *nn*, cultus, *m*
tiller (boat), clāvus, (*m*) gŭbernācŭli **(handle of the rudder)**
tilt, *v.t*, **(bend),** dēclĭno (1)
timber, mātĕrĭa, *f*
time, tempus, *n*; **(period, space of —),** intervallum, *n*, spătĭum, *n*; **(generation, age),** aetas, *f*; **(— of day),** hōra, *f*; **(at the right —),** *adv. phr*, ad tempus; **(at —s),** *adv*, interdum; **(once upon a —),** *adv*, ŏlim; **(at the same —),** *adv*, sĭmŭl; **(at that —),** *adv*, tum
timely, *adj*, opportūnus
timid, tĭmĭdus
timidity, tĭmĭdĭtas, *f*
tin, plumbum album, *n*
tincture, cŏlor, *m*
tinder, fōmes, *m*
tinge, *v.t*, tingo (3)
tingle, *v.i*, prūrĭo (4)
tinker, făber, *m*, **(artificer)**
tinkle, *v.i*, tinnĭo (4)
tiny, exĭgŭus, parvŭlus
tip, căcūmen, *n*
tip, *v.t*, **(put a point on),** praefĭgo (3); **(tip over),** verto (3)

For List of Abbreviations used, turn to pages 3, 4

tire, *v.t*, fătīgo (1); *v.i*, dēfătīgor (1 *dep*)
tired, fessus
tiresome, mŏlestus
tissue, textus, *m*
tit-bits, cūpēdĭa, *n.pl*
tithe, dĕcūma, *f*
title, tĭtŭlus, *m*
titled (of nobility), nōbĭlis
titter, *nn*, rīsus, *m*
to, *prep*, (*motion towards a place, and expressions of time*), ad (*with acc*); (*sometimes, e.g. names of towns, acc. of nn. alone*); *often dat. case can be used, e.g. indirect object after vb. to give;* (*before a clause expressing purpose*), ut; (*sometimes indicates the infinitive of a vb*), *e.g.* **to love**, ămāre
toad, būfo, *m*
toast, *v.t*, torrĕo (2); (**a person's health**), prŏpīno (1) (*with dat. of person*)
today, *adv*, hŏdĭē
toe, dĭgĭtus, *m*
together, *adv*, sĭmŭl, ūnā
toil, *nn*, lăbor, *m*
toil, *v.i*, lăbōro (1)
toilet (care of person, etc.), cultus, *m*
token, signum, *n*
tolerable, tŏlĕrābĭlis
tolerance, tŏlĕrantĭa, *f*
tolerate, *v.t*, tŏlĕro (1)
toll, *nn*, vectīgal, *n*
tomb, sĕpulcrum, *n*, tŭmŭlus, *m*
tombstone, lăpis, *m*
tomorrow, *adv*, crās
tomorrow, *nn*, crastĭnus dĭes, *m*
tone, sŏnus, *m*
tongs, forceps, *m*
tongue, lingua, *f*
tonight, *adv*, hŏdĭē nocte
tonsils, tonsillae, *f. pl*
too (also), ĕtĭam; (— **little**), părum; (— **much**), nĭmis; *comparative adj. or adv. can be used, e.g.* **too far**, longĭus
tool, instrūmentum, *n*
tooth, dens, *m*
toothache, dŏlor (*m*) dentĭum
toothed, dentātus
toothless, ēdentŭlus
toothpick, dentiscalpĭum, *n*
top, *use adj*, summus *in agreement with nn, e.g.* **the top of the rock**, summum saxum, *n*; (**summit**), căcūmen, *n*
top, *v.t*, sŭpĕro (1)
topic, rēs, *f*
topmost, summus
topography, *use phr*, nătūra (*f*) lŏci (**nature of the land**)
torch, fax, *f*
torment, *nn*, crŭcĭātus, *m*
torment, *v.t*, crŭcĭo (1)
tornado, turbo, *m*
torpid, torpens, pĭger
torpor, torpor, *m*
torrent, torrens, *m*
tortoise, testūdo, *f*
tortuous, sĭnŭōsus
torture, *nn*, crŭcĭātus, *m*
torture, *v.t*, crŭcĭo (1)
torturer, carnĭfex, *m*
toss, *nn*, iactus, *m*
toss, *v.t*, iacto (1)
total, *nn*, summa, *f*
total, *adj*, tōtus
totally, *adv*, omnĭno
totter, *v.i*, lăbo (1)
touch, *nn*, tactus, *m*; (**contact**), contāgĭo, *f*
touch, *v.t*, tango (3), attingo (3); (**move**), mŏvĕo (2)
touchy, stŏmăchōsus
tough, *adj*, lentus
toughness, dūrĭtĭa, *f*
tour, pĕrĕgrīnātĭo, *f*, ĭter, *n*
tourist, pĕrĕgrīnātor, *m*
tournament, *use* certāmen, *n*, (**contest**)
tow, *v.t*, trăho (3)
tow, *nn*, (**hemp**), stuppa, *f*
towards, *prep*, (**of direction, position**) ad (*with acc*); (**of time**), sub (*with acc*); (**emotions**), ergā, in (*with acc*); (**with names of towns**), versus (*placed after the noun*)
towel, mantēle, *n*
tower, *nn*, turris, *f*
tower, *v.i*, exsto (1)
town, urbs, *f*, oppĭdum, *n*
townsman, oppĭdānus, *m*
toy (child's rattle), crĕpundĭa, *n.pl*
toy with, *v.i*, illūdo (3)
trace, *nn*, vestīgĭum, *n*, signum, *n*
trace, *v.t*, sĕquendo invĕnĭo (4) (**find by following**)
track, *nn*, (**path**), callis, *m*; (**footsteps, etc.**), vestīgĭum, *n*
track, *v.t* (— **down**), investīgo (1); (**pursue**), sĕquor (3 *dep*)
trackless, āvĭus
tract (region), rĕgĭo, *f*; (**booklet**), lĭbellus, *m*
tractable, dŏcĭlis

trade, mercātūra, *f*; **(a particular —),** ars, *f*
trade, *v.i*, mercātūram făcĭo (3)
trader, mercātor, *m*
tradition, mĕmŏrĭa, *f*
traditional, *use phr*, trādĭtus ā māiōrĭbus **(handed down from our ancestors)**
traffic (trade, etc.), commercĭum, *n*; **(streets, etc.),** *use phr. with* frĕquento (1) **(to crowd)**
tragedy, trăgoedĭa, *f*
tragic, trăgĭcus; **(unhappy),** tristis
trail (path), callis, *m*
train, ordo, *m*; **(procession),** pompa, *f. pl*; **(of a dress),** pēnĭcŭlāmentum, *n*
train, *v.t*, instĭtŭo (3), exercĕo (2)
trainer, exercĭtor, *m*
training, *nn*, disciplĭna, *f*
traitor, prōdĭtor, *m*
traitorous, perfĭdus
tramp, *v.i*, ambŭlo (1)
trample on, *v.t*, obtĕro (3)
trance (elation, exaltation), ēlātĭo, *f*
tranquil, tranquillus, plăcĭdus
transact, *v.t*, ăgo (3)
transaction, rēs, *f*, nĕgōtĭum, *n*
transcend, *v.t*, sŭpĕro (1)
transcribe, *v.t*, transcrĭbo (3)
transfer, *nn*, **(of property),** mancĭpĭum, *n*
transfer, *v.t*, transfĕro (*irreg*)
transfix, *v.t*, transfĭgo (3)
transform, *v.t*, mūto (1)
transgress, *v.t*, vĭŏlo (1); *v.i*, pecco (1)
transgression (fault), dēlictum, *n*
transit, transĭtus, *m*
transitory, cădūcus
translate, *v.t*, verto (3)
translation (a work), ŏpus translātum, *n*; **(act),** translātĭo, *f*
translator, interpres, *c*
transmigrate, *v.i*, transmĭgro (1)
transmit, *v.t*, transmitto (3)
transparent, perlūcĭdus
transpire, *v.i*. **(get about),** vulgor (1 *pass*)
transplant, *v.t*, transfĕro (*irreg*)
transport, *nn*, *use vb. below*; **(joy),** laetĭtĭa, *f*, exsultātĭo, *f*
transport, *v.t*, transporto (1), trāĭcĭo (3)
trap, *nn*, insĭdĭae, *f. pl*; **(for animals),** lăquĕus, *m*
trap, *v.t*, *use phr*, illĭcĭo (3) in insĭdĭas **(entice into a trap)**
trappings, insignĭa, *n.pl*
trash, scrūta, *n.pl*, nūgae, *f. pl*
travel, *nn*, ĭter, *n*
travel, *v.i*, ĭter făcĭo (3)
traveller, vĭātor, *m*
traverse, *v.t*, ŏbĕo (4)
travesty (mockery), lūdĭbrĭum, *n*
tray, fercŭlum, *n*
treacherous, perfĭdus
treachery, perfĭdĭa, *f*, fraus, *f*
tread, *nn*, grădus, *m*
tread, *v.i*, ingrĕdĭor (3 *dep*); *v.t* **(— on),** calco (1)
treason, māiestas, *f*
treasure, ŏpes *f. pl*; **(hoard, treasure-house),** thēsaurus, *m*
treasure, *v.t*, **(regard highly),** magni aestĭmo (1); **(store up),** rĕcondo (3)
treasurer, praefectus, (*m*) aerārĭi **(director of the treasury)**
treasury, aerārĭum, *n*
treat, *nn*, dēlectātĭo, *f*
treat, *v.t*, **(deal with, behave towards),** hăbĕo (2); **(medically),** cūro (1); **(discuss),** ăgo (3)
treatise, lĭber, *m*
treatment, tractātĭo, *f*; **(cure),** cūrātĭo, *f*
treaty, foedus, *n*
treble, *adj*, trĭplex
treble, *v.t*, trĭplĭco (1)
tree, arbor, *f*
trellis, cancelli, *m. pl*
tremble, *v.i*, trĕmo (3)
trembling, *nn*, trĕmor, *m*
tremendous, ingens
tremulous, trĕmŭlus
trench, fossa, *f*
trepidation, trĕpĭdātĭo, *f*
trespass (crime), dēlictum, *n*
trespass, *v.i*, *use phr. with* ingrĕdi **(to enter),** *and* te (me, *etc.*), invĭto **(without your (my) permission)**
tress (hair), grādus, *m*
trial (legal), iūdĭcĭum, *n*; **(experiment),** expĕrĭentĭa, *f*
triangle, trĭangŭlum, *n*
triangular, trĭangŭlus
tribe (Roman), trĭbus, *f*; **(other),** pŏpŭlus, *m*
tribunal, iūdĭcĭum, *n*
tribune, trĭbūnus, *m*
tributary, *adj*, **(paying tribute),** vectīgālis
tributary, *nn*, **(river),** *use phr*, qui in flūmen inflŭit **(which flows into a river)**
tribute, trĭbūtum, *n*, vectīgal, *n*
trick, *nn*, dŏlus, *m*, fraus, *f*
trick, *v.t*, dĕcĭpĭo (3)
trickery, dŏlus, *m*
trickle, *v.i*, mano (1)
trickster, hŏmo dŏlōsus, fallax
tricky (dangerous), pĕrĭcŭlōsus
trident, trĭdens, *m*

tried (well —), prŏbātus
trifle, *nn*, rēs parva, *f*, nūgae, *f. pl*
trifle, *v.i*, lūdo (3)
trifling, *adj*, lĕvis
trim, *adj*, nĭtĭdus
trim, *v.t*, pŭto (1)
trinkets, mundus, *m*
trip, *nn*, (journey), ĭter, *n*
trip, *v.t*, supplanto (1); *v.i* (stumble), offendo (3), lābor (3 dep)
tripe, ŏmāsum, *n*
triple, trĭplex
tripod, trĭpūs, *m*
trite, trītus
triumph (Roman celebration of victory), trĭumphus, *m*; (victory), victōrĭa, *f*
triumph, *v.i, and v.t*, trĭumpho (1)
triumphant, victor
triumvirate, trĭumvĭrātus, *m*
trivial, lĕvis, vīlis
troop (band), mănus, *f*; (— of cavalry), turma, *f*; (—s), cōpĭae, *f, pl*
troop, *v.i*, conflŭo (3)
trooper, ĕques, *m*
trophy, trŏpaeum, *n*
trot, *nn*, lentus cursus, *m*
trot, *v.i*, lento cursu ĕo (4); (proceed on a slow course)
trouble, *nn*, (disadvantage), incommŏdum, *n*; (exertion), ŏpĕra, *f*; (commotion), tŭmultus, *m*; (annoyance), mŏlestĭa, *f*
trouble, *v.t*, (disturb), sollĭcĭto (1); (harass), vexo (1); (— oneself about), cūro (1)
troublesome, mŏlestus
trough, alvĕus, *m*
trousers, brācae, *f. pl*
trowel, trulla, *f*
truant, *nn, use phr*, qui consultō ăbest (who is absent deliberately)
truce, indūtĭae, *f. pl*
truck, plaustrum, *n*
truculent (grim), trux
trudge, *v.i, use phr*, aegrē ambŭlo (1) (walk with difficulty)
true, vērus; (faithful), fĭdus
truffle, tūber, *n*
truly, *adv*, vērē, prŏfectō
trumpery, scrūta, *n.pl*
trumpet, *nn*, tŭba, *f*, būcĭna, *f*
trumpeter, tŭbĭcen, *m*
truncheon, fustis, *m*
trundle, *v.t*, volvo (3)
trunk, truncus, *m*; (of elephant) prŏboscis, *f*; (box), arca, *f*
truss, fascĭa, *f*
trust, *nn*, fĭdes, *f*
trust, *v.t*, confĭdo (3 *semi-dep*) (*with dat. of person*), crēdo (3); (commit to), commĭtto (3)
trustworthy, trusty certus, fĭdus
truth, vērĭtas, *f*; (true things), vēra, *n.pl*; (in —), *adv*, vēro
truthful, vērax
truthfulness, vērĭtas, *f*
try, *v.i*, (attempt), cōnor (1 *dep*); *v.t*, (put to the test), tento (1); (— in court), iūdĭco (1)
trying, *adj*, mŏlestus
tub, lābrum, *n*
tube, tŭbŭlus, *m*
tuber, tūber, *n*
tubular, tŭbŭlātus
tuck up, *v.t*, succingo (3)
tuft, crīnis, *m*
tug, *v.t*, trăho (3)
tuition, instĭtūtĭo, *f*
tumble, *nn*, cāsus, *m*
tumble, *v.i*, cădo (3)
tumbler (beaker), pōcŭlum, *n*
tumour, tŭmor, *m*
tumult, tŭmultus, *m*
tumultuous, tŭmultŭōsus
tun (cask), dōlĭum, *n*
tune (melody), cantus, *m*; (out of —), *adj*, absōnus
tune, *v.t*, (stringed instrument), tendo (3)
tuneful, cănōrus
tunic, tūnĭca, *f*
tunnel, cănālis, *m*, cūnĭcŭlus, *m*
tunny fish, thunnus, *m*
turban, mĭtra, *f*
turbid, turbĭdus
turbot, rhombus, *m*
turbulence, tŭmultus, *m*
turbulent, turbŭlentus
turf, caespes, *m*
turgid, turgĭdus
turmoil, turba, *f*, tŭmultus, *m*
turn (movement), conversĭo, *f*; (bending), flexus, *m*; (change), commūtātĭo, *f*; (by —s, in —), *adv*, invĭcem, per vĭces; (a good —), offĭcĭum, *n*
turn, *v.t*, verto (3); (bend), flecto (3); (— aside), dēflecto (3); *v.i*, sē dēclīnāre (1 *reflex*); (— away), āverto (3); (— the back), *v.i*, tergum verto (3); (change), *v.i*, mūtor (1 *pass*); (— back), *v.i*, rĕvertor (3 *pass*); (— out), *v.t*, ĕĭcĭo (3); *v.i*, ĕvĕnĭo (4); (— round), *v.t*, circumăgo (3); *v.i*, circumăgor (3 *pass*)
turning, *nn*, flexus, *m*
turnip, rāpum, *n*

turpitude, turpĭtūdo, *f*
turret, turris, *f*
turtle-dove, turtur, *m*
tusk, dens, *m*
tutelage, tūtēla, *f*
tutor, măgister, *m*
twang, *nn*, sŏnĭtus, *m*
twang, *v.i*, sŏno (1)
tweak, *v.t*, vellĭco (1)
tweezers, volsella, *f*
twelfth, dŭŏdĕcĭmus
twelve, dŭŏdĕcim; (— **each**), duodeni
twentieth, vĭcēsĭmus
twenty, vīginti
twice, *adj*, bis
twig, rāmŭlus, *m*
twilight, crĕpuscŭlum, *n*
twin, *nn and adj*, gĕmĭnus
twine, *nn*, līnum, *n*
twine, *v.t*, circumplĭco (1); *v.i*, circumplector (3 *dep*)
twinge, *nn*, dŏlor, *m*
twinkle, *v.i*, mĭco (1)
twirl, *v.t*, verso (1)
twist, *v.t*, torquĕo (2); *v.i*, sē torquēre (2 *reflex*)
twit, *v.t*, ōbĭcĭo(3) (*acc. of thing and dat, of person*)
twitch, *v.t*, vellĭco (1)
twitter, *v.i*, (**chirp**), pīpĭlo (1)
two, dŭŏ; (— **each**), bĭni
two-fold, dŭplex
two-footed, bĭpes
two hundred, dŭcenti
type (**class, sort**), gĕnus, *n*; (**example**), exemplar, *n*
typical, *use adj*, ūsĭtātus (**familiar**)
tyrannical, tȳrannĭcus, sŭperbus
tyrannize, *v.i*, dŏmĭnor (1 *dep*)
tyranny, dŏmĭnātĭo, *f*
tyrant, tȳrannus, *m*

U

ubiquitous, praesens (**present**)
udder, ūber, *n*
ugliness, dĕformĭtas, *f*
ugly, dĕformis
ulcer, vŏmĭca, *f*
ulcerate, *v.i*, suppūro (1)
ulceration, ulcĕrātĭo, *f*
ulcerous, ulcĕrōsus
ulterior, ultĕrĭor
ultimate, ultĭmus
ultimatum (**to present** —) ultĭmam condĭcĭōnem ferre (*irreg*)
umbrage (**to take — at**), *v.t*, aegrē fĕro (*irreg*)
umbrella, umbella, *f*
umpire, arbĭter, *m*
un-, *prefix, often* nōn, haud, *can be used*
unabashed, intrĕpĭdus; (**brazen**), impŭdens
unabated, immĭnūtus
unable, *use vb. phr. with* non posse (**to be unable**)
unacceptable, ingrātus
unaccompanied, incŏmĭtātus
unaccomplished, infectus
unaccountable, inexplĭcābĭlis
unaccustomed, insŏlĭtus
unacquainted, ignārus
unadorned, īnornātus
unadulterated, sincērus
unadvisable (**foolhardy**), audax
unadvised, inconsīdĕrātus
unaffected (**natural**), simplex; (**untouched**), intĕger
unaided, *use adv. phr*, sĭne auxĭlĭo (**without help**)
unalloyed, pūrus
unalterable, immūtābĭlis
unambitious, hŭmĭlis,
unanimity, ūnănĭmĭtas, *f*
unanimous, ūnĭversus (**all together**)
unanimously, *adv*, ūnā vōce
unanswerable, non rĕvincendus
unanswered, *use vb.* rēsponděo (2) (**to answer**)
unappeased, implācātus
unapproachable, nōn ăděundus
unarmed, īnermis
unassailable, īnexpugnābĭlis
unassailed, intactus
unassuming, mŏdestus
unattainable, *use phr. with vb.* attĭngo (3) (**to reach**)
unattempted, īnexpertus
unauthorized, illĭcĭtus
unavailing, fūtĭlis
unavoidable, īnēvĭtābĭlis
unaware, inscĭus
unawares, *adv*, dē imprōvĭso
unbar, *v.t*, rĕsĕro (1)
unbearable, intŏlĕrābĭlis
unbecoming, indĕcōrus
unbelieving, incrēdŭlus
unbend, *v.t*, rĕmitto (3)
unbending, rĭgĭdus
unbiassed, intĕger
unbidden, iniussus
unbind, *v.t*, solvo (3)
unblemished, pūrus
unbound, sŏlūtus
unbounded, infīnĭtus
unbreakable, *use phr*, quod frangi non pŏtest (**that cannot be broken**)
unbridled, effrēnātus
unbroken, intĕger, perpĕtŭus

For List of Abbreviations used, turn to pages 3, 4

unbuckle, *v.t,* diffĭbŭlo (1)
unburden, *v.t,* exŏnĕro (1)
unburied, ĭnhŭmātus
uncared for, neglectus
unceasing, perpĕtŭus
uncertain, incertus, dŭbĭus; **(to be —),** *v.i,* dŭbĭto (1)
uncertainty, dŭbĭtātĭo, *f*
unchangeable, immūtābĭlis
unchanged, constans; **(to remain —),** *v.i,* permănĕo (2)
uncharitable, inhūmānus
uncivil, ĭnurbānus
uncivilized, incultus
uncle (father's side), pătrŭus, *m*; **(mother's side),** ăvuncŭlus, *m*
unclean, inquĭnātus
unclouded, sērēnus
uncoil, *v.t,* ēvolvo (3); *v.i,* se ēvolvĕre (3 *reflex*)
uncombed, incomptus
uncomfortable, mŏlestus
uncommon, rārus, insŏlĭtus
uncompleted, imperfectus
unconcerned, sēcūrus
unconditional, simplex; **(to surrender -ly),** mănus do (1)
uncongenial, ingrātus
unconnected, disiunctus
unconquerable, invictus
unconquered, invictus
unconscious (unaware), insciŭs; **(insensible),** *use phr,* sensu ablāto **(with feeling withdrawn)**
unconstitutional, non lēgĭtĭmus
uncontaminated, incontāmĭnātus
uncontested, *use phr,* quod in contentĭōnem non vēnit **(that has not come into dispute)**
uncontrollable, impŏtens
uncontrolled, lĭber
uncooked, incoctus
uncouth, incultus
uncover, *v.t,* dētĕgo (3)
unction, unctĭo, *f*
uncultivated, incultus; **(person),** ăgrestis
uncut (hair), intonsus, prōmissus
undamaged, intĕger
undaunted, fortis
undeceive, *v.t,* errōrem ērĭpĭo (3)
undecided, incertus; **(of a battle),** anceps
undefended, nūdus, indēfensus
undeniable, certus
under, *prep,* sub (*with abl. to denote rest, and acc. to denote motion*); infra (*with acc*); **(— the leadership of),** *use abl. phr, e.g.* tē dŭce **(— your leadership)**
underclothes, sŭbŭcŭla, *f*
under-current, flŭentum subterlăbens, *n*
underestimate, *v.t,* mĭnōris aestĭmo (1)
undergo, *v.t,* sŭbĕo (3), fĕro (*irreg*)
underground, *adj,* subterrānĕus
undergrowth, virgulta, *n.pl*
underhand, *adj,* clandestīnus
underlying (lying hidden), lătens
undermine, *v.t,* subrŭo (3)
undermost, *adj,* infĭmus
underneath, *adv,* infrā
underrate, *v.t,* mĭnōris aestĭmo (1)
understand, *v.t,* intellĕgo (3), comprĕhendo (3)
understanding, *nn,* mens, *f*; **(agreement),** conventum, *n*
undertake, *v.t,* suscĭpĭo (3); **(put in hand),** incĭpĭo (3)
undertaker, vespillo, *m*
undertaking, *nn,* inceptum, *n*
undervalue, *v.t,* mĭnōris aestĭmo (1)
undeserved, imměrĭtus
undeserving, indignus
undesirable, *use phr. with* nōn *and* cŭpĭo (3) *or* expĕto (3) **(to desire)**
undetected, tectus
undeveloped, immātūrus
undigested, crūdus
undiminished, immĭnūtus
undisciplined, inexercĭtātus
undisguised, non dissĭmŭlātus
undistinguished, ignōbĭlis
undisturbed, stăbĭlis, immōtus
undo, *v.t,* solvo (3); **(render ineffectual),** irrĭtum făcĭo (3)
undone, infectus
undoubted, certus
undoubtedly, *adv,* sĭne dŭbĭo
undress, *v.t,* vestem dētrăho (3) (*with dat. of person*)
undressed, *adj,* nūdus
undue, nĭmĭus
undulate, *v.i,* fluctŭo (1)
unduly, *adv,* (excessively), nĭmĭum
undying, immortālis
unearth, *v.t,* dētĕgo (3)
unearthly, *adv, use* terrĭbĭlis **(frightful)**
uneasiness, anxiĕtas, *f*
uneasy, anxĭus
uneducated, indoctus
unemployed, ōtĭōsus
unending, aeternus, infĭnĭtus
unenterprising, ĭners, ĭnaudax
unequal, impar, ĭnīquus
unequalled, singŭlāris

unequivocal, non dŭbĭus
unerring, certus
uneven, īnaequālis; **(of ground),** īnīquus
unevenness, īnīquĭtas, *f*
unexampled, īnaudītus, ūnĭcus
unexpected, īnŏpīnātus
unexpectedly, *adv*, ex (*or* dē) imprōvīso
unexplored, īnexplōrātus
unfailing, pĕrennis
unfair, īnīquus, īniustus
unfairness, īnīquĭtas, *f*
unfaithful, infĭdēlis, perfĭdus
unfaithfulness, infĭdēlĭtas,
unfamiliar, insŭētus
unfashionable, *use phr. with* extrā consŭētūdĭnem **(outside of custom)**
unfasten, *v.t*, solvo (3), rēfīgo (3)
unfathomable, infīnĭtus
unfavourable, īnīquus; **(omen),** sĭnister, infēlix
unfeeling, dūrus
unfeigned, sincērus, simplex
unfinished, imperfectus; **(task)** infectus
unfit, incommŏdus
unfitness, īnūtĭlĭtas, *f*
unfitting, indĕcōrus
unfix, *v.t*, rēfīgo (3)
unfold, *v.t*, explĭco (1)
unforseen, imprōvīsus
unforgiving, implācābĭlis
unforgotten, *use phr. with* mĕmor, *adj*, **(remembering)**
unfortified, immūnĭtus
unfortunate, infēlix
unfounded (groundless), vānus
unfriendliness, īnĭmīcĭtĭa,
unfriendly, īnĭmīcus
unfulfilled, irrĭtus, īnānis
unfurl, *v.t*, pando (3)
unfurnished nūdus
ungainly, rūdis
ungentlemanly, illĭbĕrālis
ungodly, incestus
ungovernable, impŏtens, indŏmĭtus
ungraceful, īnēlĕgans
ungrateful, ingrātus
unguarded, incustōdĭtus; **(speech or action),** incautus
unhappiness, mĭsĕrĭa, *f*
unhappy, mĭser, infēlix
unharmed, incŏlūmis
unhealthiness, vălētūdo, *f*; **(of place, etc.),** grăvĭtas, *f*
unheard (of), īnaudītus
unheeded, neglectus
unhesitating, confidens
unhindered, expĕdĭtus
unhoped for, inspērātus
unhorse, *v.t*, ĕquo dēĭcĭo (3) **(throw down from a horse)**
unicorn, mŏnŏcĕros, *m*
uniform, *nn*, **(military —),** hăbĭtus mĭlĭtāris, *m*
uniform, *adj*, aequābĭlis
unimaginable, *use phr*, quod mente concĭpi non pŏtest **(that cannot be conceived in the mind)**
unimpaired, intĕger
unimportant, lĕvis
uninhabitable, īnhăbĭtābĭlis
uninhabited, dēsertus
uninitiated, prŏfānus
uninjured, incŏlūmis
unintelligible, obscūrus
unintentional, non praemĕdĭtātus
uninteresting (flat, insipid), frīgĭdus
uninterrupted, contĭnŭus
uninvited, invŏcātus
union (act of joining), iunctĭo, *f*; **(— of states),** cīvĭtātes foedĕrātae, *f.pl*; **(agreement),** consensus, *m*
unique, ūnĭcus
unit (one), ūnus
unite, *v.t*, coniungo (3), consŏcĭo (1); *v.i*, sē consŏcĭāre (*1 reflex*), sē coniungĕre (*3 reflex*)
united, consŏcĭātus
unity (one), ūnus; **(agreement),** concordĭa, *f*
universal, ūnĭversus
universe, mundus, *m*
university, ăcădēmĭa, *f*
unjust, īniustus
unjustifiable, *use phr*, quod excūsāri non pŏtest **(that cannot be excused)**
unkind, īnhūmānus
unkindness, īnhūmānĭtas, *f*
unknowingly, *adj*. imprūdens
unknown, ignōtus, incognĭtus
unlawful (forbidden), vĕtĭtus
unlearned, indoctus
unless, *conj*, nĭsi
unlettered, indoctus, illittĕrātus
unlike, dissĭmĭlis (*foll. by dat. or genit*)
unlikely, non vēri sĭmĭlis **(not like the truth)**
unlimited, infīnĭtus
unload, *v.t*, exŏnĕro (1); **(goods, etc.),** expōno (3)
unlock, *v.t*, rĕsĕro (1)
unlooked for, īnexpectātus
unloose, *v.t*, solvo (3)
unlucky, infēlix
unmanageable, impŏtens; **(things),** īnhăbĭlis
unmanly, mollis
unmarried, caelebs
unmask, *v.t*, **(plans, etc.),** ăpĕrĭo (4)

unmerciful, immīsĕrĭcors
unmindful, immĕmor
unmistakable, certus
unmitigated, mĕrus
unmolested, intĕger
unmoved, immōtus
unnatural, monstrŭōsus; **(far-fetched)**, arcessītus
unnavigable, innāvĭgābĭlis
unnecessary, non nĕcessārĭus, sŭpervăcāněus
unnoticed, *use vb*, lătĕo (2) **(to lie hidden)**
unnumbered, innŭmĕrābĭlis
unoccupied (at leisure), ōtĭōsus; **(of land)**, ăpertus
unoffending, innŏcens
unopposed (militarily), *use phr*, nullo hoste prŏhĭbente **(with no enemy impeding)**
unpack, *v.t*, exŏněro (1)
unpaid, *use* rĕlĭquus **(remaining)**
unparalleled, ūnĭcus
unpitied, immīsĕrābĭlis
unpleasant, iniūcundus
unpleasantness (trouble), mŏlestĭa, *f*
unpolished, impŏlītus
unpolluted, intactus
unpopular, invĭdĭōsus,
unpopularity, invĭdĭa, *f*
unprecedented, nŏvus
unprejudiced, intĕger
unpremĕditated, sŭbĭtus
unprepared, impărātus
unpretentious, hŭmĭlis
unprincipled (good for nothing), nēquam
unproductive, infēcundus
unprofitable, non quaestŭōsus
unprotected, indēfensus
unprovoked, illăcessītus
unpunished, impūnītus
unqualified, nōn aptus; **(unlimited)**, infīnītus
unquestionable, certus
unravel, *v.t*, rĕtexo (3); **(a problem, etc.)**, explĭco (1)
unreasonable, īnīquus
unrelenting, inexŏrābĭlis
unremitting, assĭdŭus
unreserved, lĭber
unrestrained, effrēnātus
unrewarded, inhŏnōrātus
unrighteous, iniustus
unripe, immātūrus
unrivalled, praestantissĭmus
unroll, *v.t*, ĕvolvo (3)
unruffled, immōtus
unruly, effrēnātus, impŏtens
unsafe, intūtus
unsatisfactory, nōn aptus
unscrupulous (wicked), mălus
unseal, *v.t*, rĕsigno (1)
unseasonable, intempestīvus
unseemly, indĕcōrus
unseen, invīsus
unselfish (persons), innŏcens; **(actions)**, grātŭĭtus
unselfishness, innŏcentĭa, *f*
unserviceable, īnūtĭlis
unsettle, *v.t*, turbo (1)
unsettled, incertus, dŭbĭus
unshaken, immōtus
unshaved, intonsus
unsheath, *v.t*, stringo (3)
unship, *v.t*, expōno (3)
unsightly, foedus
unskilful, impĕrītus
unskilfulness, impĕrītĭa, *f*
unslaked (thirst), nōn explētus
unsociable, diffĭcĭlis
unsophisticated, simplex
unsound (of health or opinions), infirmus; **(of mind)**, insānus
unsoundness, infirmĭtas, *f*, insānĭtas, *f*
unsparing (severe), sĕvērus; **(lavish)**, prōdĭgus; **(effort, etc.)**, non rĕmissus
unspeakable, infandus
unspoiled, intĕger
unstained, pūrus
unsteadiness, mōbĭlĭtas, *f*
unsteady, instăbĭlis, vărĭus
unstring, rĕtendo (3)
unsuccessful, irrĭtus; **(person)**, infaustus
unsuitable, incommŏdus
unsuitableness, incommŏdĭtas, *f*
unsuspected, non suspectus
unsuspecting, incautus
untameable, impŏtens
untamed, indŏmĭtus
untaught, indoctus
unteachable, indŏcĭlis
untenable (position), *use phr*, quod tĕnēri non pŏtest **(that cannot be held)**
unthankful, ingrātus
unthinking (inconsiderate), inconsīdĕrātus
untie, *v.t*, solvo (3)
until, *conj*, dum, dōnec
until, *prep*, ad, (*with acc*)
untilled, incultus
untimely, *adj*, immātūrus
untiring, assĭdŭus
untold (numbers), innŭmĕrābĭlis
untouched, intĕger
untried, inexpertus
untroubled, sēcūrus
untrue, falsus
untruth, mendăcĭum, *n*

unused (**of persons**), insŏlĭtus; (**things**) intĕger
unusual, insŏlĭtus, ĭnūsĭtātus
unutterable, infandus
unveil, *v.t*, dētĕgo (3)
unwarily, *adv*, incautē
unwarlike, imbellis
unwarrantable, ĭnīquus
unwary, incautus
unwavering, constans
unwearied, indēfessus
unwelcome, ingrātus
unwell, aeger
unwholesome, grăvis
unwieldy, ĭnhābĭlis
unwilling, invītus; (**to be —**), *v.i*, nolle (*irreg*)
unwillingly, **unwillingness**, *use adj*, invītus (**unwilling**)
unwind, *v.t*, rĕtexo (3), rĕvolvo (3)
unwise, stultus, imprūdens
unworthiness, indignĭtas, *f*
unworthy, indignus, immĕrĭtus
unwrap, *v.t*, explĭco (1)
unyielding, firmus, inflexĭbĭlis
unyoke, *v.t*, disiungo (3)
up, *prep*, (**— stream or hill**), adversus (*in agreement with noun*); (**— to**), tĕnus (*with abl*)
up, *adv*, sursum; (**— and down**), sursum dĕorsum
upbraid, *v.t*, obiurgo (1)
upbraiding, *nn*, exprŏbrātĭo, *f*
uphill, *adv. phr*, adverso colle
uphold, *v.t*, sustĭnĕo (2)
uplift, *v.t*, tollo (3)
upon, *prep*, sŭper (*with acc*); (**on**), in (*with abl*)
upper, *adj*, sŭpĕrĭor; (**to get the — hand**), sŭpĕrĭor esse (*irreg*)
uppermost, *adj*, summus
upright, rectus; (**of morals**), prŏbus
uprightness, prŏbĭtas, *f*
uproar, clāmor, *m*
uproarious, tūmultŭōsus
uproot, ēvello (3)
upset, *v.t*, ēverto (3)
upset, *adj*, mōtus; (**troubled**), anxĭus
upshot, exĭtus, *m*
upside down, (**to turn —**), *use vb.* verto (3) (**to overturn**) *or* miscĕo (2) (**throw into confusion**)
upstart, nŏvus hŏmo
upwards, *adv*, sursum; (**of number, — of**), amplĭus quam
urbane, urbānus
urbanity, urbānĭtas, *f*
urchin, pūsĭo, *m*
urge, *v.t*, urgĕo (2); (**persuade**), suādĕo (2) (*with dat. of person*)
urgency, grăvĭtas, *f*
urgent, grăvis
urine, ūrīna, *f*
urn, urna, *f*
us, *obj. pron*, nos
usage, mos, *m*
use, ūsus, *m*; (**advantage**), commŏdum, *n*
use, *v.t*, ūtor (3 *dep. with abl*)
useful, ūtĭlis
usefulness, ūtĭlĭtas, *f*
useless, ĭnūtĭlis
uselessness, ĭnūtĭlĭtas, *f*
usher in, *v.t*, intrōdūco (3)
usual, ūsĭtātus, sŏlĭtus
usually, *adv*, plērumque, fĕrē
usurer, fēnĕrātor, *m*
usurious, fēnĕrātōrĭus
usurp, *v.t*, occŭpo (1); (**seize**), răpĭo (3)
usury, fēnĕrātĭo, *f*, ūsūra, *f*
utensils, vāsa, *n.pl*
utilize, *v.t*, ūtor (3 *dep. with abl*)
utility, ūtĭlĭtas, *f*
utmost, extrēmus, summus
utter, *adj*, tōtus
utter, *v.t*, dīco (3)
utterance, dictum, *n*
utterly, *adv*, omnĭno

V

vacancy, (**empty post**), lŏcus văcŭus, *m*
vacant, *adj*, văcŭus, ĭnānis
vacate, *v.t*, rēlinquo (3) (**a post**), ējūro (1)
vacation, fērĭae, *f.pl*
vacillate, *v.i*, văcillo (1)
vacillation, văcillātĭo, *f*
vacuum, ĭnāne, *n*
vagabond, erro, *m*
vagabond, *adj*, văgus
vagary, lĭbīdo, *f*
vagrant, *adj*, văgus
vague, incertus
vagueness, obscūrĭtas, *f*
vain, vānus; (**boastful, etc.**), glōrĭōsus; (**in —**), *adv*, frustrā
vainglorious, glōrĭōsus
vainglory, glōrĭa, *f*
vale, valles, *f*
valet, cŭbĭcŭlārĭus, *m*
valetudinarian, vălētŭdĭnārĭus, *m*
valiant, fortis
valid, firmus, vălĭdus
validity, grăvĭtas, *f*
valise, capsa, *f*
valley, valles, *f*
valorous, fortis

For List of Abbreviations used, turn to pages 3, 4

valour, virtus, *f*
valuable, prĕtĭōsus
valuation, aestĭmātĭo, *f*
value, *nn*, prĕtĭum, *n*
value, *v.t*, aestĭmo (1); **(— highly),** magni dūco (3) **(— little),** parvi dūco
valueless, vīlis
valve, ĕpistŏmĭum, *n*
van (vanguard), prīmum agmen, *n*
vanish, *v.i*, vānesco (3), dīlābor (3 *dep*)
vanity, vānĭtas, *f*, iactātĭo, *f*
vanquish, *v.t*, vinco (3)
vanquisher, victor, *m*
vantage-point, lŏcus sŭpĕrĭor, *m*
vapid, văpĭdus
vapour, văpor, *m*,
variability, mūtābĭlĭtas, *f*
variable, vărĭus, mūtābĭlis
variance, dissensĭo, *f*; **(to be at — with),** dissīdĕo (2) ab (*with abl*)
variation, vărĭētas, *f*
varicose, vărĭcōsus; **(a — vein),** vărix, *c*
variegated, vărĭus
variety, vărĭētas, *f*, dĭversĭtas, *f*
various, vărĭus, dĭversus
varnish, *nn*, ātrāmentum, *n*
vary, *v.i and v.t*, vărĭo (1)
vase, vās, *n*
vassal, clĭens, *m*, *f*
vast, vastus, ingens
vastness, immensĭtas, *f*
vat, cūpa, *f*
vault, fornix, *m*
vault, *v.i*, sălĭo (4)
vaunt, *v.t*, iacto (1); *v.i*, glōrĭor (1 *dep*)
vaunting, *nn*, iactātĭo, *f*
veal, vĭtŭlĭna cărо, *f*, **(calf's flesh)**
veer, *v.i*, sē vertĕre (3 *reflex*)
vegetable, hŏlus, *n*
vehemence, vīs, *f*
vehement, vĕhĕmens, ācer
vehicle, vĕhĭcŭlum, *n*
veil, *v.t*, vēlo (1), tĕgo (3)
veil, *nn*, rīca, *f*; **(bridal —),** flammĕum, *n*; **(disguise),** intĕgŭmentum, *n*
vein, vēna, *f*
velocity, vĕlōcĭtas, *f*
venal, vēnālis
venality, vēnālĭtas, *f*
vendor, vendĭtor, *m*
veneer, *nn*, *use* cortex, *m*, **(bark, shell)**
venerable, vĕnĕrābĭlis
venerate, *v.t*, cŏlo (3), vĕnĕror (1 *dep*)
veneration, cultus, *m*
venereal, vĕnĕrĕus
vengeance, ultĭo, *f*; **(to take —),** ulciscor (3 *dep*)
venial, *use phr*, cui ignosci pŏtest **(that can be pardoned)**
venison, fĕrīna cărо, *f*
venom, vĕnēnum, *n*
venemous, vĕnēnātus
vent, *nn*, spīrāmentum, *n*
vent, *v.t*, **(pour out),** effundo (3)
ventilate, *v.t*, ventĭlo (1); **(discuss, etc.),** *use vb*, prōfĕro (*irreg*) **(to bring out)**
ventilator, spīrāmentum, *n*
ventricle, ventrĭcŭlus, *m*
venture, *nn*, **(undertaking),** rēs, *f*, inceptum, *n*
venture, *v.t*, pĕrĭclĭtor (1 *dep*)
venturous, audax
veracious, vērus
veracity, vērĭtas, *f*
veranda, pŏdĭum, *n*
verb, verbum, *n*
verbal, *nn*, *see adv*, **verbally**
verbally, per verba **(by means of words)**
verbatim, *adv*, tŏtĭdem verbis **(with the same number of words)**
verbose, verbōsus
verdant, vĭrĭdis
verdict (of a person or jury), sententĭa, *f*; **(of a court),** iūdĭcĭum, *n*
verdigris, aerūgo, *f*
verge, *nn*, ōra, *f*, margo, *c*; **(on the — of)** *use phr*. minimum abest quin . . **(it is very little wanting that . . .)**
verge, *v.i*, vergo (3)
verger, appārĭtor, *m*
verification, prŏbātĭo, *f*
verify, *v.t*, prŏbo (1)
veritable, vērus
vermilion, mĭnĭum, *n*
versatile, vărĭus
versatility, ăgĭlĭtas, *f*
verse, versus, *m*
versed in, *adj*, exercĭtātus
versify, *v.i*, versus făcĭo (3)
version, *use vb*, converto (3) **(turn)**
vertebra, vertĕbra, *f*
vertical, rectus
vertigo, vertīgo, *f*
very, *adj*, *use emphatic pron*, ipse
very, *adv*, *use superlative of adj. or adv*, *e.g.* **—beautiful,** pulcherrĭmus; **—quickly,** cĕlerrĭme; *otherwise* maxĭmē, valdē, admŏdum
vessel (receptacle), vās, *n*; **(ship),** nāvis, *f*
vest, tŭnĭca, *f*

vest, *v.t,* **(invest, impart),** do (1)
vestal virgin, vestālis virgo, *f*
vestibule, vestĭbŭlum, *n*
vestige, vestĭgĭum, *n*; **(mark),** nŏta, *f*, indĭcĭum, *n*
vestry, aedĭcŭla, *f*
veteran, *adj*, vĕtĕrānus; **(— soldier),** vĕtĕrānus mīles, *m*
veterinary, vĕtĕrīnārĭus
veto, *nn*, intercessĭo, *f*
veto, *v.i*, intercēdo (3) (*with dat*)
vex, *v.t*, vexo (1), sollĭcĭto (1)
vexation, indignātĭo, *f*, dŏlor, *m*
vexatious, mŏlestus
vial, lăgēna, *f*
viands, cĭbus, *m*
viaticum, vĭātĭcum, *n*
vibrate, *v.i. and v.t*, vĭbro (1)
vibration, ăgĭtātĭo, *f*
vicarious, vĭcārĭus
vice, turpĭtūdo, *f*
viceroy, lēgātus, *m*
vicinity, vĭcīnĭtas, *f*
vicious, vĭtĭōsus; **(fierce),** fĕrus
vicissitude, vĭces, *f. pl*, vĭcissĭtūdo, *f*
victim, hostĭa, *f*, victĭma, *f*
victor, victor, *m*, victrix, *f*
victorious, victor
victory, victōrĭa, *f*
victual, *v.t, use phr*, rem frūmentārĭam prōvĭdĕo (2) **(to look after the supply of provisions)**
victuals, cĭbus, *m*
vie with, *v.i*, certo (1) cum (*with abl*)
view, *nn*, aspectus, *m*, conspectus, *m*; **(opinion),** sententĭa, *f*
view, *v.t*, conspĭcĭo (3); **(consider),** *use* sentĭo (4) **(to feel)**
vigil, pervĭgĭlātĭo, *f*
vigilance, vĭgĭlantĭa, *f*
vigilant, vĭgĭlans
vigorous, impĭger
vigour, vīs, *f*, vĭgor, *m*
vile, turpis
vileness, turpĭtūdo, *f*
vilify, *v.t*, infāmo (1), dētrăho (3)
villa, villa, *f*
village, pāgus, *m*
villager, pāgānus, *m*
villain, hŏmo scĕlĕrātus
villainy, prāvĭtas, *f*, scĕlus, *n*
vindicate, *v.t*, vindĭco (1); **(justify),** purgo (1)
vindication, purgātĭo, *f*
vindictive, *use phr*, ăvĭdus iniūrĭae ulciscendae **(eager to avenge a wrong)**
vine, vītis, *f*
vine-grower, cultor, (*m*) vītis
vinegar, ăcētum, *n*
vineyard, vīnĕa, *f*
vintage, *nn*, vindēmĭa, *f*
vintner, vīnārĭus, *m*
violate, *v.t*, vĭŏlo (1)
violation, vĭŏlātĭo, *f*
violator, vĭŏlātor, *m*
violence, vīs, *f*, vĭŏlentĭa, *f*, impĕtus, *m*
violent, vĭŏlentus, impŏtens
violet, *nn*, vĭŏla, *f*
violet, *adj* **(— colour),** ĭanthĭnus
viper, vīpĕra, *f*; *adj*, vīpĕrīnus
virago, vīrāgo, *f*
virgin, *nn*, virgo, *f*
virgin, *adj*, virgĭnālis
virginity, virgĭnĭtas, *f*
virile, vīrīlis
virtually, *adv* re ipsā
virtue, virtus, *f*, hŏnestas, *f*; **(by — of),** *use abl. case of noun alone, or use* per (*with acc*)
virtuous, hŏnestus
virulent, ăcerbus
viscous, lentus
visible (noticeable), mănifestus; *or use nn.* conspectus, *m*, **(view)**
vision, visus, *m*; **(phantom, apparition),** ĭmāgo, *f*, spĕcĭes, *f*
visionary, vānus
visit, *nn*, **(call),** sălūtātĭo, *f*; **(stay),** commŏrātĭo, *f*
visit, *v.t* vīso (3)
visitor, sălūtātor, *m*, hospes, *m*
visor, buccŭla, *f*
vista, prospectus, *m*
visual, *use phr. with* ŏcŭlus, *m*, **(eye)**
vital, vītālis; **(important),** grăvis
vitality, vīs, *f*, vīvācĭtas, *f*
vitiate, *v.t*, vĭtĭo (1), corrumpo (3)
vitreous, vĭtrĕus
vituperation, vĭtŭpĕrātĭo, *f*
vituperate, *v.t*, vĭtŭpĕro (1)
vivacious, ălăcer
vivacity, ălăcrĭtas, *f*
vivid, vīvus
vivify, *v.t*, ănĭmo (1)
vixen, vulpes, *f*
vocabulary, verba, *n.pl*
vocal, vōcālis
vocation, offĭcĭum, *n*
vociferate, *v.i*, clāmo (1)
vociferous, clāmōsus
vociferously, *adv*, magno clāmōre
vogue, mos, *m*, **(custom)**
voice, vox, *f*
voice, *v.t*, dĭco (3)
void, *nn*, ĭnāne, *n*
void, *adj*, ĭnānis; **(— of),** văcŭus (*with abl*)
volatile, lĕvis

volcano, mons qui ĕructat flammas (**a mountain which emits flames**)
volition, vŏluntas, *f*; (**of his own —**), sŭā sponte
volley (**of javelins**), tēla missa, *n.pl*
volubility, vŏlŭbĭlĭtas, *f*
voluble, vŏlŭbĭlis
volume (**book**), lĭber, *m*; (**of noise**), magnĭtūdo, *f*
voluminous, cōpĭōsus
voluntarily, *adv*, sponte (**of one's own accord**) *with appropriate pron*, mĕā, tŭā, sŭā
voluntary, vŏluntārĭus
volunteer, *nn*, mīles vŏluntārĭus, *m*
volunteer, *v.i*, (**of soldiers**), *use phr*, ultro nōmen dăre (**enlist voluntarily**)
vuluptuous, vŏluptārĭus
voluptuousness, luxŭrĭa, *f*
vomit, *nn*, vŏmĭtĭo, *f*
vomit, *v.i. and v.t*, vŏmo (3)
voracious, ĕdax, vŏrax
voracity, ĕdācĭtas, *f*
vortex, vertex, *m*
vote, suffrāgĭum, *n*, sententĭa, *f*
vote, *v.i*, suffrāgĭum fĕro (*irreg*); (**to — in favour of**), in sententĭam īre (*irreg*) (*with genit*)
voter, suffrāgātor, *m*
voting-tablet (**ballot-paper**), tăbella, *f*
vouch for, *v.t* praesto (1), testor (1 *dep*), testĭfĭcor (1 *dep.*)
voucher (**authority**), auctōrĭtas, *f*
vow, vōtum, *n*; (**promise**), fĭdes, *f*
vow, *v.t.* prōmitto (3), vŏvĕo (2)
vowel, vōcālis littĕra, *f*
voyage, *nn*, nāvĭgātĭo, *f*
voyage, *v.i*, nāvĭgo (1)
voyager, pĕrĕgrīnātor, *m*
vulgar, vulgāris, plēbēius, sordĭdus
vulgarity (**of manner, etc.**), *use phr*, mōres sordĭdi, *m.pl*
vulgarize, *v.t*, pervulgo (1)
vulnerable, ăpertus
vulture, vultur, *m*

W

wadding, *use* lānūgo, *f*, (**woolly down**)
wade, *v.i*, *use phr*, per văda īre (*irreg*) (**to go through the shallows**)
wafer, crustŭlum (**pastry**)
waft, *v.t*, fĕro (*irreg*)
wag, *nn*, (**jester**), iōcŭlātor, *m*
wag, *v.t*, quasso (1)
wage (**war**), *v.t*, gĕro (3) (bellum)
wager, *nn*, sponsĭo, *f*
wager, *v.i*, sponsĭōnem făcĭo (3)
wages, merces, *f*
waggish, făcētus
waggon, plaustrum, *n*
wagtail, mōtăcilla, *f*
wail, wailing, *nn*, plōrātus, *m*, flĕtus, *m*
wail, *v.i*, plōro (1) flĕo (2)
waist, mĕdĭum corpus, *n*
waistcoat, sŭbūcŭla, *f*, (**undergarment**)
wait, *v.i*, mănĕo (2); *v.t*, (**to — for**), exspecto (1); (**serve**), fămŭlor (1 *dep.*); (**— in ambush**), insĭdĭas făcio (3) (*with dat*)
wait, *nn*, mŏra, *f*
waiter, fămŭlus, *m*
waiting, exspectātĭo, *f*, mansĭo, *f*
waive, *v.t*, rĕmitto (3)
wake, *v.t*, excĭto (1); *v.i*, expergiscor (3 *dep.*)
wakeful, vĭgil
wakefulness, vĭgĭlantĭa, *f*, insomnĭa, *f*
walk, *nn*, ambŭlātĭo, *f*; (**gait**), incessus, *m*; (**— of life, occupation**), quaestus, *m*
walk, *v.i*, ambŭlo (1), grădĭor (3 *dep.*), incēdo (3)
walker, pĕdes, *m*
walking, *nn*, ambŭlātĭo, *f*
wall, mūrus, *m*; (**ramparts**), moenĭa, *n.pl*; (**inner —**), pārĭes, *m*
wall, *v.t*, mūnĭo (4) (**fortify**)
wallet, saccŭlus, *m*
wallow, *v.i*, vŏlūtor (1 *pass*)
walnut (**tree and nut**), iūglans, *f*
wan, *adj*, pallĭdus
wand, virga, *f*, cādūcĕus, *m*
wander, *v.i*, erro (1), văgor (1 *dep.*)
wanderer, erro, *m*
wandering, *nn*, error, *m*
wane, *v.i*, dēcresco (3)
want, *nn*, (**lack**), ĭnŏpĭa, *f*, pēnūrĭa, *f*; (**longing for**), dēsīdĕrĭum, *n*; (**failing**), dēfectĭo, *f*; (**in —**), *adj*, ĭnops
want, *v.i*, (**wish**), vŏlo (*irreg*); *v.t*, (**to lack**), cărĕo (2), ĕgĕo (2) (*with abl*); (**long for**), dēsīdĕro (1); (**desire**), cŭpĭo (3)
wanting (**to be —, to fail**), *v.i*, dēsum (*irreg*)
wanton, *adj*, lascīvus, lĭbĭdĭnōsus
wantoness, lascīvĭa, *f*
war, bellum, *n*; (**civil —**), bellum cĭvĭle, *n*; (**in —**), *adv*, bello; (**to make — on**), bellum infĕro (*irreg, with dat*); (**to declare — on**), bellum indĭco (3) (*with dat*); (**to wage —**), bellum gĕro (3)
warble, *v.i*, căno (3)
war-cry, clāmor, *m*
ward, pūpillus, *m*, pūpilla, *f*; (**district**), rĕgĭo, *f*
ward off, *v.t*, arcĕo (2)
warden, cūrātor, *m*

warder, custos, *c*
wardrobe, vestiārĭum, *n*
warehouse, horrĕum, *n*
wares, merx, *f*
warfare, mīlĭtĭa, *f*
warily, *adv*, cautē
wariness, cautĭo, *f*
warlike, *adj*, bellĭcōsus, mīlĭtāris
warm, cālĭdus; **(to be —),** *v.i*, cālĕo (2)
warm, *v.t*, cālĕfăcĭo (3)
warmly (eagerly), *adv*, vĕhementer
warmth, cālor, *m*
warn, *v.t*, mŏnĕo (2)
warning, *nn*, **(act of —),** mŏnĭtĭo, *f*; **(the warning itself),** mŏnĭtum, *n*
warp, *nn*, stāmen, *n*
warp, *v.t*, **(distort, of mind, etc.),** dēprāvo (1)
warrant, *nn*, mandātum, *n*; **(authority),** auctōrĭtas, *f*
warrant, *v.t*, **(guarantee),** firmo (1), praesto (1)
warranty, sātisdătĭo, *f*
warren, lĕpŏrārĭum, *n*
warrior, mīles, *c*, bellātor, *m*
wart, verrūca, *f*
wary, prōvĭdus, prūdens
wash, *v.t*, lăvo (1); *v.i*, lăvor (1 *pass*)
wash, washing, *nn*, lăvātĭo, *f*
wash-basin, āquālis, *c*
wasp, vespa, *f*
waspish, ăcerbus
waste, *nn*, damnum, *n*; **(careless throwing away),** effūsĭo, *f*; **(—land),** vastĭtas, *f*
waste, *adj*, vastus, dēsertus
waste, *v.t*, consūmo (3), perdo (3); **(— time),** tempus tĕro (3); *v.i*, **(— away),** tābesco (3)
wasteful, prŏfūsus
wastefulness, prŏfūsĭo, *f*
watch (a — of the night), vĭgĭlĭa, *f*; **(watching on guard),** excŭbĭae, *f.pl*
watch, *v.t*, **(observe),** specto (1); **(guard),** custōdĭo (4); *v.i*, **(not to sleep),** excŭbo (1)
watchful, vĭgĭlans
watchfulness, vĭgĭlantĭa, *f*
watchman, custos, *m*
watchword, tessĕra, *f*
water, āqua, *f*; **(fresh —),** āqua dulcis, *f*; **(salt —),** āqua salsa, *f*
water, *v.t*, rĭgo (1), irrĭgo (1)
water-carrier, āquārĭus, *m*
water-closet, lātrīna, *f*
waterfall, āqua dēsĭlĭens, *f*, **(water leaping down)**
watering-place, āquātĭo, *f*; **(resort),** āquae, *f.pl*
water-snake, hydrus, *m*
waterworks, āquaeductus, *m*
watery, āquātĭcus
wattle, crātis, *f*
wave, *nn*, unda, *f*, fluctus, *m*
wave, *v.i*, undo (1), fluctŭo (1); *v.t*, ăgĭto (1)
waver, *v.i*, fluctŭo (1) dŭbĭto (1)
wavering, *adj*, dŭbĭus
wavering, *nn*, dŭbĭtātĭo, *f*
wavy (of hair), crispus
wax, *nn*, cēra, *f*; *adj*, cērĕus
wax, *v.i*, cresco (3)
way, vĭa, *f*; **(journey),** ĭter, *n*; **(pathway),** sēmĭta, *f*; **(course),** cursus, *m*; **(manner),** mŏdus, *m*; **(habit),** mos, *m*; **(system),** rătĭo, *f*; **(in the —),** *adj*, obvĭus; **(in this —),** *adv*, ĭta, sīc; **(out of the —),** *adj*, āvĭus; **(to give or to make —),** *v.i*, cēdo (3); **(to get one's own —),** vinco (3)
wayfarer, vĭātor, *m*
waylay, *v.t*, insīdĭor (1 *dep.*) (*with dat*)
wayward, pertĭnax
we, *pron*, nos; *often expressed by* 1*st person plural of vb, e.g.* **we are,** sumus
weak, infirmus, dēbĭlis; **(overcome),** confectus; **(of arguments, etc.),** lĕvis
weaken, *v.t*, infirmo (1), dēbĭlĭto (1); *v.i*, languesco (3), dēfĭcĭo (3)
weak-hearted, pūsilli ănĭmi (**of weak heart**)
weakness, infirmĭtas, *f*, dēbĭlĭtas, *f*, lĕvĭtas, *f*
weal (the common —), bŏnum pūblĭcum, *n*; **(on skin),** vĭbex, *f*
wealth, dīvĭtĭae, *f.pl*, ŏpes, *f.pl*; **(large supply),** cōpĭa, *f*
wealthy, dīves, lŏcŭples
wean, *v.t*, lacte dēpello (3) **(remove from the milk)**
weapon, tēlum, *n*; (*pl*) arma, *n.pl*
wear, *v.t*, **(rub),** tĕro (3); **(— out),** contĕro (3); **(— a garment),** gĕro (3); *v.i*, **(last),** dūro (1)
weariness, lassĭtūdo, *f*
wearisome, lăbōrĭōsus
weary, *adj*, fessus, fătīgātus
weary, *v.t*, fătīgo (1); *v.i*, **(grow —),** dēfătīgor (1 *pass*)
weasel, mustēla, *f*
weather, tempestas, *f*
weather, *v.t*, **(endure, bear),** perfĕro (*irreg*)
weave, *v.t*, texo (3)
weaver, textor, *m*
web, tēla, *f*
wed, *v.t*, **(of the husband),** dūco (3); **(of the wife),** nūbo (3) (*with dat*)

For List of Abbreviations used, turn to pages 3, 4

wedding, *nn,* nuptĭae, *f.pl;* **(— day),** dĭes (*m*) nuptĭārum
wedge, *nn,* cŭnĕus, *m*
wedlock, mātrĭmōnĭum, *n*
weed, *nn,* herba ĭnūtĭlis, *f* **(harmful plant)**
weed, *v.t,* runco (1)
week, *use phr,* spătĭum septem dĭērum **(a space of seven days)**
weep, *v.i,* lăcrĭmo (1)
weeping, *nn,* flĕtus, *m*
weeping-willow, sălix, *f*
weevil, curcŭlĭo, *m*
weigh, *v.t,* pendo (3), penso (1); **(consider),** pondĕro (1); **(— down),** grăvo (1)
weight, pondus, *n*; **(a —),** lĭbrămentum, *n*; **(influence, etc.),** *use adj.* grăvis **(important)**
weightiness, grăvĭtas, *f*
weighty, grăvis
weir (dam), mōles, *f*
welcome, *adj,* grātus, acceptus
welcome, *nn,* sălūtātĭo, *f*
welcome! salve! (*pl.* salvēte!)
welcome, *v.t,* excĭpĭo (3)
weld, *v.t,* ferrūmĭno (1)
welfare, bŏnum, *n,* sălus, *f*
well, *adv,* bĕnĕ; **(very —),** optĭmē
well, *nn,* pŭtĕus, *m*
well, *adj,* **(safe),** salvus; **(healthy),** sānus, vălens; **(to be —),** *v.i,* vălĕo (2)
well-being, *nn,* sălus, *f*
well-born, nōbĭlis
well-disposed, bĕnĕvŏlus
well-favoured, pulcher
well-known, nōtus
well-wisher, *use adj,* bĕnĕvŏlus **(well-disposed)**
welter, *v.i,* vŏlūtor (1 *pass*)
wench, pŭella, *f*
west, *nn,* occĭdens, *m*
west, *adj,* occĭdentālis
westward, *adv,* ad occĭdentem **(sōlem)**
wet, *adj,* hūmĭdus, mădĭdus
wet, *v.t,* mădĕfăcĭo (3)
wether, vervex, *m*
wet-nurse, nūtrix, *f*
whale, bālaena, *f*
wharf, nāvāle, *n*
what, *interrog. pron,* quid? *interrog. adj,* qui, quae, quod; *relative pron,* quod, *pl,* quae; **(— for, wherefore, why),** quārē; **(— sort),** quālis?
whatever, *pron,* quodcumque; *adj,* quĭcumque
wheat, trĭtĭcum, *n*
wheel, rŏta, *f*
wheel, *v.t,* circŭmăgo (3)
wheelbarrow, păbo, *m*
wheeling, *adj,* circumflectens
whelp, *nn,* cătŭlus, *m*
when? *interrog,* quando? (*temporal*), cum (*with vb, in indicative or subjunctive mood*), ŭbĭ (*vb. in indicative*)
whence, *adv,* undĕ
whenever, *adv,* quandōcumque
where? *interrog,* ŭbĭ?; (*relative*), quā; **(— from),** undĕ; **(— to),** quō; **(anywhere, everywhere),** *adv,* ŭbĭque
whereas, *adv,* quŏnĭam
wherever, quācumque
wherefore, *adv,* quārē
whereupon, *use phr,* quo facto **(with which having been done)**
whet, *v.t.* **(sharpen),** ăcŭo (3)
whether, *conj.* (*in a single question*), num, nĕ; (*in a double question,* **whether . . . or),** ŭtrum . . . an; (*in a conditional sentence*), sīve . . . sīve
whetstone, cōs, *f*
whey, sĕrum, *n*
which, *interrog,* quis, quid; (*relative*), qui, quae, quod; **(which of two),** ŭter
while, *conj,* dum (*often foll. by. vb. in present tense indicative*)
while, *nn,* tempus, *n,* spătĭum, *n*; **(for a little —),** *adv,* părumper; **(in a little —),** brĕvi (tempŏre)
while away, *v.t,* fallo (3), tĕro (3)
whim, lĭbīdo, *f*
whimper, *v.i,* vāgĭo (4)
whimsical, rĭdĭcŭlus
whine, *v.i,* vāgĭo (4)
whinny, *v.i,* hinnĭo (4)
whip, *nn,* flăgellum, *n*
whip, *v.t,* verbĕro (1), flăgello (1)
whirl, *v.t,* torquĕo (2); *v.i,* torquĕor (2 *pass*)
whirlpool, *m,* gurges, *m*
whirlwind, turbo, *m*
whirr, *nn,* strĭdor, *m*
whirr, *v.i,* strĭdĕo (2)
whiskers, *use* barba, *f,* **(beard)**
whisper, *nn,* sŭsurrus, *m*
whisper, *v.i,* sŭsurro (1)
whispering, *adj,* sŭsurrus
whistle, whistling, *nn,* sĭbĭlus, *m*
whistle, *v.i,* sĭbĭlo (1)
white, *adj,* albus; **(shining —),** candĭdus
white, *nn,* album, *n*
whiten, *v.t,* dĕalbo (1); *v.i,* albesco (3)
whiteness, candor, *m*

whitewash, *nn,* albārĭum, *n*
white-wash, *v.t,* dĕalbo (1)
whither, (*interrog. and relative*), quo
whiz, *v.i,* strĭdĕo (2)
whiz, whizzing, *nn,* strĭdor, *m*
who, *interrog,* quis? (*relative*), qui, quae
whoever, *pron,* quĭcunque
whole, *adj,* tōtus; **(untouched),** intĕger
whole, *nn,* tōtum, *n,* ūnĭversĭtas, *f, or use adj,* tōtus, *e.g.* **the — of the army,** tōtus exercĭtus, *m.*
wholesale trader, mercātor, *m*
wholesale trading, mercātūra, *f*
wholesome, sălūbris
wholly, *adv,* omnīno
whoop, *nn,* ŭlŭlātus, *m*
whom, *acc. case of rel. pron,* quem, quam; *pl,* quos, quas
whore, mĕrĕtrix, *f*
whose, *genit. case of rel. pron,* cūius; *pl,* quōrum, quārum
why, *adv,* cur, quārē
wick, ellychnĭum, *n*
wicked, scĕlestus, mălus, imprŏbus
wickedness, scĕlus, *n,* imprŏbĭtas, *f*
wicker, vīmĭnĕus
wide, lātus; **(— open),** pătens
widen, *v.t,* dĭlāto (1); *v.i,* sē dĭlātāre (1 *reflex*)
widow, vĭdŭa, *f*
widower, vĭdŭus vir, *m*
widowhood, vĭdŭĭtas, *f*
width, lātĭtūdo, *f*
wield, *v.t,* tracto (1)
wife, uxor, *f*
wig, căpillāmentum, *n*
wild, indŏmĭtus, fĕrus; **(uncultivated),** incultus; **(mad),** āmens
wilderness, dēserta lŏca, *n.pl*
wildness, fĕrĭtas, *f*
wile, dŏlus, *m*
wilful, pervĭcax
wilfully, *adv,* pervĭcācĭter; **(deliberately),** consultō
wilfulness, pervĭcācĭa, *f*
wiliness, callĭdĭtas, *f*
will (desire), vŏluntas, *f*; **(purpose),** consĭlĭum, *n*; **(pleasure),** lĭbīdo, *f*; **(decision, authority),** arbĭtrĭum, *n*; **(legal),** testāmentum, *n*
will, *v.t,* **(bequeath),** lēgo (1)
willing, *adj,* lĭbens
willingly, *adv,* lĭbenter
willingness, vŏluntas, *f*
willow, sălix, *f*
wily, callĭdus, văfer
win, *v.i,* vinco (3); *v.t,* consĕquor (3 *dep*), ădĭpiscor (3 *dep*)
wind, ventus, *m*; **(breeze),** aura, *f*
wind, *v.t,* volvo (3)
winding, *nn,* flexus, *m*
winding, *adj,* flexŭōsus
windlass, sŭcŭla, *f*
window, fĕnestra, *f*
windward, *use phr,* conversus ad ventum **(turned towards the wind)**
windy, ventōsus
wine, vīnum, *n*
wine-cask, dŏlĭum, *n*
wine-cellar, ăpŏthēca, *f*
wine-cup, pōcŭlum, *n*
wine-merchant, vīnārĭus, *m*
wing, āla, *f*; **(of army, etc.),** cornu, *n*
winged, penngĕr
wink, *nn,* nictātĭo, *f*
wink, *v.i,* nictŏ (1); **(overlook),** cōnĭvĕo (2)
winner, victor, *m*
winning, *adj,* **(of manner),** blandus
winnow, *v.t,* ventĭlo (1)
winter, *nn,* hĭems, *f*
winter, *adj,* hĭĕmālis
winter, *v.i,* hĭĕmo (1)
wintry, hĭĕmālis
wipe, *v.t,* tergĕo (2)
wire, fīlum, *n,* **(thread)**
wisdom, săpĭentĭa, *f,* prūdentĭa, *f*
wise, *adj,* săpĭens, prūdens
wisely, *adv,* săpĭenter, prūdenter
wish, *nn,* **(desire),** vŏluntas, *f*; **(the wish itself),** optātum, *n*; **(longing),** dēsiděrĭum, *n*
wish, *v.t,* vŏlo (*irreg*), cŭpĭo (3), opto (1); **(long for),** dēsīdĕro (1)
wishing, *nn,* optātĭo, *f*
wisp, mănĭpŭlus, *m*
wistful, cŭpĭdus **(longing for); (dejected),** tristis
wit, ingĕnĭum, *n*; **(humour),** făcētĭae, *f. pl*; **(out of one's —s),** *adj,* āmens
witch, sāga, *f*
witchcraft, ars măgĭca, *f*
with, *prep,* cum (*with abl, but when denoting the instrument, use abl. case, alone*; **(among, at the house of),** ăpud (*with acc*)
withdraw, *v.i,* cēdo (3), sē rĕcĭpĕre (3 *reflex*); *v.t,* dēdūco (3), rĕmŏvĕo (2)
withdrawal, regressus, *m*
wither, *v.i,* languesco (3); *v.t,* **(parch),** torrĕo (2)
withered, flaccĭdus
withhold, *v.t,* rĕtĭnĕo (2)
within, *adv,* intus
within, *prep,* **(time and space),** intrā (*with acc*); **(time),** *use abl. case alone, e.g.* **within three days,** trĭbus diēbus

without, *prep*, sīne (*with abl*); (**outside of**), extrā (*with acc*); *when* **without** *is followed by a gerund* (*e.g.* **I returned without seeing him**) *use a clause introduced by* nĕque, quīn, ĭta . . . ut: *e.g.* rĕgressus sum, nĕque ĕum vīdi
without, *adv*, extrā
withstand, *v.t*, rĕsisto (3) (*with dat*)
witness, *nn*, (**person**), testis, *c*; (**testimony**), testĭmōnĭum, *n*
witness, *v.t*, testor (1 *dep*), testĭfĭcor (1 *dep*); (**to see**), vīdĕo (2)
witticism, făcētĭae, *f. pl*
witty, făcētus; (**sharp**), salsus
wizard, măgus, *m*
woad, vĭtrum, *n*
woe, dŏlor, *m*, luctus, *m*
woeful, tristis
wolf, lŭpus, *m*
wolfish (**greedy, rapacious**), răpax
woman, fēmĭna, *f*, mŭlĭer, *f*; (**young —**), pŭella, *f*; (**old —**), ănus, *f*
womanish, womanly, mŭlĭĕbris
womb, ŭtĕrus, *m*
wonder, mīrātĭo, *f*; (**a marvel**) mīrăcŭlum, *n*
wonder, *v.i. and v.t*, mīror (1 *dep*)
wonderful, mīrus, mīrābĭlis
wont, wonted, *adj*, sŭētus
wont, *nn*, mos, *m*
woo, *v.t*, pĕto (3), ămo (1)
wood (**material**), mātĕrĭa, *f*; (**forest**), silva, *f*
wood-collector, lignātor, *m*
wooded, sĭlvestris
wooden, ligněus
woodland, silvae, *f. pl*
woodpecker, pīcus, *m*
wooer, prŏcus, *m*
wool, lāna, *f*
woollen, lānĕus
word, verbum, *n*; (**promise**), fĭdes, *f*; (**information**), nuntĭus, *m*; **send word,** *v.t*, nuntĭo (1)
wordy, verbōsus
work, *nn*, ŏpus, *n*; (**labour**), lăbor, *m*
work, *v.i*, ŏpĕror (1 *dep*)
work, *v.t*, exercĕo (2); (**handle, manipulate**), tracto (1); (**bring about**), effĭcio (3)
worker, ŏpĭfex, *c*, ŏpĕrārĭus, *m*
workman, ŏpĭfex, *c*, ŏpĕrārĭus, *m*
workmanship, ars, *f*
workshop, offĭcīna, *f*
world, mundus, *m*, orbis (*m*) terrārum; (**people**), hŏmĭnes, *c. pl*
worldliness, *use phr*, stŭdĭum rērum prŏfānārum (**fondness for common matters**)
worm, vermis, *m*
worm-eaten, vermĭnōsus
worm (**one's way**), *v.i*, sē insĭnŭāre (1 *reflex*)
wormwood, absinthĭum, *n*
worn (**— out**), *adj*, trĭtus; (**as clothes**), gestus
worry, *nn*, anxĭĕtas, *f*
worry, *v.t*, vexo (1); *v.i*, cūrā affĭci (3 *pass*) (**to be affected by worry**)
worse, *adj*, pēior.
worse, *adv*, pēius
worship, *v.t*, vĕnĕror (1 *dep*), cŏlo (3)
worship, *nn*, vĕnĕrātĭo, *f*, cultus, *m*
worshipper, cultor, *m*
worst, *adj*, pessĭmus
worst, *adv*, pessĭmē
worst, *v.t*, vinco (3)
worth, *nn*, (**price**), prĕtĭum, *n*; (**valuation**), aestĭmātĭo, *f*; (**worthiness**), virtus, *f*, dignĭtas, *f*; (**— nothing**), nĭhĭlĭ; (**to be — much**), *v.i*, multum vălĕo (2); (*adj*) dignus
worthiness, dignĭtas, *f*
worthless, vīlis
worthy (*with noun*), dignus (*with abl*); (*with phr*) dignus qui (ut)(*with vb. in subjunctive*); (**man**), prŏbus
wound, *nn*, vulnus, *n*
wound, *v.t*, vulnĕro (1), saucĭo (1)
wounded, vulnĕrātus, saucĭus
wrangle, *v.i*, rixor (1 *dep*)
wrangle, wrangling, *nn*, rixa, *f*
wrap, *v.t*, involvo (3)
wrapper, invŏlūcrum, *n*
wrath, īra, *f*
wrathful, īrātus
wreak vengeance on, *v.t*, ulciscor (3 *dep*)
wreath, *nn*, serta, *n.pl*
wreathe, *v.t*, torquĕo (2)
wreck, *nn*, naufrăgĭum, *n*
wreck, *v.t*, frango (3)
wrecked, naufrăgus
wren, rēgŭlus, *m*
wrench away, wrest, *v.t*, extorquĕo (2)
wrestle, *v.i*, luctor (1 *dep*)
wrestler, luctātor, *m*
wrestling, *nn*, luctātĭo, *f*
wretch, perdĭtus, *m*
wretched, mĭser
wretchedness, mĭsĕrĭa, *f*
wriggle, *v.i*, torquĕor (2 *pass*)
wring, *v.t*, torquĕo (2)
wrinkle, rūga, *f*
wrinkled, rūgōsus
wrist, *use* bracchĭum, *n*, (**forearm**)
writ (**legal —**), mandātum, *n*
write, *v.t*, scrĭbo (3)
writer, scriptor, *m*; (**author**), auctor, *c*
writhe, *v.i*, torquĕor (2 *pass*)

writing, scriptĭo, *f*; (something written), scriptum, *n*, ŏpus, *n*
wrong, *adj*, falsus; (improper, bad), prāvus; (to be —), *v.i*, erro (1)
wrong, *nn*, nĕfas, *n*, peccātum *n*; (a —), iniūrĭa, *f*
wrongly *adv*, (badly), mălĕ; (in error), falso
wrong, *v.t*, fraudo (1), iniūrĭam infĕro (*irreg*) (*with dat*)
wrongful, iniustus
wroth, īrātus
wrought, confectus
wry, distortus

Y

yacht, cĕlox, *f*
yard (measurement), *often* passus, *m*, (five feet approx.) (court —), ārĕa, *f*
yarn (thread), fĭlum, *n*; (story), fābŭla, *f*
yawn, *nn*, oscĭtātĭo, *f*
yawn, *v.i*, oscĭto (1)
year, annus, *m*; (a half —), sēmestre spātĭum, *n*, (space of six months)
yearly, *adj*, (throughout a year), annŭus; (every year), *adv*, quŏtannis
yearn for, *v.t*, dēsīdĕro (1)
yearning, dēsīdĕrĭum, *n*
yeast, fermentum, *n*
yell, clāmor, *m*, ŭlŭlātus, *m*
yell, *v.i*, magnā vōce clāmo (1)
yellow, flāvus
yellowish, subflāvus
yelp, *v.i*, gannĭo (4)
yelping, *nn*, gannĭtus, *m*
yeoman, cŏlōnus, *m*
yes, *adv*, ĭta
yesterday, *adv*, hĕri; *nn*, hesternus dĭes, *m*
yet, *adv*, (nevertheless), tămen; (*with comparatives*) ĕtĭam, *e.g.* yet bigger, ĕtĭam māior; (of time; still), ădhuc
yew, taxus, *f*
yield, *v.i*, cēdo (3) (*with dat*); (surrender), sē dēdĕre (3 *reflex*)
yielding, *nn*, concessĭo, *f*
yielding, *adj*, (soft), mollis
yoke, *nn*, iŭgum, *n*
yoke, *v.t*, iungo (3)
yoked, iŭgālis; (— pair), iŭgum, *n*
yolk, vĭtellus, *m*
yonder, *adv*, illic
yore, *adv*, ōlim (once, in time past)
you, *pron*, *often not expressed*, *e.g.* you come, vĕnis; *pl*, vĕnĭtis; *otherwise use appropriate case of* tu; *pl*, vos
young, *adj*, iŭvĕnis, parvus; (child), infans; (— person), ădŏlescens
young, *nn*, (offspring), partus, *m*
younger, iūnĭor, mĭnor nātu (less in age)
young man, iŭvĕnis, *m*.
youngster, iŭvĕnis, *c*
your, yours (*singular*), tŭus; (*of more than one*), vester
yourself (*emphatic*), *use* ipse *in agreement with pron*; (*reflexive*), te; *pl*, vos
youth (time of —), iŭventus, *f*, ădŏlescentĭa, *f*; (young man), ădŏlescens, iŭvĕnis, *c*; (body of young persons), iŭventus, *f*
youthful, iŭvĕnĭlis

Z

zeal, stŭdĭum, *n*
zealous, stŭdĭōsus
zenith, *use* summus, *adj*, (top of)
zephyr, Zĕphȳrus, *m*, Fāvōnĭus, *m*
zero (nothing), nĭhil
zest, ălăcrĭtas, *f*
zodiac, signĭfer orbis, *m*, (sign-bearing orb)
zone, lŏcus, *m*

LIST OF PROPER NAMES

With Classical equivalents

Adriatic, Mărе Sŭpĕrum, *n*
Aegean, Mărе Aegaeum, *n*
Africa, Afrĭca, ae, *f*
African, *adj*, Afrĭcānus, a, um
Alps, Alpes, ĭum, *f. pl*
Antioch, Antĭŏchĭa, ae, *f*
Anthony, Antōnĭus
Apennines, Mons Apennīnus, *m*
Ardennes, Ardŭenna, ae, *f*
Athens, Athēnae, ārum, *f. pl*
Athenian, *adj*, Athēnĭensis, e
Aventine, Aventīnus, i, *m*
Babylon, Băbȳlōn, ōnis, *f*
Bath, Aquae, (*f. pl*,) Sulis
Belgium, Gallia Belgĭca, *f*
The Belgians, Belgae, *m. pl*
Black Sea, Pontus Euxīnus, *m*
Britain, Brĭtannĭa, ae, *f*
British, *adj*, Brĭtannĭcus, a, um
Caerleon, Isca, ae, *f*
Capri, Caprĕae, ārum, *f. pl*
Cyprus, Cȳprus, i, *f*
Damascus, Dămascus, i, *f*
Danube (lower part), Hister, tri, *m*;
(upper), Dānŭvĭus, ii, *m*
Ebro, Hĭbērus, i, *m*
Egypt, Aegyptus, i, *m*
Egyptian, *adj*., Aegyptĭus
Etna, Aetna, ae, *f*
Europe, Eurōpa, ae, *f*
France, Gallĭa, ae, *f*
Gaul, Gallĭa, ae, *f*
Geneva (Lake —), lacus Lĕmannus, *m*
German, *adj*, Germānus, a, um
Germany, Germānĭa, ae, *f*
Gloucester, Glevum, i, *n*
Greece, Graecĭa, ae, *f*
Greek, *adj*, Graecus, a, um
Helen, Hĕlĕna, ae, *f*
Horace, Hŏrātĭus
Ireland, Hĭbernĭa, *f*
Italy, Itălĭa, ae, *f*
Jerusalem, Hĭĕrŏsŏlȳma, ōrum, *n.pl*
Kent, Cantĭum, i, *n*
Lincoln, Lindum, *n*
Loire, Lĭger, ĕris, *m*
London, Londīnĭum, i, *n*
Lyons, Lugdūnum, i, *n*
Majorca, Bălĭāris Măior, *f*
Malta, Mĕlĭta, ae, *f*
Marseilles, Massĭlĭa, ae, *f*
Messina, Messāna, ae, *f*
Mediterranean, mărе nostrum, *n*
Provence, Prōvincĭa, ae, *f*
Pyrenees, Pȳrēnaei Montes, *m. pl*
Rhine, Rhēnus, i, *m*
Rhodes, Rhŏdos, i, *f*
Rhone, Rhŏdănus, i, *m*
Roman, Rōmānus, a, um,
Rome, Rōma, ae, *f*
Scotland, Călĕdŏnĭa, ae, *f*
Severn, Sabrīna, ae, *f*
Sicily, Sĭcĭlĭa, ae, *f*
Spain, Hispānĭa, ae, *f*
St. Albans, Vĕrŭlāmĭum, i, *n*
Syracuse, Sȳrācūsae, ārum, *f. pl*
Thames, Tămēsis, is, *m*
Tiber, Tĭbĕris, is, *m*
Tuscany, Ĕtrūrĭa, ae, *f*
Isle of Wight, Vectis, is, *f*

Names of the Winds

North, Bŏrĕas, ae, *m*
North-east, Āquĭlo, ōnis, *m*
East, Eurus, i, *m*
South-east, Vulturnus, i, *m*
South, Auster, tri, *m*, Nŏtus, i, *m*
South-west, Afrĭcus, i, *m*
West, Fāvōnĭus, i, *n*
Zĕphȳrus, i, *m*
North-west, Cōrus, i, *m*

CONCISE GRAMMAR

ALPHABET

The Latin alphabet contained twenty-three letters:

A B C D E F G H I K L M N O P Q R S T V X Y Z

Pronunciation

Although there is not complete agreement about the way in which the Romans spoke Latin, this is one method of pronunciation which many people believe to have been used by the Romans.

Vowels

ă (short a) as in "fat"; ā (long a) as in "father".
ĕ (short e) as in "net"; ē (long e) as in "they".
ĭ (short i) as in "pin"; ī (long i) as in "police".
ŏ (short o) as in "not"; ō (long o) as in "note".
ŭ (short u) as "oo" in "wood"; ū (long u) as "oo" in "mood".

Long vowels only are marked in this section. Other vowels are short, unless they are made long by two consonants or *x* immediately following them.

Diphthongs

Two vowels pronounced together to form one sound are called Diphthongs, e.g. ae, au, oe, and are pronounced as follows.

ae, as "ai" in "aisle".
au, as "ow" in "cow".
oe, as "oi" in "oil".

Consonants

These are mostly pronounced as in English, but note:

c is always hard, as in "cat".
g is always hard, as in "get".
i, when it is used as a consonant, is always pronounced as y in "yellow" e.g. *iam*, "yam".
s is always pronounced as in "son".
t is always pronounced as in "top".
v is pronounced as "w" in "wall", e.g. *servi*, pronounced "serwee".
th is pronounced as "t" and *ch* as "k".

NOUNS

Latin is a language of "endings", or, as they are sometimes called "inflections". It is usually by the ending of a noun in Latin that we can tell what its relationship is to the other words in the sentence. Nouns which have the same sets of endings are grouped together in what is known as a Declension. There are five of these in Latin, and each one is distinguished by the way in which the nouns belonging to it form their genitive singular case, e.g.

First Declension—*ae*—insul*ae*
Second Declension—*i*—mur*i*
Third Declension—*is*—reg*is*
Fourth Declension—*us*—exercit*us*
Fifth Declension—*ei*—di*ei*

The genitive is one of the six cases which each noun in Latin has. These are:

Nominative: This is used when the noun is the *subject* of the sentence, e.g. *The sailor* loves the queen.

Vocative: This is the case of the person *addressed*, e.g. *Sailor*, where are you going?

Accusative: This is used whenthe noun is the *object* of the sentence, e.g. The queen loves *the sailor*.

Genitive: This case denotes *possession*, and translates the English word "of", e.g. The dog *of the sailor*, or, *The sailor's* dog.

Dative: This is used when the noun is the *indirect object* of the sentence, and usually translates the English words "to" and "for", e.g. He gives money *to the sailor*.

Ablative: This translates the English words "by", "with", "from", "on", and "in".

These cases have different endings when they are used in the singular and in the plural.

First Declension

Most nouns of the First Declension end in "a" and are feminine, e.g *insula*, f . . . an island.

	Singular	Plural
Nom.	*insula*	*insulae*
Voc.	*insula*	*insulae*
Acc.	*insulam*	*insulās*
Gen.	*insulae*	*insulārum*
Dat.	*insulae*	*insulīs*
Abl.	*insulā*	*insulīs*

Second Declension

Some nouns in this declension are masculine, and end in "*us*" or "*er*", e.g. *mūrus*, m . . . a wall, and *ager*, m . . . a field.

	Singular	Plural	Singular	Plural
Nom.	*mūrus*	*mūrī*	*ager*	*agrī*
Voc.	*mūre*	*mūrī*	*ager*	*agrī*
Acc.	*mūrum*	*mūrōs*	*agrum*	*agrōs*
Gen.	*mūrī*	*mūrōrum*	*agrī*	*agrōrum*
Dat.	*mūrō*	*mūrīs*	*agrō*	*agrīs*
Abl.	*mūrō*	*mūrīs*	*agrō*	*agrīs*

Some nouns in this declension are neuter, and end in "*um*", e.g. *bellum*, n . . . war.

	Singular	Plural
Nom.	*bellum*	*bella*
Voc.	*bellum.*	*bella*
Acc.	*bellum*	*bella*
Gen.	*bellī*	*bellōrum*
Dat.	*bellō*	*bellīs*
Abl.	*bellō*	*bellīs*

Third Declension

In this declension are nouns of all three genders, masculine, feminine, and neuter.

(*a*) Masculine and feminine nouns are usually declined like *rex*, m . . . a king, or *cīvis*, m . . . a citizen.

	Singular	Plural	Singular	Plural
Nom.	*rex*	*rēgēs*	*cīvis*	*cīvēs*
Voc.	*rex*	*rēgēs*	*cīvis*	*cīvēs*
Acc.	*rēgem*	*rēgēs*	*cīvem*	*cīvēs*
Gen.	*rēgis*	*rēgum*	*cīvis*	*cīvium*
Dat.	*rēgī*	*rēgibus*	*cīvī*	*cīvibus*
Abl.	*rēge*	*rēgibus*	*cīve*	*cīvibus*

Parisyllabic nouns (i.e. with the same number of syllables in nominative and genitive singular) e.g. *nāvis* (nom.), *nāvis* (gen.) are declined like *cīvis*, except the following "family" nouns:

pater, m, father	*senex*, m, old man
māter, f, mother	*iuvenis*, m, young man
frāter, m, brother	*canis*, m, dog

These nouns have the same genitive plural ending as *rex*.

Imparisyllabic nouns (i.e. with more syllables in genitive than in the nominative singular case) e.g. *ōrātor* (nom.), *ōrātōris* (gen.) are declined like *rex*, except those which are monosyllabic and whose stem ends in two consonants e.g. *urbs*, *urbis*—city; *mens*, *mentis*—mind.

They have the same genitive plural ending as *cīvis*.

(*b*) Neuter nouns are declined like *mare*, n . . . the sea, or *tempus*, n . . . time.

	Singular	Plural	Singular	Plural
Nom.	*mare*	*maria*	*tempus*	*tempora*
Voc.	*mare*	*maria*	*tempus*	*tempora*
Acc.	*mare*	*maria*	*tempus*	*tempora*
Gen.	*maris*	*marium*	*temporis*	*temporum*
Dat.	*marī*	*maribus*	*temporī*	*temporibus*
Abl.	*marī*	*maribus*	*tempore*	*temporibus*

The nouns whose stems end in *ar*, *al*, *il*, are declined like *mare*, others like *tempus*.

Fourth Declension

In this declension, masculine and feminine nouns end in "*us*", e.g. *exercitus*, m . . . an army, *manus*, f . . . a hand, and neuter nouns in "*u*", e.g. *cornū*, n . . . horn.

	Singular	Plural	Singular	Plural
Nom.	*exercitus*	*exercitūs*	*cornū*	*cornua*
Voc.	*exercitus*	*exercitūs*	*cornū*	*cornua*
Acc.	*exercitum*	*exercitūs*	*cornū*	*cornua*
Gen.	*exercitūs*	*exercituum*	*cornūs*	*cornuum*
Dat.	*exercituī*	*exercitibus*	*cornū*	*cornibus*
Abl.	*exercitū*	*exercitibus*	*cornū*	*cornibus*

Fifth Declension

The nouns in this declension are all declined like *diēs*, m, or f . . . a day, or *rēs*, f . . . a thing.

	Singular	Plural	Singular	Plural
Nom.	*diēs*	*diēs*	*rēs*	*rēs*
Voc.	*diēs*	*diēs*	*rēs*	*rēs*
Acc.	*diem*	*diēs*	*rem*	*rēs*
Gen.	*diēī*	*diērum*	*reī*	*rērum*
Dat.	*diēī*	*diēbus*	*reī*	*rēbus*
Abl.	*diē*	*diēbus*	*rē*	*rēbus*

Irregular Nouns

A few of the commoner nouns which contain irregularities of inflexion are given below:

domus, f . . . house, home; *vīs*, f . . . force; *bos*, c . . . ox; *Iuppiter*, m . . . Juppiter

	Singular	Plural	Singular	Plural
Nom. Voc.	*domus*	*domūs*	*vīs*	*vīrēs*
Acc.	*domum*	*domūs* (*domōs*)	*vim*	*vīrēs*
Gen.	*domūs* (or *domī*)	*domōrum*	—	*vīrium*
Dat.	*domuī* (*domō*)	*domibus*	—	*vīribus*
Abl.	*domū* (*domō*)	*domibus*	*vī*	*vīribus*

	Singular	Plural	Singular
Nom. Voc.	*bos*	*bovēs*	*Iuppiter*
Acc.	*bovem*	*bovēs*	*Iovem*
Gen.	*bovis*	*boum*	*Iovis*
Dat.	*bovī*	*bōbus* (*būbus*)	*Iovī*
Abl.	*bove*	*bōbus* (*būbus*)	*Iove*

ADJECTIVES

In Latin, adjectives, like nouns, have different "endings", or inflections. If an adjective describes a singular masculine noun it has one set of endings, if it describes a singular feminine noun it has another set. All adjectives must agree with the noun they describe in three respects:

(*a*) Number, i.e. Singular or Plural
(*b*) Gender, i.e. Masculine, Feminine or Neuter
(*c*) Case, whichever case the noun is in.

Therefore each adjective must have three different sets of endings, in singular and plural, in order to be able to agree with masculine, feminine, and neuter nouns.

There are two main classes of adjectives in Latin.

Class I

In this class, adjectives have the endings of First and Second Declension nouns and are declined either like *bonus, -a, -um* . . . good; *asper, aspera, asperum* . . . rough; or *āter, ātra, ātrum* . . . black.

	Singular			Plural		
	MASC.	FEM.	NEUT.	MASC.	FEM.	NEUT.
Nom.	*bonus*	*-a*	*-um*	*bonī*	*-ae*	*-a*
Voc.	*bone*	*-a*	*-um*	*bonī*	*-ae*	*-a*
Acc.	*bonum*	*-am*	*-um*	*bonōs*	*-ās*	*-a*
Gen.	*bonī*	*-ae*	*-ī*	*bonōrum*	*-ārum*	*-ōrum*
Dat.	*bonō*	*-ae*	*-ō*	*bonīs*	*-īs*	*-īs*
Abl.	*bonō*	*-ā*	*-ō*	*bonīs*	*-īs*	*-īs*
Nom. Voc.	*asper*	*aspera*	*asperum*	*asperī*	*-ae*	*-a*
Acc.	*asperum*	*-am*	*-um*	*asperōs*	*-ās*	*-a*
Gen.	*asperī*	*-ae*	*-ī*	*asperōrum*	*-ārum*	*-ōrum*
Dat.	*asperō*	*-ae*	*-ō*	*asperīs*	*-īs*	*-īs*
Abl.	*asperō*	*-ā*	*-ō*	*asperīs*	*-īs*	*-īs*
Nom. Voc.	*āter*	*ātra*	*ātrum*	*ātrī*	*-ae*	*-a*
Acc.	*ātrum*	*-am*	*-um*	*ātrōs*	*-ās*	*-a*
Gen.	*ātrī*	*-ae*	*-ī*	*ātrōrum*	*-ārum*	*-ōrum*
Dat.	*ātrō*	*-ae*	*-ō*	*ātrīs*	*-īs*	*-īs*
Abl.	*ātro*	*-ā*	*-ō*	*ātrīs*	*-īs*	*-īs*

Class II

These adjectives are declined like nouns of the Third Declension. If the nominative ends in *is* (*omnis* . . . all), *er* (*ācer* . . . keen), *x* (*fēlix* . . . happy), *ens* (*ingens* . . . huge), they are declined as follows:

	Singular		Plural	
	MASC. AND FEM.	NEUT.	MASC. AND FEM.	NEUT.
Nom. Voc.	*omnis*	*omne*	*omnēs*	*-ia*
Acc.	*omnem*	*-e*	*omnēs*	*-ia*
Gen.	*omnis*	*-is*	*omnium*	*-ium*
Dat.	*omnī*	*-ī*	*omnibus*	*-ibus*
Abl.	*omnī*	*-ī*	*omnibus*	*-ibus*

	MASC.	FEM.	NEUT.	MASC. AND FEM.	NEUT.
Nom. Voc.	*ācer*	*ācris*	*ācre*	*ācrēs*	*-ia*
Acc.	*ācrem*	*-em*	*-e*	*ācrēs*	*-ia*
Gen.	*ācris*	*-is*	*-is*	*ācrium*	*-ium*
Dat.	*ācrī*	*-ī*	*-ī*	*ācribus*	*-ibus*
Abl.	*ācrī*	*-ī*	*-ī*	*ācribus*	*-ibus*

	MASC. AND FEM.	NEUT.	MASC. AND FEM.	NEUT.
Nom. Voc.	*fēlix*	*-ix*	*fēlīcēs*	*-ia*
Acc.	*fēlīcem*	*-ix*	*fēlīcēs*	*-ia*
Gen.	*fēlīcis*	*-is*	*fēlīcium*	*-ium*
Dat.	*fēlīcī*	*-ī*	*fēlīcibus*	*-ibus*
Abl.	*fēlīcī*	*-ī*	*fēlīcibus*	*-ibus*
Nom. Voc.	*ingens*	*-ens*	*ingentēs*	*-ia*
Acc.	*ingentem*	*-ens*	*ingentēs*	*-ia*
Gen.	*ingentis*	*-is*	*ingentium*	*-ium*
Dat.	*ingentī*	*-ī*	*ingentibus*	*-ibus*
Abl.	*ingentī*	*-ī*	*ingentibus*	*-ibus*

Other adjectives of the Class II are declined like *melior* . . . better, or *vetus* . . . old.

	MASC. AND FEM.	NEUT.	MASC. AND FEM.	NEUT.
Nom. Voc.	*melior*	*-ius*	*meliōrēs*	*-a*
Acc.	*meliōrem*	*-ius*	*meliōrēs*	*-a*
Gen.	*meliōris*	*-is*	*meliōrum*	*-um*
Dat.	*meliōrī*	*-ī*	*meliōribus*	*-ibus*
Abl.	*meliōre*	*-e*	*meliōribus*	*-ibus*
Nom. Voc.	*vetus*	*-us*	*veterēs*	*-a*
Acc.	*veterem*	*-us*	*veterēs*	*-a*
Gen.	*veteris*	*-is*	*veterum*	*-um*
Dat.	*veterī*	*-ī*	*veteribus*	*-ibus*
Abl.	*vetere*	*-e*	*veteribus*	*-ibus*

Adjectives with . . . *ius* in the Genitive Singular and . . . *i* in the Dative Singular

There is also a class of adjectives which, from the endings of the nominative singular, one would expect to belong to Class I. They are in fact exactly the same in declension as adjectives of Class I, except in the genitive and dative singular. The genitive has the ending-*ius* in all genders, and the dative—*i*. These adjectives are *sōlus* (alone); *tōtus* (whole); *ūnus* (one); *ullus* (any); *nullus* (not any, no one); *alius* (other, another); *alter* (one of two); *uter?* (which of two?); *neuter* (neither of two).

Singular

	MASC.	FEM.	NEUT.
Nom.	*sōlus*	*-a*	*-um*
Acc.	*sōlum*	*-am*	*-um*
Gen.	*sōlīus*	*-īus*	*-īus*
Dat.	*sōlī*	*-ī*	*-ī*
Abl.	*sōlō*	*-ā*	*-ō*

The plural is quite regular, like *bonus*.

COMPARISON OF ADJECTIVES

In English we talk of one thing being "hard", of another being "harder" and of a third thing being "hardest" of all. These are called different "degrees" of the adjective, the first being called the Positive Degree, the second the Comparative Degree, the third the Superlative Degree. In English we usually form the comparative and superlative by adding -er and -est to the adjective, e.g. harder, hardest. In Latin we add *-ior* and *-issimus* to the *stem* of the adjective. (The stem is the genitive singular without its ending). Thus positive *dūrus*—hard, genitive *dūrī*, gives comparative *dūrior*, (harder) and superlative "*dūrrissimus*", (hardest). Comparative adjectives are declined like *melior* (P. 298) and superlative adjectives like *bonus* (P. 297).

Besides "harder", *durior* can mean "too hard", and besides "hardest", *dūrissimus* can mean "very hard".

N.B. Adjectives which end in *-er* form the superlative by doubling the "*r*" and adding *-imus*, e.g.

asper—asperrimus, niger—nigerrimus
ācer—ācerrimus, celer—celerrimus

Six adjectives form the superlative by doubling the "*l*" and adding *-imus*. They are:

facilis, (easy)—*facillimus* — *difficilis*, (difficult)—*difficillimus*
similis, (like)—*simillimus* — *dissimilis*, (unlike)—*dissimillimus*
gracilis, (slender)—*gracillimus* — *humilis*, (low)—*humillimus*

Irregular Comparisons

bonus, good	*melior*, better	*optimus*, best
malus, bad	*pēior*, worse	*pessimus*, worst
magnus, great	*māior*, greater	*maximus*, greatest
parvus, small	*minor*, smaller	*minimus*, smallest
multus, much	*plūs*, more	*plūrimus*, most
senex, old	*nātū māior*, older	*nātū maximus*, oldest
iuvenis, young	*nātū minor*, younger	*nātū minimus*, youngest

When two things are compared after the comparative one may use *quam* (than), and put the two things in the same case, or omit the *quam* and put the second thing in the ablative case:

Illud est durius quam hoc (nom. sing. neut.). That is harder than this.
Illud est hoc (abl. sing. neut.) *durius*. That is harder than this.

VERBS

In Latin, when the subject of a verb is a pronoun, I, you, he, etc., it is represented by the ending or inflection only. Further, different inflections show differences of tense, e.g. Present, I am loving, *am-ō*; Future, I shall love, *am-ābō*. Verbs which have a similar set of endings are classed together into what is known as a Conjugation. There are four of these in Latin. All verbs, except irregular ones, fall into one of these conjugations, according to the termination of their present infinitive. To love, to advise, to rule, to hear, are present infinitives in English. *Am-āre, mon-ēre, reg-ĕre, aud-īre* are the corresponding infinitives in Latin. So, verbs with infinitives ending in *-āre* belong to the First Conjugation. Verbs with infinitives ending in *-ēre* belong to the Second Conjugation. Verbs with infinitives ending in *-ĕre* belong to the Third Conjugation. Verbs with infinitives ending in *-īre* belong to the Fourth Conjugation.

TABLES OF THE REGULAR VERBS

Active Voice

First Conjugation. Example, *Amō*, I love.
(From Present Stem *Am-*)

INDICATIVE MOOD	SUBJUNCTIVE MOOD
Present	*Present*
Am-ō, I love, I am loving	*Am-em*
Am-ās, you love, you are loving	*Am-ēs*
Am-at, he, she, it loves; he, she, it is loving	*Am-et*
Am-āmus, we love, we are loving	*Am-ēmus*
Am-ātis, you love, you are loving	*Am-ētis*
Am-ant, they love, they are loving	*Am-ent*
Imperfect	*Imperfect*
Am-ābam, I was loving, I used to love	*Am-ārem*
Am-ābās, you were loving, you used to love	*Am-ārēs*
Am-ābat, he, she, it was loving, he, she, it used to love	*Am-āret*
Am-ābāmus, we were loving, we used to love	*Am-ārēmus*
Am-ābātis, you were loving, you used to love	*Am-ārētis*
Am-ābant, they were loving, they used to love	*Am-ārent*
Future	
Am-ābō, I shall love	Present Participle
Am-ābis, you will love	*Am-ans*, loving
Am-ābit, he, she, it will love	Present Infinitive
Am-ābimus, we shall love	*Am-āre*, to love
Am-ābitis, you will love	Gerund
Am-ābunt, they will love	*Am-andum-ī*, loving (noun)

IMPERATIVE MOOD

Am-ā, love thou	*Am-āte*, love ye	*Am-ātō*, thou shalt love
Am-ātōte, ye shall love	*Am-ātō*, he shall love	*Am-antō*, they shall love

(From Perfect Stem *Amāv-*)

INDICATIVE MOOD	SUBJUNCTIVE MOOD
Perfect	*Perfect*
Amāv-ī, I loved, I did love, I have loved	*Amāv-erim*
Amāv-isti, you loved, etc.	*Amāv-eris*
Amāv-it, he, she, it loved, etc.	*Amāv-erit*
Amāv-imus, we loved, etc.	*Amāv-erīmus*
Amāv-istis, you loved, etc.	*Amāv-eritis*
Amāv-ērunt, or *-ēre*, they loved, *etc*	*Amāv-erint*

INDICATIVE MOOD	SUBJUNCTIVE MOOD
Pluperfect	*Pluperfect*
Amāv-eram, I had loved	*Amāv-issem*
Amāv-erās, you had loved	*Amāv-issēs*
Amāv-erat, he, she, it had loved	*Amāv-isset*
Amāv-erāmus, we had loved	*Amāv-issēmus*
Amāv-erātis, you had loved	*Amāv-issētis*
Amāv-erant, they had loved	*Amāv-issent*
Future Perfect	
Amāv-erō, I shall have loved	Perfect Infinitive
Amāv-eris, you will have loved	*Amāv-isse*, to have loved
Amāv-erit, he, she, it will have loved	
Amāv-erimus, we shall have loved	
Amāv-eritis, you shall have loved	
Amāv-erint, they will have loved	

(From Supine Stem *Amāt-*)

First Supine, *Amāt-um* Second Supine, *Amāt-ū*

Future Participle, *Amāt-ūrus*, *-a*, *-um*, about to love

Future Infinitive = Future Participle + *esse* = *Amātūrus esse*, to be about to love.

Second Conjugation. Example, *Moneō*, I warn.
(From Present Stem *Mon-*)

INDICATIVE MOOD		SUBJUNCTIVE MOOD	
Present		*Present*	
Mon-eō	*Mon-ēmus*	*Mon-eam*	*Mon-eāmus*
Mon-ēs	*Mon-ētis*	*Mon-eās*	*Mon-eātis*
Mon-et	*Mon-ent*	*Mon-eat*	*Mon-eant*
Imperfect		*Imperfect*	
Mon-ēbam	*Mon-ēbāmus*	*Mon-ērem*	*Mon-ērēmus*
Mon-ēbās	*Mon-ēbātis*	*Mon-ērēs*	*Mon-ērētis*
Mon-ēbat	*Mon-ēbant*	*Mon-ēret*	*Mon-ērent*
Future			
Mon-ēbō	*Mon-ēbimus*	Present Participle.	*Mon-ens*
Mon-ēbis	*Mon-ēbitis*	Present Infinitive.	*Mon-ēre*
Mon-ēbit	*Mon-ēbunt*	Gerund.	*Mon-endum*, *-ī*.

IMPERATIVE MOOD

Mon-ē warn thou *Mon-ēte* warn ye *Mon-ētō* thou shalt warn
Mon-ētōte ye shall warn *Mon-ētō* he shall warn *Mon-ento* they shall warn

(From Perfect Stem *Monu-*)

INDICATIVE MOOD		SUBJUNCTIVE MOOD	
Perfect		*Perfect*	
Monu-ī	*Monu-imus*	*Monu-erim*	*Monu-erīmus*
Monu-istī	*Monu-istis*	*Monu-eris*	*Monu-eritis*
Monu-it	*Monu-ērunt* or *-ēre*	*Monu-erit*	*Monu-erint*

INDICATIVE MOOD		SUBJUNCTIVE MOOD	
Pluperfect		*Pluperfect*	
Monu-eram	*Monu-erāmus*	*Monu-issem*	*Monu-issēmus*
Monu-erās	*Monu-erātis*	*Monu-issēs*	*Monu-issētis*
Monu-erat	*Monu-erant*	*Monu-isset*	*Monu-issent*
Future Perfect			
Monu-erō	*Monu-erimus*	Perfect Infinitive, *Monu-isse*,	
Monu-eris	*Monu-eritis*		
Monu-erit	*Monu-erint*		

(From Supine Stem *Monit-*)

First Supine, *Monit-um* Second Supine, *Monit-ū*

Future Participle, *Monit-ūrus, -a, -um*

Future Infinitive = Future Participle + *esse* = *Monitūrus esse*

Third Conjugation. Example, *Regō*, I rule.

(From Present Stem *Reg-*.)

INDICATIVE MOOD		SUBJUNCTIVE MOOD	
Present		*Present*	
Reg-ō	*Reg-imus*	*Reg-am*	*Reg-āmus*
Reg-is	*Reg-itis*	*Reg-ās*	*Reg-ātis*
Reg-it	*Reg-unt*	*Reg-at*	*Reg-ant*
Imperfect		*Imperfect*	
Reg-ēbam	*Reg-ēbāmus*	*Reg-erem*	*Reg-erēmus*
Reg-ēbās	*Reg-ēbātis*	*Reg-erēs*	*Reg-erētis*
Reg-ēbat	*Reg-ēbant*	*Reg-eret*	*Reg-erent*
Future			
Reg-am	*Reg-ēmus*	Present Participle.	*Reg-ens*
Reg-ēs	*Reg-ētis*	Present Infinitive.	*Reg-ere*
Reg-et	*Reg-ent*	Gerund.	*Reg-endum, -ī*

IMPERATIVE MOOD

Rege, rule thou *Regite*, rule ye *Regito*, thou shalt rule

Regitōte, ye shall rule *Regitō*, he shall rule *Reguntō*, they shall rule

(From Perfect Stem *Rex-*)

INDICATIVE MOOD		SUBJUNCTIVE MOOD	
Perfect		*Perfect*	
Rex-ī	*Rex-imus*	*Rex-erim*	*Rex-erīmus*
Rex-istī	*Rex-istis*	*Rex-eris*	*Rex-eritis*
Rex-it	*Rex-ērunt* or *-ēre*	*Rex-erit*	*Rex-erint*
Pluperfect		*Pluperfect*	
Rex-eram	*Rex-erāmus*	*Rex-issem*	*Rex-issēmus*
Rex-erās	*Rex-erātis*	*Rex-issēs*	*Rex-issētis*
Rex-erat	*Rex-erant*	*Rex-isset*	*Rex-issent*
Future Perfect			
Rex-erō	*Rex-erimus*	Perfect Infinitive, *Rex-isse*	
Rex-eris	*Rex-eritis*		
Rex-erit	*Rex-erint*		

(From Supine Stem *Rect-*)

First Supine, *Rect-um* Second Supine, *Rect-ū*

Future Participle, *Rect-ūrus, -a, -um*

Future Infinitive = Future Participle + *esse* = *Rectūrus esse*

Fourth Conjugation. Example, *Audiō*, I hear.

(From Present Stem *Aud-*)

INDICATIVE MOOD		SUBJUNCTIVE MOOD	
Present		*Present*	
Aud-iō	*Aud-īmus*	*Aud-iam*	*Aud-iāmus*
Aud-īs	*Aud-ītis*	*Aud-iās*	*Aud-iātis*
Aud-it	*Aud-iunt*	*Aud-iat*	*Aud-iant*
Imperfect		*Imperfect*	
Aud-iēbam	*Aud-iēbāmus*	*Aud-īrem*	*Aud-īrēmus*
Aud-iēbās	*Aud-iēbātis*	*Aud-īrēs*	*Aud-īrētis*
Aud-iēbat	*Aud-iēbant*	*Aud-īret*	*Aud-īrent*
Future			
Aud-iam	*Aud-iēmus*	Present Participle.	*Aud-iens*
Aud-iēs	*Aud-iētis*	Present Infinitive.	*Aud-īre*
Aud-iet	*Aud-ient*	Gerund.	*Aud-iendum, -ī*

IMPERATIVE MOOD

Aud-ī, hear thou *Aud-īte*, hear ye *Aud-ītō*, thou shalt hear
Aud-ītōte, ye shall hear *Aud-ītō*, he shall hear *Aud-iuntō*, they shall hear

(From Perfect Stem *Audīv-*)

INDICATIVE MOOD		SUBJUNCTIVE MOOD	
Perfect		*Perfect*	
Audīv-ī	*Audīv-imus*	*Audīv-erim*	*Audīv-erīmus*
Audīv-istī	*Audīv-istis*	*Audīv-erīs*	*Audīv-eritis*
Audīv-it	*Audīv-ērunt* or *-ēre*	*Audīv-erit*	*Audīv-erint*
Pluperfect		*Pluperfect*	
Audīv-eram	*Audīv-erāmus*	*Audīv-issem*	*Audīv-issēmus*
Audīv-erās	*Audīv-erātis*	*Audīv-issēs*	*Audīv-issētis*
Audīv-erat	*Audīv-erant*	*Audīv-isset*	*Audīv-issent*
Future Perfect			
Audīv-erō	*Audīv-erimus*	Perfect Infinitive, *Audīv-isse*	
Audīv-eris	*Audīv-eritis*		
Audīv-erit	*Audīv-erint*		

(From Supine Stem *Audīt-*)

First Supine *Audīt-um* Second Supine, *Audīt-ū*

Future Participle, *Audīt-ūrus, -a, um*, about to hear

Future Infinitive = Future Participle + *esse* = *Audīturus esse*

Passive Voice

First Conjugation. *Amor*, I am loved.

(From Present Stem *Am-*)

INDICATIVE MOOD	SUBJUNCTIVE MOOD
Present	*Present*
Am-or, I am being loved	*Am-er*
Am-āris (*-āre*), you are being loved	*Am-ēris* (*ēre*)
Am-ātur, he is being loved	*Am-ētur*
Am-āmur, we are being loved	*Am-ēmur*
Am-āminī, you are being loved	*Am-ēminī*
Am-antur, they are being loved	*Am-entur*
Imperfect	*Imperfect*
Am-ābar, I was being loved	*Am-ārer*
Am-ābāris (*-ābāre*), you were being loved	*Am-ārēris* (*-ārēre*)
Am-ābātur, he was being loved	*Am-ārētur*
Am-ābāmur, we were being loved	*Am-ārēmur*
Am-ābāminī, you were being loved	*Am-ārēminī*
Am-ābantur, they were being loved	*Am-ārentur*
Future	
Am-ābor, I shall be loved	Present Participle
Am-āberis (*-ābere*), you will be loved	—
Am-ābitur, he will be loved	Present Infinitive
Am-ābimur we shall be loved	*Amārī*, to be loved
Am-ābiminī, you shall be loved	Gerundive
Am-ābuntur, they will be loved	*Amandus*, *-a*, *-um*, fit to be loved

IMPERATIVE MOOD

Am-āre } be thou loved
Am-ātor }
Am-āminī, be ye loved
Am-ātor, let him be loved
Am-antor, let them be loved

Perfect Tenses

INDICATIVE MOOD	SUBJUNCTIVE MOOD
Perfect	*Perfect*
Amātus, *a*, *um*, I have been loved	*Amātus*, etc., *sim*
Amātus, etc., *es*, you have been loved	*Amātus*, etc., *sīs*
Amātus, etc., *est*, he has been loved	*Amātus*, etc., *sit*
Amātī, etc., *sumus*, we have been loved	*Amātī*, etc., *sīmus*
Amātī, etc., *estis*, you have been loved	*Amātī*, etc., *sītis*
Amātī, etc., *sunt*, they have been loved	*Amātī*, etc., *sint*
Pluperfect	*Pluperfect*
Amātus eram, I had been loved	*Amātus essem*
Amātus erās, you had been loved	*Amātus essēs*
Amātus erat, he had been loved	*Amātus esset*
Amātī erāmus, we had been loved	*Amātī essēmus*
Amātī erātis, you had been loved	*Amātī essētis*
Amātī erant, they had been loved	*Amātī essent*
Future Perfect	
Amātus erō, I shall have been loved	Perfect Infinitive
Amātus eris, you will have been loved	*Amātus esse*, to have been loved
Amātus erit, he will have been loved	
Amātī erimus, we shall have been loved	
Amātī eritis, you will have been loved	
Amātī erunt, they will have been loved	

(From Supine Stem *Amāt-*)

Past Participle Passive, *Amātus, -a, -um.* Future Infinitive Passive, *Amātum īrī,* to be about to be loved.

Second Conjugation. *Moneor,* I am warned.

(From Present Stem *Mon-*)

INDICATIVE MOOD		SUBJUNCTIVE MOOD	
Present		*Present*	
Mon-eor	*Mon-ēmur*	*Mon-ear*	*Mon-eāmur*
Mon-ēris (or *-ēre*)	*Mon-ēminī*	*Mon-eāris* (or *-eāre*)	*Mon-eāminī*
Mon-ētur	*Mon-entur*	*Mon-eātur*	*Mon-eantur*
Imperfect		*Imperfect*	
Mon-ēbar	*Mon-ēbāmur*	*Mon-ērer*	*Mon-ērēmur*
Mon-ēbāris (or *-ēbāre*)	*Mon-ēbāminī*	*Mon-ērēris* (or *ērēre*)	*Mon-ērēminī*
Mon-ēbātur	*Mon-ēbantur*	*Mon-ērētur*	*Mon-ērentur*
Future			
Mon-ēbor	*Mon-ēbimur*	Present Participle, —	
Mon-ēberis (or *-ēbere*)	*Mon-ēbiminī*	Present Infinitive, *Mon-ērī*	
Mon-ēbitur	*Mon-ēbuntur*	Gerundive, *Mon-endus, -a, -um*	

IMPERATIVE MOOD

Mon-ēre	*Mon-ēminī*	*Mon-ētor*	
		Mon-ētor	*Mon-entor*

Perfect Tenses

INDICATIVE MOOD		SUBJUNCTIVE MOOD	
Perfect		*Perfect*	
Monitus sum	*Monitī sumus*	*Monitus sim*	*Monitī sīmus*
Monitus es	*Monitī estis*	*Monitus sīs*	*Monitī sītis*
Monitus est	*Monitī sunt*	*Monitus sit*	*Monitī sint*
Pluperfect		*Pluperfect*	
Monitus eram	*Monitī erāmus*	*Monitus essem*	*Monitī essēmus*
Monitus erās	*Monitī erātis*	*Monitus essēs*	*Monitī essētis*
Monitus erat	*Monitī erant*	*Monitus esset*	*Monitī essent*
Future Perfect		Perfect Infinitive, *Monitus esse*	
Monitus erō	*Monitī erimus*		
Monitus eris	*Monitī eritis*		
Monitus erit	*Monitī erunt*		

(From Supine Stem *Monit*)

Past Participle Passive, *Monitus, -a, -um*
Future Infinitive Passive, *Monitum īrī*

Third Conjugation. *Regor,* I am ruled.

(From Present Stem *Reg-*)

INDICATIVE MOOD		SUBJUNCTIVE MOOD	
Present		*Present*	
Reg-or	*Reg-imur*	*Reg-ar*	*Reg-āmur*
Reg-eris (*-ere*)	*Reg-iminī*	*Reg-āris* (*-āre*)	*Reg-āminī*
Reg-itur	*Reg-untur*	*Reg-ātur*	*Reg-antur*

INDICATIVE MOOD

Imperfect

Reg-ēbar *Reg-ēbāmur*
Reg-ēbāris (*-ēbāre*) *Reg-ēbāminī*
Reg-ēbātur *Reg-ēbantur*

Future

Reg-ar *Reg-ēmur*
Reg-ēris (*-ēre*) *Reg-ēminī*
Reg-ētur *Reg-entur*

SUBJUNCTIVE MOOD

Imperfect

Reg-erer *Reg-erēmur*
Reg-erēris (*-erēre*) *Reg-erēminī*
Reg-erētur *Reg-erentur*

Present Participle, —
Present Infinitive, *Reg-i*
Gerundive, *Reg-endus, -a, -um*

IMPERATIVE MOOD

Reg-ere *Reg-iminī* *Reg-itor* *Reg-itor* *Reg-untor*

Perfect Tenses

INDICATIVE MOOD

Perfect

Rectus sum *Rectī sumus*
Rectus es *Rectī estis*
Rectus est *Rectī sunt*

Pluperfect

Rectus eram *Rectī erāmus*
Rectus erās *Rectī erātis*
Rectus erat *Rectī erant*

Future Perfect

Rectus erō *Rectī erimus*
Rectus eris *Rectī eritis*
Rectus erit *Recti erunt*

SUBJUNCTIVE MOOD

Perfect

Rectus sim *Rectī sīmus*
Rectus sīs *Rectī sītis*
Rectus sit *Rectī sint*

Pluperfect

Rectus essem *Rectī essēmus*
Rectus essēs *Rectī essētis*
Rectus esset *Rectī essent*

Perfect Infinitive, *Rectus esse*

(From Supine Stem *Rect-*)
Past Participle Passive, *Rectus, -a, -um*
Future Infinitive Passive, *Rectum īrī.*

Fourth Conjugation. *Audior*, I am heard.

(From Present Stem *Aud-*)

INDICATIVE MOOD

Present

Aud-ior *Aud-īmur*
Aud-īris (*-īre*) *Aud-īminī*
Aud-ītur *Aud-iuntur*

Imperfect

Aud-iēbār *Aud-iēbāmur*
Aud-iēbāris (*-iēbāre*) *Aud-iēbāminī*
Aud-iēbātur *Aud-iēbantur*

Future

Aud-iar *Aud-iēmur*
Aud-iēris (*-iēre*) *Aud-iēminī*
Aud-iētur *Aud-ientur*

SUBJUNCTIVE MOOD

Present

Aud-iar *Aud-iāmur*
Aud-iāris (*-iāre*) *Aud-iāminī*
Aud-iātur *Aud-iantur*

Imperfect

Aud-īrer *Aud-īrēmur*
Aud-īrēris (*-īrēre*) *Aud-īrēminī*
Aud-īrētur *Aud-īrentur*

Present Participle, —
Present Infinitive, *Aud-īrī*
Gerundive, *Aud-iendus, -a, -um*

IMPERATIVE MOOD

Aud-īre *Aud-īminī* *Aud-ītor* *Aud-ītor* *Aud-iuntor*

Perfect Tenses

INDICATIVE MOOD

Perfect

Audītus sum *Audītī sumus*
Audītus es *Audītī estis*
Audītus est *Audītī sunt*

Pluperfect

Audītus eram *Audītī erāmus*
Audītus erās *Audītī erātis*
Audītus erat *Audītī erant*

Future Perfect

Audītus erō *Audītī erimus*
Audītus eris *Audītī eritis*
Audītus erit *Audītī erunt*

SUBJUNCTIVE MOOD

Perfect

Audītus sim *Audītī sīmus*
Audītus sīs *Audītī sītis*
Audītus sit *Audītī sint*

Pluperfect

Audītus essem *Audītī essēmus*
Audītus essēs *Audītī essētis*
Audītus esset *Audītī essent*

Perfect Infinitive, *Audītus esse*

(From Supine Stem *Audīt-*)
Past Participle Passive, *Audītus, -a, -um*
Future Infinitive Passive, *Audītum īrī.*

IRREGULAR VERBS

Verb *Sum*, I am

(Tenses from the Present Stems)

INDICATIVE

Present

sum, I am
es, you are
est, he is
sumus, we are
estis, you are
sunt, they are

Imperfect

eram, I was
erās, you were
erat, he was
erāmus, we were
erātis, you were
erant, they were

Future

erō, I shall be
eris, you will be
erit, he will be
erimus, we shall be
eritis, you will be
erunt, they will be

SUBJUNCTIVE

Present

sim
sīs
sit
sīmus
sītis
sint

Imperfect

essem
essēs
esset
essēmus
essētis
essent

Present Infinitive
Esse, to be

IMPERATIVE

Es, be (thou)
Este, be (ye)

Estō, you shall be
Estōte, you shall be
Estō, he shall be
Suntō, they shall be

(From Perfect Stem *Fu-*)

INDICATIVE	SUBJUNCTIVE
Perfect	*Perfect*
Fu-ī, I have been or I was	*Fu-erim*
Fu-istī, you have been or you were	*Fu-erīs*
Fu-it, he has been or he was	*Fu-erit*
Fu-imus, we have been or we were	*Fu-erīmus*
Fu-istis, you have been or you were	*Fu-erītis*
Fu-ērunt or *-ēre*, they have been or they were	*Fu-erint*
Pluperfect	*Pluperfect*
Fu-eram, I had been	*Fu-issem*
Fu-erās, you had been	*Fu-issēs*
Fu-erat, he had been	*Fu-isset*
Fu-erāmus, we had been	*Fu-issēmus*
Fu-erātis, you had been	*Fu-issētis*
Fu-erant, they had been	*Fu-issent*
Future Perfect	
Fu-erō, I shall have been	Perfect Infinitive,
Fu-eris, you will have been	*Fu-isse*, to have been
Fu-erit, he will have been	
Fu-erimus, we shall have been	
Fu-eritis, you will have been	
Fu-erint, they will have been	

(From Supine Stem *Fut-*)

First Supine, wanting. Second Supine, wanting
Future Participle, *Futūrus, -a, -um*, about to be
Future Infinitive, *Futūrus esse*, to be about to be

Tables of the commoner irregular verbs are given below:

Possum	*posse*	*potuī*	—	to be able
Volō	*velle*	*voluī*	—	to wish
Nōlō	*nolle*	*nōluī*	—	to be unwilling
Ferō	*ferre*	*tulī*	*lātum*	to bear, bring
Fīō	*fierī*	*factus sum*		to become, be made
Eō	*īre*	*iī*	*itum*	to go

Ferre, (to bear) and *īre*, (to go) have many compounds which are conjugated like the basic verb given below:

Active

INDICATIVE

	Singular		*Plural*		
Present					
Pos-sum	*pot-es*	*pot-est*	*pos-sumus*	*pot-estis*	*pos-sunt*
Volō	*vīs*	*vult*	*volumus*	*vultis*	*volunt*
Nōlō	*nōnvīs*	*nōnvult*	*nōlumus*	*nōnvultis*	*nōlunt*
Mālō	*māvīs*	*māvult*	*mālumus*	*māvultis*	*mālunt*
Ferō	*fers*	*fert*	*ferimus*	*fertis*	*ferunt*
Fīō	*fīs*	*fit*	—	—	*fīunt*
Eō	*īs*	*it*	*īmus*	*ītis*	*eunt*

Imperfect

Pot-eram	*-erās*	*-erat*	*-erāmus*	*-erātis*	*-erant*
Volē-, *Nōlē-*, *Mālē-*, *Ferē-*, *Fiē-*, *I-* } *bam*	*-bās*	*-bat*	*-bāmus*	*-bātis*	*-bant*

Future

Pot-erō	*-eris*	*-erit*	*-erimus*	*-eritis*	*-erun*
Vol-, *Nōl-*, *Māl-*, *Fer-*, *Fī-* } *am*	*-ēs*	*-et*	*-ēmus*	*-ētis*	*-ent*
Ib-ō	*-is*	*-it*	*-imus*	*-itis*	*-unt*

Perfect, Pluperfect, Future Perfect Tenses are formed regularly from the Perfect Stem.

PARTICIPLE	INFINITIVE	GERUND
—	*posse*	—
Vol-, *Nōl-*, *Māl-*, *Fer-*, *I—* } *ens*	*velle*	*vol-*, *nōl-*, *māl-*, *fer-* } *endum, -ī*
	nolle	
	malle	
	ferre	
Gen. *euntis*	*fieri*	—
	ire	*e-undum*

SUBJUNCTIVE

	Singular			*Plural*	
Present					
Pos-sim	*pos-sīs*	*pos-sit*	*pos-sīmus*	*pos-sītis*	*pos-sint*
Vel-, *Nōl-*, *Māl-* } *im*	*-īs*	*-it*	*-īmus*	*-ītis*	*-int*
Fer-, *Fī-*, *E-* } *am*	*-ās*	*-at*	*-āmus*	*-ātis*	*-ant*
	Singular			*Plural*	
Imperfect					
Poss-, *Vell-*, *Noll-*, *Mall-*, *Ferr-*, *Fier-*, *Ir-* } *em*	*-ēs*	*-et*	*-ēmus*	*-ētis*	*-ent*

IMPERATIVE

Singular		*Plural*	
—	—	—	—
—	—	—	—
Nōl-ī, nōl-ītō	*nōl-ītō*	*nōl-īte, nōl-ītōte*	*nōl-untō*
—	—	—	—
Fer, fer-tō	*fer-tō*	*fer-te, fer-tōte*	*fer-untō*
Fī	—	*fī-te*	—
Ī, i-tō	*ī-tō*	*ī-te, ī-tōte*	*e-untō*

Passive

INDICATIVE

	Singular			*Plura*	
Present					
Fer-or	*fer-ris*	*fer-tur*	*fer-imur*	*fer-iminī*	*fer-untur*
Imperfect					
Fer-ēbar	*fer-ēbāris*	*fer-ēbātur*	*fer-ēbāmur*	*fer-ēbāminī*	*fer-ēbāntur*
Future					
Fer-ar	*Fer-ēris*	*er-ētur*	*fer-ēmur*	*fer-ēminī*	*fer-entur*

SUBJUNCTIVE

Present					
Fer-ar	*fer-āris*	*fer-ātur*	*fer-āmur*	*fer-āminī*	*fer-antur*
Imperfect					
Ferr-er	*ferr-ēris*	*ferrētur*	*ferr-ēmur*	*ferr-ēminī*	*ferr-entur*

IMPERATIVE

Fer-re, fer-tor *fer-tor* *fer-iminī* *fer-untor*

Gerundive: *Fer-endus* Present Infinitive: *Ferr-ī*

DEPONENT VERBS

Many Latin verbs are passive in form but active in meaning, e.g. *hortor* "I exhort"; *hortātus sum*, "I have exhorted"; *hortārī*, "to exhort". They are conjugated like ordinary passive verbs, but of course they have no passive meanings themselves. *Hortor* means "I exhort". If you want to say in Latin "I am exhorted", you have to use a different verb.

There are, however, two exceptions to the above rule.

1. Most deponent verbs still keep their active voice forms for the present and future participle, future infinitive and gerund, e.g. *morior*, "I die"; *moriens*, "dying"; *moritūrus*, "about to die"; *moritūrus esse*, "to be about to die"; *moriendum* (gerund) "dying".

2. Their gerundives are passive both in form and meaning. E.g. *hortandus*, "fit to be exhorted".

N.B. The past participle is passive in form, but active in meaning, e.g. *veritus*, "having feared".

Here is a list of some of the commoner deponent verbs:

	Present Tense	*Infinitive*	*Perfect Tense*	*Meaning*
1st conjugation	*cōnor*	*cōnārī*	*cōnātus sum*	to try
	hortor	*hortārī*	*hortātus sum*	to exhort
	vēnor	*vēnārī*	*vēnātus sum*	to hunt
2nd conjugation	*vereor*	*verērī*	*veritus sum*	to fear
	polliceor	*pollicērī*	*pollicitus sum*	to promise
3rd conjugation	*patior*	*patī*	*passus sum*	to suffer
	ūtor	*ūtī*	*ūsus sum*	to use
	morior	*morī*	*mortuus sum*	to die
	aggredior	*aggredī*	*agressus sum*	to attack
	prōgredior	*prōgredī*	*prōgressus sum*	to set out
	ingredior	*ingredī*	*ingressus sum*	to enter
	regredior	*regredī*	*regressus sum*	to return
	loquor	*loquī*	*locūtus sum*	to speak
	proficiscor	*proficiscī*	*profectus sum*	to set out
4th conjugation	*partior*	*partirī*	*partītus sum*	to share
	orior	*orīrī*	*ortus sum*	to rise

IMPERSONAL VERBS

There are certain verbs in Latin which can only be used in the third person singular and in the infinitive. They never have a personal subject but always the pronoun "it": hence they are called Impersonal Verbs. These verbs have only the third person singular *of each tense*, an infinitive, and a gerund. They may be divided into four types.

(*a*) Verbs which have an accusative of the person and a genitive of the cause:

Present	*Perfect*	*Infinitive*	*Meaning*
Miseret	*miseruit*	*miserēre*	it pities
Paenitet	*paenituit*	*paenitēre*	it repents
Pudet	*puduit*	*pudēre*	it shames
Taedet	*taeduit*	*taedēre*	it wearies
Piget	*piguit*	*pigēre*	it annoys, vexes

Example:

Pudet me huius facti, I am ashamed of this deed.

(*b*) In this class are two verbs which take a genitive of person, unless a personal pronoun is used, in which case they take the feminine ablative singular of the possessive pronoun. These verbs are *interest* (from *intersum*) and *rēfert* (from *re-fero*), both meaning "it matters", "it is important", "it is in the interests of—".

Example:

Interest civium regem bene regere. It is in the interest of the citizens that the king should rule well.

Quid id refert tua? What does it matter to you?

(*c*) Verbs taking the accusative and infinitive:

Oportet me, it behoves me; I ought
Decet me, it becomes me
Dēdecet me, it does not become me
Iuvat me, it delights me, I delight.

Example:

Oportet me hoc facere, I ought to do this
Oportuit me hoc facere, I ought to have done this.

(*d*) Verbs taking the dative and infinitive:

Licet mihi, it is permitted to me, I may
Accidit tibi, it happens to you
Libet / *Placet* } *eis*, it is pleasing to them, they are pleased.

Example:

Tibi abesse licet, you may be absent.

DEFECTIVE VERBS

There are a number of verbs in Latin which lack a considerable number of parts. The commonest of them are:

Coepī, I have begun

Perfect	Fut. Perfect	Pluperfect	Infinitive	Perf. Subj.	Pluperf. Subj
Coepī	*coeperō*	*coeperam*	*coepisse*	*coeperim*	*coepissem*

Odī, I hate

Ōdī	*ōderō*	*ōderam*	*ōdisse*	*ōderim*	*ōdissem*

Meminī, I remember

Meminī	*memineró*	*memineram*	*meminisse*	*meminerim*	*meminissem*

Nōvī, I have got to know, I know

Nōvī	*nōverō*	*nōveram*	*nōvisse*	*nōverim*	*nōvissem*

Inquam, I say

Pres. tense	*Inquam,*	*inquis*	*inquit*	*inquimus*	*inquitis*	*inquiunt*
Imperfect	—	—	*inquiēbat*	—	—	*inquiēbant*
Future	—	—	*inquiet*	—	—	—
Perfect	—	*inquistī*	*inquit*	—	—	—

Fāri, to speak

Pres. tense	—	—	*fātur*	—	—	—
Future	*Fābor*	—	*fābitur*	—	—	—

Present Participle, acc. *Fantem*; Perfect, *Fātus*.
Gerund, *Fandī*, *fando*; Gerundive, *Fandus*.

Note that *memini* and *odi* are perfect in form, but present in meaning. The tenses which are missing from these verbs can often be supplied by other verbs with the same meaning, e.g. *incipio* (begin) can supply present, future, and imperfect tenses meaning I begin, I shall begin, etc.

PRONOUNS

1. *Personal Pronouns.* Latin has pronouns to translate our English "I" and "you", but they are employed in the nominative cases, only when very emphatic.

	Singular		*Plural*	
Nom.	*ego*	I	*nōs*	we
Acc.	*mē*	me	*nōs*	us
Gen.	*meī*	of me	*nostrum, nostri*[1]	of us
Dat.	*mihĭ*	to, for me	*nōbīs*	to, for us
Abl.	*mē*	from me	*nōbīs*	from us
Nom.	*tū*	you	*vōs*	you
Acc.	*tē*	you	*vōs*	you
Gen.	*tūī*	of you	*vestrum, vestri*[1]	of you
Dat.	*tibĭ*	to, for you	*vōbīs*	to, for you
Abl.	*tē*	from you	*vōbīs*	from you

[1] *Nostrum* and *vestrum* are partitive genitives, e.g. *Unus vestrum*, one of you. *Nostri* and *vestri* are objective genitives, e.g. *memor vestri*, mindful of you.

2. *Reflexive Pronouns.* This pronoun is used when the subject of the verb is denoted as acting on itself, e.g. The enemy are slaying themselves. *Hostes se interficiunt.*

Acc.	*sē* (or *sēsē*), himself, herself, itself, themselves.
Gen.	*suī*, of himself, etc.
Dat.	*sibī*, to, for himself, etc.
Abl.	*sē* (or *sēsē*), by, with, from himself, etc.

3. *Demonstrative Pronouns.* There are two common demonstrative pronouns in Latin which mean that; *is* and *ille.* They can also mean "he", "she" or "it". *Ille* has a stronger demonstrative force than *is*, meaning "that" (over there, near him). Declined exactly like *ille* is *iste*, meaning "that over there, near you".

	Singular			*Plura*		
	Masc.	Fem.	Neut.	Masc.	Fem.	Neut.
Nom.	*is*	*ea*	*id*	*eī (iī)*	*eae*	*ea*
Acc.	*eum*	*eam*	*id*	*eōs*	*eās*	*ea*
Gen.	*eius*	*eius*	*eius*	*eōrum*	*eārum*	*eōrum*
Dat.	*eī*	*eī*	*eī*	*eīs (iīs)*	*eīs*	*eīs*
Abl.	*eō*	*eā*	*eō*	*eīs*	*eīs*	*eīs*
Nom.	*ille*	*illa*	*illud*	*illī*	*illae*	*illa*
Acc.	*illum*	*illam*	*illud*	*illōs*	*illās*	*illa*
Gen.	*illīus*	*illīus*	*illīus*	*illōrum*	*illārum*	*illōrum*
Dat.	*illī*	*illī*	*illī*	*illīs*	*illīs*	*illīs*
Abl.	*illō*	*illā*	*illō*	*illīs*	*illīs*	*illīs*

The pronoun meaning "this" is *hic, haec, hoc.*

Nom.	*hīc*	*haec*	*hōc*	*hī*	*hae*	*haec*
Acc.	*hunc*	*hanc*	*hōc*	*hōs*	*hās*	*haec*
Gen.	*huius*	*huius*	*huius*	*hōrum*	*hārum*	*hōrum*
Dat.	*huic*	*huic*	*huic*	*hīs*	*hīs*	*hīs*
Abl.	*hōc*	*hāc*	*hōc*	*hīs*	*hīs*	*hīs*

The pronoun meaning "the same" is *idem.*

	Singular			*Plural*		
	Masc.	Fem.	Neut.	Masc.	Fem.	Neut.
Nom.	*īdem*	*eadem*	*idem*	*eīdem*	*eaedem*	*eadem*
Acc.	*eundem*	*eandem*	*idem*	*eōsdem*	*eāsdem*	*eadem*
Gen.	*eiusdem*	*eiusdem*	*eiusdem*	*eōrundem*	*eārundem*	*eōrundem*
Dat.	*eīdem*	*eīdem*	*eīdem*	*eīsdem* (or *īsdem*)	*eīsdem*	*eīsdem*
Abl.	*eōdem*	*eādem*	*eōdem*	*eīsdem*	*eīsdem*	*eīsdem*

4. *Emphatic Pronoun. Ipse*, a pronoun meaning "— self", simply emphasizes the noun or pronoun to which it refers, e.g. *Puer ipse cantat.* The boy himself sings.

	Singular			*Plural*		
	Masc.	Fem.	Neut.	Masc.	Fem.	Neut.
Nom.	*ipse*	*ipsa*	*ipsum*	*ipsī*	*ipsae*	*ipsa*
Acc.	*ipsum*	*ipsam*	*ipsum*	*ipsōs*	*ipsās*	*ipsā*
Gen.	*ipsīus*	*ipsīus*	*ipsīus*	*ipsōrum*	*ipsārum*	*ipsōrum*
Dat.	*ipsī*	*ipsī*	*ipsī*	*ipsīs*	*ipsīs*	*ipsīs*
Abl.	*ipsō*	*ipsā*	*ipsō*	*ipsīs*	*ipsīs*	*ipsīs*

5. *Relative Pronouns.* The relative pronoun, "who", "which", is *qui, quae, quod.* In Latin this pronoun takes its number (singular or plural) and its gender (masc., fem., or neut.) from the word in the main clause of the sentence to which it refers (its antecedent). But its case is determined by its own clause, i.e. depending on whether it is the subject or object, etc., of the verb. The pronoun is declined as follows.

	Singular			*Plural*		
	Masc.	Fem.	Neut.	Masc.	Fem.	Neut.
Nom.	*quī*	*quae*	*quod*	*quī*	*quae*	*quae*
Acc.	*quem*	*quam*	*quod*	*quōs*	*quās*	*quae*
Gen.	*cuius*	*cuius*	*cuius*	*quōrum*	*quārum*	*quōrum*
Dat.	*cui*	*cui*	*cui*	*quibus*	*quibus*	*quibus*
Abl.	*quō*	*quā*	*quō*	*quibus*	*quibus*	*quibus*

6. *Interrogative Pronoun. Quis,* who? what? is declined in all cases except the nominative and accusative in the same way as the relative pronoun.

	Singular		
	Masc.	Fem.	Neut.
Nom.	*quis*	*quis*	*quid*
Acc.	*quem*	*quam*	*quid*

7. *Other Pronouns.* A list of other pronouns in common use is given below:

Masc.	Fem.	Neut.	Meaning
quīdam	*quaedam*	*quoddam*	a certain (person) (thing)
aliquis	*aliqua*	*aliquid*	someone, something
quivīs	*quaevīs*	*quodvīs* }	anyone you like
quilibet	*quaelibet*	*quodlibet* }	
quisque	*quaeque*	*quodque*	each
quicumque	*quaecumque*	*quodcumque* }	whosoever, whatsoever
quisquis	*quisquis*	*quidquid* }	
quisquam	*quaequam*	*quidquam*	anyone

PREPOSITIONS

In Latin prepositions help the inflections or endings of nouns, adjectives, and pronouns to show the relations between them and other words in a sentence. They are also compounded with verbs, to change the meaning of the original verb, e.g. *eo,* I go; *abeo,* I go away.

The following is a list of the prepositions used with the ablative case:
ā, ab, cum, dē, cōram, palam, ē, ex, sine, tenus, prō, prae
Nearly all other prepositions are used with the accusative case.

The following prepositions take the accusative when "motion towards" is meant, and the ablative when "place where" is meant.

in	in, on, into	*super*	upon, over
sub	under, up to	*subter*	under

CONJUNCTIONS

Conjunctions are words which join together words or sentences. The commonest of them are given, with their meanings, and in alphabetical order, below.

after	*postquam* (with verb in indicative)
and	*et, atque, ăc, -que* (joined to a word)
and . . . lest	*neu, nĕve* (with verb in subjunctive)
and . . . not	*nec, neque*
although	*quamquam* (with factual concessive clause); *quamvis* (hypothetical)
as	*ut* (with verb in indicative)
as if	*quasi*
as soon as	*cum prīmum, ut prīmum, simul ăc (atque)*
because	*quod, quia, quoniam, cum*
before	*antequam, priusquam* (with indicative when purely temporal, subjunctive when there is an additional idea of intention)
both . . . and	*et . . . et*
but	*sed, autem* (second word)
but . . . not	*neque . . . vĕro*
either . . . or	*aut . . . aut, vel . . . vel*
for	*nam, namque, enim* (second word)
for . . . not	*neque . . . enim*
however	*tamen, autem*
if	*sī* (with indicative or subjunctive, depending on the type of conditional sentence)
if not	*nisi, sī . . . non*
just as if	*tamquam sī* (with verb in subjunctive)
neither	*nec, neque*
neither . . . nor	*neque . . . neque, nec . . . nec*
nevertheless	*tamen*
or	*aut, vel;* (in questions) *an*
questions are introduced by	*ne* (joined to the first word in the sentence)
	nonne (introducing a question expecting the answer "yes")
	num (introducing a question expecting the answer "no")
since	*cum, quoniam*
so (in such a way) . . . that	*ita . . . ut*
so that (purpose)	*ut*
so that . . . never	*ut numquam* (consecutive); *nē umquam* (purpose)
so that . . . not	*ut nōn* (consecutive); *nē* (purpose)
so that . . . no-one	*ut nēmo* (consecutive); *nē quis* (purpose)
so that . . . nowhere	*ut nusquam* (consecutive); *nē usquam* (purpose)
therefore	*itaque, igitur*
until	*dum, dōnec* (with verb in indicative when purely temporal, subjunctive when there is an additional idea of purpose)
when	*cum, ubī* (temporal); *quandō* (interrogative)
where	*ubī* (relative and interrogative)
whether	*num* (introducing single indirect questions); *ūtrum* (introducing alternative indirect questions); *sīve, seu* (introducing alternative conditional sentences)
while	*dum* (usually with verb in indicative)
whither	*quō* (relative and interrogative)
why	*cur, quārē*

ADVERBS

In Latin it is easy to make adverbs from adjectives. With adjectives of Class I, simply add *-e* to the stem of the adjective to form the adverb, e.g. *benignus* (kind), genitive singular, *benigni*, adverb, *benignē* (kindly); *līber* (free), genitive singular, *līberi*, adverb, *līberē* (freely). Note these common exceptions to this rule, *subitus* (sudden), gives *subitō*; *falsus* (false), gives *falsō*; *necessārius* (necessary), gives *necessāriō*.

In adjectives of the second class, add *-iter* to the stem, e.g. *ferox*, (fierce,) genitive singular, *ferōc-is*, adverb, *ferōciter*. Note that adjectives like *prūdens* (prudent), simply add *-er* to the stem, *prūdenter*, (prudently).

Common Irregular Adverbs

bene, well	*diū*, for a long time
multum, much	*saepe*, often
magnoperē, greatly	*tandem*, at length

Comparison of Adverbs

The comparative of an adverb is simply the neuter singular of the comparative adjective. The superlative is obtained from the superlative of the adjective by changing the *-us* ending into *-e*, e.g.

	Positive	Comparative	Superlative
Adjective	*līber*, free	*līberior*	*līberrimus*
Adverb	*līberē*, freely	*līberius*	*līberrimē*
Adjective	*prūdens*, prudent	*prūdentior*	*prūdentissimus*
Adverb	*prūdenter*, prudently	*prūdentius*	*prūdentissimē*

A few adverbs are compared irregularly:

bene (*bonus*), well	*melius*, better	*optimē*, best
male (*malus*), badly	*pēius*, worse	*pessimē*, worst
multum (*multus*), much	*plūs*, more	*plūrimum*, most
magnoperē (*magnus*), greatly	*magis*, more	*maximē*, most
paulum (*parvus*), little	*minus*, less	*minimē*, least
diū, for a long time	*diūtius*, longer	*diūtissimē*, longest
saepe, often	*saepius*, oftener	*saepissimē*, oftenest

NUMERALS

	CARDINAL	ORDINAL
1	*Ūn-us, -a, -um*, one	*Prīm-us, -a, -um*, first
2	*Du-o, -ae, -o*, two	*Secund-us, -a, -um*, (*alter*), second
3	*Trēs, tria*, three	*Terti-us, -a, -um*, third
4	*Quattuor*, four	*Quart-us, -a, -um*, fourth
5	*Quinque*	*Quint-us, -a, -um*,
6	*Sex*	*Sext-us, -a, -um*
7	*Septem*	*Septim-us, -a, -um*
8	*Octō*	*Octāv-us, -a, -um*
9	*Novem*	*Nōn-us, -a, -um*
10	*Decem*	*Decim-us, -a, -um*
11	*Undecim*	*Undecim-us, -a, -um*
12	*Duodecim*	*Duodecim-us, -a, -um*
13	*Trēdecim*	*Tertius decim-us, -a, -um*, etc.
14	*Quattuordecim*	*Quart-us decim-us*, etc.
15	*Quindecim*	*Quint-us decim-us*, etc.
16	*Sēdecim*	*Sext-us decim-us*, etc.

17	*Septendecim*	*Septim-us decim-us*, etc.
18	*Duodēvīgintī*	*Duodēvīcēsim-us*, etc.
19	*Undēvīgint*	*Undēvīcēsim-us*, etc.
20	*Vīgintī*	*Vīcēsim-us*, etc.
30	*Trīgintā*	*Trīcēsim-us*, etc.
40	*Quādrāgintā*	*Quādrāgēsim-us*, etc.
50	*Quinquāgintā*	*Quinquāgēsim-us*, etc.
60	*Sexāgintā*	*Sexāgēsim-us*, etc.
70	*Septuāgintā*	*Septuāgēsim-us*, etc.
80	*Octōgintā*	*Octōgēsim-us*, etc.
90	*Nōnāgintā*	*Nōnāgēsim-us*, etc.
100	*Centum*	*Centēsim-us*, etc.
200	*Ducent-ī, -ae, -a*	*Ducentēsim-us*, etc.
300	*Trecent-ī, -ae, -a*	*Trecentēsim-us*, etc.
400	*Quādringent-ī, -ae, -a*	*Quādringentēsim-us*, etc.
500	*Quingent-ī, -ae, -a*	*Quingentēsimus*
600	*Sescent-ī, -ae, -a*	*Sexcentēsim-us*, etc.
700	*Septingent-ī, -ae, -a*	*Septingentēsim-us*, etc.
800	*Octingent-ī, -ae, -a*	*Octingentēsim-us*, etc.
900	*Nongent-ī, -ae, -a*	*Nongentēsim-us*, etc.
1,000	*Mille* (indeclinable)	*Millēsim-us*, etc.
2,000	*Duo mīlia* (followed by genitive case)	*Bis millēsim-us*, etc.
100,000	*Centum mīlia*	*Centiēs millēsim-us*, etc.
1,000,000	*Deciēs centēna mīlia*	*Deciēs centiēs millēsim-us*, etc.

	DISTRIBUTIVE	NUMERAL ADVERBS
1	*Singul-ī, -ae, -a*, one each	*Semel*, once
2	*Bīn-ī, -ae, -a*, two each	*Bis*, twice
3	*Tern-ī* (*trīn-ī*), *-ae, -a*, three each	*Ter*, thrice
4	*Quatern-ī, -ae, -a*, four each	*Quater*, four times
5	*Quīn-ī, -ae, -a*	*Quinquiēs*
6	*Sēn-ī, -ae, -a*	*Sexiēs*
7	*Septēn-ī, -ae, -a*	*Septiēs*
8	*Octōn-ī, -ae, -a*	*Octiēs*
9	*Novēn-ī, -ae, -a*	*Noviēs*
10	*Dēn-ī, -ae, -a*	*Deciēs*
11	*Undēn-ī, -ae, -a*	*Undeciēs*
12	*Duodēn-ī, -ae, -a*	*Duodeciēs*
13	*Tern-ī dēn-ī, -ae, -a*	*Ter deciēs*
14	*Quatern-ī dēn-ī, -ae, -a*	*Quater deciēs*
15	*Quīn-ī dēn-ī, -ae, -a*	*Quinquiēs deciēs*
16	*Sēn-ī dēn-ī, -ae, -a*	*Sexiēs deciēs*
17	*Septēn-ī dēn-ī, -ae, -a*	*Septiēs deciēs*
18	*Duodēvīcēn-ī, -ae, -a*	*Duodēvīciēs*
19	*Undēvīcēn-ī, -ae, -a*	*Undēvīciēs*
20	*Vīcēn-ī, -ae, -a*	*Vīciēs*
30	*Trīcēn-ī, -ae, -a*	*Trīciēs*
40	*Quādrāgēn-ī, -ae, -a*	*Quādrāgiēs*
50	*Quinquāgēn-ī, -ae, -a*	*Quinquāgiēs*
60	*Sexāgēn-ī, -ae, -a*	*Sexāgiēs*
70	*Septuāgēn-ī, -ae, -a*	*Septuāgiēs*
80	*Octōgēn-ī, -ae, -a*	*Octōgiēs*
90	*Nōnāgēn-ī, -ae, -a*	*Nōnāgiēs*
100	*Centēn-ī, -ae, -a*	*Centiēs*
200	*Ducēn-ī, -ae, -a*	*Ducentiēs*
300	*Trecēn-ī, -ae, -a*	*Trecentiēs*
400	*Quādringēn-ī, -ae, -a*	*Quādringentiēs*

500	*Quingēn-ī, -ae, -a*	*Quingentiēs*
600	*Sescēn-ī, -ae, -a*	*Sexcentiēs*
700	*Septingēn-ī, -ae, -a*	*Septingentiēs*
800	*Octingēn-ī, -ae, -a*	*Octingentiēs*
900	*Nōngēn-ī, -ae, -a*	*Nongentiēs*
1,000	*Singula mīlia*	*Mīliēs*
2,000	*Bīna mīlia*	*Bis mīliēs*
100,000	*Centēna mīlia*	*Centiēs mīliēs*
1,000,000	*Deciēs centēna mīlia*	*Deciēs centiēs mīliēs*

Ŭnus, duo, and *trēs* are declined as follows. The cardinals from *quattuor* to *centum* are indeclinable. *Ducentī, trecentī,* etc., are declined as the plural of *bonus.*

	Singular			*Plural*		
	Masc.	Fem.	Neut.	Masc.	Fem.	Neut.
Nom.	*ūnus*	*ūna*	*ūnum*	*ūnī*	*ūnae*	*ūna*
Acc.	*ūnum*	*ūnam*	*ūnum*	*ūnōs*	*ūnās*	*ūna*
Gen.	*ūnīus*	*ūnīus*	*ūnīus*	*ūnōrum*	*ūnārum*	*ūnōrum*
Dat.	*ūnī*	*ūnī*	*ūnī*	*ūnīs*	*ūnīs*	*ūnīs*
Abl.	*ūnō*	*ūnā*	*ūnō*	*ūnīs*	*ūnīs*	*ūnīs*

	Plural			*Plural*		
	Masc.	Fem.	Neut.	Masc.	Fem.	Neut.
Nom.	*duo*	*duae*	*duo*	*trēs*	*trēs*	*tria*
Acc.	*duōs*, (*duo*)	*duās*	*duo*	*trēs*	*trēs*	*tria*
Gen.	*duōrum*	*duārum*	*duōrum*	*trium*	*trium*	*trium*
Dat.	*duōbus*	*duābus*	*duōbus*	*tribus*	*tribus*	*tribus*
Abl.	*duōbus*	*duābus*	*duōbus*	*tribus*	*tribus*	*tribus*

ROMAN CALENDAR

There were twelve months in the Roman year. The Latin word for month is *mensis,* m., and the names of the months are given as adjectives, agreeing with *mensis* (understood).

Thus:

Jānuārius	January	*Jūlius* (or *Quintīlis*)	July
Februārius	February	*Augustus* (or *Sextīlis*)	August
Martius	March	*September*	September
Aprīlis	April	*Octōber*	October
Māius	May	*November*	November
Jūnius	June	*December*	December

There were three chief days in each month:

1st = *Kalendae* (Calends)
5th = *Nōnae* (Nones)
13th = *Īdus* (Ides)

but "in March, July, October, May the Nones fall on the 7th day," and the Ides 8 days later, on the 15th.

Dating

(*a*) For one of the chief days, e.g. on the first of January, use the ablative case (point of time) with the name of the month in agreement, ***Kalendis Januariis***; 13th November, ***Idibus Novembribus.***

(*b*) For the day before one of the chief days, e.g. on the 4th of January; use the word *prīdiē* (on the day before) with the chief day and the name of the month in the accusative case, *pridie Nonas Januarias*; 30th September, *pridie Kalendas Octobres*.

(*c*) For any other day, e.g. 3rd January, reckon backwards from the next chief day, in this case the *Nonae* (5th), but do so "inclusively", counting in the days at both ends. So, for days before the *Nonae*, or the *Idus*, subtract the day you require from the day on which the next chief day falls, and increase by one. For days before the *Kalendae* subtract the day you require from the number of days in the month, and increase by two. Then use the following formula: *ante diem* (ordinal number), *important day* (acc.), *name of month* (acc.).

Examples: 3rd January—*ante diem* tertium *Nonas Januarias*
26th September: *ante diem* sextum *Kalendas Octobres*.

MONEY, WEIGHTS, MEASURES

I. *Roman Money* (1)

Bronze or Copper Coinage

As—originally a bar of bronze, 1 lb in weight, later 2 ounces

Sēmis	one-half *as*
Triens	one-third *as*
Quādrans	one-quarter *as*
Sextans	one-sixth *as*
Uncia	one-twelfth *as*, *as* one ounce.

(2) Silver Coinage

Dēnārius	10 *asses*, later 16
Quīnārius	5 *asses*, later 8
Sestertius	2½ *asses*, later 4; this was the ordinary coin of the Romans, used in the reckoning of even the largest sums. Its symbol was HS.

Sestertium = 1,000 *Sestertii*.

(3) Gold Coinage

Denarius aureus (or simply "*aureus*") was the standard gold coin of the Romans, equivalent in value to 25 silver *denarii*, or 100 *sestertii*.

II. *Weights*

Libra. This was the unit of weight, the Roman pound.
Uncia. The *libra* (pound) was divided into 12 *unciae* (ounces).

III. *Measures*

Length: *Pes*. This was the unit of length, equivalent to our "foot".
Uncia. This *pes* (foot) was divided into 12 *unciae* (inches).
Passus. This was equivalent to 5 *pedes* (5 feet).
Mille Passus (pl. *milia passuum*) was one Roman mile (1,620 yards).

Area: *iugerum*, equivalent to five-eighths of an acre.

Capacity: *coclear* = a "spoonful"
cyathus = one-twelfth sextarius = 0·08 of a pint
sextārius = 0·96 of a pint
modius = 16 sextarii = 15 pints
amphora = 48 sextarii = 5 gallons 6 pints.

TIME, PLACE, SPACE

Time

(*a*) Point of time, or the time *at which* something happens, is expressed in Latin by the ablative case, e.g.

Auctumno folia sunt rubra.
In autumn the leaves are red.

(*b*) Duration of time, or the time *during which* something happens, is expressed in Latin by the accusative case, e.g.

Viginti annos Poeni cum Romanis bellabant.
During twenty years the Carthaginians waged war with the Romans.

(*c*) The time *within which* something happens (usually denoted by the word "in" or "within" in the English) is expressed in Latin by the ablative case, e.g.

Tribus mensibus redibit.
He will return *within three months.*

Place

(*a*) *Motion towards* a place is expressed in Latin by a preposition (*in*, *ad*) with the accusative case, except where names of towns or small islands, *domus* (house), and *rus* (countryside) are concerned. With these use the accusative case without a preposition, e.g.

Ad villam eo, I go to the country-house.
Romam eo, I go to Rome.

(*b*) *Motion from* a place is expressed in Latin by a preposition (*a*, *ab*, *e*, *ex*) with the ablative case, except where the names of towns or small islands, *domus* (house) and *rus* (countryside) are concerned. With these use the ablative case without a preposition, e.g.

Ab Africa navigavit, he sailed from Africa.
Rure venit, he comes from the country.

(*c*) *Place where*, *Rest in* a place is expressed in Latin by the preposition *in* with the ablative case, except where the names of towns or small islands, *domus* (house) and *rus* (countryside) are concerned. With these use the locative case, which in a singular noun of the First or Second Declension is like the genitive case, e.g. *Romae* (at Rome), *Londinii* (in London), and in all other nouns is like the ablative case, e.g. *Carthagine* (at Carthage), *Athenis* (in Athens).

N.B. at home, *domi*; in the countryside, *ruri.*

Space

Extent of space is expressed in Latin by the accusative case, e.g.

Tria milia passuum progressus est.
He advanced three miles.

Space which is the *amount of difference* between two points is expressed in Latin by the ablative case. (There is usually a comparative adjective in such a phrase.) e.g. This wall is three feet higher than that one. *Altior illo hic murus est tribus pedibus.*

TEACH YOURSELF BOOKS

FRENCH

J. Adams & N. Scarlyn Wilson

No previous knowledge of French is necessary for the reader wishing to learn the language through this book. It has been specially prepared with the beginner and his problems in mind.

Part I of this course consists of an introduction to pronunciation and a series of graded lessons thoroughly covering the groundwork of the French language. Included in each lesson are working exercises and the Key to these is in Part II along with detailed explanatory notes where every effort is made to build up the student's vocabulary as he progresses through the course. An extensive vocabulary and lists of irregular verbs are to be found at the end of the book.

As a result of studying this course, the student should emerge with a sound working knowledge of everyday French.

TEACH YOURSELF BOOKS

GERMAN

J. Adams

Intended essentially for the beginner, this complete course in contemporary German has been specially designed to enable the student to learn the language as quickly and effectively as possible.

Both the German alphabet and pronunciation are thoroughly covered in separate sections while a course of thirty carefully graded lessons leads the student through the various points of the grammar. At the same time the vocabulary is gradually built up in conjunction with the exercises to be found in each lesson.

Having thoroughly worked his way through this book, the student should emerge with a sound practical knowledge of written and spoken German.

TEACH YOURSELF BOOKS

RUSSIAN

Michael Frewin

Russian is always thought to be a very difficult language but, in fact, it is not so much difficult as different. Only half the population of the Soviet Union speaks Russian as their mother tongue – the other hundred million learn it as a foreign language and accept this as natural.

This book aims to give a good working knowledge of the language. It consists of twenty lessons, each containing a reading passage, a section to explain new grammatical points, and exercises which practise the new material in many different ways. A key to the exercises is included and, as well as the grammar notes in each lesson, a summary of all the main forms is given in the appendix.

At the end of the book, a selection of reading passages is provided which are all derived from contemporary Soviet sources and are completely unabridged. They are thus a real guide to the progress the student is making and hence a particularly valuable feature of the book.

TEACH YOURSELF BOOKS

SPANISH

N. Scarlyn Wilson

As a language of world importance, Spanish rivals French and German. There are over 115 million speakers of the language in the world, both in South America and Spain, and obviously a knowledge of Spanish is useful – not only to the student but also to the tourist and the businessman.

Because of its phonetic simplicity and the basic regularity of its grammatical forms, Spanish is a relatively easy language to learn. This book takes the reader through a series of graded lessons which have been designed both for use in the classroom and for study at home. Each lesson comes complete with exercises and translation pieces and the aim is that the reader, on working his way through the course, should have a sound command of Spanish.

'Anyone who works through this volume intelligently should be able to read and speak Spanish. No student should fail to obtain this excellent course'
Journal of the Incorporated Association of Assistant Masters

TEACH YOURSELF BOOKS

LATIN

F. Kinchin Smith

Although Latin is one of the so-called 'dead languages', its literature is still very much alive. A knowledge of Latin opens up to the reader the works of such classical writers as Cicero and Virgil.

This book offers a complete course in Latin for beginners. The student is first taken through the basic grammar and vocabulary and then introduced to the more difficult aspects of Latin. Throughout the text are to be found Latin passages for translation as well as useful exercises. Each section is clearly laid out and the aim has been to provide a course which the beginner can work through on his own and which will enable him to translate English into Latin and read Latin with ease.

A practical working course in Latin, invaluable to the beginner and the student, for use both at home and in the classroom.

TEACH YOURSELF BOOKS

ITALIAN

Kathleen Speight

A working knowledge of Italian is not difficult to acquire, and the pronunciation of the language is relatively simple and consistent.

This book offers a complete course in modern conversational Italian for beginners studying at home. Pronunciation, grammar and syntax are fully explained in easy stages illustrated by examples, and a basic grounding in the everyday vocabulary is provided.

TEACH YOURSELF BOOKS

GERMAN GRAMMAR

P. G. Wilson

This grammar is not intended for the beginner but for the student who has already made some progress with German, from working through a course such as *Teach Yourself German*.

The reader will find here a thorough and exhaustive course in German grammar. The book is so arranged that the student can not only work his way through the course and emerge with a detailed knowledge of German grammar, but also use the contents of the book as a handy form of reference in his reading and German studies in general. This book will be particularly useful to those students wishing to revise their grammar, apart from those embarking on an advanced course in German.

'A praiseworthy attempt to clarify in a practical way what is to most a rather forbidding subject'

The Times Educational Supplement

TEACH YOURSELF BOOKS

SPANISH DICTIONARY

Margaret H. Raventós

This book offers an invaluable aid for students, tourists, businessmen and all who wish to become proficient in modern Spanish.

Full Spanish–English and English–Spanish sections, each with some 25,000 entries, provide clear definitions for a wide range of words and phrases in convenient form in addition there are special sections on proper names and abbreviations in each language, and on weights, measures and currency.

'One of the best, if not the best, class dictionaries available'

Higher Education Journal

TEACH YOURSELF BOOKS

FRENCH DICTIONARY

N. Scarlyn Wilson

This dictionary provides the user with a comprehensive vocabulary for working French. With over 35,000 words in both sections, special care has been taken to include current usage including some slang. A complete list of Irregular Verbs, a selection of French Idioms and Phrases, lists of Christian Names and Geographical Places are all included. For the student of French, an extensive and workmanlike dictionary which will prove to be invaluable.

TEACH YOURSELF BOOKS

FRENCH GRAMMAR

E. S. Jenkins

This grammar is not intended for the beginner but for the student who has already made some progress with French, from working through a course such as *Teach Yourself French.*

The reader will find here a grammar course which is both thorough and exhaustive. The book is so arranged that the student can not only work his way through the course and emerge with a detailed knowledge of French grammar, but also use the contents of this book as a handy form of reference in his reading and French studies. This book will be particularly useful for those students wishing to revise their grammar, as well as for those embarking on an advanced course in French.

'An excellent book for examination revision if only for the clarity of its layout and the multiplicity of well chosen French examples'

The Times Literary Supplement